Sustainable Development in Practice

Sustainable Development in Practice

Case Studies for Engineers and Scientists

Editors

ADISA AZAPAGIC
University of Surrey

SLOBODAN PERDAN

and

ROLAND CLIFT
University of Surrey

John Wiley & Sons, Ltd

This publication is designed to provide accurate and authoritative information in regard to the subject matter covered. It is sold on the understanding that the Publisher is not engaged in rendering professional services. If professional advice or other expert assistance is required, the services of a competent professional should be sought.

Other Wiley Editorial Offices

John Wiley & Sons Inc., 111 River Street, Hoboken, NJ 07030, USA

Jossey-Bass, 989 Market Street, San Francisco, CA 94103-1741, USA

Wiley-VCH Verlag GmbH, Boschstr. 12, D-69469 Weinheim, Germany

John Wiley & Sons Australia Ltd, 33 Park Road, Milton, Queensland 4064, Australia

John Wiley & Sons (Asia) Pte Ltd, 2 Clementi Loop #02-01, Jin Xing Distripark, Singapore 129809

John Wiley & Sons Canada Ltd, 22 Worcester Road, Etobicoke, Ontario, Canada M9W 1L1

Wiley also publishes its books in a variety of electronic formats. Some content that appears in print may not be available in electronic books.

Library of Congress Cataloging-in-Publication Data

Sustainable development in practice : case studies for engineers and
scientists / edited by Adisa Azapagic, Slobodan Perdan, Roland Clift.
     p.   cm.
  Includes bibliographical references and index.
  ISBN 0-470-85608-4 (cloth : alk. paper) — ISBN 0-470-85609-2 (pbk. : alk. paper)
  1. Engineering—Research.   2. Sustainable development.   I. Azapagic, Adisa.
  II. Perdan, Slobodan.   III. Clift, R. (Roland)
  TA160.S87 2004
  620′.0028′6—dc22   2004004937

British Library Cataloguing in Publication Data

A catalogue record for this book is available from the British Library

ISBN 0-470-85608-4 (Cloth)
ISBN 0-470-85609-2 (Paper)

Typeset in 10/12 pt Times by Integra Software Services Pvt. Ltd, Pondicherry, India
Printed and bound in Great Britain by Antony Rowe Ltd, Chippenham, Wiltshire
This book is printed on acid-free paper responsibly manufactured from sustainable forestry in which at least two trees are planted for each one used for paper production.

Contents

About the Editors

Adisa Azapagic is Professor of Sustainable Engineering. Her research interests and expertise include life cycle modelling and optimisation, life cycle assessment, industrial ecology, sustainability indicators, multiple criteria decision analysis and corporate social responsibility. Azapagic is the author of over 130 publications in these areas, including a book on Polymers, the Environment and Sustainable Development also published by Wiley. She is also interested in sustainability education and is a member of the European Federation of Chemical Engineering (EFCE) Working Party on Education. She is a UNESCO/TWAS/ICSU Visiting Scientist at the Instituto Tecnológico Autónomo de México (ITAM), Mexico City.

Slobodan Perdan is a philosopher with expertise and professional interests in the areas of sustainable development, moral philosophy and sustainability education. He has written on a variety of issues concerning sustainable development, and has taught and researched a wide range of subjects including environmental philosophy, business and engineering ethics, corporate sustainability and social and political theory. Perdan is currently working as a freelance consultant having previously worked at the University of Surrey for several years.

Roland Clift is a Distinguished Professor in Environmental Technology and founding Director of the Centre for Environmental Strategy at the University of Surrey; previously Head of the Department of Chemical and Process Engineering at the University of Surrey. He is a member of the Royal Commission on Environmental Pollution, of the International Expert Group on application of Life Cycle Assessment to waste management and of the Rolls-Royce Environmental Advisory Board, and a past member of the UK Ecolabelling Board. Clift is a Visiting Professor in Environmental System Analysis at Chalmers University, Göteborg, Sweden. He has recently been awarded the Sir Frank Whittle medal by the Royal Academy of Engineering for his leading role in developing the holistic life cycle assessment of products and its use as a systematic way of incorporating environmental and social issues in engineering decisions.

About the Contributors

David Allen is the Melvin H. Gertz Regents Chair in Chemical Engineering and the Director of the Center for Energy and Environmental Resources at the University of Texas at Austin. His research interests lie in air quality and pollution prevention. He is the author of four books and over 150 papers in these areas. Allen is also actively involved in developing Green Engineering educational materials for the chemical engineering curriculum.

Lauren Basson is a post-doctoral research fellow in Chemical Engineering, University of Cape Town. Her research is focused on multiple criteria approaches to complex decision problems including management of uncertainty.

Anna Carew is a PhD student in the Department of Chemical Engineering at the University of Sydney. Her research sits in the nexus of engineering philosophy, sustainability thinking and educational theory.

James Clark holds the Chair of Industrial and Applied Chemistry at the University of York and is the founding Director of the Green Chemistry Network. His research interests cover various aspects of chemistry including catalysis and new materials.

Aaron Collett is a chemical engineering graduate from the University of Surrey. He has been working as a Research Assistant at the University on different research projects. His primary professional interest lies in professional education and training of engineers and scientists.

Richard Darton is Professor in Engineering Science at the University of Oxford. His research interests include sustainable development, separation processes and the rheology of surfaces. He worked for Shell in the Netherlands for 16 years, and in 1991 returned to the UK to initiate a chemical engineering course at Oxford, where he is now a Fellow of Keble College.

Charles Duff is the Royal Academy of Engineering Visiting Professor in Sustainable Design at the University of Surrey. He has an extensive background in environmental management in industry, including a secondment to the World Business Council for Sustainable Development.

Jeffrey Hardy holds the post of Green Chemistry Educational Associate at the University of York. His research interests lie in the field of chemicals and feedstocks from renewable raw materials and Green Chemistry practical development.

Norman Kirkby is a Senior Lecturer at the University of Surrey. His research interests include mathematical modelling of bioreactors, and more recently radiotherapy modelling. He has 20 years experience of teaching, especially thermodynamics, reaction engineering, dynamics and control.

Alan Millington is a Senior Lecturer and Director of Studies for Chemical Engineering Programmes at the University of Surrey. His research interests range from filtration to safety assessment in chemical and process engineering. Millington is particularly interested in engineering education and has extensive experience in teaching various chemical engineering subjects.

Cynthia Mitchell is a Senior Research Fellow at the Institute for Sustainable Futures at the University of Technology in Sydney. She has 15 years experience in science and engineering education and research, for which she has received national and international awards. Mitchell served two terms as President of the Australasian Association for Engineering Education.

Michael J. Nicholas is a Process Industries Regulation Officer in the Environment Agency for England and Wales. He specialises in the regulation of Major Accident Hazard sites under the COMAH regulations, along with the regulation of other industrial installations under the Integrated Pollution Control and Pollution Prevention and Control regimes. He has previously worked in the field of environmental management at Lurgi (UK) Ltd, a process contracting company.

Philippa Notten is an independent consultant in the field of Life Cycle Assessment, based in Denmark. She is co-chair of the UNEP SETAC Life Cycle Initiative on Data Quality.

Martin Pehnt is a Senior Scientist at the Institute for Energy and Environmental Research (IFEU) in Heidelberg. His research interests include technology and environmental assessment of energy and transport systems, and environmental communication. He has recently been awarded the Robert Mayer Award by the Association of German Engineers for outstanding merits in the field of science journalism and publicism, particularly with respect to engineering and energy developments.

Jim Petrie is Professor and Head of the Department of Chemical Engineering at the University of Sydney. He also serves as Director of CRESTA, the Centre for Risk, Environment, Systems Technology and Analysis, and is an Adjunct Professor at the University of Cape Town, South Africa. His main research interests are in the area of environmental systems analysis in the resources sector.

Omar Romero-Hernandez is a Professor in the Department of Industrial Engineering and Operations at the Instituto Tecnológico Autónomo de México (ITAM), Mexico City. His research interests include energy and the environment, technology and manufacturing strategy, product development and design, and operations management.

Mary Stewart is a Senior Research Fellow in the Department of Chemical Engineering at the University of Sydney, Australia. She is a member of the South African and Australasian Institutes of Mining and Metallurgy, treasurer of the Australian Life Cycle Assessment Society and co-chair of the UNEP SETAC Life Cycle Initiative working group of metals. The focus of her work is on multi-criteria decision-making for sustainable development in mining and minerals processing.

Preface

This book is about sustainable development and its implications for science and engineering practice. It is aimed at engineering and science students and educators as well as practising engineers and scientists.

An important thesis in this book is that sustainable development imposes new responsibilities on the "expert", which demand a re-examination of the professional roles of engineers and scientists. However, we also argue that the new role actually makes the profession more attractive, requiring personal skills as well as technical expertise.

Part 1 of this book explores the concept of sustainable development and its implications for technical experts. Recognising that practical interpretation of sustainable development depends on the context, Part 2 of this book is devoted to a set of case studies. These are drawn from a range of industrial sectors, including water, energy, waste, chemicals, glass and mining and minerals. All set out real practical problems. They explore the scientific and technical aspects of each problem but also consider its economic, environmental and social ramifications, to position the expert analysis in the context of sustainable development. They are intended as vehicles to develop the reflective approach to practising as a technical expert which we believe is essential for sustainable development.

We dedicate the book to our students and successors, in the hope that it will help them to play their essential role in helping everyone to have a better quality of life, now and in the future, on this beautiful little blue-green planet.

Adisa Azapagic
Slobodan Perdan
Roland Clift
Guildford, Surrey

Acknowledgements

We would like to thank those who have helped in the production of this book. First of all, we would like to thank all the contributors and we hope that they will feel that the book rewards their efforts.

The Royal Academy of Engineering supported development of several of the case studies, through its programme of Visiting Professors in Engineering Design for Sustainable Development. Adisa Azapagic is grateful to the Leverhulme Trust for a Study Abroad Fellowship which supported her sabbatical leave during which several chapters of this book were prepared. Roland Clift would like to thank his colleagues in the Centre for Environmental Strategy for providing the essential resources of listening, critically but constructively, to partially formed ideas. He is also grateful to Sue Ponsford who has typed parts of this book, displaying her usual helpfulness and patience.

Last but not least, we are thankful to the staff of John Wiley & Sons, particularly Lyn Roberts, Keily Larkins and Amanda Smith, and to Bharath Parthasarathy at Integra for their help and professionalism in producing the book.

PART 1

SUSTAINABLE DEVELOPMENT, ENGINEERS AND SCIENTISTS

1

Introduction to Sustainable Development

Slobodan Perdan

1.1 Introduction

At the beginning of the 21st century, around the world we see signs of severe stress on our interdependent economic, environmental and social systems. Population is growing – it topped 6 billion in 2000, up from 4.4 billion in 1980, and it is expected to reach 8 billion by 2025 (UNCSD, 2002). Excessive consumption and poverty continue to put enormous pressure on the environment. In many areas, the state of the environment is much more fragile and degraded than it was a few decades ago. Despite notable improvements in areas such as river and air quality in places like Europe and North America, generally there has been a steady decline in the environment, especially across large parts of the developing world (UNEP, 2002).

There are some alarming trends underway. The United Nations Environmental Programme's *GEO-2002* (UNEP, 2002) report puts them into stark figures, characteristic examples of which include:

– Around 2000 million (2 billion) ha of soil, equal to 15% of the earth's land or an area bigger than the United States and Mexico combined, is now classed as degraded as a result of human activities. About one-sixth of this, a total of 305 million ha of soils, is either "strongly or extremely degraded". Extremely degraded soils are so badly damaged that they cannot be restored.
– Around half of the world's rivers are seriously depleted and polluted.
– About 24% (1130) of mammals and 12% (1183) of bird species are currently regarded as globally threatened.

Sustainable Development in Practice: Case Studies for Engineers and Scientists
Edited by Adisa Azapagic, Slobodan Perdan and Roland Clift
© 2004 John Wiley & Sons, Ltd   ISBNs: 0-470-85608-4 (HB); 0-470-85609-2 (PB)

- Depletion of the ozone layer, which protects life from damaging ultraviolet light, has now reached record levels. In September 2000, the ozone hole over Antarctica covered more than 28 million km^2.
- Concentrations of carbon dioxide, the main gas linked with global warming, currently stand at 367 ppm or 25% higher than that 150 years ago. Concentrations of other greenhouse gases, such as methane and halocarbons, have also risen.

Other noteworthy trends include (UNDP, 2002):

- Some 80 countries, amounting to 40% of the world's population, were suffering from serious water shortages by the mid-1990s. Around 1.1 billion people still lack access to safe drinking water and 2.4 billion to improved sanitation, mainly in Africa and Asia.
- A population of 2.8 billion live on less than $2 a day, with 1.2 billion of them barely surviving on the margins of subsistence with less than $1 a day.
- Every year about 11 million children die of preventable causes, often for want of simple and easily provided improvements in nutrition, sanitation, maternal health and education.

These and a host of other trends suggest that our current development course is unsustainable. The high and increasing consumption of scarce resources and resulting pollution compounded by population growth, and the growing imbalance in development between different countries pose unacceptable risks to communities, nations and humanity as a whole. It has become clear that economic development that disregards environmental and social impacts can bring unintended and unwanted consequences, as evidenced by the threat of climate change, overuse of freshwater resources, loss of biological diversity and raising inequalities.

The concept of sustainable development has grown out of concerns about these adverse trends. In essence, it is an approach to development which focuses on integrating economic activity with environmental protection and social concerns.

1.2   Development of the Concept

The concept of sustainable development as we know it today emerged in the 1980s as a response to the destructive social and environmental effects of the prevailing approach to "economic growth". The idea originated within the environmental movement. One of the earliest formulations of the concept of sustainable development can be found in the 1980's World Conservation Strategy jointly presented by the UN Environment Programme, the World Wildlife Fund and the International Union for Conservation of Nature and Natural Resources (UNEP/WWF/IUCNNR, 1980). This early formulation emphasised that:

> For development to be sustainable, it must take account of social and ecological factors, as well as economic ones; of the living and non-living resource base; and of the long-term as well as the short-term advantages and disadvantages of alternative actions.
>
> *UNEP/WWF/IUCNNR, 1980*

It called for three priorities to be built into development policies: the maintenance of ecological processes; the sustainable use of resources; and the maintenance of genetic diversity.

However, the concept of sustainable development gained a wider recognition only after the World Commission on Environment and Development (WCED) published its report "Our common future" (also known as "the Brundtland Report") in 1987. It was this report that gave the concept the prominence it has today.

The WCED report set the benchmark for all future discussions on sustainable development. The starting point for the Commission's work was their acknowledgement that the future of humanity is threatened. "Our common future" opened by declaring:

> The Earth is one but the world is not. We all depend on one biosphere for sustaining our lives. Yet each community, each country, strives for survival and prosperity with little regard for its impacts on others. Some consume the Earth's resources at a rate that would leave little for future generations. Others, many more in number, consume far too little and live with the prospects of hunger, squalor, disease, and early death.
>
> *WCED, 1987*

To confront the challenges of over-consumption on the one hand and grinding poverty on the other, the Commission called for sustainable development, defined as "development that meets the needs of the present without compromising the ability of future generations to meet their own needs".

In order to reverse unsustainable trends, the WCED recommended the following seven critical actions aimed at ensuring a good quality of life for people around the world (WCED, 1987):

- revive growth;
- change the quality of growth;
- meet essential needs and aspirations for jobs, food, energy, water and sanitation;
- ensure a sustainable level of population;
- conserve and enhance the resource base;
- reorient technology and manage risk; and
- include and combine environment and economic considerations in decision-making.

Since the Brundtland report, a whole series of events and initiatives have brought us to the wide-ranging interpretation of sustainable development that we see today. One of the key events was, undoubtedly, the United Nations Conference on Environment and Development, more informally known as the Earth Summit, held in Rio de Janeiro in 1992. At the Earth Summit, representatives of nearly 180 countries endorsed the Rio Declaration on Environment and Development which set out 27 principles supporting sustainable development. The assembled leaders also signed the Framework Convention on Climate Change, the Convention on Biological Diversity, and the Forest Principles. They also agreed a global plan of action, Agenda 21, designed to deliver a more sustainable pattern of development and recommended that all countries should produce national sustainable development strategies.

Ten years later, in September 2002 at the World Summit on Sustainable Development (WSSD) in Johannesburg, leaders and representatives of 183 countries reaffirmed sustainable development as a central element of the international agenda. The present governments agreed to a wide range of concrete commitments and targets for action to achieve sustainable development objectives, including (WSSD, 2002):

– to halve, by the year 2015, the proportion of people in poverty;
– to encourage and promote the development of a 10-year framework of programmes to accelerate the shift towards sustainable consumption and production;
– to diversify energy supply and substantially increase the global share of renewable energy sources in order to increase its contribution to total energy supply;
– to improve access to reliable, affordable, economically viable, socially acceptable and environmentally sound energy services and resources;
– to accelerate the development and dissemination of energy efficiency and energy conservation technologies, including the promotion of research and development;
– to develop integrated water resource management and water efficiency plans by 2005; and
– to achieve by 2010 a significant reduction in the current rate of loss of biological diversity.

The Johannesburg Summit moved the sustainability agenda further, and consolidated and broadened the understanding of sustainable development, particularly the important linkages between poverty, the environment and the use of natural resources.

These political events brought sustainable development firmly into the public arena and established it as a widely accepted goal for policy makers. As a result, we have seen a proliferation of sustainable development strategies and policies, innovative technological, scientific and educational initiatives, and new legislative regimes and institutions. The concept of sustainable development now influences governance, business and economic activity at different levels, and affects individual and society lifestyle choices.

In the last three decades, a continuing debate about what sustainability truly means has produced a plethora of definitions. A wide variety of groups – ranging from businesses to national governments to international organisations – have adopted the concept and given it their own particular interpretations.

The UK government, for example, in its sustainable development strategy defines sustainable development as "the simple idea of ensuring a better quality of life for everyone, now and for generations to come" (DETR, 1999). The strategy emphasises that sustainable development means meeting the following four objectives at the same time, in the UK and the world as a whole:

– social progress which recognises the needs of everyone;
– effective protection of the environment;
– prudent use of natural resources; and
– maintenance of high and stable levels of economic growth and employment.

Most countries in the developed world and many developing countries have now incorporated sustainability into their national planning, and defined sustainable development in their national contexts. According to national reports received from governments before the WSSD in 2002, about 85 countries have developed some kind of national sustainability strategy, although the nature and effectiveness of those strategies vary considerably from country to country (UNCSD, 2002).

The concept of sustainable development has also made inroads into the business community. In the last three decades, the understanding and acceptance of sustainable development within the business community have grown significantly. Most forward-looking companies and businesses are beginning to integrate sustainability into corporate strategies and practice. They recognise that the challenge of sustainable development for the business enterprise means adopting business strategies and activities that meet the needs of the enterprise and its stakeholders today while protecting, sustaining and enhancing the human and natural resources that will be needed in the future (IISD, 1992). This way of thinking is, for instance, behind the World Business Council for Sustainable Development (WBCSD), a wide coalition of 165 international companies (including some of the world's largest corporations) united by "a shared commitment to sustainable development via the three pillars of economic growth, ecological balance and social progress". Although not all of WBCSD component corporations have exemplary environmental records, this coalition has been involved actively in the activities aimed at identifying and defining sustainable pathways for businesses.

Many professional organisations including engineering and scientific associations have incorporated sustainable development into their mission statements, statutes and codes. As an example, in their "Melbourne communiqué" representatives of 20 chemical engineering organisations from around the world committed themselves to using their "skills to strive to improve the quality of life, foster employment, advance economic and social development and protect the environment through sustainable development" (WCEC, 2001).

Finally, environmental organisations contributed significantly to the development of the concept of sustainable development. After all, sustainable development began life as one of their concepts. One of the most prominent and influential definitions comes from a "Strategy for Sustainable Living" (UNEP/WWF/IUCN, 1991), another joint publication by the UNEP, International Union for the Conservation of Nature (IUCN) and WWF, in which sustainable development is defined as "improving the quality of life while living within the carrying capacity of supporting ecosystems". In a similar vain, in its "Action for Global Sustainability", the Union of Concerned Scientists advocates that "humanity must learn to live within the limits of natural systems while ensuring an adequate living standard for all people" (UCS, 2001).

These are just some of the many formulations which have over the years increased our understanding of what sustainable development means within many different contexts. The principle of sustainable development and many of its objectives have now been widely adopted, and the agenda has moved from the question of "What does sustainable development mean?" on to the questions of "How do we achieve sustainable development?" and "How do we measure our progress towards achieving it?" Yet, in contrast to rapid progress in *developing* the *concepts* of sustainable development, progress in *implementing* sustainable development has been slow. As the WSSD demonstrated in 2002, sustainable development remains largely theoretical for the majority of the world's population.

1.3 Sustainable Development: Implementation

Sustainable development presents a framework for change rather than a list of prescriptions to achieve it. There is, however, a growing consensus that the transition to a more sustainable society requires new ways of meeting our needs which can reduce the level of material consumption and reduce environmental damage without affecting quality of life. This will require, above all, limiting the throughput of materials and energy in the economy and finding less wasteful ways of meeting needs through increasing efficiency, reusing materials and using sustainable technologies.

Moving to a more sustainable path, however, does not only require a better management of the environment. Certain minimal socio-economic conditions must also be met to ensure the necessary consensus for short-term actions and long-term stability. "Greening" industrial economies whilst ignoring the need for poverty alleviation and the redistribution of opportunity would not ensure long-term sustainability. True sustainability means ensuring a satisfying quality of life for everyone. Meeting this objective, therefore, not only requires reducing the scale of polluting activities and the excessive levels of consumption, but also calls for well-planned actions to alleviate poverty and achieve greater equity and distribution of opportunities both within and between countries.

1.3.1 Sustainable Production and Consumption

According to the Johannesburg Plan of Implementation, adopted at the 2002 WSSD, "fundamental changes in the way societies produce and consume are indispensable for achieving global sustainable development" (WSSD, 2002). There are some encouraging sings of a more sustainable production such as energy efficiency improvements and lower consumption of raw materials per unit of production in industrialised societies. The European Union, for example, achieved significant economic growth in the 1990s without notable increases in its consumption of fossil fuels. This was mainly due to a shift in production and consumption from material and energy intensive sectors to services. However, these gains in efficiency have been offset by an increase in the volume of goods and services consumed and discarded. For instance, according to the Organisation for Economic Cooperation and Development (OECD), the amount of waste generated in Europe between 1990 and 1995 increased by 10% and has continued to grow since then. It is estimated that by 2020 Europe could be generating 45% more waste than it generated in 1995 (for more details on the issue of waste, see Chapter 5).

As more natural resources are being consumed and more pollution is generated, it is becoming clear that decoupling economic growth from adverse environmental impacts, such as emissions of greenhouse gases, waste production and use of hazardous materials, holds one of the keys to sustainable development. To achieve this, companies and industries must become more "eco-efficient". The concept of eco-efficiency was developed by the WBCSD in 1991 and has become widely recognised by the business world. Eco-efficiency calls for a business to achieve more value from lower inputs of materials and energy and with reduced emissions. It applies throughout a business, to marketing and product development just as much as to manufacturing or distribution. WBCSD has identified seven elements that a business can use to improve their eco-efficiency and should be considered at each stage in production process of all goods and services (WBCSD, 1996, 2000, 2001; de Simone and Popoff, 1997). These include:

- reducing the material requirements (total mass consumed);
- reducing the energy intensity (energy consumed during every phase of production);
- reducing toxic dispersion (release of toxic substances to all media);
- enhancing material recyclability (reuse of materials or energy);
- maximising sustainable use of renewable resources (avoiding depletion of finite resources);
- extending product durability (optimising product life);
- increasing the service intensity (creating value-added while reducing environmental impacts).

A central tenet of eco-efficiency is that it requires improvement in most, if not all, of the above elements over the medium to long term, while maintaining performance with respect to the others. These seven elements may be thought of as being concerned with three broad objectives (WBCSD, 2000):

1. reducing the consumption of resources: this includes minimising the use of energy, materials, water and land, enhancing recyclability and product durability and closing material loops;
2. reducing the impact on nature: this includes minimising air emissions, water discharges, waste disposal and the dispersion of toxic substances, as well as fostering the sustainable use of renewable resources; and
3. increasing product or service value: this means providing more benefits to customers through product functionality, flexibility and modularity, providing additional services and focusing on selling the functional needs that customers actually want. This raises the possibility of the customer receiving the same functional need with fewer materials and less resources. It also improves the prospects of closing material loops because responsibility and ownership, and therefore concern for efficient use, remain with the service provider.

In short, eco-efficient companies and industries must deliver competitively priced goods and services that improve quality of life, while reducing ecological impacts and resource-use intensity to a level within the earth's carrying capacity.

One of the important question is: how much more efficient do companies and industries need to be to become more sustainable? Globally, the goal is to quadruple resource productivity so that wealth is doubled and resource use is halved. This has been described as the need to achieve a "Factor 4" increase in resource efficiency (von Weizsäcker *et al.*, 1997). Often associated with Factor 4 is "Factor 10", whose proponents argue that in the long term, a tenfold reduction in resource consumption in the industrialised countries is necessary if we are to approach sustainability (International Factor 10 Club, 1997; UNEP, 2000). The reasoning behind this is that globally, consumption needs to be halved, but that the greatest reduction should be borne by those countries that are currently the most profligate in their use of resources.

Implementing Factor 4 and Factor 10 strategies and becoming eco-efficient will require step changes in processes and products. This is unlikely to be achieved with incremental improvements. It will require truly novel approaches to the development and use of technologies, products and services. This is a huge challenge for engineers and scientists and to respond to it, we must rethink the way we design, operate and analyse industrial systems. This new way of thinking or a paradigm shift in science and engineering and the role of scientists and engineers in sustainable development are explored in more detail in the next chapter and in the subsequent case studies. Here, we turn our attention to the role of technology in achieving sustainable development.

1.3.2   Sustainable Technologies

Sustainable technologies enable humans to meet their needs with minimum impact on the environment. Many kinds of sustainable technologies already exist, ranging from direct solar and wind power to recycling. Some, such as wind and water power, were invented centuries ago. The others are much "younger", for example, the solar cell was invented in the 1950s. These technologies however have failed to become widespread largely for social and economic reasons, not technical ones. Many other technologies and practices that could reduce the environmental impacts of economic activities are also already available. For example, numerous technical means of improving the scope and rates of recycling of waste materials exist but are poorly used in many countries.

Latest technological advances such as the accelerated developments in information and communications technology could play an essential role in achieving sustainable development. Photograph by A. Azapagic.

Latest technological advances offer even greater opportunities for a more sustainable production. Just as technological progress has been a major source of economic growth over the past two centuries, so could today's technological transformations play a pivotal role in achieving sustainable development. They offer the prospect of reconciling economic development and prosperity with environmental improvement, and create new possibilities for reducing environmental impacts, improving health, expanding knowledge, stimulating economic growth and ensuring a better quality of life. Leading these transformations are the accelerated developments in information and communications technology, biotechnology and just-emerging nanotechnology.

Innovations in information and communications technology nowadays enable us to process, store and rapidly distribute enormous amounts of information. By dramatically increasing access to information and communications, these new technologies are breaking barriers to knowledge and participation, offering tremendous possibilities for improving education and political participation. They also create new economic opportunities, thereby contributing to economic growth and employment creation.

Modern biotechnology – recombinant DNA technology – is transforming life sciences. Genetics is now the basis of life sciences, and much research on pharmaceuticals and plant breeding is now based on biotechnology. The power of genetics can now be used to engineer the attributes of plants and other organisms, creating the potential for huge advances, particularly in agriculture and medicine. Biotechnology can speed up plant breeding and drive the development of new crop varieties with greater drought and disease resistance, more nutritional value and less environmental stress. Pest-resistant genetically modified (GM) crops, for instance, could reduce the need to use pesticides that can harm soil quality and human health.

Designing new drugs and treatments based on genomics and related technologies offers potential for tackling the major health challenges facing poor countries and people. The cloning of Dolly the Sheep has pushed scientific frontiers even further and will transform technology development for years to come. The mapping of the genes that comprise the human genome, together with the development of genetic screening, makes possible even the alteration of the human species itself!

To these two new technologies may soon be added a third, just-emerging nanotechnology, which promises to revolutionise medicine, electronics and chemistry. Nanotechnology is evolving from scientific breakthroughs enabling engineering and science at the molecular level, and it is promising to create smaller and cheaper devices, using less material and consuming less energy. Although research into nanotechnology is still in its infancy, it has already created single-molecule transistors, an enzyme-powered bio-molecular motor with nickel propellers, and a minute carrier able to cross from the blood to the brain to deliver chemicals to fight tumours. Future (still hypothetical) applications suggested include cheap, light materials strong enough to make space transport economical, nano-scale robots which will heal injured human tissue and remove obstructions in the circulatory system, and solar nanotechnologies which may in the future be able to provide energy to an ever-growing population.

These accelerated technological developments will undoubtedly further transform the way we live, work, communicate, produce and consume. Many products – vaccines for infectious diseases, drought-tolerant plant varieties for farmers in uncertain climates, clean energy sources for cooking and heating, Internet access for information and communications – contribute directly to sustainable development through improving health, nutrition, knowledge and living standards, reducing environmental pollution and increasing people's ability to participate more actively in the social, economic and political life of their communities. They also deliver the necessary improvement in resource efficiency and contribute to economic growth through the productivity gains they generate.

However, just as technological advance in these instances opens up new avenues for sustainable development, it also creates new risks. Every technological advance brings potential risks, some of which are not easy to predict. Nuclear power, once believed to be a limitless source of energy, came to be seen as a dangerous threat to health and the environment after the accidents at Three Mile Island in the United States and Chernobyl in Ukraine. Chlorofluorocarbons (CFCs) until recently widely used in refrigerators, aerosol cans and air conditioners caused the depletion of the ozone layer and increased danger of skin cancer for people in the countries exposed to increased ultraviolet radiation. Reliance on fossil fuels as the energy source has led to increased atmospheric carbon dioxide levels and the prospect of global warming.

As in previous developments, today's technological advances raise concerns about their possible environmental, health and socio-economic impacts. There is, for instance, a growing public unease about some aspects of information and communications technology such as the health risks associated with the use of mobile phones or the role of the Internet in facilitating drug trade networks and the dissemination of child pornography. Some concerns are also raised about the potential contribution of information technology to raising inequalities and widening the gap between the rich and the poor both at national and at global levels.

Cutting-edge biotechnological research has raised ethical concerns about the possibility of human cloning and the easy manufacture of devastating biological weapons. Serious questions have been asked about the potential risks posed by Genetically Modified Organisms (GMOs) with some concerns that they could adversely affect other species, disrupt entire ecosystems and cause risks to human health. With GM foods, the two main health concerns are that the introduction of novel genes could make a food toxic and that they could introduce new allergens into foods, causing reactions in some people. As to possible harms to the environment, the concern is that GMOs could reproduce and interbreed with natural organisms, thereby spreading to new environments and future generations in an unforeseeable and uncontrollable way. Doubt is also cast on the role of GM technology in providing the answer to food security, with the claim that technological solutions like GM crops overshadow the real social and environmental problems that cause hunger and malnutrition.

Most recently some concerns about nanotechnology have been expressed as well. Echoing in some way the concerns about biotechnology, the problem areas include the environment ("What will the new nano-materials do when they are released?") and equity ("Who will benefit – just the rich, or the poor as well?").

It has been suggested that the most effective response to technological risk is the adoption of a precautionary principle. The precautionary principle states that when an activity raises threats of harm to the environment or human health, precautionary

Nuclear power, once believed to be the solution for the society's energy needs, came to be seen as unsafe after the accidents at Three Mile Island in the United States and Chernobyl in Ukraine. Photograph courtesy of PhotoDisc, Inc.

measures should be taken even if some cause-and-effect relationships are not fully established scientifically (see Box 1.1 for more detail on the precautionary principle). Sometimes it seems to imply a generalised hostility to science and technology as such, but, more rationally, it means taking action before risks are conclusively established. It is, basically, a "better-safe-than-sorry" principle.

Box 1.1 *The precautionary principle*

Although applied more broadly, the precautionary principle has been developed primarily in the context of environmental policy. It emerged in European environmental policies in the late 1970s, and has since become enshrined in numerous international treaties and declarations. It was explicitly recognised during the UN Conference on Environment and Development (UNCED) in Rio de Janeiro in 1992 and was included in the so-called Rio Declaration. Since then, the precautionary principle has been implemented in various environmental instruments, and in particular in those related to global climate change, ozone-depleting substances and biodiversity conservation. It is, by the Treaty on European Union (1992), the basis for European environmental law and plays an increasing role in developing environmental health policies as well (Foster *et al.*, 2000). Essentially, the precautionary principle specifies that scientific uncertainty is no excuse for inaction on an environmental or health problem.

Despite its seemingly widespread political support, the precautionary principle has engendered endless controversy, and has been interpreted in different ways. In its strongest formulations, the principle can be interpreted as calling for absolute proof of safety before allowing new technologies to be adopted. For example, the World Charter for Nature (UN, 1982) states: "where potential adverse effects are not fully understood, the activities should not proceed". If interpreted literally, no new technology could meet this requirement (Foster *et al.*, 2000). Another strong formulation is set out in the 1990 Third Ministerial Declaration on the North Sea, which requires governments to "apply the precautionary principle, that is to take action to avoid potentially damaging impacts of [toxic] substances ... even where there is no scientific evidence to prove a causal link between emissions and effects". This formulation requires governments to take action without considering offsetting factors and without scientific evidence of harm.

A relatively soft formulation appears in the 1992 Rio Declaration on Environment and Development which opens the door to cost–benefit analysis and discretionary judgement. The Rio Declaration (UN, 1992) says that lack of "full scientific certainty shall not be used as a reason for postponing cost-effective measures to prevent environmental degradation".

Between these soft and strong formulations lie a wide range of other positions, which should not be surprising. The precautionary principle is still evolving, and its final character will be shaped by scientific and political processes. A range of formulations – from soft to strong – will continue to be used in different circumstances because different technologies and situations require different degrees of precaution.

However, development of science and technology is bound with risks and, as the progress of science and technology accelerates, we have to get used to dealing with risk situations. These risks deserve our full attention, but cannot be the only consideration shaping our choices of sustainable technologies. An approach to technology assessment that looked only at potential harms of technologies would be flawed. We need to make a full assessment to weigh the expected harms of a new technology against its expected benefits and compare these with the harms and benefits of existing and alternative technologies. To obtain a full picture of the risks and benefits, these assessments must be done on a life cycle basis or from "cradle to grave" (Azapagic, 2002). The life cycle approach is discussed in more detail in the Appendix at the end of the book.

Furthermore, the full technology assessment must also take into consideration the context in which specific technological risks occur. The trade-offs of technological change vary from use to use and from country to country. Different societies expect different benefits, face different risks and have widely varying capacities to handle those risks safely.

Take for example the controversy over GM foods. Opponents of the GM technology often ignore the harms of the *status quo*. European consumers who do not face food shortages or nutritional deficiencies see few benefits in GM foods; they are more concerned about possible health effects. Undernourished farming communities in developing countries, however, are more likely to focus on the potential benefits of higher yields with greater nutritional value (UNDP, 2001). As Sakiko Fukuda-Parr, the lead author of a UN Report that looked into potential benefits of new technologies for developing countries, puts it:

> You and I don't really need the tomato with longer shelf life. On the other hand, a farmer in Mali facing crop failure every three years really needs better drought-resistant crops that biotechnology can offer.

So the potential benefits that biotechnology has for the agriculture in developing countries are enormously different from the potential benefits for the agriculture in Europe or the OECD countries. Many developing countries might reap great benefits from GM foods, crops and other GMOs. For developing countries facing malnutrition, the unique potential of GM techniques for creating virus-resistant, drought-tolerant and nutrient-enhanced crops poses different choices. In their case, the risks of no change may outweigh any concerns over the potential health effects of GMOs.

Similarly, proponents of new technologies often fail to consider alternatives. Nuclear power, for example, should be weighed not just against fossil fuels but also against other – possibly preferable – alternatives such as solar power and hydrogen fuel cells. And many people argue that the use of GMOs should be weighed against alternatives such as organic farming, which in some situations could be a more suitable choice. "The golden rice" controversy is an appropriate case to consider in this context.

The GM industry claims that a rice variety, genetically modified to contain vitamin A ("the golden rice"), could save thousands of children from blindness and millions of malnourished people from vitamin-A deficiency (VAD). Yet, the golden rice could, if introduced on a large scale, exacerbate malnutrition and ultimately undermine food security because it encourages a diet based on one staple. For the short term, measures such as supplementation (i.e. pills) and food fortification are effective and cheaper. Promoting locally appropriate and ecologically sustainable agriculture and diet diversification programmes would address a wide variety of micronutrient deficiencies, not just VAD, and lead to a long-term solution.

The golden rice case highlights an important point when considering sustainable technologies: we must not fall into the trap of thinking that technological innovation is a universal remedy for our problems. To create a sustainable society, we must focus on strategies that address the root causes of our problems.

Treating the symptoms, regardless of how technologically advanced the treatment is, results only in short-term gains that may be offset by other factors. Consider, for example, the catalytic converter, a device used in cars to reduce the emissions of certain pollutants, notably carbon monoxide and hydrocarbons. Catalytic converters work well and are responsible for a dramatic decline in the pollution our cars produce. They are even responsible for a general "cleansing" of the air in many urban centres. However, the number of motor vehicles in the world has increased from 630 million in 1990 to over one billion in 2000. Continuing expansion of the population and the ever-increasing number of vehicle-miles travelled per year (increasing in the US alone by about 51 billion miles per year) could overwhelm the gains resulting from the use of catalytic converters (Chiras, 2003).

Gains from technological improvements such as the catalytic converter, a device used on cars to reduce the emissions of certain pollutants, may be offset by other factors, such as the ever-increasing number and use of cars. Photograph courtesy of University of Surrey.

Certainly, there are many examples of how technologies can help us to move to a sustainable path (such as those considered in this book!). The authors of the Factor 4 concept, for instance, give 50 examples of technologies that could be called upon to deliver the necessary improvement in resource efficiency, including ultra fuel-efficient cars and low-energy homes (von Weizsäcker *et al.*, 1997).

Technological innovations can indeed offer new, less wasteful ways of meeting our needs through efficiency improvements, reuse, recycling and substitution of natural resources. Ultimately however, sustainability will require social and institutional innovation just as much as technological innovation. It is a simple fact that as we become more efficient at producing things we will get wealthier. And as we get wealthier, we are able to produce and consume more goods and services.

1.4   Economic Growth, Environmental Constraints and Social Concerns

The latest statistics show that the annual output of the world economy grew from $31 trillion in 1990 to $42 trillion in 2000, compared to just $6.2 trillion in 1950 (UNCSD, 2003). This increase in economic activity created millions of new jobs and allowed people to consume more. World consumption has expanded at an unprecedented rate in the last century, with private and public consumption expenditures reaching $24 trillion in 1998, twice the level in 1975 and six times that of 1950. Consumption in and of itself is not bad, of course – all living things must consume to maintain their biological existence. The real sustainability issue, however, is the extent of consumption and its environmental and social impacts. And, worryingly, current global consumption and production levels appear to be 25% higher than the earth's sustainable carrying capacity (UNCSD, 2003).

Carrying capacity is defined as the maximum number of individuals of a defined species that a given environment can support over the long term. The notion of limits is fundamental to the concept of carrying capacity. Researchers and non-governmental organisations have promoted a range of new approaches, including the concepts of environmental space and ecological footprints to define these ecological limits and demonstrate the extent of our consumption.

1.4.1   Environmental Space

The concept of environmental space describes the scope for human activities by defining environmental constraints. The concept has been developed and championed by a non-governmental environmental organisation, Friends of the Earth (McLaren *et al.*, 1998; McLaren, 2003), with the aim to estimate a per capita sustainable level of consumption.

The first stage in this calculation is to estimate the world's carrying capacity: that is the total area of productive land available for agriculture; the maximum harvest of renewable resources which can be sustained without depleting the stock; the maximum rate at which the atmosphere can absorb carbon dioxide without causing long-term global warming; the maximum rate of environmental assimilation of other wastes and pollutants; and so on. The second factor is the question of distribution of this carrying capacity. At present the distribution is very unequal. According to the latest UN statistics, the 15% of the world's population living in high-income countries account for 56% of the world's total consumption, while the poorest 40%, in low-income countries, account for only 11% of consumption (UNCSD, 2003).

The concept of environmental space can then be used to set practical targets for sustainable rates of use of environmental resources that reflect real ecological limits and the need for equitable access to those resources. The extent of change needed for any one country can be illustrated by comparing the share of that sustainable production it consumes with its share of the global population.

Friends of the Earth Netherlands (1990) have made a pioneering study to calculate the implications on consumption in the Netherlands of living up to the concept of environmental space, starting with the following basic questions: "What is the environmental space for human activities in a sustainable society? How much energy and resources can we use without destroying the earth?"

The study concluded that the Netherlands is currently consuming more than its fair share of environmental space, and recommended a number of reductions in resource use. It has suggested some concrete targets for consumption reduction in the Netherlands by the year 2010, such as:

- CO_2 emissions will have to be reduced by 60%;
- water use will have to be reduced by 32%;
- meat consumption will have to decline by 60–80%; and
- timber usage will have to drop by approximately 60%.

The study also concluded that even when citizens of a developed country such as the Netherlands adapt their consumption to a level based on a fair share of the world's natural resources, they will still have a comfortable standard of living.

More recently, Friends of the Earth UK have applied the environmental space approach to its own country's economy. Unsurprisingly, the UK's consumption of key environmental resources exceeds its fair share too. With just 1% of the world's people, the UK currently uses 5% of the planet's capacity for carbon dioxide absorption, over 2% of its sustainable timber yield and almost 5% of its sustainable steel and aluminium production. In short, recognising the environmental limits and the need for a more equitable distribution of the world's resources means that the UK needs to cut its use of resources by around 80% (McLaren *et al.*, 1998). Some of the specific targets for the UK for the year 2010 include reduction of:

- energy use by 30%;
- land exploitation by 7%;
- overall water abstraction by 15%;
- timber use by 65%;
- aluminium use by 22%; and
- steel use by 21%.

Friends of the Earth UK suggest three different ways ("sufficiency strategies") by which these targets can be met:

1. a more efficient use of resources – for example by using less material to make a product, and designing it to last longer;
2. using different technologies to meet needs – for example by switching to wind and solar energy from fossil fuels; and
3. finding ways of meeting environmental space targets that meet needs directly and avoid the over-consumption that is damaging quality of life – for example energy companies could sell energy services rather than just energy – and meeting the need for warmth or lighting through a combination of energy efficiency and energy provision, and not just through providing energy.

All of these three ways, according to Friends of the Earth UK, can reduce the level of material consumption and improve the environment without affecting quality of life. However, this can happen only if sustainable technologies and best practices are adopted throughout the UK economy. This indeed is one of the main challenges of sustainable development, not only for the UK but for all other national economies in the world.

1.4.2 Ecological Footprint

Another useful tool for measuring the extent of our consumption is the ecological footprint, endorsed by many researchers, non-governmental organisations and local initiatives. The ecological footprint shows how much productive land and water is required to support a defined economy or population at a specified standard of living. Industrialised economies are considered to require far more land than they have, thus, through trade, impacting on resources in other countries. Also known as "appropriated carrying capacity", this concept too incorporates the distributional aspects of sustainable production and consumption.

Dividing all of the earth's productive land and sea by the number of people today results in an average of 1.9 ha (4.7 acres) of biologically productive space available per person. According to the latest ecological footprint studies, the world average ecological footprint is 2.3 global hectares (5.6 acres) per person (Redefining Progress, 2003). This means that humanity is currently exceeding the biosphere's ecological capacity by over 20% (using 1999 data, the latest available). Due to population increase, the capacity per person decreased by 4% from 1999 to 2002. Leaving space untouched for other species – the authors of the Brundtland Report (WCED,1987), for instance, invited the world community to set aside 12% of the biologically productive space for other species – makes the ecological deficit even larger.

The ranking of national ecological footprints shows which countries are ecologically most sustainable and which are running an ecological deficit. Among the nations of the world, the Americans have the largest ecological footprint. Estimates for the year 2002, which are based on the most recent publicly accessible United Nations statistics, show that an average American required approximately 9.6 ha to provide for his or her consumption, including all the embodied resources and the generated waste (Redefining Progress, 2003). This ecological footprint is over 5 times more than is available per person worldwide and 16 times more than the ecological footprint of an average person in Bangladesh. This should not be surprising since large "ecological deficits" are the rule for industrialised regions and countries. In fact, if everyone in the world were to live like an average person in the high-income countries, we would need 2.6 additional planets to support us all (UNCSD, 2003).

The concepts such as the ecological footprint and environmental space are not perfect measures but are useful in many ways. First, they enable us to understand better the environmental limits to human activity at the global scale. They cast light on rather worrying facts – we are overusing the earth and depleting ecological assets at an increasing rate. They send us, therefore, a clear message: we have to be less profligate in our use of non-renewable resources and thermodynamically irreversible processes if the planet is to be fit for us and for future generations to live on.

Secondly, they reveal a huge disparity in access to environmental resources and an increasing gap between the developed and developing worlds. The patterns of consumption highlighted by the ecological footprint and environmental space studies point to global inequality characterised by a growing "lifestyle divide". One side of the lifestyle divide is characterised by excesses of consumption by the minority one-fifth of the world population, which is responsible for close to 90% of total personal consumption; the other side is characterised by extreme poverty where 1.2 billion live on less than US$1 per day (UNCSD, 2002). This gap – partly a result of growing poverty and of affluence – is a serious threat to sustainable development.

An easy way of demonstrating this global inequality is by adjusting population figures to reflect energy consumption. The population of the US, at some 250 million people, is a long way behind those of India and China, with 900 million and 1.1 billion respectively. If population is adjusted by consumption, however, the figures are entirely different. In terms of consumption-adjusted population, the US exceeds India and China combined by 70% (Commission on Global Governance, 1995). This disparity in energy consumption is reflected globally – people in developed countries use almost ten times more energy per person than people in developing regions. It is not, of course, only energy consumption that is highly disproportional in global terms. It is estimated that around 80–90% of all environmental capacities are consumed by the 20% of the global population who live in industrialised countries (McLaren *et al.*, 1998).

In parallel, inequality between and within countries has also risen – the ratio of the average income of the richest to the poorest country in the world increased from 9 to 1 at the end of the 19th century to about 30 to 1 in 1960 and to more than 60 to 1 today (World Bank, 2000). Unequal access to technology, protectionism in trade, collapsing systems for the commodity exports of developing countries are all part of the existing inequality problems. Sustainable consumption is therefore inextricably linked with the question of equitable distribution of and access to available resources and opportunities.

1.5   Equity and Sustainable Development

The question of equity is at the heart of sustainable development. It focuses attention on redressing the enormous imbalances in political and economic power – between rich and poor countries and peoples, and among corporations, states, communities and generations. The Brundtland report strongly underlined that benefits and burdens from development and environmental policies should be distributed fairly among the members of society and between generations in order to promote social and economic equity. The report has repeatedly emphasised that a primary goal of sustainable development is greater equity, both within the current generation (intragenerational equity) and between generations (intergenerational equity).

1.5.1 Intragenerational Equity

One of the core principles of sustainable development is to achieve basic standards of material equity and social justice both within and between countries. Combating poverty and extending to all the opportunity to fulfil their aspirations for a better life are indispensable for achieving this aim. The Brundtland report pointed out that meeting essential needs requires not only economic growth for nations in which the majority are poor, but an assurance that those poor get their fair share of the resources required to sustain that growth (WCED, 1987). It also stated that "the world in which poverty is endemic would always be prone to ecological catastrophes", pointing to significant links between poverty and the environment. Indeed, much environmental degradation in the developing world today arises from poor people seeking the basic essentials for human life: food, water, fuel and so on. Environmental degradation, on the other hand, has serious social and economic repercussions for the poor, including unsafe water and poor sanitation causing diseases and death of millions of people and children in developing countries, and health-threatening levels of pollution in urban environment.

In addition, the poor tend to be the most vulnerable to the effects of environmental degradation. They tend to have much lower coping capacities, and therefore they are particularly susceptible to the impact of disasters, drought, desertification and pollution. As the UN intergovernmental panel on climate change (IPCC) report on the impacts of increased global temperatures points out, the poorest parts of the world will suffer most from climate change over the next century. The impacts are expected to fall "disproportionately on the poor", the report claims, because most less-developed regions are vulnerable due to a "larger share of their economies being in climate-sensitive areas" such as agriculture, and due to their low capacity to adapt to change (IPCC, 2001).

Unfortunately, the link between poverty and environment is often uncritically characterised as a "vicious circle". Population growth and inadequate resources are presumed to lead to the migration of the poor to ever more fragile lands or more hazardous living sites, forcing them to overuse environmental resources. In turn, the degradation of these resources further impoverishes them. Although this does sometimes happen as a general model, it is highly simplistic. Moreover, it often leads to policies that either protect the environment at the expense of the poor or reduce poverty at the expense of the environment. The linkages between poverty and the environment are complex and require locally specific analyses to be understood – there is no simple causal link. In many areas, the non-poor, commercial companies and state agencies actually cause the majority of environmental damage through land-clearing, agro-chemical use, water appropriation and pollution. Sometimes privileged groups force the poor onto marginal lands, where, unable to afford conservation and regeneration measures, their land-use practices further damage an already degraded environment. Indeed, unsustainable practices by the poor, such as slash-and-burn farming by displaced peasants, seriously damage tropical forests, but as Norman Myers has put it, "blaming them for deforestation is like blaming soldiers for starting a war" (Myers, 2002).

There are also many examples in which very poor people take care of the environment and invest in improving it. Based on experience from around the world, "win-win" options exist which can build better institutions and partnerships with poor people, creating more robust livelihoods and healthier environments. These options simultaneously pursue two goals: reduced poverty and enhanced environmental protection.

Take, for example, the case of indoor pollution from cooking and heating. Around one billion people are affected by problems caused by the use of traditional biomass fuels for cooking and heating. They prepare food and heat their homes with fires that burn dung, wood, crop residues, charcoal or other combustible materials. While seemingly rather harmless, these cookstoves are major causes of massive environmental destruction. Many thousands of acres of forests and other ecosystems are degraded as people seek firewood and other biomass fuels. Besides the obvious harm to the ecosystem, deforestation and plant denudation are a major cause of soil erosion. Human health suffers too as people are exposed to high levels of indoor pollution in poorly ventilated areas. Estimates suggest that indoor air pollution contributes to acute respiratory infections that kill some four million infants and children a year and decreases the overall health and life expectancy of million more women and children.

In the case of indoor pollution from cooking and heating, even a simple but well-thought change could create a win-win situation. Improving efficiency of traditional cookstoves to just 20%, for instance, can reduce the amount of firewood (ecological damage) and smoke (health impact) by half (McKinney and Schoch, 2003). Introducing a different and more appropriate technology such as a solar cookstove or oven will lead to an even better type of improvement. No biomass fuel is used, and no unhealthy smoke is produced. The solar cookstove is still relatively new, and not yet widely used. Early efforts to introduce the new technologies were unsuccessful because many social factors, such as community needs and customs, were not considered. Simple considerations such as including local artisans as stove makers could often not only make new technologies more acceptable to the local population but also produce jobs for community. Thus, simple actions such as improving cookstoves and including local artisans as stove makers will not only reduce harm to the environment and people's health but also improve living standards. It is an example where developing appropriate technologies that are needed by the poor simultaneously tackles an environmental problem and improves livelihoods of the poor. It is also a good example of how well-planned actions can break a vicious circle of poverty and environmental degradation.

It should also be noted that too often we deal with the consequences of poverty rather than the underlying causes. Archbishop Helder Camara once remarked, "When I help the poor I am called a saint, but when I ask why they are poor I am called a communist." What his remark really tells us is that true helping is not merely the palliative response of immediate compassion, but is the search for the causes of poverty and then the removal of those causes which can be removed. One need not be a communist to recognise that amongst the causes of poverty may be injustice, economic policies and so on.

In fact, the causes of poverty are often environmental in nature. For instance, environmental factors are responsible for almost a quarter of all diseases in developing countries. The poor, particularly women and children, are most affected by environmental health problems. The most important hazard, particularly for urban populations in developing countries, is faecal contamination of water and food due to poor or non-existent sewage systems and inadequate hygiene, compounded by unreliable and unsafe domestic water supply. There are other significant hazards. According to the World Health Organisation (WHO), 90% of the global burden of malaria, which is estimated to kill one in twenty children under 5 years of age in sub-Saharan Africa, is attributable to environmental factors.

Tackling the causes of poverty, including environmental ones, is one of the world's major challenges in the 21st century. As already mentioned, the Johannesburg Summit on Sustainable Development agreed on the target to halve by the year 2015 the proportion of people living in extreme poverty. But quite what this target might mean is obscured by the bewildering ambiguity with which the term "poverty" is used and by the many different indicators proposed to monitor poverty. There is no single definition of poverty. The term has been used to define the level of income obtained by households or individuals, lack of access to social services, as well as the inability to participate in society, economically, socially, culturally or politically (Maxwell, 1999). Different organisations, institutions and agencies use different concepts to describe poverty: income or consumption poverty, human underdevelopment, social exclusion, ill-being, lack of capability and functioning, vulnerability, livelihood unsustainability, lack of basic needs, relative deprivation and so on. (Maxwell, 1999).

Different concepts imply different instruments to tackle poverty. Yet, defining poverty is only a start. Only by understanding causes can we begin to design, implement and evaluate programmes to alleviate poverty. In designing poverty programmes, it is advisable to respect the understanding of poverty articulated by poor people themselves. In some cases, this may mean implementing measures to increase income. But in others, the priority may be to reduce variability of income, strengthen women's autonomy by improving the legal system, or improve the access to environmental resources and services.

Poverty is, indeed, a complex issue, and we cannot do it justice in this short chapter. Environmental issues are, of course, part of wider set of factors which contribute to making people poor. Breaking the "vicious circle" of poverty and environmental degradation is, however, critical for sustainability. There are a number of practical actions that the international community can take in addressing this issue. These actions have been recognised and summarised by the UNDP and the EU Poverty and Environment Initiative (UNDP–EU, 1999a,b):

- strengthen participation of the poor in the preparation and implementation of national and local plans, policies and strategies;
- protect the current natural asset base of the poor through protecting the access they already have to critical resources (such as entitlements to land, water, trees, pastures, fishing grounds) – especially in cases where the poor are in a weak

position to resist appropriation of these resources by other groups, and through protecting the environmental resources upon which the poor depend on for their livelihoods;

- expand the natural asset base of the poor through transferring ownership of natural assets to the poor (such as the recognition of community forest law, the creation of community forest rights or rights to other resources) and promoting pro-poor land reform;

- co-manage and co-invest in environmental services and resources with the poor through promoting and strengthening community management of environmental resources, and assisting the poor to overcome the high initial costs for receiving better-quality environmental services (such as water supply and sanitation, renewable energy and waste management);

- promote environmental infrastructure and technology that benefit the poor through a greater focus on tackling the environmental problems and hazards that impact most upon their health and livelihoods and through developing affordable and environmentally sound technologies that are needed and can be used by the poor; and

- make resource transfers to the poor through reducing subsidies for environmental services that benefit the non-poor (such as energy and water) and increasing investments in areas in which the poor live and work.

Working up such programmes will be challenging. Yet, eradicating poverty and improving quality of life of the poor in rural and urban areas is an imperative of sustainable development. How we approach these issues will play a major role in determining whether we move toward or away from more sustainable paths.

1.5.2   Intergenerational Equity

As already mentioned, the idea of sustainable development not only implies our responsibility to assist the presently needy, but also refers to our obligations to consider the well-being of future generations. Indeed, the need to safeguard the interests of future generations has been an integral part of sustainable development from the very beginning of the concept. One of the earlier UK government's documents on sustainable development states that we have "the moral duty to look after our planet and to hand it on in good order to future generations" (UK Government, 1995). This moral duty is based on the recognition of legitimate interests and rights of future generations to live in a physically secure and healthy environment, and, consequently, as the recognition of our moral responsibility to protect the natural environment to such an extent that the survival and well-being of future generations are not jeopardised (Perdan and Azapagic, 2000). The goal is for future generations to have as good a life as we have now, or better. This demand of intergenerational equity requires passing the means of survival on to future generations unimpaired and building, or at least not diminishing, the total stock of capital.

One interpretation of intergenerational equity is that the welfare of society as a whole may not be allowed to decline for the indefinite future. It is sometimes expressed as "the constant capital rule": the value of the overall capital stock must not be allowed to decline for the indefinite future. This is known as "weak" sustainability because it assumes that the forms of capital[1] are completely substitutable for each other. It does not matter what form the stock of capital takes as long as the total does not decline. While this position is consistent with intergenerational equity in demanding that equivalent or increased amounts of capital are passed to future generations, it allows the form of this capital to change. This opens the door to passing on to the next generation less of one kind of capital (e.g. natural capital) so long as there is more of another (e.g. built capital) to balance it.

However, some theorists of sustainable development argue that some ecological assets such as the ozone layer or biological diversity are not substitutable – they form "critical" natural capital and the destruction of this capital could threaten the very survival of the human race. Moreover, while most manufactured and human capital can be replaced, the loss of natural capital is often irreversible (i.e. once natural capital assets are lost it may not be possible to recreate them). This view is often called "strong" sustainability, and it demands that the equivalent stock of natural capital is preserved for future generations.

This discussion of "weak" vs "strong" sustainability is not just a theoretical concern. It goes right to the heart, for example, of why some people think there should be no economic activities in protected areas. Some people believe that certain areas should be beyond reach for any human activity that will disturb them because they contain irreplaceable critical natural or human capital (IIED and WBCSD, 2002). The ongoing theoretical debates about "weak" and "strong" sustainability should not, however, obscure the main message: the goal of sustainable development is to sustain improvements in human well-being over time and to ensure that what we do today will not deprive future generations of the means to meet their own needs.

Perhaps one way of understanding how to achieve this goal is to follow general principles of intergenerational equity. The following two principles may provide us with some guidance:

1. the principle of not closing down options for future generations (e.g. by making irreversible changes, including the elimination of species or the using up of resources); and
2. the principle of maximising future choices by making a considered judgement as to what are the most central, significant or important things to preserve and protect, for example, clean air, energy, biodiversity, cultural values and so on.

While most people accept these principles, the difficulty comes in agreeing how to apply them. In practice, the principles of intergenerational equity become entangled with the issues of intragenerational equity. In some cases, it may be possible to advance all the goals of sustainable development simultaneously: improve

---

[1] The idea of "capital" has five main forms: *built capital*, such as machinery, buildings and infrastructure; *human capital*, in the form of knowledge, skills, health and cultural endowment; *social capital*, the institutions and structures that allow individuals and groups to develop collaboratively; *natural capital*, which provides a continuing income of ecosystem benefits such as biological diversity, mineral resources, and clean air and water; and *financial capital*, the value of which is simply representative of the other forms of capital.

material well-being for this generation, spread that well-being more equitably, enhance the environment and pass on enhanced stocks of capital to future generations. In others, there may be a conflict between long-term sustainability objectives of preserving "critical" natural capital such as biodiversity and immediate imperatives of providing basic needs of the poor, for instance, through intensive agricultural development.

In many situations, our decisions will have to involve trade-offs: between different objectives and dimensions, and sometimes between the current and future generations. However, if we apply the principles of sustainable development consistently, we stand a better chance of minimising trade-offs between objectives of intra- and intergenerational equity, and finding the ways of integrating otherwise conflicting goals.

Conclusions

Sustainable development is an approach to environment and development issues, which seeks to reconcile human needs and the capacity of the environment to cope with the consequences of economic systems. Despite its deceptively simple formulations such as the Brundtland definition, sustainable development has multiple layers of meaning and some profound implications. In essence, it is a call to change our actions and to do things differently.

Sustainable development is a dynamic process that will continue to evolve and grow as lessons are learnt and ideas re-examined. Achieving its goals and objectives presents great challenges for all parts of society. Various means are available to facilitate putting sustainable development into practice. Some of these are well known; others are in experimental stages. In this introduction, we have argued that sustainable development depends both on reducing environmental destruction and on improving the quality of life of the world's poor, in ways that will not deprive future generations of means to meet their own needs.

A core principle of sustainable development is to improve human well-being and to sustain these improvements over time. This objective can be achieved by reducing excessive levels of production and consumption, that is by limiting the material and energy throughput in the human economy, through a more efficient use of resources and by addressing the challenge of poverty eradication through concerted actions which tackle the causes of poverty and ensure that available resources are used to the benefit of all.

Sustainable development requires creativity and innovation at every level: social, economic, institutional and technical. There are many favourable trends underway and new and promising developments that give us hope. Important agreements have been reached to reduce global pollution, protect biodiversity and alleviate poverty. Many countries have begun to take steps to create economies that are better for the environment. Many businesses have introduced cleaner and more eco-efficient production processes that reduce pollution and other environmental impacts, while delivering competitively priced goods and services. New technologies are also helping solve problems, as are individual actions. The public has become more aware that as individuals, we each have a right, a role and a responsibility to contribute to sustainable development. Recycling rates are increasing, and we, as consumers, are becoming ready to pay more for organic and other environmentally sound products. At the policy level, a greater attention has been paid to integrating the three conventionally separate domains of economic, environmental and social policy. A wide variety of activities ranging from consultation hearings as part of an environmental impact assessment to co-management of natural resources are indicating that institutional processes are changing too, starting to recognise that increasing public participation in decision-making is an important aspect of sustainable development. These are encouraging signs but there is still a lot more to do. In the final analysis, sustainability means securing a satisfying quality of life for everyone. We know what we have to do to achieve this goal – now it's time to do it.

References and Further Reading

Azapagic, A. (2002) Life Cycle Assessment: A tool for identification of more sustainable products and processes, pp. 62–85. In: *Handbook of Green Chemistry and Technology* (eds J. Clark and D. Macquarrie), Blackwell Science, Oxford.

Chiras, D.D. (2003) *Environmental Science: Creating a Sustainable Future*, 6th edn, Jones and Bartlett Publishers, Sudbury, MA.

Commission on Global Governance (1995) *Our Global Neighbourhood*. Oxford University Press, Oxford.

de Simone, L. and Popoff, F. (1997) *Eco-efficiency: The Business Link to Sustainable Development*. MIT, Cambridge, MA.

Declaration of the Third International Conference on the Protection of the North Sea (1990) Preamble. Final Declaration of the Third International Conference on Protection of the North Sea, 7–8 March 1990. *International Environmental Law* **658**, 662–673.

DETR (1999) A Better Quality of Life: A Strategy for Sustainable Development for the United Kingdom. Department of the Environment, Transport and the Regions: London, From: http://www.sustainable-development.gov.uk/ (March 2003).

Foster, K.R., Vecchia, P. and Repacholi, M.H. (2000) Science and the Precautionary Principle, *Science*, May 2002, 979–981.

Friends of the Earth Netherlands (1990) *Action Plan for a Sustainable Netherlands*. Vereniging Milieudefense, Amsterdam.

IIED and WBCSD (2002) Breaking New Ground: Mining, Minerals and Sustainable Development. Final Report on the Mining, Minerals and Sustainable Development Project (MMSD). International Institute for Environment and Development and World Business Council for Sustainable Development. www.iied.org/mmsd (October 2002).

IISD (1992) Business Strategy for Sustainable Development: Leadership and Accountability for the 90s. The International Institute for Sustainable Development, Deloitte & Touche and the World Business Council for Sustainable Development.

International Factor 10 Club (1997) Statement to Governments and Business Leaders. Wuppertal Institute for Climate, Environment and Energy, Wuppertal.

IPCC (2001) Climate Change 2001: Impacts, Adaptation and Vulnerability, IPCC Third Assessment Report, Cambridge University Press.

Maxwell, S. (1999) The Meaning and Measurement of Poverty. ODI Poverty Briefings 3 February 1999.

McKinney, M. and Schoch, R.M. (2003) *Environmental Science: Systems and Solutions*, 3rd edn, Jones and Bartlett Publishers, Sudbury, MA.

McLaren, D., Bullock, S. and Yousuf, N. (1998) *Tomorrow's World: Britain's Share in a Sustainable Future*. Friends of the Earth, Earthscan, London.

McLaren, D. (2003) Sustainable Europe and Environmental Space: Achieving Sustainability through the Concept of Environmental Space: A Trans European Project, Article,

Friends of the Earth, http://www.foe.co.uk/resource/articles/sustain_europe_env_space. html (March, 2003).

Myers, N. (2002) Biodiversity. Presentation to the Foreign and Commonwealth Office. March 2002, London.

Perdan, S. and Azapagic, A. (2000) Sustainable Development and Industry: Ethical Indicators. Environmental Protection Bulletin, Issue 066, May 2000, IChemE.

Redefining Progress (2003) Ecological footprint. http://www.rprogress.org/programs/ sustainability/ef/ (March 2003).

UCS (2001) Action for Global Sustainability. http://www.ucsusa.org/.

UK Government (1995) This Common Inheritance. UK Annual Report 1995. HMSO, London.

UN (1982) World Charter for Nature. U.N. GA Resolution 37/7.

UN (1992) Rio Declaration on Environment and Development. 13 June 1992 (U.N. Doc./ CONF.151/5/Rev.1).

UNCSD (2002) Implementing Agenda 21 – Report of the Secretary-General, Commission on Sustainable Development Acting as the Preparatory Committee for the World Summit on Sustainable Development, Second session, 28 January–8 February 2002, http://www. johannesburgsummit.org/html/documents/no170793sgreport.pdf.

UNCSD (2003) Action for Sustainable Development, Sustainable Production and Consumption: Fact Sheet. www.uncsd.org.

UNDP (1998) Human Development Report 1998: Consumption for Human Development, United Nations Development Programme, Oxford University Press, Oxford.

UNDP (2001) Human Development Report 2001: Making New Technologies Work for Human Development, United Nations Development Programme, Oxford University Press, Oxford.

UNDP (2002) Human Development Report 2002: Deepening Democracy in a Fragmented World, United Nations Development Programme, Oxford University Press, Oxford.

UNDP–EU (1999a) Poverty & Environment Initiative: Attacking Poverty While Improving the Environment: Practical Recommendations. http://www.unesco.or.id/prog/cii/com-index/Database/undp.htm.

UNDP–EU (1999b) Poverty & Environment Initiative: Attacking Poverty While Improving the Environment: Towards Win-Win Policy Options. http://www.unesco.or.id/prog/cii/ com-index/Database/undp.htm.

UNEP (2000) Global Environment Outlook 2000, United Nations Environment Programme, Earthscan Publications, London.

UNEP (2002) Global Environment Outlook 2002, United Nations Environment Programme, Earthscan Publications, London.

UNEP/WWF/IUCN (1991) Caring for the Earth: A Strategy for Sustainable Living. International Union for Conservation of Nature, Gland. www.iucn.org.

UNEP/WWF/IUCNNF (1980) World Conservation Strategy. International Union for Conservation of Nature and Natural Resources, Gland. www.iucn.org.

von Weizsäcker, E., Lovins, A.B. and Lovins, L.H. (1997) Factor Four: Doubling Wealth – Halving Resource Use, Earthscan Publications, London, p. 244.

WBCSD (1996) Eco-efficiency Principles from WBCSD. Eco-efficient Leadership for Improved Economic and Environmental Performance. World Business Council for Sustainable Development, Geneva.

WBCSD (2000) Eco-efficiency: Creating More Value with Less Impact. http://www. wbcsd.org/DocRoot/02w8IK14V8E3HMIiFYue/EEcreating.pdf (March 2003).

WBCSD (2001) The Business Case for Sustainable Development: Making a Difference toward the Johannesburg Summit 2002 and Beyond. World Business Council for Sustainable Development, Geneva.

WCEC (2001) Melbourne Communiqué. 6th World Congress of Chemical Engineering, Melbourne, 24–28 September 2001.

WCED (1987) *Our common future*. World Commission on Environment and Development, Oxford University Press, Oxford.

World Bank (2000) *World Development Report 2000: Attacking Poverty*. Oxford University Press, New York.

WSSD (2002) Key Outcomes of the Summit. http://www.johannesburgsummit.org (October 2002).

2

The Role of the Professional Engineer and Scientist in Sustainable Development

Cynthia A. Mitchell, Anna L. Carew and Roland Clift

Summary

The practice of sustainable development requires a new approach from engineers and scientists: participation in open-decision processes, in a role which we call the Honest Broker of technical and scientific knowledge. This new role implies a different model of professional practice and requires a different approach to teaching and learning. Forecasting the future needs to be complemented by the approach of foresighting and backcasting, where combining scientific and engineering expertise with other approaches can lead to outcomes which are impossible to conceive within one perspective.

2.1 The New Model of Teaching, Learning and Practice

Chapter 1 introduced the concept of sustainable development and explored some of its philosophical implications. This chapter moves closer to the domain of the scientist and engineer by asking: *What does sustainability mean for the technical expert?* A principal thesis of this book is that the new paradigm embodied in the concept of sustainable development in turn requires a new role for engineers and scientists; their knowledge and professional skills are unchanged, but this professional expertise needs to be deployed in ways which may be unfamiliar, even uncomfortable. But it is also

Sustainable Development in Practice: Case Studies for Engineers and Scientists
Edited by Adisa Azapagic, Slobodan Perdan and Roland Clift
© 2004 John Wiley & Sons, Ltd   ISBNs: 0-470-85608-4 (HB); 0-470-85609-2 (PB)

part of the thesis that the new demands placed on the technical specialist actually make their role less mechanical and therefore more challenging and interesting.

This chapter explores the reasons for and implications of taking on a broader social role, to introduce the general themes illustrated by the case studies in later chapters. We start with the recognition, introduced in Chapter 1, that there are constraints on what humans can do with and on the planet, represented by constraints on natural resources, techno-economic capabilities and societal needs. Chapter 1 also showed why the new organisational approaches required for sustainable development require more public participation. These concerns define a new context within which technical decision-makers must work, which in turn demands changes in accustomed professional approaches. It will often be necessary for open-decision processes to involve "non-experts"; it is primarily this new emphasis on participative decision-making which leads to the new paradigm of the role of the technical expert.

Making sustainable technical decisions is contingent on the current and likely future environmental, social and economic context within which the decision will be enacted. It is the consideration of context which makes sustainability such a double-edged sword for practitioners of science and engineering. On the one hand, considering the context and making context-appropriate technological decisions might satisfy much contemporary critique of these professions (IEAust, 1996). On the other hand, rigorous consideration of context leads us away from the safe, high ground of "objective" surety and into a swamp of wild, complex and borderless problems (Schön, 1987) populated by human beings who have their own assumptions and objectives; that is their own concept of what is "rational". Some of the case studies in this book illustrate the kind of approach which is then needed.

Furthermore, sustainability requires a systems approach (Clayton and Radcliffe, 1996). Following the work of Checkland (1981), systems are recognised as possessing "emergent properties": attributes which cannot be discerned when a system is reduced or dissected into its component parts. The devalued word "holistic" implies "looking at the whole system". The case studies presented in this book all follow the systems approach: sustainability is an integrative principle, not a specific attribute.

This chapter also outlines the approaches to teaching and learning which we believe will enable the development of the new model of technical experts. We consider some of the challenges that educators face in training graduates to take on messy, contextualised, holistic problems. Specifically, we consider four questions:

1. What are the key skills and attitudes required of the new model expert? We suggest that sustainable decision-making requires a switch from "technology advocate" to the role of "Honest Broker" of technical information.
2. What are the implications of the new model of expertise for the accustomed structures and cultures of science and engineering? We explore the idea that sustainability calls for an exploration of new models of professionalism and a capacity to work with different conceptions of "rationality".
3. Why is active learning so necessary for teaching and learning a new model of expertise? We draw connections between our description of practice as honest broking and the attributes learners can develop through engagement in active learning processes like Problem-based Learning (PBL).
4. How can "foresighting" and "backcasting" assist in shaping our new approach? We offer a case study which demonstrates the significant opportunities available

to our Honest Broker and the synergies that are possible when we engage a diversity of views to deal with complex problems.

Our intent in this chapter is to stimulate without prescribing; to model the practices and principles we advocate; to use conceptual frameworks as learning supports, rather than creativity constraints (Scott, 2002). Our aim is to demonstrate how a reflective specialist works in practice; what it means to be a self-aware expert and how a self-aware expert can contribute to the most difficult and complex questions our societies face; and how multiple perspectives can add richness and lead to better outcomes for engineering and science, and for society in general.

2.2 The New Model Expert

2.2.1 Living within the Constraints

We start our exploration of the new role of the professional engineer or scientist[1] with the idea that "humans have attained the unprecedented capacity to modify the natural environment on a global scale, and with this capacity comes the need for a new type of responsibility" (Carew and Mitchell, 2002). We might think of this capacity for modification, in broad thermodynamic terms, as a series of resource, energy and waste flows between key global systems. In Figure 2.1, we represent the human economy and associated resource flows as a series of such transfers.

Energy (or, in more correct thermodynamic terms, exergy[2]) is needed to drive the material transformations carried out within the human economy. Before the industrial revolution 150 years ago, this energy came directly or indirectly from the sun. Since the industrial revolution, we have come to rely – almost completely in industrial societies – on non-renewable fossil fuels both for direct energy supply for industrial and domestic use and for producing the fertilisers used in intensive agriculture. Supplies of fossil fuels are finite, and when they are burned the carbon dioxide, "sequestered" when the coal or hydrocarbon is formed, is put back into the atmosphere. Whether availability of carbon-based fuels or the effect of the emissions on the global climate becomes an active constraint first is a matter for debate, but either way the present level of use of carbon-based fossil fuels cannot be sustainable. An approach to a sustainable energy policy which recognises this constraint is outlined as an example later in this chapter and further explored in Chapter 9, which outlines an approach to developing technical scenarios for future energy supply.

Figure 2.1 also illustrates the general material flows through the human economy, and shows "waste" as part of the economy. Wastes from both agricultural and industrial activities can be put to beneficial use in the same or other economic activities, an approach which is becoming known as Industrial Ecology (e.g. Clift, 2001). Waste which is not immediately reused can be stored as a resource for the

---

[1] The starting point is important because it inevitably brings key issues to the fore, suppresses other elements and begins the process of narrowing those problem solutions we might consider (Crofton, 2000).
[2] The part of energy that can be converted to useful work.

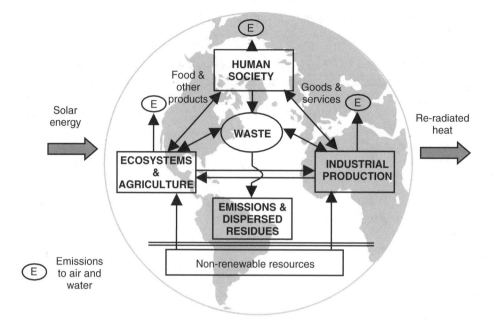

Figure 2.1   *Resource flows in the human economy (Adapted from Clift, 1995; reproduced by permission of The Royal Academy of Engineering.)*

future. We see examples of this in the reworking of old mine-tailings to extract precious metals, and in the "quarrying" of old landfills, partly to reclaim the land but also because they contain greater amounts of metal than some virgin ores. Materials are lost to the economy only when they are dispersed. However, even then they are not lost from the planet – all the human economy does is to emit them in a dilute high-entropy form.

The idea of using waste as a material resource is developed in Chapter 7 while Chapter 5 explores the idea of using waste to recover energy. To see the full environmental significance of material and energy flows, it is essential to look at the complete supply chain within an economic system. A systematic approach to carrying out such an analysis is known as life cycle thinking (e.g. Tillman and Baumann, 2003). Life Cycle Assessment (LCA) is a related tool, underpinned by life cycle thinking, which helps us identify and quantify the environmental impacts of an economic system from "cradle to grave" (see the Appendix at the end of the book). LCA is one of the tools of environmental systems analysis, an approach which uses systems thinking to examine the interactions between economic systems and the environment. Many case studies in this book take a life cycle approach to environmental analysis and illustrate the use of LCA for identifying environmentally more sustainable solutions to engineering and scientific problems. Chapter 8 uses a related but different environmental systems analysis tool, Material Flow Analysis (MFA), which enables us to understand the environmental implications of the flow of materials in the human economy.

The present behaviour of the human species is unsustainable: our use of non-renewable resources and our production of waste in support of human existence are depleting limited primary resources, whilst concurrently outstripping our planet's carrying capacity (Chapter 1). One of the primary drivers of this process of depletion is widely recognised to be the resource intensity of the high levels of consumption in the developed world. One way of expressing this resource intensity is the concept of the ecological footprint (Wackernagel and Reese, 1996), introduced in Chapter 1. The ecological footprint is an estimate of the total surface area of arable land which would be required to provide renewable resources and energy such that each person could maintain their current standard of living. This metric provides us with a sense of the share of resources taken up by individuals in different societies and cultures. Chapter 1 pointed out that the present level of global resource consumption already exceeds what the planet can sustain and that provision of the level of resource consumption enjoyed by the developed nations would require several "planet earths". Recognising the limits on resource consumption immediately raises the issue of equity in access to resources, within and between generations, which is at the heart of sustainable development. The issue of equity is explored in more detail in Chapter 1.

This resource intensity has unfortunate implications, some of which are already upon us (e.g. global climate change, loss of biodiversity, social inequity, etc.). So, how did we come to this? We would suggest that the resource intensity of our current lifestyles has resulted, in part, from decision processes which failed to account for limits and equity. Specifically:

– the limits to our global stock of non-renewable resources;
– the limits to the planet's carrying capacity (beyond which local and/or global systems would begin to change in ways we didn't like); and
– the rights of others (including future generations) to their share of these non-renewable goods, to their say in how they are used and to reasonably stable ecological, sociological and economic systems.

So one of the keys to sustainability lies in decision processes based on the principle of equity.

2.2.2 Sustainability and Transformation

The new imperatives introduced by sustainable development lead directly to the new role of the technical expert. Perhaps recognition of a new role is timely. Many groups are already calling for new models of professional practice, for example to maintain the status and authority of professional scientists and engineers, or to achieve greater diversity by encouraging the participation of women and other minority groups (IEAust, 1996). The new role in turn needs new approaches to teaching and learning which are explored later in section 2.3.

We have found it useful to represent the constraints which make sustainable development an imperative in the form of a simple Venn diagram – as illustrated in Figure 2.2. "Techno-centric concerns" represent human expertise and ingenuity – the skills we deploy as engineers and applied scientists, and the economic system within which we deploy them. "Eco-centric concerns" represent the ability of the

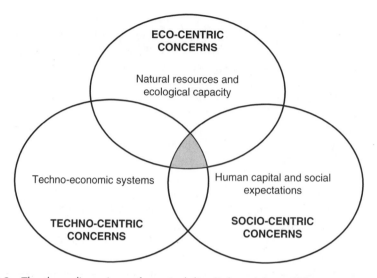

Figure 2.2   *The three dimensions of sustainability (Adapted from Clift, 1995; reproduced by permission of The Royal Academy of Engineering.)*

planet to sustain us – both the material and energy resources available to us, and the capacity of the earth to accommodate us and our emissions and wastes.[3] An important application of science is to identify and estimate these constraints. "Socio-centric concerns" represent human expectations – and aspirations – the needs of human beings to live worthwhile satisfying lives, summed up by the phrase "quality of life for everyone" (Chapter 1).

Sustainability can be thought of as the central region in the diagram where all three sets of constraints are met, while sustainable development is a trajectory which moves towards this central region. While unquestionably simplistic, Figure 2.2 reminds us that sustainable development means living equitably within all three types of long-term constraint: technology and science cannot be deployed as though they have no environmental or societal implications.[4] We would contend that traditional teaching, learning and practice in engineering and applied science have largely been confined within the techno-centric sphere. Our responsibility in decision-making has been to consider only those factors which fell within this sphere; for example, whether the technology would perform the requested task

[3] This interpretation in effect gives primacy to the economic dimension of sustainability: ecosystem sustainability is defined in instrumental terms so that the scientific analysis should estimate productivity in terms of parameters like "maximum sustainable yield". However, ecosystem sustainability can also be framed in ways that include intrinsic value, not presuming that an ecosystem is merely a "resource" to be managed. Put another way, we have presented Figure 2.2 focusing on the ability of the planet to support us, rather than on the ability of the biosphere to support itself. This conflict between different ends illustrates why the way in which a problem is framed is an important part of a decision process, and illustrates why the use of scientific analysis is dependent on the context. For further discussion of this general issue, see Owens and Cowell (2002).

[4] The debate over whether scientific knowledge can be separated from its social context is by no means new (section 2.3.2).

rapidly, reliably and cost-effectively, that is, to "do the thing right" (Holt, 1997). But the imperatives represented in Figure 2.1 refute the idea that we can continue to operate only within this constrained sphere.

The necessity of reducing our resource intensity leads us straight into the heart of the eco-centric sphere, by extending our professional responsibility for the judicious use of non-renewable resources and waste sinks. We now review the role of engineers and scientists in the scheme of transformations from the "means" represented by natural raw materials to the goal, or "ends", of sustainable satisfaction of human wellbeing.

The concept of *means* and *ends* was articulated by Daly (1973) to describe how natural capital[5] is related to human wellbeing. His intent was to situate the human economy in the context of a hierarchy of processes resting on natural resources. Twenty years later, Donnella Meadows and her colleagues selected this concept as the best-available framework for sustainable development indicators.[6] According to Meadows (1998), the goal of a sustainable society is to produce the greatest possible ends with the least possible means. Thus, Daly's means and ends hierarchy would appear to have significant standing amongst leading sustainability thinkers, and his term "wellbeing" is an acceptable proxy for sustainability.

In this context, we use the means and ends hierarchy for a different purpose: to identify the main players in each transformation. But first, the concept is described in Table 2.1.

Daly begins by acknowledging wellbeing as the ultimate purpose or end for which humans strive and natural capital as the ultimate means of attaining wellbeing. According to his model, there are three basic transformations. First, science and technology transform natural capital into built and human capital, identified as our intermediate means. Our society's political economy transforms these intermediate means to the intermediate ends of human and social capital. Finally, through philosophy and ethics, these intermediate ends are transformed to our ultimate goal of wellbeing. Daly also acknowledges that our economy focuses exclusively on the central transformation (no. 2 in Table 2.1) and systematically ignores the lower and upper transformations.

Daly described the transformations in terms of discourses. We propose to describe the transformations in terms of the primary actors because our interest is in the role of engineers and scientists in these processes.[7] Professional engineers and scientists are primarily responsible for the transformation of natural capital into built capital and human capital. Professionals working in fields such as accounting, business, commerce, economics, finance, law, government, politics, psychology and sociology transform these intermediate means to human and social capital. Finally, assisted by the actions of professionals working in fields such as history, philosophy, ethics,

---

[5] One of the five forms of capital (Chapter 1), which provides a continuing income of ecosystem benefits such as biological diversity, mineral resources, and clean air and water.

[6] Meadows explains each of the forms of capital in some detail and provides many thought-provoking ideas for what indicators we might choose to describe them meaningfully. Here, we use her descriptors to exemplify the *means* and *ends* concept.

[7] We recognise that many factors and actors influence each transformation, and that engineers and scientists could be and probably are involved in all kinds of transformations. However, for the purpose of this chapter, we focus on those primarily responsible for each transformation.

Table 2.1 *Primary actors in the transformation of natural capital to wellbeing (Daly, 1973; Meadows, 1998)*

Daly's model		Meadows's descriptors
Ends and means	**Capital**	
Ultimate means	Natural	Solar energy, biosphere, earth materials, biogeochemical cycles
		TRANSFORMATION 1
		Science and engineering transform natural capital into built and human capital
Intermediate means	Built and human	Labour, tools, factories, processed raw materials
		TRANSFORMATION 2
		Political economy transforms built capital into human and social capital
Intermediate ends	Human and social	Health, wealth, leisure, mobility, knowledge, communication, consumer goods
		TRANSFORMATION 3
		Philosophy and ethics transform human and social capital into wellbeing
Ultimate ends	Spiritual	Happiness, harmony, identity, fulfilment, self-respect, wellbeing, community, transcendence, enlightenment

cultural studies and religion, these intermediate ends are transformed into our well-being. At each transformation, the actions of the professionals are responsive to and mediated and influenced by the expressed desires of citizens.

This means-to-ends transformation shows that the technological actions of scientists and engineers are a necessary but not sufficient condition to progress from our ultimate means of natural capital to our ultimate ends of wellbeing. Meadows describes the implications of problems with each transformation. For the primary transformation, she states:

> If there is wisdom about ultimate ends but no technology for tapping ultimate means, the wisdom will rest on a foundation of physical scarcity. If technologies are destructive of the ultimate means, the entire structure will crumble at its foundations, regardless of the excellence of its upper levels.

Put another way, if the ultimate ends are not part of our collective thinking, planning and decision processes, then the tools, actions and strategies (Robèrt, 2000) we apply as engineers and scientists could well go awry. Occupying a particular position in the means–ends hierarchy infers particular responsibilities in terms of risks and decisions. In the next section, we explore different kinds of decisions and the implications for scientists and engineers.

2.2.3 Decision Processes

Sustainability asks us to step away from the role of "objective decision-maker" and enter the complex, value-laden, didactic realm of social priorities, social acceptability and participatory processes. In other words, we now need to know that we are "doing the right thing" as well as "doing the thing right" (Holt, 1997). We also need to recognise that much of the scientific knowledge which we rely on has inherent uncertainties (e.g. Chapters 3 and 12) going beyond mere statistical imprecision. All of this lies behind the need for a new approach to decision-making.

The conventional role of a technical expert has not disappeared, but the specialist must be able to recognise when the role needed is that of technical decision-maker and when it is the role which we have called *Honest Broker* (as discussed further in section 2.2.4). Figure 2.3 shows a classification of decision processes which helps to clarify the role.[8]

The key question is whether the objectives or criteria to be used in selecting one option as preferable to the others have been agreed in advance. Within a purely commercial organisation, the criteria will have been agreed, either explicitly or implicitly, for example, in terms of short- and long-term economic returns and share value, which is in turn affected by the company's reputation which depends *inter alia* on environmental performance. It is common to express environmental performance in terms of a set of quantified environmental impact categories (Clift, 2001) using, for example, LCA as a tool (as defined in the Appendix at the end of the book).

Within this broad class of decisions, to the left in Figure 2.3, there are two sub-classes depending on whether the objectives have been aggregated into a single number. For example, environmental impacts are sometimes assigned relative weights so that they can be aggregated into a single metric or "environmental score". The ecological footprint introduced in Chapter 1 is one example of an aggregated metric of environmental impact. Another common approach is to express impacts as estimates of damage costs, which can then be considered along with conventional economic costs,[9] as, for example, illustrated in the case study in Chapter 4. When

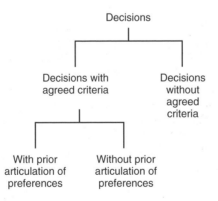

Figure 2.3   *A taxonomy of decisions*

[8] The idea behind Figure 2.3 comes from multi-objective optimisation (Cohon, 1978; Azapagic and Clift, 1999). However, the terminology has been modified to that used in Environmental Systems Analysis (e.g. Wrisberg and Udo de Haes, 2002).
[9] It should be clearly understood that we are not advocating the cost–benefit approach to decision-making except under very specific circumstances determined by the categorisation in Figure 2.3.

pre-agreed weights are attached to all the different criteria, the decision is reduced to selecting or optimising on the basis of a single parameter. This approach can be useful and valid when the decisions are routine and each individual decision has limited significance: an example is selection of material and components for a manufactured product.

For more strategic decisions such as selection between alternative investments or technical processes, it is usually considered preferable not to aggregate the objectives into a single metric because this conceals information and can lead to sub-optimal solutions. Instead, the trade-off between different criteria is considered explicitly as part of the decision process. The principal role of the technical specialist is now to present all the necessary information in a readily intelligible form, usually using various optimisation techniques. Structured approaches to multi-criteria decision analysis are widely used (Triantaphyllou, 2000; Belton and Stewart, 2002); one such approach is illustrated in Chapter 12.

The foregoing types of decision still incorporate the traditional role of the technical specialist (although where there is large uncertainty, the approach may need to be modified to use some aspects of the deliberative approach which is about to be introduced). It is the type of decision on the right of Figure 2.3, where defining the objectives or criteria must be part of the decision process, which really involves the new paradigm and requires the expert to act as Honest Broker. Substantive decisions in the public domain are likely to fall within this class. Examples include setting environmental standards (RCEP, 1998), use of land and natural habitats, and more mundane but nevertheless contentious public decisions such as road developments or waste-management facilities (see Chapter 5 for a discussion of the latter). Failure to recognise that deciding on the objectives has to be treated as part of the decision process has generated some of the most acrimonious disputes in developed countries in recent decades (Clift, 1999).

Sustainability puts even more weight on the problems which move decisions to the right of Figure 2.3. The resulting context and approach have been particularly articulated by Funtowicz and Ravetz (e.g. Funtowicz and Ravetz, 1990; Ravetz, 1997; Funtowicz *et al.*, 1999). Decisions must be made in the face of missing information and uncertainty over the confidence which can be placed on the information which is available. Decisions affect, and therefore need to involve, a broad range of stakeholders who may have different views on what attributes distinguish better from less desirable options. The systems about which decisions must be made may be complex, to the point where their behaviour may not be predictable. Furthermore, particularly when sustainability is concerned, the decision stakes are high.

Funtowicz and Ravetz have introduced a general methodology for managing complex decisions involving uncertainty and plural values; it is known as *post-normal science*. The idea is shown schematically in Figure 2.4. Decisions with low uncertainty and relatively low stakes are the conventional province of the professional engineer or scientist. When the stakes or uncertainty are higher, routine professional expertise may not be enough: specialist skill and judgement are needed, perhaps along with the willingness to take risks. Funtowicz and Ravetz call this kind of activity *professional consultancy*.

When the stakes and/or uncertainty are high, we are in the realm of post-normal science. In cases of post-normal science,

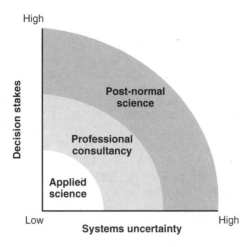

Figure 2.4 *Post-normal science (Ravetz, 1993; reprinted from FUTURES, Vol. 25, No. 7, Ravetz 'Science for the post normal age', pp. 735–755, Copyright 1993, with permission from Elsevier.)*

the contribution of all the stakeholders.... is not merely a matter of broader democratic participation... These new problems are in many ways different from those of research science, professional practice or industrial development... Quality depends on open dialogue between all those affected. This we call an 'extended peer community', consisting not merely of persons with some form.... of institutional accreditation, but rather of all those with a desire to participate in the resolution of the issue.

Funtowicz et al. (1999)

Thus the concept of post-normal science offers a paradigm for public participation in decision processes. It recognises that the knowledge needed to reach an accepted decision does not reside solely with the technical experts.[10] This is the context in which the technical expert must act as Honest Broker, to ensure that the scientific and technical information is presented clearly and without bias. The UK Royal Commission on Environmental Pollution (RCEP, 1998) has proposed a kind of deliberative decision process which Funtowicz *et al.* (1999) describe as "a sort of manual for post-normal science". Although developed as an approach to setting environmental standards, the RCEP's model can be applied much more widely to decisions in the class on the right of Figure 2.3.

2.2.4   The Technical Expert as "Honest Broker"

In essence, we see the foundation of a new model of expertise as being that of the honest broking of technical information. Sustainable science and engineering may

---

[10] The role of the "lay expert" is also the topic of a body of literature (e.g. Irwin, 2003). The extent to which procedures to implement the post-normal science approach can meet the democratic criterion of representativity is a matter for discussion (e.g. Owens and Cowell, 2002).

call on the new model expert to take an entirely new approach to professional decision-making. The new approach we envisage asks the expert to take a longer-term, broader-scale, systems perspective on environmental impacts (Crofton, 2000); to engage a range of stakeholders in consultative decision processes; and to practise personal quality assurance through self-critical and reflective practice.

We now examine the skills, knowledge and attitudes associated with these new modes of practice. Our description of the new model of expertise is not meant to be prescriptive; rather it is intended to provoke reflection and to support considered choice on the modes of practice and domains within which we might choose to operate. The foundation of the new model of expertise, honest broking, extends beyond the bounds of the traditional techno-centric preserve in Figure 2.2. Rather than deciding, designing and presenting a technological solution to a pre-defined problem, the Honest Broker is an expert who investigates and describes a range of technical options for the realisation of a desired service within the broad contextual constraints of the problem-setting. This archetype provides a range of vehicles which might transport the expert to more sustainable modes of professional practice and expands the bounds of engineering and science in three ways: moving away from singular, prescribed technology; engaging with problem formulation; and considering the problem in context.

The Honest Broker paradigm moves the technical expert away from propounding "the right answer" and towards offering a range of technological options. Investigating and communicating a range of different technological options contrasts with the more traditional role of a designer and advocate of a particular technological solution. The difficulty of fulfilling this role is not to be underestimated: it calls on the specialist to withhold judgement, to be explicit about their own values and perspective, and to accept that a wide range of stakeholder perspectives and priorities (rather than elegant technical or economical design alone) will determine the eventual decision.

Honest broking offers a platform from which technical experts may choose to brave the conceptual and emotional leap into consultative decision processes. The umbrella term "consultation" (as distinct from professional consultancy) is applied to many forms of engagement with stakeholders. These range from *informing*, through *bargaining*, to processes like *deliberation, participation* and *consensus-making*. These different approaches to consultation represent different degrees of challenge and opportunity for the technical expert. An informing approach requires little time and, more significantly, allows the specialist to maintain control over and responsibility for the decision process and outcome. Stakeholders are merely kept up to date with decisions and outcomes. At the other end of our consultation spectrum, approaches like deliberation and consensus-making present a radical and unsettling shift from some traditional modes of practice and assumptions of expertise. These approaches are more likely to recognise stakeholders as experts in their own needs and wants, and allow them substantive power in guiding decision process and determining preferred options. Some commentators suggest that the loss of decision-making power in adopting such approaches would be well compensated by the gains in public enfranchisement and more contextually appropriate decision outcomes (RCEP, 1998; Fawcett and Roberts, 2002).

A second way in which the Honest Broker paradigm expands the bounds of science and engineering is in moving beyond problem solution towards problem formulation. Approaches such as those recommended by the RCEP (1998) emphasise that "framing" the problem has to be treated as part of the decision process, to set the agenda, focus and limits to the range of solutions we might generate (Crofton, 2000). Problem solution asks us as professionals to apply our technical skills and expertise to a problem *as defined by our client*, and to come up with an appropriate solution within the financial, legislative and technical constraints of the client's operating environment. In engaging with problem formulation, the Honest Broker has the opportunity to explore a much wider range of solutions including envisioning the problem in terms of service provision as opposed to the design, operation and maintenance of a process or technology. Shifting from selling products to providing services is another paradigm shift, often seen as necessary to achieve more efficient use of resources (Clift, 2001).

A third way in which the Honest Broker presents a new paradigm lies in the expanded focus offered during problem formulation. Problem formulation asks that the specialist considers the problem in terms of its broader context – environmental, social and economic. This raises some interesting and profound "why are we here" type of questions. These might include questions about how we justify our traditional planning horizons; how we construct borders around the borderless systems in which technical problems exist; about the notions of "client" and "stakeholder"; and where we place the boundaries to a specialist's professional responsibilities and expertise. One way of engaging with these fundamental questions is through reflective

Educating a new generation of technical experts as 'Honest Brokers' at the University of Surrey. Photograph by H. Wickens.

practice (Schön, 1987). Reflective practice can operate on a number of different levels (Fien, 1996) but, in broad terms, we suggest that the new model of expertise would have the inclination and ability to reflect on, question and critique the fundamental assumptions and values which inform their day-to-day practice. This self-critical process could provide a mechanism for personal quality assurance. This process of quality assurance would take the form of heightened awareness of the role that socio-political and cultural mechanisms, subjectivity and personal values play in guiding professional decision-making (Taylor, 2002).

Honest broking questions some of the conventions and assumptions upon which we as technical experts teach, learn and practise our trade. We offer the Honest Broker as a foundation or first step towards more sustainable science and engineering. This shift to honest broking, and into the realm of a new model of expertise, may rest on more visceral questioning about the worldviews and cultures which form the often unexamined foundation to professional science and engineering practice. In the next section, we explore where some of these questions might lead.

2.3 Implications for Practice, Teaching and Learning

So far we have set out our conceptions about how natural capital is transformed to the ultimate end of sustainability, and the roles and responsibilities of engineers and scientists in that process. We have argued for the Honest Broker as the new model of expertise in engineering teaching, learning and practice. Articulating our place in the scheme of things, and describing a new model of practice, teaching and learning, is relatively easy. Working out what is required to put these ideas into practice is more difficult. The professions of science and engineering have strongly developed and well-established worldviews and cultures. These determine the nature of engineering and science practice, teaching and learning. In this section, we identify the implications of our new model for existing cultures and worldviews.

Sustainability calls for explicit inclusion of values in actions, and alignment between values and actions. This kind of thinking has many proponents outside the field of sustainability (e.g. in education, Biggs, 1999; in management, Covey, 1990; in professional practice, generally, Argyris and Schön, 1978). Argyris and Schön coined the terms "espoused theory" and "theory-in-use" to describe what we say versus what we do. They describe reflective practice as that which enables explicit consideration and articulation of the motivations behind our actions. In other words, in reflective practice, our theory-in-use is constantly evaluated against our espoused theory so that the two are at least aligned if not one and the same. In the sections that follow, we propose theories for professional practice, teaching and learning consistent with our new model of expertise, and contrast those with current espoused theories and theories-in-use.

2.3.1 Implications for Practice

Models of professional practice can be broadly categorised as having either a *social contract* or a *business orientation*. A social contract practice model (Taylor, 1995) requires the profession to hold the protection and benefit of society above all else and, in particular, above the protection or benefit of a client or colleague. We contrast this with a *business model* (Taylor, 1995) in which personal advancement, clients and colleagues are paramount. These represent the two ends of a very wide spectrum of possibilities.

The professional practice model for the Honest Broker could conceivably have elements of both. The Honest Broker model of professional practice would encourage reflective practice to explicitly recognise and appropriately integrate all three categories of constraints: ecological, social and economic, both in theory and in practice. How does this compare with current theories espoused and in use?

Many professional bodies and institutions have at their core a Code of Ethics which represents the bond between society and the profession. Codes of Ethics represent the espoused theory of professional science and engineering institutions, and tend towards a social contract model of practice. However, engineering practice appears to be largely unexamined (Green, 2002; Fawcett and Roberts, 2002) and tends towards a business model (Taylor, 1995), indicating a lack of reflection and a lack of alignment between our espoused theory and our theory-in-use. So, from this angle, the new model of expertise raises two challenges: first, we need to develop an espoused theory of professional practice that fully reflects sustainability and, secondly, we need to align our espoused theory and the theory we use in practice.

2.3.2   Implications for Teaching

In section 2.2.3, we argued that Honest Brokers must be able to discern when the kind of professional approach usually regarded as "objective" is appropriate and when subjectivity needs to be brought into play. This call, which is again neither new nor particular to the field of sustainability, demands an appreciation of the value of both perspectives. As the guardians, maintainers and purveyors of our existing body of knowledge, educators have a special responsibility in developing this ability in themselves and in our Honest Brokers in training. To explore what this implies, we review perspectives on the nature of knowledge (epistemology) in science and engineering, and the implications for teaching and training.

Placing a premium on intellectual objectivity results in the assumption that knowledge can be abstracted and codified in lectures and textbooks (Blackburn, 1971). Thus, engineering and science educators have traditionally been concerned with the transmission of an objectively defined body of knowledge and practice (Green, 2002).

Thirty years ago, in an article in *Science*, Thomas Blackburn (1971) outlined how science's claim of amorality and objectivity made it incomplete. He described the need for something "other" to create a whole, something which is contradictory without being incompatible. The result, far from being a compromise, is synergistic and therefore richer, as is elegantly demonstrated by Niels Bohr's notion of complementarity in understanding the behaviour of electrons, that is, that it is possible to conceive of an electron as both a particle and a wave. Blackburn, an ecologist, argued that complementarity was necessary to understand complex natural systems, using the terms "intellectual" and "sensuous" to describe the two halves of his whole.

We see these terms as synonyms for objectivity and subjectivity, for quantitative and qualitative understandings.

The debate over the relationship between scientific knowledge and its social context has been pursued by philosophers of science such as Ravetz (1971). However, engineer or scientist's lack of an inherent introspective or philosophic tradition means that we have tended to view the world in the precise terms of mathematical and scientific models, rather than to engage with its real "messiness" (Taylor, 2002). In our case study in section 2.4, we explain how inherent uncertainties foil our objective and predictive attempts at forecasting in precise mathematical ("objective") terms, and show how this problem can be turned to our advantage.

From an objective standpoint, industrial design is about selecting the best technology to solve a well-specified objective; social, political and economic influences compromise the ideal design (Green, 2002). Earlier, we explained that engaging with context requires us to leap into the swamp of messy, ill-defined problems. An Honest Broker would see design as an evolutionary, participatory process with clients and stakeholders, each expert in their own needs and each with a legitimate place at the decision-making table. Defining the design objectives becomes part of this process.

Even the context is messy and ill-defined. Much as we might like to retain the espoused theory that there is a "best" solution for every problem, notions of sustainability are many and varied (Chapter 1), even amongst engineering academics. This diversity is real. It reflects both our subjectivity and our lack of reflective practice, since our theory-in-use is not aligned with our espoused theory. It also demonstrates differences in our values. All of this diversity is cause for celebration, and should be made explicit in our practising, learning and teaching sustainability.

Scott (2002) makes a bold statement about the responsibility of sustainability educators for their learners and for themselves as learners. He proposes that the role of sustainability educators is to stimulate without prescribing; to use conceptual frameworks as learning supports, rather than creativity restraints; and to see themselves as learners, that is to keep an open mind on the meaning of sustainability. Scott argues that "to do less seems neglectful; to do more risks indoctrination". We see this as reflective practice in teaching.

So, a model for teaching Honest Brokers would encompass both objectivity and subjectivity, and would explain the need to develop the skills to differentiate between simple[11] problems where one right answer will suffice; complicated problems requiring contextual problem formulation where there is more than one right answer; and complex problems requiring contextual formulation as well as participatory solutions.

2.3.3   Implications for Learning

According to Scott (2002), learning how to learn is the single most important goal for sustainable development. In contrast to Scott's notions, emphasising

---

[11] Based on the problem classification hierarchy set out in section 2.2.3.

"professional objectivity" has implications for learning as well as the implications for teaching discussed in the previous section. It leads to the mistaken assumption that what is taught is the same as what is learned (Prosser and Trigwell, 1999) and rejects the idea that learning is inherently intuitive and experiential (Marton and Booth, 1997).

Scott proposes four principles for learning how to learn. We see Scott's principles as consistent with our new model of expertise, and with learning at all levels, that is learning for professional formation and learning for reflective practice and teaching. We reproduce the principles here, and link them to our arguments:

1. *Help the learner understand why consideration of sustainability is in their inter-est*:   Motivation is a key issue in facilitating quality learning.
2. *Use appropriate pedagogies for active engagement with issues*:   Active engagement is the key for engineers and scientist to make the most of their potential role in sustainable development – we suggest a model for active learning later in this chapter.
3. *Help learners gain plural perspectives*:   Professional awareness (a view to context, both ours and others) and personal awareness (a view to values, both ours and others) are essential for engineering and science to adequately play their part in the transformation of natural capital to wellbeing.
4. *Encourage learners to continue thinking about such issues beyond their formal education*:   Reflective practice is all about continuing to revisit our conceptions of the ecological, socio-political and techno-economic constraints on sustainable development.

We now explore how teachers of sustainable engineering and science might use active learning to enact some of the principles Scott proposes.

2.3.4   Active Learning, Active Teaching

The new model of expertise requires acceptance of new ways of thinking and acting. Given rapidly changing expectations of professional competence, and the fact that understanding of sustainability is still developing, learning needs to continue beyond formal education. Still following the approach articulated by Scott (2002), the appropriate teaching and learning processes for sustainability correspond to *active learning*. Active learning invites the student to "practise the art of enquiry" through dynamic interaction with what they are learning. The actively engaged student will read, speak, think, listen and do, and will develop and apply higher-order thinking skills like analysis, critique and synthesis. This approach to teaching and learning can be tailored to support personal development by encouraging reflective examin-ation of, for example, ethical frameworks and values. In contrast, *passive learning* which fits more comfortably with the concept of "professional objectivity" (Green, 2002) is often characterised as "knowledge delivery" from teacher to learner, with the learner expected to receive, absorb and recall the knowledge uncritically.

Problem-based Learning is an approach to active learning in which the student engages with real-life, complex problems. Students generally work in self-directed project teams, on problems which are open-ended but fall within a defined context. The process of addressing the problem is at least as important as the outcome, if the student is to develop a reflective approach. PBL naturally lends itself to the development of Honest Brokers.

Table 2.2 sets out a possible approach based, in part, on a model known as Reiterative PBL (Ryan, 1999) which was designed to develop the skills of effective reasoning and participative learning. The stages in this model of PBL follow the requirements of post-normal science (section 2.2.3). The first four steps address problem formulation. The students are introduced to a realistic problem defined by one or more clients (A). They then start to assess the uncertainties in the problem and its context, and identify the stakeholders who will make up the extended peer

Table 2.2   *Stages in Problem-based Learning (PBL) for the Honest Broker*

Teacher's role	Learner or project team's role
(A) Meeting the problem situation	
Teacher introduces the problem "as defined by the client" (or students are given guidance on selecting an appropriate problem) Details of problem presented as they would be in professional practice Familiarises students with expected processes (e.g. reiterative PBL, team management, reflective practice)	Learners evaluate their own knowledge, values and reasoning abilities associated with the problem Project team "takes stock" of cumulative knowledge, values and reasoning abilities Team judges likely impact of (a) and (b) on their engagement with the problem (reflective practice)
(B) Characterising the problem situation (based on section 2.2.3)	
Teacher leads discussion on assessing levels of uncertainty, and identifying stakeholders or "extended peer community" (EPC) Teacher provides a critique and feedback on team's judgements of uncertainty and identification of EPC	Project team evaluates the level of uncertainty associated with the problem situation, and identifies an EPC Team judges likely impact of individual and team values, assumptions, skills, reasoning abilities and knowledge of the problem on judgement of uncertainty and identification of EPC (reflective practice)
(C) Positioning the extended peer community	
Teacher provides guidance on investigating the values, perspectives and priorities of the EPC (mechanisms might include interviewing, role-play, literature review, Internet enquiry) Critiques position papers, etc.	Learners synthesise, justify and represent various EPC positions on the problem (mechanisms might include position papers, oral presentations) Team uses reflective practice to judge the quality of their EPC positioning
(D) Framing the problem (based on section 2.2.4)	
Teacher provides guidance on defining objectives of the problem solution and criteria by which various problem solutions might be judged Facilitates, guides or informs processes for reconciling or trading-off competing objectives	Project teams describe the objectives of the problem solution as defined by the various EPC positions (students may be asked to reconcile or trade-off competing objectives) Teams describe the criteria by which various problem solutions will be judged based on EPC positions

Critiques objectives and criteria	Teams use reflective practice to judge the quality of objectives and criteria Teams use objectives, criteria and reflection as basis for identifying what they need to learn or investigate

(E) Identifying and investigating potential solutions (based on section 2.2.4)[a]

Teacher provides guidance on the means of investigating and evaluating a range of technical and non-technical solutions (might include providing information resources, acting as technical consultant, critiquing design or analysis calculations)	Project team identifies and investigates a preliminary range of technical and non-technical solutions appropriate to satisfy the EPC's objectives Preliminary evaluation of the costs and benefits of each according to the EPC's criteria Team reflects on identification, investigation and evaluation processes

(F) Communicating potential solutions (based on sections 2.2.3 and 2.2.4)

Teacher creates realistic setting for feedback and discussion on proposed solutions (e.g. oral presentation to other learners) Facilitates diverse feedback on proposed solutions (could be by technical critique, consultant, critiquing design or analysis calculations, strategic questioning, role-play)	Project team communicates the preliminary costs and benefits of each solution in medium and appropriate language to EPC (e.g. flow diagrams, written or oral reporting, sketches) Project team gathers comments and questions on proposed solutions Identify a smaller field of "preferred options" (these may include options from outside the range of potential solutions offered by the project team) Team reflects on communication and feedback processes

(G) Reiterating the investigation into preferred options and communicating potential solutions[b]

Teacher repeats (E) and (F) providing closer critique	Project team repeats (E) at a greater level of detail and accuracy Team once again communicates costs and benefits of preferred options and seeks feedback from EPC (F)

(H) Reflective summary

	Individual learners review personal and group reflection to generate appreciation of how and what they have learned, and a sense of what they still need to learn

[a] This is the more accustomed starting point in teaching problem-solving for engineers and scientists.
[b] This step may be repeated if the teaching and learning objective is for the project teams to arrive at a final solution.

review community (B). The problem and its context are examined from the perspectives represented by this extended group (C), and the problem is framed by developing the objectives and criteria defining desirable solutions (D). Potential solutions are identified (E), and then expounded and discussed (F). Steps E and F are repeated in progressively more detail (G). Finally, the outcome and processes are reviewed (H) so that each student can identify and embed what they have learned from the experience.

Consistent with the concept of the Honest Broker, the problem is "solved" at the stage of communicating the relative merits of a range of preferred options. We draw attention to this for two reasons. One is that this may feel like an uncomfortable stopping place for engineers and scientists in training and for their teachers who may be accustomed to providing *one right answer*. Another reason is that the point of this kind of learning is not to find the right answer, but rather to find the "right" questions and to develop the capacity and inclination to answer those questions in an insightful, critical and consultative way.

A shift to PBL may be challenging. Part of this challenge arises from the adjustment required in educators and learners' mind-sets: moving away from more traditional modes of teaching, learning and assessment asks teachers and learners to adopt new roles and take on potentially unaccustomed responsibilities (Little, 1999). As is apparent from Table 2.2, the locus of responsibility for learning rests much more firmly with the student. The teachers' responsibilities change from "knowledge delivery" to facilitator, consultant, critic, client, stakeholder and troubleshooter. The way in which a teacher deploys these new roles will vary depending on the problem, desired learning outcomes, educational setting and the stage of development of the learners. This represents a challenging shift for teachers of science and engineering, who may be skilled at and derive great satisfaction from the more accustomed process of delivering "objective" knowledge.

Importantly, PBL for the Honest Broker engages the learner in the problem and context prior to theoretical or formal learning. This approach follows an inductive model of learning (Farrell and Hesketh, 2000) and contrasts with the deductive approach more commonly used in engineering and science education. The deductive approach assumes that the learner can have nothing meaningful to contribute to addressing a problem until they have mastered the theory (fundamentals first, application second). In contrast, the inductive approach recognises that no learner arrives at a learning situation as an "empty vessel", and also uses the problem as a vehicle to define and reinforce theoretical learning (Farrell and Hesketh, 2000).

Learning by case studies is consistent with and follows the PBL approach. In the rest of this book, through the case studies, students, professionals and teachers are encouraged to learn and teach actively by critique, participation and communication, and reflective thinking. But before we invite you to sample some of these studies in Part II of the book, we return to the Honest Brokers for the final discussion on their role in sustainable development.

2.4   The Honest Broker in Practice: Back to the Future

We have argued that sustainability represents a range of desired future states of the planet, part of the full range of possible futures. In this section, we bring together this vision with humanity's fascination with predicting the future. We then explore what happens when our Honest Broker responds by setting out to forecast or foresee the future. To balance the limitations of forecasting, we introduce the concept of foresighting and backcasting, and show that they can work well together for our new model of expertise. We conclude this section with a case study concerned with climate change and energy policy, exemplifying the role of engineers and scientists in collaboration with other disciplines and perspectives. The case study involves actors from all three of the means–ends transformations introduced in section 2.2.2. Our intent is to demonstrate the role of the Honest Broker and the powerful synergies that are possible when we engage a diversity of views to deal with complex problems.

2.4.1   The Limits of Prediction (or Flaws in the Crystal Ball)

Humans have always sought to predict the future, although the responsibility for doing this has been shared, in variable degrees, between religion and science. Since the first development of the scientific paradigm as a way of viewing and understanding the world, science has been concerned with prediction. Global climate change models are one of the most recent scientific expressions of our desire to know the future.

Our ability to predict the future, particularly with complex mathematical models, is constrained by fundamental uncertainties. These uncertainties take on particular forms when dealing with complex societal issues over long periods of time, such as the wide-ranging changes required in industrialised societies in order to achieve sustainable development, and the long time required (at least several decades) to implement such changes. Building on Dreborg (1996), Robinson (2003) proposes three sources of these uncertainties: the limitations of our knowledge concerning system conditions and dynamics (uncertainty in Dreborg's terms); the certainty of innovation and surprise (Dreborg terms this "indeterminacy"); and the intentional nature of human decision-making.[12] For "natural" systems such as the global climate, indeterminacy must include the case of non-linear dynamic systems which show chaotic behaviour, and are therefore inherently unpredictable when they can switch from one state to another.

Engineers and scientists are already adept in developing, applying and interpreting models. The key differences in modelling for sustainability lie in going beyond causal thinking in the relationships we model, making the assumptions which underpin our models both explicit and open to change, and engaging with multiple perspectives on the context and the personal and professional values inherent in the system under study.

Forecasting is the process of predicting how a system is likely to develop, based on current and historical behaviour often with some sensitivity analysis to assess the uncertainty in the predictions. Inasmuch as forecasting uses formulaic modelling, it is at the core of objectivist engineering and science practice, teaching and learning. Forecasting is most effective when the system is relatively stable and the planning horizon is relatively short. It is generally unreliable when major discontinuities are possible, the planning horizon is long (typically 10 years or more for the kind of

---

[12] The question of intentionality in human action has long been a topic of study in the history of philosophy and science. There are essentially two schools of thought: causal and teleological. Dreborg (1996) presents an insightful discussion on how both are meaningful in the context of future studies and sustainability.

system of concern for sustainable development) or when interdependencies between system elements or the system's environment are likely to change.

For complicated and complex problems, the effectiveness of forecasting is constrained by the uncertainties inherent in our models. Although forecasting often incorporates sensitivity analyses, these are limited by the first two sources of uncertainty explained above: limitations in our understanding of the systems we are modelling; and our inability to predict the results of innovation or some kinds of change. These limitations imply that forecasting deals poorly with context. Earlier, we argued that recognising and working with the context of a problem is one of three fundamental expansions necessary for the Honest Broker in practice. The third source of uncertainty suggests that forecasting deals poorly with values. Reflecting on, respecting and engaging with the personal and professional values of ourselves and others represent the other two expansion dimensions for our new model of expertise. The importance of values for the Honest Broker in practice is demonstrated clearly in the case study presented in Chapter 13.

2.4.2   Complementary Futures

The most likely short-term future, foretold by forecasting, may not be the most desirable future. Whereas forecasting starts from now and tries to project forward, *foresighting* is an approach which starts by projecting future scenarios, typically presented as narratives of possible future states. The application of this approach to energy systems is illustrated in Chapter 10.

The complementary approach of *backcasting* is the process of working back from these scenarios to ask what needs to be done now to increase the chances of reaching a desirable future scenario, to reduce the probability of realising an undesirable scenario, or to initiate changes necessary for comfortable transition to a range of future scenarios.

The combination of foresighting and backcasting enables feasibility and desirability to be incorporated into explorations of the future. In the terms used earlier in this chapter, when compared with forecasting, foresighting provides a qualitatively different starting point, and so includes a qualitatively different problem formulation and solution set. The process begins by articulating one or more desirable futures, often distinctly different from the present or from forecasts, and is then concerned with finding feasible paths back from the future to the present. So, the solutions generated are independent of current dominant trends, and therefore the feasible paths will likely require both marginal and step changes in the system. Incorporating desirability and feasibility into an analysis of the future provides a means of explicitly engaging with values and context respectively, precisely the dimensions into which the Honest Broker needs to expand in practice, teaching and learning.

Foresighting and backcasting synthesise qualitative and quantitative analyses – the approach meets Blackburn's call for complementarity in approaching complex problems. Backcasting focuses on the implications of alternative futures, and in so doing requires explicit exploration of the necessary qualitative measures, such as policy frameworks, power relationships, cultural traditions and implementation strategies, as well as quantitative modelling based on scientifically determined relationships. In other words, the paths to desirable futures are determined by engaging with actors involved in all transformations in the means–ends spectrum, and will probably require marginal and step changes in both qualitative (policy, power, culture) and quantitative terms (scientific and engineering formulations).

Forecasting and foresighting are complementary in planning for the future (Robèrt, 2000; Mitchell and White, 2003). We argue for two maxims for action directed towards sustainability: "pick the low hanging fruit" and "challenge existing assumptions". Picking the low hanging fruit has a short-term focus, is interested in highly predictable outcomes and is consistent with forecasting. It is what engineers and scientists do well now, and provides the organisational cash flow and reflective space to focus on long-term challenges. Challenging existing assumptions has a long-term focus, is interested in desirable futures and is enabled by foresighting.

Using forecasting and foresighting iteratively is necessary for sustainable development. The kinds of answers provided by these two approaches are entirely dependent on the kinds of assumptions we build into our models. For example, when a forecast suggests that a resource demand is about to outstrip supply, the traditional approach is to increase supply. In the water sector, this translates to new dams, reservoirs, pumps and pipes. A more sustainable approach would investigate different scenarios, for example, to meet new demand by reducing existing demand and effectively increasing the efficiency of the existing infrastructure. In the water sector, this could mean providing water-efficient appliances to existing customers.

The role of scientists and engineers in foresighting and backcasting the future is therefore one of the Honest Broker, the reflective self-aware modeller, engaging with and respectful of diverse worldviews but pointing out what is possible in the techno-economic arena.

2.4.3 Energy: the Changing Climate

We now illustrate the concept of combining scientific and engineering expertise with other approaches by a specific case: an influential study by RCEP (2000) on climate change and energy supply. A very simplified account of the RCEP's argument follows.

The study started by reviewing scientific evidence on the threat of global climate change, caused by human emissions of greenhouse gases into the atmosphere. The principal greenhouse agent is carbon dioxide produced by burning carbon-based fossil fuels (section 2.2.1). In terms of the approaches discussed in this chapter, the analysis involved the use of quantitative climatic models to forecast the likely effect of different emission levels, validating the analysis as far as possible by reviewing historical evidence on atmospheric temperature and composition. However, uncertainty in the predictions is inherent, primarily because the global atmosphere is a non-linear dynamic system. Recognising the significance of the predictions, the report concludes "... the world is now faced with a radical challenge of a totally new kind which requires an urgent response". The uncertainty is also recognised, but with the need for precautionary action.[13] "By the time the effects of human activities on

[13] This represents a specific application of the Precautionary Principle (Box 1.1).

the global climate are clear and unambiguous it would be too late to take preventive measures." The most effective and immediate preventive measure must be to reduce global emissions of greenhouse agents, primarily carbon dioxide. Quantitative modelling, carried out by the Intergovernmental Panel on Climate Change (IPCC),[14] led to the conclusion that the concentration of carbon dioxide in the atmosphere should not exceed 550 ppm, roughly twice the level which existed before the industrial revolution. This figure was proposed to avoid the risk of major changes in climatic patterns, for example, caused by changes in ocean circulation. Thus the analysis deliberately avoided very uncertain forecasts which assume continuous change by considering constraints imposed by the need to avoid discontinuous change. However, it was recognised that even this "cap" on atmospheric carbon dioxide would probably lead to major changes in the biosphere due, for example, to changes in temperature zones and sea level. The calculations enabled the limits on atmospheric concentration to be expressed as limits on total global emissions of carbon dioxide by the year 2050.[15]

Up to this point, the analysis clearly explored the eco-centric constraints of Figure 2.2, using forecasting and foresighting. The next step in the RCEP's analysis moved into the socio-centric lobe of Figure 2.2, deploying ethical arguments to address how the tolerable emissions might be allocated among the inhabitants of the planet. "Our view is that an effective, enduring and equitable climate protocol will eventually require emission quotas to be allocated to nations on a simple and equal per capita basis." The policy recommendation was that "nations emission quotas (should) follow a contraction and convergence trajectory". Applying this general principle to the specific case of the UK led to the conclusion that "UK carbon dioxide emissions (must) be reduced by almost 60% from their current level by mid-century".

The analysis now moved into the techno-economic lobe of Figure 2.2 to investigate how the proposed policy could be reconciled with technical feasibility. This was essentially an exercise in backcasting. Four quantitative scenarios were developed to show how a reduction of 60% might be achieved, without using technologies which could be criticised as speculative. The conclusion was that appropriate combinations of efficiency improvements in energy use[16] and new technologies for the supply and conversion of energy from low-carbon sources could achieve the 60% target without reverting to a pre-industrial way of life.

The strength of the argument derives in part from its three "legs" corresponding to the three components of sustainability. Necessarily, the analysis combined different disciplinary perspectives. The success of the process underlines the imperative of involving a range of primary actors in taking decisions about transforming ultimate means (natural capital) to satisfy ultimate ends (wellbeing), as discussed in section 2.2.2. It was possible for the RCEP to say: "In this report we illustrate ways in which the UK could cut its carbon dioxide emissions by 60% by 2050. Achieving this will

---

[14] An international expert body set up following the 1992 Rio Conference (Chapter 1).

[15] The year 2050 was chosen because not even the most enthusiastic advocates of nuclear fusion thought the technology would be available by that year.

[16] These scenarios included systematic use of low-grade heat, something which has never been widespread in the UK (as in other countries with a major nuclear component in their energy sector). Promotion of Combined Heat and Power (CHP) is now part of UK energy policy.

require vision, leadership, and action which begin now." In other words, the proposals are possible; the question is whether the political will exists.

About $2\frac{1}{2}$ years after publication of the RCEP report, the recommendation was accepted in a White Paper setting out UK energy policy. The UK government is now advocating the 60% reduction target as a policy to be embraced by the European Union as a whole, as an important step towards sustainability. The problem and its possible solution have been framed; more detailed decisions and concrete action must now follow.

Conclusions

In this chapter, we started from the concept of sustainable development and interpreted it as a set of constraints on what humans can do on and with the planet. Three types of constraint are recognised: techno-economic, ecological and social. All three sets of constraints must be satisfied in the long term for a system to be sustainable. Engineers and scientists have a particular role in sustainable development in devising, designing and implementing ways to use the means represented by natural resources to meet the ends of satisfying human needs and improving the quality of life. However, this requires the technical expert to step away from the familiar role of "objective decision-maker" and take on the role of Honest Broker of scientific and technical information in deliberative decision processes. This kind of process, needed when the decision is very significant and the uncertainty in the scientific information is high, is known as post-normal science. The role of Honest Broker implies a new model of professional practice: based on a social contract rather than business imperatives. Recognising this new role has, in turn, implications for the education and training of engineers and scientists. PBL, a form of active learning, is well suited to the demands of post-normal science. It should equip engineers and scientists to participate in the kind of process which is emerging as an important approach to managing sustainable development: foresighting and backcasting.

This and the preceding chapter have attempted to explain why sustainable development is an imperative and why the new context changes the demands on and the role of the technical expert. Succeeding chapters set out specific case studies, which exemplify various aspects of the new demands and role.

References

Argyris, C. and Schön, D. (1978) *Organizational Learning*, Addison-Wesley, Massachusetts.

Azapagic, A. and Clift, R. (1999) The Application of Life Cycle Assessment to Process Optimisation. *Comp. & Chem. Eng.*, **23**, 1509–1526.

Belton, V. and Stewart, T.J. (2002) *Multi Criteria Decision Analysis*, Kluwer Academic Publishers, Boston.

Biggs, J. (1999) *Teaching for Quality Learning at University: What the Student Does*. The Society for Research into Higher Education and Open University Press, Buckingham, United Kingdom.

Blackburn, T. (1971) Sensuous-Intellectual Complementarity in Science, *Science*, **172**, 1003–1007.

Carew, A.L. and Mitchell, C.A. (2002) Characterising Undergraduate Engineering Students' Understanding of Sustainability, *European Journal of Engineering Education*, **27**(4), 349–361.

Checkland, P.B. (1981) *Systems Thinking, Systems Practice*, John Wiley & Sons, Chichester.

Clayton, A.M.H. and Radcliffe, N.J. (1996) *Sustainability: A System Approach*, Earthscan, London.

Clift, R. (1995) The Challenge for Manufacturing, pp. 82–87. In: *Engineering for Sustainable Development*, ed. J. McQuaid, The Royal Academy of Engineering, London.

Clift, R. (1999) Public Sector Decisions and the Limits to Technological Assessment. *Proc. Second International Symposium on Incineration and Flue Gas Treatment Technologies. Combustion*, 4–6 July 1999, Sheffield University, UK. IChemE, Rugby.

Clift, R. (2001) Clean Technology and Industrial Ecology, pp. 411–444 (Chapter 16). In: *Pollution: Causes, Effects and Control*, ed. R.M. Harrison (4th edition), Royal Society of Chemistry, London.

Cohon, J.L. (1978) Multiobjective Programming and Planning. In: *Mathematics in Science and Engineering*, Academic Press, New York.

Covey, S. (1990) *The Seven Habits of Highly Effective People*, Simon and Schuster, New York.

Crofton, F. (2000) Educating for Sustainability: Opportunities in Undergraduate Engineering, *Journal of Cleaner Production*, **8**, 397–405.

Daly, H. (1973) *Toward a Steady State Economy*, WH Freeman and Company, San Francisco.

Dreborg, K. (1996) Essence of Backcasting, *Futures*, **28**, 813–828.

Fawcett, A. and Roberts, P. (2002) The Institution of Engineers, Australia – At the turn, Remaking for Relevance, *Transactions of Multidisciplinary Engineering*, GE**25**, 51–63.

Farrell, S. and Hesketh, R. (2000) An Inductive Approach to Teaching Heat and Mass Transfer. In: *Proceedings of the American Society for Engineering Education Annual Conference*. Session 2213. June 2000, Missouri.

Fien, J. (1996) Reflective Practice: A Case Study of Professional Development for Environmental Education, *The Journal of Environmental Education*, **27**(3), 11–20.

Funtowicz, S.O. and Ravetz, J.R. (1990) *Uncertainty and Quality in Science for Policy*, Kluwer, Academic Publishers, Dordrecht.

Funtowicz, S.O., Martinez-Alier, J., Munda, G. and Ravetz, J.R. (1999) *Information Tools for Environmental Policy under Conditions of Complexity*. Environmental Issues series no. 9, European Environment Agency, Copenhagen.

Green, M. (2002) Educating the New Engineer, *Transactions of Multidisciplinary Engineering*, GE**25**, 39–50.

Holt, J.E. (1997) *The Future of Engineering Practice and Education*. Discussion paper. Department of Mechanical Engineering, The University of Queensland, Australia.

IEAust (1996) *Changing the Culture: A Review of Engineering Education in Australia*, The Institution of Engineers, Australia. Canberra, Australia.

Irwin, A. (2003) *Citizen Science; A Study of People, Expertise and Sustainable Development*, Routledge, London.

Little, S. (1999) Preparing Tertiary Teachers for Problem-based Learning, pp. 117–124 (Chapter 12). In: *The Challenge of Problem-Based Learning*, eds D. Boud and G. Feletti (2nd edition), Kogan Page, London.

Marton, F. and Booth, S. (1997) *Learning and Awareness*, Lawrence Erlbaum Associates, New Jersey.

Meadows, D. (1998) *Indicators and Information Systems for Sustainable Development: A Report to the Balaton Group*. The Sustainability Institute Vermont.

Mitchell, C.A. and White, S. (2003) Forecasting and Backcasting for Sustainable Urban Water Futures, *Water*, **30**(5), 25–30.

Owens, S. and Cowell, R. (2002). *Land and limits: Interpreting Sustainability in the Planning Process*, Routledge, London.

Prosser, M. and Trigwell, K. (1999) *Understanding Learning and Teaching: The Experience in Higher Education*. The Society for Research into Higher Education and Open University Press, Buckingham, United Kingdom.

Ravetz, J.R. (1971) *Scientific Knowledge and its Social Problems*, Clarendon Press, Oxford.

Ravetz, J.R. (1997) The Science of 'What-If?', *Futures*, volume **29**(6), 533–539.

Ravetz, J.R. (1993) Science for the Post Normal Age. *Futures*, **25**(7), 735–755.

RCEP (1998) Setting Environmental Standards. 21st Report of the Royal Commission on Environmental Pollution, The Stationery Office, London.

RCEP (2000) Energy – the Changing Climate. 22nd Report of the Royal Commission on Environmental Pollution, The Stationery Office, London.

Robèrt, K.-H. (2000) Tools and Concepts for Sustainable Development, How Do They Relate to a Framework for Sustainable Development, and How Do They Relate to Each Other? *The Journal of Cleaner Production*, **8**(4), 243–254.

Robinson, J. (2003) Future Subjunctive: Backcasting as Social Learning, *Futures*, **35**, 839–856.

Ryan, G. (1999) Ensuring that Students Develop an Adequate, and Well-structured, Knowledge Base, pp. 125–136 (Chapter 13). In: *The Challenge of Problem-Based Learning*, eds D. Boud and G. Feletti (2nd edition), Kogan Page, London.

Schön, D. (1987) *Educating the Reflective Practitioner*, Jossey-Bass Publishers, San Francisco.

Scott, W. (2002) *Sustainability and Learning: What Role for the Curriculum?* University of Bath Inaugural Lecture, April 2002. Available at http://www.bath.ac.uk/cree/home.htm.

Taylor, E. (1995) Professional Values and Attitudes, *Australasian Journal of Engineering Education*, **6**(2), 145–150.

Taylor, E. (2002) *The Illusion of Control*, Central Queensland University Engineering Dean's Inaugural Lecture, September 2002 (Rockhampton, Australia).

Triantaphyllou, E. (2000) *Multi-criteria Decision Making Methods: A Comparative Study*, Kluwer Academic Publishers, Dordrecht.

Tillman, A.-M. and Baumann, H. (2003) *The Hitchhikers Guide to LCA*, Studentlitteratur, Lund, Sweden.

Wrisberg, N. and Udo de Haes, H.A. (eds) (2002) *Analytical Tools for Environmental Design and Management in a Systems Perspective*, Kluwer, Dordrecht.

Wackernagel, M. and Reese, W. (1996) Our Ecological Footprint: Reducing Human Impact on the Earth, *Population and Environment*, **17**, 195–215.

PART 2
CASE STUDIES

3

Waste Water Management: Identifying Sustainable Processes

Adisa Azapagic, Charles Duff and Roland Clift

Summary

Water is one of the main prerequisites of life on earth. However, fresh water is becoming a scarce resource in many parts of the world. At the same time, industrial and human activities generate large amounts of waste water. To prevent damage to the environment and also to increase the availability of fresh water, waste water must be treated before being discharged into the environment.

The question we are asking here is how to do it in the most sustainable way. We use the case of sewage, waste water generated by our everyday activities, to illustrate which processes could be used and which criteria should be considered in assessing the level of sustainability of these processes. The case study is based around a typical Sewage Treatment Plant (STP) which uses a biological treatment process. The efficiency of this process depends on the provision of dissolved oxygen to the incoming waste water stream. There are several alternative ways of providing oxygen and we explore technical, environmental, economic and social aspects of the different alternatives. The aim is to show which criteria engineers and scientists should consider in identifying more sustainable alternatives for waste water treatment.

3.1 Sources of Fresh Water

Water is vital to all forms of life, and indeed to social and economic activity. And yet so many people in the world lack access to clean water and sanitation which leads to

Sustainable Development in Practice: Case Studies for Engineers and Scientists
Edited by Adisa Azapagic, Slobodan Perdan and Roland Clift
© 2004 John Wiley & Sons, Ltd   ISBNs: 0-470-85608-4 (HB); 0-470-85609-2 (PB)

preventable diseases and death for many people. Some of the global issues associated with the availability of fresh water and sanitation are highlighted in Box 3.1.

In the past, the supply of fresh water (at least in the Northern Hemisphere) has been considered inexhaustible and, like fresh air, it has been treated as virtually a 'free' good. But now, there are signs that the demand for fresh water is approaching the limits of supply; according to some estimates, a global water supply crisis is

---

Box 3.1   *Water: key facts (UN, 2003a)*

- More than one billion people lack access to a steady supply of clean water. There are 2.4 billion people – more than a third of the world's population – who do not have access to proper sanitation.
- More than 2.2 million people, mostly in developing countries, die each year from diseases associated with poor water and sanitary conditions.
- 6000 children die every day from diseases that can be prevented by improved water and sanitation.
- Over 250 million people suffer from water-related diseases every year.
- About 70% of all available fresh water is used for agriculture. Yet because of inefficient irrigation systems, particularly in developing countries, 60% of this water is lost to evaporation or is returned to rivers and groundwater aquifers.
- More and more of the world is facing water shortages, particularly in North Africa and western and South Asia.
- Water use increased sixfold during the last century, more than twice the rate of population growth.
- Water losses due to leakage, illegal water hook-ups and waste total about 50% of the amount of water used for drinking in developing countries.
- About 90% of sewage and 70% of industrial wastes in developing countries are discharged without treatment, often polluting the usable water supply.
- Freshwater ecosystems have been severely degraded: about half the world's wetlands have been lost and more than 20% of the world's 10 000 known freshwater species are extinct.
- In areas such as the United States, China and India, groundwater is being consumed faster than it is being replenished, and groundwater tables are steadily falling. Some rivers, such as the Colorado River in the western United States and the Yellow River in China, often run dry before they reach the sea.
- The task of carrying water in many rural areas falls to women and children, who often must walk miles each day to get water for their family. Women and girls also tend to suffer the most as a result of the lack of sanitation facilities.
- At any time, half of the world's hospital beds are occupied by patients suffering from water-borne diseases.
- During the 1990s, about 835 million people in developing countries gained access to safe drinking water and about 784 million gained access to sanitation facilities.

projected to occur between 2025 and 2050, although much earlier for some individual countries (UN, 2003a). Hence, attention is now being focused more sharply on the prudent use of water and on more effective methods for treating and recovering it after use. As water is no longer free nor freely available, it is becoming clear that we can no longer afford to discard fresh water as though it is a waste product.

Although there are large quantities of water on earth, very little of that is available for human consumption. Of the world's total water supply, 99.4% is in the oceans or frozen in bodies of ice (Philip, 2000). Most of the rest circulates through the rocks beneath our feet as ground water (0.587%). Water in rivers and lakes, in the soil and in the atmosphere together make up only 0.013% of the world's total water.

The supply of fresh water on land is dependent on the hydrological or water cycle, which is ultimately driven by the heat from the sun. The major steps of the hydrological cycle are shown in Figure 3.1. The cycle starts with the evaporation of water from seas, oceans and open water courses. This water vapour collects in the atmosphere and is precipitated as rain, snow, sleet, hail or dew. At this stage, the water can be considered 'fresh' and largely free from contamination. On reaching the surface, this fresh water percolates through soils and rock layers, or runs off directly to water courses and eventually returns to the sea.

Water is continuously abstracted, directly from these water courses, from land, or from wells or bore holes, to sustain natural vegetation and animal life, and for human agricultural, industrial and domestic purposes. As shown in Figure 3.2, it normally has to be treated before use to make it safe for human and other consumption. After use, water becomes contaminated with various substances and must be treated again before it can be returned to the environment safely. This water is then available again for abstraction and, as illustrated in Figure 3.2, its life cycle starts again.

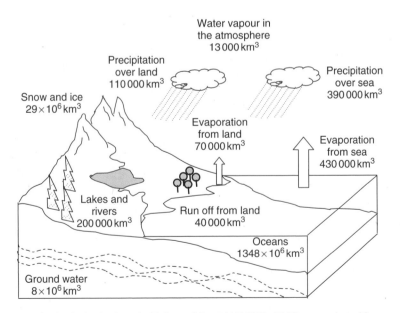

Figure 3.1   *The hydrological cycle (Adapted from WBCSD, 1998; reproduced by permission of Albert S. Fry.)*

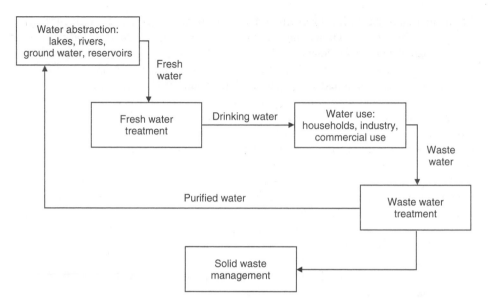

Figure 3.2   *Water life cycle: from water abstraction through water treatment to its return to the environment*

One of the challenges in water management is to increase the 'residence' time during which a given amount of fresh water remains available and 'fresh', that is usable. Storing water in reservoirs is a standard means of achieving this. However, this option is becoming increasingly disputed in view of widespread concern over the potential social and environmental impacts of certain new reservoir projects. Some of these impacts are related to the large land area required for the reservoirs, the local environmental disturbances and in many cases the need to relocate the local population living at the planned site. Reservoirs are also very expensive and can take up to 20 years to construct. In some countries such as the UK, it is almost impossible to obtain planning permission for the construction of a new water reservoir.

The problem of retention of fresh water is also exacerbated by deforestation in many regions. This can drastically reduce freshwater residence time, as the rainwater can no longer be retained in soils and the root systems of plants, and is rapidly lost through flash floods. Flash floods, which are now occurring more frequently due to climate changes, have a further effect of washing soil away into water courses, leaving the land bare, arid and infertile.

A similar phenomenon occurs in urban locations. Buildings, roadways and concreted areas such as car parks prevent rainwater percolating into the subsoil and from there finding natural pathways into water courses. Rather, it is conducted into artificial and impermeable drainage systems which are prone to storm flooding and overloads. With no opportunity for natural dispersion, this waste water must be fed into waste water treatment plants which must consequently be designed for larger throughputs than would otherwise be necessary.

Questions

1. How much water is there on earth? How much of that can be used as drinking water?
2. Why is the supply of fresh water diminishing if the water is constantly cycling on earth?
3. Explain the link between climate change and loss of fresh water.
4. Describe the freshwater situation in your country.
5. Why do you think it appears to be so difficult to provide clean water and sanitation in developing countries? How would you solve this problem?
6. In many countries, consumption of bottled water is higher than tap water used for drinking and people often pay much more for bottled water than for tap water. For example, in the USA, people spend from 240 to over 10 000 times more per litre for bottled water than they typically do for tap water. And yet, a study in the United States found that bottled water is not necessarily safer than the tap water as it contains chemicals and bacterial contamination (NRDC, 1999). What is the situation in your country with respect to consumption of bottled versus tap water?

3.2 Water Consumption

Demand for fresh water depends on a country's level of economic development. In developing regions of the world, people use far less water per capita than in developed regions (Hinrichsen *et al.*, 1998). For example, in Africa people use on average 47 l of water per day for personal use and in Asia, 85 l/day (Clarke, 1991). In contrast, comparable water use in the UK is estimated at 150 l/day (Water UK, 2003) and in the US, 400 l/day (EPA, 2003). The amount of water required for basic human needs is between 20 and 50 l/day.

On a worldwide basis, agriculture accounts for about 69% of all annual water withdrawals; industry, about 23%; and domestic use, about 8% (Hinrichsen *et al.*, 1998). However, these figures vary according to the level of economic development of a country and the climate. For example, as shown in Table 3.1, in Norway 68% of fresh water is consumed by industry, 3% by agriculture and 27% by domestic and commercial activities. On the other hand, in less developed countries with hotter climates (e.g. India and Egypt), water usage is dominated by agricultural irrigation practices.

Table 3.1 *Sectoral use of fresh water in selected countries (Reproduced by permission of World Resources Institute, 2001.)*

Country	Agricultural (%)	Industrial (%)	Domestic and commercial (%)
China	77	18	5
Egypt	86	8	6
India	92	3	5
France	12	73	15
Norway	3	68	27
Germany	0	86	14

Questions

1. How much water do you use per day? How does that compare with the average consumption in your country? What could you do to reduce the use of water?
2. How can people be encouraged to reduce water consumption? What should governments do to promote reduced water usage?
3. How could water be recycled in households to reduce the use of fresh water?

3.3   Sources and Measures of Water Pollution

3.3.1   Sources of Water Pollution

Agriculture is considered to be the largest contributor to water pollution, due to run-off into water courses from farmyard wastes, slurry, and profligate use of fertilisers and pesticides. Industry is also a large polluter generating waste water which often contains oils, chemicals, metals and other polluting substances. In developed countries, industrial effluents are closely monitored by the regulatory agencies and consents must be obtained before they are permitted into water courses or sewerage systems. Furthermore, for economic reasons, industry is now recycling progressively higher proportions of its process water on-site, thereby reducing its need for fresh supplies.

Waste water from households and commercial use (sewage) is contaminated largely with organic pollution and pathogenic bacteria. Unlike industrial waste water, sewage is normally not treated at source, but fed through the sewerage system to be purified at a Sewage Treatment Plant (STP). The key objective of the treatment is to reduce or remove the organic pollution and render harmless any toxic materials and pathogenic organisms. Following successful treatment of the pollution, the treated water should be fit for return to reservoirs or other watercourses, and from there, for further use. However, in many mainly developing countries sewage water is discharged into the environment untreated, causing contamination of fresh water and various diseases (Box 3.1).

3.3.2   Measures of Water Pollution

The main indicators of water pollution are Biochemical Oxygen Demand (BOD), Chemical Oxygen Demand (COD), Total Solids (TS), Total Suspended Solids (TSS) and the amount of nutrients, primarily nitrogen and phosphorus. Both BOD and COD are measures of water pollution caused by organic substances – the higher the BOD and COD, the more polluted the water. BOD is a measure of the organic carbon in the waste water which is biodegradable, while COD measures the total organic carbon, both biodegradable and non-biodegradable. BOD is expressed as the amount of dissolved oxygen in milligrams per litre (mg/l) of waste water, consumed by micro-organisms to biodegrade organic carbon over a certain period of time. BOD_5 is often used to measure the amount of dissolved oxygen consumed by micro-organisms during a period of five days. COD is expressed as the amount of oxygen consumed from a specified oxidising agent (usually potassium permanganate) for complete oxidation of the organic carbon to from carbon dioxide and water. Typically, COD can be two or three times higher than the BOD.

Total solids comprise suspended, colloidal and dissolved solids. TSS is a measure of the suspended material (non-settleable), mostly of organic content. Nitrogen and phosphorous compounds can also be present in waste water. They are classified as nutrients. If discharged with waste waters, they can cause overfertilisation of the water and stimulate 'blooms' of algae. The growing algal biomass depletes the oxygen dissolved in water and can lead to fish kills. This process is known as eutrophication. As an illustration, Table 3.2 shows typical values of BOD, COD, TSS and other measures of pollution for sewage.

Questions

1. What parameters define water quality? Why is the maintenance of water quality important?
2. In what ways do industrial and domestic activities impact on freshwater systems? What are the major sources and effects of water pollution on the environment?

Table 3.2 *Typical characteristics of raw urban waste water (Kiely, 1996; reproduced with permission of The McGraw-Hill Companies.)*

Parameter	Measure	Total (mg/l)
Physical	Total solids (TS)	740
	Total suspended solids (TSS)	300
	Temperature	10–20 °C
	pH	
	Colour	Fresh – grey; old – black
	Odour	
Chemical – Organic	Carbohydrates	
	Proteins	
	Lipids	
	Fats, oils, grease	100
	BOD (Biological oxygen demand)	250
	COD (Chemical oxygen demand)	500
	TOC (Total organic carbon)	160
	Alkalinity	100
	Grit	
	Heavy metals	
Chemical – Inorganic	Nutrients N, P	N = 40; P = 9
	Chlorides	
	Sulphur	
	Hydrogen sulphide	
	Gases	
Microbiological	Bacteria	
	Algae	
	Protozoa	
	Viruses	1000–10 000 units/l
	Coliforms	100–1000 million/l .

3.4   Waste Water Treatment

In this chapter we are concerned with sewage treatment, so we will now limit our discussion to the treatment of this type of waste water. Note that the terms 'waste water' and 'sewage' are used interchangeably and, for the purposes of this chapter, they have the same meaning.

The contaminants of sewage are primarily organic, so that the main treatment process is directed at the removal of organic substances. In a modern STP, physical, chemical or biological processes are used to treat water in a series of stages, including:

– pre-treatment: physical and/or chemical
– primary treatment: physical
– secondary treatment: biological
– tertiary treatment: physical and/or biological

Waste water pre-treatment removes large floating objects, oils and greases, while primary treatment allows water to settle for several hours in a settling tank, mainly to remove suspended solids. Secondary treatment is based on biological processes which use micro-organisms to biodegrade the polluting organic matter. The purpose of the tertiary treatment is to remove the nutrients and any suspended solids remaining after the secondary treatment.

In the case study to follow, we will concentrate on the biological treatment. Biological treatment can be carried either in the presence or absence of oxygen.

A waste water treatment plant. Photograph courtesy of PhotoDisc, Inc.

In most STPs, water treatment is carried out in the presence of oxygen which micro-organisms utilise to oxidise the organic pollution to form CO_2 and H_2O. Anaerobic processes are carried out in the absence of oxygen with different strains of bacteria which reduce organic pollutants to methane. Further discussion will be focused on aerobic biological processes which are the subject of our case study.

3.4.1 Aerobic Treatment of Waste Water

As illustrated in Figure 3.3, waste water entering a typical STP is first pre-treated to remove larger solid objects and then fed into a primary settlement tank. Here, a proportion of suspended solids (typically 30%) settle by gravity and are removed as 'primary sludge'. The waste water is then ready for secondary biological treatment in an aeration tank. The aeration tank acts as a biological reactor in which the 'activated' sludge is mixed with waste water in the presence of oxygen. The activated sludge consists of micro-organisms which use organic matter in the water as food to generate more microbial cells, while at the same time converting the organic pollution into CO_2 and water:

$$\text{Organic matter} + O_2 + \text{nutrients} \xrightarrow{\text{Micro-organisms}} \text{new biomass} + CO_2 + H_2O$$

This is an oxidation reaction which consumes dissolved O_2. If the oxygen demand of the waste (BOD) is high enough, it may deplete all the O_2 in the water and may lead to an anaerobic water body. As the micro-organisms rely on the dissolved oxygen for their metabolism, lack of oxygen may destroy the activated sludge and impede the breakdown of organic pollution in the waste water.

As the digestion proceeds, the mass of activated sludge is continuously washed through the aeration tank into a sludge-separation tank. After settlement, the clarified water is drawn off for further (tertiary) treatment or is returned directly to the environment. Part of the settled activated sludge is removed for disposal, but the majority of it is recycled as Returned Activated Sludge (RAS). This ensures that sufficient biomass is available in the aeration tank to enable full digestion of the pollutants in the new influent waste water. The micro-organisms in the sludge

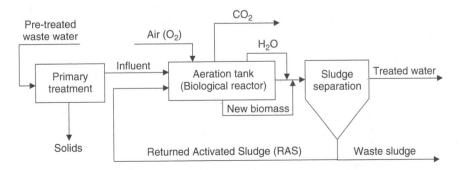

Figure 3.3 *Typical layout of a sewage treatment plant (STP) using aerobic process*

progressively die off and are themselves digested, but the nutrients in the new influent sustain the growth and activity of the biomass as a whole.

Pumps recirculate the sludge continuously for mixing with new waste water and further oxygenation. At each pass of the RAS, a proportion of the pollutants associated with it are broken down or digested, purifying the waste water, renewing the RAS and releasing the by-products. A steady state is established, the net effect being a balance between the incoming biomass, the new growth, effluent biomass and the waste sludge:

$$\text{Influent biomass} + \text{New biomass} = \text{Effluent biomass} + \text{Waste sludge}$$

The biomass in the influent and effluent water can be neglected so that the new biomass is discharged as waste sludge, while the amount of RAS in circulation remains roughly constant when the characteristics of the influent waste water are constant.

The task of the STP operators is to adjust and control the amount and flow rate of the RAS and the aeration process so that they match the BOD and flow rate of the incoming waste water. At the same time, they must take account of the regulator's requirements regarding the quality of the treated water on its final release.

As already mentioned, waste activated sludge is one of the by-products of the biological treatment which needs to be disposed of. In many countries, sewage sludge is dumped at sea. Up to 1998, this was also a standard practice for sludge disposal in many parts of Europe but it has been banned by recent legislation so that alternative methods of disposal have had to be found. The options for sludge disposal include the use of sludge on agricultural land as a fertiliser and soil conditioner, and incineration for energy recovery. However, neither of these two options has been widely accepted, the former due to health concerns over the pathogenic organisms remaining in the waste sludge and the latter due to health and pollution risks associated with incineration (see Chapter 5 for a case study on incineration).

Questions

1. The micro-organisms in the activated sludge are susceptible to the variations in the operating condition of the aeration tanks. What conditions must be maintained to ensure that they are not killed?
2. How is the sewage treated in your area? Is tertiary treatment of water standard practice in your country?
3. How is the activated sludge disposed of in your country? Which sludge disposal options are sustainable?

3.5   Alternatives for Aeration

As noted in the previous section, the key limiting factor in aerobic waste water treatment is the provision of sufficient amount of oxygen dissolved in water in the aeration tank, to ensure complete breakdown of the polluting organic material by the activated sludge. Several aeration techniques can be used for this purpose, including mechanical aeration, coarse-bubble aeration and fine-bubble or jet aeration.

3.5.1 Mechanical Aeration

Mechanical aeration is the simplest aeration method carried out by surface agitators and is still widely used. In the most common systems, paddles are fixed on a horizontal spindle mounted at or just below the surface of the aeration tank (Figure 3.4). The spindle is rotated causing the paddles to stir the top layers of waste water and sludge. The paddles entrap air bubbles and submerge them below the surface. Some of the oxygen present in these air bubbles dissolves in water and is available for the aerobic process.

3.5.2 Bubble Aeration: Coarse Bubbles

Aeration by agitating the surface layers of the sludge and the overlying water is less efficient than methods which involve greater mixing throughout the whole body of the aeration tank and so allowing more time for oxygen from air bubbles to dissolve. One method for achieving this is to pump in air through perforated pipes (spargers) located at the bottom of the tank. This technique is illustrated in Figure 3.5. The air rises through the tank to the surface in the form of a stream of coarse bubbles with diameter of around 3–5 mm. This sets up circulation patterns in the water which aid better mixing. The bubbles spend several tens of seconds in the liquid, enabling a proportion of the oxygen in the bubbles to dissolve in the solution and allowing the digestion process to proceed.

Figure 3.4 *Mechanical aeration: paddle aerator*

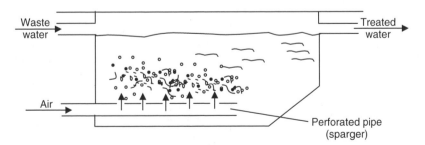

Figure 3.5 *Bubble aeration: coarse bubbles*

3.5.3 Jet Aeration: Fine Bubbles

A further improvement of the aeration process is to extract a stream of water from the aeration tank and then pump it back into the bottom layers of the water/activated sludge mix under higher pressure (Figure 3.6). As the stream passes through the surface of the tank, it entrains air which is forced into the bulk of the tank in the form of fine bubbles with diameter of 1.5–2 mm. This has two advantages: more air, and hence oxygen, can be delivered per unit time, and the smaller bubble size leads to increased area of contact between the air and the water. The rate of the transfer of the oxygen in gaseous form to the oxygen in solution depends on the interfacial area between gas and liquid: the finer the bubbles, the greater the contact area per unit mass of O_2. This is explained in more detail in Box 3.2.

Box 3.2   *Aeration and oxygenation*

In order to react with the polluting organic matter, oxygen must be dissolved in the waste water. This requires a mass transfer process, in which oxygen passes from the gas phase into the liquid phase. The rate at which this occurs depends on:

1. the contact area between the gas (air) bubble and the liquid;
2. the resistance to mass transfer through the gas/liquid interface.

In a dirty liquid like waste water, the resistance to mass transfer through the gas/ liquid interface is caused mainly by a film of contaminants which collect on the surface of the gas bubbles; this varies from application to application, and can usually be estimated only with the benefit of experience. However, the contact area between the gas bubble and the liquid depends on the bubble size. Small bubbles like those in water treatment systems (or a glass of sparkling mineral water) are spherical. If the bubble diameter is d (m), then the volume V of one bubble is $\pi d^3/6$ (m^3) and its surface area A is πd^2 (m^2). Therefore, the contact area per unit volume of gas (air) is:

$$a = A/V = (\pi d^2)/(\pi d^3/6) = 6/d(\text{m}^2/\text{m}^3)$$

that is the smaller the bubbles, the greater the contact area, and hence the area for mass transfer.

   The above refers to the rate of mass transfer from the gas to the liquid. The total oxygen transfer also depends on the residence time of the bubbles in the liquid, as they rise from the bottom of the tank to the surface. For small spherical bubbles, the rise velocity is proportional to the square of the diameter, d^2, so that the residence time for a given liquid depth is inversely proportional to the square of the bubble diameter. This means that a smaller bubble would rise slower thus remaining longer in contact with the water; this further increases oxygen utilisation. Generally, the smaller the bubble the better because smaller bubbles have more surface area and stay in the liquid for longer.

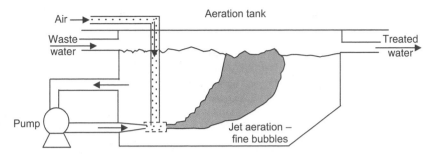

Figure 3.6 *Jet aeration: fine bubbles*

Questions

1. Summarise the main differences between mechanical aeration, coarse-bubble aeration and jet aeration.
2. Why is jet aeration more efficient in bringing oxygen to the waste water?

3.6 Using Oxygen Instead of Air

Only 21% of air consists of oxygen. Consequently, the use of pure oxygen rather than air in the aeration process has an immediate attraction: it would speed up the reaction because more oxygen would be available per unit mass of pollutant and per unit time. This also suggests that a smaller amount of gas, that is oxygen, needs to be delivered to the aerobic tank. However, unlike air, pure oxygen is not available freely in the environment, so it has to be generated. This is done commercially by air-separation processes which separate oxygen from the nitrogen and trace gases present in the air. These processes are costly and generate environmental impacts. Therefore, as we will show in the case study below, an evaluation of oxygen-based systems has to take into account both the economic and environmental costs of obtaining pure oxygen, as well as where, how and in what quantities the air separation is carried out.

3.6.1 Jet Aeration with Oxygen: Vitox[TM] Process

The Vitox[TM] process is a particularly efficient oxygenation system developed by the UK-based company BOC. This system is equivalent to the fine-bubble jet aeration system described in 3.5.3. As illustrated in Figure 3.7, a stream of mixed waste water and RAS is extracted from the aeration tank and pumped through a venturi[1] under

---

[1] A duct with a reduced cross-sectional area; the section with the reduced cross-sectional area is known as venturi throat.

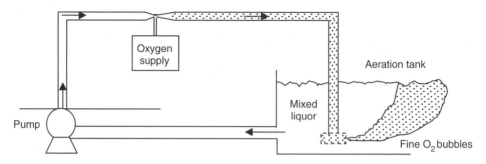

Figure 3.7 *Jet aeration with oxygen: the Vitox^{TM} system*

a pressure of 2–3 bar. Oxygen is injected at the throat of the venturi and in contact with the high-speed water flow it is broken down into small bubbles. The oxygen continues to travel along with water through the pipe to the bottom of the tank. When the water and oxygen enter the tank through an expansion nozzle, the bubbles are shattered into millions of rapidly dissolving micro-bubbles which are then available for biological digestion.

In the Vitox^{TM} system, the gas/liquid contact area is highly increased and the oxygen passes into the solution with an efficiency of around 95%. In other words, only 5% of the delivered oxygen is wasted and discharged to the atmosphere. The flow of fine bubbles both promotes the dissolution of oxygen and creates highly efficient mixing.

Questions

1. Explain why oxygen-based aeration systems are more efficient in treating waste water than air-based systems.
2. Explain the role of the venturi in delivering oxygen to the waste water. Why is the oxygen injected at the venturi throat?
3. Does the increased aeration efficiency justify the use of pure oxygen which must be produced industrially? Why?

3.6.2   Production of Oxygen

As mentioned above, pure oxygen is produced by air-separation processes, which separate oxygen and nitrogen from the air. Two types of air-separation techniques are used:

1. cryogenic separation (by cooling): utilising the different boiling points of liquefied gases present in the air; and
2. Pressure Swing Adsorption (PSA): utilising different rates and affinity of adsorption of the components of the air.

Descriptions of these two types of air-separation process are given in Boxes 3.3 and 3.4 respectively.

Cryogenic separation yields liquid oxygen, while PSA generates gaseous oxygen. Oxygen can be transported to an STP in either form, in pressurised or refrigerated road tankers. However, whichever option is chosen, the oxygen will be injected into the waste water stream at the STP in gaseous form because liquid O_2 vaporises on release from the container. The choice between the liquid and gaseous forms depends on a number of factors including financial and energy costs. Furthermore, there are significant variations in the economies of scale[2] between these options: there is, for example, a choice between a small-scale air-separation plant situated on the STP site and a larger-scale plant located elsewhere, where the oxygen has to be transported to the STP. These options have different environmental, economic and social costs as shown in the case study which follows.

Box 3.3   *Cryogenic air separation*

This process involves liquefaction of air, followed by distillation to separate it into its components, mainly nitrogen and oxygen. The filtered air is first compressed and cooled in a heat exchanger. Next, the air is passed through adsorbent beds and coolers to remove impurities such as carbon dioxide and hydrocarbons. The air is then passed into a distillation column where oxygen and nitrogen are separated by using their different boiling points. An oxygen-rich liquid exits from the bottom of the column, and the liquid nitrogen exits from the top. The liquid gases are stored in pressurized containers before being delivered to the customer. Cryogenic air-separation units are most suitable for high volume demand (from 100 to several hundred tones of oxygen per day) and for high-purity applications.

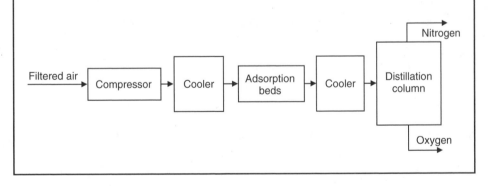

---

[2] The economies of scale refer to the relationship between the size of a chemical plant and its capital and operating costs. (Capital costs are costs incurred to build the plant while the operating costs are those incurred by running the plant. The latter include the costs of raw materials, energy and workforce.) Normally, the larger the capacity of an industrial plant, that is the larger the economies of scale, the lower the capital and operating costs per unit of throughput.

Box 3.4   *Adsorption*

The adsorption process used for air separation is known as PSA. The principle of the operation is that the oxygen in the incoming air is separated by adsorption at high pressure (1.5–4 bar), and is then released from the adsorbent at the atmospheric or sub-atmospheric (vacuum) pressure. Hence the name 'swing' adsorption. The process operates on a repeated cycle with two basic steps, adsorption and regeneration of the adsorbent. During regeneration, the oxygen is released and collected and the impurities are cleaned from the adsorbent, so that the bed will be available again for the adsorption step. Zeolites are most commonly used as the adsorbents of oxygen. The typical output capacity of a large-scale PSA unit is 20–80 t O_2/day.

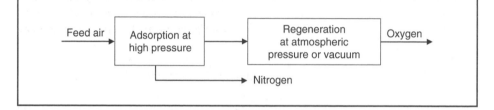

Questions

1. What is the main difference between the cryogenic air-separation process and separation by PSA?
2. What are the zeolites used in PSA? Why are they used?

3.7   Case Study: Identifying Sustainable Aeration Processes

We will now consider a typical aerobic STP. The aim of the case study is to evaluate different aeration technologies on the relevant process, economic, environmental and social criteria, and choose the most sustainable technique.

3.7.1   Waste Water Treatment Plant

The plant considered here treats waste water generated in a town with a population of around 48 000 people. The waste water is produced at an average rate of 200 l per person per day with an average BOD_5 of 400 mg O_2/l. However, the flow rates of waste water may vary substantially depending on the time of day, the season and the weather. In this case study we assume constant flow rates. The plant operates continuously 24 h/day.

The layout of the plant is shown in Figure 3.8. In the primary treatment stage, 480 t of primary sludge (settled solids/waste water mixture) are removed. The

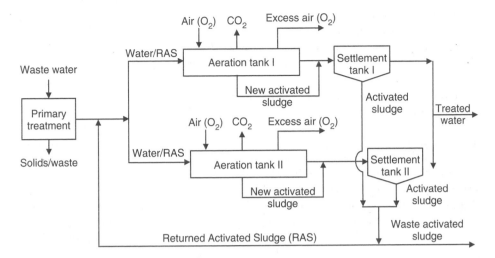

Figure 3.8   *Flow diagram of the sewage treatment plant*

remaining waste water is mixed with 6720 t/day of RAS and pumped into the aeration tanks. There are two aeration tanks of equal size and the water/RAS mixture is split equally between them. Each tank is approximately 50-m long, 10-m wide and 3-m deep and is divided into five 10 m cells by concrete baffles which encourage further mixing of the sludge and water as it circulates through the system.

On exiting the aeration tanks, the two sludge/water streams are fed into two secondary settlement tanks. From each of the settlement tanks, a stream of 4320 t/day of purified water is discharged into the local river with a residual BOD_5 of 15 mg O_2/l. The balance from each of the secondary settlement tanks is drawn off and combined into one stream. Of this, 6720 t/day are returned as RAS for blending with new influent after primary settlement. The remainder is the waste activated sludge, which must be disposed of in an appropriate way.

Questions

1. Perform a mass balance on the plant by using the given flows to calculate all the remaining flows that have not been specified above. Write all the flow rates on the flow diagram.
2. Given the average BOD_5 value of the waste water of 400 mg O_2/l, calculate the amount of oxygen in t/day needed for complete digestion.
3. What is the overall BOD reduction efficiency?
4. The concentration of dissolved oxygen in the local river before the treated water is discharged is on average 9 mg O_2/l. If the river flow rate is 1.5 m³/s and the treated water is discharged with a residual BOD_5 of 15 mg O_2/l, find out if the dilution of the treated effluent with river water is sufficient to ensure that the oxygen level in the river water is not significantly lowered.

3.7.2 Process Considerations

To be able to choose the best aeration technology from the technical point of view, we need to consider two important process parameters: aeration efficiency and energy requirements for aeration. In the following sections, we discuss these two parameters for both the air- and oxygen-based aeration systems.

Aeration Efficiency

Aeration or oxygen utilisation efficiency measures how efficiently an aeration technology delivers oxygen to the waste water. It is expressed as the percentage of oxygen delivered which dissolves in solution. The rate of dissolution depends on a number of parameters, of which the most important is the initial bubble size (Box 3.2). Typical values for oxygen utilisation efficiency of the different aeration systems are given in Table 3.3.

In other words, of all the oxygen delivered by the paddle aerator, for example, only 5–6% is available and utilised for the digestion process, with the rest being discharged into the atmosphere. The Vitox^{TM} system, on the other hand, utilises 95% of oxygen delivered and discharges only 5% into the environment.

Energy Efficiency of Aeration

Apart from the energy required to pump the waste water, energy is also required to power the aeration process, whether turning the spindle of a paddle aerator or pushing the water through a venturi in the Vitox^{TM} system. The energy efficiency of the aeration process is measured as the amount of oxygen dissolved per unit of energy supplied. This is termed the 'oxygenation efficiency'. Table 3.3 shows the values for oxygenation efficiency of the air- and oxygen-based systems. For example, a paddle aerator can provide 0.06–0.67 kg of dissolved O_2 per MJ of energy used whilst the Vitox^{TM} system can deliver up to 1.11 kg O_2/MJ. Expressed another way, a paddle aerator requires between 1.5 and 16.7 MJ of energy per kg of dissolved oxygen. For the Vitox^{TM}, this energy ranges from 0.9 to 1.45 MJ/kg O_2.

Table 3.3 *Oxygenation utilisation and oxygenation efficiency for air- and oxygen-based systems*

	Oxygen utilisation efficiency (%)	Oxygenation efficiency (kg O_2/MJ)
Air-based systems		
Paddle aerator	5–6	0.06–0.67
Coarse-bubble diffusers	5–6	0.25–0.33
Fine-bubble diffusers	11–18	0.42–1.00
Oxygen-based systems		
Vitox^{TM} system	95	0.69–1.11

Question

1. Compare the different aeration techniques shown in Table 3.3 using both the respective lowest and highest efficiency values, and the average values. What can you conclude: which aeration system or systems may be preferable from the technical point of view? Why?

3.7.3 Economic Considerations

The Cost of Aeration Technologies

Of major significance in the selection between alternative aeration (and any other) technologies is the question of cost – both capital and operating. The capital costs of the aeration technologies considered here include the construction and installation while the operating costs mainly depend on the amount of energy they require for their operation as well as on the maintenance costs. As discussed below, in the case of the Vitox^{TM}, the costs of oxygen generation and use must also be taken into account in calculating the operating costs. Table 3.4 ranks the four aeration technologies according to their operating and capital costs, with the costs increasing from 1 to 4.

The Cost of Oxygen

For the oxygen-based systems, we also need to consider the costs of generating oxygen by air separation. These costs are determined by the energy used to separate the oxygen and nitrogen and the size of the air-separation plant (economies of scale). Typical energy requirements for different sizes of the cryogenic and PSA processes are given in Table 3.5.

Table 3.4 *Capital and operating costs of aeration systems*

	Capital costs	Operating costs
Paddle aerator	3–4[a]	4
Coarse-bubble diffusers	1–2[a]	3
Fine-bubble diffusers	3–4[a]	1–2[a]
Vitox^{TM} system	1–2[a]	1–2[a]

[a] sharing 1st and 2nd or 3rd and 4th place

Table 3.5 *Energy requirements and operating costs of air-separation plants*

	Energy requirement (MJ/kg O_2)	Operating costs relative to the large-scale cryogenic unit
Cryogenic separation		
Large scale (600 t O_2/day)	1.1	1
Small scale (140 t O_2/day)	1.8	3
Pressure swing adsorption		
Large scale (70 t O_2/day)	3.7	5
Small scale (9 t O_2/day)	6.0	7

These data show that large-scale plants are more cost- and energy-efficient than equivalent smaller plants. For example, a small-scale cryogenic separation unit is three times more expensive to run per unit of oxygen produced than a larger-scale process (Smith and Armond, 1973). A similar relationship is found for the energy used. For comparison, a small-scale PSA uses around 20 times more energy to produce 1 kg of oxygen than is required to boil 1 l of water.

The energy used in air separation not only affects the operating costs of the air-separation plant but also contributes to environmental impacts. We will now consider environmental criteria and examine how they affect the choice of the aeration technology.

Questions

1. Why is a larger air-separation plant less expensive per unit oxygen produced than a small-scale plant?
2. What can you conclude about the link between the process energy, costs and the economies of scale of air-separation plants?
3. Compare the energy use and operating costs of different air-separation plants. Which option would you choose and why?
4. What do you conclude by comparing the relative ranking of capital and operating costs for different aeration technologies: which one would you choose and why?

3.7.4   Environmental Considerations

Energy Use

The energy (electricity) used by different aeration technologies at the STP is shown in Table 3.3. Comparison of these figures would point to the conclusion that the Vitox^{TM} technology is preferred over the other three aeration techniques. However, if we add the electricity used to generate oxygen (Table 3.5), then the choice is no longer so clear and other aeration technologies become more competitive.

When considering energy use and the associated environmental impacts, we have to take into account not only the energy used by the aeration technologies at the STP site but also the impacts from the whole life cycle of electricity generation. The life cycle of energy generation includes extraction of fossil fuels, their refining and combustion of fuels to convert heat into electricity. This is known as a life cycle approach (see the Appendix at the end of the book), which must be adopted in assessing the environmental impacts of any process or product to ensure that we have not ignored potentially large impacts in different life cycle stages. For example, the use of electricity has no environmental impact at the point of use, so that all environmental impacts are generated prior to the use stage. If we were to ignore them, then we would be ignoring around 30% of the world emissions of CO_2 and the associated global warming impact.

Questions

1. Which air-separation process do you think is most sustainable with respect to energy requirements and the associated environmental impacts?
2. Calculate the total energy use for the Vitox^{TM} technology, taking into account the energy used for oxygen generation in different air-separation plants as well as the energy used by the technology itself at the STP. Compare these results with the energy used by the other aeration technologies. Which option would you choose on the basis of energy use and the associated environmental impacts?
3. Calculate the following:

   (a) emissions of CO_2 associated with the energy required to produce 1 kg of O_2 in the large-scale cryogenic plant and in the small-scale PSA unit and compare the results; and
   (b) calculate the global warming potential per year from this emission of CO_2, given the oxygen demand in the STP per day and the Vitox^{TM} oxygen utilisation efficiency.

To simplify the analysis, assume the following:

- the energy used is electricity generated from natural gas;
- heating value of natural gas is $36.6\,MJ/m^3$ and its density is $0.59\,kg/m^3$;
- the efficiency of conversion of heat from natural gas to electricity is 40% (i.e. you will recover only 40% of the heating value of the gas as electrical energy);
- natural gas is 100% methane (CH_4); and
- complete oxidation (burning) of simple hydrocarbon fuels forms only CO_2 and water; that is, for a hydrocarbon fuel with the general composition C_nH_m, the stoichiometric reaction is:

$$C_nH_m + \left(n+\frac{m}{4}\right)O_2 \longrightarrow nCO_2 + \left(\frac{m}{2}\right)H_2O$$

4. Apart from CO_2 emissions and the associated global warming potential, what other environmental impacts from the energy use you would expect to be important? Take a life cycle approach in identifying these impacts.

Transport of Oxygen

If the oxygen-based system is chosen for the STP, we would have two options for providing the oxygen: one is to source oxygen from a large-scale plant situated away from the STP and transport liquid oxygen in pressurised containers to the STP; the other is to generate oxygen in a smaller-size plant based at the STP and avoid transportation.

In this case study, we assume that a large-scale cryogenic unit is located 200 km from the STP. The oxygen is delivered by road tanker which uses 0.5 MJ of energy per kg of oxygen delivered for the round trip (i.e. for 400 km). Given the daily demand of oxygen at our STP and the capacities of the cryogenic and PSA plants (Table 3.5), the only small-scale process that we can consider here is the PSA plant with capacity up to $9\,t\,O_2/day$. One of the questions that arise is: would a smaller-size plant based at the STP be a more sustainable option than the oxygen sourced and transported to the STP from a larger cryogenic unit?

Questions

1. What is the total energy used by the large-scale cryogenic plant to produce and deliver 1 kg of oxygen to the STP?
2. How does that compare with the energy required by an on-site small-scale PSA plant?
3. What can you conclude from the point of view of energy consumption: is transport an important consideration in this case?
4. What can you conclude: is a smaller-size plant based at the STP a better option than the large-scale plant situated away from the STP? Why?
5. In addition to energy consumption, what other environmental impacts are attributable to transport?
6. List some of the impacts of transport in general on the environment, economy and society.

3.7.5   Social Considerations

The main social considerations associated with the aeration technologies considered in this case study are noise and odour. In the case of Vitox^{TM}, transport of oxygen can also have some social impacts.

Odour and Noise

Odour may be a problem encountered at STPs if there is even a slight oxygen deficit. There are two reasons for this. One is that, under anaerobic conditions, hydrogen sulphide (H_2S) is generated, which not only has an unpleasant odour but is harmful to health. Volatile Organic Compounds (VOC), present as organic pollutant in the waste water, can also cause odour at STPs. VOCs evaporate easily in the aeration tank due to the turbulence and the elevated temperatures associated with the biological digestion. Both problems are treated with an increased level of oxygen supply which prevents H_2S generation and binds VOCs to the sludge enabling their digestion. Hence, with an aeration technology which enables efficient delivery of oxygen to the water, the odour problem can be eliminated.

Noise can also be an issue in some aeration technologies. For example, typical noise level from the paddle aerator is between 70 and 110 dB (equivalent to the level of noise in night clubs). Compared to the other three aeration technologies, Vitox^{TM} is quieter. However, the equipment used to generate oxygen may have an associated noise problem. So, if a small-scale PSA plant is situated at the STP, noise may be increased and thus offset the benefit of the quieter Vitox^{TM} technology.

Questions

1. Why might noise and odour be important social considerations?
2. Who is most likely to be affected?

3. How might the affected people react to these nuisances?
4. If the Vitox^{TM} technology is chosen for the STP, what social impact do you think the deliveries of oxygen would have on the population living nearby the STP?

Other Social Considerations

In addition to noise, odour and transport, there are wider social issues to be considered in relation to any STP. They include:

- the service provided by the STP and the benefits it yields;
- the social acceptability of STP and the 'NIMBY' syndrome (not-in-my-back-yard);
- planning permission and consultation processes involving the local population;
- land use for the waste water treatment plant and possible displacement of local population.

Questions

1. What 'social' service is provided by an STP? What are the benefits of treating the waste water?
2. If STPs provide benefits to society, why is there lack of these facilities in developing countries? How could this problem be overcome?
3. People usually reject proposals for siting of a sewage treatment (or any other) plant in their neighbourhood. This is known as the 'NIMBY' syndrome. (You may wish to read Chapter 5 for a typical case of the NIMBY syndrome.) What are your views as an engineer or scientist on such reactions by the local communities?
4. How would you respond if a company proposed to build a sewage treatment (or a chemical) plant in your neighbourhood, near your home? Why?

3.7.6 Choosing the Aeration Technology

We have now examined the technical, economic, environmental and social aspects of the four alternative aeration technologies. Our final question is: based on the findings for all these criteria, which of the aeration technologies is most sustainable? Follow the questions below to find an answer.

Questions

1. Calculate:

   (a) the amount of air that has to be supplied for the different aeration technologies and the amount of unutilised oxygen that escapes into the atmosphere; comment on the consequences of supplying these amounts of air and of the escaped oxygen;
   (b) the daily energy requirement in MJ/day for operating each of the aeration processes at the STP.

To compare the different processes, it is important to identify a common basis; in this case, this is the daily oxygen demand for complete digestion of influent pollution. However, all the processes do not have the same oxygen utilisation rates, and this must be taken into account. For the purposes of your analysis, assume the worst-case scenario (i.e. the lowest values) for oxygen utilisation and oxygenation efficiency.

2. List all considerations relevant for choosing an aeration technology. On the basis of the results obtained, rank the processes in order of their desirability. You may want to represent these in a table, assigning a number to each technology to indicate the order of preference on a scale from 1 to 4 (e.g. number 1 indicates the best technology and 4, the worst); this ranking should be done for each of the considerations listed.
3. Make a decision on the most sustainable aeration technology, assuming that you are Head of Engineering and Science Division in a company. Justify your choice.
4. Now assume that you are, in turn:

   (a) a local authority councillor;
   (b) a local resident; and
   (c) an environmental activist

   and make a decision on the most sustainable technology in each role. Justify your choice by discussing what considerations would be important for you in each of the roles in choosing the best technology and explain why.
5. What can you conclude in terms of how different considerations influence different 'actors' in society (i.e. engineers and scientists, local authorities, local residents and environmentalists) in choosing the most sustainable technology?
6. How would the choice of the aeration technology be affected depending on whether its application is in a developed or developing country? Which of the aeration technologies are appropriate for application in a developing country? Why?

Conclusions

Security of water supply is one of the most important problems that must be addressed urgently within the context of sustainable development. At the political level, the international community must find ways of bringing clean water to millions of people who currently lack this basic life resource. At the practical level, technological solutions for providing clean and safe water are relatively simple and easily available. However, not all of them are appropriate, particularly for developing countries, and not all of them are sustainable. Therefore, one of the tasks for us, engineers and scientists, in the context of sustainable development is to identify and design the most appropriate and sustainable water technologies.

We have chosen a case study on an aerobic waste water treatment plant to illustrate how this could be done at the practical level. By considering the relevant technical, economic, environmental and social criteria in turn, we have shown how the choice of the most sustainable aeration technology changes for different sets of sustainability criteria. The challenge for engineers and scientists is to balance these competing criteria in order to make an appropriate decision on the 'best' technology. In doing so, engineers and scientists must also appreciate that the choice of the most sustainable option will depend not only on the 'hard' engineering and scientific facts but also on the 'soft' opinions of the other stakeholders. As we argued in Chapter 2, learning not only to understand and accept these 'soft' issues but also to communicate the 'hard' facts to 'non-experts' is an important part of the paradigm shift in engineering and science. Subsequent case studies show why.

Acknowledgements

Part of the case study presented in this chapter has been developed with financial support from the Royal Academy of Engineering (RAEng) within its scheme 'Visiting Professors in Sustainable Design'. The authors gratefully acknowledge the support of the RAEng.

References and Further Reading

Binnie, C., M. Kimber and G. Smethurst (2002) *Basic Water Treatment*. The Royal Society of Chemistry, London.

Clarke, R. (1991) *Water: The International Crisis*. Earthscan, London, 193pp.

EPA (2003) Ground Water Primer. http://www.epa.gov/seahome/groundwater/src/faq.htm#2 (October 2003).

Gleick, H.P., W.C.G. Burns, E.L. Chalecki, M. Cohen, K.K. Cushing, A.S. Mann, R. Reyes, G.H. Wolff and A.K. Wong (2003) *The World's Water: The Biennial Report on Freshwater Resources: 2002–2003*. Island Press. Washington.

Hammer, M. and M. Hammer Jr (2000) *Water and Wastewater Technology* (International Edition). Prentice Hall. Englewood Cliffs, N.J. USA.

Hinrichsen, D., B. Robey and U.D. Upadhyay (1998) How Water is Used? Population Reports. Volume XXVI, Number 1, September 1998. The Johns Hopkins School of Public Health, Baltimore, Maryland, USA. http://www.infoforhealth.org/pr/m14/m14chap2_2.shtml (October 2003).

Kiely, G. (1996) *Environmental Engineering*. McGraw-Hill Co., London.

Novotny, D.W. (2003) *Water Quality: Prevention, Identification, and Management of Diffuse Pollution*. John Wiley & Sons, Inc.

NRDC (1999) Bottled Water: Pure Drink or Pure Hype? National Resources Defence Council. http://www.nrdc.org/water/drinking/bw/bwinx.asp (October 2003).

Philip, G. (2000) *Philip's World Atlas*. George Philip Ltd, London.

Smith, K.C. and J.W. Armond (1973) Adsorption as a Technique for Gas Separation, *Cryotech 73 Proceedings*, 101–106.

Tchobanoglous, G., F. Burton and H.D. Stensel (2002) *Wastewater Engineering: Treatment and Reuse*. McGraw-Hill Series in Civil and Environmental Engineering. McGraw-Hill Education.

Twort, A.C., D.D. Ratnayaka and M.J. Brandt (2000) *Water Supply*. Butterworth-Heinemann.

UN (2003a) Water: A Matter of Life and Death. Fact sheet. http://www.un.org/events/water/factsheet.pdf (October 2003).

UN (2003b) Water for People – Water for Life: United Nations Water Development Report 2003. United Nations, New York.

Water UK (2003) Environmental Indicators for UK Water Industry. http://admin.
  evolvingmedia.co.uk/users/files/1FinalReport0102.PDF (October 2003).
WBCSD (1998) Industry, Fresh Water and Sustainable Development. World Business Coun-
  cil for Sustainable Development, April 1998.
WRI (2001) World Resources 2000–2001 – People and Ecosystems: The Fraying Web of Life.
  Report prepared by the United Nations Development Programme (UNDP), the United
  Nations Environment Programme (UNEP), the World Bank, and the World Resources
  Institute. http://www.wri.org (October 2003).

4

Integrated Prevention and Control of Air Pollution: The Case of Nitrogen Oxides

Adisa Azapagic, Charles Duff and Roland Clift

Summary

Air quality in many parts of the world is poor due to emissions of various pollutants such as sulphur dioxide (SO_2), nitrogen oxides (NO and NO_2), volatile organic compounds (VOCs), particulates and so on. Many air pollutants remain in the atmosphere for long periods of time and often travel long distances thus affecting both the local and the global environment. In addition to causing global warming, acidification and other environmental effects, air pollution can also affect human health. Therefore, addressing the problem of air pollution is an important issue in sustainable development. This chapter uses a case study of nitrogen oxides (NO_x) generated in the manufacture of nitric acid to illustrate how engineers and scientists can help tackle the problem of air pollution in a more sustainable way. Taking the life cycle approach to Integrated Pollution Prevention and Control (IPPC), the case study shows how to balance the three components of sustainable development in search of the Best Available Technique (BAT) for reducing air pollution.

4.1 Global Atmosphere

The atmosphere surrounding the earth is critically important for the survival of humans and most other species, not just because it contains the oxygen we need to

Sustainable Development in Practice: Case Studies for Engineers and Scientists
Edited by Adisa Azapagic, Slobodan Perdan and Roland Clift
© 2004 John Wiley & Sons, Ltd   ISBNs: 0-470-85608-4 (HB); 0-470-85609-2 (PB)

breathe but also because it provides a barrier to harmful radiation from the sun and plays a major role in maintaining the surface temperature of the planet – if the earth had no atmosphere, the mean surface temperature would be about 30 °C lower than that at present (Harrison, 1997; RCEP, 2000) and would be uninhabitable for most living organisms, including humans. Thus, preserving the quality of the atmosphere is literally vital for sustaining life on earth.

And yet, human and industrial activities affect the quality of the atmosphere on an everyday basis, causing global, regional and local air pollution. Two major global effects observed in the past few decades are global warming and ozone layer depletion. Both phenomena affect the temperature balance of the earth and are linked to the observed climate change as described briefly below.

4.1.1   Global Warming

The mean temperature at the surface of the earth is determined by the balance between energy received from the sun and energy re-radiated back into space. The atmosphere allows most of the incoming radiation to reach the surface of the earth. However, because the earth is at much lower temperatures than the sun, the re-radiated energy is in the form of longer-wavelength infrared radiation which is partially absorbed and retained by some gases in the atmosphere (RCEP, 2000). The effect is exactly analogous to that in a greenhouse, where the glass transmits short wavelength incoming radiation but traps much of the re-radiated energy. The constituents of the atmosphere

Floods, as well as droughts, are only some of the extreme effects linked to climate change caused by human activities. Photograph courtesy of USDA.

which absorb the emitted radiation are known as greenhouse gases. The principal greenhouse gas is carbon dioxide (CO_2). Other significant greenhouse gases are methane (CH_4), water vapour and nitrous oxide (N_2O). Other gases, although present in small concentrations, are nevertheless potent heat absorbers and therefore contribute to the greenhouse effect: they include chlorofluorocarbons (CFCs), hydrofluorocarbons (HFCs), other halons and tropospheric ozone[1] (O_3).

Human activities have caused a large measurable increase in the concentration of greenhouse gases in the atmosphere. Although there is some uncertainty in the predictions, the general scientific consensus is that the enhanced greenhouse effect is causing a rise in average global temperature which is likely to cause major changes in climatic patterns (as discussed in Chapter 2). Consequently, as the Intergovernmental Panel on Climate Change predicts, a rise in mean global temperatures of between 1.4 and 5.8 °C could be expected by the end of 21st century (IPCC, 2001).

Although on an equal mass basis CO_2 is a less potent global warming agent than the other greenhouse gases (e.g. 1 kg of methane has about 21 times the global warming potential of 1 kg of CO_2, averaged over 100 years), the quantity of CO_2 emissions is so large that it remains the main contributor to global warming. In 2003, global emissions of CO_2 from fossil fuel emissions alone are estimated at 25×10^9 t/yr. The emissions of CO_2 have been increasing since the industrial revolution 150 years ago, leading to 25% increase in the CO_2 atmospheric concentration which today stands at 367 ppm. One of the main sources of CO_2 emissions is combustion of fossil carbon-based fuels – coal, oil and gas – used for energy generation and transport. From a technical point of view, it may be possible to reduce emissions of CO_2 through improved energy efficiency, use of non-fossil fuel-based sources of energy and by sequestering part of the CO_2 to prevent or at least delay its release (RCEP, 2000). At a political level, various international agreements and protocols have been signed in an attempt to slow down the climate change caused by human activities. For example, a Framework Convention on Climate Change was established by the United Nations at the Rio Earth Summit in 1992. This was followed by the Kyoto Protocol of 1997, by which nations committed themselves to varying levels of reduction of their emissions of greenhouse gases. A number of subsequent conferences on climate change have been concerned with negotiations on emission reduction targets for different countries. Progress is slow and any future success of the climate change agreements will be a telling indicator of commitment of the international community to sustainable development. However, even the full Kyoto commiments are only a small fraction of the reductions needed to stabilise the global climate (see section 2.4.3 in Chapter 2).

4.1.2 Ozone Layer Depletion

The second global air-pollution phenomenon that is also linked to climate change is depletion of the ozone layer. The majority of ozone is located in the upper part of the

---

[1] Ozone generated in the lower layer of the atmosphere known as troposphere. This is the layer immediately above the ground, stretching up to 10 km above the earth.

atmosphere (stratosphere) at an altitude of 10–50 km above the earth; this is known as the *ozone layer*. It filters the incoming harmful ultraviolet (UV) radiation which would otherwise affect humans, for example, by causing eye disorders and skin cancers. The ozone layer is depleted easily by halogens (chlorine, bromine and fluorine) bound in organic compounds such as CFCs, carbon tetrachloride, methyl chloroform, hydrochlorofluorocarbons (HCFCs) and halons. These compounds have been used in many applications including refrigeration, air conditioning, foam blowing, cleaning of electronic components and as solvents and fire-inhibiting medium. Because they are chemically inert and therefore persistent, they easily reach the stratosphere where, under the influence of the UV radiation, they dissociate to release the halogen atoms. They then react quickly with ozone to create oxygen molecules and atoms thus destroying the molecules of ozone. Due to these reactions, the ozone layer has been thinning during the past few decades. The worst cases of the ozone layer depletion have been recorded above the Antarctic, but major ozone layer losses have also been occurring in the Northern Hemisphere.

The problem of ozone depletion has been addressed by the international community through a number of international agreements, most notably through the Montreal Protocol of 1987 and its numerous amendments. In fact, this is one of the most successful cases in global cooperation related to the environment. The Montreal Protocol was signed by over 180 countries, endorsing proposals to phase out the production and use of 96 different ozone-depleting substances. For developed countries in general, the phase-out programme will be largely completed by 2010; longer periods have been permitted for developing countries. If the international protocols and agreements are adhered to, global ozone losses and the ozone 'hole' are predicted to recover by about 2045. Otherwise, the UNEP estimates that without the phase-out programme the harmful UV radiation in Northern Europe would double, leading to 19 million more cases of skin cancer and 130 million more cases of eye cataracts (UNEP, 2000).

Questions

1. What is the usual composition of clean air? Compare this with the composition of air in the area you live. What do you conclude – is your surrounding air polluted? When do we consider the air to be polluted?
2. Describe the mechanisms of global warming and ozone layer depletion. Which substances have the greatest global warming and ozone-depleting potential respectively?
3. Why is the ozone loss greater above the Antarctic than the Arctic when the ozone-depleting substances are released mainly in the Northern Hemisphere?
4. How can CFCs get to the stratosphere if they are heavier than air?
5. What consequences are expected from climate change caused by global warming? What is the influence of ozone layer depletion on climate change?
6. Which countries are the greatest emitters of greenhouse gases? Are they signatories to the Kyoto Protocol?
7. Summarise the requirements of the Kyoto and Montreal Protocols. What is the commitment of your country to these Protocols?
8. Are international agreements such as the Kyoto and Montreal Protocols legally binding? What happens if the signatories do not comply with these agreements?
9. What are the options for reducing emissions of CO_2?

10. Which renewable energy systems would lead to a reduction in CO_2 emissions? Which of these systems are used in your country and what is their percentage contribution to the total energy generation in your country?
11. Which substances have replaced CFCs and other halogenated carbons? Are they more sustainable than the original substances? Why?

4.2   Regional Air Pollution

In addition to the global effects, human activities also cause regional air pollution and associated environmental degradation. One such effect is water and soil acidification caused by emissions of acid gases into the atmosphere. The acid gases, which include SO_2, NO, NO_2 and ammonia (NH_3), are dispersed in the atmosphere and can travel long distances before being deposited on the ground or in waterways. Deposition can be by both wet and dry mechanisms. The former occurs when the acid gases are washed out by rain; this phenomenon is known as acid rain. Dry deposition occurs by direct uptake of acid gases by vegetation and soil.

The following atmospheric reactions may be expected for SO_2 and NO_x respectively:

$$SO_2 + \frac{1}{2}O_2 \rightarrow SO_3$$

$$SO_3 + H_2O \rightarrow H_2SO_4$$

$$NO_2 + OH \rightarrow HNO_3$$

$$NO_2 + O_3 \rightarrow NO_3 + O_2$$

$$NO_3 + RH \rightarrow HNO_3 + R$$

$$NO_3 + NO_2 \leftrightarrow N_2O_5$$

$$N_2O_5 + H_2O \leftrightarrow 2HNO_3$$

where RH is a hydrocarbon.

Once deposited, acid gases can reduce the pH of water or soil to values as low as 3. Thus they can cause great physical damage to crops, forests, watercourses and to the external surfaces of buildings. Acidification can also leach (dissolve) metals from soils and clays into solutions which are sufficiently concentrated to be toxic to freshwater fish and other species. Further environmental damage from deposition of nitrogen-containing gases such as NO_x, and NH_3 occurs due to nutrient enrichment of terrestrial and aquatic ecosystems with resulting increase in growth of biomass. As mentioned in Chapter 3, this effect is known as eutrophication. In aquatic systems, eutrophication causes increased growth of algae which cloud the water and block sunlight, causing underwater grasses to die, thus destroying habitats and food for many aquatic organisms. Furthermore, when the algae die and decompose, they deplete oxygen dissolved in the water and so kill other organisms such as fish and crabs.

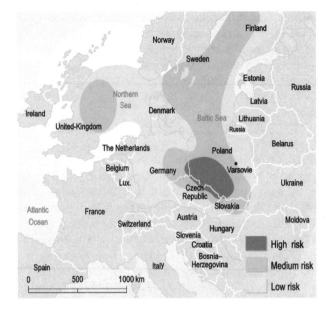

Figure 4.1   *Regions in Europe affected by acid rain (UNEP GRID-Arendal, 2001; reproduced by permission from GRID-Arendal Associate.). Source*: Hatier (1993) (ed.) European Atlas of Environment and Health. Website: www.grida.no/db/maps/prod/level3/id_1177.htm

Figure 4.1 shows the areas in Europe affected by acid rain. Some of these countries are affected mainly due to 'imports' of SO_2 and NO_x from the other countries in the region. For example, Sweden and Norway 'import' much more acid gases from Poland, Germany and the UK than they themselves generate (EMEP, 1999).

The largest source of acid gases is the combustion of fossil fuels for energy generation and transportation. Other significant sources of NO_x emissions include industrial processes such as manufacture of nitric acid and fertilisers. Ammonia is emitted from agricultural activities such as storage of manure, soil fertilising, animal husbandry and so on.

Although the SO_2 and NO_x emissions in Europe have been decreasing steadily during the past decade, emissions in other regions, especially in some parts of Asia, are a major and growing problem. Both the environmental and the economic impacts have already been observed: for example, the World Bank has estimated China's overall annual forest and crop losses due to acid rain at US$5000 million (UNEP GRID-Arendal, 2001).

To reduce and slow down the effects of acid gases and some other air pollutants, the international community has promulgated a Convention on Long-Range Trans-boundary Air Pollution (UNECE, 2003). The Convention obliges the signatory countries to reduce and prevent air pollution through the use of Best Available Technology (BAT) that is economically feasible (NSCA, 2003).

Questions

1. Describe the mechanisms of acid rain and eutrophication respectively. What are the effects of these two environmental impacts?

2. List the major world anthropogenic emission sources of SO_2 and NO_x and their estimated contributions to the total emissions of these pollutants in tonnes per year. What is the percentage contribution of your country to these global emissions?
3. What options exist for the prevention and clean-up of acidic emissions?
4. List the most important legislation concerned with emissions of SO_2 and NO_x from large combustion and industrial plants in your country.
5. Which air pollutants are included in the UNECE Convention on Long-Range Transboundary Air Pollution (LRTAP)? What are the targets for these pollutants?
6. The Convention on LRTAP uses the concept of 'critical loads' to prevent damage to the environment and human health. Find out the meaning of this concept.
7. What obligations does your country have under the Convention on LRTAP?

4.3 Local Air Pollution

In many parts of the world, particularly in large cities, the local atmosphere is becoming increasingly polluted from local industrial activities, road vehicles and household heating. A wide variety of substances can contribute to local air pollution, most notably SO_2, NO_x, CO_2, CO, VOCs, unburned hydrocarbons and solid particles of dust, ash and soot. In addition to causing the global and regional effects discussed in the preceding sections, the combined effect of these pollutants can cause a number of local air-pollution effects. Of these, 'winter' and 'summer' smog are the two effects most often encountered in the urban atmosphere.

The main constituents of winter smog are SO_2 and particles, whose emissions increase in the winter months in the areas which use coal for heating; hence the name. The synergistic effect of particles and SO_2 can have a deleterious impact on the environment and particularly on human health. A direct link between these pollutants and increased illness and mortality was first established in the 1950s in London where, in one week alone, 4000 people died due to the prolonged winter-smog episodes.

Summer or photochemical smog, on the other hand, occurs in the summer months due to the reactions between NO_x, VOCs and unburned hydrocarbons in the presence of UV radiation from the sun. These pollutants, emitted mainly from vehicles, react to generate photochemical oxidants such as peroxylacetylnitrate and tropospheric ozone. Photochemical smog and photo-oxidants can cause respiratory problems and eye irritation in humans and can also affect vegetation through oxidation processes. Tropospheric ozone can also act as a greenhouse gas.

Questions

1. What is the difference between 'winter' and 'summer' smog? Explain the mechanism by which they are generated.
2. What is the difference between stratospheric and tropospheric ozone? Are they generally beneficial or generally harmful? Explain the role of NO_x in the generation of tropospheric ozone.

3. What are the major sources of air pollution in your town or city? Find out how much SO_2, NO_x and particles they emit per year.
4. Describe air-pollution legislation in your country and list the major acts which regulate air pollution.
5. How would you deal with the problem of air pollution in urban areas?
6. Transport in cities is one large source of air pollution. How would you improve the transport situation in your town/city? What would be more sustainable transport option than currently used in your city?
7. Which arguments would you use to persuade the local government in your town/city to adopt and develop more sustainable transport policies?

4.4 Health Effects of Air Pollution

One of the reasons for our concern about air quality lies in the effects of air pollution on human health. Some of these effects are immediate and obvious, whilst the others can develop over time. In either case, it is not easy to establish a direct link between air pollution and human health effects because of the many other factors that also have an influence.

There have been many studies over the years which aimed to obtain reliable data and estimates on the actual effects of air pollution on human health. For example, an EU study (Spix *et al.*, 1998) analysed a number of epidemiological studies carried out in 15 large cities across the EU. The study concluded that the rate of hospital admissions does vary depending on the state of the atmosphere: increases of $50\,\mu g/m^3$ in NO_2 levels above the background level were estimated to lead, within hours or a few days, to an increase of 2.6% in hospital admissions for asthma treatment. The same increase in NO_2 levels leads to a 1.9% increase in admissions for lung conditions. A UK-based study showed that mortality rates follow a similar trend: deaths from all causes (excluding external causes such as accidents) are increased by 3.5% for every increase of $100\,\mu g/m^3$ in daily average NO_2 level (COMEAP, 1998). The same study estimated that in the urban areas in the UK the number of extra hospital admissions related to increased NO_2 and tropospheric ozone levels is 8700 and 9900 per year respectively.

Air pollution costs not only human health and lives, but also money. Another UK report estimated that in 1996/1997 the cost of admissions to hospitals for respiratory diseases related to air pollution cost Government (and the tax payer) in total £566 million or £1400 per person per spell in hospital (Department of Health, 1999). These estimates were based on 407 000 hospital admissions during that year, with an average length of stay of 7.7 days. The report also concluded that the relationship between pollution and health was linear and reversible over the pollution ranges considered so that reductions in pollution levels would reduce both hospital admissions and premature deaths. Table 4.1 summarises these reductions and the estimated health and cost benefits of the three pollutants – particulate matter (PM10)[2], SO_2 and tropospheric ozone – for which the information is most

---

[2] Particulates that are less than $10\,\mu$ in diameter.

Table 4.1 *Reduction of concentration of air pollutants and the resulting health and costs benefits (Reproduced with permission from Department of Health, 1999, © Crown.)*

	Effect per µg/m^3 reduction of pollutant (based on urban population)		
	Particulate matter (PM10)	Sulphur dioxide	Tropospheric ozone (summer only)
Number of premature deaths avoided per year	340	270	170
Number of hospital admissions avoided per year (respiratory diseases)	280	180	145
Annual average savings for the 'tax payer' (1996 prices)	£0.62 m	£0.43 m	£0.37 m

reliable. The figures suggest that 780 fewer people would die per year from air pollution-related illnesses and this could potentially save £1.42 million of tax payers' money per year.

However, it should be stressed that there is still a large uncertainty in these estimates, in terms of both the actual relationship between pollution and human health and the estimated costs to society. Therefore, there is an ongoing debate regarding the environmental, economic and ethical aspects of air pollution and some of the questions raised include the following.

Questions

1. Taking the precautionary principle into account, can we afford not to act now and wait until the scientific facts on the effects of pollution are more certain?
2. What are the losses to the economy and society through the days off work because of the health effects of air pollution? Is the position different if the patients are younger or older, working or not working?
3. From the ethical point of view, is it correct to evaluate the health effects of pollution on humans by estimating economic costs, in effect putting monetary value on human life? Does it mean that if people are not employed (young or elderly), therefore not costing the economy through the days off work, their lives are less 'valuable' than lives of those which are employed?
4. If the UK Government spends £566 million on hospital treatment for respiratory disorders, how much is it worth spending on policies for preventing and reducing air pollution – less, the same or more? Why?
5. Should the pollution-related healthcare costs be recovered from general taxation and/or from those who need health treatment, or should they be recovered from polluters? If the latter, how should this be done?
6. Can individual polluters be identified and the responsibility for pollution allocated? Take into account that there are several different groups of polluters: for

example, a relatively few operators of large industrial sites and a large number of consumers and car drivers.
7. How should the level of pollution fines be set? What account should be taken of the polluter's ability to pay? What if the polluter has no other option (e.g. an alternative to the private car for commuting)?

4.5 Air Pollution Prevention and Control

Protecting human health and the environment from pollution demands action at both international and national levels. As we mentioned in the preceding sections, a number of international agreements and protocols have been put in place to protect the environment from air pollution, including the Montreal (UNEP, 2003) and Kyoto (UNFCCC, 2003) Protocols and the UNECE Convention on Long-Range Transboundary Air Pollution (LRTAP) (UNECE, 2003). At the EU level, numerous directives regulate air pollution from industrial installations and motor vehicles (NSCA, 2003). In addition to these, in most countries national legislation regulates to a differing degree emissions to air from industrial and other activities. In the USA, for example, the Clean Air Act sets strict emission limits for a number of pollutants including SO_x, NO_x and particulates (EPA, 2003).

A sustainable approach to combating air pollution must be based on Integrated Pollution Prevention and Control (IPPC). This means that air quality protection must not be achieved by polluting the other two environmental media – water and land. For example, removing air pollutants from power plant flue gas is often carried out by absorption in a liquid, which then requires further treatment and disposal of the liquid effluent. This in effect transfers pollution from air to water.

The IPPC approach to industrial pollution has more recently been integrated within the EC legislation on environmental pollution and is now enshrined in the Directive on IPPC (EC, 1996). This is a major new legislation in the EU aimed at reducing environmental pollution from industrial activities in an integrated fashion and, if properly applied and enforced, could potentially lead to reduced pollution and improved industrial sustainability. It is therefore interesting for us to explore further the IPPC approach and the requirements of the IPPC Directive. We will then introduce a case study to illustrate how this approach can be used to prevent and reduce air pollution from nitrogen oxides.

The IPPC Directive is based on three main principles:

1. the environment as a whole must be protected;
2. pollution prevention has priority over pollution control;
3. in protecting the environment, environmental, economic and social impacts must be balanced.

1. The first IPPC principle is based on a life cycle approach and demands consideration of whole supply chains (Nicholas *et al.*, 2000). As illustrated in Figure 4.2, this means that the impact of an industrial installation on the environment should be assessed by taking into account both on- and off-site activities.

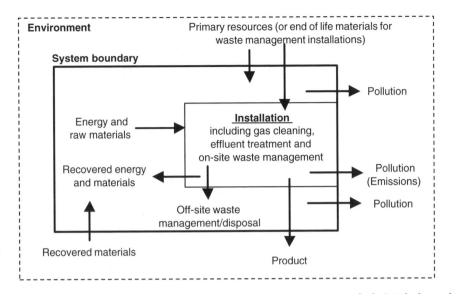

Figure 4.2   *The first IPPC principle: protection of the environment as a whole (Nicholas et al., 2000; reproduced by permission of The Institution of Chemical Engineers.)*

For example, on-site considerations include emissions from the installation itself as well as from any gas cleaning, effluent treatment and waste management, and post-closure site restoration. The off-site considerations should include the sources and types of raw material and energy, off-site waste disposal and any materials or energy recovered from the installation and used elsewhere. Such an approach avoids shifting of environmental impacts upstream or downstream in the supply chain and ensures that the impact on the environment as a whole has been minimised.

2. The second principle in the IPPC Directive acknowledges that pollution prevention is a more sustainable approach than pollution clean-up. Therefore, to protect the environment as a whole, pollution control should be considered only when all prevention options have been exhausted. Some examples of pollution prevention options include the use of sustainable raw materials and energy, process optimisation, waste minimisation and recycling. Pollution control is based on clean-up techniques which normally require further treatment and disposal of effluents and solid wastes generated in the clean-up process. The second IPPC principle is illustrated in Figure 4.3.

3. The third IPPC principle requires that in choosing and assessing pollution prevention and control options, environmental and socio-economic costs are to be considered and balanced. This means that protection of the environment should be achieved at a reasonable economic cost, using technically feasible and socially acceptable options.

The IPPC Directive requires that most industrial installations be designed, operated, maintained and decommissioned according to the above three principles.

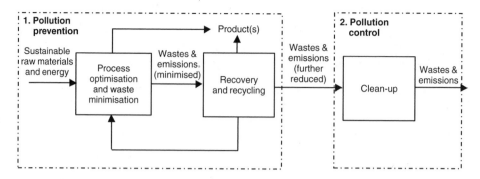

Figure 4.3   *The second IPPC principle: pollution prevention has priority over pollution control*

Table 4.2   *The meaning of the term BAT (Adapted from EC, 1996.)*

Best	Available	Techniques
Most effective in achieving a high general level of protection of the environment as a whole.	Developed on a scale which allows implementation in the relevant industrial sector, under economically and technically viable conditions, taking into consideration the costs and advantages, as long as they are reasonably accessible to the operator.	Include both the technology used and the way in which the installation is designed, built, maintained, operated and decommissioned.

Application of these principles should lead to a choice of the BAT for a particular installation. As regulated by the Directive, to obtain or keep a permit to operate, operators of industrial plants must demonstrate that their installation is BAT. The meaning of the term BAT is summarised in Table 4.2. We will now explore how the IPPC approach can be applied to identify BAT for prevention and control of NO_x emissions from one of the large potential sources of these pollutants – the manufacture of nitric acid.

Questions

1. Give an overview of the development of air pollution-related legislation in your country and comment on its effectiveness in protecting air quality.
2. Which stages in the life cycle of an installation must be considered within the IPPC Directive?
3. Which industrial sectors are regulated by the IPPC Directive? Why do you think these sectors have been included under the IPPC Directive?

4.6   Case Study: Identifying BAT for the Prevention and Control of NO$_x$ Emissions

Nitric acid (HNO$_3$) is an important raw material used in many sectors, including the fertiliser, plastic, explosive and metal industries. The majority of HNO$_3$ plants produce medium-concentration acid (57–70 wt%). As explained further below, medium-concentration HNO$_3$ is mostly produced by oxidation of ammonia followed by absorption of NO and NO$_2$ (NO$_x$) in weak nitric acid. Due to process inefficiencies, not all of the NO$_x$ is converted into the acid so that without the appropriate control measures, relatively high emissions of NO$_x$ could be released into the atmosphere. Typical uncontrolled emissions in the tail gas leaving the absorption tower are between 1000 and 1500 mg/m^3. In addition to NO$_x$, some nitrous oxide (N$_2$O) can also be released from the manufacture of HNO$_3$.

We consider here the case of an existing nitric acid manufacturing plant as originally described by Kniel *et al.* (1996). The plant produces 720 t/day of 56% acid and emits 107 kg NO$_x$ per hour (1432 ppm). The flow diagram of the plant is given in Figure 4.4. This is an old plant and when it was built no pollution prevention or control systems were required to reduce NO$_x$ emissions. However, the IPPC Directive has been put in place in the meantime so the plant must be modified to comply with the Directive or it will be closed down. Therefore, the company needs to apply the IPPC approach and identify BAT for NO$_x$ emission prevention and control for their particular conditions.

The HNO$_3$ manufacturing process is relatively complex and there are a number of pollution prevention and control options that can be used to reduce NO$_x$ emissions. Therefore, before we can apply the IPPC approach and identify BAT for the specific conditions of this plant, we will first need to understand both the HNO$_3$ process and the pollution prevention and control techniques. These are described next.

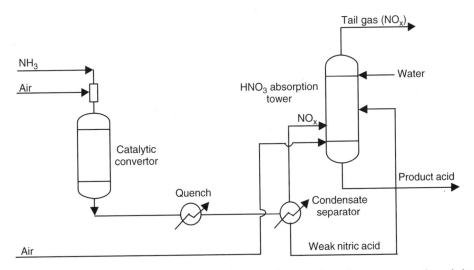

Figure 4.4 *A simplified flow diagram for the manufacture of medium-concentration nitric acid (EA, 2001)*

4.6.1 Nitric Acid Manufacture

As shown in Figure 4.4, the HNO_3 manufacturing process used in the plant involves the following steps:

1. catalytic oxidation of ammonia (NH_3) to nitrogen monoxide (NO);
2. oxidation of nitrogen monoxide to the dioxide (NO_2); and
3. absorption of NO_2 in water to produce medium-concentration HNO_3 accompanied by the release of NO_x.

1. In the oxidation (combustion) stage, ammonia and air are passed through a catalytic converter. The ammonia is oxidised to nitric oxide (NO) according to the equation:

$$4NH_3 + 5O_2 \longleftrightarrow 4NO + 6H_2O \qquad (4.1)$$

There are simultaneous side reactions which are undesirable because they reduce the yield of NO:

$$4NH_3 + 3O_2 \longleftrightarrow 2N_2 + 6H_2O \qquad (4.2)$$

$$4NH_3 + 4O_2 \longleftrightarrow 2N_2O + 6H_2O \qquad (4.3)$$

The nitrogen (N_2) and nitrous oxide (N_2O) products of the side reactions pass through the remaining parts of the process almost unchanged and are discharged through the stack into the atmosphere. The ammonia oxidation process is highly exothermic, and the yield of NO is dependent on temperature and pressure: the lower the temperature and pressure, the higher the yield. Optimum temperatures and pressures for catalytic oxidation are in the range of 800–950 °C and 3–5 bar and the NO yield is around 96%. This plant is operated at 900 °C and 4 bar.

2. The exit gases from the catalytic converter are cooled in the cooler-condenser to around 50 °C. During this stage some of the NO oxidises to NO_2:

$$2NO + O_2 \longleftrightarrow 2NO_2 \qquad (4.4)$$

The oxygen required for oxidation is provided through an excess air supply at the convertor inlet. However, the oxidation reaction is not completed until the gases enter the absorption section.

Water produced by ammonia oxidation reactions (4.1)–(4.3) is condensed in the cooler-condenser and it absorbs nitrogen dioxide formed in reaction (4.4) to form a weak nitric acid. This acid is then transferred to the absorption tower (Figure 4.4).

3. The NO and NO_2 gases are then passed from the cooler-condenser section into the absorption tower. In the counter-current flow with water, they are absorbed to yield nitric acid according to the following reaction:

$$3NO_2 + H_2O \longleftrightarrow 2HNO_3 + NO \qquad (4.5)$$

In addition, the undesired reverse of reaction (4.4) can take place simultaneously in the gas and liquid phases. Minor formation of nitrous acid can also occur:

$$NO + NO_2 + H_2O \longleftrightarrow 2HNO_2 \tag{4.6}$$

The absorption process is limited by the concentration of NO_2 in the absorption tower which, on the other hand, is limited by the reaction kinetics between O_2 and NO (reaction 4.4). When all the NO_2 generated in that way is spent, the rate of absorption then depends on the amount of NO liberated in reaction (4.5). A summary of the general absorption and mass transfer principles can be found in Appendix 4.A.

Both NO oxidation and NO_2 absorption are assisted by increasing the pressure and decreasing the temperature. Hence, high nitric acid yields can be achieved at medium to high pressures in the absorption tower (3–11 bar) and at low temperatures. This plant operates at 3.25 bar and 10 °C. To increase the residence time and contact area between the gas and the liquid, a packed absorption tower is used. A general description of packed towers is given in Appendix 4.A.

The NO_x tail gas from the absorption tower is currently discharged into the atmosphere. However, to comply with the IPPC Directive, the plant has to be modified to accommodate the appropriate pollution prevention and control measures. These measures are discussed in the following sections.

Questions

1. What influences the yield of nitric acid? Why is it important to maximise its yield?
2. Oxidation of NO to NO_2 starts during cool-down of gases leaving the convertor in the cooler-condenser section. Explain why the oxidation reaction is not completed in this stage.
3. Why are the reaction (4.6) and the reverse of reaction (4.4) undesirable in this process?
4. The rate of NO oxidation to NO_2 as given by reaction (4.4) is limited by the partial pressures (i.e. concentrations) of NO and O_2. Assuming the equilibrium to be fully established, write down the equation for calculating the partial pressure of NO_2, given the partial pressures of NO and O_2. Explain what that equation means.

4.6.2 Pollution Prevention and Control of NO_x Emissions

A number of pollution prevention and control techniques can be used to reduce NO_x emissions from the manufacture of nitric acid. The pollution prevention methods involve optimisation of the design and process parameters while the control options include clean-up techniques such as absorption into sodium hydroxide and reduction to nitrogen with hydrogen or natural gas.

Pollution Prevention: Process Design and Operation

NO_x emissions from the manufacture of nitric acid can be prevented by a good design and optimised operation of the absorption tower. The important engineering and process parameters that determine the efficiency of absorption include:

- pressure and temperature in the absorber;
- reaction volume and residence time;
- gas–liquid contact area; and
- partial pressures (concentrations) of nitrogen monoxide and oxygen.

Table 4.3 summarises the relationship between NO_x emissions and the operating parameters in the absorption tower. Further details on the fundamentals of absorption can be found in Appendix 4.A.

Thus, it is possible to minimise NO_x emissions by identifying an optimum range for the operating parameters. For instance, operating the absorption tower at 8 bar and 10 °C can bring the emissions of NO_x down to 400 mg/m^3. Another way to minimise the emissions is to increase the Number of Transfer Units (NTU) to provide the additional reaction volume and residence time (Appendix 4.A). This in effect means increasing the height of the absorption tower or adding a second tower in series. This technique is known as extended or enhanced absorption.

Pollution Prevention: Extended Absorption

If Extended Absorption (EA) is used, it is more likely that a second absorption tower would be installed rather than making the original absorber taller. If that is the case, the tail gas from the first tower is directed to the base of the second tower and flows counter-current to a chilled-process water feed to form weak nitric acid. This weak acid is then recycled to the upper part of the first tower absorbing the rising NO_x gases from the ammonia oxidation stage and producing the product acid at the tower bottom. To minimise the size of the second tower, the incoming gas has to be pressurised and additional cooling provided in the tower. Further increases in the efficiency can be achieved by injection of pure oxygen into the tower to speed up the oxidation process of NO to NO_2.

After a certain contact time between the gaseous NO_x and the water–weak nitric acid solution, the efficiency of the absorption process decreases as the concentration of NO_x in the solution rises and the driving force decreases. For that reason, even at high pressures and extended residence times, some NO_x will remain in the gaseous

Table 4.3 *NO_x emissions as a function of process parameters in the absorption column*

Process parameter	Parameter change	NO_x emissions
Pressure	Increase	Decrease
Temperature	Increase	Increase
Reaction volume/residence time	Increase	Decrease
Gas–liquid contact area	Increase	Decrease
Concentration of NO and O_2	Increase	Decrease

phase. Therefore, the tail gas from nitric acid plants will always contain a certain amount of NO_x gases and some clean-up technique will have to be used to reduce the NO_x emissions further. In the next sections, we review and compare some of the NO_x clean-up techniques.

Pollution Control: Absorption into Sodium hydroxide

Sodium hydroxide (NaOH) is an effective absorbent of NO_x. The absorption process is accompanied by a chemical reaction (chemisorption) in which NO and NO_2 react with NaOH to form sodium nitrite:

$$NO + NO_2 \rightarrow N_2O_3 \tag{4.7}$$

$$N_2O_3 + 2NaOH \rightarrow 2NaNO_2 + H_2O \tag{4.8}$$

While NO does not absorb in NaOH readily, NO_2 reacts with NaOH to form sodium nitrate and nitrite according to the equation:

$$2NO_2 + 2NaOH \rightarrow NaNO_2 + NaNO_3 + H_2O \tag{4.9}$$

The rate of reaction and absorption efficiency depends on many parameters, including the ratio of NO to NO_2, concentration of NaOH, temperature and pressure (Katima *et al.*, 1992, 1993). For example, if the NO and NO_2 are present in equal (stoichiometric) amounts and pressure is in excess of 4.5 bar, the process can be very efficient, reducing NO_x in the tail gas from 1200 to 400 mg/m^3. If the NO and NO_2 are in off-stoichiometric proportions, the absorption process is impeded.

The resulting sodium nitrite–nitrate solution is a liquid effluent and as such may present a disposal problem; hence the absorption process can be considered BAT only if the effluent can either be utilised (e.g. as a product) or eliminated without causing further environmental pollution (EA, 2001). This clean-up technique is unlikely to be capable of reducing NO_x to acceptable emission levels on its own. Furthermore, from the economic point of view, the costs of NaOH and the pumping energy provide further disincentive to select this pollution control technique as BAT.

Pollution Control: Non-selective Catalytic Reduction (NSCR)

A reducing agent, normally hydrogen or natural gas, is injected into the tail gas of the absorption tower to react with the chemical substances present in the gas, including NO, NO_2 and N_2O. Therefore, NSCR is capable of removing both NO_x and N_2O. To improve the removal rates, the reduction reactions are carried out using a platinum catalyst. If hydrogen is used, the NO_x and N_2O are reduced to nitrogen and water, as shown by the following summary reaction:

$$6H_2 + O_2 + NO_2 + NO + N_2O \rightarrow 2N_2 + 6H_2O \tag{4.10}$$

However, if natural gas is used, then carbon dioxide is also generated and released with the tail gas:

$$2CH_4 + O_2 + 2NO_2 + 2N_2O \rightarrow 2CO_2 + 4H_2O + 3N_2 \tag{4.11}$$

An excess of reducing agent is necessary to ensure reducing conditions. The minimum operating temperature for hydrogen is $200\,°C$ but typically the process is operated at $300\,°C$. If natural gas is used as the reducing agent, the optimum operating temperature is between 480 and $550\,°C$.

These reactions are exothermic so that the gas leaves the catalyst bed at an elevated temperature (up to $750\,°C$). This heat can be utilised in a heat exchanger or turbine to generate steam or power. NSCR is capable of eliminating 90% of NO_x and 70% of N_2O originally present in the tail gas.

Pollution Control: Selective Catalytic Reduction (SCR)

Similar to NSCR, the SCR process also reduces NO_x to nitrogen and water. However, whilst in NSCR the reactions involve various gaseous species, here the reducing agent, ammonia, reacts selectively with NO_x, and other gases do not participate in the reactions.

The ammonia is injected into the tail gas of the absorption tower and passed through beds of solid catalyst pellets (such as vanadium oxide, V_2O_5) at elevated temperatures, generally above $250\,°C$. This technique can remove over 95% of NO_x. The summary reaction can be represented by the following equation:

$$5NO + 7NO_2 + 14NH_3 + O_2 \rightarrow 13N_2 + 21H_2O \tag{4.12}$$

A small amount of ammonia can pass through the catalyst beds unreacted and be released into the atmosphere. This is known as 'ammonia slip' and can be as high as $10\,mg/m^3$ of the tail gas.

Questions

1. In addition to NO_x and N_2O emissions, what other releases to air, water and land can be expected from nitric acid manufacture? What environmental impacts these releases can cause?
2. Explain why the process parameters listed in Table 4.3 have the stated effect on the NO_x absorption efficiency (i.e. why increasing the operating pressure increases the efficiency? etc.).
3. Explain the idea behind extended absorption. What is the link between the NTU in the HNO_3 absorption tower and the NO_x emissions?
4. How would you calculate the required height of the absorption column to increase the HNO_3 production yield and reduce the emissions of NO_x from the manufacture of nitric acid? What information and data would you need to do that?

5. The efficiency of NO_2 absorption to produce HNO_3 can be increased further by increasing pressure. Discuss the advantages and disadvantages of pressurised systems in terms of their technical complexity, environmental impacts (including noise) and economic costs.

6. Discuss the advantages and disadvantages of supplying pure oxygen instead of air for oxidation of NO in the HNO_3 absorption tower. Address the following issues:

   (a) What are the advantages of using pure oxygen instead of air in terms of oxidation efficiency, gas flow rates, column volume and so on?

   (b) As discussed in Chapter 3, unlike air, oxygen does not come for free – it has to be produced by separating nitrogen from air. This is usually done in a large-scale cryogenic process (separation by cooling). What are the implications of this in the context of IPPC (i.e. taking into account all life cycle stages associated with this process option)?

7. Assume annual production of nitric acid of 500 000 t with NO_x emissions of 10 kg NO_2/t acid. If scrubbing with sodium hydroxide is used to reduce the emissions of NO_x, calculate the amount of waste liquid effluent generated by reaction (4.8) in t/yr that would have to be treated and disposed of. Assume the absorption efficiency is 95%. Note that the emissions of NO_x are expressed as NO_2. How would the effluent be treated and where would it be disposed of?

8. IPPC requires consideration of wider impacts of an activity, which means consideration of a number of life cycle stages of a process. In the case of NO_x scrubbing using sodium hydroxide, what parts of the life cycle must be included for BAT assessment? Analysing this system, explain why absorption of NO_x in NaOH is unlikely to represent BAT.

9. NSCR is quite efficient in reducing the emissions of NO_x from the manufacture of nitric acid. However, it also generates additional environmental impacts. Identify these impacts for hydrogen and natural gas as reducing agents and explain the origin of these impacts.

10. Calculate the amount of carbon dioxide in t/yr generated in the NSCR process which removes 2 t NO_2/day from the nitric acid tail gas using natural gas. Calculate the potential for global warming from these CO_2 emissions. Compare that with the global warming avoided by the removal of the equivalent amount of N_2O/day from the same tail gas. What do you conclude?

11. Use the example in the previous question to calculate the equivalent acidification impact that would be avoided by the removal of NO_x with the NSCR process. Compare this avoided impact with global warming generated through the use of natural gas to remove the NO_x. What do you conclude? How should we approach situations like these, where reducing one environmental impact causes another?

12. What are the main environmental and safety concerns associated with the SCR process?

13. Why is it important to minimise ammonia 'slip' from the SCR process for NO_x control?

4.6.3   Balancing Environmental and Economic Costs

Now that we are familiar with the nitric acid manufacturing process and the pollution prevention and control techniques, we can apply the IPPC approach described in section 4.5 to identify BAT for reducing the emissions of NO_x from the plant considered in our case study.

To be able to apply the IPPC and BAT requirements, we will have to compare the techniques in terms of the following:

- efficiencies in reducing the emissions of NO_x;
- ease of application and availability;
- on-site environmental impacts (i.e. those arising from the technique itself);
- off-site environmental impacts associated with the manufacture of raw materials, energy generation and use; and
- economic costs.

To help them in their choice of BAT, the company has summarised the advantages and disadvantages of the pollution prevention techniques in Table 4.4. Furthermore, they have presented data on the costs of NO_x removal for the EA, NSCR and SCR. These are compared with a plant with no control of NO_x emissions (base case) in Table 4.5. However, these cost data refer to a new plant producing 1000 t/day of nitric acid so that they cannot be used directly for the existing plant. Nevertheless, the data will provide some guidance to the company with respect to the economic costs of pollution prevention and control.

The data in Table 4.5 represent average annualised costs expressed in terms of additional cost of NO_x reduction, compared to the base case. The table shows that each of the options reduces the final emissions significantly compared to the base case. These data are also illustrated in Figure 4.5. The figure shows that, once a high level of control has been achieved, the cost of attaining still further NO_x emission reduction rises very rapidly. It could be argued that with 98.5–98.8% reduction attained, extra gains in the removal efficiency would be approaching the limits of 'reasonable cost'. This means that, purely on a cost basis, a combination of extended absorption and selective catalytic reduction (EA + SCR) or extended absorption and non-selective catalytic reduction (EA + NSCR) would be ruled out as BAT; the EA would be chosen as BAT. However, from the environmental perspective, the EA is not as efficient in reducing the NO_x emissions as, for example, NSCR and SCR (Table 4.4). Therefore, from an environmental point of view, it would appear that a combination of EA and SCR is BAT. In an attempt to balance both environmental and economic criteria, it could be argued that the cost of this option is reasonable given its environmental efficiency, so that the choice of this option could be justified as BAT.

However, the disadvantage of SCR is that it does not remove N_2O while NSCR does. The question for the company is: does the removal of this potent global warming agent justify the high costs of NSCR?

Table 4.4 Comparison of techniques for NO_x prevention and control

Technique	On-site environmental releases/impacts					Exit NO_x level (mg/m^3)	Features
	Air[a]	Water	Land	Energy	Raw Materials		
Process design and operation (including high pressure)	None	None	None	Compressors, cooling	None	>400	Clean technology, easy to implement if done at an early design stage
Extended Absorption (EA)	None	None	None	Pumping, compressors, cooling, O_2 generation (if used)	Water	205–410	Recovery of product; high retrofit cost, moderate if part of original design
Sodium hydroxide scrubbing	None	Nitrate/ nitrite effluent	None	Pumping	NaOH	400	Liquid effluent, BAT if $NaNO_2$ can be recovered
NSCR	CO_2	None	Catalyst disposal	Compressors; gas preheating; potential for energy recovery	Fuel or H_2	205	Removes N_2O; high capital cost; difficult to retrofit
SCR	NH_3 'slip'	None	Catalyst disposal	Gas preheating	NH_3	100	Can be retrofitted; N_2O is not removed

[a] In each case, emissions to air exclude the NO_x emissions that remain untreated in the tail gas.

Table 4.5 *Comparison of annualised costs for NO$_x$ pollution prevention and control (EA, 2001)*

Technique	Residual NO$_x$ (kg NO$_2$/t of acid)	NO$_x$ removed (%)	Cost (£/t acid)
None ('base case')	9.7	0	0
EA	0.5	94.8	230
EA + SCR	0.15	98.5	880
EA + NSCR	0.12	98.8	1850

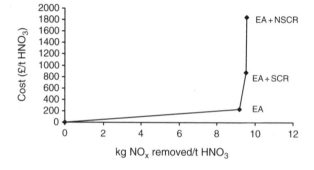

Figure 4.5 *Annualised NO$_x$ prevention and control costs (Adapted from EA, 2001; reproduced by permission of the Environment Agency.)*

Questions

1. What would be your answer to the above question on the comparison between SCR and NSCR?
2. Analyse the data shown in Tables 4.4 and 4.5 and Figure 4.5, and make your own choice of BAT for NO$_x$ prevention and control. Explain and justify your choice.
3. The social implications of the pollution prevention and control techniques have not been considered above. Can you identify them for each option? Do the social considerations change your choice of BAT?

4.6.4 Choosing BAT

After considering the design of the plant and feasibility of the different options, the company has decided to consider two alternatives in more detail:

– modification of the absorption tower to enable operation at higher pressure (HP); and
– installation of an ammonia-based SCR plant.

The company has estimated that increasing pressure in the absorption towers to 7.3 bar could reduce NO_x releases from the current 1432 ppm down to 230 ppm, while SCR would reduce the NO_x emissions from the current levels to 100 ppm. However, SCR would require 1358 kg/day of ammonia. Their next task is to find out which of these two options represents BAT.

Question

1. Why do you think the company has chosen to consider these two options and not any other described above?

Choosing BAT: Environmental Considerations

Adopting the life cycle approach, the company has carried out Life Cycle Assessment (LCA) to compare the environmental impacts of these two NO_x prevention and control options with the existing plant design. They followed the LCA methodology described in the Appendix at the end of the book. The LCA results, normalised to the base case, are summarised in Figure 4.6. It is apparent from the results that operation of the absorption tower at high pressure (HP) is environmentally preferred over the other two options. On the other hand, using the SCR technique reduces some of the impacts compared to the base case but at the expense of some other impacts, notably depletion of fossil fuels and the ozone layer, which are slightly increased. Furthermore, using SCR has no effect on the global warming potential which remains the same as for the base case.

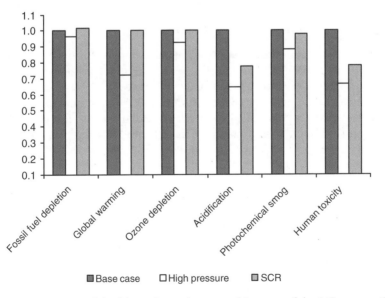

Figure 4.6 *Comparison of the life-cycle environmental impacts of the NO_x prevention and control options (Based on data from Kniel et al., 1996.)*

The environmental analysis would therefore point to the conclusions that the HP option is BAT for this nitric acid plant. However, SCR is 2.3 times more efficient in removing the NO_x and should not be disregarded as an option at this stage. Furthermore, the company still has to examine the socio-economic implications of each of these two plant modifications. That is their next task.

Questions

1. Consider the LCA results shown and answer the following questions:
   (a) Why do you think the SCR option has higher fossil fuel and ozone depletion than the base case?
   (b) The fact that SCR is better for some impacts but worse for the others when compared with the base case makes it more difficult to choose BAT. If you as a plant operator had to choose between these two options, which one would you choose? Justify your choice by discussing the 'significance' of global impacts (such as ozone depletion and fossil fuel depletion) and regional and local impacts (such as acidification and photochemical smog).

2. Based purely on environmental considerations, which process out of the three options (base case, HP and SCR) would you choose as BAT? Explain why.
3. Compare now the SCR and HP options in terms of the level of NO_x emissions that they can achieve. Which process would you as an operator choose? Why?
4. Combine both the environmental impacts and the levels of NO_x emission that each option can achieve and make an overall choice of BAT. Justify your choice by taking into account the IPPC principles.

Choosing BAT: Socio-economic Considerations

The capital and operating costs estimated by the company for the base case, HP and SCR are summarised in Table 4.6. The operating costs include the costs of raw material and energy, while the revenue includes proceeds from the sales of nitric acid and from energy recovery. The SCR option has the highest annual costs because it does not recover any additional acid to increase revenue whilst consuming additional raw materials (ammonia) and energy. The HP modification, on the other hand, increases the efficiency of absorption and therefore increases nitric acid production

Table 4.6 Comparison of costs for the NO_x prevention and control options (Based on data from Kniel et al., 1996.)

	Revenues and costs (million £, 1997 values)		
	Base case	Base case + HP	Base case + SCR
Capital cost	7.48	8.98	8.03
Total annual revenue	4.89	4.96	4.90
Annual costs	2.42	2.31	2.76
Annual profit	2.47	2.65	2.14

rates. The net operating costs of the HP modification are consequently lower than for the base case.

Based on the data in Table 4.6 and on the removal efficiencies of the two options, it is possible to calculate the 'Marginal Abatement Cost' (MAC) of NO_x pollution prevention and control. Note that the term 'abatement' (or reduction of emissions) includes both prevention and control. The MAC is defined as the increase in costs of abatement for a unit decrease in pollutant emissions. The MACs for SCR and HP, relative to the base case, are shown in Table 4.7. Only the operating costs are considered because the capital costs over the 25–30-year plant lifetime are going to be insignificant.

The results show that the MAC for the HP modification is −£92/ppm. This means that installing an HP option would result in a saving of £92/ppm NO_x removed compared with the base case. The reason for this is the surplus energy generated and increase in acid production through the increased rate of absorption. Conversely, the MAC for SCR is £255/ppm, which means that installing an SCR plant would increase the running costs by £255/ppm NO_x removed.

In addition to the MACs, which are internal to the company, it is also necessary to try to estimate the external costs associated with the damage to society of *not* preventing the emissions of NO_x. This is known as a 'Marginal Damage Cost' (MDC) and is defined as a change (increase or decrease) in economic damage to the whole society attributable to emissions of pollutants. MDCs are often referred to as 'externalities' or 'external costs'.

Combined internal and external costs give a full picture of the economic and social impacts of an emission and its prevention. However, calculating external costs is very difficult and at present there is no agreed methodology on how to do this. As discussed in section 4.4, some estimates in the UK are based on the costs to the national health system incurred through the hospital admissions related to increased pollution by NO_x (e.g. the cost of £1400 per person per one-week stay in hospital).

For the purposes of this case study, however, an estimated MDC of £700/t of NO_x emissions will be used (Hodge, 1995). This includes the costs of damage due to water acidification, damage to buildings, crops and forests and health costs (e.g. hospital admissions). Because of the large uncertainty in estimating the externalities, this figure should be used with caution and for indicative purposes only, rather than as a reliable and absolute estimate.

The total MDCs for the base case and the two NO_x emission control options are shown in Table 4.8. The results, which depend heavily on the figure assumed for the external cost of damage caused by NO_x emissions, show that SCR has the lowest

Table 4.7 *Marginal abatement costs (MAC) for NO_x emissions*

	HP	SCR
Removal efficiency	84%	93%
NO_x removed	1202 ppm	1332 ppm
Difference in operating costs between the plant modification and the base case	−£0.11 million (= £2.31 m − £2.42 m)	£0.34 million 0(= £2.76 m − £2.42 m)
MAC (operating)	−£92/ppm (= −£0.11 m/1202 ppm)	£255/ppm (= £0.34 m/1332 ppm)

Table 4.8 *Marginal damage cost (MDC) due to NO$_x$ emissions*

	Base case	HP	SCR
NO$_x$ releases (kg/h)	107	16.8	7.3
NO$_x$ releases (t/yr)	749	117.6	51.1
	(= 0.107 t/h ×7000 h)	(= 0.0168 t/h × 7000 h)	(= 0.0073 t/h × 7000 h)
Reduction in NO$_x$ emissions (t/yr)	–	631.4 (= 749 t/h – 117.6 t/h)	697.9 (= 749 t/h – 51.1 t/h)
Reduction of damage by NO$_x$ reduction (£/yr)	–	441 980 (= 631.4(t/h)/£700/t)	488 530 (= 697.9(t/h)/£700/t)
MDC due to NO$_x$ emissions (£/yr)	524 300 (= 749 t/yr ×£700/t)	82 320 (= 117.6 t/yr × £700/t)	35 770 (= 51.1 t/yr × £700/t)

external economic damage due to NO$_x$ emissions. The reason for this is that it is more effective in reducing the emissions of NO$_x$ than the HP modification.

Questions

1. Choose your preferred NO$_x$ prevention or control option considering the internal (MAC) and external costs (MDC) shown in Tables 4.7 and 4.8 by assuming the following roles:

   (a) plant operator;
   (b) Environment Agency inspector;
   (c) Government minister for the environment and social affairs.

   Justify your choice and explain the rationale for decision-making for each case.

Choosing BAT: The Whole Picture

The final step for the company is to carry out an integrated evaluation of the options on the technical, environmental, economic and social criteria. As we have seen from the above results, the final choice of BAT will involve balancing of these criteria, as one option is better for some and worse for the other sustainability aspects. This will require some value judgements by the company to decide which of these criteria are more important to them. They will then have to justify their choice and convince the regulator that the option they have chosen is indeed BAT which provides a more sustainable solution to the problem of NO$_x$ emissions.

Questions

1. List all criteria relevant for choosing BAT in the above case study. On the basis of the results obtained, rank the three options in order of their desirability. You may wish to create a ranking table, assigning a number to each technology to indicate the order of preference on a scale from 1 to 3 (e.g. number 1 indicates the best option and 3, the worst); this ranking should be done for each of the criteria you have listed.

2. Identify BAT for the conditions of this case study, assuming that you are Head of Engineering and Technology Division in a company. Justify your choice.
3. Now assume that you are:

   (a) local authority councillor;
   (b) local resident;
   (c) environmental activist;
   (d) Environment Agency inspector; and
   (e) Government minister for the environment and social affairs
       and choose BAT.

   Justify your choice by discussing what considerations would be important to you in each of the roles in choosing the BAT and explain why.

4. What can you conclude in terms of how different considerations influence different stakeholders (i.e. companies, local authorities and residents, the regulator and the government) in choosing BAT?

Conclusions

Improving air quality requires an integrated life cycle-based approach to ensure that the most sustainable options for pollution prevention and control have been identified. This case study demonstrates how this can be done at the practical level by applying the IPPC principles as defined by the EC Directive on IPPC. We have chosen the case of NO_x as one of the globally present pollutants, to illustrate that the choice of BAT for pollution prevention and control depends on many sustainability aspects and that the choice of BAT must be based on an integrated assessment of these aspects. The case study clearly illustrates that considering a limited number of decision criteria and drawing the system boundary too narrowly can result in the selection of a less sustainable pollution reduction technique. Furthermore, it shows that pollution prevention is not necessarily always the most sustainable option and that each technique must be assessed for the particular conditions for which BAT is being sought.

Identifying and choosing BAT is not an easy task, particularly if one technique is better for one set of criteria but worse for the others. Often, a compromise has to be made and engineers and scientists have to make decisions by using value judgements and trading-off different considerations. In doing so, they must be aware of the value system of the other stakeholders as their decisions will be scrutinised and may need to be justified. Pollution affects everyone and decisions on the protection of human health and the environment must therefore involve everyone – the role of engineers and scientists is to ensure that their choice of pollution reduction techniques does indeed protect everyone affected.

Acknowledgements

Part of the case study presented in this chapter has been developed with financial support from the Royal Academy of Engineering (RAEng) within its scheme 'Visiting Professors in Sustainable Design'. The authors gratefully acknowledge the support of the RAEng.

Appendix 4.A: Mass Transfer in Gas–Liquid Contacting

Packed towers are widely used devices for contacting gas and liquid streams, usually to absorb one or more components from the gas into the liquid or to desorb from the liquid to the gas; that is to carry out mass transfer operations. Figure 4.A.1 illustrates a typical packed absorption tower. The packing is often of specially shaped plastic or ceramic components and its role is to maximise the contact between the liquid and the gas by providing an extended surface across which the transfer can take place. Absorption towers are usually operated in a way that the two phases flow counter-current to each other: the liquid passes down through the tower by trickling over the surface of the packing, while the gas passes upwards in the passages through and between the packing elements.

In the following summary, the analysis is carried out in terms of the mole fraction of the transferred species in the two phases: x and y. Exactly analogous equations can be written in terms of the partial pressure of the gas and concentration of the liquid. This summary is also limited to the case of a linear equilibrium relationship (which means, in practice, relatively dilute mixtures) represented by:

$$y^* = m \cdot x \tag{4.A.1}$$

where y^* is the gas mole fraction in equilibrium with the liquid at mole fraction x. The equations are written for absorption; the case of desorption merely requires a few signs to be changed.

Per unit area of gas–liquid surface at any level in the tower, the overall rate of mass transfer N (i.e. the mass transfer flux) depends on the local departure from equilibrium (i.e. the mass transfer driving force, $y-y^*$) and on the overall mass transfer coefficient K_y:

$$N = K_y(y - y^*) \tag{4.A.2}$$

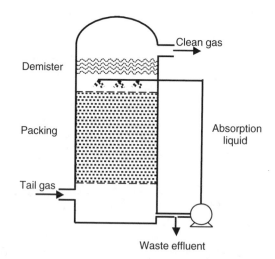

Figure 4.A.1 *Schematic representation of a typical packed absorption tower*

If the interfacial area per unit packed volume is a, then the local rate of absorption per unit packed volume is:

$$r = N \cdot a = K_y \cdot a(y - y^*) \tag{4.A.3}$$

We use mass balances to describe the composition changes in the two phases as they pass through the tower. Suppose the molar flow rates per unit cross-sectional area are G and L, and the mole fraction at the bottom and top of the tower are respectively (x_B, y_B) and (x_T, y_T). From the mass balance over the whole tower (Figure 4.A.2):

$$Gy_B + Lx_T = Gy_T + Lx_B \tag{4.A.4}$$

From the mass balance over the surface shown in Figure 4.A.2, from the base of the tower to a level at distance z below the top of the packing, we have:

$$Gy_B + Lx = Gy + Lx_B$$

or

$$(y - y_B) = L(x - x_B)/G \tag{4.A.5}$$

which is the equation of the *operating line* relating gas and liquid compositions in contact with each other.

Figure 4.A.3 shows a differential slice across the column. Per unit column area, the volume of the slice is dz. Therefore, from equations (4.A.3) and (4.A.1), the rate of transfer from the gas to the liquid in the slice is:

$$\begin{aligned} rdz &= Nadz = K_y a(y - y^*)dz \\ &= K_y a(y - mx)dz \end{aligned} \tag{4.A.6}$$

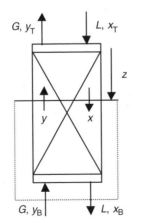

Figure 4.A.2   *A graphical representation of packed absorption tower*

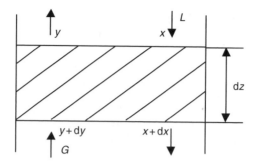

Figure 4.A.3   *Differential element of an absorption tower*

From the mass balance over the differential element:

$$G(y + \mathrm{d}y) = Gy + r\mathrm{d}z$$

which rearranges to:

$$\mathrm{d}y/\mathrm{d}z = r/G = K_y a(y - mx)/G \qquad (4.A.7)$$

From equation (4.A.7), it is now possible to calculate the total height of packing, H, and therefore the height of column needed to reduce the gas phase mole fraction from y_B to y_T:

$$H = \int_0^H \mathrm{d}z = \frac{G}{k_y a} \int_{y_T}^{y_B} \frac{\mathrm{d}y}{(y - mx)} \qquad (4.A.8)$$

The first term on the right hand side in equation (4.A.8) is a property of the packing, dependent on the gas and liquid flow rates; it is called the *height of a transfer unit* (HTU). The integral is a measure of the difficulty of the absorption operation, and is independent of the packing properties; it is called the *number of transfer units* (NTU) characterising the operation.

The integral for NTU can be evaluated using the operating line (equation 4.A.5) to eliminate x. Using R to denote mG/L:

$$NTU = \int_{y_T}^{y_B} \frac{\mathrm{d}y}{(y - mx)} = \int_{y_T}^{y_B} \frac{\mathrm{d}y}{(1 - R)y + Ry_B - y_B}$$

$$NTU = \frac{1}{1 - R}[\ln\{(1 - R)y + Ry_B - y_B\}]_{y_T}^{y_B}$$

Further algebraic manipulation reduces this to:

$$NTU = \frac{1}{1 - R} \ln \left[\frac{y_B - y_B}{y_T - y_T} \right] \qquad (4.A.9)$$

where $y_B^* = mx_B$ and $y_T^* = mx_T$.

Notation

a	Interfacial area per unit packed volume
G	Molar gas flow rate per unit tower area
H	Overall height of packing
K_y	Overall mass transfer coefficient, with driving force expressed in terms of gas phase mole fraction
L	Molar liquid flow rate per unit tower area
m	Slope of equilibrium line
N	Mass transfer flux from gas into liquid
R	Gradient of operating line, mG/L
r	Rate of absorption per unit packed volume
x	Mole fraction of transferred component in liquid
x^*	Liquid mole fraction in equilibrium with y
x_B	Liquid mole fraction at the bottom of the tower
x_T	Liquid mole fraction at the top of the tower
y	Mole fraction of transferred component in gas
y^*	Gas mole fraction in equilibrium with x
y_B	Gas mole fraction at the bottom of the tower
y_T	Gas mole fraction at the top of the tower
z	Distance below top of packing

References and Further Reading

COMEAP (1998) Quantification of the Effects of Air Pollution on Health in the United Kingdom. Committee on the Medical Effects of Air Pollutants, Department of Health, The Stationary office, London.

Department of Health (1999) Economic Appraisal of the Health Effects of Air Pollution. Ad-Hoc Group on the Economic Appraisal of the Health Effects of Air Pollution, The Stationary Office, London.

EA (2001) Inorganic Acids and Halogens, IPC Guidance Notes IPC S2 4.03. Environment Agency for England and Wales, http://www.environment-agency.gov.uk/commondata/105385/ipcs2403.html (October 2003).

EC (1996) Council Directive 96/61/EC of 24/9/96 Concerning Integrated Pollution Prevention and Control, *Official Journal of the European Communities L257 10 October 1996.* http://europa.eu.int.

EMEP (1999) Deposition and Transboundary Fluxes for SO_x. European Evaluation and Monitoring Programme, http://www.emep.int/areas/fluxtrend/sox_EMP.html (October 2003).

EPA (2003) Clean Air Act 1990. The US Environmental Protection Agency. http://www.epa.gov/oar/oaqps/peg_caa/pegcaain.html (October 2003).

EPA (2001) Ozone depletion, http://www.epa.gov/ozone (October 2003).

Harrison, R.M., ed. (1996) *Pollution: Causes, Effects and Control*, 3rd edition. The Royal Society of Chemistry, Cambridge.

Harrison, R.M., ed. (1997) *Understanding Our Environment*. The Royal Society of Chemistry, Cambridge.

Hodge, I. (1995) *Environmental Economics: Individual Incentives and Public Choices*. Economics today series, Macmillan, Basingstoke.

IPCC (2001) Climate Change 2001: The Scientific Base. Intergovernmental Panel on Climate Change, http://www.ipcc.ch (September 2003).

Katima, J.H.Y., Azapagic, A. and Handley, D. (1992) Nitrogen Oxides Absorption into Sodium Hydroxide Solution in a Packed Column: Effect of NaOH Concentration. *IChemE Trans. B*, **70**, 39–43.

Katima, J.H.Y., Azapagic, A. and Handley, D. (1993) Absorption of Nitrogen Oxides into Sodium Hydroxide Solution in a Packed Tower: Effect of Gas Flow Rate and Temperature. *IChemE Trans. B*, **71**, 50–56.

Kniel, G.E., Delmarco, K. and Petrie, J.G. (1996) Life Cycle Assessment Applied to Process Design: Environmental and Economic Analysis and Optimisation of a Nitric Acid Plant. *Environmental Progress*, **15**(4), 221–228, Winter 1996.

NASA (2001) Atmospheric Chemistry Data and Resources, http://daac.gsfc.nasa.gov/CAMPAIGN_DOCS/ATM_CHEM/ac_main.html (October 2003).

NETC (1998) Chemistry of Atmospheric Pollutants. National Environmental Technology Centre, http://www.aeat.co.uk/netcen/airqual/networks/kinetics.html (October 2003).

Nicholas, M.J., Clift, R. Walker, F.C. Azapagic, A. and Porter, D.E. (2000) Determination of 'Best Available Techniques' for Integrated Pollution Prevention and Control: A Life Cycle Approach. *IChemE Trans. B*, **78**(3), 193–203.

NSCA (2003) *Pollution Handbook 2003*. National Society for Clean Air and Environmental Protection, Brighton.

RCEP (2000) Energy: The Changing Climate. 22nd report of the Royal Commission on Environmental Pollution. HMSO, London.

Spix, C., Anderson, H.R., Schwartz, J., Vigotti, M.A., Letertre, A., Vonk, J.M., Touloumi, G., Balducci, F., Piekarski, T., Bacharova, Lj., Tobias, A., Ponka, A. and Katsouyanni, K. (1998) Short-term Effects of Air Pollution on Hospital Admissions of Respiratory Diseases in Europe: a Quantitative Summary of APHEA Study Results. (Air Pollution and Health: A European Approach). EU Project in the Environment and climate Programme, http://europa.eu.int/comm/research/success/en/env/ 0267e.html (October 2003).

UNECE (2003) Convention on Long-range Transboundary Air Pollution. United Nations Economic Commission for Europe. http://www.unece.org/env/lrtap (September 2003).

UNEP (2000) Backgrounder: Basic Facts and Data on the Science and Politics of Ozone Protection, http://www.unep.ch/conventions/info/ozone/backgrounder.htm (October 2003).

UNEP GRID-Arendal (2001) Acid Rain in Europe, UNEP GRID-Arendal, http://www.grida.no/db/maps/prod/level3/id_1177.htm (October 2003).

UNEP (2003) The Montreal Protocol on Substances that Deplete the Ozone Layer. UNEP, http://www.unep.org/ozone/montreal.shtml (October 2003).

UNFCCC (2003) The Convention and Kyoto Protocol. The United Nations Framework Convention on Climate Change, http://unfccc.int/resource/convkp.html (October 2003).

5

Municipal Solid Waste Management: Can Thermodynamics Influence People's Opinions about Incineration?

Norman Kirkby and Adisa Azapagic

with a contribution from

Omar Romero-Hernandez[1]

Summary

Municipal Solid Waste (MSW) management is one of the most important and challenging issues for sustainable development. It is also one of the most controversial issues and is the subject of an ongoing debate between different stakeholders. A particularly 'difficult' issue is MSW incineration which has in many countries become a socially unacceptable option for dealing with solid waste. On the other hand, the increasing amounts of waste each year demand an immediate and practical solution to the problem which currently cannot be solved by recycling alone. This chapter addresses the problem of MSW and after an introduction to this vast and complex subject presents a case study related to using MSW for energy generation. The subject of the case study is a proposal by a waste management company for an Energy-from-Waste (EfW) plant. The study shows the complexity and a multidisciplinary nature of the problem by guiding the reader through the issues involved, from

---

[1]Omar Romaro-Hernandez contributed the material related to the case study in Mexico City, given in Box 5.7.

Sustainable Development in Practice: Case Studies for Engineers and Scientists
Edited by Adisa Azapagic, Slobodan Perdan and Roland Clift
© 2004 John Wiley & Sons, Ltd   ISBNs: 0-470-85608-4 (HB); 0-470-85609-2 (PB)

the technical and design aspects, through environmental assessments of different technologies to social concerns of the stakeholders. Through that, the case study examines the role of thermodynamics, engineering design, scientific assessments and people's opinions in decision-making for a more sustainable MSW management.

5.1 Introduction

Management of household and commercial waste, collectively known as Municipal Solid Waste (MSW), is one of the major challenges of sustainable development. As societies are becoming wealthier, they are creating more and more waste so that the amount of waste is growing each year. For example, in 1990, each individual in the world produced on average 250 kg of MSW or around four times our body weight, generating in total 1.3×10^9 t of solid waste (Beede and Bloom, 1995). Ten years later, this amount of waste almost doubled, reaching 2.3×10^9 t produced worldwide. In the European Union (EU) countries, over 250×10^6 t of municipal waste are produced each year and with the annual growth of 3%, MSW has outpaced the GDP growth over the last decade.

With each person producing on average 500 kg of solid waste per year, developed countries generate on average twice as much MSW as countries in the developing world (Table 5.1). In the UK alone, every person generates ten times their own body weight as household waste every year.

By 2020, the OECD estimates we could be generating 45% more waste than we did in 1995. Obviously, we must reverse this trend if we are to avoid being submerged in rubbish. The EU, for example, wants to reduce the quantity of waste going to landfill by 20% from 2000 to 2010, and by 50% by 2050. Currently, 67% of solid waste is landfilled in the EU countries.

Solid waste creates a number of problems. First, large amounts of waste generated each year require large space for its storage and disposal. MSW is currently predominantly disposed of in landfills and in many countries landfill space is at a premium as the amount of land available for these purposes is diminishing. Secondly, landfilling waste generates a number of environmental problems, including emissions of carbon dioxide (CO_2) and methane (CH_4) into the atmosphere and

Table 5.1 *Municipal solid waste generation in the world (Adapted from Rand et al., 2000; reproduced by permission of WorldBank.)*

Area	Range (kg/capita · year)	Mean (kg/capita · year)	Growth rate (%)
OECD-total	263–864	513	1.9
North America		826	2.0
Japan		394	1.1
OECD-Europe		336	1.5
Europe (32 countries)	150–624	345	n/a
8 Asian capitals	185–1000	n/a	n/a
South and West Asia	185–290	n/a	n/a
Latin America and the Caribbean	110–365	n/a	n/a

leaching of chemicals into the soil and groundwater. Landfilling also represents a waste of valuable resources which could otherwise be recycled to recover materials or energy. For example, it has been estimated that in the UK alone, the MSW generated annually has a potential energy value equivalent to 30×10^6 t of coal which is around 10% of the UK's primary energy demand. Only about 1.5% of that energy potential is currently utilised (Barron, 1995).

Therefore, the main challenge associated with the MSW is how to manage the waste in the most sustainable way. Following the widely adopted waste management hierarchy shown in Figure 5.1, it is clear that reducing waste generation in the first place is the most sustainable option. However, the wealthier societies in particular have not been very good at achieving this goal so far and at present we are left with an ever increasing pile of waste each year. Reusing and recycling waste to recover materials would also be a sustainable way to deal with the problem of MSW; however, various factors such as lack of appropriate technologies, high costs of collection, sorting and recycling of waste as well as insufficient public participation make recycling difficult (Azapagic *et al.*, 2003). A further MSW management option is to recover energy from waste, for example, through incineration. The final and the least desirable option is to incinerate the waste without energy recovery or to landfill it.

This chapter explores one of the options for MSW management – energy recovery by incineration, which can be used when all other more desirable options in the waste management hierarchy have been exhausted. This option is particularly interesting to explore in the context of sustainable development for several reasons. First, from a thermodynamic point of view, recovering energy from waste is a more sustainable option than the currently most practised MSW management option – waste landfilling. Secondly, if an appropriate incineration technology is chosen and if it is designed properly, energy recovery by incineration could be economically profitable as well as environmentally safe. However, incineration is one of the areas where the public tends to mistrust or reject assurances over the reliability of some technological options and over associated risks to human

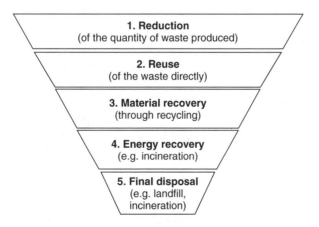

Figure 5.1   *Solid waste management hierarchy in a decreasing order of desirability*

health and the environment (Clift, 1999). For exactly this reason, in most countries in Europe and in the USA, it is now almost impossible to obtain planning permission for a new incinerator.

Therefore, the case study presented here poses an important question: can thermodynamic and other technical considerations persuade the public that energy recovery by incineration of waste could be a sustainable option for MSW management? The case study is based on a real design and a planning application for a new MSW incinerator in England; however, to preserve confidentiality, the names of the place and the company are not mentioned.

Prior to introducing the case study, we give a brief overview of MSW management options in general and specific practices around the world. This is followed by an overview of the technical, environmental, economic and social aspects of energy recovery by incineration, to help the reader understand the scope of the problem and the main sustainability issues involved in the case study.

5.2   Integrated MSW Management

MSW comprises waste from households and commercial activities and includes waste paper, glass, plastics, food scraps and garden waste and other, normally, non-hazardous types of waste. Examples of a typical composition of MSW are shown in Figure 5.2.

Sustainable management of MSW demands an integrated approach based on the waste management hierarchy shown in Figure 5.1. It is unlikely that any one single waste management option will be sufficient to deal with the problem of MSW, so that we will normally need to consider a combination of several options. Some of these options are shown in Figure 5.3. Clearly, the first and most preferable option is prevention and reduced generation of MSW. Waste prevention is closely linked with influencing consumers to demand greener products and less packaging.

If generation of waste cannot be prevented, as many of the materials as possible should be recovered, preferably by recycling. Many countries have introduced

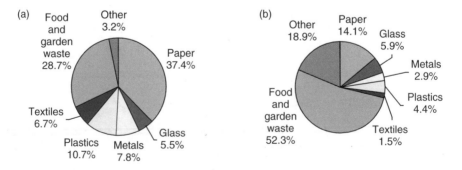

Figure 5.2 *Examples of typical MSW composition by material: (a) MSW in the USA (Based on the data from EPA, 2002.); and (b) MSW in Mexico (Based on the data from SEDESOL, 1999.)*

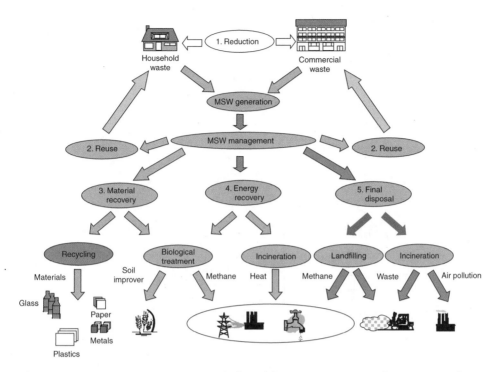

Figure 5.3   *MSW management options (Adapted from Romero-Hernandez et al., 2003.)*

recycling targets for materials recovery. For example, the European Commission (EC) has defined recovery and recycling targets for packaging waste (EC, 1994), end-of-life vehicles (EC, 2000a) and electrical and electronic waste (EC, 2003a).

A further option for materials recovery is aerobic composting of organic waste such as food scraps and garden waste, to produce minerals and humus which can be used as soil improvers. Anaerobic digestion of organic waste, on the other hand, generates biogas – methane – which can be used to generate either heat or electricity. This is the next option in the MSW management hierarchy related to energy recovery. Further energy recovery options include incineration to generate heat or electricity or both (Figure 5.3).

Final disposal of waste by landfill or incineration without energy recovery should be used only as a last resort. Both these methods need close monitoring because of their potential to cause environmental damage. However, it is also important to bear in mind that the other waste management options, such as materials and energy recovery, will also generate some environmental impacts, due to the collection and transportation of waste, recycling processes, incineration and other related activities. Applying life cycle thinking (see the Appendix at the end of the book) can help us identify the environmental impacts associated with each of the waste management alternatives from 'cradle to grave' and choose the most sustainable options. The life cycle of the integrated MSW management is outlined in Figure 5.4.

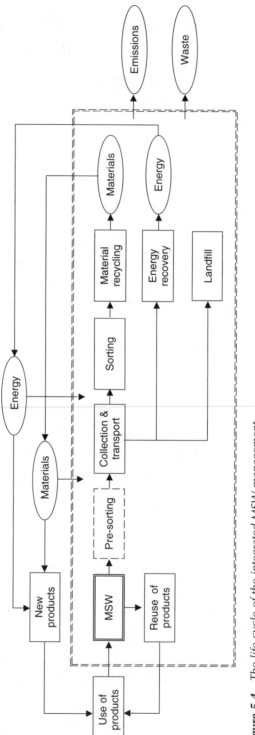

Figure 5.4 *The life cycle of the integrated MSW management*

To help us understand the current trends, the following section gives a brief overview of the MSW management practices in different regions of the world.

5.2.1   MSW Management in the EU

The EU countries generate in total around 250×10^6 t of MSW each year. Table 5.2 shows the amount and the composition of waste in different EU countries. The waste management systems in the EU are designed around the waste management hierarchy described in section 5.1. However, there is some variation in the waste management priorities within the EU countries: for example, the northern European nations give the recovery of materials a higher priority than energy recovery, while France considers them as equal. Figure 5.5 shows the percentage of different MSW management options used in some of the EU countries.

Table 5.2   *MSW generation and composition by weight in Europe in 1999 or the latest available year (EC, 2003c)*

	Amount (1000 t)	Paper	Textiles	Plastics	Glass	Metals	Food and garden waste	Other
Belgium	5 462	17	4	6	3	4	20	46
Denmark	3 141							
Germany	44 390							
Greece	3 900	18	4	10	3	3	51	11
Spain	24 470	21	5	11	7	4	44	8
France	37 800	25	3	11	13	4	29	15
Ireland	1 933	33	2	10	6	3	24	22
Italy	26 846							
Luxembourg	184							
Netherlands	9 359	28	2	5	6	3	39	17
Austria	5 270	24	3	15	9	7	29	13
Portugal	4 364							
Finland	2 510	33	2	3	2	5	33	22
Sweden	4 000							
UK	28 000							
Iceland	189							
Norway	2 650	36	4	9	3	4	30	14
Switzerland	4 555							
Bulgaria	3 197	11	4	7	6	4	41	27
Cyprus	369	29	7	12	1	2	42	7
Czech Republic	3 365	8	2	4	4	2	18	62
Estonia	569							
Hungary	4 376	20	5	15	4	3	31	22
Latvia	292	14	3	7	8	4	48	16
Lithuania	1 236	1	1	0	2	19	40	37
Poland	12 317							
Romania	5 699	18	6	10	6	5	53	2
Slovak Republic	1 700	13	3	9	6	8	26	35
Slovenia	1 024	15		10	5	7	32	31

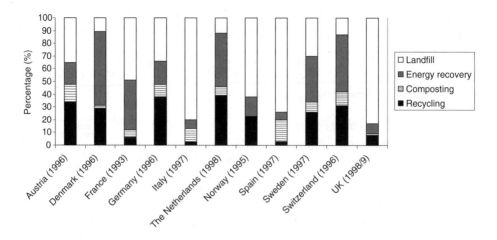

Figure 5.5 *MSW management in the EU (Based on the data from EC, 2003c.)*

Overall, the recycling rates are increasing in the EU countries, with the amount of landfilled waste falling steadily. An example of this trend is shown in Figure 5.6 for the UK. The data show an increase in recycling and composting of waste (by 55%) and in incineration with energy recovery (by 41%) in the period 1996–2002; however, over the same period, the total amount of waste increased by 15% so that the amount of waste sent to landfill decreased only by 8%.

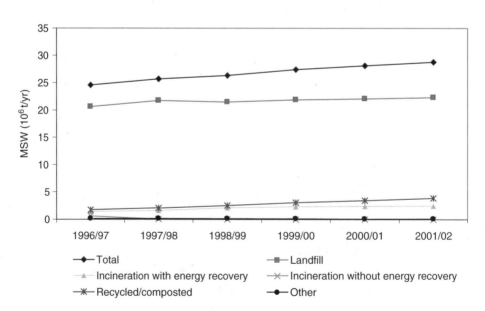

Figure 5.6 *MSW generation and management in the UK from 1996 to 2002 (Based on the data from DEFRA, 2003.)*

Waste management is legislated extensively at the EU level and legislation is based on the following main principles, known as 'five Ps' (EC, 2003b):

1. *Prevention principle*: waste prevention and minimisation should be given the highest priority.
2. *Proximity principle*: waste should be disposed of as close as possible to where it is produced.
3. *Producer responsibility principle*: waste producers should bear full 'cradle to grave' (Figure 5.4) responsibility for any damage caused by the waste that they produce.
4. *Polluter pays principle*: polluters (including waste producers), rather than society in general, should bear the full cost of the safe management and disposal of waste.
5. *Precautionary principle*: waste management strategies should not pose risks (if there is even a small chance of a major problem, then that option should be avoided).

Some examples of the EC legislation in the area of waste management include the directives on environmental impact assessment, incineration, landfilling, packaging waste, electronic and electrical waste equipment and end-of-life vehicles. Some of the waste-related directives are listed in Box 5.1. The responsibility for the implementation of these directives rests with the national governments of the member countries. A number of the EU waste directives and many national waste laws and regulations are linked to the planning processes so that most waste management programmes and facilities require a planning permission before they can be built. The authority for granting the planning permissions varies widely within the EU. For example, in countries like France this process is highly centralised, while in the UK most decisions are made by the local authorities for the region where the planning application has been made.

5.2.2 MSW Management in the USA

As shown in Figure 5.7, approximately 232×10^6 t of MSW were generated in the United States in 2000, or 2.05 kg per person each day (EPA, 2002). The recovery rate for material recycling (including composting) was 30.1%, or around 0.63 kg per person per day, with the highest recycling rates achieved for paper, non-ferrous metals and garden waste (Table 5.3). Of the remaining waste, 14.5% was incinerated for energy recovery and 55.3% was landfilled. It is predicted that the amount of MSW in the USA will grow by 1.6% by weight annually from 2000 to 2010, twice the predicted growth of the population (EPA, 2002).

The US Environmental Protection Agency (EPA) has adopted the integrated waste management hierarchy similar to that in the EU. The hierarchy includes the following three components, listed in order of preference (EPA, 2002):

1. source reduction (or waste prevention), including reuse of products and on-site, or backyard, composting of yard trimmings;
2. recycling, including off-site, or community, composting; and
3. disposal, including waste combustion (preferably with energy recovery) and land-filling.

Box 5.1   *EU legislation on solid waste (EC, 2003b)*

Waste Framework
- Framework Directive on Waste (Council Directive 75/442/EEC as amended by Council Directive 91/156/EEC).
- Hazardous Waste Directive (Council Directive 91/689/EEC as amended by Council Directive 94/31/EC).

Specific Wastes
- Disposal of waste oils (Council Directive 75/439/EEC).
- Directives on waste from the titanium dioxide industry (Council Directives 78/176/EEC, 82/883/EEC and 92/112/EEC).
- Batteries and accumulators containing certain dangerous substances (Council Directive 91/157/EEC).
- Packaging and packaging waste (Council Directive 94/62/EC).
- The disposal of polychlorinated biphenyis (PCB) and polychlorinated ter-phenyls (PCT) (Council Directive 96/59/EC).
- Protection of the environment, and in particular of the soil, when sewage sludge is used in agriculture (Council Directive 86/278/EEC).

Processes and Facilities
- Reduction of air pollution from existing municipal waste-incineration plants (Council Directive 89/429/EEC).
- Reduction of air pollution from new municipal waste-incineration plants (Council Directive 89/369/EEC).
- Incineration of hazardous waste (Council Directive 94/67/EC).
- Directive on the Landfill of Waste (Council Directive 99/31/EC).

Transport, Import and Export
- The supervision and control of shipments of waste within, into and out of the European Community (Council Regulation EEC No 259/93).
- Rules and procedures applying to shipments of certain types of wastes to non-OECD countries (Council Regulation No 1420/1999 and Commission Regulation No 1547/99).

Although the EPA encourages the use of strategies that emphasise the top of the hierarchy whenever possible, all three components remain important within an integrated waste management system.

Most states and provinces in the USA have solid waste management plans that define the goals and agenda for regional waste management action within the integrated waste management hierarchy. Some laws require local governments to set up recycling centres or programmes that will achieve specific levels of recycling; other laws impose recycling responsibilities on industries and businesses.

Local governments have primary responsibility for managing MSW in the USA. However, there are minimum national-level design and operating standards for landfills, incineration and materials recovery facilities which must be adopted at the state level and implemented by local governments and private firms (UNEP,

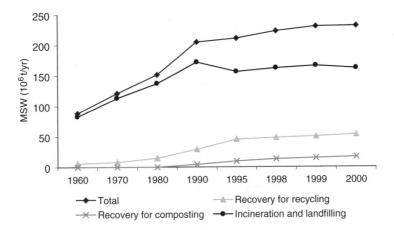

Figure 5.7 *MSW generation and management in the USA from 1960 to 2000 (Based on the data from EPA, 2002.)*

Table 5.3 *Generation and recovery of materials in MSW in 2000)*

Material	Generated (10^6 t)	Recovered (10^6 t)	Recovered (%)
Paper and paperboard	86.7	39.4	45.4
Glass	12.8	2.9	23.0
Steel	13.5	4.6	34.0
Aluminium	3.2	0.9	27.4
Other non-ferrous metals[a]	1.4	0.9	66.9
Plastics	24.7	1.3	5.4
Rubber and leather	6.4	0.8	12.2
Textiles	9.4	1.3	13.5
Wood	12.7	0.5	3.8
Other materials	4.0	0.9	21.3
Food, other[b]	25.9	0.7	2.6
Garden waste	27.7	15.8	56.9
Miscellaneous inorganic wastes	3.5	<0.05	<0.05
Total MSW	231.9	69.9	30.1

[a] Includes lead from lead-acid batteries.
[b] Includes recovery of paper for composting.

Original source: Franklin Associates, Ltd.

1996). In some states and provinces, the economic and environmental pressures of waste disposal are causing the responsibility for waste management to shift from the local to the state/provincial level.

5.2.3 Asia and Pacific

Solid waste management policies and practices in the countries in Asia and the Pacific are normally related to the level of public awareness of and interest in the waste issues and to the existing quality of the environment. Waste management is much more advanced in the industrialised countries of the region than in the developing countries. In Japan and Australia, for example, laws and regulations have banned the disposal of substances such as batteries, waste oil, tires, CFC gases, PCBs and so on (UNEP, 1996). There is a mandatory deposit/take-back requirement for some goods such as mercury oxide batteries, aluminium and plastic containers, tires and non-degradable plastic bags. In Japan, to ensure that separation of wastes is carried out properly, households are required to use transparent plastic bags for waste disposal so that collection crews can see the contents. A major issue for MSW planning in these countries is public resistance to the siting of disposal facilities (UNEP, 1996).

The most common MSW management problems in developing countries of the region are financial constraints, outdated legislation and its inadequate enforcement as well as the shortage of experienced specialists in the field. The additional problem is that in many cases, the new waste regulations are directly copied from industrialised countries without any serious study of the social and economic conditions, the technology, the level of skill required and the local administrative structure. As a result, they prove to be unenforceable (UNEP, 1996). To help overcome this problem, the UNEP has defined a set criteria for the evaluation of MSW management options (Box 5.2) to guide decision-makers in choosing the most appropriate waste management alternative or a combination of alternatives for their specific conditions.

Box 5.2 *Criteria for evaluation of waste management options (UNEP, 1996)*

For each technology or policy under consideration, decision-makers should ask a number of questions designed to facilitate comparison of the available alternatives:

- Is the proposed technology likely to accomplish its purpose in the circumstances where it would be used? More specifically, is it technologically feasible and appropriate, given the financial and human resources available?
- Focusing on the financial aspects of the practice, is it the most cost-effective option available?
- What are the environmental benefits and costs of the practice?
- Could the environmental soundness of the proposed practice be significantly enhanced by a small increase in costs? If so, do the environmental benefits justify budgeting for these costs?
- Conversely, would it be possible to significantly reduce the cost of the practice with only a small detriment to environmental soundness? If so, should that cost-reducing option be chosen, perhaps with the aim of more fruitfully investing society's resources in environmental quality improvement or toward other ends?
- Is the practice administratively feasible and sensible?
- Is it practical in the given social and cultural environment?
- How would specific sectors of society be affected by the adoption of this technology or policy? Do these effects promote or conflict with overall social goals of the society?

In many large cities in the developing countries, a particular problem is MSW management in the poor areas or 'slum cities' which are often treated by authorities as illegal and denied waste collection services. In many such places, the accumulation of waste in open areas represents a health hazard.

Municipalities in most South Asian countries operate under the health, environment or local government ministries of the central or regional governments. In the central part of the region and in some countries in the north, health ministries are expanding to oversee more directly municipal corporations. In the Indian subcontinent, on the other hand, there is a movement toward decentralisation, with municipalities being expected to raise their own funds and take on more responsibilities (UNEP, 1996).

5.2.4   Africa

Similar to the problems in other developing countries, MSW management in African countries is also constrained by a lack of financial resources, trained staff and poor enforcement of legislation. Responsibility for MSW management in African countries rests either with the Ministry of Environment, the Ministry of Health or the Ministry of Planning and Development. Under the national ministry, various municipal agencies are responsible for planning and urban affairs in the country's major cities. Inefficient administration is often quoted as one of the reasons for poor waste management practices in Africa (UNEP, 1996).

5.2.5   Latin America and the Caribbean

In this region, MSW technologies are fairly well developed but the quality of services is dependent on improving the present management systems (UNEP, 1996). Throughout the region, local governments are responsible for management of solid wastes within their jurisdiction. However, enforcement programmes are practically non-existent as legislation on MSW management is weak and the local governments lack resources.

Questions

1. Compare the typical composition of MSW in the USA, the EU countries and Mexico. What do you conclude in terms of the materials used in the households in these countries? Compare these with the waste composition in your country and discuss any differences.
2. Based on the typical composition of MSW in the USA, the EU countries and Mexico, which MSW management options shown in Figure 5.3 would be the most suitable for each type of MSW? Why? Which options would be suitable for the waste composition in your country?

3. Find out how much MSW is generated in your town or city and in your country, and how much of that is recycled for materials and energy recovery and how much is landfilled.
4. Taking the life cycle approach (Figure 5.4), describe the life cycles of each of the MSW waste management options shown in Figure 5.3 and discuss the advantages and disadvantages of each.
5. Describe the MSW management hierarchy in your country (if any) and discuss the current waste management practices.
6. Use the UNEP's evaluation criteria in Box 5.2 and the MSW management options shown in Figure 5.3 to devise an integrated MSW management strategy for your town or city. Justify your choice of MSW options. Do they correspond to the current practice? Discuss any differences.

5.3   Energy Recovery from MSW

The previous two sections have provided an introduction and an overview of the problem of MSW and options for its integrated management. As the subject of this chapter and the case study is energy recovery from MSW by incineration, we will now focus on this waste management option to understand the general technical and sustainability issues associated with it before we examine on a specific case study how they apply in practice.

A typical design of an EfW plant. Photograph by A. Azapagic

5.3.1 Technical Considerations

As illustrated in Figure 5.8, an Energy-from-Waste (EfW) plant typically comprises the following parts:

- waste handling facility, including waste reception and pre-treatment;
- incinerator and boiler;
- energy recovery and energy generation plant;
- air pollution control plant; and
- ash treatment facility.

As shown in more detail in the block diagram in Figure 5.9, depending on the type of incineration technology, fuel pre-treatment can include sorting and/or mixing and shredding of waste. Incineration involves burning of waste at high temperatures (normally from 980 to 1090 °C) to generate heat. The heat can then be recovered as hot water or as steam by heating water in the boiler. The hot water can be used directly or in a district-heating system whilst the steam can be utilised directly or it can be used to turn a turbine which drives a generator to produce electricity. The type of energy recovered determines the total energy efficiency of the plant and therefore influences its economic and environmental sustainability. As shown in Table 5.4, combined heat and power (CHP) plants are the most efficient systems recovering up to 85% of the original energy contained in the waste. Generating electricity alone on the other hand recovers only 35% of energy.

In addition to the useful product – heat, electricity or both – the incineration process also generates flue gases, containing various air pollutants, such as carbon oxides (CO and CO_2), sulphur oxides (SO_2 and SO_3), nitrogen oxides (NO and NO_2), hydrogen chloride (HCl), heavy metals and dioxins and furans. A certain amount of ash is also generated, equivalent to about one quarter of the original weight of the waste and approximately 90% of its volume. Both the flue gases and the ash must be treated in an appropriate way before they can be discharged into the environment.

To choose and design a sustainable EfW system, we must take into account a number of technical factors including waste composition and its energy content, type of incineration technology and energy recovery system. These factors are discussed briefly below.

Waste Composition and Characteristics

One of the most important factors to consider in recovering energy from MSW is its suitability for combustion. The following chemical and energy properties determine whether the waste is suitable for combustion:

- moisture content;
- flammable fraction (volatile matter + fixed carbon);
- content of elements (C, H, O, N, S);
- non-combustible fraction (ash); and
- lower and higher heating values.

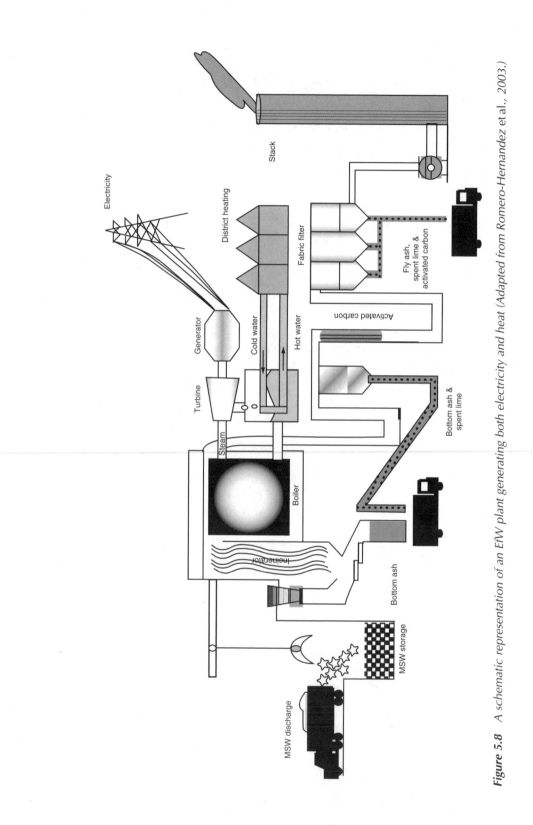

Figure 5.8 A schematic representation of an EfW plant generating both electricity and heat (Adapted from Romero-Hernandez et al., 2003.)

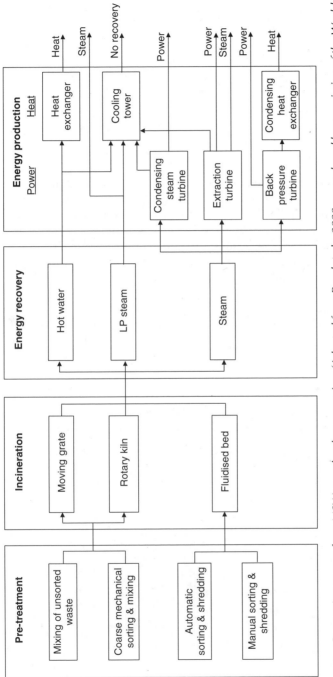

Figure 5.9 Generating energy from MSW: a technology overview (Adapted from Rand et al., 2000; reproduced by permission of the World Bank.)

Table 5.4   *Energy efficiency of different EfW systems*

Energy system	Energy recovery (%)		Overall efficiency[a] (%)
Heat only	Heat	80	80
Steam only	Steam	80	80
Power only	Power	35	35
Combined steam and power	Steam	75	35–75
	Power	35	
Combined heat and power (CHP)	Heat	60–65	85
	Power	20–25	

[a] Efficiency defined as usable energy related to the energy content (lower heating value) of waste.

The waste is theoretically suitable for combustion without additional fuel when the moisture content W < 50%, the ash content A < 60% and the content of carbon C > 25% (Rand *et al.*, 2000). This 'combustible' region is represented by the shaded area in the Tanner diagram shown in Figure 5.10.

The lower and the higher heating values determine how much thermal energy can be recovered from the waste. The higher heating value (HHV) of MSW can be determined from the following equation:

$$HHV = 337C + 1419(H_2 - 0.125O_2) + 93S + 23N \qquad (5.1)$$

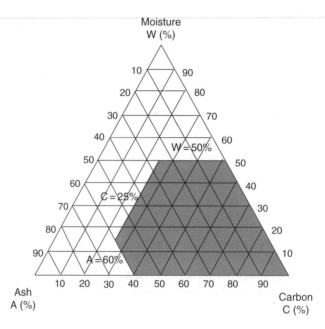

Figure 5.10   *Tanner triangle for assessment of combustibility of MSW (Rand et al., 2000; reproduced by permission of the World Bank.)*

where:

    HHV   higher heating value (MJ/kg) (heating value without water and ash)

    C, H, O, S, N   percentage by weight of each element obtained by ultimate analysis

Typically, the HHV of MSW is about 20 MJ/kg (Kiely, 1996).

    The lower heating value (LHV) of waste can be calculated as:

$$LHV = HHV \times B - 2.445W \qquad (5.2)$$

where:

    LHV   lower heating value (MJ/kg)

    B   flammable fraction (volatile matter + fixed carbon) by weight obtained in proximate analysis

    W   moisture content fraction by weight obtained in proximate analysis

An alternative formula for calculating the LHV of MSW has been proposed (Kiely, 1996):

$$LHV = 0.051(F + 3.6CP) + 0.352 \, (PLR) \qquad (5.3)$$

where:

    F   percentage of food by weight

    CP   percentage of cardboard and paper by weight

    PLR percentage of plastic and rubber by weight

Typical LHV and HHV for MSW are given in Table 5.5. Obviously, the higher the heating values, the higher the amount of energy that can be recovered from waste. Table 5.6 shows that the production of steam drops dramatically with a decrease in the heating value of MSW as well as with the increase in moisture and the fraction of incombustibles in the waste. In addition, the amount of energy recovered will also depend on the type of EfW technology chosen and on the incinerator design. These factors are discussed next.

Table 5.5 *Typical energy content of MSW (Kiely, 1996; reproduced with permission of McGraw-Hill.)*

Material	% by weight				MJ/kg	
	Moisture	Volatiles	Fixed carbon	Ash	LHV	HHV
Paper and card	10.2	76	8.4	5.4	15.7	18.7
Plastics	0.2	96	2	2	32.7	37.1
Textiles	10	66	17.5	6.5	18.3	22.7
Glass	2	–	–	96–99	0.2	0.15
Food	70	21	3.6	5	4.2	16.7
Metals	2.5	–	–	94–99	0.7	0.7

Table 5.6   *Steam production related to the quality of MSW as a fuel (Vesilind* et al., *2002; reproduced with permission of Thompson Learning.)*

MSW composition	LHV (kJ/kg)				
	15 000	14 000	11 500	9300	7000
Moisture (%)	15	18	25	32	39
Non-combustibles (%)	14	16	20	24	28
Combustibles (%)	71	66	55	44	33
Steam generated (t/t MSW)	4.3	3.9	3.2	2.3	1.5

The Energy-from-Waste Technologies

There are many types of incineration plants currently in use for energy recovery from MSW but they can be divided into three general categories (UNEP, 1996):

1. mass-burn plants;
2. modular plants; and
3. refuse-derived fuel (RDF) plants.

Mass-burn systems generally consist of either two or three combustion units ranging in capacity from 50 to 1000 t per day per unit. Hence, the total mass-burn plant capacity ranges from about 100 to 3000 t/day. These plants can accept waste that has undergone little pre-processing other than the removal of oversized items, such as refrigerators and sofas. Most of the mass-burn systems generate both electricity and heat.

Modular combustors have relatively small capacities burning between 5 and 120 t of waste per day. Typical plants have between one and four units for a total plant capacity of about 15 to 400 t/day. The majority of modular units produce steam as the only energy product. Because of their small capacity, modular combustors are generally used in smaller communities or for commercial and industrial operations. On average, investment (capital) costs per tonne of capacity are lower for modular units than for mass-burn and RDF plants (UNEP, 1996).

Refuse-derived fuel (RDF) refers to solid waste that has been mechanically processed to produce a storable, transportable and more homogeneous fuel for combustion. A large majority of RDF combustion facilities generate electricity. On average, capital costs per tonne of capacity are higher for RDF combustion units than for mass-burn and modular units (UNEP, 1996). The production of RDF is relatively more common in the USA and Scandinavia, where it is co-fired with other wastes, but less so in other EU countries.

In addition to the established incineration-based EfW technologies, two new MSW thermal treatment techniques are being investigated: pyrolysis and gasification. The former involves decomposition of MSW by heating with no oxygen and the latter with a reduced amount of oxygen, compared to the normal combustion conditions. The products of pyrolysis and gasification include carbon monoxide, hydrogen, oils, tars, carbon and non-combustible residues. Carbon monoxide and hydrogen (also known as 'syngas') can be used either as fuels or raw materials (e.g. for methanol production) whilst oils, tars, carbon and the other products can be used as raw materials in different industrial sectors. Therefore, pyrolysis and gasification comprise both materials and energy recovery. Although there are more than 100 facilities operating or ordered around the world, some of which have been in operation for 5 years (Juniper, 2003), these technologies are currently considered as unproven.

With regard to the incinerator designs, there are three common types (Figure 5.9):

1. moving grate or mechanical stoker;
2. fluidised bed; and
3. rotary kiln.

The majority of mass-burn incinerators have a moving-grate design. The moving grate pushes the waste through the incinerator and deposits the ash in the tank at the bottom of the incinerator. A typical design of a moving-grate incinerator is shown in Figure 5.11. This technology is well developed and commercially available from

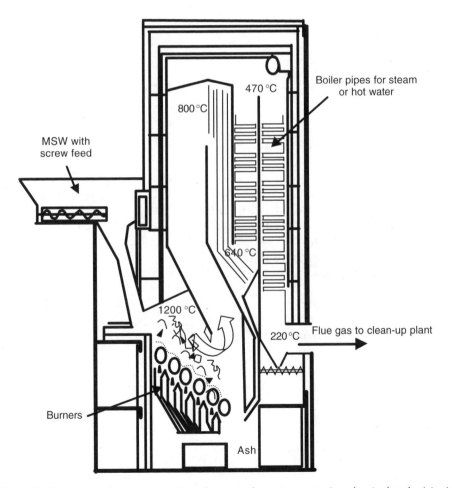

Figure 5.11 *Schematic representation of a typical moving-grate (mechanical stoker) incinerator (Azapagic et al., 2003; published with the permission of John Wiley & Sons Ltd.)*

Table 5.7 Comparison of fluidised-bed and moving-grate incinerators (Adapted from White et al., 1995; published with the permission of Kluwer.)

	Moving-grate incinerator	Fluidised-bed incinerator
Max. capacity	1200 t/day	350 t/day
Combustion		
Mixing	Mild agitation	Turbulent
Burn-out	Often incomplete	Complete
Air ratio	1.8–2.5	1.5–2.0
Load	200–250 kg/m$^2 \cdot$ h	400–600 kg/m$^2 \cdot$ h
Fuel size	75 cm	50 cm
Combustion residue		
Unburnt carbon	3–5% by wt.	0.1% by wt.
Volume	Larger	Smaller
State	Wet	Dry
Iron recovery	Difficult	Easy
Fly ash		
Volume	Smaller	Larger
Unburnt carbon	3–7% by wt.	1% by wt.
Flue gas		
Volume	Larger	Smaller
NO$_x$ control	Post-combustion	In-combustion

a number of manufacturers. It is the dominant technology with many plants providing heat, electricity or both.

In a fluidised-bed combustor, instead of a grate supporting the waste, the furnace contains a bed of sand on an air distribution system. The air keeps the sand bed and the waste fluidised and so increases mixing and combustion efficiency. The fluidised-bed design is particularly suited for RDF, as these types of incinerator require pre-processing of waste. A comparison of the technical performance of a fluidised-bed and a moving-grate incinerator is given in Table 5.7.

In a rotary-kiln combustor, waste is rotated in a cylindrical furnace as it burns; the air is supplied through the perforations along the length of the furnace to ensure complete combustion. Rotary kilns provide the most turbulence of any grate system and thereby enhance the rate and completion of combustion. This technology is not widely used for MSW management (White *et al.*, 1995).

Questions

1. Draw a flow diagram of a typical EfW facility and describe each part.
2. Why is a CHP plant so much more efficient than a plant that generates electricity only? In your opinion, what is the reason that CHP plants are still relatively rare compared to the electricity-generating plants?
3. Which characteristics of waste must be considered in determining its suitability for energy recovery?

4. What is the difference between HHV and LHV? Write down the formulae for calculating both HHV and LHV.
5. What is the difference between the proximate and ultimate analysis of waste? If you have a chemistry background, describe how each type of analysis can be carried out.
6. List the main incineration technologies and describe the suitability of each depending on the amount of waste to be treated.
7. Describe the difference between incineration, pyrolysis and gasification of MSW.
8. What are the main differences between a moving-grate furnace and a fluidised-bed combustor? Which one would you choose based on their technical performance?
9. Suppose that your friend who has no engineering or science background has asked you to explain how an EfW plant operates. Using words and sketches, explain on one A4 page how such facilities work from taking the waste in to generating electricity.

5.3.2 Environmental Considerations

As we have already mentioned, incineration of MSW can be environmentally damaging mainly because of the air pollution and solid waste (bottom and fly ash) generated during the combustion process. Dust, heavy metals, dioxins and furans as well as acid gases, such as SO_x, NO_x and HCl, are some of the air pollutants that can be present in the flue gas. Dioxins and furans in particular are a subject of an ongoing debate and opposition of the public to incineration due to the potential of dioxins and furans to cause cancer. CO_2 is also generated in the combustion of MSW, thus contributing to global warming and climate change. The composition of waste, incineration technology and the combustion conditions all influence the formation of these pollutants. Typical air emission levels from MSW incinerators before flue gas treatment are shown in Table 5.8.

Liquid effluents and water pollution can also be generated in cases where the treatment of flue gases involves the use of an absorption liquid.

Table 5.8 *Typical emission levels from MSW incinerators before flue gas clean-up (Kiely, 1996; reproduced with permission from McGraw-Hill.)*

Pollutant	Typical emissions $(mg/m^3$ at 9% $O_2)$
Dust	1500–1800
SO_2	400
HCF	500
HF	5
NO_x	300
CO	100
Organic vapours	5
Hg vapours	0.05–0.5
Ni + As + Pb + Cr + Cu + Mn	0.05–0.5

Clearly, energy recovery from MSW can be considered a sustainable option only if the environmental impacts of incineration do not exceed the benefit of energy recovery. Hence, it is important to minimise the potential environmental damage from incineration by preventing and controlling air and water pollution as well as by a responsible disposal of the bottom and fly ash. The following section gives an overview of the techniques used for the prevention and control of pollution from incineration.

Air Pollution Prevention and Control

The following air pollutants can be generated in the combustion of MSW:

- nitrogen oxides, NO_x (NO and NO_2);
- sulphur oxides, SO_x (SO_2 and SO_3);
- carbon oxides, CO_x (CO and CO_2);
- particulate matter, PM (dust and particles of various sizes);
- metals, metalloids and their compounds;
- halogens and their compounds, including HCl and HF; and
- organic compounds, including dioxins and furans.

Discussion of the formation mechanisms and control of these pollutants is outside the scope of this chapter. The interested reader can consult, for example, Theodore (1990), Kiely (1996) and Vesilind *et al.* (2002) for an overview of the subject.

Two types of measures can be used to control air pollution from combustion of MSW: primary and secondary. The primary measures are those used in the furnace to prevent the formation of the pollutants and the secondary use clean-up technologies to remove air pollutants.

Primary measures: in-combustion control

The formation of pollutants such as particulates, NO_x, CO, hydrocarbons (HCs), including dioxins and furans, can be reduced significantly by controlling the combustion conditions within the furnace and the boiler. These measures can, for example, include:

- a control system for the supply of primary and secondary air (to control emissions of CO, NO_x and dioxins); and
- control of temperature and residence times in the combustion chamber, boiler and flue treatment units (to prevent formation of dioxins and NO_x).

For example, running the incinerator with a lower excess of air decreases the amount of nitrogen oxides formed during combustion by lowering the flame temperature and the amount of nitrogen and oxygen available for the formation of NO_x; however, this measure also increases the amount of CO and HCs due to the incomplete combustion. Table 5.9 lists several of the primary measures and summarises their effects on NO_x, CO, HCs and dioxins, as well as on the bottom ash (clinker) and energy efficiency. The control mechanisms for dioxins, furans and heavy metals are summarised in Box 5.3. A technically minded reader may wish to consult a paper by

Table 5.9 *Effect of primary measures (in-combustion control) on the formation of air pollutants*

Primary measure	Furnace temperature	O_2	CO and HCs	Total NO_x $(NO + NO_2)$	Remark
Low excess air	Decrease	Decrease	Increase	Decrease	Reduced bottom ash burn-out and increase of dioxins; reduced potential for recycling of bottom ash
Increased excess air	Decrease	Increase	Decrease	Increase	Improved bottom ash burn-out but the furnace temperature must be controlled carefully to prevent formation of dioxins
Increased air preheat	Increase	No effect	Decrease	Increase	Improved bottom ash burn-out and decrease of dioxins; increased potential for recycling of bottom ash
Less air preheat	Decrease	No effect	Increase	Decrease	Reduced thermal efficiency
Load reduction (lower MSW throughput)	Decrease	No effect	No effect	Decrease	Reduced thermal efficiency

Acharya *et al.* (1991) which provides a good overview of the dioxin formation and control mechanisms.

Secondary measures: cleaning up the air pollution from incineration
As illustrated in Figure 5.8, a flue gas treatment system can include a combination of the following:

– scrubbers for the removal of acid gases such as HCl, HF, SO_2;
– cyclones, electrostatic precipitators or fabric filters for fly ash removal;
– activated carbon for the removal of heavy metals and dioxins;
– selective catalytic reduction (SCR) of NO_x with ammonia; and
– selective non-catalytic reduction (SNCR) of NO_x with ammonia or urea.

The choice of a particular type of equipment and treatment method will depend on many factors including their removal efficiency, capital and operating costs as well as the ease of operation and maintenance. The average removal efficiencies of some of the control techniques are summarised in Table 5.10. Further detail on the air pollution control equipment can be found, for example, in Theodore (1990), Theodore and Buonicore (1994) and Vesilind *et al.* (2002). Some of the NO_x control methods were also discussed in Chapter 4.

Box 5.3   *Controlling emissions of dioxins, furans and heavy metals*

Dioxins and furans represent a combination of a number of organic compounds called polychlorinated dibenzodioxins (PCDD) and polychlorinated dibenzofurans (PCDF) respectively. There are two primary mechanisms responsible for the presence of dioxins and furans in flue gases formed during incineration:

1. direct emissions from materials containing dioxins and furans introduced into the incinerator as part of the waste feed, which have not been removed before being fed to the furnace or which are not destroyed during combustion; and
2. formation by *de novo* synthesis from chlorinated precursors including PVC and polychlorinated biphenyls. This process typically occurs as the combustion gas is cooled or passed through the flue gas clean-up equipment, or both.

The formation of dioxins and furans can be minimised by controlling waste feed rate and its composition, combustion temperature (minimum of 850 °C), residence time of the flue gas in the combustor, CO and HC levels and so on. As an additional measure to remove dioxins and furans formed during the combustion process, the flue gas can be passed over the activated carbon.

To prevent *de novo* synthesis of dioxins and furans, the combustion gases should be cooled rapidly to below 200 °C before entering the flue gas clean-up equipment and the residence time in the cooler regions of the stack should be limited to less than two minutes. Cooling the gas also has the advantage of causing the low-volatility metals (antimony, arsenic, beryllium and chromium) and semi-volatile metals (lead and cadmium) to condense out, along with some of the heavier organics, thus promoting the removal of the heavy metals from the flue gas.

Solid Waste Disposal: Bottom and Fly Ash

Two types of ash are generated in incineration of MSW: bottom and fly ash. The bottom ash consists of the ash-part of the burnable materials such as paper and plastics and the incombustible matter such as glass and metals. The mixture of ash and the partially fused residues from the furnace is often referred to as clinker. A small fraction of the bottom ash ends as fly ash which comes off in the flue gas. Typically, burning one tonne of MSW generates 200 kg of bottom ash and 30–40 kg of fly ash (Kiely, 1996).

The main environmental concern associated with the bottom and fly ash is the generation of heavy metals and dioxins. For example, some of the heavy metals such as lead remain in the bottom ash while the more volatile mercury concentrates in the fly ash. However, while the heavy metals in the bottom ash are not prone to leaching, they seem to be more leachable in the fly ash. Furthermore, dioxins and furans are concentrated in the fly ash so that the fly ash should be disposed of only in secure landfills. However, until recently, fly ash has often been used in bonded asphalt and

Table 5.10 *Removal efficiency of different air control equipment*

	Efficiency	Remark
	Acid gases	
Scrubbers		Relatively simple designs and
Dry	Up to 65%	inexpensive; the need to dispose of
Semi-dry	~70%	the spent adsorption/absorption
Wet	>90%	medium
	Particulate matter	
Dry cyclones	Up to 90% for particles >5 μ	Simple design and inexpensive, can operate at high temperatures and pressures; ineffective for smaller particles; pressure drop 100–2000 Pa
Fabric filters	Up to 99.9% for particles >1 μ 90% for particles <1 μ	Require high capital costs and regular maintenance; sensitive to acid gases; pressure drop 1000–2000 Pa
Electrostatic precipitators	Up to 99% for particles >1 μ Up to 99.99% for particles <1 μ	Require high capital costs and regular maintenance; pressure drop ~250 Pa; efficient with very small particles, down to 0.01 μ
	Nitrogen oxides	
Selective non-catalytic reduction (SNCR)	30–65%	Optimum temperature 900–1090 °C; maintaining the optimum temperature is difficult; emissions of ammonia ('slip') and N_2O into the atmosphere
Selective catalytic reduction (SCR)	80–90%	Optimum temperature 300–400 °C; safety problems with handling anhydrous ammonia; ammonia 'slip'

other road products (UNEP, 1996). This practice has been discontinued in many countries as awareness has grown of the presence and the leachability of the toxic constituents of these materials, particularly dioxins. The bottom ash could be utilised with care, for example, in road construction.

Questions

1. List the air pollutants that are generated by incineration of MSW and describe the mechanisms for their formation.
2. Describe the methods for primary and secondary control of the air pollutants you listed in the previous question and discuss their advantages and disadvantages.
3. How can *de novo* synthesis of dioxins and furans be prevented?
4. Applying life cycle thinking and using the information on the primary and secondary air pollution techniques summarised in Tables 5.9 and 5.10 respectively, which techniques would you choose to control air pollution from MSW incineration? Explain and justify your choices.

Environmental Legislation

Most countries have very strict environmental legislation for the control of gaseous, liquid and solid discharges from MSW incineration. For example, in the EU, proposals for new EfW plants are subject to at least six EC Directives, including:

1. Integrated Pollution Prevention Control (IPPC) Directive (Chapter 4);
2. Environmental Impact Assessment (EIA) Directive (Chapter 6);
3. Framework Directive on Waste;
4. Landfill Directive;
5. Waste Incineration Directive; and
6. Ambient Air Framework Directive.

In addition to the EC regulations, EfW activities are also subject to national legislation in each EU country. The situation is no less complex in other regions, including the USA, Australia and Japan. Therefore, attempting to give an overview of MSW-related legislation worldwide would not be feasible for the purposes of this chapter. Given that our case study is based in the EU region and specifically in the UK, we will discuss the relevant legislation later within the case study. The interested reader based in the EU region or in the USA can consult the EC website (EC, 2003c) and US EPA (EPA, 2002) respectively for a more comprehensive overview of environmental legislation for MSW management and EfW plants. Here, we continue by considering the economic factors related to energy recovery from MSW.

Questions

1. Describe the legislative framework for MSW management and EfW plants in your country.
2. If you were to make an application for a planning permission for a new EfW plant in your town, which authority would you apply to? What kind of documentation would you have to prepare?

5.3.3 Economic Considerations

The EfW plants require high capital investments as well as operating and maintenance costs. Hence, the resulting cost per tonne of waste incinerated can be rather high compared to the other options such as landfilling. For example, in the USA, incineration costs range from about $400 to 550 per tonne of waste while landfilling costs are between $60 and 270 (McKinney and Schoch, 2003). These costs are much lower in developing countries; for example, in Southeast Asia the incineration costs range from $25 to 100 per tonne of waste with an average costs of $50/t, while the landfilling costs range from $10 to 40 (Rand *et al.*, 2000). The following sections give a brief overview of the capital and operating costs in different countries.

Capital Costs

Capital costs of an EfW plant depend on a wide range of factors including the type and size of combustor, waste throughput, heating value of the waste, type of energy recovered as well as environmental legislation. Figure 5.12 shows the influence of the size of the plant on the capital costs: the smaller plants are more expensive per tonne of waste incinerated than the higher-capacity plants. For example, an EfW facility which burns 500 t/day of waste costs on average £6000/MW which is 1.5 times more expensive than a facility burning 2000 t/day of MSW.

At present, building a typical mass-burn incinerator in the USA that can treat around 500 t/day of waste would cost around $120 million, whilst the plant treating 2000 t/day would cost between $160 and 200 million. Capital costs of EfW plants in the EU countries are shown in Table 5.11. The costs are based on the 1990 data so that the costs for the latter years are the projections rather than the actual data.

Operating Costs

Operating costs include fixed and variable costs. The former comprise cost of administration and salaries while the latter include costs of chemicals for the flue gas cleaning system, cost of electricity (which will be offset if the plant is producing electricity), cost of water and handling of waste water and cost of residue disposal. Additional operating costs are related to maintenance, which comprise costs to maintain the equipment and the buildings. Finally, waste collection and transportation also contribute to the total operating costs. For example, the average operating costs in Europe are around £70/t (Juniper, 2003) or £140 000/MW (EC, 2003c). The average transportation costs are around £10/100 km.

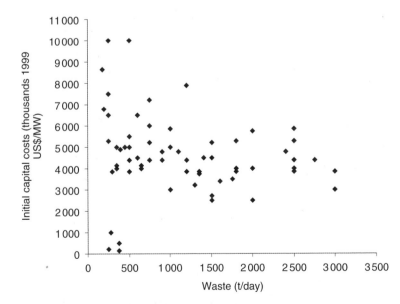

Figure 5.12 *Capital costs of EfW plants in the USA for different plant capacities (Based on the data from EIA, 2001.)*

Table 5.11 Costs and technical performance of EfW plants (Adapted from EC, 2003c.)

Parameter	1980	1985	1990	1995	2000	2005	2010
Typical unit size (MWe)	4–7	4–11	5–18	10–27	11–29	15–30	15–30
Availability factor (%)	80	80	85	85	90	90	90
Fuel efficiency (%)	14	16	18	20	22	23	24
Energy consumption rate (% of output)	10	10	12	12	15	15	15
Construction time (years)	2	2	2	2–3	2–3	2–3	2–3
Economic lifetime (years)	20	20	20	20	20	20	20
Capital cost (£[1990]/kW)	3153–3941	3448–3621	2759–3678	1931–2483	1856–2445	1343–2359	1276–2241
Operation and maintenance cost (£[1990]/kW)	268–315	234–280	184–245	145–166	131–151	116–129	110–123
Fuel cost (£[1990]/kWh)	–(0.01–0.03)	–(0.01–0.06)	–(0.01–0.07)	–(0.01–0.09)	–(0.01–0.1)	–(0.02–0.1)	–(0.02–0.1)
Cost of energy derived from above data, using 8% discount rate (pence[1990]/kWh)	6–8	2.3–8	1–7.5	0.9–7.5	0.5–3.7	0.47–3.26	0.47–2.8

Conversion rate: £1 = 2.145 ECU (1990).

The operating costs of EfW plants are offset by an income from the energy recovered and through the tipping fees, which are paid by the local authorities to the operators of EfW plants to treat the waste.

Assumptions underlying the cost and technical performance data for MSW incinerators:

1. During the 1980s a significant proportion of the facilities (about 35%) were just incinerators (no power recovery) and, compared to later facilities, with low throughput capacities. Further, the gas cleaning equipment was rudimentary – usually only dust control. Power generation efficiencies were also low (about 350 kWh/t compared to 500 kWh/t for modern plant). Capital costs per kW are therefore comparatively high.
2. The newer facilities require a greater capital investment because of gas cleaning requirement and so on, but have increased throughput to be more cost-effective, and are more efficient power generators – hence the lowering of costs on a per kW basis.
3. The fuel cost is negative as this is effectively the waste disposal fee which, in the early years, was relatively low about £2–9 (1990)/t, but now ranges from £5 to 42 (1990)/t. In future, the lower costs are expected to rise more quickly than the higher ones such that by 2010 the costs will range from £14 to 52 (1990)/t.
4. The impact of this increase in waste disposal cost, taken together with better power generation efficiencies and lower capital costs per kW, is to reduce the energy costs from a high value of about 8 pence(1990)/kWh to a value in the range 0.47–2.8 pence(1990)/kWh in the future.

Externalities

The capital and operating costs are known as 'internal' costs and they represent direct costs associated with incineration. However, it is also important to know the total cost of waste management to the environment and society. These are known as 'externalities' and take into account environmental damage caused by a waste management option. However, they are very difficult to estimate and are associated with a large uncertainty because there is no agreed methodology yet which can estimate the monetary value of environmental pollution, loss of human life associated with that pollution and so on. Nevertheless, some estimates of externalities have been made and these are listed in Table 5.12. These data should be interpreted

Table 5.12 *Estimates of externalities of landfill and incineration (The UK Government, 1995; © Crown.)*

Waste management option	Externalities (£/t waste)
Incineration with energy recovery	−£4.00
Incineration without energy recovery	£5.00
Landfill with energy recovery	£1.00
Landfill without energy recovery	£3.50

with care and only as a relative indication of what it might cost the environment and society to incinerate the waste rather than to landfill it. The estimated externalities include emissions of greenhouse gases (methane and carbon dioxide), acid gases (sulphur dioxide and nitrogen oxides), volatile organic compounds (VOCs), lea-chates, transport-related impacts and pollution displacement from the energy recovery. The emissions of dioxins from incinerators are not included. The negative values for incineration with energy recovery show the importance of pollution displacement which would have been otherwise generated through the use of conventional fuels.

For example, a municipal incinerator which burns 135 000 t of MSW a year, producing heat of about 34 MW for 3500 dwellings, saves around 170×10^6 kWh of fossil fuel energy and 30 000 t of carbon dioxide each year, which would have been produced by burning a fossil fuel.

Questions

1. Explain how capital and operating costs can be calculated for an EfW plant.
2. Use the cost data given in Figure 5.12 and Table 5.11 to compare the costs of incineration in the USA and Europe. What do you conclude?
3. What are the capital and operating costs of EfW plants in your country? Discuss the sources and reliability of the cost data.
4. Explain the meaning of 'externalities' in the context of MSW management and particularly the EfW option. How are these externalities calculated?

5.3.4 Social Considerations

There are a number of stakeholders associated with EfW systems and their interests and concerns must be taken into account when considering a proposal for a new EfW plant. As shown in Table 5.13, in addition to the EfW plant operators, the EfW stakeholders include local communities, citizens, NGOs, waste-handling companies and energy producers. Scavengers are also important in developing countries as they are involved in collection and sorting of waste for reuse and recycling.

The interests and concerns raised by these stakeholders are often at the opposite ends. For example, the waste-handling and EfW plant operators have an active interest in building new EfW facilities as they wish to maintain or expand their business.

On the other hand, community groups, neighbours, NGOs and the general public are likely to be against proposals for new EfW plants. In fact, public acceptability of incineration is a very important issue and is often the main obstacle to building new EfW plants. There are two main reasons for this: the not-in-my-back-yard (NIMBY) syndrome; and the concern related to pollution from incineration and the impacts on human health and the environment. Dioxins and furans are in particular a subject of a continuing debate between the proponents and opponents of EfW systems over the levels of emissions and the related human toxicity. The issue of dioxins is very serious indeed and, as illustrated recently in the UK, it can have very serious consequences (Box 5.4).

Table 5.13 *Typical stakeholders for the EfW systems*

Stakeholders	Stakeholder interests	Possible stakeholder influence
Neighbours and community groups	Concerned that the proposed EfW plant would lead to an increase in noise, dust, traffic and visual impact and a reduction in property prices; on the other hand, interested in increased employment opportunities	Delay, change in specification of the EfW plant and/or refusal of the planning permission due to protests
NGOs	Interested in reducing the impact of waste management on the environment; primarily promoted minimisation of waste and recycling	Delay, change in specification of the EfW plant and/or refusal of the planning permission due to protests
Scavengers	Concerned that changed waste management practices may affect or eliminate their source of income	Scavengers' activities may affect the properties and amounts of waste; in some countries they have a strong political influence opposing EfW plants
Waste-handling companies	Interested in collection and transport of waste for EfW plants in order to maintain or expand their business	Can dictate the collection, transportation and tipping fees and increase the operating costs of EfW plants
EfW operators	Wish to maintain or expand their business; interested in reliable and increasing waste streams	Can lobby local authorities and influence the planning process
(Large) energy producers	Opposition to purchase energy from smaller external producers (such as EfW plants)	Can be a barrier to the sale of energy at local market prices; can dictate the price of energy

Furthermore, some stakeholders object to the visual impact, odour and noise from the EfW facilities, increased transport activities in their area associated with waste handling and the effect on their property value. On the other hand, the local communities may also be interested in the new employment opportunities that the EfW systems provide, both during their construction and operation.

In many countries, the opposition by some groups of stakeholders to new incineration plants is very strong and can often lead to a refusal of the planning permission for a new plant. These groups advocate waste minimisation and recycling instead, and argue that new incinerators encourage increased consumption and waste generation. However, one problem with waste minimisation and recycling is that it has so far failed to reduce the amount of solid waste significantly because of the lack of public participation and recycling facilities. A recent survey on public perception of MSW and recycling carried out in the UK confirms that recycling is important but will not on its own be able to achieve the targets for reducing the amount of MSW that is disposed of in landfills (Box 5.5).

Therefore, we have to find alternative ways of dealing with the growing amount of MSW, and EfW may be one of these alternatives within an integrated waste management strategy. However, this can be an alternative only if EfW plants can be designed and operated in a sustainable way. The following case study illustrates what needs to be taken into account in an attempt to achieve this goal by considering the relevant technical, environmental, economic and social issues. It also illustrates the complexity of the problem which involves a number of stakeholders with different and often opposing interests. Starting with the choice of technology and design of the plant, the case study guides the reader through the environmental, economic and social assessments of the EfW plant, as required by the planning application process in many countries. Read on to find out which stakeholder group – the proposers or the opponents – won the argument and if the planning application for this EfW plant has been successful. Prior to presenting the case study, it is interesting to get an insight into the current use of EfW systems around the world.

Box 5.4   *Dioxin pollution: the case of the Byker incinerator in Newcastle, UK*

The following Guardian (2003) article illustrates the scope of the problem and the controversy caused by the use of mixed bottom and fly ash from the Byker incinerator as a 'soil improver' over the allotments in Newcastle upon Tyne in the northeast of England.

'Dioxins in city may be worst case in UK
David Hencke, Westminster correspondent, Guardian
Tuesday, Feb 13, 2001

The spreading of poisoned incinerator ash over allotments in Newcastle upon Tyne's poorest area was one of the worst cases of dioxin contamination in Britain, an independent investigator said yesterday.

The consumption of eggs, poultry and vegetables produced on 22 allotments in the city was banned last year after 2000 t of incinerator ash was spread in Byker, in the constituency of the agriculture minister, Nick Brown.

The report, by Alan Watson, an independent scientist, was commissioned by residents. Separate reports by the environment agency and the food standards agency released last night confirmed high levels of metal contamination and the presence of high levels of dioxins – which can cause cancer – in the eggs of hens raised on the allotments. The Environment Agency has also revealed that the allotments were already highly polluted before the ash was spread. A fourth report, by Newcastle University, analysed the findings.

The disclosure of the findings, which had been held back for six months, provoked a big row between residents and the city council at a meeting in Byker last night. Newcastle council and the Newcastle and North Tyneside health authority have agreed to continue the ban on the consumption of eggs and poultry raised on the allotments as "a precautionary measure". But they claimed that, although the level of dioxins was high, it was not a serious danger to health.

Last year the council removed all the ash – which had been there for up to 8 years – from the allotments, footpaths and bridleways in the city. Toddlers were prevented from playing on the allotments in case they ate the ash.

The council and Cambridge-based Combined Heat and Power face 19 charges between them of illegally disposing of toxic waste.

Dr Watson's report said: "The contamination of allotments in Newcastle by high levels of dioxins and heavy metals from the Byker incinerator could be one of the most serious dioxin contamination events in the UK ... this is because it is nearly unprecedented to have high levels of dioxin-contaminated material being introduced so directly on to land used for personal food supplies including eggs for a large number of people."

He accused the food standards agency and environment agency of not doing a thorough job. He said they had failed to assess the dioxin intakes of children under the age of 10 and had ignored the effect of dioxins on people who might have eaten the contaminated hens. He said there could be other contaminated sites in Newcastle that had not been identified. "In at least some of the cases the allotments will need to be cleared completely, with new topsoil being supplied."

Last night Newcastle council condemned Dr Watson's findings. A spokesman said: "He is the only person who seems to have drawn such a conclusion – neither the food standards agency nor the environment agency are saying that the risk to health is so serious."

The reports from the two agencies and the analysis by Newcastle University all confirm heavy contamination. The University revealed that severe soil contamination with heavy metals and arsenic was found in more than half the allotments – and warned that other sources as well as the incinerator could be responsible. It also found that many of the eggs tested had dioxin levels "well in excess of levels found in supermarket barn eggs".

Both the environment agency and the food standards agency thought that people would have to have consumed huge quantities of produce to run a serious risk.'

Box 5.5   *Public perception of MSW and recycling (EA, 2002c)*

This survey, carried out by the Environment Agency in England and Wales, found out the following:

- On the whole, people would participate in recycling if the councils provided a means of sorting waste for recycling, but time is an issue.
- 28% people feel that they do not have time to sort their rubbish – a view that is most strongly held among younger, convenience food-using people.
- Potential for waste is exacerbated by two-for-one offers in supermarkets, usually economising triumphs over environmental responsibility – even among environmentally responsible people.

Box 5.5 *Continued*

- On the whole, people do not think that recycled products are of inferior quality, but a third do perceive them as being more expensive than non-recycled products.
- People see the point in recycling and claim to mend or repair broken/worn out possessions and buy more durable products.
- It seems that willingness to mend/repair and purchase more durable products is economy- not conscience-driven.
- Though people know that avoiding products with lots of packaging will significantly reduce waste, relatively few do so.
- Significant recycling is limited to newspapers and glass – items that are easily recycled because the council either collects or provides street-recycling points.
- Although people recycle newspapers (58%), only a small proportion (33%) recycle cardboard boxes.
- Hardly anyone recycles plastic packaging (11%), a greater, yet still small (22%), proportion recycle plastic bottles. This compares with 60% for glass bottles and 35% for drinks cans. Charging by amount of rubbish produced was unpopular – 58% opposed such an idea.
- 90% would be certain or very likely to sort rubbish for recycling if their local council provided containers. Similar proportions claim that they would sort if they were charged varying amounts of £10/yr to £100/yr, suggesting that fees may do little to increase participation.

Conclusions of the survey

- The concept of sorting and recycling is favourably received by the public – the majority claim they would recycle more if they were provided easier means to sort rubbish.
- The public has a reasonable degree of knowledge of recycling issues, but remain uncertain as to the environmental advantages and disadvantages of landfilling versus incinerating, and how to dispose of more 'difficult' products such as paint, household chemicals and pesticides.
- However, there is a significant minority, of between a fifth and a quarter, who are not willing to participate in responsible waste management. These tend to be younger, non-environmentally committed, time-starved people, those living in rented accommodation and more elderly households.

Questions

1. Emissions of dioxins are one of the main objections of the public to incineration and EfW plant. However, dioxins are also emitted from open fires such as home fireplaces. It is known that the effect of fireplaces on human health is greater than that of incinerators (why?). Discuss why you think that people

accept this health risk to enjoy a romantic evening by the fireplace and yet object to the incinerators.

2. Comment on the Byker incinerator case. What is your view on the affair? Explain and justify your position.

3. In protest against the practice of using bottom and fly ash rather than disposing of it safely, Greenpeace have recently occupied the incinerator in Edmonton in England and shut it down. This resulted in the government enquiry into the practice of using the ash from this plant for making bricks to construct a local housing estate. Visit the Greenpeace website in the UK and find out more about the affair. What is your view on the Greenpeace action? Explain and justify your position.

4. You are the managing director of an EfW plant. Your plant manager calls you at home in the early morning in panic to inform you that several members of Greenpeace have climbed the stack of the plant and chained themselves to it. The press has already arrived at the site. What actions do you take?

5.3.5   EfW Plants Worldwide

EfW Plants in the EU

As shown in Table 5.14, there is a wide variation in the EU countries in their reliance on MSW incineration, ranging from 8% in the UK up to 48% in Denmark (EC, 2003b). Most incineration plants recover energy either in the form of steam used for district heating or as electricity or both. The production of RDF is another type of energy recovery system in operation in Europe. There are a number of recycling and RDF-producing installations in operation.

As in many other regions, incineration is a very contentious issue in Europe with a growing public opposition to building new incinerators, mainly because of health concerns associated with air emissions from incineration of mixed waste (as discussed in sections 'Air Pollution Prevention and Control' and 'Social Considerations'). In the EU countries, the incinerators are fitted with the pollution control equipment which in most cases includes scrubbers to remove acid gases and either electrostatic precipitators or baghouse filters to capture particulates and heavy metals. The EU is enforcing severe emission standards for all types of incinerators, along with rules for protecting the health and the safety of workers (see Box 5.1 for some examples of the EC directives related to incineration).

Incinerators in Eastern Europe are often older ones that usually do not have adequate, or in some cases any, environmental controls (UNEP, 1996). Eastern European cities, other than major ones, have wastes that cannot be incinerated without auxiliary, usually fossil, fuel.

EfW Plants in the USA

Most of the MSW incinerators in the USA recover energy in the form of steam, which is used either to drive a turbine to generate electricity or directly for heating or cooling. In the mid-1990s, there were about 168 waste-to-energy facilities in the USA

Table 5.14   *The state of MSW incineration in Europe, USA and Japan in the early 1990s (White et al., 1995; published with permission by Blackie Academic & Professional (now Kluwer))*

Country	No. of incineration plants	% of MSW incinerated	Energy recovery (% of capacity)	Type of energy recovery
Austria	2	8.5	100	
Belgium	25	54	30	HW/ST/EL
Czech Republic		4	77	
Denmark	38	65	100	District heating
Finland		2	100	
France	170	42	72	ST/HW/EL
Germany	49	34	43 plants	EL/ST/HW
Greece	0	0	–	
Hungary	0	0	–	
Ireland	0	0	–	
Italy	94	18	33	HW/EL
Luxembourg	2	69	100	EL
Netherlands	8	35	6 plants	EL/ST/HW
Norway		20	89	
Poland	0	0	–	
Portugal	0	0	–	
Slovak Republic		6		
Spain	23	6	5 plants	ST/EL
Sweden	23	56	100	District heating
Switzerland	30	80	72	
UK	34	8	37	HW/EL
USA	168	16	128 plants	
Japan	1873	74	Most plants	District heating/EL

HW – hot water; ST – steam; EL – electricity; given in order of level of use.

which managed about 10–16% of the MSW stream (Table 5.14). However, the amount of solid waste processed in the incineration facilities varies significantly by region. For example, the northeastern US currently incinerates and recovers energy from over 40% of its solid waste, while many states incinerate less than 2% of the solid waste they generate (UNEP, 1996). The relatively recent development of regional landfills with inexpensive disposal capacity has made it more difficult for capital-intensive EfW plants to compete.

As in Europe and elsewhere, similar public concerns exist in the USA regarding the environmental and health risks from incineration plants. The air pollution control laws and regulations have been strengthened in recent years to specifically address these concerns and reduce potential impacts from air emissions. The major air emission control technologies employed in the USA are fabric filters, electrostatic precipitators and scrubbers.

EfW Plants in Asia and Pacific

Modern incinerators recovering energy in the form of steam for heating and for electricity generation are currently in service only in cities of more industrialised countries such as Australia, Hong Kong, Japan, Singapore, South Korea and Taiwan (UNEP, 1996). For example, Singapore has three incinerators which burn 90% of the daily 5800 t of MSW collected and generate 60 MW of electrical energy, some of which is used to run incinerator operations.

There are 1873 incinerators in Japan; Tokyo alone has 13 (Table 5.14). Some Japanese cities have integrated their MSW incinerators in community complexes with indoor gardens, meeting halls, second-hand shops and offices of NGOs. Hong Kong, on the other hand, has had to close its incinerators because they could not meet the prescribed air pollution standards. In South Korea, there is a strong local opposition to incinerators and authorities are exploring ways to resolve such conflicts. It is likely that incineration will remain popular in cities like Singapore and Tokyo as there is a lack of landfill sites. Even there, however, there is a controversy about greenhouse and other gases released by incineration.

High capital investment, high operating and maintenance costs, lack of trained operators and stringent air pollution control regulations have severely limited the use of incineration for disposal in the less-developed countries of the region (UNEP, 1996). A further difficulty is that waste in the low-income economies is generally low in combustibles such as paper and plastic, so incinerators need additional, often fossil, fuel.

In rare cases where incinerators do exist (e.g. Thailand, China, Indonesia), they have mainly been imported from developed countries and are causing many problems as they are not suitable for local conditions. For example, some incinerators are not operated at a high enough temperature to destroy pathogens and contribute to air pollution due to lack of environmental controls. Furthermore, MSW in these countries is often too wet so that it must be dried, often for days, before it can be incinerated.

In cities of developing countries, open burning of refuse is common in landfill sites as well as in households. This contributes to air pollution in cities and towns. Some authorities encourage this backyard burning as it reduces the amount of MSW they have to collect (UNEP, 1996).

EfW Plants in Africa

There are very few incineration plants in Africa. One energy recovery plant was recently constructed in Tanzania with foreign assistance (UNEP, 1996). The main obstacles to expanding the incineration capacity in Africa include high costs, lack of infrastructure, local technical capacity to maintain and service the facilities, the availability of basic spare parts and the effective implementation of a monitoring programme to protect public health from plant emissions. The composition of waste, which consists of around 70% of putrescibles (food scraps, garden and other organic waste) and is therefore inappropriate for incineration, also suggests that this waste disposal method is not suitable for the countries in Africa.

EfW Plants in Latin America

Virtually no incinerators operate in Latin America or the Caribbean, although there have been a number of feasibility studies. To date, however, the costs of this technology are far too high to be considered by local governments as an appropriate waste management technology (UNEP, 1996).

Questions

1. Why do you think the waste in developing countries has a higher content of putrescibles (e.g. food scraps) than the waste in developed countries?
2. Given a high proportion of putrescibles in African and some other countries, which MSW options do you think are more appropriate for these countries?
3. Find out how many incinerators (if any) there are in your country and what kind of energy (if any) they recover. What is the position of different stakeholders on EfW plants in your country?

5.4   Case Study: A Proposal for a new EfW Plant

This case study is based on a real proposal for a new EfW plant in England. The following describes the development of the case, from technical design, through sustainability assessments to the final decision of the local authority on whether to grant the planning permission. The names of the place and the actors are not mentioned to preserve confidentiality.

5.4.1   The Problem

A County Council (CC) in England is considering various options for MSW management. Following the waste management hierarchy discussed in sections 5.1 and 5.2, the CC has already put in place the schemes for the waste reduction and materials recovery through recycling. However, although improving, these schemes are not reducing significantly the amount of MSW disposed of in the regional landfills. Currently, out of almost 600 000 t of MSW generated each year within the county, only 13% is recycled and the remaining 87% is landfilled. Even if the recycling rates are increased to the target of 25% set by the EU, the county will still have 450 000 t of waste per year to treat or dispose of by other means.

   In the meantime, the region is running out of the landfill space, with the predictions that the last licensed landfill site will reach its capacity in 3 years' time. It is unlikely that a new landfill site will be opened due to the increasing objections by the public to new landfill facilities. The CC is therefore willing to consider energy recovery as one of the longer-term options that could help it deal with the increasing amounts of waste generated each year. However, the CC is aware that this is going to be a very contentious issue as the local population and other stakeholders are likely to oppose the proposal for an EfW plant, particularly as this would be the first incinerator in the whole county.

   Nevertheless, given its own pressures related to MSW management, the CC has identified an existing industrial site as a possible location for an MSW incinerator and has invited a reputable, locally based waste management company 'WEnergise' to put together a proposal for an EfW plant. The company's task is to design a sustainable EfW system which will be able to handle 225 000 t of waste per year.

   To accomplish this task, WEnergise has put together a design team consisting of three engineers and an environmental scientist. In addition, the company lawyer has been made available to the design team for guidance and advice on the planning process and environmental legislation. Furthermore, the company has also contracted an environmental consultancy firm to help the design team with the environmental assessments of the proposed plant as required by the relevant EU and UK legislation.

Having examined a number of options, the design team has put forward a design for an EfW plant generating on average 20 MW of electricity. The team has also considered the use of heat for district heating in addition to electricity generation but has decided against it because of the lack of district-heating infrastructure. However, they have designed the plant so as to enable an easy modification, should district heating become a feasible option at a later stage.

In putting the proposal together, the team has evaluated the level of sustainability of the following six design options:

- *Base case*   Moving-grate furnace with SNCR for NO_x removal and semi-dry removal of acid gases;
- *Option 1*   Fluidised-bed furnace with dry removal of acid gases;
- *Option 2*   Moving-grate furnace with SNCR for NO_x removal and dry removal of acid gases;
- *Option 3*   Moving-grate furnace with semi-dry removal of acid gases;
- *Option 4*   Moving-grate furnace with SNCR for NO_x removal and wet removal of acid gases; and
- *Option 5*   Moving-grate furnace with SCR for NO_x removal and semi-dry removal of acid gases.

As required by the EU Directives on IPPC and EIA, the design team has assessed these options with the help of the environmental consultancy on the technical, economic, environmental and social performance and has concluded that the base case is the most sustainable EfW option. Following this decision and as required by the EU and UK law, WEnergise has submitted the required documentation to the CC for a planning permission, including an application for the IPPC Authorisation and the EIA Statement.

As expected by both the CC and the WEnergise, the proposal has attracted a considerable public interest with the local residents vigorously opposing the proposal and organising an anti-incinerator movement. As a result, the CC has solicited written opinions from the various stakeholders to try to resolve the issue. The following sections recount this whole process, from the technical design of the incinerator, through the sustainability assessment of the options to the issues raised by the public and other stakeholders, and the final decision of the CC on whether to grant a planning permission for this EfW application. The reader is invited to participate in this process by challenging both the technical design and sustainability assessment of the plant carried out by the WEnergise team and the environmental consultancy as well as the arguments and opinions of the other stakeholders.

Because of its complexity and 'richness', the case study is structured in a way that the readers with different backgrounds can concentrate on the sections that are of more interest to them. Non-engineers and non-scientists may wish to skip the technical section and concentrate on the sustainability issues and the objections raised by the public and other stakeholders, which are explored further below.

Questions

1. If you were the managing director of WEnergise and had to put a design team together to design an EfW plant, which professions would you want to include in the team and why?
2. Use Table 3.13 to identify the stakeholders for the proposed EfW plant and try to predict their position on the proposal.

5.4.2   Overview of the Base Case Design

The base case design of the EfW plant as proposed by the WEnergise design team is shown in Figure 5.13. The proposed plant consists of four parts:

1. waste handling facility;
2. incinerator and energy recovery plant, including the incinerator, turbine and generator;
3. air pollution prevention and flue gas treatment plant; and
4. bottom ash treatment facility.

As this is a complex system, the team has built the design step by step, by first considering each part separately and then connecting and optimising them into an integrated design. The design process is discussed in more detail further below.

Waste Handling Facility

This part of the plant consists of the waste reception and storage areas. The waste will be weighted on arrival and then tipped into the storage bunker. Waste in the bunker will be mixed regularly to homogenise it, identify non-combustible items and avoid malodorous (anaerobic) decomposition.

Incinerator and Energy Recovery Plant

Waste from the storage bunker will be transferred by overhead cranes to the feed hoppers of the mass-burn moving-grate incinerator. To be able to process the predicted throughput of 225 000 t/yr of waste, the team has chosen two incinerator units with a total capacity of 28.6 t/h or 14.3 t/h each. With an estimated average LHV of 98 000 kJ/kg, this amount of waste will be generating 20 MW of electricity.

Air Pollution Prevention and Control Plant

In this proposed design, SNCR will be used to remove nitrogen oxides by injection of either aqueous ammonia or dry urea into the incinerator. The formation of dioxins and furans during combustion will be prevented by an online control of the combustion temperature and the residence time of the flue gas in the combustor as well as by a subsequent rapid cooling of the combustion gases to below 200 °C to prevent

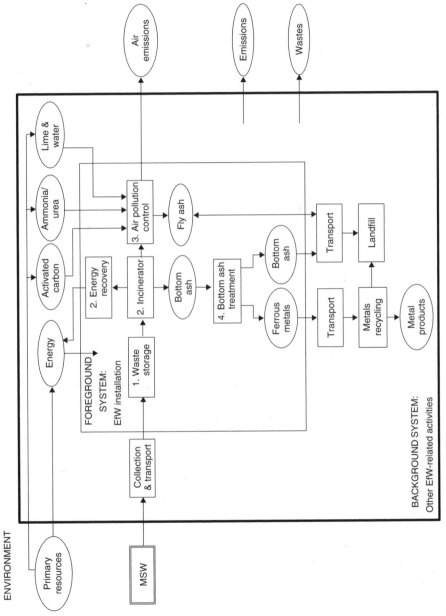

Figure 5.13 Block diagram of the proposed EfW plant from 'cradle to grave' (excluding construction of the plant)

formation of these pollutants by *de novo* synthesis. Acid gases such as SO_2, HCl and HF will be scrubbed in a semi-dry cyclone with lime slurry [$(CaOH)_2$]. Some of the larger particulates will also be removed in the cyclone while the fly ash particles will be removed in a fabric filter following the semi-dry cyclone. The design team has estimated that, depending on the composition of the waste, the amount of fly ash captured will be around 8300 t/yr, all of which will be disposed of in a licensed landfill.

In addition to these air pollution control measures, activated carbon will be injected into the flue gas between the cyclone and the filter to remove mercury and other metals as well as any dioxins formed during the flue gas treatment. Further amounts of these pollutants will also be adsorbed in the filter on to the lime particles some of which remain in the flue gas after the treatment in the cyclone. The cleaned flue gas will then be discharged through a 70-m high flue stack.

Bottom Ash Treatment Facility

Depending on the waste composition, the plant will produce on average 47 800 t of bottom ash residue per year. The ash will comprise approximately 25% by weight or 8% by volume of the original waste and will contain less than 3% unburnt carbon.

The ash will be discharged from the bottom of the incinerator by an ash discharger onto vibrating conveyors, which will deliver the ash residue into residues bunker. A drum magnet arranged over the conveyor will extract ferrous materials which will then be recycled. The following sections discuss the proposed design in more detail, considering technical, economic, environmental and social criteria.

5.4.3   Technical Considerations

The design team is well aware that burning MSW to recover energy poses many technical challenges. Some of these are related to its variable composition, heating value and water content, which influence the amount of energy that can be recovered as well as the flue gas emissions and related requirements for pollution prevention and control. Therefore, they first have to determine these variables and the extent to which they may vary so that the designed plant can cope under the different operating conditions.

The next task for the design team is to estimate the following thermodynamic parameters:

- total heat released by combustion of the waste;
- efficiency of the turbine and the efficiency of energy conversion – from heat into electricity;
- material and energy balances of the plant, including the flow rates of the steam.

The following section shows how some of these parameters have been calculated by the team. Due to space limitations, it is not possible to discuss the calculations in detail so that in most cases only the final result estimated by the team is given. However, the reader is invited to complete the calculations and check the accuracy of the results obtained by the design team. Some prior knowledge of physics and thermodynamics is necessary to follow the discussion and carry out the calculations. Furthermore, the reader should be familiar with the air pollution clean-up techniques and technologies, which are also discussed in this section. The less technically inclined reader may wish to skip this section and go directly to the sections which discuss economic and environmental issues associated with this case study.

Waste Arisings and its Composition

The average amount of waste that will be available for collection and incineration has been supplied to the team by the CC and this is estimated at 225 000 t of MSW per year. Figure 5.14 shows the expected average composition of the MSW while Tables 5.15 and 5.16 give the results of proximate and ultimate analyses respectively carried out by the WEnergise laboratory using a number of waste samples. The design team has used these data on the Tanner triangle (Figure 5.10) to determine whether the waste is suitable for combustion. Using the results of LHV and HHV for each component of the waste shown in Table 5.15, the team has estimated that LHV of waste is about 9800 kJ/kg and the HHV is around 19 600 kJ/kg.

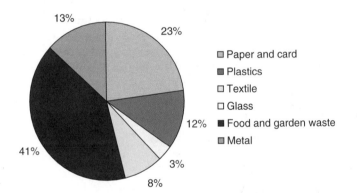

Figure 5.14 *Average composition of the MSW to be burnt in the EfW plant (composition by weight)*

Table 5.15 *Composition of waste by weight on a wet basis (proximate analysis) and its energy content*

	Composition (% by wet weight)				Heating value (MJ/kg)	
	Moisture	Volatiles	Fixed carbon	Ash	LHV	HHV
Paper and card	6	80	11	3	15.5	24
Plastics	0.1	97	2	1	32.7	39
Textile	6	70	21	3	18.3	23
Glass	1	0	0	99	0.2	0.2
Food and garden waste	55	40	3	2	4.2	21
Metal	4	0	0	96	0.7	1

Table 5.16   *Composition of waste on a dry basis (ultimate analysis)*

	Composition (% by dry weight)					
	Carbon	Hydrogen	Oxygen	Nitrogen	Sulphur	Ash
Paper and card	57.5	6	30	0.3	0.2	6
Plastics	68	7	23	0	0	2
Textile	67.8	4	18	5	0.2	5
Glass	0.5	0.1	0.3	0.1	0	99
Food and garden waste	60	6	26	2.5	0.5	5
Metal	1.5	0.6	1.8	0.1	0	96

Questions

1. Use the results of the proximate and ultimate analyses shown in Tables 5.15 and 5.16 to find on the Tanner diagram (Figure 5.10) the point which defines this waste. What do you think the design team concluded about suitability of the waste for incineration?

2. Examine the waste composition and heating values of the waste given in Figure 5.14, Tables 5.15 and 5.16 and answer the following questions:

   (a) Which materials in the MSW will contribute to the energy generation and which materials have little energy value?
   (b) Use the data in Tables 5.15 and 5.16 to check that the design team has calculated correctly the lower and the higher heating values for the waste composition given in Figure 5.14.
   (c) Use equations (5.1)–(5.3) to check how well the LHV and HHV that you calculated above agree.

3. How does the waste composition shown in Figure 5.14 differ from the waste composition in your region? Is the waste in your region suitable for incineration and energy recovery? Why?

The Incineration and Energy Recovery Plant: Designing for Energy Efficiency

As already mentioned, to be able to process 225 000 t/yr of waste, the design team has chosen the incinerator with a total capacity of 28.6 t/h of waste. This capacity is based on an estimated availability of the plant for 7867 operating hours per year. Two incineration units will be used, each with the capacity of 14.3 t/h of waste. The waste will be incinerated in the presence of 47.6 t/h of primary air and 31.7 t/h of secondary air. The primary air will be heated to about 100 °C in the furnace air preheater before entry into the furnace; secondary air will go directly into the furnace without preheating. To ensure maximum oxidation of dioxins and other organic pollutants, after the last injection of air the flue gas will be held at the temperature above 850 °C for at least two seconds in the presence of at least 6% of oxygen.

For these operating conditions, the team has estimated the total heat release at 77.9 MW. This heat will be utilised in the boiler to raise steam. However, the team knows that this is well in excess of the heat load that will actually be passed to the steam due to heat losses. Furthermore, they also have to take into account situations whereby some very wet or otherwise incombustible waste has been fed into the incinerator so that the use of additional fuel (oil or natural gas) may be necessary. The thermodynamic cycle of one design variation of the incinerator and energy recovery plant proposed by the design team is shown in Figure 5.15. Their design is based on the assumptions described below.

The heat due to combustion raises supersaturated high-pressure (HP) steam in the boiler at 400 °C and 40 barg. The steam is then passed through a two-stage turbine: a high-pressure (HP) and a low-pressure (LP) stage. The isentropic efficiencies of the two stages of the turbine are assumed to be identical and equal to 0.838. Intermediate-pressure (IP) steam which is produced between the two turbine stages is at 147 °C and 2.6 barg. This steam can be bled off and used in other process units such as an open-feed or closed-feed boiler water heater and in a furnace air preheater. Altern-atively, the IP steam can be reheated in the furnace before its entry into the LP turbine, to increase the overall efficiency of energy conversion. The design shown in Figure 5.15 considers the latter option, with a reheat of the IP steam to 380 °C. This option requires additional piping between the turbine hall and the boiler, which must be of a sufficiently large diameter because of the lower fluid density and the need to control the pressure drops by controlling the fluid velocity.

The IP steam is expanded through the LP turbine to an air-cooled condenser operating at 0.1 bara and 46 °C. Note that all condensers in this design are air-cooled because of the lack of local supply of water for direct cooling purposes. Further-more, there is insufficient space at the site for a wet tower and the visible plume would be unacceptable. The condensed steam, that is the boiler water, is then pumped back into the boiler.

Applying the equations given in Appendix 5.A, the design team has calculated that the required flow rate of the HP steam is 18.6 kg/s. With the estimated heat loads on the condenser of -45.15 MW and on the boiler of 65.15 MW, the overall efficiency of electricity generation is equal to 30.7%.

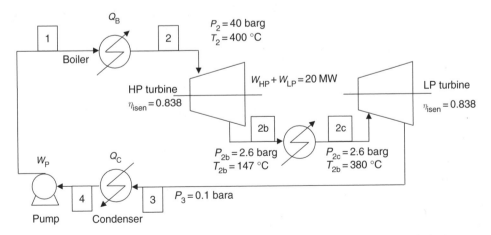

Figure 5.15   *The thermodynamic cycle for the incinerator and energy recovery plant*

In an attempt to improve the overall thermal efficiency, the design team has considered using the previously mentioned design variation, regarding the use of the IP steam for preheating the boiler water, including:

- an open-feed heater whereby the steam is injected live into the boiler feed water at atmospheric pressure to decrease the amount of dissolved air in the boiler feed water and to increase the temperature of the water going into the boiler from 46 to 100 °C; however, the penalty for this is a small loss of flow rate through the LP turbine;
- a closed-feed heater to preheat the boiler water up to about 137 °C; and
- the IP steam sub-cooling to about 56 °C to take the advantage of the fact that IP steam is condensed at about 46 °C so that more energy can be recovered from the steam.

The design team has summarised its findings for each of these design variations in Table 5.17. The results demonstrate that it is possible to increase energy efficiency by several percents through careful design. Further improvements are possible by condensation of the hot flue gases to recover the latent heat as they have to be cooled down to below 200 °C before entering the air pollution control system. However, these improvements are relatively small for the design effort involved. They can also lead to cost penalties because of the loss of the steam flow and the additional piping and heat transfer area required. On the other hand, much more substantial efficiency improvements would be achieved if the plant were to generate both the electricity and the heat for district heating. In that case, the overall efficiency of the system could be above 75%. However, as already mentioned, the lack of the district-heating infrastructure makes this option currently infeasible.

Having examined the energy efficiency results in Table 5.17 and considered the cost implications of each of the design variations, the team has decided to use the design that combines the boiler water preheat in a closed-feed heater and the IP preheat in the furnace.

Table 5.17 *Comparison of different design options with respect to the use of IP steam*

	Furnace preheat	Open-feed heater	Closed-feed heater	Steam sub-cooling
Assumptions	IP steam at 147 °C and 2.6 barg; heated to 380 °C; $\eta_{isen} = \eta_{HP} = \eta_{LP} = 0.838$	IP steam at 147 °C and 2.6 barg; $\eta_{isen} = \eta_{HP} = \eta_{LP} = 0.838$; Temp. of boiler feed water increased from 46 to 100 °C	IP steam at 147 °C and 2.6 barg; water heated to 137 °C; $\eta_{isen} = \eta_{HP} = \eta_{LP} = 0.838$; Temp. of boiler feed water increased from 46 to 137 °C	IP steam at 147 °C and 2.6 barg; steam sub-cooled to 56 °C and condensed at 46 °C
HP steam flow rate (kg/s)	18.6	22.8	24.0	23.6
Reduction of steam flow in the LP turbine (%)	–	9	17.9	15.4
Efficiency of energy conversion (%)	30.7	31.4	31.7	32.1

Questions

1. Show that burning 28.6 t/h of waste with the LHV of 9800 kJ/kg will release 77.9 MW of heat.
2. If the EfW plant is producing 20 MW of electricity and 15% of that is used to run the plant, calculate the net export of electricity from the site.
3. Calculate how much coal is saved each year in a power station, equivalent to the net exported electricity generated by burning MSW. Repeat the same calculation for oil and natural gas. Use the following LHVs of the fuel and the heat-to-electricity conversions:

   (a) Coal   LHV $= 17 \,\text{MJ/kg}$, $\eta = 33\%$;
   (b) Oil   LHV $= 42 \,\text{MJ/kg}$, $\eta = 40\%$; and
   (c) Gas   LHV $= 35 \,\text{MJ/m}^3$, $\eta = 42\%$.

4. Discuss the implications of burning wet waste and the use of additional (fossil) fuel to maintain combustion of the wet waste.
5. Given the total amount of waste to be burnt per day, which incineration technology would you chose (see section 'The Energy-from-Waste Technologies') and with how many units? Is your choice different from the choice of the WEnergise team?
6. Why is it desirable to preheat the primary air before combustion? How would you preheat it?
7. List and discuss the advantages and disadvantages of water- and air-cooled condensers. Why is the visible plume generated by water-cooled condensers unacceptable?
8. Start your design of the EfW plant considered in this case study by using a simple, modified Rankine cycle given in Appendix 5.A.
9. Now consider a more realistic case than that given in Appendix 5.A and calculate the pressure and thermal losses between the boiler and the turbine. Assume that the steam will leave the boiler at 400 °C and 40 barg but will arrive at the turbine at 385 °C and 38.5 barg. Estimate the following:

   (a) the increase in steam flow required to maintain the turbine power output;
   (b) the rate of heat loss from the HP steam pipe;
   (c) the boiler and condenser heat loads; and
   (d) the effect on the overall thermal efficiency.

10. Returning to the simple design case considered in Appendix 5.A, that is neglecting the losses considered in question 9, estimate:

    (a) the increase in steam flow required to maintain the turbine power output;
    (b) the heat loss from the turbine;
    (c) the boiler and condenser heat loads; and
    (d) the effect on the overall thermal efficiency.

11. Draw the enthalpy–entropy diagram for the design shown in Figure 5.15.
12. Consider different uses of the IP steam and use the assumptions summarised in Table 5.17 to calculate the changes in the thermal efficiencies for different design options. Discuss the advantages and disadvantages of each option with respect

to thermal efficiencies, flow rates of the steam and the cost implications. Which combination of the IP steam uses would you choose? Is your choice different from that of the WEnergise design team? Justify your choice.

13. Now design the configuration which combines both the closed-feed heater and the IP steam preheat in the furnace. In this design, also take into account a more realistic case where the temperature and pressure of the HP steam will be reduced to 385 °C and 38.5 barg before entry into the HP turbine. What is the energy efficiency of the process now?

14. How is the low pressure (0.1 bara) in the air-cooled IP steam condenser maintained (see the design shown in Figure 5.15)?

15. Compare the amounts of steam you calculated for different design options with the engineering 'rule of thumb' for steam production given in Table 5.6. How well do your result agree with these data? What do you conclude: can you use this 'rule of thumb' for future preliminary estimates?

16. Improve your design further by recovering the additional heat by cooling the flue gas to 190 °C. How much heat can you recover and what is the overall gain in the energy efficiency by this design modification? To answer this question, you will have to find out the exit temperature of the flue gas and for that you will have to carry out the energy balance on the incinerator. Use the figure below and the following steady-state equation for the energy balance calculation:

$$H_{MSW} + H_w = H_{fg} + H_s + H_v + H_{ash} + H_r$$

where:

H_{MSW}	heat generated by MSW (MJ/h)
H_w	heat in the water (MJ/h)
H_{fg}	heat out in the flue gases (MJ/h)
H_s	heat out in the steam (MJ/h)
H_v	heat out as latent heat of vaporisation (MJ/h)
H_{ash}	heat out in the ash (MJ/h)
H_r	heat loss due to radiation (MJ/h)

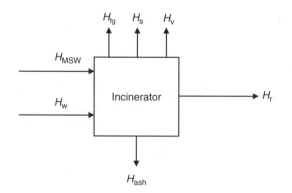

Assume that 5% of the heat input is lost due to radiation and that exit temperature of ash is 800 °C; the specific heat of ash is 0.84 kJ/kg °C.
17. Calculate the overall system efficiency assuming that the EfW plant is a CHP
plant producing 15 MW of electricity and using the rest of the available heat for
district heating. Assume 50% heat losses in the distribution system.

The Air Pollution Prevention and Control Plant: Designing for Environmental Protection

In addition to designing for energy efficiency, the design team must also make sure
that the plant is optimised on environmental performance. The design team has
identified that the following air pollutants will be formed in the combustion process:

- nitrogen oxides (NO and NO_2);
- sulphur oxides (SO_2);
- carbon oxides (CO and CO_2);
- hydrogen chloride and hydrogen fluoride (HCl and HF);
- particulates (fly ash);
- heavy metals and their compounds; and
- organic compounds including dioxins and furans.

To prevent the formation and control the emissions of these pollutants, the team has
decided to combine both the primary and the secondary measures for the prevention
and control of air pollutants (see section 'Air Pollution Prevention and Control' for
an overview of these measures). The layout of this design of air pollution prevention
and control plant is given in Figure 5.16.

Primary measures
After a careful consideration of the options and their effects on the air pollutants as
summarised in Table 5.9, the team has chosen the primary air preheating option to

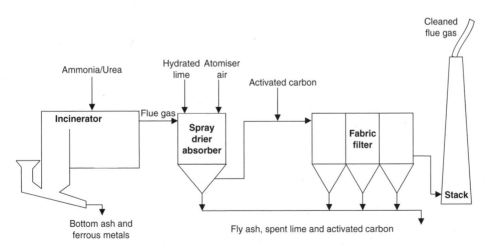

Figure 5.16 *The air pollution prevention and control plant*

reduce the formation of CO and HCs, including the dioxins, and to improve the potential for bottom ash recycling (e.g. in the construction applications). However, the preheating of air will increase the formation of NO_x, which will be controlled by SNCR, as explained below.

Furthermore, the constant movement of the grate will continuously rotate the burning waste, enabling the formation of a homogenous bed and promoting the burn-out of waste. This will in turn ensure the destruction of dioxins, furans and other VOCs and improve the potential for recycling the furnace bottom ash.

Secondary measures
As shown in Figure 5.16, the proposed flue gas clean-up plant comprises:

- SNCR of NO_x to nitrogen and water by injection of ammonia or urea into the boiler;
- semi-dry scrubber for removal of acid gases with lime slurry;
- fabric filters for removal of particulates (fly ash);
- system for removal of waste/recycled product from the filters and the absorber; and
- injection of activated carbon to remove dioxins, furans and metals.

After the rapid cooling of the flue gas within the boiler, the gases exit the boiler and enter a cyclone spray dryer where a lime slurry is atomised into the gas stream. The temperature of the flue gas will be carefully maintained at 130–150 °C by water injection, to prevent the formation of dioxins by *de novo* synthesis. The temperature drop may also cause condensation of certain metals, for example, mercury, and organic compounds onto the lime particles. Some lime particles will be collected at the bottom of the cyclone while the finer particles will be collected onto a fabric filter which is installed downstream from the semi-dry system. The expected lime usage is between 15 and 21 kg/t of waste burnt, depending on the HCl content.

However, before the flue gas is passed into the fabric filters to collect the fly ash, activated carbon is injected upstream of the filter to promote the removal of dioxins, gaseous mercury and some other heavy metals. Depending on the content of the acid gases, the operating temperature of the filter will be held around 140 °C or slightly above the acid dew point to prevent the condensation of the acid gases and the resulting damage to the filter fabric.

Questions

1. Consider the effects of different primary measures on the formation of the pollutants shown in Table 5.9. Which of these measures would you use to control pollution from the EfW plant considered in this case study and why? Is your choice different from the choice made by the design team? If so, why?
2. Which secondary air pollution measures would you choose and why? Discuss their advantages and disadvantages.
3. Why is the acid dew point important for the operation of fabric filters? Find out how the content of acid gases such as SO_2 and HCl affect the acid dew point. What happens if the acid dew point is above 200 °C and how does that affect the design of the air pollution control plant?

5.4.4   Environmental Considerations

Having designed the EfW plant, the next task for the WEnergise team is to carry out an environmental assessment of its proposed design. Since the proposed EfW plant is subject to both the IPPC and the EIA Directives, the team has to identify and quantify all potential releases to air, water and land from the construction and operation of the plant, together with the measures that will be used to prevent or reduce these releases. The team's assessment carried out in collaboration with the contracted environmental consultancy is summarised in the sections below. You may wish to consult Chapter 4 for the requirements of the IPPC Directive and Chapter 6 (Box 6.1) which outlines the EIA process to be able to follow the discussion easier.

Both the IPPC and the EIA Directives require quantification of environmental impacts during the construction and operation of the plant. Although the information required by the IPPC and EIA is similar and the project proposers can use parts of the IPPC documentation for the EIA and vice versa in their application for a new EfW plant, further work is needed for both types of applications and normally involves a significant effort to carry them out. Space precludes detailed considerations of both types of application so we start here by examining in more detail the IPPC requirements and conclude by giving a summary of these and the EIA findings at the end of this section.

The environmental consultancy has advised the WEnergise design team that one of the requirements of the IPPC Directive is that the emissions and discharges of the prescribed and other substances resulting from the proposed EfW installation into the environment should be prevented or controlled by using Best Available Technique (BAT). They have explained that BAT should be based on the balance between environmental benefits and economic costs, and should consider the impacts of both the foreground system (i.e. the installation) and the background system (i.e. other related activities). Furthermore, the team has been made aware that identification of BAT must be based on a life cycle approach, including the use of energy and raw materials and pollution from both the foreground and the background systems as shown in Figure 5.17 (note that this diagram is based on a more detailed system outline shown earlier, in Figure 5.13). The reader may wish to consult Chapter 4 for more detail on IPPC and BAT assessment. It should be noted that Figure 5.17 represents a modification of Figure 4.2, which shows a general interpretation of the system boundaries and the life cycle stages considered within the IPPC.

The Foreground System: The EfW Plant

Energy and raw materials
In addition to generating energy, the EfW plant will use some energy to run the pumps, air-cooling fans, conveyors, air pollution control equipment and so on. The design team has estimated that the plant will use 15% of the energy generated.

The raw materials will include lime, water, ammonia or urea and activated carbon. The estimated quantities of the raw materials that will be used in the EfW plant are listed in Table 5.18.

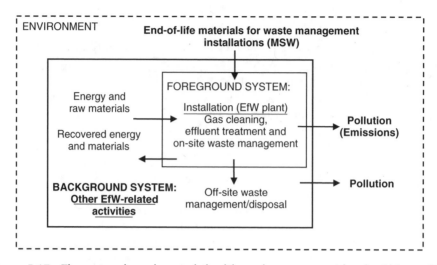

Figure 5.17 *The system boundary and the life cycle stages considered within an IPPC application for a new EfW plant (Adapted from Nicholas et al., 2000; published with the permission of the Institute of Chemical Engineers.)*

Table 5.18 *Raw materials used in the EfW plant*

Raw material	Quantity (t/yr)
Towns water	74 250
Lime	3 375–4 500
Activated carbon	100
Ammonia	370

Gas cleaning, effluent treatment and on-site waste management
The emissions of the prescribed substances into air will be controlled by the air pollution prevention and control plant described in section 'The Air Pollution Prevention and Control Plant: Designing for Environmental Protection'.

Pollution (emissions)
Air pollution   To estimate the air emissions from the EfW plant, the WEnergise design team and the environmental consultancy have used two main sources of information:

1. the average air emission factors for the construction and operation of an EfW plant, as shown in Table 5.19;
2. the limits on air emission from incinerators as prescribed by the EC Waste Incineration Directive and summarised in Table 5.20.

Using the maximum emission limits listed in Table 5.20, the team has estimated the total annual air emissions which are summarised in Table 5.21.

To ensure that the emission of the air pollutants will not result in a significant decrease in air quality around the plant as required by the Ambient Air Framework Directive on the Air Quality Standards (AQS) (see Table 5.22 for the AQS

Table 5.19 *Average emissions from EfW plants during construction of the plant and from combustion (EC, 2003c)*

Air pollutant	Emission factor (kg/TJ)
Combustion	
CO_2 (non-biomass)	99 850
SO_2	697
NO_x	843
Particulates	73
VOCs	47
Construction	
CO_2	1 251
SO_2	10
NO_x	4

Table 5.20 *Air emission limit values from incinerators: Waste Incineration Directive 2000/76/EC (EC, 2000b)*

(a) Daily average values (mg/m^3)		
Total dust		10
Total organic carbon		10
Hydrogen chloride		10
Hydrogen fluoride		1
Sulphur dioxide		50
NO and NO_2 expressed as NO_2		
existing plant with capacity exceeding 6 t/h or a new plant		200
existing plant with capacity of 6 t/h or less		400
(b) Half-hourly average values (mg/m^3)		
Total dust		30
Total organic carbon		20
Hydrogen chloride		60
Hydrogen fluoride		4
Sulphur dioxide		200
NO and NO_2 expressed as NO_2		
existing plant with capacity exceeding 3 t/h or a new plant		400
(c) Average values over sample period (mg/m^3)	min. 30 min	max. 8 h
Hg	0.05	0.1
Cd + Tl	0.05 (total)	0.1 (total)
Sb + As + Pb + Cr + Co + Cu + Mn + Ni + V	0.5 (total)	1 (total)
(d) Average values over sample period		min. 6 h, max. 8 h
Dioxin and furans		0.1 ng/m^3 (total)
Carbon monoxide		
Daily average value		50 mg/m^3
10-minute average value		150 mg/m^3
Half-hourly average values taken in any 24-h period		100 mg/m^3

Table 5.21 Assessing the significance of different air emission categories to identify BAT for air pollution prevention and control

Substance	Maximum daily mean release (g/s)	Maximum yearly mean release (kg/yr)	Long-term contribution				Short-term contribution			
			Process contribution, PC (µg/m³)	Environmental assessment level, EAL (µg/m³)	1% of EAL (µg/m³)	Significant	Process contribution, PC (µg/m³)	Environmental assessment level, EAL (µg/m³)	10% of EAL (µg/m³)	Significant
Particulate matter (PM)	0.434	12 290	0.11	40	0.4	No	0.5	50	5	No
Hydrogen chloride (HCl)	0.434	12 290	0.11	20	0.2	No	5.7	800	80	No
Hydrogen fluoride (HF)	0.0434	1 230	0.011	–	n/a	n/a	0.57	250	25	No
Sulphur dioxide (SO₂)	2.168	61 400	0.56	50	0.5	Yes	47	267	26.7	Yes
Nitrogen oxides (as NO₂)	8.674	245 660	2.24	40	0.4	Yes	96	200	20	Yes
Cadmium (Cd)	0.0022	62	0.0006	0.005	0.00005	Yes	0.028	1.5	0.15	No
Mercury (Hg)	0.0022	62	0.0006	0.25	0.0025	Yes	0.028	7.5	0.75	No
Antimony (Sb)	0.022	623	0.006	5	0.05	No	0.0028	150	15	No
Arsenic (As)	0.022	623	0.006	0.2	0.002	Yes	0.0028	15	1.5	No
Lead (Pb)	0.022	623	0.006	0.5	0.005	Yes	0.0028	n/a	n/a	n/a
Chromium (as CrVI)	0.022	623	0.006	0.1	0.001	Yes	0.0028	3	0.3	No
Cobalt (Co)	0.022	623	0.006	0.2	0.002	Yes	0.0028	6	0.6	No
Nickel (Ni)	0.022	623	0.006	1	0.01	No	0.0028	30	3	No
Vanadium (V)	0.022	623	0.006	5	0.05	No	0.0028	1	0.1	No
Carbon dioxide	3.6	102 895 000	–	n/a	n/a	n/a	n/a	n/a	n/a	n/a
Dioxins and furans	4.34E–09	0.0001	1.12E–09	n/a	n/a	n/a	n/a	n/a	n/a	n/a

Table 5.22 *Environmental quality standards for air pollutants – the Ambient Air Framework Directive (99/30/EC)*

Substance	Reference period	EC Directive (99/30/EC) Limit value	EC Directive (99/30/EC) To be met by	UK Air Quality Regulations Standards Limit value	UK Air Quality Regulations Standards To be met by
Sulphur dioxide	Hourly mean	350 μg/m^3 Exceeded no more than 24 times a year	1 Jan 2005	350 μg/m^3 Exceeded no more than 24 times a year	31 Dec 2004
	Daily mean (24 h)	125 μg/m^3 Exceeded no more than 3 times a year	1 Jan 2005	125 μg/m^3 Exceeded no more than 3 times a year	31 Dec 2004
	15-minute mean			266 μg/m^3 Exceeded no more than 35 times a year	31 Dec 2005
Particulate matter (PM10)	Daily mean (24 h)	50 μg/m^3 Exceeded no more than 35 times a year	1 Jan 2005	50 μg/m^3 Exceeded no more than 35 times a year	31 Dec 2004
		50 μg/m^3 Exceeded no more than 7 times a year	1 Jan 2010		
	Annual mean	40 μg/m^3 20 μg/m^3	1 Jan 2005 1 Jan 2010	40 μg/m^3	31 Dec 2004
Nitrogen dioxide	Hourly mean	200 μg/m^3 Exceeded no more than 18 times a year	1 Jan 2010	200 μg/m^3 Exceeded no more than 18 times a year	31 Dec 2005
	Annual mean	40 μg/m^3	1 Jan 2010	40 μg/m^3	31 Dec 2005
Ozone		120 μg/m^3 Exceeded no more than 20 days a year averaged over 3 years	1 Jan 2010		

Table 5.22 *Continued*

Substance	Reference period	EC Directive (99/30/EC)		UK Air Quality Regulations Standards	
		Limit value	To be met by	Limit value	To be met by
	Daily maximum of running 8-h mean			$100\ \mu g/m^3$ Not exceeded more than 10 times a year	31 Dec 2005
Carbon monoxide	8-h mean Running 8-h mean	$10\ \mu g/m^3$	1 Jan 2005	$11.6\ \mu g/m^3$	31 Dec 2003
Benzene	Annual mean Running annual mean	$5\ \mu g/m^3$	1 Jan 2010	$16.25\ \mu g/m^3$	31 Dec 2003
Lead	Annual mean	$0.5\ \mu g/m^3$	31 Dec 2004	$0.5\ \mu g/m^3$ $0.25\ \mu g/m^3$	1 Jan 2005 31 Dec 2008
1,3-Butadiene	Running annual mean			$2.25\ \mu g/m^3$	31 Dec 2003

in the EU and UK), the design team has carried out air dispersion modelling to calculate the ground concentrations of the emitted air pollutants. The results are shown in Table 5.23, also indicating the percentage of contribution of the plant to the ground concentrations of the prescribed pollutants, relative to the prescribed AQS.

Water pollution   No process water will be released from the plant during normal operation so that no liquid effluent will be released into the surface or ground water except for the sewage which will be discharged directly into the sewer.

Land pollution   The main types and quantities of solid waste that will arise from the combustion process are given in Table 5.24.

The expected composition of the bottom and fly ash estimated by the design team is shown in Table 5.25. Ferrous metals will be recycled in the background system, therefore they will not be disposed of as waste. Bottom ash can be recycled; however,

Table 5.23   *Summary results of the air quality impact assessment for the proposed EfW plant*

Substance	Reference period	Ground air concentration ($\mu g/m^3$)	UK Air Quality Standard (AQS) ($\mu g/m^3$)	Percentage of the AQS (%)
Sulphur Dioxide	Hourly mean	22	350	6.3
	Daily mean (24 h)	6	125	4.8
	15-minute mean	47	266	18
Particulate matter (PM10)	Daily mean (24 h)	0.3	50	0.6
	Annual mean	0.11	40	0.3
Nitrogen dioxide	Hourly mean	48	200	24
	Annual mean	1.12	40	2.8
Benzene	Running annual mean	0.11	16.25	0.7
Lead (+other heavy metals)	Annual mean	0.006	0.5	1.2
			0.25	2.4

Table 5.24   *Solid wastes arising and materials recovered from the EfW plant*

Material	Quantity (t/yr)
Bottom ash	47 800
Fly ash	8 300
Spent lime	4 000
Ferrous metals	28 000
Activated carbon	100

Table 5.25 Expected composition of the bottom and fly ash

Major constituents	Bottom ash (% by weight)	Fly ash (% by weight)
Aluminium as Al_2O_3	7.2	2.3
Calcium as CaO	14.0	47.6
Copper as CuO	0.2	
Iron as Fe_2O_3	9.7	7.9
Lead as PbO	0.1	0.4
Magnesium as MgO	1.6	0.7
Phosphorous as P_2O_5	5.3	2.0
Potassium as K_2O	1.0	1.0
Silicon as SiO_2	42.9	5.4
Sodium as Na_2O	3.1	1.2
Titanium as TiO_2	0.8	0.4
Zinc as ZnO	0.1	1.4
Chloride as Cl	0.1	11.8
Sulphate as SO_3	0.2	0.6
Sulphate as SO_2	<0.1	0.6
Hydroxide as OH		11.5
Other, including heavy metals	0.2	0.3

initially at least, it is envisaged that the bottom ash will be landfilled together with the fly ash, spent lime particles and activated carbon.

Questions

1. Use the air emission results in Table 5.21 and air emission limits according to the EC Directive on Incineration shown in Table 5.20 to calculate the volume of the flue gas from the incinerator in m^3/h (R: $156\,240\,m^3/h$).
2. Use the CO_2 emission factors shown in Table 5.8 and the LHV you calculated in question 2 in section 'Waste Arisings and its Composition' to calculate the emissions of CO_2 and the equivalent contribution to global warming by the EfW plant. Note that by convention the biomass-derived CO_2 is not counted in the total emission of CO_2. The biomass-derived CO_2 in the case of MSW is considered to be the CO_2 emitted as a result of incineration of paper and cardboard, and food and garden waste. The global warming potential of CO_2 is equal to 1 kg $CO_{2\,eq}$/kg CO_2.
3. According to the USA EPA (1999) the average emissions of methane and carbon dioxide from decomposition of waste in landfills are 113 kg/t and 311 kg/t of MSW respectively. Calculate the contribution to global warming by landfilling of the 225 000 t/yr of waste. Use the global warming potential of methane over 100 years, equivalent to 21 kg CO_2 equiv./kg CO_2. Compare that with the global warming from incineration of the same amount of waste, which you calculated in the previous question. What do you conclude in terms of this impact – is it better to landfill or incinerate?

4. Use the CO_2 emission factors below to calculate the savings or the increase in the CO_2 emissions from MSW incineration, compared to the electricity generated by a mix of fuels, including the nuclear energy, and the electricity produced using coal only. What do you conclude? Is MSW incineration a better option for generating electricity in terms of the emissions of CO_2?

	CO_2 emission $(kg/MW_{th})^a$	Efficiency of electricity generation (%)
Electricity (mix of different fuels, including nuclear energy)	166	38
Coal	300	33

[a] Note that by convention the CO_2 emission factors are shown for the primary energy (i.e. per MW_{th}), which means that you need to divide these factors by the efficiency (fraction, not percentage) of electricity generation to obtain the emission of CO_2 per MW of electricity (MW_{el}).

5. Use the results in Table 5.25 to calculate the total yearly amounts of individual components of the bottom and fly ash what will have to be disposed of.
6. Use Figure 5.13 to show the inputs and outputs of materials and energy into and out of the EfW system, as well as their flows through the system.
7. Compare the predicted ground air concentrations of different pollutants with the UK AQS, both given in Table 5.23. Do you think that air pollution from the proposed EfW plant is going to be significant? Why?

The Background System: Other Related Activities

Recovered energy and materials
The plant will generate 20 MW of electrical energy, all of which will be sold to the national grid, except for the energy used to run the plant, which has been estimated at 15% of the total energy generated.

On average, around 28 000 t of ferrous metals will be recovered from the plant and sold to a metal recycling company. As already mentioned, bottom ash could also potentially be reused but currently it is envisaged to landfill it.

Off-site waste management and disposal
As already mentioned, 47 800 t/yr of bottom ash and 8300 t/yr of fly ash will have to be disposed of in a landfill. The ash will be transported together with the spent lime particles and activated carbon to the nearby landfill site every five days to reduce the impact of transport on the neighbourhood.

Pollution: emissions to air, water and land
Various emissions to air, water and land will be released in the background system. These include the emissions related to the collection and transport of waste to the foreground system, recycling of metals and disposal of the bottom and fly ash as well

as the spent lime and activated carbon. Further impacts include the upstream impacts associated with the life cycle of the transport, recycling and waste disposal systems.

Questions

1. List the air and water emissions and solid waste that will be generated in the background system associated with this EfW plant. How easy would it be to quantify these emissions?
2. Which impacts do you think are more significant: those from the foreground or those from the background system? Why?
3. If you have access to a Life Cycle Assessment (LCA) software, carry out an LCA of this EfW plant. Divide your system into the foreground and background and compare the impacts from each. What do you conclude?
4. On the basis of technical design and environmental assessment of the EfW plant carried out by the design team, do you think the planning permission for this plant should be granted? Justify your decision.

BAT Appraisal of Air Pollution Control Options

To justify the choice of the base case design of the EfW plant as the BAT among the six options considered, the design team has had to carry out a full BAT appraisal as prescribed by the IPPC Directive. For these purposes, they have followed the IPPC H1 Guidance on Environmental Assessment and Appraisal of BAT for different air pollution control options (EA, 2002a). The results of the appraisal are shown in Tables 5.21–5.27. The BAT appraisal process is illustrated in Figure 5.18 and summarised in Box 5.6.

Comparison between the options is based on 'significant' air, water and land impacts which are identified following the procedure explained in Box 5.6. As shown in Tables 5.21 and 5.26, the team has found that the significant air pollution criteria on which the different options should be assessed are:

- sulphur dioxide (SO_2);
- nitrogen oxides (as NO_2);
- cadmium (Cd);
- mercury (Hg);
- arsenic (As);
- lead (Pb);
- chromium (as CrVI); and
- cobalt (Co).

As the options are similar for the other environmental impacts including waste, global warming potential, noise, odour and visual impact as well as the potential for accidents, the team has not compared them on these impacts. Therefore, the team has based their comparison between the options on the environmental

Table 5.26 *Long- and short-term environmental quotients for air pollutants for the base case design*

'Significant' substance	Long-term Environmental quotients			Short-term environmental quotients		
	EAL	PC	EQ = PC/EAL	EAL	PC	EQ = PC/EAL
Sulphur dioxide (SO$_2$)	50	0.56	0.011	267	47	0.176
Nitrogen oxides (as NO$_2$)	40	2.24	0.056	200	96	0.48
Cadmium (Cd)	0.005	0.0006	0.120	1.5	0.028	0.019
Mercury (Hg)	0.25	0.0006	0.002	7.5	0.028	0.004
Arsenic (As)	0.2	0.006	0.030	15	0.0028	0.000
Lead (Pb)	0.5	0.006	0.012	n/a	0.0028	n/a
Chromium (as CrVI)	0.1	0.006	0.060	3	0.0028	0.001
Cobalt (Co)	0.2	0.006	0.030	6	0.0028	0.000
Total EQ$_{air}$			0.322			0.680

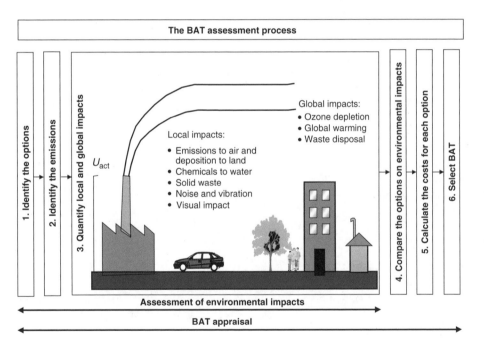

Figure 5.18 *BAT appraisal of EfW options under the IPPC regulations (Adapted from EA, 2002a.)*

quotient for air (EQ$_{air}$) alone (see Box 5.6 for calculation of EQ$_{air}$). These results indicate that Option 5 is BAT, with the EQ$_{air}$ 54% lower than the proposed base case design (Table 5.27). Option 5 also has the lowest potential for tropospheric ozone creation (see Chapter 4 for more detail on tropospheric ozone formation).

However, in terms of energy use, Option 5 uses 45% more energy than the base case. With respect to this criterion, Option 2 is BAT.

To be able to make a final decision on BAT, the design team has to also examine and assess the total costs of the options. However, prior to discussing this BAT criterion, they have summarised their findings on the environmental sustainability of the proposed EfW plant in Tables 5.28 and 5.29. This summary matrix shows the environmental impacts from both the construction and the operation of the plant as required by the EIA.

Table 5.27   BAT appraisal of different design options for the EfW plant

	Options					
	Base	1	2	3	4	5
Furnace						
Moving grate	X		X	X	X	X
Fluidised bed		X				
Air pollution control						
SNCR for NO_x removal	X		X		X	
SCR for NO_x removal						X
Dry removal of acid gases		X	X			
Semi-dry removal of acid gases	X			X		X
Wet removal of acid gases					X	
Total power used (kWh/t waste)	75	80	71	74	88	109
Energy use relative to the base case (%)	0	7	−5	−1	17	45
Total annualised cost of options in £k	7200	7560	7308	7056	7416	8244
Total cost relative to the base case (%)	0	5	1.5	−2	3	14.5
Average air environmental quotient [$EQ_{air} = (EQ_{air\ long\ term} + EQ_{air\ short\ term})/2$]	0.50	0.79	0.57	0.73	0.43	0.23
Average air environmental quotient relative to the base case (%)	0	58	14	46	−14	−54
Photochemical ozone creation potential (POCP), teethylene/yr	983	1590	1131	1141	835	467
POCP relative to the base case (%)	0	62	15	16	−15	−52

Box 5.6   *Summary of the BAT options appraisal process (EA, 2002a)*

1. *Identify the options*   This step involves description of the options to be compared (see section 5.4.1 for the description of the options for the proposed EfW plant).

2. *Identify the emissions*   The aim of this step is to produce an inventory of sources and releases of polluting substances in each option. Due to space limitation, the results of this step are shown for air pollutants of the base case option only in Table 5.21 as maximum daily mean releases in g/s. They are referred to as 'Release Rate' (RR).

For the air pollution, the so-called effective height of release from the stack must be calculated using the formula:

$$U_{\text{eff}} = 1.66\,H\left(\frac{U_{\text{act}}}{H} - 1\right) \tag{1}$$

where:
   U_{eff} effective height of release of the flue gas and air pollutants (m);
   H height of the tallest building within five stack heights (m);
   U_{act} actual height of the stack (m).

The effective stack height will then be used to calculate the ground concentrations of air pollutants. The reference conditions for releases to air from point sources are: temperature 273 K (0 °C); pressure 101.3 kPa (1 atmosphere) with no correction for water vapour or oxygen.

The next step is to quantify local and global impacts associated with each option and then to identify those impacts which are significant and for which the options should be compared. The significance of each impact is assessed by comparison with the available benchmark values for that impact.

Again, due to space limitations, we consider here only the methodology for air. The estimates of impacts are based on the ground concentrations of the air pollutants. These emissions are referred to as 'Process Contribution' (PC) and are expressed in $\mu g/m^3$. They can be obtained either by using sophisticated mathematical dispersion modelling or by the simplified method developed by the Environment Agency, using the formula:

$$PC = DF \times RR \tag{2}$$

where:
   PC   process contribution ($\mu g/m^3$)
   DF   dispersion factors ($[\mu g/m^3]/[g/s]$), expressed as the maximum average ground level concentration per unit mass RR, based on annual average for long-term release and hourly average for short-term releases. A table of DF is provided below; linear interpolation can be used for stacks of different heights than those given in the table.
   RR   release rate (g/s)

Box 5.6*   *Continued

Effective height of release (U_{eff})	Dispersion factor, DF [(μg/m^3/(g/s)]	
	Long term: maximum annual average	Short term: maximum hourly average
0	148	3900
10	32	580
20	4.6	161
30	1.7	77
50	0.52	31
70	0.24	16
100	0.11	8.6
150	0.048	4.0
200	0.023	2.3

Air pollution PCs obtained for the proposed EfW plant by air dispersion model-ling are summarised in Table 5.21. Two types of PCs are distinguished: long and short term. The former are based on the annual averages and the latter, on the hourly averages. The PCs are considered to be 'significant' if:

PC$_{long\ term}$ >1% of the long-term environmental benchmark;
PC$_{short\ term}$ >10% of the short-term environmental benchmark.

The environmental benchmarks are based on either Environmental Quality Standards (EQS) or Environmental Assessment Levels (EAL), depending on the availability of the data. Like PCs, both the EQS and the EAL are expressed as the long- and short-term values. The EAL for the air pollutants relevant to this case study are shown and compared with the PCs in Table 5.21.

3. *Quantify local and global impacts*   The next step involves listing all substances emitted to air that have not been screened as insignificant. This should be done for long-term emissions only. The PCs should then be normalised for each substance against the appropriate benchmark, either EQS or EAL for that sub-stance using the formula:

$$EQ_{substance} = PC_{substance}/EAL_{substance}$$

The normalised values $EQ_{substance}$ are then summed up for all air pollution substances to obtain a total cumulative air impact:

$$EQ_{air} = EQ_{substance1} + EQ_{substance2} + \cdots$$

The results of these calculations for the proposed EfW plant are shown in Table 5.26. A similar methodology is also used to quantify emissions to air, depositions on land and for water emissions. The IPPC also provides guidance on calculating the impacts of noise, odour and accidents, visual impact, the photochemical ozone creation potential (POCP) and global warming potential. Further details on these methodologies can be found in EA (2002a). The EA has also developed a freely available software to help with the calculations of the impacts.

4. *Compare the options on environmental impacts* The aim of this step is to compare the overall performance of each option for all the environmental considerations assessed in step 3, to identify which option has the lowest impact on the environment as a whole. The appraisal results for the proposed EfW plant for the air pollutants are given in Table 5.27.

  If it is obvious which option is better, then the appraisal process can stop here. If however, the applicant wishes to justify their choice on the basis of costs, then they should proceed to the next step.

5. *Calculate costs for each option* The aim of this module is to estimate the costs of implementing each of the options carried forward from step 4, so that a balanced judgement of the costs of controlling releases of pollution against the environmental benefits can be made. Both capital and operating costs should be considered and the total expressed as annualised costs. The guidance note explains the methodology in detail (EA, 2002a). The costs of different air pollution control options for the proposed EfW plant are compared with the environmental performance in Table 5.27.

6. *Select BAT* The aim of this module is to identify the BAT from the candidate options, by balancing the environmental benefits of each option against the costs of achieving them. In our case, the base option has been identified as BAT by the design team.

Overall, based on their findings and the summary matrix, the design team has concluded that the negative environmental impact from the proposed EfW plant would be insignificant. In the worst case, the plant will have a slight impact on the air quality, land use and the landscape. On the other hand, they believe that the plant would have a significant positive impact on waste management.

Table 5.28 *Environmental impacts from the construction of the combustion plant*

Aspect	Impacts during the construction stage		
	Impact	Nature	Significance
Geology, ground and surface water	Change to the run-off characteristics of the site	–	No or negligible impact
	Mobilisation of contaminants	–	No or negligible impact
	Localised excavation of the ground water	–	No or negligible impact
Waste management	Disruption to existing waste management operations during construction	–	No or negligible impact
Ecology	Temporary loss of habitat for certain bird species	–	No or negligible impact
	Temporary loss of water bodies and marshy grassland at application site	–	No or negligible impact
	Temporary disturbance to wildlife using the site	Adverse	Slight
Air quality	Dust arising from construction	Adverse	Slight
Noise	Noise arising from construction	Adverse	Slight
Transport	Additional traffic generation for periods during construction	Adverse	Slight
Cultural heritage	Potential damage to or destruction of archaeological features or deposits	Adverse	Slight
	Increased knowledge of the archaeology of the area	Beneficial	Moderate
Socio-economic	Reduction in unemployment within the construction sector	Beneficial	Slight
Land use	The land which is within an industrial site is currently not used for any other purpose	–	No or negligible impact
Landscape	Temporary effect of construction activity on landscape character and views	Adverse	Slight

Table 5.29 *Environmental impacts from the normal operation of the plant*

Aspect	Impacts from the plant operation		
	Impact	Nature	Significance
Geology, ground and surface water	Changes to surface water drainage	–	No or negligible impact
Waste management	Sustainable change to long-term waste management within the county	Beneficial	Significant
	Disposal of ash residue within the context of sustainable strategy for the county	–	No or negligible impact
Ecology	Provision of enhanced habitat for certain bird species	Beneficial	Slight
	Provision of replacement for aquatic habitat	Beneficial	Slight

	Build-up of pollutants within the defined habitat	Adverse	No or negligible impact
Air quality	Net reduction in greenhouse gases	Beneficial	Slight
	Slight increase in atmospheric pollution but remaining well within relevant guidelines and standards both individually and cumulatively	Adverse	Slight
	Emission from lorry traffic	–	No or negligible impact
Noise	Noise from lorry traffic	–	No or negligible impact
	Net change in the noise environment as a result of the operation of the site	–	No or negligible impact
Transport	Increase in vehicle movements at the site	Adverse	Slight
	Number of lorry movements during an average weekday	–	No or negligible impact
Cultural heritage	Archaeological potential	–	No or negligible impact
	Impact on the town's conservation area	–	No or negligible impact
Socio-economic	Reduction in unemployment in the local area	Beneficial	Slight
	Creation of skill shortages or wage increase	–	No or negligible impact
Land use	Conformity with development plan policy but some conflict over non-statutory guidance	Beneficial	Moderate
	Perception of impact from the adjacent industrial estate and the recreational park	Adverse	Slight
Landscape	Effect on landscape character and views from the existing industrial estate	Beneficial	Moderate
	Effect on landscape character and views from within the site itself	Beneficial	Slight
	Effect on landscape character of the river corridor and adjacent residential areas and views from the nearby nature reserve and river corridor	Adverse	Moderate
	Effect on views from residential areas	Adverse	No or negligible impact/slight

Questions

1. If the actual height of the stack for the proposed incinerator is 70 m, use formula (1) in Box 5.6 to calculate the effective height of the stack, that is the height at which the flue gas and the air pollutants will be released into the environment taking into account the specifics of the site where the incinerator would be situated. The height of the tallest building within five-stack heights is 38 m.
2. The PC to the air emissions have been calculated using air dispersion modelling software. In cases where such software is not available, then, according to the IPPC guidance notes, PC can be calculated using formula (2) in Box 5.6. Use this

formula and the DF shown in the table in the box to calculate the PCs for different air pollutants and compare your results with those of the design team shown in Table 5.21. How well do the results agree?

3. Compare your results for PCs with the EAL given in Table 5.26 to determine the significance of the pollutants that will then be used for BAT appraisal of the six air pollution control options. Which air pollutants are significant in your case? Do your result correspond to the results of the design team?

4. Use your results to calculate the Environmental Quotients (EQ) for the significant air pollutants using the following formula:

$$EQ_{substance} = PC_{substance}/EAL_{substance}$$

5. Now calculate the total environmental burden for both long- and short-term releases as:

$$EQ_{air} = EQ_{substance1} + EQ_{substance2} + \cdots$$

Compare your result for the base case design with that of the design team. Are the results similar? If not, explain the differences.

6. Use the emission factors in Table 5.8 to estimate the total yearly emissions of the air pollutants from the proposed EfW plant. Compare these figures with the estimated annual releases shown in Table 5.21 and calculate the required efficiency of the air pollution control plant to maintain the Release Rates(RRs) at the level required by the EU Incineration Directive. Do you think these efficiencies are realistic? Comment on the ability of the operator to maintain the emissions of the air pollutants at the level required by the EU Incineration Directive (Table 5.20).

7. How does your base case design compare with the other five options with respect to the air environmental quotient, EQ_{air}? Which option would you choose if you were to consider the air pollution alone? Justify your choice.

5.4.5   Economic Considerations

Plant Costs

The annualised plant costs for the six design options investigated by the design team are given in Table 5.27. The costs include the initial capital and financing costs (which are theoretically spread over the estimated life of the technology) and the maintenance and supply costs, taking into account the revenue gained from energy recovery. The team has estimated that the base case design would cost £7.2 million per year. The least expensive option is Option 3 which is 2% cheaper than the base design. However, this option is 14% worse in air pollution than the base design and is therefore not a BAT candidate. On the other hand, the environmentally best Option 5 is 14.5% more expensive than the base case and would be difficult to be justified as BAT. On balance, taking into account both the environmental and the cost criteria, the design team believes it can justify its choice of the base case design as BAT and is confident that it can convince the CC that its choice conforms to the BAT principles.

The final step that remains to be carried out by the design team before they can submit their application for the IPPC authorisation and planning permission is a social assessment of its proposed plant. These considerations are discussed next.

5.4.6   Social Considerations

Employment

The design team has estimated that the proposed plant will result in the creation of a number of temporary construction jobs as well as permanent jobs during the operation of the plant. The number of construction workers that will be working on site in any one month is estimated at around 320 over the 3-year period of construction. Once fully operational, the plant is predicted to create around 55 new permanent jobs for people within the local labour market.

Human Health Impact Assessment

In order to assess the potential public health implications of the release of the pollutants from the proposed EfW plant, the design team has considered the possible pathways for these substances into the human population, through the atmosphere (inhalation) and through contaminated vegetation or food (ingestion), including milk and beef from locally reared cattle.

A key aspect of health impact assessment is a dose estimate for the exposed population. Because of the large uncertainty in determining the exposure dose, it is common practice to take a precautionary principle and assume a worst-case scenario of a hypothetical individual exposed to a maximum dose from all sources over a normal lifetime of 70 years. The design team realises that this approach will produce an overestimate but will also guarantee that if under these circumstances the health impact is insignificant, then it will also be insignificant under the realistic actual dose conditions.

The results of the dose estimates carried out by the design team for the dioxins and furans are shown in Table 5.30. The estimated intake from the EfW source is 0.02 pg/day of dioxins and furans. The World Health Organisation (WHO) defines tolerable daily intake (TDI) of dioxins and furans between 70 and 280 pg I-TEQ/day for a 70 kg adult. The contribution from the EfW plant is therefore between 0.007 and 0.03% of the TDI.

Table 5.30 *Uptake of dioxins and furans via inhalation, vegetation and locally produced food (milk and beef)*

	Estimated daily intake (pg/kg · day)	Tolerable Daily Intake (TDI)(pg/kg · day)	Percentage of TDI (%)
Inhalation	2.86E − 04	1–4	0.007–0.03
Vegetation	1.8E − 02	1–4	0.45–1.8
Milk	1.28E − 03	1–4	0.03–0.13
Beef	8E − 05	1–4	0.002–0.008

The estimated intake of dioxins and furans from the ingestion pathway through vegetation consumption is 0.018 pg/kg · day, which represents 0.45–1.8% of the TDI. The dioxin uptake via locally produced cattle, that is through milk and beef is estimated at 1.28 and 0.08 pg/kg · day respectively, which represents 0.03–0.13 and 0.002–0.008% of the TDI respectively.

The total daily intake of the metals is estimated to be 0.12 µg/day. The US EPA reference doses (RD) for the metals that will be emitted from this EfW is equal to 131 mg/day, so that the contribution from the EfW plant is less than 0.0003%. Using these estimates, the design team has concluded that the potential human health impacts are insignificant under the worst assumed conditions and that they will therefore be even more insignificant under the actual dose conditions.

Odour and Noise

The MSW management facilities must be designed so as to control the odour that is generated by decomposition of MSW. The design team has ensured that the design of the plant enables odorous materials to be processed rapidly to prevent decomposition and the production of odours. Containment of any odour that may develop will be achieved by the maintenance of a negative pressure in the hall. This will be achieved by the combustion air fans drawing air from the bunker hall into the furnace to feed the combustion process. As a result, potential odour arising from the tipping, mixing and furnace loading operation will be retained within the bunker or sent into the furnace rather than escaping to the outside.

Regarding the noise levels, the background noise is already relatively high due to the proximity of a busy motorway in the area where the EfW plant is proposed to be built. The traffic levels are likely to increase regardless of the proposed development because of the increased influx of population in the area, therefore leading to a gradual increase in the background noise. However, the proposed EfW plant is likely to contribute further to the traffic as well as to the noise levels, both during the construction and operation phases. The design team claims that the plant has been designed to ensure that the noise levels generated are below the level that could be heard at the nearest housing at the quietest part of the night or day. This has been achieved by placing many of the noisier operations, such as fans and condensers, inside a single building and using silencers in other parts of the process.

Visual Impact

The proposed development could have a visual effect on both the local landscape and the views from important viewpoints. The local landscape is characterised by a diverse landscape with open, rolling heathland and coniferous woods. The river corridor is generally attractive with mature trees which prevent long-distance views. Heavily populated areas also exist, with development focused on transport corridors. The landscape quality is affected, however, by the nearby motorway, the electricity pylons, mobile-phone masts and the industrial estate. The latter, which is the proposed siting of the EfW plant, is influenced by the usual character of the industrial sites – it is generally unattractive and dominated by the car parks, open storage and so on. Resembling an aircraft or a space ship, the architectural design of the EfW plant itself is very modern, almost futuristic, and in that respect the plant would stick out from the surrounding industrial buildings and particularly from the nearby housing estates with red-brick terraced houses. The stack although not particularly tall would be visible from various viewpoints in the area.

Transport

The design team has estimated that the construction and operation of the EfW plant will lead to a slight increase in traffic. In the construction phase, this increase will be around 2.5% compared to the current situation. It is predicted that when fully operational, the development will generate 1300 heavy-goods vehicle movements during weekdays with a total of 85 on Saturdays.

Cultural Heritage

The area has a number of archaeological sites and remains from the Neolithic, Bronze, Iron and Roman periods. Field evaluations will be undertaken during construction works to ensure that none of the archaeological sites is damaged. The team anticipates no effects on these sites during the operation phase.

Questions

1. Describe the human health effects of the air pollutants that will be emitted from the proposed plant. What are the main exposure pathways for the public for each of these pollutants emitted from an EfW plant? Discuss in particular the effects of VOCs, dioxins and furans.
2. Use the results in Tables 5.21 and 5.23 and the estimated atmospheric exposure doses given in section 'Human Health Impact Assessment' to determine if the human health effects from the air pollution are likely to be significant. Discuss your conclusions.
3. Using the predicted process contribution (PC) of $1.12 \times 10^{-9}\,\mu g/m^3$ by dioxins and furans and a total metal concentration of $0.006\,\mu g/m^3$ and assuming a typical pulmonary ventilation rate of $20\,m^3/day$, calculate the total lifetime dose (over 70 years) to a hypothetical individual from the atmospheric exposure route. Do you think these amounts are significant? Why?
4. Examine the predicted composition of the bottom and fly ash given in Table 5.25. Which of the components are harmful to the humans and the environment and how would you dispose of the ash?
5. In your opinion, is the daily number of heavy-goods vehicle movements (1300) needed to deliver waste to the EfW significant? Why? How would you organise transport logistics so that the impact of waste deliveries is reduced?
6. Summarise and discuss the social impacts from the EfW plant, both positive and negative. Are there any impacts that the design team has not considered that you think are important?

5.5   Final Considerations: Stakeholders' Views and the Decision

Having prepared very detailed assessments in support of the planning and the IPPC authorisation application as described above in a summarised form, WEnergise has submitted the documentation to the CC. The application has quickly attracted attention of a number of stakeholder groups in the local area who by law have access to the planning application documentation. The stakeholder groups included the local residents, NGOs and political parties. The following summarises their views on the proposed development.

5.5.1   Local Residents

Having examined the application in some detail, the local residents formed an association and started a very active campaign against the proposed EfW plant. Their objections included the following:

- the plant will be visually intrusive with its dimensions of 138×101 m, 40-m high, with the stack 70-m high;
- it will cause deterioration of the air quality in the area, particularly due to the increase in the concentrations of NO_x and particulate matter;
- it will put the health of local residents at risk due to the emissions of dioxins and heavy metals;
- it will increase noise due to the air cooling condensers;
- it will generate odours including ammonia;
- it will generate further solid waste and ash residues;
- it will generate heavy traffic flows, increasing an already high congestion in the area;
- it will pose a threat to the economy of the town because businesses and employees would be deterred by a large polluting industrial installation;
- it will undermine the recreational and amenity value of the river corridor and the local nature reserve;
- it would prejudice recycling by burning material that is capable of being recycled;
- the proposed design has not been proven to be the BAT as it has to be assessed alongside waste minimisation, recycling, composting, digestion and other techniques, using LCA;
- the plant would waste energy because of the lack of CHP generation, which is an absolute requirement and its absence places this application low down the waste hierarchy; and
- waste from other regions would be imported to be burnt in this plant.

The local residents have stressed that they believe that the incinerator is the wrong solution and the location is too sensitive. They have argued that they want to reduce waste and recycle instead. They have demanded that the CC initiates kerbside collections of waste that would be pre-sorted to help the recycling process. They have also demanded a moratorium on incineration in the county. Furthermore, the residents have demanded to be consulted on waste policy in the county before any decision is taken on the need for, let alone the location of, an incinerator. They have concluded their objections to the development by asking that this application be refused and more environmentally acceptable and sustainable waste solutions be explored.

5.5.2   Other Stakeholders

The local residents have been supported by both the environmental NGOs and an opposition political party. The NGOs have argued that incineration wastes resources, causes pollution and does not solve the problem of landfill as ash still has to be disposed of. They too wanted to see the waste strategy based on a properly resourced kerbside-recycling system and other sustainable waste management initiatives.

The opposition political party wanted consideration of the alternative technologies for EfW plants, including pyrolysis. Like the local residents and the NGOs, they also wanted to see the recycling rate improve to meet the government's target of 25% waste recycled.

5.5.3   The County Council Decision

Having received over 20 000 letters of objection from the local residents and the other stakeholders, the proposal for the EfW plant has been rejected by the CC. The explanation given is that the proposal involves built development on a substantial scale and form, which will have a significant adverse material impact on the adjacent river, green-belt town centre and nearby residential and business properties. It would also have a negative visual effect.

Questions

1. Analyse the stakeholders' views on the proposed EfW plant and summarise their objections. In your opinion, which of the raised points are 'right' and which are 'wrong'? In answering this question, try to put yourself in the role of each of the stakeholder groups.
2. What could have the design team and WEnergise done to ensure that the planning permission is granted? Where do you think they went wrong?
3. If you were the managing director of WEnergise, what would you do to ensure that the company obtained the planning permission for this EfW plant?
4. There is another case of an EfW plant in England – SELCHIP, situated in southeast London. The proposers of this CHP plant were very successful in their proposal for the development and the project was granted the planning permission without much opposition by the local communities. Find out how this project developed and the reasons why the proposal for the plant was successful. Compare and contrast the case of SELCHIP with the case study presented in this chapter. What are the main differences and what is the lesson that we can learn from both of these cases?

Box 5.7   *An alternative case study: MSW and energy recovery systems in Mexico City*

(prepared by Omar Romero-Hernandez)

Together with the problems of water supply and air pollution, the issue of MSW in Mexico City is one of the most serious sustainability problems. With an estimated 20 million people living in Greater Mexico City, this is one of the largest cities in the world which continues to grow with an estimated 1100 newcomers each day. The 'inner' city, Federal District (FD) Mexico City alone has more than 8.7 million people with the population density of around 6000 people/km². As this overpopulation grows, so does the amount of solid waste generated. According to the Government, per capita production of MSW in Mexico City averages 1.3 kg/person.day (Semarnat, 2001), which represents almost 12 000 t of MSW generated every day in the FD alone and over 25 000 t/yr in Greater Mexico City (Munoz and Arciga, 2000). The latter is enough to completely cover with rubbish two countries of the size of the Netherlands each year. Currently, only a small percentage (5–10%) of the total MSW generated in Mexico City is recovered and reused, and this includes mainly paper, cardboard, metals and glass. The rest of the waste is destined for final disposal in landfills.

The task for the local governments is massive in terms of the collection, transport and management of MSW. A particular problem is a serious lack of landfill space in the city. Currently, there are three active landfills: Santa Catarina, San Juan de Aragon and Bordo Poniente. Two of these landfills have reached capacity and are just about to be closed. It is estimated that the third landfill (Bordo Poniente) will reach its capacity in a few years' time (Munoz and Arciga, 2000).

Therefore, there is an urgent need to identify alternatives other than landfilling for MSW management in Mexico City. One option is to increase recycling and the local governments are looking into the ways to encourage separation of waste at source and increase recycling rates. Currently, the waste is separated and collected for recycling mainly by scavengers, who play a major role in this process. However, the conditions in which the scavengers operate are not sustainable: they live and work in the landfills and are constantly exposed to health and other hazards. Furthermore, they earn very little from their activities as these operations are 'owned' by a few people at the top of the 'waste management pyramids'. At the same time, the amount of MSW reaching the landfills is not decreasing despite these recycling activities and the space problem persists.

Another alternative to reduce the amount of waste being landfilled would be to consider the energy recovery schemes. Currently, there are no EfW plants in Mexico City. One obstacle to building these plants here are the relatively high capital costs. Furthermore, the public and the NGOs are opposed to these developments, for the same reasons that were discussed in section 5.3.4. In fact, the opposition is so strong that the Congress is currently considering introducing legislation which would ban waste incineration in Mexico City. However, the other two energy recovery options – anaerobic digestion of waste and methane recovery from landfills – have not been explored here either and neither of these facilities exist in Mexico City. Hence, currently no one knows which – if any – energy recovery options would be most feasible and sustainable for this city. Therefore, there is a need for a feasibility study and a sustainability assessment of different energy recovery options for Mexico City. This is your task.

Questions

1. Carry out a feasibility study and sustainability evaluation of energy recovery options for Mexico City by doing the following:

   (a) consider the treatment of 100 t/day of MSW with the composition shown in Table 1;
   (b) carry out a preliminary design of:
       – an EfW electricity generation plant; and
       – a plant for anaerobic digestion of MSW to recover methane considering environmental and other relevant legislation in Mexico related to these facilities; an example of air pollution legislation for combustion facilities is given in Table 2;
   (c) carry out the appropriate sustainability assessments for the Mexico City conditions, following the template used in the main case study; and
   (d) discuss your findings and identify the most sustainable technique with respect to the technical, economic, environmental and social considerations.

2. How many of the EfW and/or anaerobic digestion facilities would FD Mexico City need to deal with the problem of MSW? Is this feasible?
3. How feasible would it be to consider recovery of methane from the existing landfill sites?
4. List any obstacles you see to installing energy recovery schemes in countries like Mexico. What could be done to promote such schemes if they were shown to be sustainable?

Table 1 *Composition and energy content of waste in Mexico City*

Components	MSW composition (% by weight)					Heating value (MJ/kg)	
	Average composition	Moisture	Volatiles	Fixed carbon	Ash	LHV	HHV
Paper and cardboard	17.3	6	80	11	3	15.5	24
Plastics	5.4	0.1	96.9	2	1	32.7	39
Textile	1.8	6	70	21	3	18.3	23
Glass	7.3	1	0	0	99	0.2	0.2
Food and garden waste	64.6	55	40	3	2	4.2	21
Metals	3.6	4	0	0	96	0.7	1

Box 5.7   Continued

Table 2   *Emission limits for air pollutants from combustion facilities in Mexico City*

Plant capacity	Emissions limits					
	Particulates		SO_2		NO_2	
MJ/h	mg/m^3	$kg/10^6\,kcal$	mg/m^3	$kg/10^6\,kcal$	mg/m^3	$kg/10^6\,kcal$
Up to 5250	n/a	n/a	550	2.04	n/a	n/a
5250 to 43 000	75	0.106	550	2.04	190	0.507
43 000 to 110 000	60	0.805	550	2.04	110	0.294
Higher than 110 000	60	0.085	550	2.16	110	0.294

This case study is available in full from the author of this textbox, as published in: Lázaro-Ruiz, A. and P. Ruiz-López (2002). Estudio Integral de Factibilidad para Implementar Procesos que Transforman Residuos Sólidos Municipales en Energía Eléctrica. Instituto Tecnológico Autónomo de México, ITAM. México (in Spanish).

Conclusions

MSW is an important problem for sustainable development which can be solved only by taking an integrated approach to waste management. Ideally, we need to avoid generating waste in the first place as this, in addition to reducing the use of resources, also avoids the need to deal with the waste. However, whilst we should strive to minimise waste generation as much as possible, on the practical level, it looks unlikely that we will succeed completely, at least not in the short term so that the problem of waste will persist for some time to come.

We have different possibilities to deal with the waste once it has been generated, including the use of waste to recover materials or energy. Alternatively, we can dispose of waste in landfills, which of course is the least sustainable option. Which option we choose to deal with MSW will depend on many factors including technical, economic, environmental and social. In this case study, we have tried to illustrate the complexity of the problem and some of the factors which determine sustainability and acceptability of an MSW management option. Admittedly, we have chosen one of the most controversial options that is there for waste management – but we have done so on purpose. The lesson to be learnt from this case is that engineers and scientists can produce technically, economically and even environmentally the most efficient designs possible but if they are deemed socially unacceptable, these designs will never become real installations.

Appendix 5.A: Estimating Thermodynamic Variables for Energy Recovery from Waste – A Simplified Example

This example considers a simple, modified Rankine cycle to demonstrate how the basic thermodynamic variables can be calculated to assist the reader in developing more complex designs of EfW plants, such as the one in the case study considered in this chapter.

Using the conditions in the case study, the simplified cycle operates on steam between the pressures of 40 barg (at the boiler outlet and turbine inlet) and 0.1 bara (at the turbine outlet). The single-stage turbine, which is assumed to be reversible and adiabatic, that is isentropic, generates 20 MW of shaft power. The Low Pressure (LP) steam is condensed in a condenser, after which the water is pumped back into the boiler to raise steam by the heat obtained from burning the waste.

Following the simplified process flow diagram in Figure 5.A.1 and the corresponding enthalpy–entropy (h–s) diagram, the following properties and variables can be calculated, as shown below:

- the flow rate of steam required;
- the heat loads on the boiler and the condenser;
- the overall thermal efficiency for this process; and
- the Carnot efficiency.

In performing the calculations, the following assumptions have been made about this process:

- no pressure drops in the pipework;
- no heat losses from the pipework;
- the turbine is isentropic;
- the steam is at 400 °C;

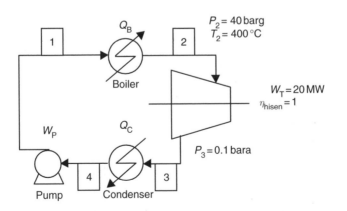

Figure 5.A.1   *The simple Rankine cycle*

– no power is required to maintain the condenser vacuum; and
– the boiler feed water pump consumes no power.

(i) Steam flow rate

The flow rate of steam can be calculated by application of the Steady Flow Energy Equation (SFEE) to the steam flowing through the turbine (see Figure 5.A.2 for a simplified steam cycle used in this example to explain the estimation of the steam flow rate). The SFEE states:

$$Q_T - W_T = m_s(h_3 - h_2 + ke_3 - ke_2 + pe_3 - pe_2) \tag{5.A.1}$$

In this case study, we are assuming that the turbine is reversible and adiabatic, that is isentropic. This means that the heat load Q_T will be zero or negligible. The pipework can be positioned and sized to minimise the change of kinetic (ke) and potential (pe) energy, hence equation (5.A.1) reduces to:

$$-W_T = m_s(h_3 - h_2) \tag{5.A.2}$$

Since the turbine power output W_T is known (20 MW), we can calculate the mass flow rate of the steam, m_s, if we can calculate specific enthalpies h_2 and h_3 of the inlet and effluent streams respectively. The specific enthalpy of the inlet stream, h_2, can be determined from the pressure ($P_2 = 40$ barg ≈ 41 bara), and the temperature ($T_2 = 400\,°C$) using thermodynamic charts, tables or software. Hence, $h_2 = 3212\,kJ/kg$.

Assuming the turbine to be isentropic, the calculation of the effluent stream from the turbine can be carried out by recognising that:

$$s_3 = s_2 \tag{5.A.3}$$

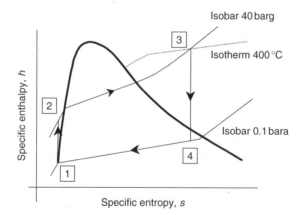

Figure 5.A.2   *The enthalpy–entropy diagram for the simplified Rankine cycle*

The specific entropy can be determined from the same sources as the specific enthalpy. Hence, $s_2 = s_3 = 6.756\,\text{kJ/kg} \cdot \text{K}$. We can now calculate other properties of this stream; for instance, $h_3 = 2140\,\text{kJ/kg}$ and the quality (or dryness fraction) is 0.8141.

So, from equation (5.A.2):

$$m_s = \frac{W_T}{(h_2 - h_3)} = \frac{20\,000}{(3212 - 2140)} = 18.66\,\text{kg/s} \qquad (5.A.4)$$

(ii) *The heat loads on the boiler and condenser*
Let us assume that the water from the condenser is a saturated liquid at 0.1 bara, and not sub-cooled. Therefore, from thermodynamic data, $h_1 = 191.8\,\text{kJ/kg}$. Applying the SFEE (equation 5.A.1) to the condenser:

$$Q_C - W_C = m_s(h_4 - h_3 + ke_4 - ke_3 + pe_4 - pe_3) \qquad (5.A.5)$$

This time, we note that condensers do not transfer energy by work with the surroundings as the turbine does! Again we can hope that carefully designed pipe-work will eliminate the changes in kinetic and potential energies, hence equation (5.A.5) reduces to:

$$-Q_C = m_s(h_4 - h_3) = 18.66(191.8 - 2140) = -36.35\,\text{MW} \qquad (5.A.6)$$

In this case, we have a negative heat load because the energy interaction by heat transfer with the surrounding is resulting in the loss of energy by the system.

We could now apply the SFEE again to the boiler, to calculate the heat load on the boiler. However, we could approach the problem from the other end by reminding ourselves that the plant as a whole is assumed to be a closed system, and the first law for a closed system applies:

$$\sum Q - \sum W = \Delta U \qquad (5.A.7)$$

In this case, the change in internal energy is known since the material in the system is returned to its initial state by progress around the closed-process loop, so $\Delta U = 0$, so that equation (5.A.7) can be written as:

$$Q_B + Q_C - W_T = 0 \qquad (5.A.8)$$

hence:

$$Q_B = W_T - Q_C = 20 - (-36.35) = 56.35\,\text{MW} \qquad (5.A.9)$$

(iii) *The overall thermal efficiency*
The thermal efficiency can be calculated as:

$$\eta_{th} = \frac{W_T}{Q_B} = \frac{20}{56.35} = 35.5\% \qquad (5.A.10)$$

This means that out of every 100 kJ released by combustion, only 35.5 kJ will be transformed into the useful work by the turbine shaft while 64.5 kJ will be released to the environment as waste heat.

(iv) *The Carnot efficiency*

As a comparison with the thermal efficiency, we can now calculate the Carnot efficiency. The Carnot efficiency, is the maximum efficiency that any ideal reversible process could possibly have working between these temperatures, can be calculated for this process from the temperature of the steam entering the turbine and the temperature of the steam in the condenser. From thermodynamic data, the saturation temperature at 0.1 bara is 45.81 °C. Hence, the Carnot efficiency is given by:

$$\eta_{Carnot} = 1 - \frac{T_C}{T_B} = 1 - \frac{45.81 + 273.15}{400 + 273.15} = 52.61\% \qquad (5.A.11)$$

You may wish to consider the following question here: why is the overall thermal efficiency not equal to the Carnot efficiency, given that the turbine is isentropic, that is there are no losses?

It is also interesting to note that the saturation temperature at 40 bara is 251.9 °C. We could therefore greatly increase the efficiency by supplying steam to the turbine at this temperature, since then most of the boiler heat load could be supplied isothermally by causing just the phase change without the subsequent superheating. However, the problem here is that turbines do not respond well to phase changes occurring as the droplets of liquid, as they form, hit and damage turbine blades. Steam turbines do operate just in the two-phase region but not so far that the droplet size starts to damage the internals of the machine.

(v) *Isentropic efficiency*

The above considerations assume ideal conditions, where the turbine isentropic efficiency is unity. However, in real life, the isentropic efficiency is lower than unity and can be calculated using the following formula, using the notation shown in Figure 5.A.1:

$$\eta_{isen} = \frac{W_T}{W_{T,ideal}} = \frac{h_3 - h_2}{h_{3i} - h_2} \qquad (5.A.12)$$

where, $W_{T,ideal}$ is the work that would be achieved by the turbine if the expansion was ideal; h_3 is the enthalpy of the stream at real conditions, while h_{3i} is the enthalpy of the same stream if the expansion is ideal. In the above example, h_3 was in fact h_{3i}. In normal practice, the isentropic efficiency of a steam turbine is about 84%.

References and Further Reading

Acharya, P., DeCiccco, S.G. and Novak, R.G. (1991) Factors that Can Influence and Control the Emissions of Dioxins and Furans from Hazardous Waste Incinerators. *J. Air Waste Manage. Assoc.*, **41**(12), 1605–1615.

Azapagic, A., Emsley, A. and Hamerton, I. (2003) *Polymers, the Environment and Sustainable Development*. John Wiley & Sons, Chichester.

Barron, J. (1995) *An Introduction to Waste Management*, 2nd edn. Chartered Institution of Water and Environmental Wastes, London.

Beede, D.N. and Bloom, D.E. (1995) Economics of the Generation and Management of Municipal Solid Waste. NBER Working Papers 5116, National Bureau of Economic Research, Inc. http://netec.mcc.ac.uk/WoPEc/data/Papers/nbrnberwo5116.html (Aug. 2003).

Clift, R. (1999) Public Sector Decisions and the Limits to Technological Assessment. *Proc. Second International Symposium on Incineration and Flue Gas Treatment Technologies. Combustion.* 4–6 July 1999, Sheffield University. UK, IChemE, Rugby.

DEFRA (2003) Municipal Waste Management Statistics 2001/2. http://www.defra.gov.uk/environment/statistics/wastats (Aug. 2003).

EA (2000) Waste Statistics for England and Wales. The Environment Agency for England and Wales. http://www.environment-agency.gov.uk/subjects/waste (Aug. 2003).

EA (2002a) Integrated Prevention and Control. Environmental Assessment and Appraisal of BAT. Horizontal Guidance Note H1. The Environment Agency for England and Wales, Environment and Heritage Service, and Scottish Environmental Protection Agency. 6 July 2003. www.environment-agency.gov.uk. (Aug. 2003).

EA (2002b) Solid Residues from Municipal Waste Incinerators in England and Wales, May 2002. www.environment-agency.gov.uk.

EA (2002c) Environment Agency Household Waste Survey 2002. The Environment Agency for England and Wales. http://www.environment-agency.gov.uk/subjects/waste (Aug. 2003).

EC (1994) Council Directive 94/62/EC of 20 December 1994 on Packaging and Packaging Waste. *Official Journal of the European Communities*, No. L365, 10–23.

EC (1999) Council Directive 1999/31/EC of 26 April 1999 on the Landfill of Waste. *Official Journal of the European Communities*, No. L182, 1–19.

EC (2000a) Directive 2000/53/EC of the European Parliament and of the Council of 18 September 2000 on End-of-Life Vehicles. *Official Journal of the European Communities*, L269, 0034–0043 (21 Oct. 2000).

EC (2000b) Directive 2000/76/EC of the European Parliament and of the Council of 4 December 2000 on the Incineration of Waste. *Official Journal of the European Communities*, L332, 0091–0111 (28 Dec. 2000).

EC (2003a) Directive 2002/96/EC of the European Parliament and of the Council of 27 January 2003 on Waste Electrical and Electronic Equipment. *Official Journal of the European Communities*, L37/24 (13 Feb. 2003).

EC (2003b) Handbook on the Implementation of EC Environmental Legislation. Section 4: Waste Management Legislation. European Commission, Brussels. europa.eu.int/comm/environment/enlarg/ handbook/waste.pdf (Aug. 2003).

EC (2003c) Municipal Solid Waste Combustion. http://europa.eu.int/comm/energy_transport/atlas/htmlu/mswtech.html (Aug. 2003).

EIA (2001) The Impact of Environmental Regulation on Capital Costs of Municipal Waste Combustion Facilities: 1960–1998. Renewable Energy In: *2000: Issues and Trends*. Energy Information Administration, Department of Energy, USA, February 2001. http://www.eia.doe.gov/cneaf/solar.renewables (Sept. 2003).

EPA (1999) *State Workbook: Methodologies for Estimating Greenhouse Gas Emissions*, Chapter 5. Second Edition. Environmental Protection Agency, USA.

EPA (2002) Municipal Solid Waste in the United States: 2000 Facts and Figures. Executive Summary. Office of Solid Waste and Emergency Response (5305W), EPA530-S-02-001, June 2002. www.epa.gov/osw (Aug. 2003).

Juniper (2003) *Pyrolysis and Gasification of Waste*. Juniper Consultancy Services Ltd, Gloucestershire, England.

Kiely, G. (1996) *Environmental Engineering*. Chapter 14: Solid Waste Treatment. McGraw-Hill, Maidenhead, England.

McKinney, M.L. and Schoch, R.M. (2003) *Environmental Science: Systems and Solutions*, 3rd edn. Chapter 18. Jones and Bartlett Publishers, Boston.

Munoz, F. and Arciga, M. (2000) Municipal Solid Waste Evaluation as a Source of Energy in Mexico City. Instituto de Ingenieria, UNAM, Mexico City, 5 pp. Available at: http://wire0. ises.org/wire/doclibs/SWC1999.nsf/0/4e6b6cadb4ea67f4c1256920003d6200?OpenDocument (15 Sept. 2003).
Nicholas, M.J., Clift, R., Walker, F.C., Azapagic, A. and Porter, D.E. (2000) Determination of 'Best Available Techniques' for Integrated Pollution Prevention and Control: A Life Cycle Approach. *IChemE Trans. Part B*, **78**(3), 193–203.
NSCA (2003) Pollution Handbook 2000. National Society for Clean Air and Environmental Protection. Brighton.
Rand, T., Haukohl, J. and Marxen, U. (2000) Municipal Solid Waste Incineration: Requirements for a Successful Project. World Bank Technical Paper no. WTP462. http://www-wds. worldbank.org (Aug. 2003).
Romero-Hernández, O., Lázaro-Ruiz, A. and Ruiz-López, P. (2003) 'Feasibility Evaluation to Incorporate Waste-to-Energy Processes in Mexico'. Working Paper. Instituto Tecnológico Autónomo de México, ITAM. México.
Semarnat (2001) Minimización y Manejo Integral de los Residuos Sólidos. Secretariat for the Environment and Natural Resources (SEMARNAT), México.
SEDESOL (1999) Situación Actual del Manejo de los Residuos Sólidos en México. Secretariat for Social Development (SEDESOL), México.
The UK Government (1995) Making Waste Work. A Strategy for Sustainable Waste Management in England and Wales. HMSO, London.
Theodore, L. (1990) *Air Pollution Control Waste Incineration*. John Wiley & Sons Inc., 405pp.
Theodore, L. and Buonicore, A. (eds) (1994) *Air Pollution Control Equipment: Selection, Design, Operation and Maintenance (Environmental Engineering)*. Springer Verlag, USA.
UNEP (1996) International Source Book on Environmentally Sound Technologies (ESTs) for Municipal Solid Waste Management (MSWM). UNEP, Nov. 1996. http://www.unep. or.jp/ietc/estdir/pub/msw/index.asp (August 2003).
Vesilind, P.A., Worrell, W.A. and Reinhart, D.R. (2002) *Solid Waste Engineering*. Brooks/ Cole Thompson Learning, USA.
White, P.R., Franke, M. and Hindle, P. (1995) *Integrated Solid Waste Management: A Life Cycle Inventory*. Blackie Academic & Professional, London.

6

Process Design for Sustainability: The Case of Vinyl Chloride Monomer

Adisa Azapagic, Alan Millington and Aaron Collett

Summary

Designing more sustainable processes is an important part of achieving sustainable development. However, a key challenge in Process Design for Sustainability (PDS) is to translate the general principles of sustainable development into design practice. Currently, there is no general methodology for PDS and almost no practical experience. This chapter therefore sets out to develop a methodology for PDS and to illustrate a case study of the Vinyl Chloride Monomer (VCM) process of how it could be applied in practice. Underpinned by life cycle thinking, the methodology guides process designers step-by-step through different design stages; from project initiation, through preliminary to detailed design, to help them design more sustainable processes by integrating technical, economic, environmental and social considerations. The case study shows how to identify relevant sustainability criteria, how to assess the level of sustainability of a particular process design and how to use the obtained information to make the design more sustainable.

6.1 Design, Systems and Life Cycles

Traditionally, process design has been guided by technical and micro-economic considerations to ensure that new plants are 'fit for purpose' and that they maximise economic returns to a company. However, it is now becoming increasingly obvious

Sustainable Development in Practice: Case Studies for Engineers and Scientists
Edited by Adisa Azapagic, Slobodan Perdan and Roland Clift
© 2004 John Wiley & Sons, Ltd   ISBNs: 0-470-85608-4 (HB); 0-470-85609-2 (PB)

that modern plants and facilities can no longer be designed on the basis of these two types of criteria alone, and that the other two dimensions of sustainability – environmental and social – must also become an integral part of design.

Designing sustainable chemical plants requires consideration of all three components of sustainability: economic viability, environmental protection and social responsibility. Photograph courtesy of PhotoDisc, Inc.

Some of the environmental (e.g. emissions) and social (e.g. safety) criteria are already integrated into design procedures. For example, some design and flowsheeting packages, such as CHEMCAD (Chemstations, 2003), enable calculation of environmental impacts of a process, including global warming, ozone depletion, acidification and so on. However, this is still often done as an 'after-thought', once the technical and economic components of the design have been finalised. Such an approach can lead to a suboptimal environmental performance of the plant because design choices are more limited in the later stages of design and may not allow consideration of more environmentally sustainable process alternatives. Moreover, even if included in the design stage, environmental criteria are usually considered at the minimum level required by legislation and are almost invariably related to direct environmental interventions from the plant without considering the upstream or downstream impacts. Thus, the designer can design a plant which reduces the environmental impacts from that particular process, but increases the impact upstream, perhaps through a choice of unsustainable energy and materials, or downstream, for example, through waste management and disposal.

Therefore, designing sustainable processes, plants and facilities requires a systems approach whereby sustainability is not considered as an 'add on' but is systematically integrated into the design. This means that in addition to the traditional technical and economic factors, environmental and social components must be considered simultaneously during design (Figure 6.1). This is by no means a trivial task and will require not only a range of 'hard' science and engineering skills but also the use of 'soft' theories and approaches, drawing on the knowledge and input from environmental and social scientists. Therefore, a multidisciplinary approach to design is essential.

Process engineers are familiar with the systems approach because this is the approach that underpins design: the process of interest is defined as a system around which a system boundary is drawn to include all of its constituent elements and their interactions (Figure 6.2). However, traditionally the system boundary is drawn around the process itself, usually without considering any upstream or downstream activities. For example, although material and energy inputs into the process and waste and emissions from the process are accounted for in design, their upstream origin and downstream destination are usually not included within the system boundary. As already mentioned, this can lead to a design which optimises the performance inside the system boundary but is suboptimal outside it.

Furthermore, design is often focused on the operation stage and is usually not concerned with the other stages in the life cycle of the plant, that is construction and decommissioning. However, these stages can often have large economic, environmental and social impacts. For example, decommissioning of chemical plants can be costly and environmentally challenging, particularly for polluting processes. Not accounting for the full life-cycle of the plant during design can potentially lead to much higher economic, environmental and social costs at the end of the plant's useful life. Nuclear plants are a typical example: when they were designed some decades ago, costs of decommissioning and nuclear waste management were not fully accounted for. This has afforded us a relatively cheap electricity but has put a huge burden on society to deal with the

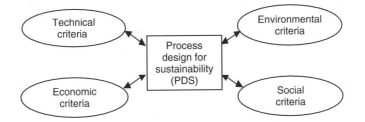

Figure 6.1 *Criteria considered in process design for sustainability*

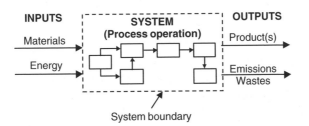

Figure 6.2 *The systems approach and system boundary assumed in conventional process design*

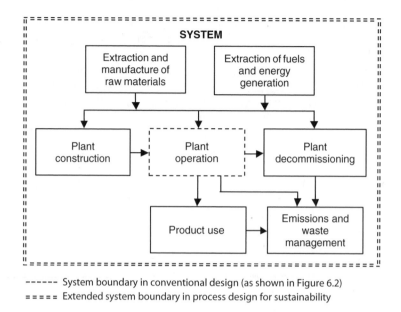

------ System boundary in conventional design (as shown in Figure 6.2)
===== Extended system boundary in process design for sustainability

Figure 6.3 *Process design for sustainability: the extended system boundary encompassing the life cycles of process and product*

consequences of the nuclear waste management. As a result, nuclear facilities are now deemed socially unacceptable in many countries and no new plants are allowed to be built.

To avoid these and similar problems in future, process designer must consider the whole life-cycle of a plant, from construction through operation to decommissioning (Figure 6.3). However, designer's responsibility does not finish there. The drive for broader corporate social responsibility (Azapagic, 2003) also demands from the process designer to consider the life cycle of the product to be made by the plant, including its use and subsequent disposal. This is known as a life cycle approach to process design (Azapagic, 1999, 2002). It is also often referred to as a 'cradle to grave' approach because it follows all activities associated with a process from the extraction of raw materials ('cradle') to decommissioning and waste management ('grave'). The life cycle approach and a broader system boundary are now increasingly being required by legislation, for example by the EU Directive on Integrated Pollution Prevention and Control (IPPC) (EC, 1996). The use of the life cycle approach as required by the IPPC has been discussed in Chapters 4 and 5.

Questions

1. What is meant by 'process design for sustainability'?
2. What is the systems approach? Why is it important for process design?
3. Explain why it is important to integrate technical and economic with environmental and social criteria in process design for sustainability.
4. What are the advantages of process design for sustainability and what might be the difficulties associated with it?

5. What is meant by 'life cycle approach to process design'? Why is it important to take a life cycle approach in design for sustainability?
6. Design for sustainability requires multidisciplinary team work. Which disciplines do you think need to work together in designing more sustainable processes? Explain why and what kind of knowledge and skills these disciplines bring together. What might be the difficulties of working in multidisciplinary teams?
7. Give some examples of sustainability criteria that you think could be relevant in process design.

6.2 Process Design for Sustainability

Approaches to design vary and no two designers will design a complex process in exactly the same way, following exactly the same steps. However, regardless of the approach, the design process normally involves the following stages:

1. project initiation;
2. preliminary design;
3. detailed design; and
4. final design.

As shown in Figure 6.4, each of these four stages consists of a number of steps. Detailed explanation of the design procedure and these steps is beyond the scope of this chapter; the interested reader can find excellent descriptions in, for example, Ulrich (1984), Douglas (1988), Ray and Johnston (1989), Sinnott (2000) and Seider *et al.* (1999). Instead, we give a brief overview of the major stages in conventional design but discuss in more detail the sustainability aspects of design. Figure 6.4 shows the design stages related to sustainability and conventional design. Final design is not considered here as it would not normally involve further sustainability considerations.

6.2.1 Project Initiation

Identifying the Need

All engineering projects, and therefore process designs, are typically initiated as a result of an identified (social) need or economic opportunity. For example, a chemical company may identify a consumer need for a certain product which can be produced profitably. The role of the designer is to create a process or product that will fulfil this need. In the context of sustainable development, however, this need must be fulfilled in a socially and environmentally responsible way, while at the same time providing economic benefits to the company which manufactures the product. It is important to emphasise here again that economic benefits are an integral part of sustainable development and if an activity is not economically viable then it cannot be sustainable.

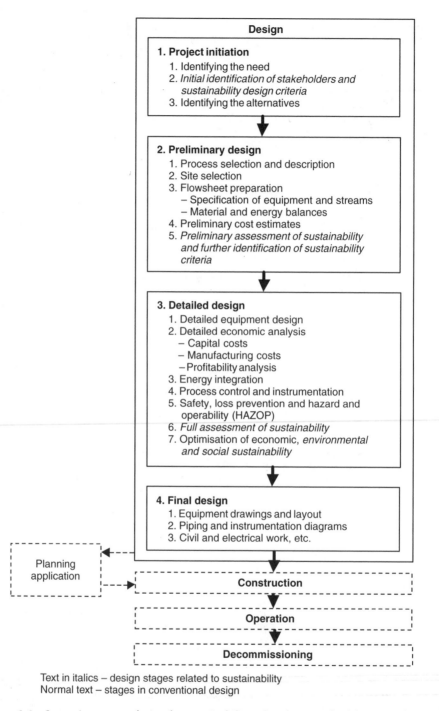

Design

1. Project initiation
    1. Identifying the need
    2. *Initial identification of stakeholders and*
       sustainability design criteria
    3. Identifying the alternatives

2. Preliminary design
    1. Process selection and description
    2. Site selection
    3. Flowsheet preparation
       – Specification of equipment and streams
       – Material and energy balances
    4. Preliminary cost estimates
    5. *Preliminary assessment of sustainability*
       and further identification of sustainability
       criteria

3. Detailed design
    1. Detailed equipment design
    2. Detailed economic analysis
       – Capital costs
       – Manufacturing costs
       – Profitability analysis
    3. Energy integration
    4. Process control and instrumentation
    5. Safety, loss prevention and hazard and
       operability (HAZOP)
    6. *Full assessment of sustainability*
    7. Optimisation of economic, *environmental*
       and social sustainability

4. Final design
    1. Equipment drawings and layout
    2. Piping and instrumentation diagrams
    3. Civil and electrical work, etc.

Planning application

Construction

Operation

Decommissioning

Text in italics – design stages related to sustainability
Normal text – stages in conventional design

Figure 6.4 *Stages in process design for sustainability, also showing the life cycle of a plant from design to decommissioning*

Thus, the designer is confronted with the sustainability challenge at the outset of the project. How successfully that challenge is tackled will depend on many factors. Some of these will be 'external' and outside the designer's control; for example, physical and thermodynamic laws will limit process efficiencies and hence the level of environmental sustainability. Other, 'internal', factors, such as the choice of process and operating conditions will be under the control of the designer; however, the limitation here may be the designer's skills and experience.

Initial Identification of Stakeholders and Sustainability Design Criteria

As discussed in the preceding section, design for sustainability requires a systems approach based on life cycle thinking. Thus, identification of sustainability design criteria must be done by considering all activities in the system from 'cradle to grave' (Figure 6.3). At this initial stage of the project specification, when it is still not clear which design alternatives exist and what sustainability issues may be relevant for each alternative, particularly when designing completely new processes, the designer can only identify and use sustainability design criteria that are generally applicable to most processes. Some examples of these criteria that can be used to evaluate and screen the alternatives in the next design step are listed in Table 6.1. In identifying the specific sustainability criteria, the designer must be aware of the relevant groups of stakeholders associated with the particular process and the sustainability issues that will be of interest to them. Typically, the stakeholders will include employees of the company which will own and operate the plant, investors, neighbouring communities and citizens, non-governmental organisations (NGOs) and government. Each stakeholder group will have their own interests in the life cycle of the project and these interests will often be at the opposite ends (Azapagic, 2003). The designer must be aware of these issues and try to balance them appropriately throughout the design.

Table 6.1 *Sustainability design criteria considered in process design for sustainability, in addition to technical variables*

Economic criteria	Environmental criteria	Social criteria
Micro-economic	Energy use	Provision of employment
Capital costs	Water use	Employee health and safety
Operating costs	Water discharge	Citizens' health and safety
Profitability	Solid waste	Customer health and safety
Decommissioning costs	Abiotic reserve depletion	Nuisance (odour, noise,
Macro-economic	Global warming	visual impact and transport)
Value-added	Ozone depletion	Public acceptability
Taxes paid, including	Acidification	
'green' taxes (e.g. carbon tax)	Summer smog	
Investment (e.g. pollution	Eutrophication	
prevention, health and	Human toxicity	
safety; decommissioning;	Eco-toxicity	
and ethical investments)		
Potential costs of		
environmental liability		

In addition to the technical design variables, some of the sustainability criteria listed in Table 6.1 are already used routinely in conventional design, particularly the micro-economic (e.g. costs and profits) and some of the environmental (e.g. energy and water use) and social criteria (e.g. employee health and safety). Others such as value-added, ethical investments and provision of employment are usually not addressed in the conventional design and particularly not within the extended system boundary from 'cradle to grave'. The interested reader can consult Azapagic and Perdan (2000) for a more detailed discussion on process-related sustainability criteria. Here we give only a brief overview of the economic, environmental and social criteria in general and then illustrate their use on the VCM case study later in section 6.3.

It should be noted that sustainability criteria are considered at the qualitative level only at this stage, by identifying advantages and disadvantages of different alternatives, with respect to these criteria. They will be translated into the more concrete and largely quantitative measures of sustainability performance in the preliminary stage of design, as discussed further in section 6.2.2.

Economic criteria

Economic viability of industrial activities is at the heart of sustainable development. Only competitive and profitable enterprises are able to make a long-term contribution to sustainable development by generating wealth and jobs and through that contributing to social welfare. Therefore, the aim of designers is to design profitable processes and facilities which will benefit both the company and society at large. Hence, two types of economic criteria are relevant for process design for sustainability: micro- and macro-economic criteria. The former are related directly to the economic performance of the company and include the usual financial measures such as capital and operating costs, cash flow and return on capital. Macro-economic criteria demonstrate social responsibility of the company which owns the process through the financial returns to society from taxes paid and other socially responsible investments, including investments in pollution prevention and health and safety, ethical investments, investment in decommissioning and so on.

Environmental criteria

Quantifying emissions and wastes from processes has already become an integral part of design, mainly because of the legislative constraints imposed on the operation of chemical processes. However, the emissions and wastes are rarely translated into the potential environmental impacts, which is what ultimately matters. For example, the emissions of CO_2 generate the greenhouse effect which contributes to global warming whilst the emissions of SO_2 and NO_x contribute to acidification (see Chapters 3 and 4 respectively, for more detail on environmental impacts). The environmental impacts listed in Table 6.1 are the typical environmental sustainability criteria considered in environmental analysis of industrial activities. In the context of process design for sustainability, the environmental impacts should be considered from 'cradle to grave' (Figure 6.3) using Life Cycle Assessment (LCA) as a tool. The environmental criteria listed in Table 6.1 are also considered routinely in LCA studies. The LCA methodology is outlined in the Appendix at the end of the book, which also shows how to translate the environmental burdens – that is the use of energy and materials, and emissions to air, water and land – into potential environmental impacts.

Social criteria

Social accountability is related to wider responsibilities that companies have to employees and to communities in which they operate. The social criteria listed in Table 6.1 take into account the interests of both the employees and the neighbouring communities by addressing health and safety issues associated with the construction, operation and decommissioning of the plant, as well as with the product use and post-use waste management. Furthermore, they also take into account potential nuisance that the plant can cause to the neighbouring communities through unpleasant odour, noise and visual impact as well as through transportation activities associated with the construction and operation of the plant. Associated with these criteria is the public acceptability of the plant and the product and the so-called 'social licence to operate'. Without the public acceptability, it will not be possible to proceed with the project however good the design is so that the public acceptability issues must be considered at an early design stage. The issue of public acceptability and its influence on engineering projects has been addressed in detail in Chapter 5.

This initial choice of sustainability design criteria will be further refined in the later stages of design. It is possible that some of the criteria will become redundant, while additional criteria emerge as the design progresses. It is therefore important that the designer is fully aware of the dynamic nature of the design process and is able to use a flexible approach which enables incorporation of new criteria as well as elimination of criteria which initially appeared relevant but later turn out to be of no importance for that particular design configuration.

Identifying the Alternatives

In many cases there will be a number of alternative solutions to the design problem. These will include alternative processing routes, technologies, raw materials, energy sources and so on. To identify feasible design solutions, it is necessary to describe the alternatives and specify the processing routes, the availability of technologies, raw materials, products and by-products. The sustainability criteria identified in the previous stage are then used to evaluate the alternatives by identifying their main advantages and disadvantages and screening out those that are less promising at this stage.

This initial screening is often done on a qualitative basis and requires experienced designers. Simple flowsheets can be used to make initial comparisons between the alternative processes. A large number of alternatives may require a more formal approach, perhaps using a simple table or a decision tree to rank the suitability of an alternative for each of the initially identified design criteria. For a smaller number of alternatives, screening can be carried out through discussions among a group of informed and interested stakeholders. Ideally, the outcome of this stage should be the identification of the most promising alternative; however, in practice, it is more likely that there will be several feasible and potentially sustainable process alternatives. The final process selection is then made in the next, preliminary design stage.

Questions

1. Use the Brundtland definition to explain the link between sustainable development and initiation of a design project.
2. Draw your own list of sustainability criteria that you think should be used in process design for sustainability and compare it with those listed in Table 6.1. Explain any differences.
3. Explain the link between the micro- and macro-economic design criteria. Support your explanations with examples.
4. Explain the links between economic, environmental and social design criteria. Give examples which illustrate these links.
5. Why is it important to identify sustainability criteria before specifying the design alternatives? What would happen if we did it the other way round?

6.2.2   Preliminary Design

Design problems are usually solved by first developing very simple design configurations and then adding successive layers of detail. There are a number of approaches to doing this, the review of which is outside the scope of this chapter. One of the approaches widely used in conventional design is the hierarchical method developed by Douglas (1988), whereby the design is developed by following a certain decision hierarchy; starting from the selection of a continuous or batch process, through the development of the input–output and recycle structure of the flowsheet, to the development of the general structure of the separation system and the heat exchanger network. This is then followed by a preliminary economic evaluation to enable a more detailed development of the process.

In design for sustainability, in addition to the economic evaluation, the system is also evaluated on environmental and social sustainability (Figure 6.4). This then enables final identification of sustainability criteria which will be used in detailed design. These stages are described briefly below, with emphasis on the stages related to sustainability.

Process Selection and Description

The final selection of an appropriate process is an important decision which will determine all the subsequent work (Ray and Johnston, 1989). It is therefore important that this decision is made by considering as many decision criteria as possible, using the technical, economic, environmental and social criteria identified in the preceding design stage. The final choice will usually be based on a trade-off between the advantages and disadvantages of the alternatives, as it is unlikely that any one process will posses all the positive and no negative sides.

The chosen process should then be described in sufficient detail to enable the flowsheet preparation in the next design step. This should include a description of the chemistry involved in different stages, the operating conditions of the process, the feeds and energy used, and intermediates, products and by-products produced.

The type of emissions and solid wastes should also be specified. However, prior to that, it is important to choose the appropriate site for the proposed plant.

Site Selection

The issue of site selection only arises in the design of completely new plants and is not a consideration for process additions to an existing integrated plant (apart from where exactly on the existing site it is going to be built). Selection of an appropriate site for a future process development is important for several reasons. First, from the operational and economic point of view, it is important that the site is accessible, has fundamental infrastructure and is close to the raw material, utility and the labour supply as well as that it is reasonably well connected to the anticipated markets. Secondly, it is important that the site is suitable from the environmental and social points of view so that the proposed plant does not cause opposition from the public and planning authorities. For example, the proposed development could be close to a nature or recreational spot or too close to the local communities. In many countries an Environmental Impact Assessment (EIA) of new and modified processes is required by law so that the designer must take into account the requirements of the EIA in choosing an appropriate site in order to minimise the relevant environmental and social impacts. In the European Union (EU), for instance, EIA is regulated by the EC Directive 97/11/EC (EC, 1997). An example of an EIA statement for a proposed engineering project is given in Chapter 5, in Tables 5.28 and 5.29.

Flowsheet Preparation

Flowsheet is a process blueprint, which shows the process sequence, individual equipment, material and energy balances and serves as a framework for cost estimation. Different flowsheeting packages are available to assist in flowsheet preparation and process simulation; some examples include ASPEN PLUS (Aspen Technology, 2003), CHEMCAD (Chemstations, 2003) and HYSIM (Hyprotech, 2003). Further detail on flowsheet preparation can be found in, for example, Ulrich (1984), Sinnott (2000) and Seider *et al.* (1999).

Preliminary Cost Estimates

This stage involves a preliminary calculation of capital and operating costs which are normally within ±20–30% of the actual costs (Ray and Johnston, 1989). This information is used to determine the economic feasibility of the chosen process or to help choose between design alternatives. Detailed and more accurate cost estimates are only required in the detailed design, after the design and sizing of all equipment and specification of pipework and instrumentation have been completed. Further discussion on cost estimates is outside the scope of this chapter and the interested reader can consult, for example, Ulrich (1984) and Sinnott (2000) for a more detailed account of costing and economic analyses of chemical processes.

Preliminary Assessment of Sustainability and Further Identification of Sustainability Criteria

As we have already mentioned, the qualitative sustainability criteria identified in the first design stage need to be translated into the appropriate measures of economic, environmental and social performance. These measures of performance are usually referred to as sustainability indicators or metrics. The quantitative indicators can be expressed in monetary, mass, energy or other suitable units, whilst the qualitative indicators are presented as descriptive statements. For example, the profitability criterion is usually translated into the economic indicators such as cash flow and net present value, which are expressed in monetary units. On the other hand, the criterion 'public acceptability' would be represented by a set of qualitative indicators which describe the issues of concern raised by the neighbouring communities, NGOs and other stakeholders. Further reading on industry-related sustainability indicators can be found, for example, in Azapagic and Perdan (2000) and IChemE (2003).

Assessing economic sustainability

The economic evaluation in conventional design is normally based on the micro-economic indicators, such as net present value, discounted cash flow analysis, returns on capital invested and so on. This evaluation is carried out for the whole lifetime of the plant, normally 25–30 years. These indicators are also used in the design for sustainability; however, as shown in Table 6.1, here the additional economic indicators must also be considered, including costs of decommissioning, value-added costs of pollution prevention and environmental liabilities. In many cases these costs will be difficult to estimate, particularly the future decommissioning costs and costs of potential environmental liability. Nevertheless, it is important that they are considered at this stage, albeit at a very crude level, as this analysis may help to improve the economic sustainability of the plant.

In conventional process design if the preliminary economic evaluation is favourable, the project is then authorised either on the basis of that information or after a further, more detailed budgeting estimate (with an accuracy of ±10–15%). However, in design for sustainability, before the project can proceed to the detailed design, it is necessary to evaluate the process on the other two dimensions of sustainability: environmental and social.

Assessing environmental sustainability

Environmental sustainability of a process can be assessed using two types of quantitative indicators: environmental burdens and impacts. The former include the use of materials and energy, emissions to air and water, and the amount of solid waste. They are obtained directly from the flowsheet and material and energy balances. The information on the burdens can then be used to calculate the environmental impacts as shown in the Appendix at the end of the book.

As discussed in section 6.1, in process design for sustainability the environmental burdens and impacts are calculated within an extended system boundary, drawn from 'cradle to grave' (Figure 6.3). LCA is a tool that is now routinely used to estimate and evaluate the burdens and impacts from 'cradle to grave'. The environmental impacts listed in Table 6.1 are typically included in LCA studies (see the Appendix at the end of the book).

By quantifying a range of environmental burdens and impacts, LCA not only enables evaluation of the overall level of environmental sustainability, but also helps to identify the most significant impacts for a particular process design. It also helps in the identification of 'hot spots' in the system, that is the parts of the system with highest contribution to the environmental impacts that should be targeted for improvements in the detailed design stage.

An LCA software and database will normally be required for the assessment of environmental sustainability. More detailed account of using LCA for process design and optimisation can be found in Azapagic (1999).

Assessing social sustainability
Social sustainability criteria can be translated into both quantitative and qualitative indicators (Table 6.1). For example, provision of employment and some health and safety issues can be expressed in quantitative terms as 'number of employees' and 'number of injuries' respectively. Others can only be expressed qualitatively, for example, the visual impact of the plant on different people. Dealing with qualitative information can be challenging in process design where most information is quantitative and where decisions are based mainly on quantitative data. However, for most of the socially related criteria that are relevant in process design, various quantitative methods have been developed. For example: to evaluate a health hazard related to the toxicity of materials used in the manufacture of chemicals, we use the LD50[1] values or Occupational Exposure Limits (OEL); or to calculate a potential safety risk from fire and explosion, we can use Dow Fire and Explosion Index (Sinnott, 2000); and so on.

As in environmental analysis, evaluation of social sustainability also enables identification of the most significant design criteria and identification of the 'hot spots' in the system. This information is fed into the next detailed stage of design.

Questions

1. List the steps involved in preliminary design and briefly describe each. Which of these steps are related to sustainability?
2. Which process variables would you need to include in describing the selected process in detail?
3. Why is the site selection important? Why is it important to select the site before the design of flowsheets starts?
4. Using the Douglas's (1988) approach to conceptual design, describe the decision hierarchy used in preliminary design and flowsheet preparation.
5. What is included in the estimation of capital and operating costs? How do we know if a process design is economically viable?
6. Describe the procedure for sustainability process assessment. Why is it carried out and what are the outcomes?
7. What is the difference between sustainability design criteria and sustainability indicators? How can the criteria be translated into the indicators?

---

[1] LD50: Lethal dose at which 50% of the test animals are killed.

8. How can we deal with the qualitative social indicators in the quantitatively based design process? How would you go about it?
9. Examine the sustainability metrics developed by the IChemE (2003). These sustainability indicators are suitable for use by chemical and process companies to assess their level of sustainability. Which of these indicators could also be relevant for assessing sustainability of chemical processes? Discuss your findings.

6.2.3 Detailed Design

After all the preliminary work has been completed, the detailed design work can begin. In conventional design, this stage will normally involve:

1. detailed equipment design, including reactors, distillation columns, heat exchangers and so on;
2. detailed economic analysis (with an accuracy of ± 5–10%), including capital and manufacturing cost estimation, and profitability analysis;
3. energy integration;
4. process control and instrumentation; and
5. safety, loss prevention and hazard and operability (HAZOP), and Control of Substances Hazardous to Health (COSHH) assessments.

Space precludes further discussion of these design steps; the interested reader can find more detail on the subject in, for example, Sinnott (2000), and Ray and Johnston (1989). Here we continue to discuss the design stages related to sustainability.

Full Assessment of Sustainability

In design for sustainability, before the work on the detailed design can proceed further, one additional step must be carried out: a full assessment of process sustainability. This involves an integrated assessment of economic, environmental and social performance and is aimed at ensuring that all relevant sustainability criteria have been identified so that they can be addressed appropriately. As a full assessment is based on the preliminary assessment already carried out, it will normally not involve much more additional work. Detailed economic assessment and some aspects of the social assessment will have been carried as part of the conventional detailed design (e.g. steps (2) and (5) respectively) so that the additional amount of work is negligible. The environmental assessment will require a more detailed LCA study which, once carried out, requires only a marginal effort, particularly if an LCA software is used. These data are then used in the next design stage, which is aimed at optimising the system to improve its overall performance.

Optimisation of Economic, Environmental and Social Sustainability

Although the purpose of design is to produce an optimal solution to the design problem so that some process optimisation is applied throughout, it may also be necessary to use more formal optimisation approaches in detailed design to fine-tune the final flowsheet. There are a number of optimisation techniques in use, ranging from simple analytical methods to sophisticated mixed-integer nonlinear programming (e.g. Edgar and Himmelblau, 1988; Floudas, 1995). The general procedure in optimisation is to define an objective function and optimise the system on it, subject to a range of constraints, including materials and energy balances, and capacities and operating conditions. In conventional process design, the main aim is to minimise costs and maximise profitability so that the objective functions are defined as costs and profit. In design for sustainability, the additional objective functions must be considered to reflect the environmental and social aspects of process performance. The environmental objectives are usually defined as environmental burdens or impacts (such as those listed in Table 6.1) which must be minimised (Azapagic, 1999). Similarly, the social objectives are defined to include the relevant social indicators so that the social benefits from the process can be maximised. However, formulating some of the social objectives may be difficult, for example, those related to health effects and external costs of pollution (see Chapter 4 for discussion on health effects and externalities).

Therefore, optimisation for sustainability is a complex and challenging task, both mathematically and also in terms of how we deal with social objectives and priorities. The mathematical challenge is to develop robust procedures for solving multi-objective optimisation problems, that is the models where a number of objectives must be considered and optimised simultaneously. This is a task for scientists and engineers. However, dealing with social objectives and priorities is not a challenge that can or should be tackled by engineers alone; it is a challenge which requires participation and involvement of all relevant stakeholders and must be addressed in a wider social context.

Questions

1. Give a brief overview of the steps included in the detailed process design.
2. What is involved in detailed sustainability assessments? Why is it necessary to have a detailed assessment if the preliminary assessment has already been carried out? What is the outcome of a detailed assessment?
3. Which optimisation techniques are used for process optimisation?
4. What is the difference between conventional process optimisation and optimisation for sustainability?
5. What are the main challenges in process optimisation for sustainability?
6. The discussion here has been focused on process design for sustainability. How would you apply this methodology to product design? Discuss any differences between the two approaches.

6.2.4 Final Design

As shown in Figure 6.4, detailed design is followed by final design which involves preparation of equipment drawing and plant layout, piping and instrumentation diagrams, civil and electrical work and so on. The intrested reader can find more detail on final design in Sinnott (2000).

6.3 Case Study: Integrating Sustainability Considerations in the Design of the Vinyl Chloride Monomer (VCM) Process

The methodology for process design for sustainability outlined in the preceding sections is now illustrated on a case study of a VCM plant. The case study aims to illustrate what kind of sustainability criteria are relevant and should be considered in process design; how to carry out sustainability assessment of the process; how to identify 'hot spots'; and how to make design choices to improve the level of process sustainability.

This is a hypothetical study, based on the type of design projects set by the Institution of Chemical Engineers (IChemE) as the final part of the Institution's qualifying examinations for professional chemical engineers. Because this is a hypothetical study, it should be borne in mind that some of the assumptions and design decisions may not necessarily be realistic. However, we believe that this is not a serious limitation because our objective is to illustrate the design for sustainability approach rather than concentrate on the detail. For the same reason, the case study goes only as far as the preliminary design with some discussion of the detailed design related to sustainability assessment and optimisation. As in the previous sections, the emphasis is on the design steps that are concerned with sustainability rather than on the conventional design stages as it is assumed that the reader is familiar with the latter.

6.3.1 Project Initiation

Identifying the Need

With over 25×10^6 t of VCM produced per year worldwide, the VCM industry is well established. Virtually all VCM produced globally (99%) is used for the production of polyvinyl chloride (PVC) so that the demand for VCM is closely linked with the demand for PVC. Following a growing worldwide demand for PVC, mainly in the USA and in the Far East, it is estimated that the world consumption of VCM will increase at an average annual rate of 4.5% (Jebens and Kishi, 2000). At this rate, it is projected that the global production of VCM in 2004 will grow to over 30×10^6 t. In 2000, the market price of VCM was around €540/t (The Innovation Group, 2000) making the total production worth around €13.5 billion in 2000 with a potential to increase to over €16 billion in 2004.

However, VCM and PVC are highly cyclical industries in terms of price and profitability. When conditions are favourable, that is when the raw material (ethylene and chlorine) prices are low and the selling price of VCM is high, the industry is very profitable. Such conditions only occur about every fourth year. Hence, it may not be very profitable to build a stand-alone plant producing solely VCM. To reduce the financial risk, it is often better to integrate the VCM plant either upstream into the production of ethylene (and co-products) and chlorine/caustic soda, or downstream into the PVC production. However, the PVC business is also very competitive, particularly in Western Europe, where it has to compete with imports from the lower cost areas such as Eastern Europe and the Middle East. In addition to this, as discussed later in this case study, many environmental NGOs in Europe and some other regions are campaigning for the ban on the PVC products because of the potential of PVC to cause human health and environmental damage.

Nevertheless, the current increasing worldwide demand for PVC is set to increase the demand for VCM so that there appears to be a (social) need for its increased production. Although financially and environmentally it can be a risky business, an international PVC company called PlasticFuture has carried out a pre-feasibility study and believes that they can design a plant to produce VCM profitably by integrating the VCM process with the existing plant for the production of PVC situated in the UK. The PVC plant is on an industrial site where two other companies produce chlorine and ethylene, the raw materials used in the production of VCM. PlasticFuture have therefore decided to initiate the project and have put a multidisciplinary design team together to help them realise this opportunity. The company's Board of Directors is committed to sustainable development and they give the design team a simple but ambitious brief.

The project
'Design a plant to produce VCM in the most sustainable way. The capacity of the plant should be 15 000 kg/h with a projected annual output of 130 000 t/yr.'

Questions

1. Find out who are the largest producers of VCM and where they are situated. What is the average output for these VCM plants? How does that compare with the capacity that PlasticFuture is designing for? Can you work out from the VCM capacity their production capacity for PVC?
2. Why do you think a company like PlasticFuture would want to build their own VCM plant?
3. Who are the main competitors to PlasticFuture in terms of PVC in the UK and in Europe? Do you think they will be able to compete with the producers in Eastern Europe and the Middle East?
4. How do you think the increased recycling of PVC would affect the VCM producers and particularly the company like PlasticFuture?
5. Find out why environmental NGOs are campaigning for the ban on PVC products.

Initial Identification of Stakeholders and Sustainability Design Criteria

The first task for the design team is to produce a list of stakeholders and initial sustainability criteria that will guide their decision-making in preliminary design. As explained in section 6.2, at this stage it is still not clear which process alternatives exist so that the design team decide to use the general sustainability criteria listed in Table 6.1 as the decision-making criteria for screening the alternatives. These will be refined further in the preliminary design after an initial sustainability assessment (section 6.3.2).

Questions

1. List sustainability criteria that you would use in design of the VCM process. How are your criteria different from the criteria used by the PlasticFuture team?
2. List the relevant stakeholders for their process. Which sustainability criteria are likely to be important to each group of the stakeholders?

Identifying the Alternatives

The VCM processing route is well established so that there are few choices to be made at this stage with respect to the processes, technologies and raw materials. As shown in a simple block diagram in Figure 6.5, VCM is produced from ethylene (or ethane) and chlorine in five main steps:

1. *Direct chlorination*:   Reaction of ethylene (or ethane) and chlorine to produce ethylene dichloride (EDC).
2. *Oxy-chlorination*:   Reaction of recycled HCl with ethylene (or ethane) and oxygen (or air) to yield more EDC.
3. *EDC purification*:   Removal of impurities from EDC to minimise the by-products from the cracking process as well as corrosion of the equipment.
4. *EDC cracking*:   Pyrolysis of EDC to produce VCM and HCl.
5. *VCM purification*:   Separation of VCM, HCl and uncracked EDC after which VCM is taken out as a product and HCl and EDC are recycled back into the process.

The VCM process is explained in more detail further on. Here, however, we concentrate on the process alternatives.

   Although the process for VCM production is well established and is carried out according to the above description, several process alternatives are used or are being investigated with the aim of improving production efficiencies, costs, health, safety

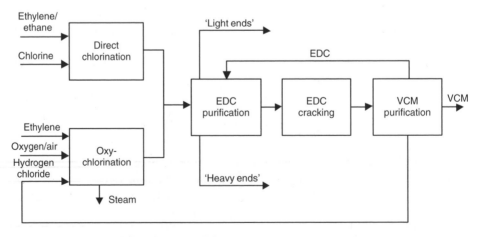

Figure 6.5 *Simplified flow diagram of the VCM process*

and environmental performances. Here, for illustration, we concentrate on the alternatives related to the:

- feedstocks; and
- processes.

Feedstock alternatives
One of the feedstock-related alternatives is to replace the expensive ethylene with a relatively inexpensive ethane feedstock in the direct chlorination stage (Clegg and Hardman, 1998; Marshall *et al.*, 2001). However, this alternative can lead to a loss of ethane, mainly through its combustion and the formation of CO_2 (Clegg and Hardman, 1998).

Another feedstock-related alternative is to use air instead of pure oxygen in the oxy-chlorination stage. Using air could be advantageous economically as air is available freely while oxygen must be produced by an air separation process (Chapter 3) and paid for. However, there are certain advantages to using pure oxygen in the process. These include smaller equipment size, lower energy use, lower operating temperature, and higher process efficiencies and product yield.

Processes alternatives
One of the problems in direct chlorination is that EDC can be easily contaminated either by iron (from the $FeCl_3$ catalyst) or through the formation of β-trichloroethane (generated in further chlorination of EDC). To control this contamination, two different processes are possible:

1. sub-cooling, where EDC is maintained below its normal boiling temperature (at 60 °C); and
2. boiling, where EDC is maintained at the normal boiling point (84 °C).

The sub-cooled process produces EDC with less β-trichloroethane but is iron-contaminated. The boiling process generates more β-trichloroethane but EDC can, in principle, be obtained iron-free. The boiling process would eliminate the need to wash and dry the EDC stream, which must be done before cracking if it contains iron. However, because of the higher proportion of β-trichloroethane in the boiling process, the reactor needs to be constructed from a material that is resistant to erosion and corrosion, as opposed to the sub-cooled process where the carbon steel can be used.

Therefore, before proceeding on to the preliminary design stage, the task of the design team is to make a choice between the alternative feedstock materials and direct chlorination processes, using the sustainability criteria identified in the previous step.

Questions

1. Find out and compare the costs of ethylene and ethane. What would be the saving in operating costs from using ethane rather than ethylene for an annual production of VCM of 130 000 t/yr? Assume complete conversion of ethylene/ethane into VCM.

2. What are the disadvantages of using ethane? In your opinion, does the cost-saving justify the use of ethane, regardless of the disadvantages?
3. Describe the process differences between an air- and an oxygen-based system. What are the advantages and disadvantages of the two alternatives?
4. Apply life cycle thinking to decide which of the following alternatives would be more sustainable:

   (a) the ethylene- or ethane-based process; and
   (b) the air- or oxygen-based system.

   Discuss and justify your choices for each alternative. You may wish to consult Chapter 3 for the air-separation processes to produce oxygen.
5. Discuss the equipment, energy use, costs, and health and safety implications of the sub-cooling and boiling process alternatives in direct chlorination. Which one appears to be favourable and why?
6. An activated carbon bed is normally used to strip EDC and traces of the other hydrocarbons present in the process water from both the direct chlorination and oxy-chlorination sections. An alternative technology to this is to use a live steam stripping for this purpose. Describe these two processes and discuss their differences. Which option is in your opinion more sustainable and why?
7. Use the preliminary sustainability criteria to evaluate the alternative feedstock materials and process options in direct chlorination. You may wish to use an example table shown below to represent relative advantages and disadvantages of the options as '+' and '−' respectively.

Alternatives	Economic criteria			Environmental criteria			Social criteria
	Capital cost	Operating cost	...	Air emissions	Water emissions	...	...
Ethylene/ Ethane	no difference	− +	...	...	...		...	...
Oxygen/ Air	+ −	− +	...	...	...		...	...
Sub-cooling/ Boiling	... ...	... ...	...	... ...	... ...		...	... ...

8. Based on your analysis and evaluation of the alternatives, which feedstock and process options would you choose? Explain how you made your choices, particularly if one alternative scored better for some criteria but worse for the others.

6.3.2 Preliminary Design

Process Selection and Description

Having considered and traded off the advantages and disadvantages of the alternative process feeds, the design team decide to choose ethylene over ethane and oxygen over air. They also decide to choose the sub-cooled over the boiling reactor. Their next task is to describe the process in enough detail to enable preparation of the more detailed flowsheets.

Question

1. Compare your choice of the feedstocks and processes with those of the Plastic-Future design team. Are they different? If so, explain your choices and why you think the design team made their choices.

VCM process description
As shown in Figure 6.5, VCM is produced first by reacting ethylene and chlorine to make EDC, followed by cracking of EDC to obtain equimolar amounts of VCM and HCl. The process is carried out according to the following summary reaction:

$$C_2H_4 + Cl_2 \longrightarrow C_2H_4Cl_2 \longrightarrow C_2H_3Cl + HCl$$

Chlorination   EDC   Cracking

As already discussed, EDC is produced in both direct chlorination and oxy-chlorination of ethylene. These stages and the relevant process variables are described in more detail below.

Direct chlorination   Gaseous ethylene and chlorine are reacted to produce EDC, by the following reaction:

$$C_2H_4 + Cl_2 \rightarrow C_2H_4Cl_2$$

This highly exothermic reaction occurs in liquid EDC in the presence of iron chloride ($FeCl_3$) as a catalyst and, as already discussed, can be carried out in either a sub-cooled or boiling reactor. This design considers a sub-cooled reactor where the reaction occurs at the temperature of $60\,^\circ$C. Due to further chlorination, β-trichloroethane is also formed:

$$C_2H_4Cl_2 + Cl_2 \rightarrow C_2H_3Cl_3 + HCl$$

The sub-cooling process will generate iron contamination but the amount of β-trichloroethane will be reduced.

The reaction of ethylene and chlorine proceeds very rapidly. The rate limiting factor is believed to be the solution of ethylene in EDC. Therefore the reactor, whether sub-cooled or boiling, must be designed to provide adequate residence time for the gas dissolution. This is commonly achieved by using bubble column reactors with the reacting gases being introduced separately into the reactor through small orifices and at a high sparging velocity ($\sim$100 m/s). To ensure the complete reaction, the process is also operated in the presence of a slight excess amount of ethylene (0.5–1.0%) relative to the amount of chlorine.

With respect to the vent gases, precautions must be taken against a breakthrough of chlorine due to loss of ethylene feed or any other reason. It is normal to provide a large scrubbing tower with sodium hydroxide solution permanently recycled through it and capable of neutralising the full chlorine inventory in the system. Furthermore, the presence of oxygen in the chlorine feed is a flammability hazard, which must be eliminated by using a suitable inert.

Questions

1. Why is the formation of β-trichloroethane highly undesirable?
2. The formation of β-trichloroethane is dependent on three major variables:

   (a) temperature of reaction;
   (b) presence of the $FeCl_3$ catalyst; and
   (c) amount of dissolved O_2.

   Find out and discuss how these process variables affect the formation of β-trichloroethane.
3. Discuss the advantages and disadvantages of the sub-cooled and the boiling processes for the direct chlorination stage.
4. Discuss the environmental, health and safety issues that are associated with direct chlorination. What are the potential risks from this process?
5. How can the flammability risk from the presence of oxygen in the chlorine feed be reduced? Which inerts would you use for these purposes?

Oxy-chlorination   In this stage, ethylene and hydrogen chloride (recycled from the VCM purification stage) react with oxygen to produce EDC and water. The exothermic reactions take place in either a fixed- or a fluidised-bed reactor with a cupric chloride ($CuCl_2$) catalyst on an alumina support:

$$C_2H_4 + 2HCl + \frac{1}{2}O_2 \rightarrow C_2H_4Cl_2 + H_2O$$

In addition to EDC, other chlorinated hydrocarbons are also formed: 'light ends' ($CHCl_3$, CCl_4, C_2H_5Cl, $C_2H_2Cl_2$ and C_2HCl_3) and 'heavy ends' ($C_2H_3Cl_3$, $C_2H_2Cl_4$ and C_2Cl_4). These impurities are removed by distillation, in the EDC purification stage (Figure 6.5).

In addition to the main oxy-chlorination reaction, a direct oxidation of ethylene to CO_2 also occurs, although this reaction only accounts for a few per cent of the ethylene converted. Catalyst activity increases with temperature but an increased temperature favours oxidation to CO_2 at the expense of oxy-chlorination. There is thus an optimum temperature which depends on the type of reactor chosen. A fluidised-bed reactor is normally operated at temperatures of 220–245 °C (and pressures of 150–500 kPa), while a fixed-bed reactor is operated at 230–300 °C (and 150–1400 kPa). Temperature in fluidised-bed reactors is controlled by internal cooling coils and in fixed-bed reactors by multitube heat exchangers.

The choice of the material of construction used for the reactor is one of the most important decisions to be made in designing this part of the process due to the complex erosion and corrosion mechanisms that occur in oxy-chlorination. Although running the reactor above the dew point of the gas mixture can help reduce the effects of corrosion, experience shows that corrosion occurs at temperatures well above the theoretically calculated dew point. The key parameter is the partial pressure of steam in the product gas mixture because this controls the gas dew point. The reactor must contain means of properly introducing the main feeds bearing in mind the necessity not to premix ethylene and oxygen outside the reactor.

On leaving the reactor the gases have to be quenched and condensed and the residual HCl neutralised, normally with sodium hydroxide. The organic and aqueous phases are separated, the former is then sent to an azeotropic drying column and the latter to a stripping column to recover dissolved EDC. Catalyst particles, entrained into the reactor exit gases, must also be removed and recycled to the reactor before the gas is discharged into the atmosphere.

If an air-based process is chosen, the vent gases leaving the system will need to pass through the equipment to recover as much EDC as possible before being vented to the atmosphere. If an oxygen-based process is chosen most of the vent gases will be recycled to the reactor to achieve the desired gas partial pressures and only a small amount is vented after cleaning to maintain pressure. The CO_2 and the excess water vapour produced in the reactor are also vented to the atmosphere.

Questions

1. Write down the reaction for direct oxidation of ethylene to CO_2. Why is this reaction undesirable from both the process and environmental points of view? How can the formation of CO_2 be minimised?
2. Discuss the differences between the fluidised- and fixed-bed reactor with respect to the operating temperature and direct oxidation of ethylene. Given the exothermic reaction, which reactor type would be more appropriate and why?
3. Why oxygen and ethylene must not be premixed outside the reactor?
4. How would you remove the catalyst particles from the reactor exit gases? Why is this cleaning-up process necessary?
5. Discuss the advantages and disadvantages of the air- and oxygen-based systems with respect to the reactor vent gases.
6. Discuss the environmental, health and safety issues that are associated with oxy-chlorination. What are the potential risks associated with this process?

EDC purification   The EDC must be treated to remove impurities before being converted into VCM in the cracking stage. The cracking process is highly susceptible to inhibition and fouling by trace impurities in the feed so that EDC must be of a very high purity, normally greater than 99.5% by weight. It is also important that the EDC is dry (containing less than 10 ppm H_2O) in order to prevent downstream corrosion.

The EDC from direct chlorination is already of high purity (99.5% wt) so that little further purification is required. If a sub-cooled reactor is chosen, as is the case in this design, the EDC product must be washed to remove iron chloride. This is preferably done in two stages, the first stage using water and the second dilute sodium hydroxide. In each stage the volumes of aqueous and organic phases continuously in contact should be approximately equal. The wet EDC must then be dried by azeotropic distillation. If a boiling reactor is chosen there is no need to wash the EDC, hence no drying is required. However, the products from the boiling reactor have to be processed in a distillation column to remove β-trichloroethane.

The EDC from the oxy-chlorinator is much less pure than the EDC from direct chlorination as it contains chlorinated hydrocarbons and water which must be removed by distillation. However, prior to distillation, the EDC must be washed with water and then with a sodium hydroxide solution to remove any chlorine impurities. The wet EDC stream is then sent to the azeotropic distillation column, to be dried together with the wet EDC from a sub-cooled direct chlorinator.

In the distillation process, the EDC is processed to separate the hydrocarbons with the low ('light ends') and high boiling points ('heavy ends'). As shown in Figure 6.5, the 'light ends' are taken off from the top of the distillation column while the EDC is collected with the 'heavy ends' at the bottom. This stream is then passed to a second distillation column. The 'heavy ends' are collected at the bottom while the EDC is taken off at the top of the column and passed to the cracking section of the plant.

Questions

1. Why is it necessary to use the azeotropic distillation for drying the EDC?
2. List the gaseous and liquid effluents from the EDC purification stage. Discuss the possible treatment and disposal options and the environmental implications of each.

EDC cracking   In this stage, EDC is first vaporised and then normally cracked by pyrolysis into VCM and HCl. This is an endothermic reaction, normally carried out as a homogeneous non-catalytic gas phase reaction at an elevated temperature (475–525 °C) and pressure (1.4–3.0 MPa) in a direct-fired furnace. This reaction can be summarised as:

$$C_2H_4Cl_2 \rightarrow C_2H_3Cl + HCl$$

A significant group of by-products are also formed during cracking, including acetylene, chloroprene and dichlorobutenes. Vinylidene chloride is also formed by partial pyrolysis of the β-trichloroethane impurity in the EDC feed. Empirical data indicate that ratio of β-trichloroethane converted to EDC is roughly 0.4.

The aim of cracking is to produce the VCM as pure as possible by minimising the formation of the by-products. A number of process parameters influence the formation of the by-products in cracking. They include operating pressure, the level of impurities (especially iron) in the EDC feed, residence time of gases in the cracking reactor and the material used for the tubes in the reactor. However, the fractional conversion of EDC per one pass through the reactor (known as 'depth of crack') is the dominating parameter. The quantity of by-products formed per tonne of VCM made increases rapidly as the depth of crack increases. Some of these by-products foul the tubes of the reactor, reducing the rate of heat transfer and increasing the pressure drop to such an extent that the reactor must be shut down for cleaning or 'decoking'.

Therefore, a low depth of crack is desirable to minimise by-product formation. However, a low crack implies increased steam usage later in VCM purification. This means that there will be an optimum depth of crack, which is normally between 0.53 and 0.63. This crack, combined with a gas residence time of around 2–30 s results in a cracking selectivity to VCM of greater than 99%.

Questions

1. Find out how the operating pressure, the level of impurities in the EDC feed, the residence time of gases in the cracking reactor and the tube wall material used in the reactor influence the formation of by-products. What are the optima for these operating parameters?
2. Which fuels would you use in the cracking furnace? Why?
3. To minimise the by-product formation and reactor coking, it is important to quench the cracker effluent gases quickly. To save energy, this is normally achieved by direct contact with the cold EDC liquid. Explain the cooling mechanism and how you would carry out this energy integration in the most cost and environmentally efficient way?
4. The Le Chatelier principle suggests that because the cracking reaction involves break-up of one molecule (EDC) and the formation of two molecules (VCM and HCl), a low operating pressure is desirable. Why is this a misleading statement?
5. Which parameters have to be considered in determining the appropriate operating pressure in the cracking section?
6. Discuss the environmental, health and safety issues that are associated with cracking. What are the potential risks from this process?

VCM purification   The mixture of VCM, HCl and uncracked EDC obtained from the EDC cracking is then separated to obtain pure VCM product. The purification is carried out by rapidly cooling the hot gases and then passing the two-phase mixture to distillation columns to separate the components. Normally, the HCl is removed first as an overhead product and returned back into the process to be utilised in the oxy-chlorination stage. This is followed by the separation of the VCM and EDC in a second column. The EDC is then recycled back into the process for further utilisation, while the VCM product is sent to storage.

Questions

1. Why is it necessary to rapidly cool the hot gases from the EDC cracking?
2. The HCl taken off the top of the distillation column is passed through a condenser which is normally refrigerated. Which refrigerant would you choose for these purposes and why? Discuss the environmental, health and safety implications of the chosen type of the refrigerant.
3. Identify all major gaseous, liquid and solid waste streams from the whole VCM process and discuss their potential impact on the environment if released. Which of these will have to be treated before their release into the environment and how do you propose to do that?

Site Selection

This VCM process will be a part of an integrated installation which also produces PVC. As already mentioned, the (hypothetical) plant is situated in the UK so that its design, construction and operation will be subject to the UK and EC legislation. This means that, amongst others, the design team will have to take into account the EC Directive on the Integrated Pollution Prevention and Control (IPPC) (EC, 1996), which requires the use of Best Available Techniques (BAT), and the UK Government IPC requirements (see Chapters 4 and 5 for more detail on the IPPC/IPC and BAT requirements). The plant will also be subject to an Environmental Impact Assessment (EIA), according to the EC Directive 97/11/EC (EC, 1997) so that a detailed EIA will have to be prepared after the design has been finalised and submitted to the competent authority as a part of the application for a planning permission. The EIA process and the EC Directive are briefly described in Box 6.1.

Therefore, in preparing the flowsheets and producing a preliminary design of the plant, the design team will have to consider the BAT and EIA requirements in order to minimise the environmental and social impacts of the proposed plant. It is important that these aspects are considered at the preliminary design stage to minimise the design time and costs, which could otherwise increase considerably if the plant did not comply with these requirements and had to be re-designed at a later stage.

Box 6.1   *Environmental Impact Assessment (EIA)*

The purpose of EIA is to determine and to evaluate the potential, environmental and socio-economic impacts of a proposed development. EIA is compulsory in many countries including the EU countries, USA, Japan, Australia and Canada.

According to the EC Directive on EIA (EC, 1997), the following elements should be included in an EIA:

- alternative processes;
- characteristics of the proposed process;
- review of the existing state of the environment;
- prediction of the state of the environment in the future with and without the proposed project;
- consideration of methods for reducing or eliminating negative impacts;
- preparation of an Environmental Impact Statement (EIS); and
- monitoring of the actual impact of the project (if the planning permission is granted).

The EIA should consider the following stages in the life cycle of the project:

- construction;
- normal plant operation;
- abnormal plant operation (start-up, shut-down and emergencies); and
- transport and other associated activities.

Questions

1. Detail the relevant legislation affecting VCM plants in your country.
2. If you are based in the EU region, discuss the general requirements of the IPPC Directive (EC, 1996). Compare and contrast the requirements of the EIA Directive (EC, 1997).
3. Which projects require an EIA according to the EC EIA Directive? Why does this proposed project require one?
4. How would you go about preparing an EIA for this plant following the legislative requirements in your country? Which activities in the life cycle of the project should be considered and what information would you need to carry out an EIA?
5. According to the EIA requirements in the EU (or your country), which environmental aspects of the normal and abnormal (start-up, shut-down and emergencies) operations should be considered in the case of the proposed VCM plant?

Flowsheet Preparation

The next task for the design team is to prepare the process flowsheets. This will involve specifying the equipment and streams and performing the mass and energy balances. Having examined the process, the chemistry and the process variables, the team decide to work towards the design specification given in Box 6.2.

Box 6.2   Design specification

Feeds

Ethylene   8.0 bara and ambient temperature containing up to 400 ppm v/v ethane

Chlorine   Available either as cell gas at 3.0 bara containing:
  Oxygen   2.0% v/v;
  Nitrogen   0.5% v/v;
  Hydrogen   0.1% v/v; and
  Carbon dioxide 0.15% v/v,
  or as re-vapourised liquid at 3.0 bara which can be assumed 100% pure

Oxygen   Purity better than 99% v/v

Product

VCM   Should contain not more than 100 ppm by weight total impurities.

Intermediate stream

EDC   As cracker feed should have a minimum purity of 99% w/w, specific impurity maxima are:
  C_1 lights   2000 ppm w/w;
  C_2 light   4000 ppm w/w;

Box 6.2   *Continued*

	C₄ lights	100 ppm w/w;

                C$_4$ lights   100 ppm w/w;

                C$_2$ heavies   1000 ppm w/w with up to 500 ppm w/w β-trichloroethane;

                C$_4$ heavies   50 ppm w/w;

                Water   0.002 mole%; and

                Fe   1 ppm w/w.

HCl   Separated from cracked gas should contain less than 200 ppm w/w VCM.

EDC   Separated from cracked gas should contain less than 200 ppm w/w VCM.

Utilities

LP steam	3.1 bara and 155 °C	Towns water	8.0 bara and 20 °C max.
IP steam	15.0 bara and 225 °C	Cooling water	4.0 bara and 22 °C
HP steam	42.4 bara and 270 °C		
Natural gas	4.5 bara and 35 °C containing:		

          94% v/v methane;

          4% v/v ethane; and

          2% v/v nitrogen.

Emissions, effluents and solid waste

All gaseous emissions, liquid effluents and solid wastes must be below the limits prescribed by legislation. Best Available Technique (BAT) should be used for the prevention and control of environmental pollution.

The team are using the flowsheeting software CHEMCAD (Chemstations, 2003) and after several iterations have produced a detailed process flowsheet which is shown in Figure 6.6. To simplify the analysis for the purposes of this writing, this flowsheet is simplified and shown as a process flow diagram (PFD) in Figure 6.7. The simplified mass balances and energy requirements in the process are shown in Table 6.2; they correspond to the simplified PFD given in Figure 6.7. A summary of the input materials and utilities and the output of gaseous and liquid flows from the process is shown in Table 6.3. Because of the high content of the chlorinated hydrocarbons, including dioxins and furans, the waste streams must be treated before they can be discharged into the environment. In this design, incineration is chosen as a method to destroy the chlorinated hydrocarbons. However, care must be taken to design and operate the incinerator so as to prevent further formation of dioxins during and after the incineration. Furthermore, because of the chlorine present, HCl is also formed during the combustion process. The flue gas from the incinerator therefore must be cleaned up before being discharged into the environment. The design team choose a sodium hydroxide scrubber for these purposes, which will absorb HCl, CO_2 and NO_x.

Like the HCl from the incinerator flue gas, the aqueous HCl stream from the EDC purification is also neutralised with sodium hydroxide. Therefore, after the treatment of the gaseous and liquid streams, in theory, very few pollutants would be discharged

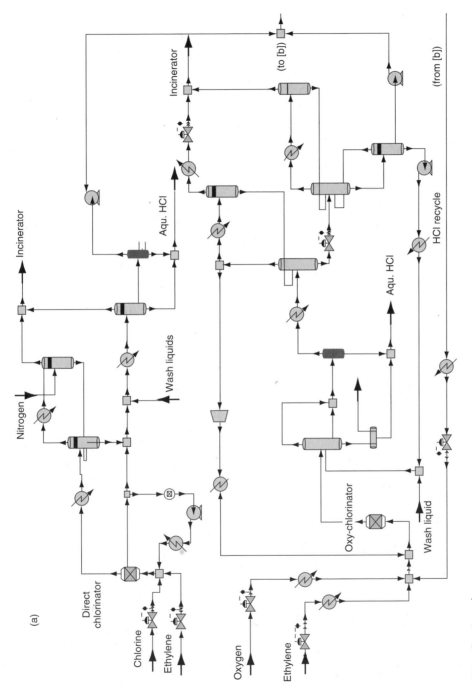

(a)

Incinerator

Nitrogen

Incinerator

Direct
chlorinator

Chlorine

Ethylene

Aqu. HCl

Wash liquids

(to [b])

Oxygen

Ethylene

Oxy-chlorinator

Wash liquid

Aqu. HCl

HCl recycle

(from [b])

Figure 6.6 Continued

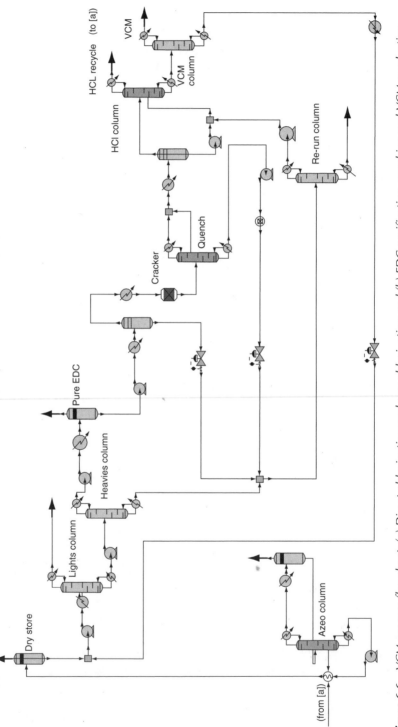

Figure 6.6 VCM process flowsheet: (a) Direct chlorination and oxy-chlorination and (b) EDC purification, cracking and VCM production

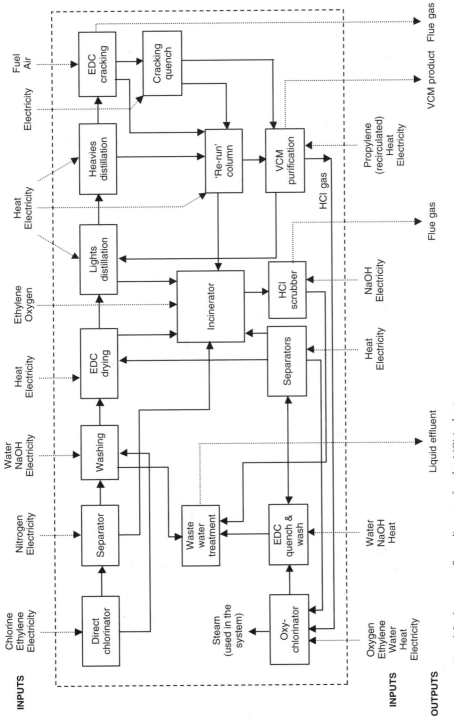

INPUTS

Chlorine
Ethylene
Electricity

Nitrogen
Electricity

Water
NaOH
Electricity

Heat
Electricity

Ethylene
Oxygen

Heat
Electricity

Heat
Electricity

Fuel
Air

Electricity

INPUTS

Oxygen
Ethylene
Water
Heat
Electricity

Water
NaOH
Heat

Heat
Electricity

NaOH
Electricity

Propylene
(recirculated)
Heat
Electricity

OUTPUTS

Steam
(used in the
system)

Liquid effluent

Flue gas

HCl gas

Flue gas

VCM product   Flue gas

Direct
chlorinator

Separator

Washing

EDC
drying

Lights
distillation

Heavies
distillation

EDC
cracking

Cracking
quench

'Re-run'
column

VCM
purification

Incinerator

HCl
scrubber

Separators

Waste
water
treatment

EDC
quench &
wash

Oxy-
chlorinator

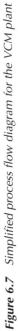

Figure 6.7   Simplified process flow diagram for the VCM plant

Table 6.2 Simplified material balances and energy requirement in the VCM process (Basis: production of 15 000 kg/h VCM.)

	Material in	kg/h	Material out	kg/h	Energy use (MJ/h)
Direct chlorination					
Direct chlorinator	Chlorine	9 204	'Direct' EDC	12 530	746
	Ethylene	3 625	'Direct' HCs	299	
Oxy-chlorination					
Oxy-chlorinator	Oxygen	2 493	'Oxy' EDC	19 792	5 664
	Ethylene	3 479			
	HCl recycle	8 959			
	CO_2 recycle	4 861			
EDC purification					
Separators (direct chlorinator)	'Direct' HCs	299	'Direct' EDC	108	73
	Nitrogen	840	'Separators' HCs	1 032	
Washing (direct chlorinator)	'Direct' EDC	12 638	NaCl	353	10
	NaOH (100%)	1	'Direct' EDC	12 646	
	Water	360			
EDC quench & wash (oxy-chlorinators)	'Oxy' EDC	19 792	'Oxy' EDC	20 857	1 155
	Water	90	NaCl	2 778	
	NaOH (100%)	176			
	Water recycle	3 577			
Separators (oxy-chlorinator)	'Oxy' EDC	20 857	'Oxy' EDC	11 899	324
			'Oxy' HCs	519	
			Water recycle	3 577	
			CO_2 recycle	4 861	
EDC drying	'Direct' EDC	12 646	'Dry' HCs	5	3 808
	'Oxy' EDC	11 899	'Dry' EDC	24 522	
Lights distillation	'Dry' EDC	24 522	Light ends	247	29 499
	EDC recycle	24 842	EDC & heavy ends	49 118	
Heavies distillation	EDC & heavy ends	49 118	'Pure' EDC	48 270	49 878
			Heavy ends	848	
EDC cracking					
EDC cracker	'Pure' EDC	48 270	'Cracked' EDC	48 270	33 192
Cracking quench	'Cracked' EDC	48 270	Quench heavies	750	611
			VCM & HCl	47 520	
'Re-run' column	Quench heavies	750	'Re-run' heavies	283	1 020
	Heavy ends	848	'Re-run' VCM & HCl	1 315	
VCM purification	VCM & HCl	47 520	VCM	15 034	20 535
	'Re-run' VCM & HCl	1 315	EDC recycle	24 842	
	Refrigerant (propylene; recirculated)	0.17	HCl Recycle	8 959	
			Refrigerant (propylene; recirculated)	0.17	
Waste water treatment	'Direct' NaCl	352	Treated waste water	3 130	n/a
	'Oxy' NaCl	2 778			

Incinerator	'Oxy' HCs	519	Flue gas containing:	2672	n/a
	'Separators' HCs	1 032	HCl	443	
	'Dry' HCs	5	CO_2	1 153	
	Light ends	247	Chlorine	3	
	'Re-run' heavies	283	Chlorinated HCs	Traces	
	Oxygen	576	NO_x	$8.5 \cdot 10^{-3}$	
	Ethylene & ethane	10	Water vapour	110	
			Nitrogen & oxygen	963	

Table 6.3 Summary of the materials and energy used in the VCM process (Basis: production of 15 000 kg/h VCM.)

	Direct chlorination	Oxy-chlorination	EDC purification	Cracking and VCM purification	Total
Chlorine (kg/h)	9 204				9 204
Ethylene (kg/h)	3 625	3 479	10		7 104
Oxygen (kg/h)		2 493	576		3 069
Sodium hydroxide[a] (100%) (kg/h)	1	176			177
Nitrogen (kg/h)	840				840
Water (kg/h)	360	90			450
Electricity (MJ/h)	746	474	1 835	7 451	10 506
Heat (natural gas) (MJ/h)		5 190	82 440	47 907	135 537

[a] Sodium hydroxide used in the scrubber to treat the incinerator flue gas is not included in this table.

into the environment. Assuming high absorption efficiencies in the scrubber, there would be almost no discharges of gaseous pollutants (although in reality, some HCl and CO_2 would still be released). The only liquid discharge would be the waste water containing salts after the neutralisation of HCl and absorption of CO_2. In addition to this, some solid waste will also be generated periodically, from the spent catalysts and the activated sludge from the waste water treatment plant.

Questions

1. Use the design specifications in Box 6.2 to generate your own VCM process flowsheet. How does your design differ from the one shown in this case study? Explain the differences.
2. Carry out material and energy balances for your design. Specify material and energy inputs and potential discharges to the environment.
3. Identify and quantify the gaseous, liquid and solid streams generated in the process which must be treated before being discharged into the environment.
4. Explain what you have done to minimise the use of materials and energy and to prevent emissions to the environment.

5. Write down the reactions in the NaOH scrubber where the flue gas from the incinerator is cleaned-up. Calculate the required amount of NaOH for the absorption of HCl, CO_2 and NO_x. Assuming the absorption efficiencies to be 95%, calculate the emissions of HCl and CO_2 to the atmosphere. Is the absorption efficiency of 95% realistic?

6. Dioxins and furans are formed in the manufacture of VCM and this is a concern because they are carcinogenic. Use the stream and components specification lists in your design to find out where in the process the dioxins and furans are generated and at what level. Are their concentrations below the limit allowed by legislation in your country? If not, how would you reduce the amount of dioxins reaching the environment?

7. Incineration has been used in this case study to prevent the emissions of hydrocarbons into the environment. However, incineration of chlorinated hydrocarbons can not only destroy but also generate dioxins. Explain how you would design and run the incinerator so that the dioxins are not formed during or after the combustion.

8. In addition to the dioxins, incineration also generates carbon dioxide and nitrogen oxides. Considering only the quantities, use the components list to compare the amount of hydrocarbons destroyed in incineration to the amount of CO_2 generated. Is the incineration justified? Can we use the quantities alone to make such a comparison? Why?

9. Now, compare the potential environmental impacts from the emissions of the hydrocarbons if discharged directly into the atmosphere with the impacts of CO_2 and dioxins (if formed) generated during incineration. Is the incineration still justified? Is it possible to compare these different impacts? If so, explain how you have compared them. If you think they cannot be compared, then explain why.

Preliminary Cost Estimates

The design team use the process flowsheets and the material and energy balances to carry out a preliminary economic assessment of the proposed design. Following the specification for economic assessment given in Box 6.3, the team calculate the capital and operating costs which are shown in Tables 6.4–6.7.

Capital costs

The design team use the Coulson and Richardson's guide to chemical engineering design (Sinnott, 2000) and the IChemE's (1998) guide to capital cost estimation to calculate the capital costs. They include the cost of equipment, buildings, facilities, construction and so on. Their results are summarised in Table 6.4, which shows that the delivered cost of the equipment is around £6 023 000. Using the calculated Lang factor[2] of 4.56, the team find out that the total capital cost is around £27 468 500. Adding 20% for tankage and 10% for off-site investments, brings the total capital cost to £35 709 000.

---

[2] The Lang factors allow scaling of the equipment items cost to calculate costs of piping, instrumentation, buildings, facilities, off-sites, engineering/construction, plant capacity and contingency.

Box 6.3   *Economic basis for design (Sept 2002 prices)*

Feeds
Chlorine (as cell gas)   £76/t
Ethylene   £305/t
Oxygen   £32/t

Product
VCM   £315/t

Utilities
NaOH (50% solution) ·   £60/t   Electricity   £38/MWh
Nitrogen   £23/t   Heat (natural gas) £1.37/GJ
Water   £0.37/m^3
Cooling water   £0.07/m^3

Other Information
Equipment shipping costs   8%
Tankage investment   20% of on-site investment costs
Off-site investment   10% of on-site investment costs
Corporation tax rate   30%
Depreciation allowance   100% in 1st year of operation
Operating personnel   5 shifts
Labour cost (one-shift position)   £300 000 (incl. overheads)
Annual maintenance cost   3% of capital costs
Other annual costs (supplies,
rates, supervision, administration, etc.)   2.6% of capital costs

Operating costs
Using the specification in Box 6.3, the design team calculate the fixed and variable operating costs as shown in Tables 6.5 and 6.6 respectively. The former includes the cost of labour, maintenance and other annual costs such as overheads, while the variable costs include the cost of raw materials and utilities. The team work under the assumption that each year the plant would be shut down for three days for routine maintenance and every third year it would require a major shut down, assumed to last 21 days. This means that in a normal year there will be 8688 hours of operation whilst in a major shut-down year, the plant will operate for 8256 hours. The team also assume that a plant of this size will need four operators per shift, with each shift position costing £300 000 per year. The PVC plant has a combined heat and power plant (CHP) run on natural gas so that the steam will be supplied from the CHP. Therefore, the team use the cost of natural gas to calculate the cost of the steam (although, in reality, the cost of steam would be higher than the cost of natural gas).

  Therefore, it will cost £35 709 000 to build the plant and around £31 874 000/yr to operate it in a normal-operation year. This gives the design team a basis for the economic evaluation of the plant which involves calculating the cash flow, the break-even point and the profit that the plant will make over a certain period of time. The

Table 6.4 *Summary of the equipment and total capital costs*

Equipment items	Cost (£)
Pumps	1 386 643
Packed columns	51 951
Distillation columns	227 087
Heat exchangers	1 090 539
Tanks	308 073
Drums	290 412
Reactors	862 821
Incinerator	142 810
Compressors	22 332
Quenches	101 946
Refrigeration unit	828 889
Catalysts	263 252
Total equipment costs	**5 576 755**
Total delivered cost of equipment (assuming shipping costs at 8% of the equipment costs)	**6 022 895**
Estimated capital costs (using the Lang factor of 4.56)	27 468 468
Total capital costs (including 20% for tankage and 10% for off-site investments)	**35 709 000**

Table 6.5 *Fixed operating costs*

	Cost (£/yr)
Annual maintenance	1 071 270
Other annual costs	928 435
Labour	1 200 000
Total	**3 199 705**

economic evaluation is carried out in the next design step, as a part of the preliminary sustainability assessment.

Questions

1. Using the economic data and assumptions made in this study, carry out your own estimates of the capital and operating costs, based on your design. How do they compare with the costs obtained by the PlasticFuture design team? Discuss any major differences in costs.
2. This design does not include the operating costs associated with the incinerator scrubber. How would the operating costs change if these costs were included?
3. The estimate of the use of heat in this design is based on the cost of natural gas rather than the actual cost of steam. Assuming the cost of HP steam of £5.5/GJ and the cost of IP of £4.3/GJ, calculate the real cost of heat supply.

Table 6.6 *Variable operating costs*

Raw materials and utilities	Amount	Cost	Normal-operation year (£/yr)	Shut-down year (£/yr)
Chlorine	9 204 kg/h	£76	6 077 291	5 775 105
Ethylene	7 104 kg/h	£305	18 824 463	17 888 440
Oxygen	3 069 kg/h	£32	853 231	810 805
Total raw materials			**25 754 985**	**24 474 350**
Sodium hydroxide[a] (50% solution)	354 kg/h	£60/t	184 533	175 357
Nitrogen	840 kg/h	£23/t	167 852	159 506
Process water	450 kg/h	£0.35/m³	1 370	1 300
Cooling[b] water	1 000 m³		350	350
Electricity	10 506 MJ/h	£38/MWh	963 470	915 563
Heat (natural gas)	135 537 MJ/h	£1.36/GJ	1 601 462	1 521 831
Total utilities			**2 919 037**	**2 773 907**

[a] Not including the amount used in the scrubber to treat the incinerator flue gas.
[b] Cooling water is recirculated, so the figure shown is an approximate total requirement over the life time of the plant.

Table 6.7 *Summary of annual operating costs (fixed and variable)*

	Normal-operation year (£/yr)	Shut-down year (£/yr)
Fixed costs	3 199 705	3 199 705
Raw materials	25 754 985	24 474 350
Utilities	2 919 037	2 773 907
Total	**31 873 727**	**30 447 962**

4. What is your confidence level in the estimated costs? How does that compare with the usual 20–30% confidence level for the preliminary costs? What would you do (if anything) to improve the accuracy of the costs at this stage?

Preliminary Assessment of Sustainability and Further Identification of Sustainability Criteria

As discussed in section 6.2, before proceeding from a preliminary to a detailed design, it is first necessary to assess the level of sustainability of the proposed process design. This involves assessments of the economic, environmental and social sustainability, as illustrated below.

Assessment of economic sustainability
Using the economic sustainability criteria listed in Table 6.1 to evaluate the plant on economic sustainability, the team's first task is to carry out a profitability analysis. For these purposes, they make the following assumptions. The design and construction phase of the plant will take 3 years: the total fixed capital for the plant will

be spent at a rate of 10% in the first year, then 30% and finally 60% in the third year. Also spent in the third year is the working capital for the project, which is spent on items like stocks of raw materials and for building up a product inventory and as such, this money is recoverable at the end of the project. This figure is assumed at 15% of the fixed capital.

The plant will start producing VCM at the beginning of year four, incurring the operating costs but also bringing income from the sales of the product. Assuming the sale price of £315/t VCM, the projected income is £41 050 800 per year for a normal-operation year and £39 009 600 per year for a year with a major shut-down. The profit from this income is subject to a corporate tax at a rate of 30%, although tax rebates may be claimed to account for the depreciation in value of the plant. The major shut-downs will also incur a cost every 3 years, which is taken to be 30% of the annual maintenance costs.

Using the above assumptions, the design team carry out the discounted annual cash-flow analysis to obtain the Net Present Value (NPV) of the plant, showing the pay-back time and the overall profit at any given time during the lifetime of the plant. The NPV profile for a discount (interest) rate of 6% is shown in Figure 6.8. The figure shows that, at the assumed interest rate, the plant has a pay-back time of just over 10 years and after 18 years, it will be making an overall profit of around £24 240 000.

The results of the cost and profitability analyses are summarised in Table 6.8. In addition to these, the team also calculate the value added[3] to find out how much the operation increases the value of purchases from other companies including raw

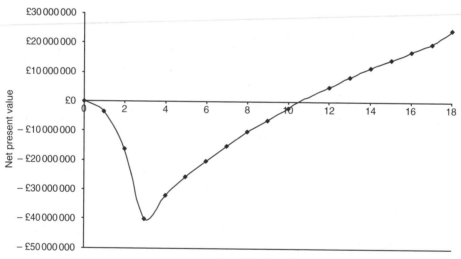

Figure 6.8   *Net present value for the first 18 years of the project (assumed discount [interest] rate: 6%)*

---

[3]Value added by the operation is the value of sales less the cost of goods, raw materials (including energy) and services purchased.

Table 6.8 *Using economic indicators to evaluate the level of economic sustainability of the VCM plant (based on the normal-operation year)*

Economic criteria	Value
Total capital costs	£35 709 000
Operating costs	£31 873 727/yr
Profitability (as NPV)	
Break-even point	10 y
Profit after 18 years	£24 235 730
Value added	£12 376 778/yr
Value added per unit value of sales	£0.30/£
Value added per unit amount of product	£95/t
Taxes	
Income tax (@30%)	£2 753 000/yr
Climate change levy tax	CHP plants exempt
Landfill tax	£~10 000/yr
Investment (as % of capital investment)	
Pollution prevention	1%
Health and safety	2%
Decommissioning	Uncertain (from 5–30%); not accounted for
Potential costs of environmental liability (as % of capital investment)	Potentially large

materials, energy, goods and services. For this design, the value added amounts approximately to £12 377 000 per year, or £95 per tonne of VCM produced. Per unit value of sales, the value added is £0.30/£.

The other information that the team wishes to analyse is profit-related tax, and also the 'green' taxes, which have been introduced by the government to protect the environment. The corporate tax paid on the profits at the rate of 30% is equal to £2 753 000 per year. They also estimate the Climate Change Levy (CCL) that taxes the industrial users in the UK for the use of fossil-fuel-derived energy. Electricity use is taxed at 0.43 pence/kWh while using natural gas costs 0.15 pence/kWh so that the total cost to the company from the CCL would be around £600 000 per year. However, the team are relieved to find out that the use of CHP is exempt from the CCL. In addition to the CCL, the team also calculate the cost of landfill tax which, at approximately £10 000, is relatively small and reflects a relatively small amount of solid waste being landfilled.

Finally, the team analyse the investments and find out that, by design, approximately 1% of the capital will have been invested in the environmental protection and 2% into health and safety. The former does not include the costs of the incinerator scrubber so that this figure is expected to be higher when the (high) costs of sodium hydroxide and energy have been added. Furthermore, the design does not take the decommissioning costs into account, but the team estimate that they could add anything from 5–30% to the cost of the investment (Hicks *et al.* (2000)). Although decommissioning should have been considered in the preliminary design, because of the lack of reliable information, the team are unable to incorporate these costs at this stage and decide to address this issue later, in the detailed design.

Thus, based on their findings, the design team decide that the project is economically (just) sustainable. However, they realise that there is a potential to improve the design to reduce costs and improve profitability. This will be their task in the detailed design, whereby the preliminary design will be optimised on costs. However, prior to that they still need to evaluate the project on the other two dimensions of sustainability.

Questions

1. Carry out an evaluation of economic sustainability of your design and compare your results with the results obtained in this case study. Which design is more economically sustainable, yours or that of the PlasticFuture? Why?
2. The break-even point of the PlasticFuture's plant is 10 years which is a relatively long time. How would you reduce this time to increase the profitability of the plant and therefore its economic sustainability?
3. The economic analysis performed by the PlasticFuture is only for 18 years of the plant's life. What profit could be expected over 25 years, which is an assumed lifetime of a chemical plant? What would the profitability look like with a different interest rate, say 8 or 10%? Which interest rate is more realistic to use in your country?
4. The PlasticFuture preliminary design does not take into account the costs of decommissioning. Can you include that in your design? Is there enough information available to carry out these estimates and can you use 'guesstimates'? Discuss your findings and reliability of the results.
5. Calculate the costs of scrubbing the incinerator effluent. What do you conclude – are the incineration and scrubbing justified economically? If not, how else would you prevent releases of chlorinated hydrocarbons and HCl into the environment?
6. Find out which 'green' taxes are used in your country and calculate the costs to the project. What design improvements could you implement to decrease or avoid paying these taxes?
7. Use the economic sustainability indicators used by the PlasticFuture design team to make an overall evaluation of your design. Do you think the plant as designed is going to be economically sustainable? Discuss your findings.

Assessment of environmental sustainability
As discussed in section 6.1, in process design for sustainability, environmental sustainability should be assessed from 'cradle to grave', using LCA. The design team have used the data from the mass and energy balances and the simplified PFD in Figure 6.7 to perform an LCA study of the proposed VCM plant. Using the methodology given in the LCA Appendix, they consider the life cycle environmental impacts of the raw materials and utilities (including energy) and the impacts from the VCM plant itself. A simplified life cycle flow diagram of the VCM plant is shown in Figure 6.9. To help them identify the 'hot spots', the team divide the system into the 'foreground' and 'background' subsystems. The former is the VCM plant itself whilst the latter includes the raw materials and utilities. The LCA results are shown in Figure 6.10. The functional unit is defined as 'the

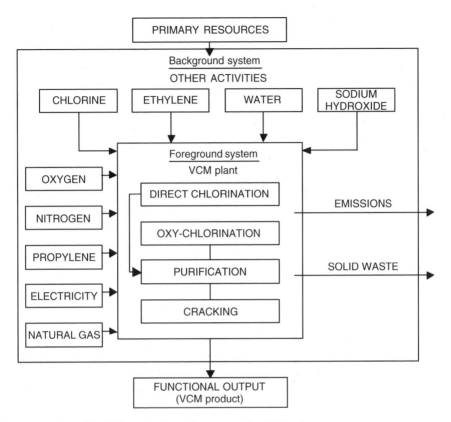

Figure 6.9   *Simplified life cycle flow diagram of the VCM plant*

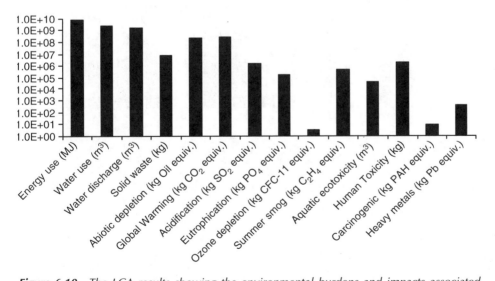

Figure 6.10   *The LCA results showing the environmental burdens and impacts associated with the proposed VCM design (All burdens and impacts expressed per functional unit '130 000 t/yr VCM produced'.)*

production of 130 000 t/yr of VCM' and the system boundary is from 'cradle to gate', that is from the extraction of primary resources to the point where the VCM is produced and ready to leave the 'factory gate'. The design team use PEMS LCA software (Pira, 2000) to carry out the LCA of the VCM plant. The LCA environmental impacts of the foreground system are calculated using the design data while the impacts from the background subsystem are calculated using the PEMS database.

The LCA results are given in Figure 6.10. The environmental burdens and impacts shown in the figure represent environmental indicators, which correspond to the environmental criteria identified earlier in the design process and listed in Table 6.1. In addition to these, the design team use further environmental indicators, to ensure that all relevant environmental criteria have been identified. Out of these, two further environmental indicators appear to be relevant: carcinogenic potential related to VCM (as discussed in the section 'social sustainability' below) and the amount of heavy metals emitted from the system into the environment. They are also shown in Figure 6.10.

The next task for the design team is to identify the 'hot spots' in the system, that is the parts of the VCM system that contribute most to the impacts. Their findings are given in Figure 6.11, which indicate that the 'hot spots' are in the background subsystem and are mainly related to the life cycles of chlorine, ethylene and energy generation (electricity and heat). The impacts from the foreground system are relatively low as there are few direct discharges from the plant into the environment.

To help them link the environmental and economic sustainability criteria and assess the level of environmental and economic sustainability in a more integrated

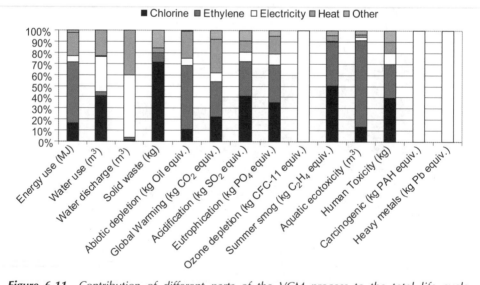

Figure 6.11 *Contribution of different parts of the VCM process to the total life cycle environmental impacts. Note: 'Chlorine', 'ethylene', 'electricity' and 'heat' represent the life cycles of chlorine, ethylene, electricity and heat; and 'Other' includes the foreground system and the life cycles of all other parts of the VCM system shown in Figure 6.9, apart from chlorine, ethylene, electricity and heat*

Table 6.9 *Using environmental indicators to assess the level of environmental and economic sustainability of the VCM plant*

Environmental criteria	Expressed per tonne of VCM	Expressed per value added (£)
Energy use	62 484 MJ	658 MJ
Water use	19 474 m³	205 m³
Water discharge	11 254 m³	118 m³
Solid waste	53 kg	0.6 kg
Abiotic reserves depletion	1502 kg oil equiv.	15.8 kg oil equiv.
Global warming	2029 kg CO_2 equiv.	34 kg CO_2 equiv.
Acidification	11 kg SO_2 equiv.	0.1 kg SO_2 equiv.
Eutrophication	1 kg PO_4 equiv.	0.01 kg PO_4 equiv.
Ozone depletion	2.5×10^{-5} kg CFC-11 equiv.	2.6×10^{-7} kg CFC-11 equiv.
Summer smog	3 kg C_2H_4 equiv.	0.03 kg C_2H_4 equiv.
Aquatic ecotoxicity	0.3 m³	3.2×10^{-3} m³
Human toxicity	14 kg	0.15 kg
Carcinogenic potential	6.7×10^{-5} kg PAH equiv.	7.1×10^{-7} kg PAH equiv.
Heavy metals	2.9×10^{-3} kg Pb equiv.	3.1×10^{-5} kg Pb equiv.

manner, the design team also calculate the LCA impacts of the VCM plant per tonne of VCM produced and per unit value added, calculated at £95/t (Table 6.8). These results are shown in Table 6.9. For example, these results reveal that to make a tonne of VCM product, on a life cycle basis, it is necessary to use 62.5 GJ of energy which depletes 1.5 t of fossil fuels (expressed as oil equivalents) and generates 2 t of CO_2. Linking the environmental and economic performance, for every pound of value added per tonne of VCM, 658 MJ of energy is used, depleting 15.8 kg of oil eq. and generating 34 kg of CO_2 emissions.

Having analysed and discussed the results, the design team proceed to the final stage of sustainability assessment to find out if their proposed design is sustainable from a social point of view.

Questions

1. Carry out an LCA of your VCM plant configuration and compare the results with the results obtained by the PlasticFuture design team. Discuss and explain any differences between your and their results. Which design is more environmentally sustainable, yours or theirs? Why?
2. Calculate the LCA impacts per tonne of VCM produced (in t/kg, m³/kg or MJ/kg) and then per unit value added (t/£, m³/£ or MJ/£). Compare your results with the respective results shown in Table 6.9 and discuss any differences.
3. How do you think different LCA databases used to calculate the environmental impacts from the background system (e.g. for ethylene, chlorine and energy generation) influence the total LCA results?
4. Draw flow diagrams to show the life cycles of the raw materials and energy generation.

5. Identify the 'hot spots' in the system. Explain why you consider them to be the 'hot spots' and discuss their relative contribution to the total impacts.
6. Identify the sources of each environmental impact for each 'hot spot'. For example, where does in the life cycle of ethylene does aquatic toxicity come from? Or, which part of the life cycle of chlorine is responsible for solid waste?
7. Based on the LCA results, which environmental impacts do you consider to be most significant? Why? Explain how you identified the 'significant' impacts.
8. Which parts of the VCM system contribute most to the most significant impacts? What do you conclude from these results: which parts of the system should be targeted for improvements? How would you do that?
9. Using the economic and environmental criteria and the results of the LCA and economic analysis so far, is it possible to make any conclusions at this stage on whether this design is sustainable? If so, what do you conclude? If not, why?

Assessing social sustainability
To assess social sustainability of their proposed design, the design team use the social criteria listed in Table 6.1. Their (mainly qualitative) findings are shown in Table 6.10 and are discussed below. Some of these preliminary findings will serve as a starting point for a detailed safety and loss prevention studies, including HAZOP, in the following, detailed design stage.

Provision of employment   The team have already found out in the economic analysis that the proposed VCM process will provide full-time employment to 20 operators over the lifetime of the plant. In addition to this, an estimated 25 full-time contractors would be employed during the construction phase which is projected to last for 3 years.

Employee health and safety   Occupational health and safety is an important issue for any chemical plant, but particularly in the case of VCM. In addition to the usual health and safety concerns such as injuries, fatalities, exposure to noise and vibration, there are several other issues that the design team need to consider here. First, production of VCM requires the use of hazardous materials, such as chlorine, ethylene, sodium hydroxide and oxygen so that the design must ensure that the risks from these materials are minimised.

Secondly, exposure to VCM has been linked to liver and other types of human cancer (Rahde, 1992). For this reason, the occupational exposure limits for VCM

Table 6.10   *Using social indicators to assess social sustainability of the proposed VCM design*

Social criteria	Issues addressed
Provision of employment	Plant operators and contractors
Employee health and safety	Injuries, fatalities, noise, VCM exposure
Citizens' health and safety	Emissions into the environment, VCM exposure
Customer health and safety	VCM exposure
Nuisance	Odour, noise, visual impact
Public acceptability	VCM, PVC and dioxins

have been reduced significantly over the years from several thousands mg/m^3 in the 1940s and 1950s to today's value of 2.6 mg/m^3 or 1 ppm (expressed as eight hours time weighted average, TLV-8h TWA). The short-exposure limit (15 min) must not exceed 5 ppm; direct contact with liquid VCM must be avoided. Although these are operational issues, the preliminary and then later the detailed design must ensure that the exposure to and contact with VCM are minimised as far as possible.

This is particularly important as the design team are aware that exposure to VCM and the associated occupational hazards are still a subject of dispute between the industry, government and NGOs. For example, in the Veneto region in Italy, three chemical companies producing chlorine, VCM and PVC are being prosecuted for the death of 157 and poor health of over one hundred employees. It is alleged that the deaths and poor health are due to a long-term exposure to VCM. In addition to these charges, the companies are also accused for the environmental damage caused to the Venice lagoon, due to the emissions of dioxins, furans and other toxic substances.

Dioxins and furans are another health and safety concern associated with the production of VCM. Exposure to these substances can cause cancer and other toxicological effects. As already mentioned, the manufacture of VCM generates a certain amount of dioxins (mainly contained in the 'heavy ends') which must be destroyed or minimised in the waste streams. The design team have for that reason chosen to incinerate the waste streams with chlorinated hydrocarbons and dioxins but they are also aware of the fact that incineration can generate further amounts of dioxins (as discussed in Chapter 5). They have therefore made sure that the design and operating conditions in the incinerators are such that the formation of dioxins is prevented.

Citizens' health and safety   The design team must also make sure that exposure to VCM of the general public living in the vicinity of the plant is prevented or minimised. Some studies suggest that daily VCM inhalation rates range from 4 µg to more than 100 µg per person per day for populations living in the immediate vicinity of VCM plants (ECETOC, 1988). Therefore, the design must ensure that the loss of the VCM product through evaporation is minimised.

Customer health and safety   All the VCM produced will be used on-site for the manufacture of PVC so that the customer in this case is the PlasticFuture company itself. In addition to the safe storage of the VCM product which the team must build into the design, they also need to be aware of the downstream customer health and safety issues. For example, as VCM is a human carcinogen, it is important that PVC contains as little residual monomer as possible. During the latter part of the 1970s, the production process was significantly improved to address this problem so that now PVC is routinely produced with less than 5 ppm of VCM.

Nuisance   The design must also ensure that noise, odour and visual impact of the plant are minimised to prevent causing nuisance to the neighbouring public. Because this VCM plant is an addition to an existing plant on an industrial estate, the design team estimate that the additional noise and odour levels will be relatively small and will probably not cause significant public nuisance. The visual impact will be minimal as the plant will blend in with the other surrounding installations.

Public acceptability   As discussed in detail in Chapter 5, public acceptability is one of the most important factors which can ultimately determine whether an industrial installation gets a planning permission or keeps its licence to operate. The design team are aware that some of the above concerns, such as citizens' health and safety issues and nuisance, may cause objections to building the proposed plant. They therefore must ensure that the above issues are addressed adequately in the design so that the objections to the planning proposal are minimised.

However, there are also public acceptability issues further downstream in the life cycle of VCM, related to PVC. Many people object to the production and use of PVC because it will eventually end up as waste and, if incinerated, it can contribute to the formation of dioxins. This is one of the main reasons for the public objection to incineration so that in many parts of the world it is now almost impossible to obtain a planning permission to build a new incinerator (as shown in the case study in Chapter 5).

Therefore, envisaging that the objections to PVC incineration could lead to a reduced demand for PVC and hence VCM, the design team decide to build into the design a possibility for PVC recycling. They then need to revisit the flowsheet to make the necessary design modifications. This is their next task before proceeding to the final design stage.

This is where we leave our design team but before we do that, let us briefly have a look at what the rest of their job will be before they hand it over to the planning application team.

Questions

1. List and discuss the health and safety hazards associated with the materials used in the VCM production.
2. What are the dioxin emissions' limit in your country?
3. At which operating conditions can the formation of dioxins from incinerators be prevented?
4. How would you prevent the loss of the VCM product so that the exposure of the public to VCM is prevented?
5. What can the VCM plant designer do to ensure customer health and safety?
6. Because this VCM plant is going to be integrated into an existing installation, the additional noise, odour and visual impact may not be significant to cause nuisance. Discuss how this would change if the plant were a stand-alone installation in a country side, surrounded by villages. What would be the main objections by the neighbouring communities to building the plant?
7. Find out why Greenpeace is opposed to the VCM and other chlorine-related industries. Do you agree with their view? Why?
8. As an engineer or a scientist, what could you do to reduce the environmental, health and safety concerns associated with the VCM and PVC? Based on that, how would you try and argue your 'case' to Greenpeace?
9. Based on all of the above consideration, carry out a social sustainability assessment of your VCM design and discuss the results.

10. How would you re-design the VCM plant to allow for recycling of waste PVC? What modifications would be necessary for that? You may wish to consult the book by Azapagic *et al.* (2003) for the PVC recycling technologies.

6.3.3   Detailed and Final Designs

After completing the preliminary design, the team begin to work on detailed design. As discussed in the beginning of this chapter, this design stage will involve detailed equipment design and economic analysis, process control and instrumentation, and safety and loss prevention, including HAZOP studies. The team will then carry out a full sustainability assessment to ensure that all relevant sustainability factors have been identified and addressed appropriately in the design. These findings can then be used to further optimise the design on the economic, environmental and social performance. This will require a choice of the appropriate objective functions to reflect the most significant sustainability issues, as identified in the sustainability assessments. The team will have to think carefully not only how to tackle mathematically this complex multi-objective nonlinear optimisation problem but also how to formulate some of the social objectives. Design optimisation is by no means a trivial task and can take considerable time and resources to perform. However, it is also a powerful approach which can help the design team to identify the most sustainable design out of a number of feasible design options.

Having identified it, the team is then ready to proceed to the final design stage to produce equipment drawings and layout, piping and instrumentation diagrams and so on. They then handover the project to the planning application team and, if their design is successful in obtaining the planning permission, to the construction team.

Questions

1. Carry out a detailed design of one or more parts of the VCM plant. If feasible, combine your work with the work of the rest of your design team to produce an overall detailed design of the VCM plant.
2. How would you perform the optimisation of your design? List the main steps in optimisation and describe how you would carry each one for your VCM design. You may wish to use the books by Edgar and Himmelblau (1988) and Floudas (1995) for optimisation theory and Lakshmanan *et al.* (1999) for a VCM optimisation case study.
3. How would you choose the objective functions for optimisation? Why?
4. How would you use the optimisation results to identify the most sustainable design? Why?
5. Describe the planning process in your country. Link that with the Environmental Impact Assessment (EIA) requirements discussed earlier within the site selection step and discuss the role of EIA in the application process.
6. What would you do as a member of the design team to make sure that the planning application is successful?

Acknowledgements

The authors are grateful to Graziella Morona, a Socrates exchange student from the University of Padova for her help with this case study.

References and Further Reading

Aspen Technology (2003) ASPEN PLUS. Aspen Technology Inc., Cambridge, Mass. http://www.aspentec.com.

Azapagic, A. (1999) Life Cycle Assessment and Its Application to Process Selection, Design and Optimisation. *Chemical Engineering Journal*, **73**, 1–21.

Azapagic, A. (2002) Life Cycle Assessment: A Tool for Identification of More Sustainable Products and Processes, pp. 62–85. In: *Handbook of Green Chemistry and Technology* (Clark, J. and D. Macquarrie, eds), Blackwell Science, Oxford.

Azapagic, A. (2003) Systems Approach to Corporate Sustainability: A General Management Framework. *IChemE Trans. B*. **81**(Part B), 303–316.

Azapagic, A. and Perdan, S. (2000) Indicators of Sustainable Development for Industry: A General Framework. *Trans. IChemE (Proc. Safety Envir. Prot.), Part B*, **78**(B4), 243–261.

Azapagic, A., Emsley, A. and Hamerton, I. (2003) *Polymers, the Environment and Sustainable Development*. John Wiley & Sons, Chichester.

Chemstations (2003) CHEMCAD. Chemstations Inc., Houston, http://www.chemstat.net.

Clegg, I. and Hardman, R. (1998) Vinyl chloride production process. Patent: US5728905.

Douglas, J.M. (1988) *Conceptual Design of Chemical Processes*. McGraw-Hill, New York, 601pp.

EC (1996) Council Directive 96/61/EC concerning Integrated Pollution Prevention and Control, *Official Journal of the European Communities* L257 (10/10/96).

EC (1997) Council Directive 97/11/EC of 3 March 1997 amending Directive 85/337/EEC on the Assessment of the Effects of Certain Public and Private Projects on the Environment. Official Journal No. L073 (14/03/1997).

ECETOC (1988) The Mutagenicity and Carcinogenicity of Vinyl Chloride: A Historical Review and Assessment. Technical Report No. 31, European Chemical Industry, Ecology and Toxicology Center (ECETOC), Brussels. (Quoted in: Rahde, A.F. (1992). Vinyl Chloride International Programme on Chemical Safety, IPCS Poisons Information Monograph 558, 1992 (http://www.inchem.org/ documents/pims/chemical/pim558.htm).

Edgar, T.E. and Himmelblau, D.M. (1988) *Optimization of Chemical Processes*. McGraw-Hill, New York.

Floudas, C.A. (1995) *Nonlinear and Mixed-integer Optimization: Fundamentals and Applications*. University Press, Oxford.

Hicks, D.I., Gittenden, B.O. and Warhurst, A.C. (2000) Design for Decommissioning: Addressing the Future Closure of Chemical Sites in the Design of New Plant. *Trans. IChemE*, **78**(Part B), November 2000, 465–479.

Hyprotech (2003) HYSIM. Hyprotech Ltd, Calgary, http://www.hyprotech.com.

IChemE (1998) *A Guide to Capital Cost Estimating*. IChemE, Rugby.

IChemE (2003) The Sustainability Metrics: Sustainable Development Progress Metrics Recommended for the Use in Process Industries, Institution of Chemical Engineers, Rugby.

Jebens, A. and Kishi, A. (2000) Vinyl Chloride Monomer (VCM). CEH Report. http://ceh.sric.sri.com/Public/Reports/696.6000/ (9 March 2003).

Lakshmanan, A., Rooney, W.C. and Biegler, L.T. (1999) A Case Study for Reactor Network Synthesis: The Vinyl Chloride Process. *Computers & Chemical Engineering*, **23**, 479–495.

Marshall, K., Henley, J., Reed, D., Walko, L., Jones, M., Olken, M., Clarke, W. and Hickman, D. (2001) Process for Vinyl Chloride Manufacture from Ethane and Ethylene with Secondary Reactive Consumption of Reactor Effluent HCl. US Patent No. WO0138272, 31 May 2001.

Pira (2000) PEMS 4.7, LCA software and database. Pira International Ltd, Leatherhead.

Rahde, A.F. (1992) Vinyl Chloride International Programme on Chemical Safety. IPCS Poisons Information Monograph 558, http://www.inchem.org/documents/pims/chemical/pim558.htm.

Ray, M.S. and Johnston, D.W. (1989) *Chemical Engineering Design Project. A Case Study Approach.* Gordon and Breach Science Publishers, London, 357pp.

Seider, W.D., Seader, J.D. and Lewin, D.R. (1999) *Process Design Principles. Synthesis, Analysis and Evaluation.* John Wiley & Sons, New York, 824pp.

Sinnott, R.K. (2000) *Coulson & Richardson's Chemical Engineering*, Vol. 6 (Design), 3rd ed., Pergamon Press, Exeter.

The Innovation Group (2000) www.the-innovation-group.com/welcome.htm (last accessed 14 March 2003).

Ulrich, G.D. (1984) A Guide to Chemical Engineering Process Design and Economics. John Wiley & Sons, New York, 472pp.

7

Towards Sustainable Chemical Manufacturing: Polylactic Acid – A Sustainable Polymer?

James H. Clark and Jeffrey J.E. Hardy

Summary

Polymer materials, such as polyethylene, polystyrene and polypropylene, are ubiquitous in today's society, being used in various products including packaging, buildings and cars. Most of these polymers are derived from non-renewable fossil resources, such as crude oil and natural gas. For various reasons, recycling and reuse of polymer materials are limited so that the majority of the polymers are landfilled at the end of their useful life. In addition to creating large amounts of non-biodegradable solid waste, this represents a loss of valuable non-renewable resource. Furthermore, legislation in the EU and other countries is being increasingly tailored towards limiting disposal of polymers (and other materials) by landfill. Therefore, alternative, more sustainable ways of producing and disposing of polymers will have to be found. This case study examines economic, environmental and social implications of one such alternative: a possibility to substitute the non-biodegradable polymers derived from non-renewable resources with a biodegradable polymer, polylactic acid (PLA). The sustainability implications of the life cycle of PLA are compared and contrasted with the life cycle of conventional polymers to identify more sustainable options for the future.

7.1 Polymers in Today's Society

The majority of polymers in use today are thermoplastic and thermoset polymers. With 75% of the total polymer consumption, five thermoplastic materials dominate

Sustainable Development in Practice: Case Studies for Engineers and Scientists
Edited by Adisa Azapagic, Slobodan Perdan and Roland Clift
© 2004 John Wiley & Sons, Ltd   ISBNs: 0-470-85608-4 (HB); 0-470-85609-2 (PB)

the market: polyethylene (PE), polypropylene (PP), polyvinyl chloride (PVC), polystyrene (PS) and polyethylene terephthalate (PET) (Azapagic *et al.*, 2003). Therefore, the focus in this chapter is on the thermoplastic polymers so that we will use the term 'plastics' interchangeably with the term 'polymers' to refer to these materials.[1]

The history of plastics goes back to the mid-19th century when the first thermoplastic resin, celluloid, was produced by reaction of the renewable raw material, cellulose, with nitric acid. Natural polymers such as rubber were in common use for the next 100 years but the real breakthrough for the large-scale commercialisation of plastics came as a result of Second World War. At this time, natural polymers were in short supply and large-scale use was found first for low-density polyethylene (LDPE) (developed in 1932/33 by ICI) and then PS (developed in 1937). In the 1950s, the other major synthetic plastics – high-density polyethylene (HDPE) and PP – were developed for large-scale manufacture.

Today, plastics are ubiquitous in modern society, being used in numerous large-volume products including packaging, textiles, pipes, cars, furniture, aircraft, foams and floor coverings. The largest of these by far is packaging which accounts for some 35% of the total (Figure 7.1) of over $100\,000 \times 10^6$ t/yr worldwide (Gomez, 1997; SUFRES, 1998; Stevens, 2002). The packaging plastics are used in films, sheets, bags, bottles, sacks and foams.

Improvements in the properties of the plastics and the use of thinner and tougher materials can lead to a reduction in the weight of plastic required, for example in carrier bags. Weight-benefits through the use of plastics are of enormous importance in the automobile industry where the weight of a car can be reduced by 100–200 kg through the replacement of conventional metallic materials in parts such as fuel

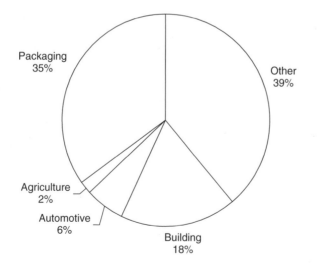

Figure 7.1   *World plastics consumption by weight by sector*

---

[1] Strictly speaking, not all polymers are plastics though plastics must be polymeric.

tanks, bonnets, bumpers, seats, insulation and so on. This has a direct beneficial effect on fuel consumption, which can partially offset the negative effects of the use of non-renewable resources for plastics manufacture.

The use and disposal of plastic packaging generates large amounts of waste each year. Photograph courtesy of Digital Vision.

Ninety percent of the plastic materials used today are synthesised using non-renewable fossil resources although, remarkably, this only accounts for about 4% of the total production of oil (the vast majority being used as a source of energy). Some of the key reasons for the continuing (and growing) large-scale usage of plastics are:

- they are low-density solids enabling the manufacture of light-weight objects;
- they can be moulded into different shapes;
- many plastics are of low cost; and
- most plastics have high corrosion resistance, are durable and have low thermal and electrical conductivities.

Additionally, plastics can be used to manufacture composite materials, which have added strength through the incorporation of other materials, notably glass, carbon and silica. Composite materials can have excellent technological properties and have become essential to major industries including aerospace, sports equipment and high performance cars.

In recent years new and exciting applications for plastic materials include computing, communication and other electronic devices as well as in artificial organs and medical implants. We can safely assume that the future will continue to see new and important applications for these remarkable materials.

Questions

1. The per capita consumption of plastics in Western Europe increased from ca. 1 kg in 1960 to 70 kg in 2000. Do you expect this level of growth of usage to continue and how do you expect the distribution of plastic usage shown in Figure 7.1 to change in the future? Why?
2. What are the main issues associated with the manufacture and use of plastic materials? In your opinion, what would be the alternatives to these types of material?

7.2 Major Types of Polymers in Common Use

Polymers are long-chain molecules composed of a large number of identical repeating units $-(Y)_n-$, where Y is the repeating unit and n is the number of units which must be large enough so that there are no variations in the polymer macroscopic properties with small changes in n. Most commercial polymers are synthetic materials made by polymerisation of monomers. This includes mixtures of monomers that give copolymers whose properties depend on the individual monomers and their relative proportions and sequencing. As shown in Figure 7.2, it is usually possible to prepare various types of copolymers including block, alternating, graft and random.

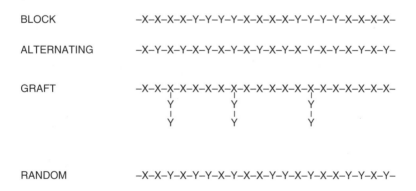

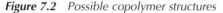

Figure 7.2   *Possible copolymer structures*

Polymers are normally classified according to the type of polymerisation used in their manufacture or their thermal behaviour. With respect to polymerisation type, *addition* and *condensation* polymers can be identified. Additional polymerisation occurs by sequential incorporation of monomers into a growing chain. The resulting polymers have the same chemical composition as the monomers and include PE, PS and PVC. Condensation polymerisations occur with elimination of small molecules such as water and give products including nylon-6,6 and PET. Regarding their thermal properties, two types of polymers are distinguished (Figure 7.3).

Thermoplastics undergo softening when heated to a particular temperature due to the absence of strong bonds between polymer chains. This property is particularly useful for recycling as it enables reprocessing of waste plastics by heating and remoulding. As already mentioned, the most important commercial plastics in this category are PE (both low and high density), PP, PS, PVC and PET. These represent the largest group of commercial plastics (ca. 75% worldwide) with the PE and PP accounting for almost a half of the overall total of plastics manufacturing (Azapagic *et al.*, 2003).

Thermosets, on the other hand, have strong covalent bonds between chains (Figure 7.3) leading to three-dimensional networks so that, once set, they cannot be remoulded. This is an obvious limitation to their potential for reuse. Commercially important thermosets include polyurethanes, epoxy resins and phenol-formaldehyde resins.

These important commercial plastics are traditionally manufactured from non-renewable fossil raw materials. The conventional production routes involve the large-scale manufacture of key monomers including ethylene (for PE), propylene (for PP), styrene (for PS), and ethylene glycol and terephthalic acid (for PET). The monomers are then polymerised normally at high temperatures (and pressures) and in the presence of a catalyst. These production routes are illustrated schematically in Figure 7.4 (Azapagic *et al.*, 2003).

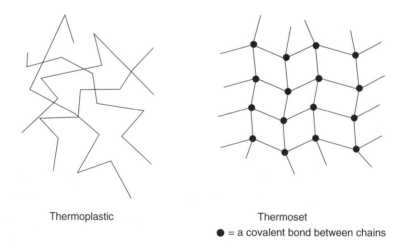

Thermoplastic   Thermoset

● = a covalent bond between chains

Figure 7.3   *Schematic structures of thermoplastic and thermoset polymers*

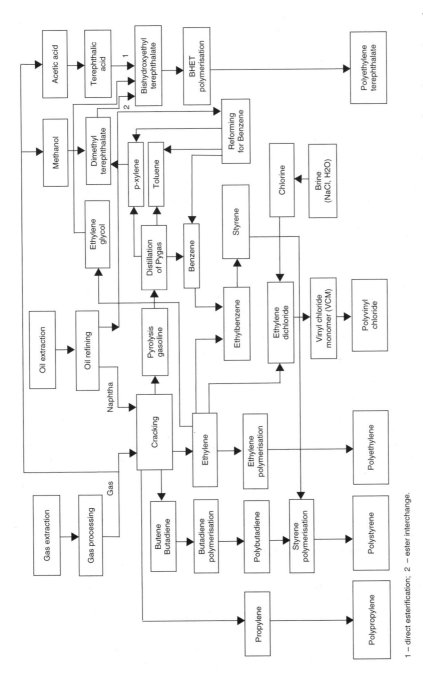

1 – direct esterification; 2 – ester interchange.

Figure 7.4 *Conventional production routes for polymers from extraction of raw materials to commodity products (Azapagic et al., 2003; reproduced with permission from John Wiley & Sons Ltd.)*

Questions

1. Apply life cycle thinking and describe the production processes for the five major plastic materials, that is PE, PP, PS, PVC and PET from the extraction of raw materials ('cradle') to the point where the commodity plastics leaves the production plant ('gate'). You may consult the Appendix at the end of the book for an introduction to life cycle thinking and a related tool, Life Cycle Assessment (LCA).
2. What is the primary raw material used for the manufacture of today's plastics? Discuss the implications of using this type of raw material for sustainable development.
3. Identify the likely resource demands and other environmental impacts in the plastics production processes.
4. Which environmental impacts do you think are most significant in the manufacture of conventional plastic materials? Why?

7.3 Sustainability Issues Associated with Polymer Materials

There are a number of reasons why the use of today's commercial polymers is unsustainable. Low polymer recycling rates mean that the majority of polymer 'waste' is landfilled. In addition to creating large amounts of non-biodegradable solid waste, this also leads to a loss of valuable non-renewable resource. Although there is a considerable effort to increase the polymer recycling rates, the potential for recycling is limited by a number of economic, environmental and social factors. These include the difficulties in collecting and separating the waste plastics from the end-user, the costs of building and operating the recycling facilities and potential environmental impacts from recycling. Technical factors also limit recycling; for example, the introduction of various additives to improve the polymer properties leads to contamination of polymer materials and makes their recycling difficult.

Some of these issues are discussed in more detail below. For further reading on the topic of sustainability issues associated with commercial polymers, the reader can consult the book by Azapagic *et al.* (2003).

7.3.1 The Use of Non-renewable Resources

The reliance on non-renewable feedstocks in making the plastic materials makes their entire life cycle unsustainable due to a diminishing resource being converted into a product that often has a single use and creates a waste with a very long lifetime. Alternatives need to be brought on line rapidly because they will probably need to overtake non-renewable feedstocks within approximately 30–40 years. Agricultural renewable resources have the potential to become a sustainable source of raw materials for the plastics industry. It is estimated that less than 1% of the ca. 7×10^{10} t/yr of renewable carbon produced in the biosphere is sufficient to meet the total worldwide demand for plastics (Gradel, 2002).

7.3.2   Additives

The potential for recycling waste plastics is limited by the common occurrence of various additives in commercial plastic products (Aguado and Ferrane, 1999) added to improve the polymers properties such as stability and appearance. Once in a landfill, some of these additives can pose an environmental hazard due to their possible leaching into the soil and the underground water. These additives are in addition to substances that may have been carried into the product from the polymerisation process, notably metallic catalysts and promoters as well as any impurities and reaction by-products. However, these species have not traditionally been considered to be a problem as long as they do not cause an unacceptable deterioration in the product properties. The main classes of additives are:

- plasticisers, such as trialkyl phosphate, which are low molecular weight organic compounds used to make the plastic more flexible at lower temperatures by lowering the polymer glass transition temperature;
- fillers, such as silica, are inert materials used to reduce cost and improve processability;
- blowing agents, such as fluorocarbons, are volatile compounds which are used to expand the plastics by forming gases after mixing;
- thermal stabilisers and antioxidants, such as hindered phenols, are organic compounds used to protect the polymer from the effect of temperature and oxygen during processing;
- flame retardants, such as polybromoorganics, include organic and inorganic compounds used to inhibit polymer decomposition on heating;
- light stabilisers, such as aromatic compounds, are organic or inorganic compounds that absorb light and so retard photochemical degradation of the polymer; and
- colorants, such as azo compounds, are organic and inorganic dyes which give colour to the materials.

The economic viability and environmental benefit of recycling plastics to useful chemicals can be severely hindered by the presence of these additives. Additives can form hazardous by-products, leave toxic residues and react with the chemicals produced in the recycling process.

7.3.3   Plastic Waste

The increasing use of plastics in modern society coupled with the reduced useful lifetime of many consumer products brought about by continuous product innovation and intensive marketing has led to a rapid increase in the volume of plastic waste (Aguado and Ferrane, 1999). Much of this is found in domestic refuse with some 63% of the plastic waste in Western Europe being in the form of municipal solid waste (MSW) mixed with a wide variety of other solid wastes (Aguado and Ferrane, 1999). It is interesting to note that this high proportion is largely due to the short lifetime of packaging compared to other major sources of plastic such as electronic goods, household items, electrical devices, buildings and cars. The proportion of MSW that is plastics is about 10% by weight (see Chapter 5 for further discussion on MSW composition) but the low density of plastic products adds considerably to the total waste volume.

Some of the sustainability issues associated with the generation of plastic wastes include:

- most plastic materials are resistant to degradation, remaining in the landfill sites for a long time and causing a steady increase in the demand for further landfill sites;
- there is a risk of fires and highly polluting emissions from landfill sites containing large quantities of organic materials;
- there is also a potential for contamination of soil and underground water table due to the leaching of additives;
- the low density of most plastic materials leads to added collection and transportation costs which limit the economic viability of recycling of plastic wastes (only consider just the fact that only one tonne of plastic is recoverable from 20 000 bottles!); and
- plastics are often commingled with other materials making their recovery costly and difficult to achieve at a useful level of purity.

7.4   Improving Sustainability of Polymer Materials

Based on the issues highlighted in the previous section, it could be argued that the current use of polymer materials is unsustainable. Therefore, we need to rethink our approach to manufacturing and using these materials to improve their sustainability. There are a number of options that could be considered here, including:

1. Reduction in the consumption of raw materials though improvements in the manufacturing processes and the product design. Examples here include the use of lighter weight food containers and the use of thinner plastic films, as well as the use of improved catalysts in polymerisations.
2. Reuse of materials, for example, through multiple use of containers such as bottles and bags, which can be encouraged at an individual consumer level.
3. Recycling, allowing wastes to be reintroduced into the consumption cycle. This can involve mechanical or chemical (feedstock) recycling with the latter involving breaking the polymer down into smaller units for chemical or fuel production.
4. Energy recovery is meant to be applied when recycling is not viable and incineration can generate energy from the waste combustion heat. However, the release of toxic gases such as those produced in the incineration of chlorine-containing plastics is a cause of concern (Chapters 5 and 6).

The final option is to landfill non-recyclable plastic waste. However, the above hierarchy of options is far from reality for many countries, with the vast majority of plastic wastes still being disposed of in landfill sites (Aguado and Ferrane, 1999). Targets for reducing the amount of plastics that is landfilled, such as those set by the EU Packaging Directive (EC, 1994), can indeed reduce the environmental damage caused by plastics and preserve the valuable non-renewable resources. However, as already mentioned, there are major difficulties with recycling and reuse not least because of the complexity of waste mixtures which makes separating out the plastics very difficult, but because of the increasing consumer demand for new products.

Material substitution is another option that could be employed to make plastic materials more sustainable. In this case other materials capable of providing the equivalent function would replace plastics. For example, paper, glass or aluminium could replace the plastics used for packaging. However, some argue (e.g. Gebauer and Hofmann, 1993) that case of packaging substitution would not be more sustainable as it would lead to an increase in weight (to over 400%), volume (200%) and costs (200%) of the materials required as well as in the energy consumed (over 20%).

The use of plastics rather than conventional materials in cars also appears to be more environmentally sustainable. For example, the replacement of 200–300 kg of conventional materials in a modern car by plastics would lead to a reduction in the fuel demands by 750 l over 150 000 km driven. In the EU, this would correspond to a saving of 12×10^6 t of oil and 30×10^6 t of CO_2 emissions every year (SUFRES, 1998).

Therefore, it would appear that plastic materials do have certain advantages over other materials so that it is realistic to assume that they will continue to be used in future for various applications. Thus, it would be interesting to examine other types of polymeric materials which appear to be more sustainable than the conventional polymers. One option is novel, biodegradable polymer materials made from renewable raw materials. In addition to providing the functional properties similar to the conventional polymers, the use of such materials would help overcome the problem of depletion of non-renewable resources and generation of solid waste with long lifetimes. This option is examined in our case study.

Questions

1. Why is the use of commercial plastic materials unsustainable? List the main economic, environmental and social reasons for that.
2. How could the use of commercial plastics be made more sustainable?
3. What are the polymer recycling rates in your country? How does that compare with the recycling rates in the EU, US and Japan?
4. List the main technical, economic, environmental and social factors that limit plastics recycling. What can be done to overcome these limiting factors?
5. Why are the additives in plastics a concern?
6. List the options for increasing the sustainability of plastic materials?
7. List and describe the methods for polymers recycling. For more information on this topic, you may use the book by Azapagic *et al.* (2003).

7.5   Case Study: Towards Sustainable Polymer Materials

Recent research has shown the potential for substantially increasing the rate of biodegradation of conventional plastics. Reported methods include the incorporation of photolabile additives which generate radical species on prolonged exposure to sunlight and initiate depolymerisation (Symphony Environmental Ltd, 2003). Another method is to incorporate sugar-type units into polyolefins so as to make the plastics 'sweeter' for microorganisms (Galgali *et al.*, 2002). These are interesting ideas and initiate a welcome increase in research activity in this area, but there are uncertainties associated with biodegradation (e.g. the availability of light in a landfill site). Further-more, they do not solve the problem of depletion of non-renewable fossil resources.

A different approach to solving some of the sustainability issues associated with plastics is to increase the use of polymers derived from renewable raw materials (RRM) which in many cases can result in the production of biodegradable polymer materials. There are several families of biodegradable polymers made from RRMs including polyhydroxyalkanoates and polylactic acid (REFS). Due to space limita-tions, it is not possible to describe these in any detail here; for further reading on this topic, the reader may wish to consult the book by Stevens (2002).

In this next section we present a case study of one type of biodegradable polymer that can be derived from an RMM. This particular case study considers polylactic acid (PLA), synthesised from lactic acid. PLA is of considerable interest as it has physical polymeric properties that lie somewhere between those of polypropylene (PP) and polyethylene terephthalate (PET). However, its main advantage over these polymers is that it is completely biodegradable. It is an interesting material to study as the monomer (lactic acid) can be synthesised from both a non-renewable fossil resource and a renewable feedstock. Both process routes, as it will be shown, have positive and negative features.

Questions

1. What are the advantages of biodegradable polymers over the polymers derived from fossil resources? Explain why.
2. How can the conventional fossil-based polymers be made biodegradable? Is this in your opinion an advantage over the non-biodegradable polymers? Why?

7.5.1 Lactic Acid

Lactic acid (2-hydroxypropionic acid) is the most widely occurring hydroxycarboxylic acid. It is present in many foodstuffs (e.g. it is the primary component in the taste of sour milk) and it is also a constituent in animal blood and muscle tissue. It is a versatile chemical and traditionally has found uses (Hofvendahl and Hahn-Hägerdal, 2000):

- as an acidulant, flavour enhancer and preservative in the food, pharmaceutical, leather and textile industries;
- for the production of organic chemicals;
- as a low toxicity solvent; and
- for polymerisation to PLA.

Some of the lactic-acid-derived products are shown in Figure 7.5. The routes to the production of lactic acid will be discussed further below.

Lactic acid is optically active and exists as two stereoisomers (as shown in Figure 7.6). Both isomers are extremely soluble in water and water-miscible organic solvents but are insoluble in other organic solvents. Traditionally, it has been complicated to resolve (separate) the optical isomers, especially on the large scale. Separation and purification of lactic acid is generally achieved by repeated distillation.

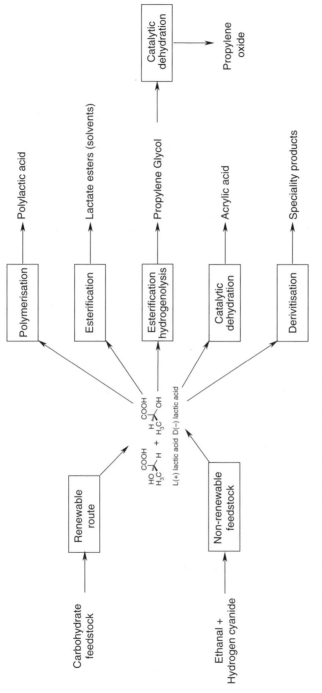

Figure 7.5 Some of the major products derived from lactic acid

L(+) lactic acid   D(−) lactic acid

Figure 7.6   *The optical isomers of lactic acid*

Questions

1. What uses has the lactic acid found so far? Why?
2. Which raw materials are used in the production of lactic acid? Which type of the raw material is in your opinion more sustainable? Explain why.

Production of Lactic Acid from Non-renewable Fossil Resources

As already mentioned, approximately 10% (or 8000 t/yr) of the world's demand for lactic acid is currently derived from the non-renewable fossil-based feedstock. The main manufacturers are Sterling Chemicals in the USA and Musashino in Japan. The chemical reactions leading to the synthesis of lactic acid are shown in Figure 7.7 and the manufacturing process is outlined in Figure 7.8.

   Taking a life cycle approach and looking at the manufacturing process from 'cradle to gate', that is from the extraction of raw materials to the production of the lactic acid (see the Appendix at the end of the book), the process can be divided

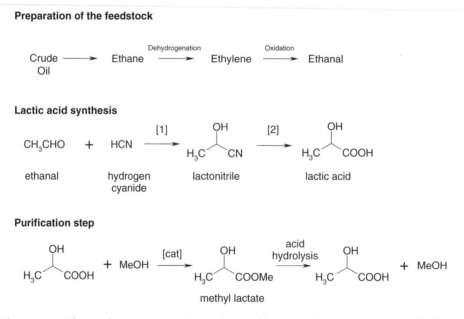

Figure 7.7   *Chemical reactions in the synthesis of lactic acid using non-renewable fossil-based feedstock*

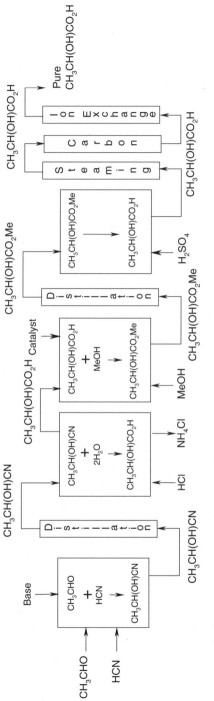

Figure 7.8 *Manufacturing process for lactic acid based on the non-renewable fossil feedstock*

into three stages: preparation of the feedstock, synthesis of lactic acid and its purification. Preparation of the feedstock involves extraction of crude oil and its refining to produce, among other products, ethane. Ethane is then used to make acetaldehyde (ethanal) which is used as a raw material in the second stage of lactic acid manufacture. The first stage is normally not carried out at the lactic acid manufacturing site but is included here to show that the primary resource for making the lactic acid is a fossil-based feedstock.

The second, synthesis stage itself involves two steps (Figures 7.7 and 7.8). Step [1] is a catalytic reaction of acetaldehyde with hydrogen cyanide in the liquid phase under atmospheric conditions to produce lactonitrile (acetaldehyde cyanohydrin) which acts as an intermediate. The lactonitrile intermediate is then isolated and purified by distillation.

As shown in Figure 7.7 and in more detail in Figure 7.8, step [2] is a hydrolysis step catalysed by sulphuric and or hydrochloric acid at around 100 °C, producing a crude lactic acid and ammonium salt (sulphate or chloride) as a by-product (Lester, 1996).

In order to produce pure lactic acid in the third, purification, stage the crude lactic acid is esterified with methanol in the presence of an acid or basic catalysis and then purified by distillation. The methyl lactate ester (a valuable product in its own right) is hydrolysed under acidic conditions to lactic acid and methanol (which is recycled). Finally, the lactic acid is purified by distillation (steaming) to yield high-purity lactic acid.

Step [1] of lactic acid synthesis (Figure 7.7) is an efficient step with an atom utilisation of 100%, while step [2] has a lower atom utilisation of around 60%. Esterification and hydrolysis are both efficient processes.

Questions

1. Describe the process for the production of lactic acid derived from non-renewable fossil resource.
2. Identify the main economic, environmental and social issues associated with this process.
3. As shown in Figure 7.8, in step [1] of the synthesis reaction, lactonitrile is synthesised from the reaction of acetaldehyde and hydrogen cyanide ($HCN_{(g)}$). What are the risks and hazards associated with $HCN_{(g)}$ and how would they be minimised in a plant-scale operation?

Production of Lactic Acid from Renewable Resources

This process route is based on renewable resources such as molasses, corn syrup or sugar, which act as a source of carbohydrates used for the production of lactic acid. The manufacturing process consists of two stages: fermentation and purification of the lactic acid. The process is represented diagrammatically in Figure 7.9.

In the fermentation stage, the carbohydrates are converted into lactic acid by homolactic organisms of the genus *Lactobacillus* at elevated temperatures under anaerobic conditions. Proteinaceous and other complex nutrients are required by the bacteria for lactic acid production and can be provided by sources such as yeast extract and corn steep liquor.

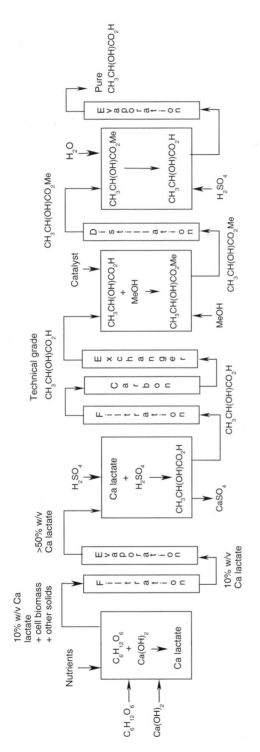

Figure 7.9 *Manufacturing process for the lactic acid derived from renewable resources*

Ca Lactate = $(CH_3CH(OH)COO^-)_2Ca^{2+}$

In general, the components involved in the fermentation process are:

1. *A suitable carbohydrate source*:   Substrates that have been used include corn, potato and rice starch, molasses, whey, cane sugar and beet sugar and dextrose (Kirk and Othmer, 1978; Datta *et al.*, 1995). The use of a carbohydrate source depends upon its price, availability and purity.
2. *Homolactic bacteria of the strain Lactobacillus*:   Common organisms are *L. delbrueckii, L. bulgaricus* and *L. leichmanii*. *Lactobacillus delbrueckii* has a thermophilic strain which exhibits optimum activity at approximately 50 °C and at a pH of 5.0–5.5. Fermentation at elevated temperatures avoids the need for the sterilisation of the growth medium by an autoclave step, which is normally required for most mesophilic fermentation systems. Instead, this system is sterilised by a simple pasteurisation step under pressure (Kirk and Othmer, 1978).
3. *Proteinaceous and other complex nutrients*:   These are required by the bacteria for the fermentation to occur and are provided by the addition of sources such as corn steep liquor or yeast extract (Datta *et al.*, 1995).
4. *Calcium carbonate*:   Calcium carbonate is added to produce calcium lactate, the calcium salt of the lactic acid in the broth which will be used in the separation stage to recover the lactic acid. Calcium lactate helps to keep the pH of the solution within the operating limit of 5.0–5.5, so as not to affect adversely the bacteria. However, in order to keep calcium lactate in solution, the concentration in the broth (an aqueous solution containing calcium lactate, microbial cells, proteinaceous material and other dissolved material) must be limited to 10% w/w. Keeping calcium lactate in solution is desirable as it allows the simple separation of the product from the insoluble materials in the broth, such as the cell biomass (i.e. the bacteria).
5. *Water*:   Fermentation reactions are generally run in aqueous media with a high dilution. The reason for this is that quite often the products of fermentation are toxic to the organisms and at high concentration would cause the process to slow down or stop altogether.

Fermentation is a batch process requiring between 4 and 6 days for completion. The following reaction describes the fermentation process:

$$C_6H_{12}O_6 + Ca(OH)_2 \xrightarrow{\text{Bacteria}} (CH_3CH(OH)COO^-)_2Ca^{2+}$$

Glucose   Calcium   Calcium lactate
         hydroxide

The calcium lactate yields are approximately 90% (w/w) based on the glucose contained in the carbohydrate source employed (Datta *et al.*, 1995). Currently, the best systems have a high yield (>90%) from carbohydrate source, together with a high product concentration (90 g/l). The best organism strains are stable and have a high productivity (>2 g/l/h of calcium lactate). The nutrients are derived from cheap sources such as corn steep liquor. Finally, the process has low energy and cooling demands because the fermentation is carried out under anaerobic conditions.

In the purification stage, the broth is filtered to remove solid materials (such as cell biomass) and then concentrated by evaporation of water to approximately 50% (w/w).

The concentrated solution is then treated with sulphuric acid to recover the lactic acid. The calcium released in this reaction precipitates as calcium sulphate, which is then removed by filtration to yield a low-value waste product, gypsum. Purification of the lactic acid can be described by the following reactions:

Production of acid from calcium lactate

$$(CH_3CH(OH)COO^-)_2Ca^{2+} + H_2SO_4 \longrightarrow CH_3CH(OH)CO_2H$$

Purification of acid as ester

$$CH_3CH(OH)CO_2H + MeOH \longrightarrow CH_3CH(OH)CO_2Me$$

Formation of pure lactic acid

$$CH_3CH(OH)CO_2Me \overset{H_2SO_4}{\longrightarrow} CH_3CH(OH)CO_2H$$

Approximately one tonne of calcium sulphate is produced per tonne of lactic acid. The crude lactic acid is further purified by treatment with activated carbon (to remove organic impurities) and by ion exchange (to remove heavy metals picked up from the feedstock). The lactic acid produced at this stage can be further evaporated to produce technical grade and food grade lactic acid; however, the product is not heat-stable and has limited uses because of this.

To produce a highly pure final product (for use in organic synthesis and as a monomer), it is necessary to produce the lactate ester. This is carried out in a similar way to the lactic acid process based on the non-renewable resource described earlier: the lactic acid is reacted with methanol or ethanol to produce the ester, which is recovered by distillation, hydrolysed by water and evaporated to yield the pure, heat-stable, final product. The alcohol released on hydrolysis is recycled.

Questions

1. Assuming an ideal fermentation process with the yield of 95% (w/w) based on the starch content of corn (30% w/w), the maximum concentration of calcium lactate tolerated in solution of 100 g/l and the productivity of 3 g/l/h of calcium lactate, find out:

   (a) How much corn, water and calcium carbonate is required to make one tonne of lactic acid?
   (b) How long does it take to make one tonne of lactic acid?

2. What are the major sustainability issues associated with the lactic acid process based on a renewable resource?
3. Discuss the advantages and disadvantages of producing the gypsum as a by-product in the purification stage of the production of the lactic acid.
4. Compare and contrast the sustainability issues for the lactic acid processes based on the non-renewable and renewable resources.

New Technological Advances

The majority of the technological advances that are expected to impact upon the sustainability of lactic acid manufacture from renewable resources are expected to arise in product purification. In this section we discuss two such techniques: the replacement of calcium carbonate with ammonium salts and the use of membranes for purification of the lactic acid.

Using ammonium instead of calcium salts

Ecochem (a DuPont–ConAgra partnership) has explored a process change, which could improve the economic sustainability of lactic acid manufacture. The innovation involves the avoidance of the production of calcium sulphate by the use of an ammonium salt instead of calcium carbonate in the initial fermentation stage. It is proposed that the waste ammonium salt could be sold as a low-cost fertiliser, improving the economics as well as environmental performance of the overall process (Datta *et al.*, 1995).

Questions

1. From a sustainability point of view, what are the advantages of producing a fertiliser as a by-product compared to a dedicated production of fertilisers?
2. Discuss the advantages and disadvantages of using the ammonium instead of calcium salts. Is gypsum a 'better' by-product than a nitrogen-based fertiliser or vice versa? Why?

Purification with membranes

New separation processes for lactic acid manufacture have been made possible through recent advances in membrane-based separation and purification technologies, particularly in the fields of ultra- and micro-filtration and electrodialysis. In a novel process which is not yet commercialised, the formation of calcium sulphate is avoided as the lactate is separated from the ammonium salt by electrodialysis. The process is shown diagrammatically in Figure 7.10.

In this process, fermentation occurs as described in the previous section. In the separation stage, the solution (containing large cell particles, microbial cells, calcium lactate salt and other dissolved materials) is then strained through a screen [3] where larger cell particles are removed. The calcium lactate salt solution, which also contains smaller microbial cells and other dissolved material, then enters the electro-dialysis unit. In the electrodialysis cells, the solution is subjected to an electrical current, which selectively causes the lactate anions to pass through an anionic-permeablen membrane into an ammonium lactate solution that circulates through the system. The feed solution minus the lactate ions is recirculated back to the fermentation tank where it can be used to produce further lactate salt. The concentrated ammonium lactate solution is then passed through the water-splitting electrodialysis apparatus where the ammonium lactate is converted to lactic acid. The collected lactic acid is passed through an ion exchanger to remove further impurities to yield a concentrated, high-purity lactic acid product (containing <1% proteinaceous

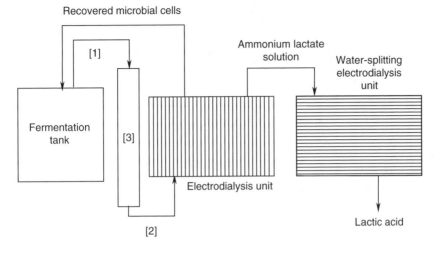

[1] Large cell particles, microbial cells, lactate salt, other dissolved material.
[2] Microbial cells, lactate salt, other dissolved materials.
[3] Screen to filter out larger particles.

Figure 7.10   *Purification of lactic acid by electrodialysis*

impurities). The ammonium containing effluent is recycled back to the electro-dialysis cells.

Questions

1. What are the major technological hurdles that need to be overcome in the production of lactic acid from a renewable resource?
2. Discuss how the recent technological advances can improve the economic and environmental sustainability of the lactic acid production?
3. The electrical power requirement for the electrodialysis steps is approximately 1 kWh/kg of lactic acid produced. If we assume that the concentration of the lactic acid in solution after the electrodialysis is 50% (w/v) in aqueous solution, how does this compare in power requirements to the necessity to evaporate the water to produce a 50% (w/v) in the conventional purification process. Take into account that at the end of the fermentation process a 10%(w/v) solution of calcium lactate is produced. Base your calculation on one tonne of lactic acid.

7.5.2 Polylactic Acid

Poly-3,6-dimethyl-1,4-dioxan-2,5-dione (herein referred to as PLA) is not a new polymer; it has been known since 1932 (Lunt, 1998). Simply removing the water from a concentrated solution of lactic acid can produce Low Molecular Weight PLA (LMWPLA). However, an LMWPLA has poor mechanical qualities so that at that point the polymer had no appreciable uses. High Molecular Weight PLA (HMWPLA) was first produced by DuPont (Lowe, 1954); however, at this stage hydrolytic instability of aliphatic polyester polymers was seen as a negative point (whereas biodegradability is today seen as an advantage) and research was discontinued. The only recorded use of PLA as a saleable product prior to recent developments is as a copolymer for uses in the medical and controlled-release (a material that slowly releases an active ingredient, such as a pesticide or a pharmaceutical product over a specific period of time) fields.

The advances in the lactic acid fermentation process, as we have discussed earlier, have a potential to reduce the cost of lactic acid. This, along with the biodegradability of PLA, has rekindled interest in the production of HMWPLA. In particular, Cargill-Dow has recently opened a 140 000 t/yr plant manufacturing HMWPLA from lactic acid derived from a renewable resource. In the next section we will examine this process in some detail.

Cargill-Dow HMWPLA Process

The chemistry and the process for the manufacture of HMWPLA from lactic acid derived from a renewable resource are shown schematically in Figures 7.11 and 7.12 respectively.

The feedstock used for the production of PLA is an aqueous solution of approximately 15% (w/v) lactic acid. The lactic acid is first concentrated in the evaporator to 85% (w/v) evaporating the water, which is then recycled back into the process.

The concentrated lactic acid is then transferred to the prepolymer reactor where more water is evaporated. This results in the polymerisation of lactic acid to

Reaction scheme

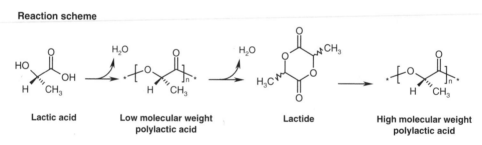

Lactic acid   Low molecular weight   Lactide   High molecular weight
                 polylactic acid   polylactic acid

Figure 7.11   *Chemical reactions in the production of high molecular weight PLA*

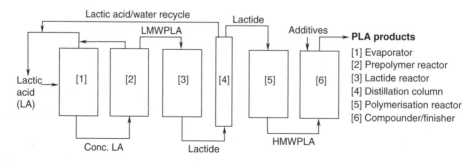

Lactic acid/water recycle   Lactide   Additives   → **PLA products**

LMWPLA

Lactic
acid
(LA)   [1]   [2]   [3]   [4]   [5]   [6]

Conc. LA   Lactide   HMWPLA

[1] Evaporator
[2] Prepolymer reactor
[3] Lactide reactor
[4] Distillation column
[5] Polymerisation reactor
[6] Compounder/finisher

Figure 7.12   *The Cargill-Dow process for the manufacture of PLA acid*

LMWPLA with the molecular weight between 400 and 2500. Because this is a condensation reaction, extra water is produced which must be removed.

The LMWPLA is then mixed with a catalyst (tin oxide or another appropriate catalyst) in a holding tank, which is held at a temperature where the LMWPLA remains in liquid form. From there, the LMWPLA is transferred to the lactide reactor to be catalytically depolymerised into the lactide, which is constantly removed, driving the equilibrium towards further lactide formation. The lactide has the potential to be one of three optical isomers, the L-, D- and meso-lactide, as shown in Figure 7.13.

You may remember from the discussion before that lactic acid exists as either L- or D-optical isomer. The majority of fermentation processes produce predominantly the L-isomer. Therefore, the lactide will predominantly be the L-type. However, under certain reaction conditions the lactic acid present in the reactor will begin to racemise, that is convert from one optical isomer into another, and thus some of the D-lactic acid will be formed. The presence of both L- and D-type of lactic acid will lead to the formation of some of the meso-lactide and possibly the D-lactide (Figure 7.13). As we will see later, this can have a profound effect on the physical properties of HMWPLA. Racemisation can be avoided by optimising the operating conditions in the reactor.

The lactide is then passed through a condenser to remove impurities, such as lactic acid and water, which may be recycled back to one of the evaporator steps. This is followed by a distillation step to separate the lactide from LMWPLA and lactic acid impurities, after which the lactide is transferred into the polymerisation reactor. In the reactor, a catalyst is added to facilitate polymerisation of the lactide to HMWPLA. As in the prepolymer reactor, the catalyst here is also tin-based (typical catalysts include tin-2-ethylhexanoate, tin octanoate and tetraphenyltin). A typical value of the molecular weight of the HMWPLA is 70 000; however, this value can be altered depending on process parameters. In the final stage, additives (such as plasticizers, flame-retardants, etc.) are added in the compunder/finisher to produce the final grade of polymer required for the desired application.

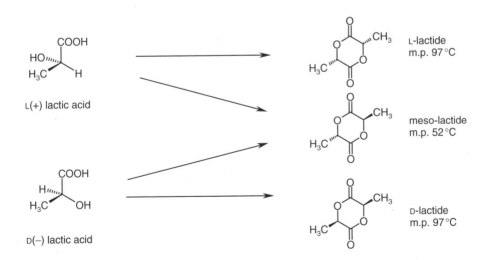

Figure 7.13 *Optical isomers of lactide*

PLA Properties

The properties of PLA will be determined by its intended application. One important property is its crystallinity, which will depend on the optical composition of the polymer. The use of pure lactide (L- or D-lactide) results in a highly crystalline polymer with a melting point of around 180 °C. The introduction of meso-lactide reduces the melting point to 130 °C and produces a more amorphous (less crystalline) polymer. In some applications, such as fibres and films, high crystallinity is desirable because the final products have greater chemical stability, higher strength and improved heat set compared to less crystalline PLA. However, from a processing point of view, a polymer which melts at a lower temperature, is also attractive as the transformation process is less energy-intensive and polymer degradation through hydrolysis and oxidation is reduced, as this process is temperature-dependant.

With respect to this and other physical properties, the HMWPLA is similar to polystyrene and PET. In particular, the PLA exhibits the following properties (Lunt, 1998):

- good flexural modulus (better than polystyrene);
- good resistance to fatty foods and dairy products (equivalent to PET);
- excellent flavour and aroma barrier;
- good heat sealability;
- excellent clarity and gloss for films (exceeds PET); and
- high surface energy allowing easy printability.

Furthermore, the properties of PLA can be changed by the inclusion of additives or by copolymerisation with another monomer. One example of an additive used is the plasticiser tri-acetyl *n*-butyl citrate, which is derived from a renewable resource. The use of this material means that film products can be blown and cast from the resultant polymer. This is important as it means that the entire product can be considered wholly renewable. Were the additives are sourced from a non-renewable resource, then this would not be the case.

Some of the properties of a PLA/ε-caprolactone copolymer are compared with the polystyrene properties in Table 7.1. Poly-ε-caprolactone is a biodegradable polymer, which is made from fossil fuel-derived ε-caprolactone. As Table 7.1 shows, the physical properties of the PLA copolymer are very close to those of polystyrene.

The wide range of properties of PLA means that it potentially can be used for several applications. In particular, it is anticipated that it will have two major uses (Cargill-Dow, 2003):

1. *Packaging* PLA can be formed into optically clear plastic packaging materials through a range of traditional techniques. In particular, it can be used in the consumer packaging, food packaging and also in serviceware (such as biodegradable plastic cups); and
2. *Fibres* PLA can be made into fibres which have natural flame-retardant properties. It can be used for apparel (clothing), carpet fibres, as a filler in furnishings and clothing, non-wovens and also in specialised industrial uses such as agrotextiles and specialist filtration media.

Table 7.1 *Comparison of the properties of PLA and polystyrene (Reprinted from FEMS Microbiology Reviews, Vol. 16, Datta et al., 'Technological and economic potential...', pp. 221–231, ©1995, with permission from Elsevier.)*

Parameter	Polystyrene	L-lactide/ε-caprolactone copolymer (95%/5%)
Tensile strength (psi)	7 000	6 900
Elongation (%)	2	1.6
Hardness, shore D	85	90
Specific gravity$^{20/4}$	1.08	1.26
DTA m.p. (°C)	130–200	160–170
Ease of moulding (°C)	Excellent	Good
Weather resistance	Good	Fair
Mineral acid	Resistant	Resistant
Caustic	Resistant	Attacked

Questions

1. What are the most important physical and chemical properties of PLA? How do these compare with the properties of PET and polystyrene?
2. Which applications could the PLA be used for? What polymer characteristics are required for these applications?
3. How do the additives or a copolymer change the properties of PLA?
4. Based on the discussion so far, summarise the main advantages of using PLA over other plastic materials?

Biodegradability of PLA

As we mentioned earlier, the hydrolytic instability of PLA was originally considered to be a drawback to its large-scale production. Today, however this hydrolytic instability, or biodegradability, is considered a major positive feature of this polymer. Essentially, the biodegradation pathway is through breaking the ester bonds between monomer units through a mechanism involving water adsorption. The rate of ester cleavage is dependent on the humidity and temperature. Microorganisms are not involved in the degradation pathway until the molecular weight of the polymer is reduced to approximately 10 000 (Lunt, 1998). This two-step mechanism differs slightly from the biodegradation process of other biodegradable polymers, where the degradation pathway is generally associated with the microorganisms only. For PLA this means the rate at which degradation occurs can be controlled by a control of the temperature and humidity that the polymer is exposed to. For instance, in a solution of water at 4 °C, PLA takes 123 months to start to biodegrade; and at 70 °C PLA takes 3.5 days to start to biodegrade. At 60 °C under composting conditions PLA takes 45 days to fully decompose (Lunt, 1998).

Question

1. From what you have learnt so far, which type of polymer appears to be more sustainable – the PLA or the conventional polymers? Why?

7.5.3   Sustainability Considerations: PLA or Conventional Plastics?

Environmental Considerations

Cargill-Dow, currently the sole industrial-scale manufacturers of HMWPLA, have recently carried out a Life Cycle Assessment (see the Appendix at the end of the book) of their product made by the process outlined in Figure 7.12. The PLA, licensed as Natureworks[TM], is manufactured in the USA at their facility in Blair, Nebraska (Vink *et al.*, 2003). In this study, the life cycle impacts of PLA manufacture have been compared to the impacts of conventional polymers derived from non-renewable resources.

Simplified life cycle flow diagrams for PLA and PET are outlined in Figures 7.14 and 7.16 respectively. As shown in the figures, the system boundary for both systems is drawn from 'cradle to gate' to include all activities from the extraction of raw materials to the production of the polymer. The basis for comparison is 1 kg of polymer produced.

In the case of PLA, the 'cradle' is growing and harvesting the corn crop while the 'gate' is the point at which the polymer is produced and ready to be delivered to the customer. The corn is grown in the USA in the same region where the PLA plant is based. In this process, the dextrose used in the fermentation process is produced only from corn starch. The dextrose is produced by an enzymatic hydrolysis step, where the polymer is broken down into smaller fragments by the action of α-amylase. For more details on the PLA manufacturing process assessed here, refer Figure 7.14.

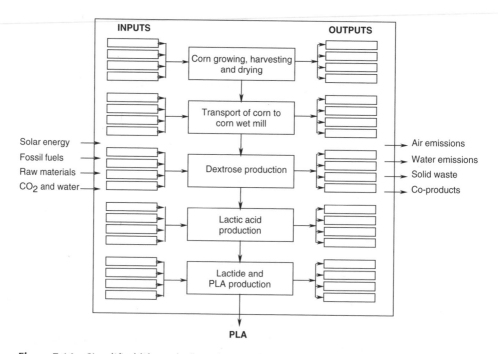

Figure 7.14   *Simplified life cycle flow diagram for PLA from 'cradle to gate'*

The life cycle of PET on the other hand starts with the extraction of crude oil, followed by its cracking and distillation to produce *p*-xylene (see 1 – direct esterification; 2 – ester interchange in Figure 7.4), which is then used as a raw material in the production of PET. Ethylene glycol, also used as a raw material in this process (Figure 7.15), is derived from either ethene (through reaction to ethylene oxide) or from formaldehyde (in reaction with carbon monoxide). Thus, like *p*-xylene, ethylene glycol is also made from a non-renewable fossil-based feedstock. The simplified life cycle flow diagram for the production of PET is shown in Figure 7.16. Selected life cycle impacts of the two polymers are compared in Figure 7.17 (Vink *et al.*, 2003).

As can be seen from the environmental impacts in Figure 7.17, PLA as manufactured currently has a greater energy demand and higher water usage compared

Formation of PET

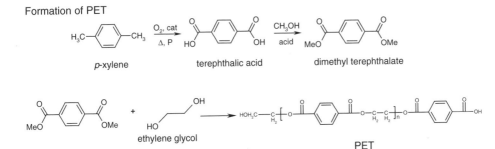

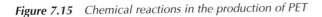

Figure 7.15 *Chemical reactions in the production of PET*

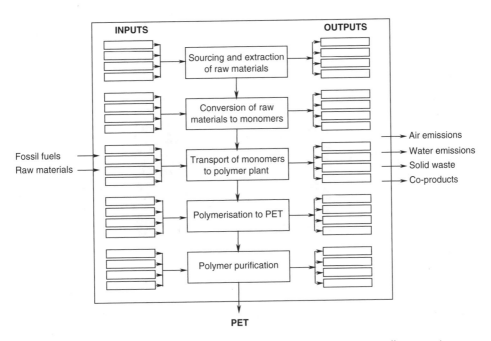

Figure 7.16 *Simplified flow diagram for the production of PET from 'cradle to gate'*

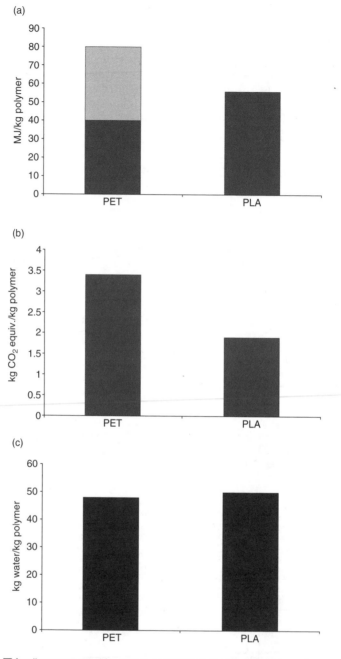

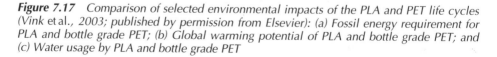

■ fossil resource used for energy generation in the life cycle of the polymer
▨ fossil resource used as a chemical feedstock to make the polymer

Figure 7.17 *Comparison of selected environmental impacts of the PLA and PET life cycles (Vink et al., 2003; published by permission from Elsevier): (a) Fossil energy requirement for PLA and bottle grade PET; (b) Global warming potential of PLA and bottle grade PET; and (c) Water usage by PLA and bottle grade PET*

to PET. However, because fossil-based feedstock is not used in the production process, the overall demand for fossil-based resources in the life cycle of PLA is lower, resulting in a lower overall contribution to global warming compared to PET.

To improve the level of environmental sustainability of the PLA life cycle, several modifications could be made to the PLA product system. These include:

1. the carbohydrate feedstock could be produced from a lignocellulosic feedstock such as corn stover (by-product of the corn industry);
2. the proteinaceous nutrients could be produced from the corn feedstock (such as corn steep liquor);
3. waste corn material (such as the straw, stover, etc.) could be used as a fuel to produce heat or electricity in the PLA manufacture; and
4. the energy for the production of PLA could be sourced from a renewable energy source such as wind power.

The effect of these four modifications on the total energy use and the associated global warming potential from the PLA system is shown in Figure 7.18.

Questions

1. The life cycle flow diagrams for the PLA and PET shown in Figures 7.14 and 7.16 respectively are incomplete as they do not include the individual inputs and outputs from each step of their respective processes. Complete both diagrams by specifying the inputs and outputs in each process step, including possible emissions and wastes.
2. Analyse the agricultural system that supports the production of corn from the life cycle perspective. What would be the main environmental and social impacts associated with a significant increase in the production of corn for non-food purposes?
3. Compare the life cycle impacts of PLA and PET shown in Figure 7.17. What do you conclude: which of the two polymers might be environmentally more sustainable?
4. Analyse the results in Figure 7.18 which shows the effect of the four PLA system modifications listed above on the energy use and global warming potential from PLA. What do you conclude – if these modifications are implemented, is PLA more environmentally sustainable for these impacts than PET? How feasible do you think these changes are?
5. What other changes could be made to the PLA product system that could potentially improve the environmental sustainability of the overall system?
6. With a particular emphasis on the feedstocks used in both the PLA and PET (and other conventional plastics) processes, comment critically on the relative reliability of supply of these feedstocks. Support your discussion by examples.
7. Compare and contrast the PET and PLA systems from 'cradle to gate' by drawing up a table of advantages and disadvantages for each system.

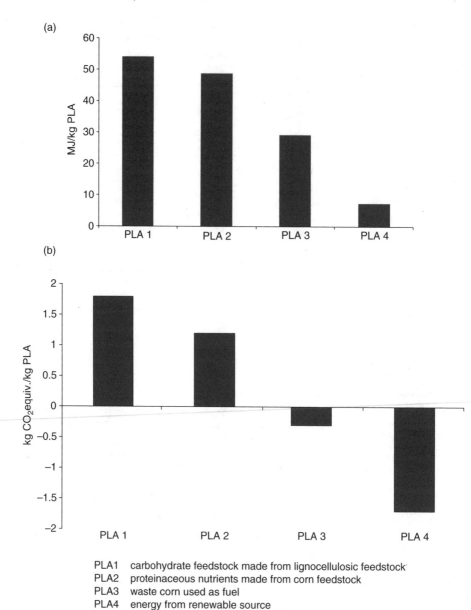

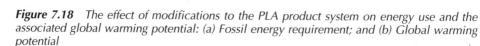

PLA1   carbohydrate feedstock made from lignocellulosic feedstock
PLA2   proteinaceous nutrients made from corn feedstock
PLA3   waste corn used as fuel
PLA4   energy from renewable source

Figure 7.18   *The effect of modifications to the PLA product system on energy use and the associated global warming potential: (a) Fossil energy requirement; and (b) Global warming potential*

Economic Considerations

We have already mentioned that there is a large potential market for lactic-acid-derived products. The range of products that can be manufactured from lactic acid is shown schematically in Figure 7.5.

However, compared to the conventional polymers, lactic acid is currently too expensive to be competitive. The cost of lactic acid production from a renewable feedstock is estimated at >$1/kg (~£0.8/kg) while the production costs of polylactic acid are estimated to be higher than $2/kg and perhaps as high as $4/kg. The market price of conventional fossil feedstock-based polymers, such as polyethylene is around $1.5/kg. Therefore, it is important to reduce the manufacturing costs of lactic and polylactic acids to increase their economic sustainability and thus their potential markets.

Theoretical studies based on experimental work have shown that the competitive target for the cost of lactic acid production is around $0.55/kg (Datta, 1995). This estimate was based on a renewable feedstock system incorporating many of the technological advances discussed earlier. It is also estimated that the costs of the production of polylactic acid can be reduced to <$2/kg through technological advances, reduced feedstock cost and the economies of scale. However, PLA production based on a renewable feedstock is still sensitive to seasonal variations in the cost of the carbohydrate source.

Questions

1. What factors affect the cost of the carbohydrate feedstock? How can this effect be minimised?
2. Could genetic modification (GM) of plants be used to reduce the cost of the feedstock? What are the issues associated with GM? You may consult Chapter 1 for further information on the GM debate.
3. Based on what you have learnt in this case study and on your background reading describe what you consider to be the major process improvements and innovations that will lead to a reduction in the cost of lactic and polylactic acid manufacture.
4. Draw a process flowsheet visualising how you perceive (based on current technology and any innovations you deem sensible) the optimum process for the production of PLA from lactic acid derived from a non-renewable feedstock.

Social Considerations

It is becoming widely acknowledged that products and companies must be assessed through a triple bottom line concept, which takes into account the economic, environmental and social performance (Chapter 11). In this case study we have examined both the environmental and economic considerations of PLA production, but not the social implications. Some of these social issues are explored in this section.

PLA can be considered a new polymeric material to the non-medical market and is therefore an unfamiliar product. The fact that PLA is also biodegradable, which can be considered an advantage in many respects, could be a critical marketing issue. For instance, if the product were to be used as a supermarket carrier bag, biodegradability would be something of great advantage compared to PE. However, if the product were to be used as a robust and long-lasting construction material (such as a window frame) then the 'will it last long enough before it starts degrading' syndrome would be prevalent amongst consumers. In launching a new and unfamiliar product such as PLA issues like these are absolutely critical.

The feedstock used by Cargill-Dow for PLA manufacture is genetically modified (GM) corn (has a higher than normal starch content). In the USA this is perfectly acceptable and would cause no overt problems. In Europe, however, this is a serious issue as GM foods and crops are viewed much more sceptically and it is quite likely (under current legislation) that companies would be unable to sell PLA made from GM corn starch within Europe. You may consult Chapter 1 for further discussion of the issue of GM food.

If PLA can be made in an environmentally sound manufacturing process, in so much as there is clear evidence that it has a substantially lower environmental impact compared to its competitor products (such as PET) then this could be used as a positive selling point. Whether this 'environmental edge' will lead to greater sales is ultimately dependent upon whether the market it is being sold in can be considered pro-environmental sustainability or neutral (as we assume that no market is overtly anti-environmental sustainability). A pro-environmental sustainability-led market will purchase the product based on its lower environmental footprint. A neutral market will ultimately buy the product only if it is either cheaper or more effective in a given use.

This leads to a further important issue, the cost of the final product. Cost will be critical, as a market will only be prepared to pay a certain premium for environmental performance (how much is dependent on the given country). Therefore, a new product, however 'environmentally friendly', could find itself simply too expensive to have a significant market impact.

Question

1. How should biodegradable plastics be marketed in order to increase its use? Discuss whether you think that they should be marketed as a competitively priced alternative to current plastics or whether they should be marketed as a more expensive, but 'environmentally friendly' alternative? Design a short (250 word maximum) press release based on your argument which could be released at the launch of a PLA product (of your choice).

Conclusions

Is it preferential to manufacture a plastic that will biodegrade in landfill conditions rather than one that will persist for many years? Is it more sustainable if a plastic is derived from a renewable feedstock rather than a non-renewable fossil-based feedstock? These are the sort of questions that have been posed in this case study – not to try and find a right or wrong answer, but rather to highlight the important sustainability issues and encourage life cycle thinking in considering these issues.

This case study puts the problems with the current plastics manufacturing industry into perspective and puts forward PLA as a potential solution to some of the sustainability issues associated with plastic materials. It is hoped that at the end of this exercise the reader will have an appreciation of the numerous issues associated with introducing a novel biodegradable plastic into an established market. It is not simply the case that a product will succeed because it can be branded 'sustainable' or 'green', but rather that it must be technologically sound, economically viable, as well as environmentally and socially acceptable.

Glossary

Autoclave   A strong steel vessel designed to work at high temperature and pressure. Often used for sterilising.

Crystallinity   Orientation of the disordered long-chain molecules of a polymer into repeating patterns. Degree of crystallinity effects stiffness, hardness, low temperature flexibility and heat resistance.

Electrodialysis   Dialysis at a rate increased by the application of an electric potential across the dialysis membrane, used especially to remove electrolytes from a colloidal suspension.

Flexural modulus   The ratio, within the elastic limit, of the applied stress on a test specimen in flexure to the corresponding strain in the outermost fibres of the specimen.

Mesophilic fermentation systems   A system where the bacteria performs best at a temperature between 25 and 45 °C.

Optical Activity   The ability of certain substances to rotate the plane of plane-polarised light as it passes through a crystal, liquid or solution. The property occurs when the molecules of a substance are asymmetric, existing in two different structural forms that are mirror images of each other (called optical isomers or enantiomers). One optical isomer will rotate the plane of polarised light in one direction, the other will rotate it by an equal amount in the opposite direction. An equimolar (equal proportion) of the optical isomers is called a *racemic mixture*. An organic molecule with an optically active centre is said to have a *chiral centre*. Lactic acid has a chiral centre.

Pasteurisation   A sterilisation process carried out by heating. The temperature and pressure required are generally lower than that used in an autoclave step.

Proteinaceous   Substances having a protein base, such as animal leather.

Stereoisomers   If two molecules have the same formula and structural groups, but differ in the arrangement of the groups, then they can be considered stereoisomers. Lactic acid exists as two stereoisomers.

Sterilisation   A high temperature (and sometimes pressure) treatment carried out to destroy microbes. Often carried out in an autoclave.

Thermophilic bacteria   Bacteria that is tolerant to heat, often requiring heating for maximum efficiency (bacteria work best at temperatures above 45 °C).

References

Aguado, J. and Ferrane, D. (1999) Feedstock Recycling of Plastic Wastes, Clark, J.H. ed., RSC Clean Technology Monographs, Cambridge.

Aldrich, 2003–2004, Handbook of Fine Chemicals and Laboratory equipment. Sigma-Aldrich, Dorset.

Azapagic, A., Emsley A. and Hamerton I. (2003) *Polymers, the Environment and Sustainable Development*. Wiley and Sons, Chichester.

Cargill-Dow (2003) Natureworks™ PLA, www.cargilldow.com, site last accessed on 27/08/03.

Cowie, J.M.G. (1991) *Polymers: Chemistry and Physics of Modern Materials*, 2nd Edition, Blackie Academic and Professional, London.

Datta, R. (1989) Recovery and Purification of Lactate Salts from Whole Fermentation Broth by Electrodialysis. United states Patent no. 4,885,247.

Datta, R., Tsai, S.-P., Bomsignore, P., Moon, S.-H. and Frank, J.R. (1995) Technological and Economic Potential of Poly (lactic acid) and Lactic Acid Derivatives. *FEMS Microbiology Reviews*, **16**, 221–231.

EC (1994) Council Directive 94/62/EC of 20 December 1994 on Packaging and Packaging Waste. *Offic. J. Eur. Communities*, L **365**, 10–23.

Galgali, P., Varma, A.J., Puntambekar, U.S., Digambar, V. and Gokhale, D.V. (2002) Towards Biodegradable Polyolefins: Strategy of Anchoring Minute Quantities of Monosaccharides and Disaccharides onto Functionalized Polystyrene, and their Effect on Facilitating Polymer Biodegradation. *Chem. Commun.*, No. **23**, 2884–2885.

Gebauer, M. and Hofmann, U. (1993) Proceedings of Recycle 1993, Davos, Switzerland.

Gomez, R. and Gil, J.R. (1997) Les Plasticos y el Tratamiento de sus Residues, UNED, Madrid.

Gradel, T.E. (2002) Green Chemistry and Technology, Clark, J.H. and Macquarrie, D.J. eds, Blackwell, Oxford.

Gruber, P.R., Hall, E.S., Kolstad, J.J., Iwen, M.L., Benson, R.D. and Borchardt, R.L. (1992) Continuous process for manufacture of lactide polymers with controlled optical purity, US Patent 5,142,023.

Hofvendahl, K. and Hahn-Hägerdal, B. (2000) *Enzyme and Microbial Technology*, Factors Affecting the Fermentative Lactic Acid Production from Renewable Resources, **26**(2–6), 87–107.

Kirk, R.E. and Othmer, D.F. (1978) *Encyclopedia of Chemical Technology*, 3rd Edition, Vol. 13, pp. 80–90.

Lester, T. (1996) Chem. Bytes, e-zine magazine, www.chemsoc.org/chembytes/ezine/1996/leser.htm (27/08/03).

Lowe, C.E. (1954) Preparation of high molecular weight polyhydroxyacetic ester, US Patent 2,668,162 (to DuPont).

Lunt, J. (1998) Polymer Degradation and Stability, **59**, 145–152.

Nikles, S.M., Piao, M., Lane, A.M. and Nikles, D.E. (2001) Green Chemistry, **3**, 109–113.

Stevens, E.S. (2002) *Green Plastics – An introduction to the New Science of Biodegradable Plastics*. Princeton University Press, Princeton, New Jersey.

SUFRES Conseil for APME (1998) Plastics: A material of Choice for the 21st century, APME, Brussels.

Symphony Environmental Ltd (2003) Chemistry and Degradation Process, www.degradable.net, site last accessed on 27/08/03.

Vink, E.T.H., Rabago, K.R., Glassner, D.A. and Gruber, P.R. (2003) Applications of Life Cycle Assessment to Natureworks™ Polylectide (PLA) Production. *Polymer Degradation and Stability*, **80**(3), 403–419.

8

An Industrial Ecology: Material Flows and Engineering Design

David T. Allen

Summary

The materials used in industrialised economies average 40–80 t/person per year. Whether we express this personal consumption as a tonne per week or a body weight per day, it amounts to staggering quantities of materials, most of which are used once, then discarded. An alternative to designing industrial systems that use materials once is to design industrial ecosystems that mimic the mass conservation properties of natural ecosystems. In industrial ecosystems, the wastes and by-products from one industrial process would be used as the raw materials for another. Are such systems realistic? Do they exist now? How could they be designed? This chapter will address these questions, which will be among the science and engineering challenges for the next century.

8.1 Introduction

[Selected passages in this Chapter are reproduced from an article in *Chem. Eng. Progress*, Nov. 2002, 40–45]

A compelling image, which reinforces basic concepts of sustainability, is our planet's appearance from space. The planet appears as a brightly lit jewel of colour, isolated in a black, vacuous expanse. It is a powerful image because it highlights the fact that the biosphere is an isolated system with finite amounts of materials. Vast amounts of energy are available, but only if we utilise solar energy rather than harvesting energy derived from materials.

Sustainable Development in Practice: Case Studies for Engineers and Scientists
Edited by Adisa Azapagic, Slobodan Perdan and Roland Clift
© 2004 John Wiley & Sons, Ltd   ISBNs: 0-470-85608-4 (HB); 0-470-85609-2 (PB)

One of the most significant challenges for future generations of engineers and scientists will be to convert these and other very general concepts of sustainability into principles of design for our built environment. Many of these design principles are appearing in the emerging field of Industrial Ecology. In its most common usage, the term "Industrial Ecology" refers to the idea that nature (specifically, nature at its higher levels of organisation such as communities and ecosystems) can serve as a useful metaphor for industrial systems. Drawing on biological analogies may help industry become more efficient and more sustainable. A commonly cited example is the flow of nutrients (materials) in natural ecosystems, where waste from one organism becomes the food for others, creating a web of interrelated processes that effectively recycle nutrients on a continuous basis. Industrial ecologists view this as a potential model for industrial systems where the waste from one process becomes the feedstock for the next. Applied more broadly, the term encompasses the analysis of industrial systems, using tools analogous to those used in the analysis of ecosystems, to gain insight into the role that technologies, companies or industry sectors play within the so-called "industrial ecosystems".

Perhaps the most powerful images evoked by the phrase "Industrial Ecology" are those of industrial systems that mimic the mass conservation properties of natural ecosystems. Chemical processes in an ideal industrial ecosystem would use the wastes and by-products of other processes, and the entire industrial system would require only energy inputs and no mass inputs. Are such systems realistic? Do they exist now? How could they be designed? This chapter will address these questions, which will be among the science and engineering challenges for the next century. But before examining the details of these systems, it is useful to characterise the magnitude and basic structure of the flows of materials at regional, national and global scales.

8.2   An Overview of Material Flows

Extraction and use of materials at regional, national and global scales have been tracked for more than a century. In the United States, systematic efforts to track mineral and commodity flows began in the 19th century, and have been gradually expanded to include additional material flows, such as environmental emissions. These mineral and commodity material flow data have been used to answer questions such as:

> Where were the metals and construction materials needed to supply the growth of manufacturing, cities, housing and highways? Where were the energy resources to keep transportation moving, keep the machinery turning, and keep us warm in winter and cool in summer? Where were the alternate sources of supply or substitutes for strategic materials?
>
> *National Research Council, 2003*

Material flow data, collected to answer questions about resource use, focused primarily on material inputs to the economy and the primary industrial processing of minerals and metals. It is beyond the scope of the chapter to present a comprehensive description of the US material flows, but readers interested in this information can find data on total material flows (Adriaanse *et al.*, 1997; Matthews *et al.*, 2000), flows of specific materials (US Geological Survey, 2003), and flows within industrial sectors

(US Census of Manufactures, 2003) in recent literature. Today, however, new types of issues are being addressed with material flow data. These include:

What fuel infrastructures should a next generation transportation system rely on? What are the economic, material flow, energy flow and environmental implications of nanotechnologies and biotechnologies? What should be the disposition of electronic products at the end of their useful life?

National Research Council, 2003

Answering these types of questions requires both data on commodity material and mineral flows entering the economy, and information on the wastes, emissions and recycling structures. Data that enable this new generation of analyses are just emerging. Therefore terminology and data-analysis frameworks are still evolving. One set of terminology is shown in Figure 8.1.

As shown in Figure 8.1, material flow analyses are performed on defined systems. The system boundary might be the geopolitical boundaries of a nation, the natural boundaries of a river's drainage basin, or the technological boundaries of a cluster of industries. The headings for the system inputs and outputs used in Figure 8.1 suggest that the system is a nation, but these inputs and outputs (domestic extraction, imports and exports) could be labelled feedstocks and products, and the system would then appear to be a cluster of industries.

Figure 8.1 also identifies material inputs, material outputs, releases to the environment and material storage and cycling within the system as components of the

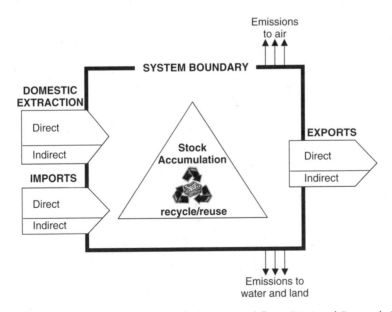

Figure 8.1 *Conceptual framework for analysing material flows (National Research Council, 2003; reprinted with permission from Materials Count: the Case for Material Flows Analysis (2003) and The Greening of Industrial Ecosystems (1994) by the National Academy of Sciences, courtesy of the National Acadamies Press, Washington, DC.)*

material flow analysis. The system inputs and outputs are divided into direct and indirect flows. Direct flows are those that are normally accounted for in scientific and engineering analyses, such as fuels, minerals, metals and water. The indirect, or hidden, flows shown in Figure 8.1 are composed of materials such as mining over-burdens and soil erosion from agricultural operations. These hidden material flows do not enter the economic system, yet occur as the result of economic activity. Within the system, stocks are accumulated and materials are reused and recycled. As flows internal to the system are re-engineered to incorporate more reuse and recycling, releases to air, water and land can be reduced and demands for inputs are reduced.

8.2.1 Magnitudes of Material Flows

Using the framework outlined in Figure 8.1, overall material flows at national scales can be examined. In most industrial economies, per capita material use is approximately 40–80 t/yr. As shown in Figure 8.2, the hidden flows defined in Figure 8.1 constitute a significant fraction of the total material displacement of industrial economies, but in general, there is relatively little information available about these flows. In the United States, the extraction of metals and minerals, including fossil fuels, erosion and infrastructure excavation, contribute significantly to the hidden flows (Adriaanse *et al.*, 1997).

Of the materials that directly enter the US economy annually, roughly 7–8 t per capita can be considered as additions to material stocks. These stock additions are primarily materials associated with housing, and the construction and maintenance of transportation infrastructure. These material flows constitute roughly 10% of all material flows (hidden and direct) and roughly a third of the direct material inputs to the economy. Addition of durable goods is a relatively minor contributor to total material flows and somewhat counter-intuitively, most material flows in the United States are domestic (Matthews *et al.*, 2000).

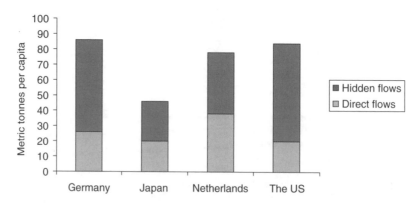

Figure 8.2 *Total annual material usage, per capita in industrial economies (Based on data from Adriaanse et al., 1997.)*

Questions

1. What materials make up the bulk of direct and indirect flows?
2. Why are there differences of upto a factor of two between different industrialised nations in the amount of materials used per capita?

8.2.2 Wastes as Raw Materials

As documented above, most of the 40–80 t of material, per capita, used by the US each year passes through the economic system and appears as waste or emissions. Over the past decade, summaries of waste flows in the United States have been published by a number of authors (e.g. Allen and Jain, 1992; Allen and Rosselot, 1997 and references cited therein) and those summaries will not be repeated here. Instead, our focus will be on the potential reprocessing and reuse of these materials and identifying the type of information that is necessary to assess whether wastes really can be used as raw materials.

One of the most important pieces of information needed in assessing the potential for reusing materials in waste streams is the composition of the material. As shown in Figure 8.3, the value of a resource is proportional to the level of dilution at which

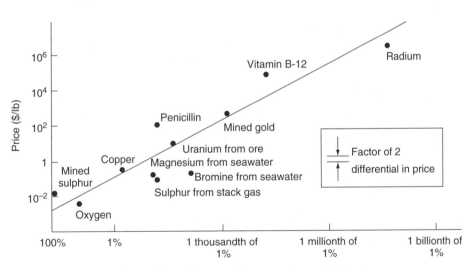

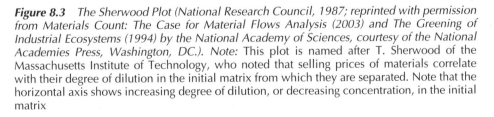

Figure 8.3 *The Sherwood Plot (National Research Council, 1987; reprinted with permission from Materials Count: The Case for Material Flows Analysis (2003) and The Greening of Industrial Ecosystems (1994) by the National Academy of Sciences, courtesy of the National Academies Press, Washington, DC.). Note: This plot is named after T. Sherwood of the Massachusetts Institute of Technology, who noted that selling prices of materials correlate with their degree of dilution in the initial matrix from which they are separated. Note that the horizontal axis shows increasing degree of dilution, or decreasing concentration, in the initial matrix*

valuable materials are present. Materials that are present at very low concentration can be recovered only at high cost, while materials present at high concentration can be recovered economically. Therefore, in evaluating whether wastes might be mined as raw materials, it is necessary to determine both the mass and the concentration of valuable materials in the waste.

As a simple case study of evaluating the potential use of industrial wastes as raw materials, consider the flows of metals in hazardous waste streams. The Sherwood plot (Figure 8.3) shows that whereas materials such as gold and radium can be recovered from raw materials that are quite dilute in the resource, materials such as copper can be recovered economically only from relatively rich ores. The price of a metal can therefore be used to estimate the approximate concentration at which the metal can be recovered from a waste stream. The approximate concentration at which metals can be effectively recovered from wastes can then be compared to the actual concentrations of the materials in the wastes. Allen and Behmanesh (1994) used this criterion to assess whether metals in hazardous waste streams in the US could be more effectively recycled and reused. Hazardous wastes were chosen because detailed data existed on their compositions, flow rates and fates. Surprisingly, many hazardous waste streams contain relatively high concentrations of metals. Approximately 90% of the copper and 95% of the zinc found in hazardous wastes are at a concentration high enough to recover. Table 8.1 shows that the situation for copper and zinc is not unusual. In fact, for every metal for which data existed, recovery occurred at rates well below rates that would be expected to be economically viable.

This very focused analysis, which was initially performed in 1994 (Allen and Behmanesh, 1994), led to the conclusion that many opportunities existed for recovering materials from wastes. There are limitations to the analysis, however.

Table 8.1   *Percentage of metals in hazardous wastes in the US that can be recovered economically (as estimated by Allen and Behmanesh, 1994)*

Metal	Theoretically recoverable (%)	Recycled in 1986 (%)
Sb	74–87	32
As	98–99	3
Ba	95–98	4
Be	54–84	31
Cd	82–97	7
Cr	68–89	8
Cu	85–92	10
Pb	84–95	56
Hg	99	41
Ni	100	0.1
Se	93–95	16
Ag	99–100	1
Tl	97–99	1
V	74–98	1
Zn	96–98	13

The analysis focused only on hazardous wastes, where legal liability concerns may limit the desire to recycle. The identification of "recyclable" streams was simplistic. It ignored issues related to economies of scale (i.e. processing geographically dispersed, heterogeneous waste streams may be more expensive than extracting a relatively homogeneous ore from a single mine). Nevertheless, the analysis indicated that resources are not effectively recovered from many waste streams. One of the primary barriers to using wastes as raw materials is a lack of critical information on waste streams. While a large number of data sources are available on waste streams, they lack critical information that is needed to assess whether waste streams might be reused. Data on the composition of wastes, their location and co-contaminants are rarely available, yet are critical to evaluating the potential use of wastes as raw materials. For example, no updated data (post-1986) on metal concentrations in hazardous wastes are available to update the information in Table 8.1. Nevertheless, this simple case study illustrates the potential for finding uses for wastes as raw materials.

Question

1. In a free market economy, why would valuable materials be discarded as wastes?

8.2.3   Tracking Specific Materials

Another approach to identifying potential uses of wastes as raw materials is to follow material flows (as opposed to waste flows) and to examine how the materials are incorporated into products or dissipated into the environment. The flows of silver in the San Francisco Bay area provide an interesting case study of this approach (Kimbrough *et al.*, 1995).

Because of its ecotoxicity, very strict waste water discharge limits are placed on silver in the San Francisco Bay area. Yet, despite these strict limits, silver discharges were still a problem, and the source of the problem did not become clear until the material flows of silver were examined.

In the United States, approximately 4000 t of silver are consumed annually. Slightly over 50% of this usage is in photographic and radiographic materials, and a large fraction of this silver becomes part of a waste stream, typically as silver halides in developer solutions. The silver halides in developer solutions are typically at concentrations high enough to be regulated and high enough to be economically recycled. Yet, a large fraction of developer solution is not recycled because it is generated, in quantities of 5 gall./month or less, by small waste generators (primarily medical and dental offices). In California these small waste generators could economically recycle the silver in their developing solution, however, to do so would have required paying a regulatory fee of around $125 to pick up the spent developer solution. If assaying and refining fees were added to the hauling cost, the total transaction cost became about $200. So, a silver waste generator had to process over $200 worth of silver to make recycling economical. This would mean processing approximately 250 gall. of developer with a silver loading of 1 g/l. Because most facilities generated only about 5 gall. of developer per month, storing enough solution for economical recycling was impractical. A variety of on-site silver recovery technologies are available and could be alternatives to hauling silver off-site for recovery. Until recently, however, small generators in California that treated such waste on site had to obtain permits that cost approximately $1000 for the first year and $500 each year thereafter. This meant that the generator had to recover the silver present in an approximately 1250 gall. of developer fluid just to recoup the first year's permitting fee. The easiest solution was to simply send spent developer solution down the drain.

In this example, regulatory fees presented a significant barrier to silver recovery for medical and dental offices, but restructuring the regulatory approach for these generators resulted in a significant increase in silver recovery. Only by tracking the flows of silver were policy-makers able to identify actions needed to reduce silver discharges.

Another example of the potential value of following flows of materials is the case of mercury. In this case the goal is to remove mercury, as much as possible, from industrial systems. As shown in Figure 8.4, mercury use has decreased dramatically in recent years, however, residual releases of mercury still occur. In the Unites States, to reduce mercury emissions further, releases of mercury in the stack gases of coal-fired power plants are likely to be controlled. It is anticipated that reducing mercury releases from coal-fired power plants will reduce the atmospheric deposition of mercury, and therefore the concentration of methyl mercury in aquatic systems and sediments, and the accumulation of mercury in the food chain. Figure 8.4 also shows an overview of mercury flows into the environment in the United States.

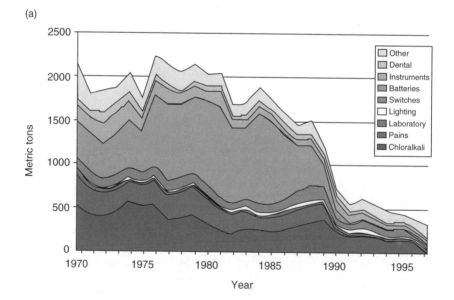

Figure 8.4 *Continued*

(b)

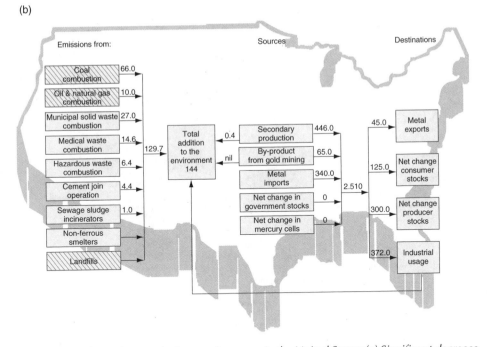

Figure 8.4   *Industrial use and releases of mercury in the United States: (a) Significant decrease in the industrial use of mercury; and (b) Sources of mercury release into the environment. (Sznopek and Goonan, 2000)*

In this assessment, mercury releases from coal-fired power plants are now the dominant source of releases.

These are national average flows, however, and there are gaps in the information. Therefore, in order to get a more complete picture of the flows of mercury that could lead to bioaccumulation, more complete data at a regional level are needed. The New York Academy of Sciences (de Cerreño *et al.*, 2002) performed such a study for the New York Harbor. The watershed that feeds the New York Harbor is shown in Figure 8.5 and the sources of mercury releases into the watershed are shown in Figure 8.6.

Figure 8.6 shows that the majority of mercury entering the Harbor comes through waste water, and Figure 8.7 shows the distribution of contributors to mercury in waste water. The surprising finding from this study is that mercury in waste waters, associated with the use of mercury containing dental amalgams, is the largest contributor to mercury loadings in New York Harbor. The policy consequence of this finding is that reducing mercury emissions from coal-fired power plants, which may be an effective strategy at a national level, is not likely to be effective in significantly reducing mercury in New York Harbor. Instead, policies designed to educate and change the practices of dentists and hospitals may be the most cost-effective approach.

These simple case studies have demonstrated that material flows in industrial economies are substantial, that wastes may have the potential to be used as raw

Watersheds of the Hudson River Basin

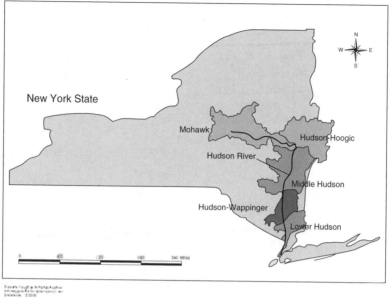

Figure 8.5   *Watershed for the New York Harbor/Hudson River used as the system boundary in examining mercury flows (de Cerreño et al., 2002; © 2002 New York Academy of Sciences.)*

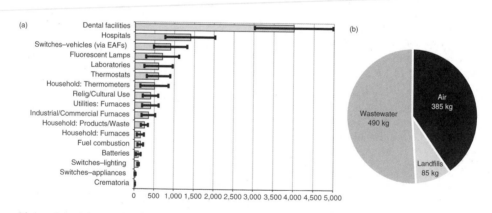

Figure 8.6   *Mercury in the New York Harbor: (a) Relative magnitudes of mercury sources (all media); and (b) Relative contribution to methyl mercury by emissions from air, water and land (de Cerreño et al., 2002; © 2002 New York Academy of Sciences.)*

materials, and that insights gained from analysing material flows at regional and national scales can provide important material policy insights. This motivates a more detailed analysis of local, regional and national material flows; section 8.3 describes some local-scale engineering systems analyses of the use of wastes as raw materials

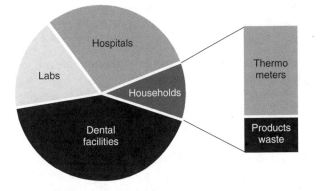

Figure 8.7 *Sources of mercury emissions to waste waters in the Hudson River drainage (de Cerreño et al., 2002; © 2002 New York Academy of Sciences.)*

and briefly describes some of the scientific and engineering tools that are available for these analyses.

Questions

1. What policies might be used to reduce mercury flows into New York Harbor?
2. Can the data on mercury flows entering New York Harbor be generalised to other regions?
3. Using the information available in online reports from the US Geological Survey (available at http://minerals.usgs.gov/minerals/pubs/mcs/), develop a material flow analysis for mercury in the United States.

   (a) Determine all sources of inputs.
   (b) Identify the relative fractions of mercury use that are employed in durable products and that are released into the environment.
   (c) Determine if the masses into and out of the system are in balance.
   (d) What policy strategies might most effectively reduce mercury concentrations?

4. Using the information available in online reports from the US Geological Survey (available at http://minerals.usgs.gov/minerals/pubs/mcs/), develop a material flow analysis for arsenic in the United States.

   (a) Determine all sources of inputs.
   (b) Identify the relative fractions of arsenic use that are employed in durable products and that are released into the environment; estimate the lifetime of durable products and estimate the stocks of arsenic present in these products.
   (c) Determine if the masses into and out of the system are in balance.
   (d) What policy strategies might most effectively be used to reclaim the arsenic in durable products, preventing their release into the environment?

5. Using the information available in on-line reports from the US Geological Survey (available at http://minerals.usgs.gov/minerals/pubs/mcs/), develop a material flow analysis for cadmium in the United States.

   (a) Determine all sources of inputs. Is cadmium mined directly or is it a by-product of other mining operations?
   (b) Identify the relative fractions of cadmium use that are employed in durable products and that are released into the environment; estimate the lifetime of durable products and estimate the stocks of cadmium present in these products. Does cadmium enter the environment through use in products in which it is not intentionally added?
   (c) Determine if the masses into and out of the system are in balance.
   (d) What impact would reducing the use of cadmium in durable goods likely have on cadmium flows? (Recall your answer to Part (a))
   (e) What policy strategies might most effectively be used to reduce the release of cadmium into the environment?

8.3   Material Flows: Engineering and Scientific Analyses and Tools

The previous section described analyses performed at national and regional scales, and demonstrated, in principle, potential uses of material flow information. However, changing the designs of products and processes so that the industrial system more closely resembles a highly networked, mass conserving, natural ecosystem requires much more detailed analyses. The remainder of this chapter will describe case studies of emerging industrial ecosystems, and some of the engineering and scientific tools that are emerging to guide industrial ecosystem development.

8.3.1   Case Studies[1]

The case studies of emerging industrial ecosystems are drawn from the work of the US Business Council for Sustainable Development. Interested readers can view their website for more information (www.usbcsd.org). A case study from the United States involves a group of facilities in north Texas led by the Chaparral Steel Company. As described by the US BCSD:

> In the early 1990s, managers of Chaparral Steel began exploring synergies between the company's operations and the operations of its parent company, Texas Industries, a manufacturer of Portland cement. One of the most successful synergies discovered was the potential for steel slag to be used as a raw material for the cement. The steel slag contained dicalcium silicate (calcined lime), formed by the high temperatures of the steel-making process and also a building block of Portland cement. By using the steel slag instead

---

[1] Text of section 8.3.1 is reproduced by permission of United States Business Council for Sustainable Development.

of purchased lime, which would then have to be heated to calcination, Texas Industries reduced the energy requirements and related emissions (CO_2, NO_x, SO_2) of the cement making process. Profits for both companies also increased.

US BCSD, 2003

Additional by-product synergies, as these material and energy exchanges are called by the US BCSD, are listed in Table 8.2. Another case study of by-product synergy can be found in Alberta, Canada. As noted by the US BCSD (2003), Alberta has

more than 60 percent of Canada's proven reserves of conventional crude oil, 85 percent of its natural gas, 63 percent of its coal, and all of its oil sands reserves. It has one of the world's most productive agricultural economies and its third largest primary economic sector is forestry. The challenge was to find ways of ensuring that this natural resource-based economy remains competitive and productive in an increasingly global economy.

Two important aspects of the Alberta situation emerged. First, the participants were relatively homogeneous – many had similar by-products. Secondly, Alberta's economy on a whole was largely extractive, with relatively low raw materials costs, which limits and creates significant competition for potential by-product synergies. Within the oil and gas sector, which was heavily represented in the project, it was evident that most of the "low-hanging fruit" had already been picked, and that the exploitation of new synergies would require a committed effort, and the involvement of new participants and business relationships.

During the BPS [By-product synergy] project, representatives of two facilities, a Weyer-haeuser Kraft mill and a Husky refinery, discovered that the spent caustic (NaOH with contaminants) from the refinery could potentially be used in the Kraft process to make up for Na losses. The idea was tested, negotiated and implemented in January 2000. The refinery trucks that were transporting spent caustic to injection sites began shipping the material to Weyerhaeuser's plant for reuse instead. The savings for the two companies was estimated at $300,000 per year plus significant operation and maintenance savings at Weyerhaeuser.

A total of 25 possible synergy opportunities were selected by the participants to pursue under five main classifications: energy, inorganics, sulphur and high-sulphur coke, indus-trial gases and eco-industrial parks. The project required the participating companies to rethink the notion of what constitutes waste, and what can, in fact, be reused.

Many more examples of emerging by-product synergies, from around the world could be cited, however, these two examples sufficiently illustrate the potential profitability of redesigning industrial networks so that they are more mass-efficient than current systems.

Question

1. Identify chemical processes that produce and consume hydrochloric acid or chlorine. Identify possible reprocessing and reuse networks for industrial uses of HCl.

Table 8.2 Annual cost and environmental benefits of successful synergies

Implemented synergies	Ecological/Biological	Energy savings	Residue reduction	Cost savings
CemStar® 130 000 t of steel slag used in place of lime (single plant operation)	Reduced SO_2 (acid rain) through coal displacement	Displacement of 11 800 t of coal used to calcined lime	130 000 t of steel slag not landfilled; *Emission reductions from coal displacement* 65 000 t CO_2, 800 t of NO_x and 33 t of hydrocarbons	*Steel producer* Value added to steel slag; Reduced/eliminated slag; and treatment/disposal costs *Cement producer* Less costly raw material; Calcination is not required $\rightarrow$ energy consumption and associated emissions for cement production are reduced
Auto Shredder Residue (ASR) 120 000 t of ASR mined for metal reclamation and ASR remaining after metal recovery used for power generation	Reduced SO_2 (acid rain) through coal displacement	18 000 t of metals (Al, Cu, Mg, Sn) recovered from ASR and not mined; 98 000 t of carbon-based ASR displaces 66 000 t of coal for power generation	120 000 t of ASR not landfilled; Energy savings associated with metal recovery vs mining prevent 151 000 t of CO_2 emissions; and SO_2 emissions reduced by substitution of ASR for coal	*ASR producer* Reduction/elimination of ASR disposal fees; Increased revenue from recovered metals; and Revenue from sale of ASR as alternative fuel *ASR consumers* Lower cost, less energy intensive method of obtaining metals; and Lower cost fuel

Graphite/Copper sludge £37 500 (17 t) of sludge saved from landfills and municipal water systems	Landfill biota not exposed to toxicity of copper waste	£18 750 (9 t) of copper recovered and not mined	£37 500 (17 t) of graphite/copper sludge not landfilled; 412 500 gall. (1.6×10^6 l) of graphite-/copper-tainted waste water not released to municipal waste water treatment	Sludge producer Reduced/eliminated waste disposal fees; Revenue from sale of sludge to copper extraction company
				Metal recovery company Lower cost source of copper

8.3.2   Engineering and Scientific Tools

Designing for mass efficiency is not a new idea, of course. It has been practised for decades by chemical engineers and very sophisticated tools are available foroptimising mass use within processes (e.g. El-Halwagi, 1997). These traditional approaches to engineering design, however, tend to focus on modelling and optimisation of flows *within a process* rather than the flow of materials and energy *between processes*. Of course, the distinction between these problems is a subtle one, depending in large part on where the "box" is drawn around the process. Traditional tools of mass optimisation will almost certainly prove essential in moving to the next scale of process integration, but the design of industrial ecosystems is also likely to require the development of entirely new tools, some of which are just now emerging.

Perhaps the most mature and certainly the most widely cited industrial ecology design and analysis tool in the United States is Bechtel's (now Nexant's) Industrial Materials Exchange (IME) tool. The IME is intended to aid in the identification and analysis of the so-called "by-product synergies" (opportunities to use wastes from one product as feedstocks for another process). Unlike the other tools discussed here, the IME is not available to users outside Nexant, which views the tool as a valuable asset for aiding their engineers and planners in designing more profitable and more tightly integrated industrial facilities.

The IME tool has been used in several high-profile industrial ecosystem projects, including the Brownsville/Matomoros Regional Industrial Symbiosis project, and the Tampico, Mexico effort facilitated by the Business Council for Sustainable Development – Gulf of Mexico (US BCSD, 2003).

A tool which is conceptually similar to the IME is the US EPA's Designing Industrial Ecosystems Tool (DIET) tool kit, developed in cooperation with Environmental Protection Agency (EPA) by Clark University and Industrial Economics Inc., a Boston (USA) consulting firm. This prototype industrial ecology tool kit is designed to help users identify, screen and optimise by-product utilisation opportunities at the regional scale. The tool kit consists of three interrelated components:

1. The Facility Synergy Tool (FaST) is a database application which helps a user identify potential matches between non-product outputs (NPOs) and the material and energy requirements of common industrial processes. This allows the user to quickly identify potential by-product synergies between facilities. The tool can also be used to identify the types of industrial partners that should be recruited to serve as "sinks" for waste streams from existing facilities.
2. The Designing Industrial Ecosystems Tool uses the by-product synergy matches identified in the FaST database tool as inputs to a linear programming model which generates optimum scenarios for industrial synergies. DIET allows the user to simultaneously optimise the system for environmental, economic and employment objectives.
3. RealityCheck™ is a screening tool used to identify potential regulatory, economic and logistical constraints (barriers) to by-product utilisation opportunities. Though originally designed as an integral part of the industrial ecology tool kit, it can be used as a stand-alone tool.

The DIET tool kit illustrates a potential approach to the design and optimisation of eco-industrial parks by helping the user to identify and evaluate potential by-product synergies within an existing regional network of industrial facilities. Unfortunately, EPA has no current plans to complete the development of the tools.

One of the practical barriers to the widespread implementation of waste water stream utilisation schemes is the high cost of transporting the materials from their source to other facilities that may be able to use the materials as feedstocks. Since the cost of transporting these materials can often be prohibitive, it seems reasonable to expect that the tools used to design industrial ecosystems should be able to take transportation costs into account. Unfortunately, this is not always the case.

An interesting exception is an industrial ecology planning tool developed at the University of Texas. The tool incorporates a Geographic Information System (GIS) to help identify feasible water reuse networks and to allow transportation costs to be explicitly included in the optimisation of these networks. Once a user has entered information about facilities in the region of study into the GIS, the model matches waste water characteristics of facilities with the feedwater requirements of other facilities in the region. By matching streams with compatible water quality criteria, the model identifies feasible water reuse opportunities within the region of study. Since any individual waste water stream may have several potential uses, the feasible matches are passed to a linear programming module to calculate the optimal water reuse scenario.

This tool was used to identify and optimise water use and reuse opportunities within a complex of approximately 20 different industrial facilities at the Baytown Industrial Complex in Pasadena, Texas (Keckler and Allen, 1998; Nobel and Allen, 2000). In this relatively simple example, economically feasible water reuse networks were identified that had the potential to reduce total freshwater use by more than 90% while simultaneously reducing water costs by 20%. The tool was developed using commercial "off-the-shelf" GIS software and a widely available mathematical optimisation package. And, although the tool was developed specifically to illustrate the optimisation of industrial water reuse networks, the underlying approach can be extended to other industrial materials with relatively little additional effort.

It should be pointed out that none of these tools are widely available. Industrial ecology is still in its infancy and many of the tools that have been developed are prototype versions built to illustrate or explore key ideas about how to use the industrial ecosystem metaphor to design large-scale systems. Of the tools discussed here, only the IME tool appears to be in current use, and that is primarily used as an in-house design tool by Nexant and its partners to add value to its consulting practices. So while industrial ecology may provide a rich framework for designing large-scale industrial networks, those wishing to apply the concepts may need to do much of the upfront tool development work themselves.

Conclusion

This chapter has focused on material flows in industrial systems, and in particular, has raised the concept of ideal industrial systems, where wastes and by-products are reprocessed and reused such that the entire industrial system requires only energy inputs and no mass inputs. Questions raised at the beginning of the chapter included: Are such systems realistic? Do they exist now? How could they be designed?

While true zero-emission/no-mass requirement industrial systems are not yet a reality, and the analysis tools for developing such designs are in their infancy, engineering design is evolving in that direction. Further evolution will occur only if the next generation of engineers and scientists builds new sets of analysis tools and develops better data on the flows of materials at regional and national scales.

References

Adriaanse, A., Bringezu, S., Hammond, A., Moriguchi, Y., Rodenburg, E., Rogich, D., and Schutz, H. (1997) *Resource Flows: The Material Basis of Industrial Economies*, World Resources Institute, Washington, DC.

Allen, D.T. and Jain, R. (eds) (1992) Special issue on industrial waste generation and management, *Hazardous Waste and Hazardous Materials*, 9(1): 1–111.

Allen, D.T. and Behmanesh, N. (1994) "Wastes as Raw Materials", in *The Greening of Industrial Ecosystems*, B.R. Allenby and D.J. Richards (eds), National Academy Press, pp. 69–89.

Allen, D.T. and Rosselot, K.S. (1997) "Wastes and Emissions in the United States", Chapter 2 in *Pollution Prevention for Chemical Processes*, Wiley, New York.

de Cerreño, A.L.C., Panero, M. and Boehme, S. (2002) "Pollution Prevention and Management Strategies for Mercury in the New York/New Jersey Harbor", New York Academy of Sciences, New York, May, http://www.nyas.org/scitech/harbor/.

Ehrenfeld, J. and Gertler, N. (1997) "Industrial Ecology in Practice, The evolution of interdependence at Kalundborg", *Journal of Industrial Ecology*, 1(1): 67–80.

El-Halwagi, M.M. (1997) *Pollution Prevention through Process Integration*, Academic Press, San Diego.

Keckler, S.E. and Allen, D.T. (1998) "Material Reuse Modeling: A Network Flow Programming Approach", *Journal of Industrial Ecology*, 2(4): 79–92.

Kimbrough, D.E., Wong, P.W. and Allen, D.T. (1995) "Policy Options for Encouraging Silver Recycling", *Pollution Prevention Review*, 5(4): 97–101.

Matthews, E., Amann, C., Bringezu, S. Fisher-Kowalski, M., Huttler, W., Kleijn, R., Moriguchi, Y., Ottke, C., Rodenburg, E., Rogich, D., Schandl, H., Schutz, H., Van der Voet, E. and Weisz, H. (2000) *The Weight of Nations*, World Resources Institute, Washington, DC.

National Research Council (1987) *Separation and Purification: Critical Needs and Opportunities*, National Academy Press, Washington, DC.

National Research Council (2003) *Materials Count: The Case for Material Flows Analysis*, National Academy Press, Washington, D.C.

Nobel, C.E. and Allen, D.T. (2000) "A Model for Industrial Water Reuse: A Geographical Systems Approach to Industrial Ecology", *Transactions of the Institution of Chemical Engineers, Part B: Safety and Environmental Protection*, 78: 295–303.

Sznopek, J.L. and Goonan, T.G. (2000) "The Materials Flow of Mercury in the Economies of the United States and the World", US Geological Survey Circular 1197, June.

US Business Council for Sustainable Development (USBCSD) (2003) "Examples of By-Product Synergies", http://www.usbcsd.org/byproductsynergy.htm.

US Census of Manufactures (2003) 1992 data, http://www.census.gov/prod/1/manmin/92mmi/92manuff.html.

US Geological Survey (2003) Mineral and commodity surveys, available at http://minerals.usgs.gov/minerals/pubs/mcs/.

9

Scenario Building and Uncertainties: Options for Energy Sources

Richard Darton

Summary

In order to develop a strategy for the future, we must have some view of that future in which our current decisions and actions, the components of our strategy, will bear fruit. In this case study we consider how distinct views of the future – scenarios – can be put together so as to influence strategic decisions, and explain how they are used. We concentrate on the key factors which are both highly important and very uncertain. A number of scenarios relevant to global energy supply are discussed, which underline the importance both of technological development and societal change.

9.1 Sustainability and the Need to Look Ahead

As discussed in Chapter 1, many different definitions of sustainability have been offered, but they all have in common that the desire of those of us alive now to enjoy a high standard of living should somehow be balanced against the needs of those who will come after us. Two immediate and difficult questions arise:

1. can we predict what the future consequences of our present decisions and actions will be; and
2. what will be the needs of future generations that we need to take account of now?

Sustainable Development in Practice: Case Studies for Engineers and Scientists
Edited by Adisa Azapagic, Slobodan Perdan and Roland Clift
© 2004 John Wiley & Sons, Ltd   ISBNs: 0-470-85608-4 (HB); 0-470-85609-2 (PB)

The concept of sustainability thus challenges us to think about the future, not in some vaguely inquisitive way, but with sufficient clarity to alter the choices we are making today. As discussed in section 2.4, this is a difficult task. Following on from that discussion, we introduce here some techniques to help us structure our thinking about the future. Our objective is not to predict the future – an impossible task – but to make our current decisions and strategies robust and in tune with various possible future developments, as far as this is possible.

9.2   Thinking about the Future

Human beings have always wanted to know the future. Early attempts at forecasting were based on mystical inspiration or the ability to interpret various signs (the relative positions of the planets, the appearance of a chicken's entrails when thrown on the ground or the position of tea-leaves in a cup). The value of such methods is questioned by those who cannot see the causality (why *should* they work?) but the casting of horoscopes is still a big business for newspapers and magazines, and they are widely read, if not equally widely believed.

Scientists and engineers are, of course, used to extrapolating into future time. The correct prediction by the Oxford professor of geometry Edmund Halley in 1705 that the comet named after him, Halley's comet, would return in 1758 was a triumph for the Newtonian system of mechanics, and a historically famous prediction. Halley himself had died in 1742. Such successful applications of the scientific method have given us the confidence to believe that if we can identify the physical and chemical laws operating in a particular situation, we can forecast how the situation will develop as time passes.

We have even learnt to accommodate uncertainty in such predictive modelling. In some places weather forecasts are now given in these terms "a 30% chance of some rain during the day", acknowledging that the physical laws at work are too complicated at present for us to be certain of the prediction. When human affairs are concerned though, the *scientific* basis for prediction vanishes and we are frequently reduced to educated guesswork. We may hire a consultant – hoping perhaps that the guesswork will be more educated and thus more likely to prove correct.

Complex systems can, of course, be modelled, and governments use models of the economy to forecast important features such as their borrowing requirement, and rates of economic growth. These forecasts are then frequently used to help determine policy, notwithstanding the fact that they are often found later to have been wrong in the predictions made.

Many assessments of sustainability contain elements of forecasting, and are thus susceptible to all the known problems of foretelling the future. The model may be wrong, accidents can happen (including unforeseen geological, biological, technical, meteorological or societal events), the current status may be misunderstood so that the extrapolation starts from the wrong point. Our experience with predictions that have gone wrong in the past should have taught us to be wary: whatever happened to the "paperless office", or nuclear power so cheap as to furnish unlimited free electricity?

In practice though, our thinking about the future mostly relies on guesswork which is heavily influenced by experience of the past, and which envisages a single outcome. For the small decisions of daily life this is usually sufficient ("The traffic is light at this time of day so the journey will take about 30 minutes"), and if we have guessed wrong we shrug our shoulders and bear the consequence.

This type of guessing about the future, which is based on short-range extrapolation of the present, is a habit of our daily lives that we tend to carry over into inappropriate situations without thinking.[1] In particular for large decisions affecting our business or long-term prosperity, extrapolation and therefore planning on only a single outcome can be extremely risky. The failure of our expectation can have very serious consequences: the financial pages of almost any newspaper will be found to carry stories about companies whose incorrect expectation of some feature of the business environment, such as sales volume, raw material price, the reliability of new technology, or the behaviour of competitors or customers, has brought them into difficulty. We need a more rational approach.

9.3 General Approach to Formulating Strategies

9.3.1 The Problem and its Time Horizon

We will consider the general problem of formulating a strategy which will comprise (a) making decisions and (b) inaugurating actions, in the present. This strategy must take proper account of possible future developments. The objective of the strategy will need to be specified. The problem could be as simple as making a single decision about a matter of personal choice, or as complex as formulating a business plan for the varied activities of a multinational company. In all cases the "problem" is the formulation of the strategy.

It will also be important to specify the time horizon – the period of time for which the strategy is to be effective. We may think that our problem is easier if the time horizon is short because there is then less time for unexpected developments and we may feel more secure in extrapolating current trends. We should be careful of this way of thinking: unexpected events can happen at any time, simply because they are unexpected! Also, by concentrating on the assumed incremental changes of short-time horizons we can lose sight of the major changes that are far more important. We should ensure that the time horizon is sufficient to include the timescales of the slowest change processes that are relevant to the strategy. For example, if the problem involves government policy on renewable energy, the time horizon will need to be several tens of years because of the immense investment needed to make changes in energy and transport infrastructure. That is not to say that all the possible changes and innovations will work on the same timescale, but that if the time

---

[1] Only in certain defined situations are most people accustomed to think of alternative outcomes, by buying insurance against damage to person or property for example, though insurance company statistics show that many people do not even take this simple measure. The ultimate disregard of future eventualities is perhaps failure to make a will, which is equally common.

horizon is too short, we will miss the effects of those processes that work more slowly.

The general approach we adopt here is thus first to determine the time horizon – the period of time for which our view of the future needs to be drawn. Then we think hard about our problem, to identify what we would like to know about the future exactly, and why – to identify the strategy factors that will affect our decision-making. We rate these factors in terms of uncertainty and importance. We then use the scenario technique to examine ways in which the key factors may change within the time horizon. Finally, we feed the result of this analysis back to evaluate the possible consequences of current decisions and actions so that we can improve our strategy.

9.3.2   Focusing on the Things We Really Need to Know – the Strategy Factors

We have already remarked that some elements of the future can be forecast quite accurately, if the physical laws which govern the circumstances (like gravity determining the movements of the planets) are well understood. Most aspects of strategy and decision-making though, have to be decided upon with much vaguer ideas about cause and effect. In coming to grips with this sea of uncertainty, it is of great importance to decide what it is that we would like to know. That is, we need to select the strategy factors which will influence and guide us. This can be more difficult than it appears – on closer inspection it may well turn out that some of the things we would like to know do not actually affect the decisions we have to take now.

For example, suppose we are trying to decide whether to go for a walk which will last two hours, and we do not want to get wet. In this simple example, the strategy factor is "total local rainfall over the next two hours" – if we only could know the value of this single factor in advance, the decision would be simple.

Now suppose we are facing a somewhat bigger problem – we own a shop selling outdoor-clothing and sports equipment, and we have to decide what goods to buy to stock our shop for the summer season. Our time horizon is around six months because virtually all the stock has to be sold during this time, in order to make way for the winter range of goods that will be brought in at the end of the summer. An important factor determining how willing our customers will be to spend money in our shop will be their feeling that they have money to spare – what is often called in shorthand, "consumer confidence". Let us suppose that analysis of the business reveals three further factors that will affect our sales – fashion, competition and local interest. If our suppliers introduce new product lines and promote them heavily with national advertising, we know that we will be able to sell a lot of these products because they will be seen as fashionable and desirable. Competition is provided by the local supermarkets who can easily undercut our prices. However, the supermarkets only ever buy a limited range of products – those that they can sell quickly and with little customer service. For these product lines though, if the supermarkets do decide to stock them, our own sales will be substantially reduced. The local interest is supplied by a local sporting star who is playing in the national open tennis championship. If she should be successful, then sales of the tennis equipment that she advertises will rise substantially. As shop-owners we have thus identified four strategy factors:

1. consumer confidence;
2. promotion campaigns by suppliers;
3. the stocking of our product lines by local supermarkets; and
4. success of local tennis star in national championship.

In our assessment of the business, it is these four factors which, if we could only know them in advance by some magical means, would enable us to make a perfect decision – that is, a decision which would enable performance to meet its objective perfectly. In the case of the shop-owner, this objective could be the achievement of a target return on the capital employed, say, or the increase in value of the business.

In coming to the short-list of four strategy factors we may have rejected many other possible candidates. Let us consider some possibilities:

- *Number and quality of staff serving in the shop*:   This is an important feature of the business, but one that we have, normally, under our own control. It does not therefore impact the decision, in that, having made our choice of stock, we choose and train the staff appropriately.
- *The weather*:   Are there grounds for expecting that the six-month time horizon will yield any different weather from an average summer? If not, then we will simply have to use our expertise to order appropriately for the local climate (in the UK, rather changeable).
- *Disaster*:   the shop is struck by lightning, attacked by thieves, drowned in a flood, etc. Again, are there any grounds for expecting that the risk of disaster is increasing? The possibility should certainly be considered, but it is probably better handled by another measure, like buying insurance rather than by changing purchasing strategy. The possibility of disaster is thus one of the strategy factors that does not affect our decision of what to buy. (Though having considered the possibility, we may feel that the way we run the business should be adjusted. For example, if there is a genuine concern about theft, we might choose not to have all the new stock delivered to the premises at the same time.)

9.3.3   Uncertainty and Importance of Strategy Factors

In the first of the above examples, the possibility of rain falling within the next two hours determined our decision, and this factor is therefore rated as highly important. In most places such a short-term forecast can be made with a reasonable degree of accuracy so that its uncertainty level could be rated as low. This combination of importance and uncertainty is shown in Figure 9.1(a).

In the second example, illustrated in Figure 9.1(b), each of the key factors will have its own uncertainty/importance ranking, and assessing this is a matter of judgement. The following arguments were used to assign the rankings shown in

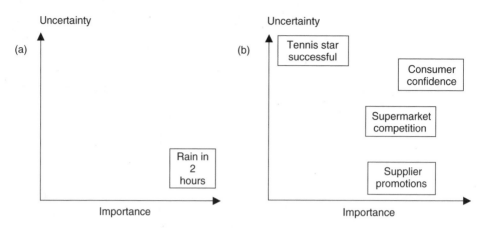

Figure 9.1   *The uncertainty and importance of strategy factors: (a) affecting the decision on going for a walk; and (b) affecting the purchasing strategy for a shop*

Figure 9.1(b). Consumer confidence will affect our total turnover, so it is highly important. It is affected by a wide range of influences, such as taxation and interest rates, house prices, unemployment rates and so on, some of these factors being national, and some regional or local in character. For this reason, it is not easy to predict how consumer confidence will change. Our estimate will be based on current trends, with the proviso that many of the influencing factors can change significantly over a six-month period, and public sentiment is anyway hard to predict – a terrorist bomb or a good football result can equally affect the public mood, in different ways. The degree of uncertainty is therefore rated as moderate-to-high. Promotion campaigns by suppliers will greatly affect the sales of some product lines, but we can find out about them in advance simply by asking the suppliers, who are not likely to change their minds. We could also ask the local supermarkets if they are proposing to stock our product lines, but they are not likely to tell us, and anyway their decisions are taken at short notice, long after we have done our own ordering. Fortunately, only a few product lines will be affected, and we can predict to some extent which lines they will probably be, from our knowledge of their suppliers, and their customer profile. The success of our local tennis star must be rated as very uncertain, but again this will only affect a limited range of goods (tennis equipment).

   In the first example, only a single strategy factor was of importance. Naturally, as the complexity of the decisions increases, the number of strategy factors increases as well. A good deal of analysis and imagination is then needed to be sure that we have captured all the relevant factors. Even so, we have not (yet) decided on our course of action, only structured our thinking about the problem. The important factors are those that we have placed on the right-hand side of the Uncertainty/Importance (U/I) diagram, and those requiring particularly careful attention are the factors in the upper right quadrant, as these are both highly important and very uncertain.

Questions

1. Describe a decision that you have taken, that you found difficult. List the factors which had an influence on the decision, and grade them in terms of importance from "least important" to "very important". Assign uncertainties to each factor ranging from "low" to "high". Did you take steps to reduce the uncertainty of any of the factors? Was there extra information that you would have liked to have had before you took the decision?

2. You own and run a business, manufacturing moulded plastic cups, plates, cutlery and containers for sale to restaurant chains, fast food outlets and catering companies. Forty per cent of your product is exported, and the rest is sold nationally. Your raw material is plastic, mainly polystyrene and polyvinyl chloride, supplied in particle form by various chemical companies. Your objective is to maximise the economic value of your company. Your time horizon is 5 years, since in 5 years' time you plan to sell the business and retire on the proceeds. Select around 10–15 factors which in your opinion will have an effect on your business over the next 5 years, and perform an Uncertainty/Importance analysis to identify the key factors which would influence your business strategy.

9.4 Dealing with Uncertainty: The Scenario Approach

9.4.1 What is a Scenario?

We saw above, in the clothing shop example, that some of the uncertainty concerning strategy factors could be reduced by research. In that example we were able to deduce, at least partially, the likely actions of local supermarkets from our knowledge of their business. We suppose that this knowledge results from previous research into the activities of our competitors. In the case of our own suppliers we could even remove the uncertainty about their plans completely, simply by asking them – very easy research! It obviously makes sense to reduce our uncertainty about strategy factors by acquiring more information, where this is feasible.[2] However, even the best information available will still leave us with some strategy factors, which have a high degree of uncertainty. Will consumer confidence be high or low over the next six months, and will it go up or down?

What we should not do with highly uncertain factors is guess how they will turn out, and base a strategy on that single guess – this is the policy of betting on a single horse to win a race. As remarked earlier, the financial press (and the bankruptcy courts) are full of stories about people who did just that. Neither should we attempt to define extreme positions and ten average them out, as this is really tantamount to guessing. Similarly, it is not satisfactory to assume that a factor will have the same value over the time horizon as it did over the same period last year or in the last

---

[2] We must be very careful to draw a distinction between the reduction in uncertainty that arises from obtaining hard information (e.g. what the definite plans for sales promotion are, revealed by our supplier) and the much less reliable information contained in consultant's or expert's opinion.

decade – at least not a factor which we have classed as highly uncertain. A more subtle and oblique approach is called for, and the one we shall develop here is based on making scenarios.

In the scenario approach we step back from the problem, and attempt to paint a number of self-consistent "portraits" in words of the different ways in which the different future worlds addressed in the strategy might develop. The particular part of the world, in which we are interested, is the part that both affects, and is affected by our strategy.[3] Each scenario is thus both a separate and distinct view of a possible future, and includes one or more paths by which the future can be reached (van der Heijden, 1996; Schwartz, 1998).

Since these futures are not extrapolations of current trends, there is no need to reconcile different opinions about the present, though the threads of the scenarios that are developed must be recognisable in the present situation. The scenarios can therefore be rich in incorporating a wide spread of experience about the present. We do not assign a probability to the likelihood of a particular scenario occurring. The future will in any case be different to any single scenario, of that we can be sure. The contrast of this approach with forecasting is shown in Figure 9.2. The differences between forecasting, foresighting and backcasting have also been discussed in Chapter 2.

We see that in making a forecast the main problem is in selecting the correct rules – those that govern the path into the future. The result is a convergent and mathematically sophisticated model, in which doubts about the result tend to be played down, perhaps by incorporating statistical information. In effect the technicians who assembled the model are those determining policy because the strategy chosen can

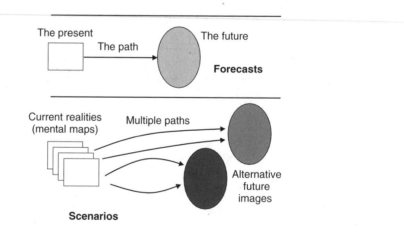

Figure 9.2 *Forecasts and scenarios compared (Dorton, 2003; reproduced by permission of the Institution of Chemical Engineers)*

[3] This, fortunately, limits the magnitude of the challenge facing us. We only need consider those parts of future worlds of relevance to our problem. Thus in tackling the decision on going for a walk, we only had to consider the rainfall in the local area. In stocking our shop, we only had to consider the sports/clothing business. We must be careful when drawing the boundaries and defining the things to be considered, not to leave important elements out, but also not to make the problem unnecessarily large.

be tested against the future forecast to predict how the strategy will turn out. ("If you do X, then Y will result. Is that what you really want?") The philosophy of forecasting assumes that it is both possible and useful to attempt to predict the future. Of course, forecasting does have a role to play, in cases where the causality (i.e. the rules connecting the present and the future) is in little doubt. We must be sure though, that this condition is fulfilled. In most of the interesting problems facing us, particularly in the context of sustainable development, it will not be.

The scenario approach to strategy formulation supposes, on the contrary, that it is neither possible nor useful to predict the future, and that we must therefore learn to manage the uncertainty. Scenario development is thus a thinking tool that focuses on the most important and uncertain strategy factors, and challenges us to consider various alternative outcomes. Whereas forecasting uses our analytical capabilities, scenarios demand our creativity and imagination.

After we have devised our scenarios, then we have to judge the effect of our strategies, and this can include quantitative analysis, as described in the next section.

The scenario approach is in harmony with the precautionary principle (discussed in Chapter 1). We cannot know what the future will bring, but we can take steps to plan for different eventualities. This is the objective of scenario-driven planning.

9.4.2   Targeting Key Strategy Factors

With respect to the analysis of strategy factors made earlier, it is essential that the scenarios have something to say about these, and particularly about the factors that have been ranked as both highly important and very uncertain. The idea is that the scenarios are used to challenge the strategy, as we develop it, to see how it performs in various possible future worlds.

With regard to our clothing shop example, the Uncertainty/Importance analysis shows that the scenarios need to say something about consumer confidence, and the policy of the local supermarkets. The scenarios must therefore address the local economic situation – employment, housing, the effects of national taxation and economic policy; and how these might change over the summer months for the sort of people we expect to be our customers; how the customers might react to the provision of low-cost goods by supermarkets; and how supermarkets might exploit the market. The scenarios we might make should arise out of our knowledge of these things. Two or three different scenarios are needed, to cover a range of possible futures, and these should be linked to some identifiable, self-consistent themes. As an example, consider the following preliminary brief sketches (the statements refer to possible future events):

1. *Booming Business (BB)*   Local employment expands as planned and new factories start operations in the spring. Housing demand rises. Local supermarket announces it will expand into home furnishings and furniture. The new public sports centre, which has no shops (and which can thus be expected to generate demand which it is not itself supplying), opens in time for the summer season and is an immediate success with a full programme of events.

2. *National Hesitation (NH)*   Opening of planned new factories is delayed until autumn as economy slows down. Increase in interest/mortgage rates reduces consumer confidence. Sports centre opens for the summer season but struggles to attract members. Supermarkets compete hard to maintain market share, exploiting every sales opportunity.

Clearly, these two scenarios each suggest different effects on the key strategy factors. When the scenarios are fully described and analysed, we should be able to make some clear statements about possible trends in these factors. Our conclusions are summarised briefly in Table 9.1.

Our knowledge of our own business should now enable us to estimate what the best purchasing policies would be, for both the overall volume of stock and the different lines, for the two different scenarios. We can also judge what the consequences would be of choosing to order stock for one scenario, when in fact the other one came about. Of course, we do not know in advance which scenario might be correct, or indeed whether some quite different set of events might happen. However, the analysis does expose what some of the problems and opportunities will be associated with any particular purchasing strategy.

For example, if we decide to purchase for the high business growth of BB, any element of the trend to NH will leave us with unsold stock and possible competition from the supermarkets in selected lines. There may be arrangements we can make in advance to deal with these eventualities, for example by negotiating resale of unsold stock to a discount store at the end of the season, or by entering some agreement with the local supermarkets or sports centre to promote joint sales of some goods. On the other hand, if we decide to purchase for the more difficult conditions of NH, and the market turns out better than expected, we will have to deal with unsatisfied demand. Again, there may be various ways of accommodating this, by taking options on mid-season deliveries of new stock, or by purchasing more of the stock that has a longer shelf-life, and which could thus be carried over into next season if it remained unsold. Either way, the consideration of the scenarios:

- does not make any decisions for us; it only demonstrates clearly what the consequences and opportunities are, relevant to the different strategies that we have thought up; and
- it does challenge us to use our ingenuity and knowledge of the problem to think "outside the box" to generate solutions and options.

Table 9.1   *Shop-owner scenarios: influence on key strategy factors*

Key strategy factor	Scenario	
	Booming Business (BB)	National Hesitation (NH)
Consumer confidence	High and rising	Falling
Supermarket competition	Minor	Aggressive

9.4.3   The Features of a Good Scenario

Clearly, the usefulness of the scenarios in the process of developing and testing a strategy is dependent on their quality, the extent to which they encapsulate various possible trends, and the imagination with which they have been thought through. A scenario which is a limp extrapolation of the current situation is not of much practical use – it must cause us to test the assumptions and extrapolations on which our strategy is based.

A good scenario is also one which picks out and develops features of the current scene. To this end, a high degree of awareness of current developments is obviously important – newspapers and broadcasting are good traditional sources of information on technical, social and political trends, and with the World Wide Web as well, there is no shortage of information: the challenge is to select a group of ideas that can be put together into a coherent scenario which addresses the key strategy factors. A scenario must be more than a set of independent assumptions.

Having invented a good scenario, it can then be put to work, using all the modelling and forecasting skills that we can summon up, to make quantitative estimates for those of our strategy factors for which this is appropriate, and possible. These calculations, which must come with all the usual warnings about their being contingent on the validity of the models, and that they refer solely to the scenario examined, nevertheless help us to flesh out the future images that we have initially described only in words.

As an example of this, consider the three basic Global Energy Scenarios of the World Energy Council (WEC), originally produced in 1990 with a time horizon of 2050 (WEC and IIASA, 1995):

1. Case A describes a *High Growth* world, in which economic growth is robust so that, despite significant improvement in energy efficiency, energy consumption grows strongly.
2. Case B describes a *Middle Course*.
3. Case C describes an *Ecologically Driven* future, in which countries collaborate in non-fossil fuel development, and a moderate economic growth is fuelled by an increasingly efficient energy supply, with maximum use of technology innovation.

The way that a number of key strategy factors change under these different scenarios can be tabulated, as we did above in the case of the clothing shop scenarios, in Table 9.1. The difference with the analysis shown in Table 9.2 is that the scenarios now have been further worked through and, where possible, numerical values have been assigned to the key factors.

Further development of the basic scenarios devised by the WEC and the International Institute for Applied Systems, Analysis (IIASA) has led to a number of subdivisions. Not surprisingly, for a problem as large as this, there are an enormous number of alternatives that one could consider.

For example, in exploring the option for increased use of non-fossil fuel, many different assumptions are possible about how the use of nuclear energy might develop. This is partly a question of technology (the potentials for cleaner, easier, cheaper, nuclear power generation, and proven, reliable waste disposal), and partly

Table 9.2 *Global energy scenarios: influence on key factors (WEC and IIASA, 1995; reproduced by permission of the World Energy Council, London.)*

Key strategy factors	Case A High growth	Case B Middle course	Case C Ecologically driven
World Population in 2050 in billion	10.1	10.1	10.1
World economic growth to 2050 per annum	2.7%	2.2%	2.2%
Energy intensity improvement to 2050 per annum	medium −1.0%	low −0.7%	high −1.4%
Primary energy demand in 2050 (Gtoe[a])	25	20	14
Resource availability			
Fossil	high	medium	low
Non-fossil	high	medium	high
Technology costs			
Fossil	low	medium	high
Non-fossil	low	medium	low
Technology Dynamics			
Fossil	high	medium	medium
Non-fossil	high	medium	low
CO_2 emission constraint	no	no	yes
Carbon emissions in 2050	9–15 Gt	10 Gt	5 Gt
Environmental taxes	no	no	yes

[a] gigatonne of oil equivalent.

a question of attitudes in society (to risk, to complicated technology, and to the association with nuclear weapons programmes). Consideration of this point highlights the aspect of geography, since these problems will certainly be viewed differently in different parts of the world. Summaries such as that presented in Table 9.2 represent the result of an averaging/integration process, by which the consequences of the scenario for each country or region are evaluated, and then all the individual consequences are gathered into the overall picture. The huge geographical variations in economic development, and every other aspect of society always have to be kept in mind when looking at global energy scenarios.

Questions

1. The WEC and IIASA scenarios shown in Table 9.2 offer a number of key strategy factors that will be of importance to any consideration of global energy strategy. Suggest some additional factors that might be of interest to a multinational oil company planning its operations with a time horizon of 10 years. Can anything be said about the importance and uncertainty of these additional factors and how they might change in the period upto the planning horizon?
2. Different parties will assess the importance and uncertainty of strategy factors differently. Consider the following participants in the debate about the need

to restrain the use of fossil fuels so as to reduce the emission of carbon dioxide:

(a) the US government;
(b) the government of a small island state which will become submerged and uninhabitable if sea levels rise due to global warming; and
(c) a group of activists concerned about environmental issues.

Taking the position of each of these groups in turn, draw up a list of strategy factors for an appropriate time horizon, and assign importance and uncertainty ratings to them. Discuss the significance of the differences, for the position that each might take in debate and negotiation on this issue.

9.5   Energy Scenarios: Glimpsing the Future?

Current significant sources of primary energy[4] are

– oil;
– coal;
– natural gas;
– nuclear; and
– hydroelectricity.

In some parts of the world, local energy demand is satisfied by:

– traditional biomass (mainly wood, or animal waste products);
– wind-power; and
– geothermal energy.

Other renewable energy sources that are being developed (Boyle, 1996) are:

– wave power;
– solar (both for direct thermal energy, and through photovoltaic conversion);
– crops grown for use as fuel.

Energy sources, such as wind, can be called renewable since the use of a certain quantity of energy from the source does not deplete the amount available for future generations. Non-renewables, such as coal, on the other hand, are taken from finite reserves. The pattern of supply from various different sources is known as the "energy mix". Note that primary energy is frequently transformed, before it is consumed by the end-user. For example, in the UK now, nearly all coal is burnt in power stations and converted into electricity. Much electricity also comes from oil and gas combustion, and some from other sources, so that the electricity actually used by the consumer derives from a range of primary energy sources. There are

[4] By "primary energy" we mean the energy released by, or extracted from, a natural energy source.

inevitably losses in conversion of energy from one form to another, and these losses are part of the cost of having the energy in a more convenient form.

The utilisation of scenarios to help develop and test strategic options was perhaps first exploited by military planners in war games, but the major application by business has been in the area of energy supply. This may be for historical reasons because of early work with the technique by Shell, but the global energy picture is particularly well suited to scenario analysis. The lead times for investment are long because of the considerable effort needed to develop new coal mines, and new oil and gas reservoirs to the stage of production, and the complex nature of refinery and gas processing facilities. Investments in large-scale hydroelectricity also require planning and construction times of many years. On the other hand, the energy supply/demand balance has shown itself to be susceptible to sudden shocks, due to war, accident, political and organisational change.

Figure 9.3 shows the world oil demand from 1960 to 2000, for the geographical area excluding centrally planned economies and Eastern Europe (for which reliable data were previously not available). Except in the period before 1973, the demand for this major commodity, which now satisfies around 40% of primary energy demand has moved in a rather irregular way. Even before 1973 when demand was steadily rising from year to year, industry experts continually underestimated the rate of growth.

For the whole energy market (all sources of energy) the interaction of supply and demand is thus highly complex, with a great many factors influencing the supply/demand balance.

Two Shell scenarios for the period upto 2050 – "Dynamics as Usual" and "Spirit of the Coming Age" – consider the implications of two different possible routes to a more sustainable energy system (Shell International Limited, 2001). Both scenarios take oil and coal to remain as major sources over this period, and the third major fossil fuel, natural gas, plays a larger role in what is an increasingly diverse supply system. As the world population grows from six to nine billion over this period of 50 years, the scenarios envisage a quadrupling of world GDP in real terms.

In "Dynamics as Usual", social priorities for clean, secure and sustainable energy shape the supply system. There is an initial explosive growth in energy demand as major developing countries seek rapid economic growth. In all markets there are

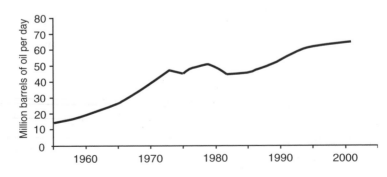

Figure 9.3 *World oil demand (excluding centrally planned economies and Eastern Europe)*

advances in communications and materials technologies which enable much more efficient energy usage. The result is shown in Figure 9.4(a). The total annual demand for primary energy increases over this period from 407 to 852 × 10[18] J,[5] and renewable energy comes to supply around one-third of demand.

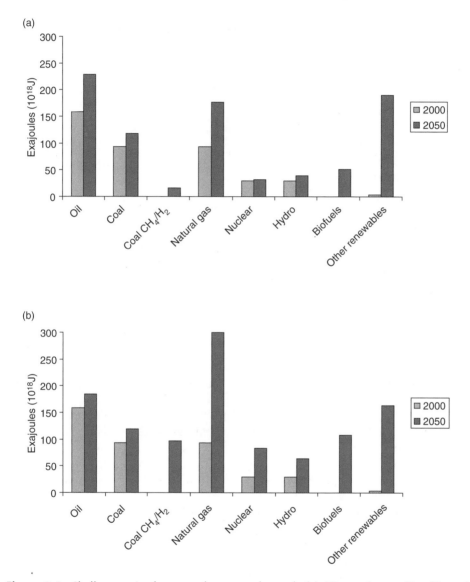

Figure 9.4 *Shell scenario for annual energy demand: (a) "Dynamics as Usual"; and (b) "Spirit of the Coming Age" (Shell International Ltd, 2001; published with permission from Shell International Ltd.)*

---

[5] In both these Shell scenarios, electrical energy from nuclear, hydro, wind, wave and solar sources is expressed as thermal equivalents.

In "Spirit of the Coming Age", the efficiency gains from new technology are fewer, and the annual energy usage increases to 1121×10^{18} J. Ingenious ways of supplying fuel are developed to meet consumer needs, particularly the continuing need for personal mobility. As shown in Figure 9.4(b), natural gas plays an even greater role, and there is a significant supply of energy from hydrogen (from coal or natural gas reforming) used in fuel cells. Biofuels, from plants grown sustainably, again become an important energy source, as do other renewables. In this scenario, the sources of primary energy become much more diverse than they were in 2000.

Questions

1. With reference to the current sources of primary energy mentioned in this section, identify situations and communities in which primary energy sources are used without further conversion. For each case, say whether you think that the energy usage is sustainable.
2. What is your country's current profile of energy sources for domestic and industrial purposes? Consider what portion of energy comes directly from gas, electricity and other sources. What is the distribution of primary sources for electricity generation, that is what fraction comes from gas, oil, coal, hydro, wind, solar, biomass and so on?
3. What are the main sustainability impacts (economic, environmental and social) associated with each of these sources of primary energy? Distinguish between impacts apparent at a global, regional and local scale.
4. What would be the main advantages and disadvantages accompanying a shift away from fossil fuel-based energy to renewable forms of energy?

9.6   Implications of Different Energy Scenarios for Sustainable Development

Energy supply is of course hugely important to our way of life and economic development, and its impact on the environment has come to be more appreciated in recent years. The global energy situation is thus directly linked to the three major components of sustainability – society, economy and environment. In this section, we consider some future consequences for sustainability, derived from scenarios made for the global energy situation.

In constructing our scenarios, we put many thoughts about the possible future into them. It is thus never correct to suppose that the scenarios themselves are making predictions, since features of the scenario only result from the assumptions made in the first place. Nevertheless, by making a coherent vision of a possible future, various insights can be teased out, which might not have been obvious from the bare bones of the original world picture.

Clearly, scenarios which address the future demand and supply of energy need to consider the possible development of new sources, but the way in which societies might develop is also a crucial strategy factor. Will people adapt their lifestyle to a more sustainable model? Attitudes are important of course, but technology also has a role to play here. For example, new computer and communications technologies could have a similar impact on lifestyle as the automobile had in the 20th century – only people would need to travel less because information can be transferred so much more easily; advanced materials technology and design could mean that goods and equipment are lighter and require less materials and energy in production and use. Carbon fibres could replace steel, and cars could become many times more fuel-efficient.

In their "Business as usual" scenario, the International Energy Agency (IEA) (Priddle, 1999) considered a world in which no policies (such as those stipulated by the Kyoto Protocol) were adopted to reduce energy-related emissions of greenhouse gases.[6] The consequence of this scenario was that, whilst energy demand grew by 65% between 1995 and 2020, CO_2 emissions increased by 70%. However, the IEA itself has pointed out (Priddle, 1999) that the future will not be "Business as usual", since the Kyoto Protocol obliges signatories to reduce emissions of greenhouse gases over this period, and policies are gradually being adopted to initiate this change. About 90% of the world's energy is currently supplied by fossil fuels, and the carbon dioxide generated in combustion of these fuels is virtually all discharged into the atmosphere. How quickly and effectively action can be taken to reduce these emissions is of course a hugely important unknown feature of the energy scene, and a major difference between many of the energy scenarios now being produced.

The UN's Intergovernmental Panel on Climate Change (IPCC) has collected many of the forecasts from various scenarios, and, as shown in Figure 9.5 they represent a very wide range of possibilities (Nakicenovic and Swart, 2000). This figure demonstrates one of the features of scenario planning – it is not a forecasting tool. Figure 9.5 shows that almost any prediction of carbon dioxide emissions can be found in the IPCC database of scenarios.

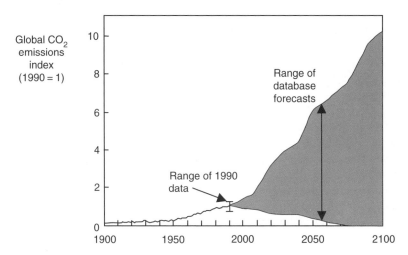

Figure 9.5   *Global carbon dioxide emissions (Based on the data from Nakicenovic and Swart, 2000.)*

---

[6] The International Energy Agency (IEA) regularly updates its World Energy Outlook. The reader is referred to the IEA website for more recent publications.

The strength of these scenarios is thus not in forecasting, but rather in the clarity of the vision that they reveal to the parties involved in energy supply, including governments. They allow these parties to appreciate what the consequences might be of particular courses of action (or inaction). In this the scenario technique has been very successful, as the publication of these various pictures has drawn attention to the link between energy supply and global warming, and helped to direct international policy development. This has resulted in various moves to encourage the use of renewable energy, such as the imposition of "carbon taxes" in some countries to penalise the use of fossil fuels, and the introduction of incentives for generators of electricity from wind and other renewable sources.

Energy scenarios like those shown in Figure 9.4, show that a potential shortfall in energy supply within the planning horizon of industry and governments could arise if too much demand is made on the finite supplies of oil and gas. The scenarios of Figure 9.4 show how this might be addressed through developing renewables to bring supply and demand into balance. Attempting to meet this shortfall by increasing coal production (Business as usual) would have significant (intolerable?) impact on global levels of carbon dioxide, and thus on global warming. This has stimulated the search for new energy sources, which must play an increasingly important role as the 21st century progresses (Boyle, 1996). One such emerging energy technology – fuel cells – is discussed in the next chapter.

Several of the scenarios have considered how the explosive growth of global communications, by telephone, television and Internet, might change society. There are huge consequences for the sort of jobs that people do, the companies they work for, and the tasks they perform, as commercial and technical information becomes much more readily accessible. There may also be more subtle shifts of power in society, as future generations will be able to decide how they want to live their lives not just by reference to local conditions, but with a vastly improved knowledge of affairs elsewhere in the world. We do not yet know how this will affect aspirations, but these scenarios portray worlds where, for the first time, development issues will be discussed in the light of truly global and public information exchange. The consumers and users – members of the public – who are the stakeholders in so many engineering projects, will be well informed of the issues, and by means of the same communication channels, will be able to express their opinions and influence decisions.

One of the major strategy factors for these long-term energy scenarios is the rate at which living standards rise in the less developed countries. Similarly, another important strategy factor is the extent to which industrialised countries can continue to improve their living standards if they pursue greater sustainability through reducing resource consumption and energy intensity. *Factor 4* (von Weizsäcker *et al.*, 1998) illustrates some approaches to this problem, giving 50 examples which demonstrate a fourfold improvement in resource usage (Chapter 1). Technology has a key role to play of course, but any new technology has to be economically viable. It may be that people will expect their governments to use fiscal and other measures to support sustainable technology which is not yet commercially viable.

With regard to the energy-based industries themselves, the Shell scenarios indicate some areas in which they might develop over the next 50 years. It is evident that throughout this period we will still be distilling oil to make fuel, though biomass grown in sustainably managed plantations could become the new source of feedstock for the distillation. Alternative sustainable fuels could include hydrogen for fuel-cell-powered cars or for generation of electricity, made by reforming bio-oil with subsequent sequestration of carbon dioxide.

Sustainably grown biomass may also support a manufacturing industry extracting and transforming biopolymeric or other natural products to replace those chemicals currently made by a petrochemical route. New industries will have arisen, associated with alternative energy sources, such as photovoltaics, fuel cells and wind farms. A snapshot of the city streets of 2050 would look as strange to us as do photographs of 1950. The challenge to scenario-makers is to be able to imagine these images 50 years before they occur.

Question

1. Assume the following roles and carry out the tasks as described:

    (a) You are a senior energy adviser to the Government. Devise an energy strategy for the country, acceptable to the electorate which will promote sustainable development.
    (b) You are the Chief Executive Officer of your City Council. Devise a strategy to implement the principles of sustainable development within the city.

Note: All elements of a coherent strategy will be driven by the same vision. Make sure you identify the levers available (e.g. legislation, investment, setting of standards, training, public opinion, taxation and tax breaks, etc.) and decide how each will be used. Consider the external pressures and other possible constraints on your actions. Consider also the influence of possible external events and other uncertainties. Where possible back up your strategy with facts and figures.

Conclusions

The notion of sustainability requires us to look into the future, both to envisage what the consequences will be of our present decisions and actions, and to consider the needs of those future generations who will be affected by them. Our problem is one of formulating a strategy, given that we do not know how the future will turn out. We have shown that our natural habit of guessing, based on limited extrapolation of the present, is not adequate for serious problems. Forecasting is useful only in those special circumstances where chain of cause and effect is known. In the scenario planning technique described here, we do not attempt to predict the future, but sketch a number of different ways in which the world might develop, and then consider our strategy in the light of these different scenarios. The objective, compatible with the precautionary principle, is to develop a strategy that is robust in a number of possible future worlds.

The scenario technique is widely used by those considering problems of energy supply, its interaction with the environment, and its effect on social and economic development. Through the use of simple examples we have exposed how the scenarios need to address those key strategy factors that we would, ideally, like to know in advance, and particularly those factors that are both highly important and very uncertain.

Finally, we have considered a number of published global energy scenarios, discussing what key strategy factors they address, and what sort of future worlds they envisage. Consideration of these scenarios underlines the important effects of international agreements on greenhouse gas emissions, of the commercial development of renewable energy sources and new technology, and of changes in lifestyle and human aspirations.

References and Further Reading

Boyle, G. (1996) *Renewable Energy*, Oxford University Press, Oxford.

BP (2003) Statistical Review of World Energy. Annual Reports. http://www.bp.com/centres/energy/index.asp.

Darton, R. (2003) Scenarios and Metrics as Guides to a Sustainable Future: The Case of Energy Supply. *IChemE Trans. B*, 81(B5), 295–302.

de Wit, B. and Meyer, R. (1998) *Strategy: Process, Content, Context*, 2nd ed. International Thomson Publishing Company, London.

Houghton, J. (1997) *Global Warming*, 2nd ed. Cambridge University Press, http://www.ipcc.ch/.

Houghton, J.T., Ding, Y., Griggs, D.J., Noguer, M., van der Linden P.J. and Xiaosu, D. (eds) (2001) Climate Change 2001: The Scientific Basis, Cambridge University Press (Contribution of Working Group I to the Third Assessment Report of the Intergovernmental Panel on Climate Change (IPCC)).

Jackson, T. (1993) *Clean Production Strategies – Developing Preventive Environmental Management in the Industrial Economy*. CRC Press, Boca Raton.

Jennings, J. (1987) *Sustainable Development – the Challenge for Energy*, Shell International Ltd, London.

Johnson, G. and Scholes, K. (2002) *Exploring Corporate Strategy*, 6th ed. Financial Times Prentice Hall, Harlow England.

Nakicenovic, N. and Swart, R. (eds) (2000) IPCC Special Report on Emissions Scenarios, Cambridge University Press.

Priddle, R. (1999) Achieving Sustainable Energy – The Challenge. *Renewable Energy World* 2(3), 23–29.

Schwartz, P. (1998) *The Art of the Longview: Planning for the Future in an Uncertain World*. John Wiley, Chichester.

Shell International Limited (2001) *Energy Needs, Choices and Possibilities, Scenarios to 2050*, Shell International Ltd, London.

Sorensen, B. (2000) *Renewable Energy: Its Physics, Engineering, Use, Environmental Impacts, Economy and Planning Aspects*, Academic Press, New York.

van der Heijden, K. (1996) *Scenarios*, John Wiley, Chichester.

von Weizsäcker, E., Lovins, A.B. and Lovins, L.H. (1998) *Factor Four, Doubling Wealth, Halving Resource Use*, Earthscan, London.

WEC and IIASA (1995) Global Energy Perspectives to 2050 and Beyond, World Energy Council and International Institute for Applied Systems Analysis, London.

10

Fuel Cells in Stationary Applications: Energy for the Future?

Martin Pehnt

Summary

Fuel cells represent an old invention which has yet to make a major contribution to the energy economy. However, the time is now ripe for fuel cells to enter widespread use to help reduce emissions of carbon dioxide and other gases emitted from the conventional energy systems based on fossil fuels. In stationary applications, fuel cells offer the possibility of much more efficient generation of electrical power from natural gas or hydrogen. However, assessment of true benefits of fuel cells must be based on a life cycle approach in which the whole supply chains related to fuel cell systems are considered. This includes fuel extraction, its processing, distribution, conversion into electricity or heat, and energy delivery and use. This chapter and the case study explore some of the benefits of using fuel cells in stationary applications and discuss the life cycle environmental implications of these installations. Economic and social factors influencing commercialisation of fuel cells are also addressed.

10.1 Energy Today: Why a Substantial Transformation is Necessary?

Greenhouse gas emissions in the European Union (EU) fell between 1990 and 2001, however, energy-related emissions fell considerably less than expected (EEA, 2002). Current trends seem to indicate that the European greenhouse gas reductions will fall well short of the reduction target of 8% agreed by the Kyoto Protocol, even though

Sustainable Development in Practice: Case Studies for Engineers and Scientists
Edited by Adisa Azapagic, Slobodan Perdan and Roland Clift
© 2004 John Wiley & Sons, Ltd   ISBNs: 0-470-85608-4 (HB); 0-470-85609-2 (PB)

the Kyoto targets fall far short of the reductions necessary to stabilise the global climate (Chapter 2).

Fossil and nuclear fuels still dominate electricity production. Unless major changes in the worldwide energy and climate policy occur, global society will still – and increasingly – rely on fossil fuels (Figure 10.1). This is mainly due to the increasing energy demand in developing countries. As the World Energy Outlook (2002) points out, more than 60% of the increase in world primary energy demand until 2030 will come from developing countries (IEA, 2002). China, already the world's second-largest energy consumer, will be a major contributor to that increase. China's energy economy is heavily dependent on coal.

For Europe, dependence on fossil and nuclear energy also implies dependence on external energy resources. According to the EU Green Paper on security of energy supply (EU, 2000), 50% of the primary energy requirements are already imported. If current trends persist, the predictions are that this will rise to 70% of the total European energy demand.

When analysing future energy situation, it is important to consider not only energy required for heat and power generation, but also for transportation. Here again, the problem is an ever increasing demand, particularly in developed countries: there is an almost linear relationship between income and distance travelled per capita. With increasing economic activity in developing countries, the use of vehicles is set to continue growing.

The consequences of the rising energy consumption are potentially serious and irreversible. One consequence is that the CO_2 emissions from burning fossil fuels, that is oil, gas or coal, will increase significantly, thus enhancing the anthropogenic

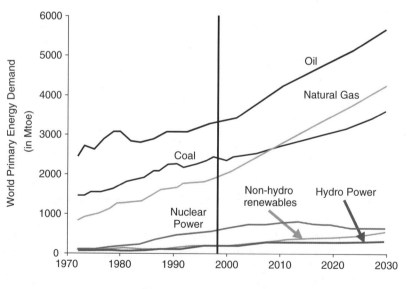

[Mtoe = megatonnes of oil equivalents]

Figure 10.1 Past and future world primary energy demand according to the reference scenario "Business as usual" (Based on data from IEA, 2002; © OECD/IEA, 2002.)

greenhouse effect (Chapter 4). Carbon dioxide concentration in the atmosphere has already increased by one-third in the past 150 years. By some estimates, the surface temperature of the earth has risen within the last century by 0.6 °C. The 1990s were the warmest years since the weather record began.

There are many more indicators pointing at a climate change on a global level. The Intergovernmental Panel on Climate Change (IPCC) estimated recently that a further global warming of between 1.4 and 5.8 °C by the end of the 21st century is possible. The consequences of this could be drastic: spread of infectious diseases, water shortages, droughts and famine, changing vegetation, soil erosion, pressure for population migration and so on.

However, global warming is only one of the impacts associated with energy supply. Other environmental impacts also arise from the increasing demand for services, mobility, electricity, communication or heating. These impacts arise through the whole life cycle from primary fuel extraction, through its processing, distribution, conversion into electricity or heat, to energy delivery and use. Some of these impacts, such as acidification caused by nitrogen oxides and sulphur dioxide emitted from power plants (Chapter 4), have been reduced considerably in many developed countries over the last 10 years. In Europe, for instance, SO_2 emissions fell by almost 60%. Several factors have contributed to this positive trend, including the use of cleaner fuels (natural gas) instead of coal, improved combustion and energy efficiency, flue gas treatment as well as an increased share of renewable energy sources. However, other impacts, such as oil tanker spills and the accumulation of radioactive waste, continue to damage our environment.

Questions

1. Identify the environmental and social impacts associated with the life cycle of electricity generation (i.e. from fuel extraction, through processing, distribution, conversion to electricity delivery and use). Compare these impacts for electricity generated using different fossil (coal, oil, gas) and nuclear fuels. What do you conclude?
2. What measures could be taken to reduce the environmental impacts of electricity supply? Identify examples for each source of electricity analysed in the previous question. Try to rank your suggestions according to feasibility, costs and potential for the reduction of environmental impacts.

10.2   Fuel Cells: An Old Invention

There are numerous approaches to reduce energy demand and therefore impact on the environment. However, even if we concentrate on the supply side and take demand as constant, there are still a number of options to reduce environmental impacts associated with energy supply. One possibility is to introduce an efficient, clean energy converter. The fuel cell is often promoted as such a device.

One hundred years ago, the electrochemist Wilhelm Ostwald presented his vision of the 20th century as the century of electrochemical, combustion-free energy conversion. In the age of coal, his credo "no smoke, no soot" seemed unrealistic. However, 70 years before Ostwald's statement, the British amateur chemist William Grove and the German Christian Friedrich Schönbein – the latter better known for discovering ozone – had already developed the fuel cell, a device converting the energy of a fuel into electricity without combustion.

One century later, we are much closer to Ostwald's vision. Today, fuel cells are seen by many as a particularly promising technology for clean energy generation and have already attracted much attention, both from industry and the public.

10.2.1   How does a Fuel Cell Work?

Fuel cells are electrochemical devices which convert chemical energy of the reaction between a fuel (typically hydrogen) and oxygen (normally from air) directly into electrical energy (as direct current, DC). As shown in Figure 10.2, a fuel cell consists of two electrodes which are interspersed with an electrolyte: fuel is oxidised on the anode and oxygen is reduced on the cathode. The role of the electrolyte is to separate the fuel and oxygen to avoid an uncontrolled explosive reaction. Bipolar plates, mounted on the outside of each electrode, feed the fuel and oxygen to the electrodes,

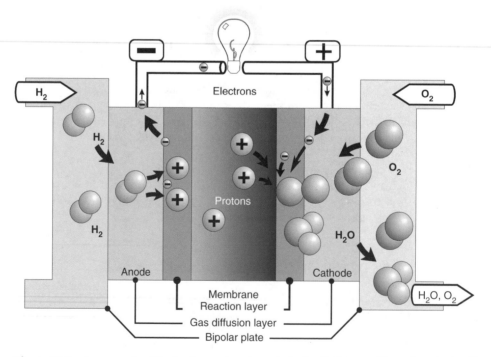

Figure 10.2   *An example of the basic construction of a fuel cell: Polymer Electrolyte Fuel Cell (PEFC)*

collect the electrons and remove the heat of reaction. To achieve higher power outputs, fuel cells typically consist of a number of single cells connected in series. This is called a fuel cell stack.

The reaction between hydrogen and oxygen in the fuel cell generates water and results in an enthalpy change:

$$H_2 + \frac{1}{2}O_2 \rightarrow H_2O_{liq.} + \Delta H \quad \Delta H = -286 \, kJ/mol$$

The change of enthalpy ΔH which characterises the "energy of the reaction" can only partially be transformed into electrical energy. The maximum possible electrical energy that can be obtained is given by the change of Gibbs free energy of formation ΔG. At the pressure of $P = 101\,325\,Pa$ and temperature of $T = 298.15\,K$, ΔG for this reaction is equal to $-237\,kJ/mol$. According to the Gibbs function, the difference between ΔH and ΔG is given by $T \cdot \Delta S$ (where T is the temperature in the fuel cell and ΔS is the change of entropy in the reaction). Therefore, the maximum (or "ideal efficiency") thermodynamic efficiency of the fuel cell is given by:

$$\eta_{fc} = \frac{\Delta G}{\Delta H} = 1 - T \cdot \frac{\Delta S}{\Delta H} \qquad (10.1)$$

That means that with increasing temperature, the efficiency[1] of fuel cell decreases.

The efficiency of fuel cell also depends on cell voltage and current density. The theoretically possible open circuit voltage of a fuel cell is determined by ΔG according to the following equation:

$$E_0 = -\frac{\Delta G}{n_e \cdot F} \qquad (10.2)$$

where F is the Faraday constant ($96\,485\,A \cdot s/mol$) and n_e is the number of electrons. At the standard conditions ($P = 101\,325\,Pa$ and $T = 298.15\,K$), E_0 is $1229\,V$. However, the theoretically achievable voltage is reduced through various losses in the system. In the fuel cell areas with low current densities, activation losses result from the slow rate of reaction on the surface of the electrodes. In the region of medium current density, Ohmic losses reduce the cell voltage, and at high current densities mass transport effects lower the voltage. An example of the resulting change in the cell/stack efficiency (which is proportional to the voltage) with current density of the cell is shown in Figure 10.3.

In addition to the efficiency of the fuel cell and the stack, we also need to consider the efficiency of the whole fuel cell system. The fuel cell system includes fuel and oxygen preparation for use in the stack, power conditioning (conversion

---

[1] It is important to note that the thermodynamic efficiency theoretically achievable in a fuel cell is much higher than (the Carnot) efficiency that is theoretically achievable in a combustion process or "heat engine" (the Carnot efficiency was discussed in Appendix 5.A).

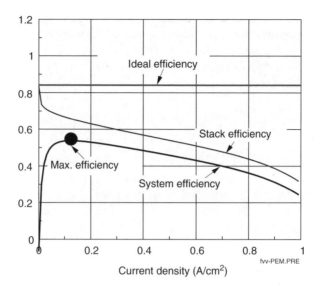

Figure 10.3 *Theoretical efficiency of the PEFC fuel cell stack and the overall system efficiency as a function of the current density*

from DC to AC current) and heat management system as well as the fuel cell stack. For instance, in systems where hydrogen is derived from natural gas, the gas has to be extracted, cleaned and reformed into hydrogen before it can be fed into the stack. Each of these parts of the system use energy and that influences the overall energy efficiency.

Questions

1. Explain the principles of design and operation of a fuel cell in your own words.
2. Describe the differences between fuel cells and conventional power converters. What potential advantages and disadvantages might result from these differences?

10.2.2   Types of Fuel Cells

Fuel cells can be categorised according to the electrolyte used. As described in Box 10.1, there are six types of fuel cell:

1. Alkaline Fuel Cells (AFC);
2. Polymer Electrolyte Fuel Cells (PEFC), also known as Proton Exchange Membrane Fuel Cells (PEMFC);
3. Direct Methanol Fuel Cells (DMFC);
4. Phosphoric Acid Fuel Cells (PAFC);
5. Molten Carbonate Fuel Cells (MCFC); and
6. Solid Oxide Fuel Cells (SOFC).

Box 10.1 *Fuel cell types*

Alkaline Fuel Cell (AFC)   Alkaline fuel cells use KOH as electrolyte. The charge transfer in the electrolyte is based on OH^- ions. At the anode, these ions react with hydrogen:

$$H_2 + 2OH^- + 2e^- \Rightarrow 2H_2O \qquad \text{(anode)}$$

At the cathode, new OH^- ions are formed:

$$\frac{1}{2}O_2 + H_2O \Rightarrow 2OH^- + 2e^- \qquad \text{(cathode)}$$

AFCs operate at temperatures around 80 °C and have high efficiencies because oxygen reduction in alkaline electrolytes is rapid. One problem with the AFC is that the electrolyte reacts with the CO_2 which is present in the feed air to form carbonates which foul the electrodes. Due to the advances in PEFC technology, the AFC has been neglected in the recent year.

Polymer Electrolyte Fuel Cell (PEFC) (or Proton Exchange Membrane Fuel Cell [PEMFC])   In the PEFC, the electrolyte consists of a proton conducting membrane. This membrane is similar to Polytetrafluoroethylene (PTFE or Teflon). Unlike the AFC, in the PEFC the protons (H^+) are the charge-transfer ions. The overall reaction is:

$$H_2 \Rightarrow 2H^+ + 2e^- \qquad \text{(anode)}$$

$$\frac{1}{2}O_2 + 2H^+ + 2e^- \Rightarrow H_2O \qquad \text{(cathode)}$$

The PEFC operates at low temperatures (around 80 °C) to avoid melting of the membrane. Therefore, it requires a catalyst to promote the reactions. Typically, platinum group metals are used for this purpose. As they are very sensitive to carbon monoxide or sulphur contamination, the feed gas must be cleaned appropriately. Water management can be a problem in PEFC.

Direct Methanol Fuel Cell (DMFC)   DMFC is similar to PEFC except that methanol is used as a fuel instead of hydrogen:

$$CH_3OH + H_2O \Rightarrow CO_2 + 6H^+ + 6e^- \qquad \text{(anode)}$$

$$1\frac{1}{2}O_2 + 6H^+ + 6e^- \Rightarrow 3H_2O \qquad \text{(cathode)}$$

The problems with DMFC include high amounts of catalysts required, and the cross-over (passage) of methanol through the membrane.

Box 10.1   *Continued*

Phosphoric Acid Fuel Cell (PAFC)   PAFCs use phosphoric acid as electrolyte. Due to the acid conditions in the cell, the protons (H^+) are transferred through the electrolyte. The partial reactions are thus identical to those in the PEFC. The PAFC operates at 200 °C and is therefore less sensitive to carbon monoxide than the PEFC. The PAFC is the only fuel cell type that has been produced commercially in larger numbers for stationary applications.

Molten Carbonate Fuel Cell (MCFC)   In MCFC, carbonates (Li_2CO_3, K_2CO_3) are used as electrolyte. These cells are operated at 650 °C. The electrodes consist of nickel materials. Carbonate ions which are produced at the cathode are conducted through the electrolyte:

$$CO_2 + \frac{1}{2}O_2 + 2e^- \Rightarrow CO_3^{2-} \quad \text{(cathode)}$$

At the anode, the H_2 reduces these ions to CO_2:

$$H_2 + CO_3^{2-} \Rightarrow H_2O + CO_2 + 2e^- \quad \text{(anode)}$$

To supply the CO_2 required at the cathode, the CO_2 from the anode off-gas is recycled back. One problem with MCFC yet to be solved is corrosion of the electrolyte materials. In addition, the electrodes degrade because the nickel from the electrodes enters the melt and causes short circuits.

The Solid Oxide Fuel Cell (SOFC)   The SOFC operates at the highest temperatures of all fuel cell types. The electrolyte is a ceramic made of zirconia doped with yttrium which conducts oxygen ions at above 750 °C:

$$H_2 + O^{2-} \Rightarrow H_2O + 2e^- \quad \text{(anode)}$$

$$\frac{1}{2}O_2 + 2e^- \Rightarrow O^{2-} \quad \text{(cathode)}$$

In both MCFC and SOFC, gases containing CH_4 and CO can be used directly as a fuel. In the low and medium temperature fuel cells, a reformer converts natural gas or other hydrogen containing gases into hydrogen.

The type of electrolyte dictates the operating temperatures in the fuel cell. Thus PEFC and AFC are operated at low-temperatures (at around 80 °C); PAFC is a medium-temperature (200 °C) while the MCFC and SOFC are high-temperature cells (operated at 650 °C and >750 °C respectively). Although higher operating temperatures of MCFC and SOFC result in decreasing thermodynamic efficiencies

(Equation 10.1), the better kinetics as well as the option to use the high-temperature exhaust gas (e.g. in turbines or for heat supply) more than offset this efficiency reduction. In addition, high-temperature fuel cells offer the advantage of internal reforming, that is the heat produced in the electrochemical reaction is simultaneously used for reforming natural gas or other fuels into hydrogen, thus decreasing the required cooling effort while efficiently using the heat. Furthermore, high-temperature fuel cells have lower purity requirements for the fuel. Whereas AFCs are sensitive to CO_2 and PEFCs to CO impurities, in high-temperature fuel cells CO_2 acts as inert gas only, and CO can even be used as a fuel.

10.2.3   Advantages and Applications of Fuel Cells

From the discussion above, two main environmental advantages of fuel cells as energy converters become obvious. On the one hand, fuel cells offer higher efficiencies of conversion into electrical power and thus reduce the amount of fuel required for the production of electricity. This is the *efficiency advantage* of fuel cells.

In addition, the electrochemical nature of the reaction, the low temperature of the reforming reaction and the necessity for removing impurities in the fuel (such as sulphur) result in extremely low local emissions – an important feature especially in highly populated (urban) areas. There is no open flame and no combustion involved except for the small burner (to combust unused hydrogen) with extremely low emissions. Furthermore, compared to the conventional energy systems based on fossil fuels, fuel cells generate lower CO_2 emissions, even when hydrogen is derived from fossil fuel. These are the *emission advantages* of fuel cells.

But besides these obvious environmental advantages, other advantages may emerge. These advantages depend on the specific application of fuel cells. Fuel cells can essentially be used in:

– *Stationary applications*:   Fuel cells can be used in small systems for domestic energy supply, in larger units for the simultaneous supply of electricity and heat to a district heating system or in large systems for industrial cogeneration. In the long term, the use of fuel cells for more centralised electricity production is of interest, particularly in combination with a gas (or steam) turbine which uses the energy contained in the off-gas. In stationary systems, small distributed power plants help to open up the potential for combined heat and power generation (CHP). Table 10.1 identifies some further potential drivers to use fuel cell systems for stationary applications.

– *Mobile applications*:   Fuel cells are attractive energy sources for powering electric drive trains in passenger cars, busses, heavy-duty vehicles, ships, trains or aeroplanes. In mobile applications, for instance, using fuel cells to replace batteries in electric vehicles increases the driving range and eliminates the need for the gear mechanism.

– *Portable applications*:   Small hydrogen fuel cell systems could be used to replace diesel generators or rechargeable batteries. The cost of fuel cells in these applications is relatively low and offers a potential for further environmental benefits, such as elimination of heavy-metal containing batteries.

Table 10.1 *Some advantages of using fuel cells in stationary applications*

Environmental
- higher efficiency, lower CO_2 emissions and resource consumption
- reduced air pollution
- reduced noise and vibration
- simple fuel switching to use less carbon intensive and renewable fuels
- possibility of "simpler" CO_2 sequestration
- possibility to generate hydrogen from renewable resources.

Technical
- high power to heat ratio
- heat levels suitable to industrial and cooling applications
- lower transmission losses due to distributed generation
- modularity and flexibility of installation
- good partial load characteristics and dynamic response
- lower maintenance costs and increased durability due to a reduced number of moving parts
- reduced requirements for pollution prevention equipment.

Energy supply
- Increased reliability of distributed generation
- Compensation for increased shares of fluctuating renewable energy sources
- New options for supply of back-up power
- Reduced vulnerability of the energy system
- New business opportunities for energy companies
- Enhanced competition through new opportunities for IPP.

Miscellaneous
- low thermal radiation (particularly suitable for military applications)
- opportunity to promote small-scale cogeneration
- possibility to provide energy in remote areas, particularly in developing countries.

Questions

1. It has taken more than 100 years since its invention for the first practicable fuel cell to be developed. What might have hindered the development of fuel cells this long? Think of the competing inventions (Werner, Siemens, Benz, Edison), but also of historical developments.
2. Discuss and explain possible drivers for fuel cell technology as presented in Table 10.1. Try to identify further advantages not listed here.
3. Why do distributed (smaller scale) fuel cells, and any kind of distributed generation, reduce transmission and distribution losses? Consider that the losses are proportional to the square of the current, to the resistivity (which is a function of temperature and thus again the current), the length of the cable and the inverse of the cross-section of the cable. Typical grid losses are in the order of 6% of the electricity generated, but they can vary between 3 and 15%. Given the relationship above, when would the electricity provided by fuel cells be most beneficial: as a base, medium or peak load? Is the grid loss reduction higher on a non-windy summer day or a cold winter night?
4. Given the information in Table 10.1 and section 10.2.3, consider the specific motivation of different nations to introduce fuel cells in mobile or stationary

applications. What might be the key driver for the following countries to introduce this innovative energy converter:

(a) United States, and particularly California;
(b) Iceland;
(c) Europe;
(d) China; and
(e) African countries.

If you are uncertain, try to find out about the key problems related to energy
supply and the key environmental issues in the respective countries or regions.

5. The World Energy Outlook 2002 (IEA, 2002) highlights that 1.6 billion people
    have no access to electricity and four out of five of these live in rural areas. Lack
    of energy leads to substantial health risks, for example toxic indoor fumes from
    biomass stoves (Chapter 1), transportation of fuel wood over large distances,
    lack of electricity for water pumps, refrigeration and for hospitals. How could
    fuel cells help to provide energy in such areas? Where do you see the main barriers
    for this?

10.3   Case Study: Fuel Cells for Distributed Power Generation

In the following case study, we consider the use of fuel cells for distributed power
generation to find out if they are more sustainable than the conventional power
plants. We will concentrate on a CHP production, also known as cogeneration (Box
10.2). We will first carry out an environmental evaluation of this fuel cell system and
then examine economic and social implications of its use for distributed power
generation.

Box 10.2   *What is cogeneration?*

In conventional power plants, only a fraction of the primary fuel input is converted into electricity. The waste heat has to be disposed of and heats up rivers or
the air. In cogeneration systems, this heat is not dissipated, but used for various
purposes. In industrial cogeneration systems, steam may be generated, agriculture
products may dried, breweries supplied with heat or galvanising baths heated. In
heating cogeneration, the thermal energy is used for space heating and domestic
warm water supply.

Various technologies exist for cogeneration, including steam and gas turbines
and reciprocating engines. More innovative systems include micro-turbines, Stirl-
ing engines or fuel cells.

10.3.1   Environmental Considerations

In this case study we assume that in the next 20 years, stationary fuel cells will mainly be fuelled with hydrogen generated from natural gas. We focus our attention on the emissions of CO_2 and CH_4 as the two most important greenhouse gases generated by the fossil-based energy systems used currently.

As already mentioned, comparison between fuel cells and the conventional energy systems must be based on a life cycle approach. We will therefore carry out a (simplified) Life Cycle Assessment (LCA) to quantify the global warming potential from the life cycle of the whole fuel cell energy system. We will then compare this global warming potential with the conventional energy systems to find out if fuel cells are truly more sustainable with respect to greenhouse gases. The analysis is based on the production of 1 kWh of electricity. You may wish to read the Appendix on the LCA methodology to help you follow the analysis and carry out the necessary calculations.

A simplified life cycle of the fuel cell system for stationary applications considered here is shown in Figure 10.4. Therefore, in our analysis we will cover the whole supply chain from the exploration and extraction of natural gas, through its processing and delivery to the power plant to the manufacture and the use of the fuel cell system. Note that the blank spaces in Figure 10.4 have been left for you to fill in the results of your calculations using the basic data given in Box 10.3 and the assumptions made in the case study.

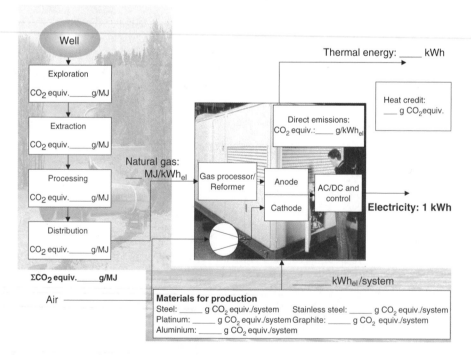

Figure 10.4   *Simplified life cycle of a stationary fuel cell*

***

Box 10.3   *Some units and properties needed for the case study*

$1 \text{ kWh} = 3.6 \text{ MJ} = 3.6 \times 10^6 \text{ J}$
$1 \text{ TJ} = 10^6 \text{ MJ}$

Global warming potential of CH_4: 21 kg CO_2 equiv./kg (see the Appendix at the end of the book)
  CO_2 emission factors for combustion of diesel and natural gas:

Diesel	74 g CO_2/MJ
Natural gas	59 g CO_2/MJ
Lower heating value of natural gas: 38 MJ/Nm^3	

All efficiencies and energy data refer to the lower heating value (LHV) of a fuel (see Chapter 5 for an explanation of LHV).

***

Questions

1. It was mentioned that CO_2 and CH_4 are typically the most important greenhouse gases emitted from the energy systems. Consider, however, energy crops as an energy source. Why are the emissions of CO_2 from the combustion of energy crops less important? Which other greenhouse gas gains in importance? Why? (Taking a life cycle approach, consider the agricultural activities necessary to support the growth of energy crops, e.g. the use and production of manure.)
2. When biomass is used to provide fuel for a fuel cell, its life-cycle CO_2 balance is almost zero (why?) The same result is found for biomass-derived fuel used in internal combustion engine. This would point to the conclusion that the high efficiency of the fuel cell system is of no importance for reducing greenhouse gases because for both the fuel cell and internal combustion systems, these emissions are very low if they use biomass-derived fuel. Why is in this case the fuel cell still of great advantage compared to the internal combustion engine?

Natural Gas Supply

Let us start our analysis of the life cycle of the fuel cell system with the supply of natural gas to the fuel cell power plant. Bringing natural gas to the fuel cell involves the following activities.

Exploration drillings
We assume here that for drilling one-metre hole, 0.01 TJ of diesel fuel is used (combusted) by the drilling equipment. Combustion of 1 MJ of diesel leads to 74 g of CO_2 emissions plus 10 g CO_2 for the production of 1 MJ of diesel. Each m^3 of natural gas may require 4×10^{-6} m drilled.

Natural gas extraction

For extraction, we assume an energy consumption of 1×10^{-9} TJ diesel for each m^3 of natural gas. As for the exploration stage, the CO_2 emissions per MJ diesel used can be assumed to be in total 84 g CO_2/MJ, including diesel production. Due to leakages, 0.1% of the gas extracted is emitted into the air at a rate of 0.6 kg CH_4/m^3 of raw natural gas.

Natural gas processing

Gas processing involves drying and desulphurisation and requires the use of energy and materials. For simplicity we will only take into account the energy requirement. The assumption is that 0.1% of the total amount of gas brought in for processing is combusted to produce heat and electricity required for this step.

Natural gas distribution

As a final step, the natural gas is distributed to the customer. The distribution is by pipeline and the assumption is that 2% of the gas has to be combusted per 1000 km pipeline length to run the pipeline compressors. In our example, we suppose that the power plant is situated in continental Western Europe with 20% of the natural gas brought from Norway (distance of 600 km), 20% from the Netherlands (200 km), 20% from Germany (100 km) and 40% from Russia (5500 km). Due to pipeline leaks, 200 kg CH_4 is emitted per TJ of natural gas sourced from Russia; for all other countries this leakage is at the rate of 2 kg CH_4/TJ of natural gas delivered.

Once the natural gas has reached the destination country, no further energy for distribution is required. Just the opposite: some gas suppliers even generate electricity using the pressure gradient from the high-pressure pipeline to the low-pressure distribution system. Due to a large number of valves, smaller pipes and other infrastructure-related factors, the methane leakage from distribution networks in some countries can be rather high. We assume here modest values of 3 kg CH_4 emissions for delivering 1 TJ natural gas in the high-pressure, 4 kg in medium-pressure and 5 kg in low-pressure pipelines.

Questions

1. Calculate and add up all CO_2 and CH_4 emissions, respectively, for the fuel supply of 1 MJ natural gas to a private household. Convert the CH_4 emissions into CO_2 equivalents using the global warming potential (GWP) given in Box 10.3. Enter the results in Figure 10.4.
2. What are the "hot spots" of the natural gas supply according to the results obtained in the previous question? Which other greenhouse gases should have been considered in these calculations?
3. What factors might influence the high gas leakage rates for the Russian pipelines? Can these leakages be reduced or eliminated?

Production of the Fuel Cell System

Production of the fuel cell system is very complex and cannot be investigated in detail in this case study. The interested reader can consult Pehnt (2002) for more detail on the subject. However, to get a feel for the relative importance of the production stage in the whole life-cycle of the fuel cell system we will consider a simplified PEFC fuel cell power plant with the output of $200\,kW_{el}$. Such a system, which can weigh 14 t, consists of thousands of different components and materials so that a detailed LCA is very complicated. For the sake of simplicity, let us assume that the system consists of 70% steel, of which 20% is stainless steel; 20% aluminium, 10% graphite, and 3 g platinum catalyst per kilowatt electric power; 90% of the platinum used in the fuel cell stack is sourced from recycled platinum.

Supplying these materials is associated with many environmental impacts because the materials have to be extracted, cleaned, processed, transported and formed into components. As we are focusing on the greenhouse gases here, we assume the following emissions of CO_2 equiv. per tonne of material used in the fuel cell system:

- $1500\,kg\,CO_2$ equiv./t of conventional steel;
- $3600\,kg\,CO_2$ equiv./t of stainless steel;
- $15\,kg\,CO_2$ equiv./kg of graphite;
- $26\,000\,kg\,CO_2$ equiv./kg of primary (virgin) platinum; and
- $3000\,kg\,CO_2$ equiv./t of aluminium.

Except for platinum, all data for CO_2 equiv. emissions are based on a mixture of primary and recycled materials. For simplicity, we assume secondary platinum as "impact free".

Further CO_2 (and other) emissions are generated from the use of electricity for the manufacture of all fuel cell components. In this case study we assume that a total of $20\,000\,kWh$ in used for these purposes, with an average CO_2 emission factor of 480 g of CO_2 equiv./kWh (average European electricity mix).

Questions

1. Calculate the CO_2 equiv. emissions from the simplified production process of the fuel cell as described above and enter the results in Figure 10.4. Now calculate the CO_2 equiv. emissions per kWh_{el} by dividing the emissions from the production of the fuel cell system by the kWh_{el} produced over its lifetime. Assume an average lifetime of 20 years for the system and a yearly electricity production of 5000 h. Neglect at this stage that the fuel cell stack has a shorter lifetime than the rest of the system.
2. Which life cycles stages can be considered as "hot spots"? Where might improvements be possible?
3. Assume that 10% of the power capacity in your country would be supplied by PEFC. Using the platinum recycling rate of 90% and a life time of 20 years (ignoring the fact that the stack has to be replaced within this lifetime), what would the annual national demand for platinum be? Compare this to the world

reserves (see for instance the website: http://minerals.usgs.gov). When would the world reserves be exhausted? Consider which non-technical factors influence platinum recycling rate. What happens in the initial growth phase when an increasing number of fuel cells enter the market?

4. What happens if, additionally, 10% of the vehicles in your country are equipped with similar fuel cells (assume that in mobile applications, 1 g platinum/kW is sufficient). Do you think that in mobile applications, similar recycling rates can be achieved?

5. What are the competing demands for platinum in other sectors? What follows for future platinum prices? Develop strategies to deal with the issue of platinum under the assumptions used in the previous two questions.

6. If you look at the different fuel cell types in the Box 10.1 and the materials mentioned therein, which of these materials might on a first glance – without considering the amount needed in fuel cells – be scarce? Discuss how that might influence the potential for fuel cell applications.

Operation of the Fuel Cell System

The term "operation" refers to the conversion of natural gas into electricity and heat. What sounds so simple is actually the interaction of various complex processes. First, the natural gas has to be converted into a gas acceptable to the fuel cell. Whereas high-temperature fuel cells can deal with natural gas directly and convert it internally (inside the stack) into hydrogen, low-temperature fuel cells such as the PEFC used in our case study cannot deal with such gas mixtures. Therefore, the gas has to be desulphurised (because sulphur destroys the catalysts) and then reformed, that is converted into hydrogen. Different processes can be used for reforming, but steam reforming is the most common method. The reforming process is carried out according to the following reaction:

$$CH_4 + H_2O + \text{heat} \Rightarrow CO + 3H_2 \text{ (synthesis gas)}$$

Because CO damages the platinum catalysts, it must be removed by the "shift" reaction:

$$CO + H_2O \Rightarrow CO_2 + H_2$$

The hydrogen gas must be further cleaned before being introduced into the fuel cell.

All this processing obviously uses energy. Furthermore, oxygen has to be supplied to the cathode of the fuel cell. In many systems, the air must be compressed to increase the oxygen partial pressure. This air compressor is very often one of the main "parasitic" power consumers of the system and might require 10 or 15% of the electrical output of the stack. For our calculations, we assume an efficiency of 80% for the full fuel processing system which, for simplicity, is taken to be more or less constant with varying current densities.

To calculate the stack efficiency, we will assume that designed current density of the fuel cell is $0.4\,A/cm^2$ (Figure 10.3) and that the system operates close to that current density all the time.

Finally, the DC current has to be converted into AC. This is accomplished in an AC/DC converter which typically has very high efficiencies. In our case we assume that the efficiency is 96%.

Our cogeneration system produces both electricity and heat, with the heat used for district heating. The amount of heat that can be extracted depends strongly on the circumstances, particularly on the temperature of the return flow from the heating system. PEFCs are low-temperature fuel cells, so the heat that can be supplied to a household or a district heating system is limited to about 80 °C. In high-temperature fuel cell systems, the heat can be used in the form of steam for industrial purposes or even to drive a gas turbine. The manufacturers' mid-term target for the thermal efficiency is 40%.

Questions

1. Calculate the electrical efficiency of the system by multiplying the efficiencies together. Compare your result with the "efficiency curve" in Figure 10.3. How close is your result to that shown in the figure? (Bear in mind that this is a simplified analysis, so the result may not be precisely the same as in Figure 10.3.)
2. The system efficiency curve in Figure 10.3 goes to zero at zero current density. What have we neglected so far that could explain this effect?
3. Calculate the amount of useful heat output produced per kWh electricity using the target thermal efficiency of 40%.
4. Assuming that the system is operated at 0.4 A/cm^2 all the time and taking the electrical efficiency as calculated in question 1, calculate the life cycle CO$_2$ equivalents. Follow the following steps:

   – with the system electrical efficiency found in question 1, calculate the amount of natural gas necessary to produce 1 kWh of AC current;
   – multiply the CO$_2$ equivalent emissions of natural gas supply (section "Natural Gas Supply") with that amount;
   – add the specific emissions for the production of one fuel cell power plant as determined in section "Production of the Fuel Cell System";
   – calculate the amount of CO$_2$ emissions generated in the reformer. This is easy to calculate: each C atom from the natural gas converted in the reformer ultimately leads to CO$_2$ emissions (see the reforming and shift reactions). Thus we can take the CO$_2$ factor of 59 g CO$_2$/MJ natural gas; and
   – enter all the results in Figure 10.4.

5. Compare the significance of the fuel supply, production of the system and operation stages. What do you conclude – which parts of the system are significant with respect to the CO$_2$ equivalents (i.e. global warming)? In vehicle applications, the production of the system is more significant. Why?
6. What are the advantages and disadvantages of shifting the operating point of a fuel cell power plant from higher to lower current densities? To answer this question, look at Figure 10.3 again. Assuming that the natural gas price may rise in future due to scarcer resources, what does that mean for the rating of such a system?

7. What have been your major problems in carrying out this simplified LCA? What further research have you done to overcome these problems?
8. Comment on the issue of data quality. How robust is the information derived? What could you do if some data points are not reliable? How could you ensure that the statements derived are sufficiently robust?

Dealing with the Co-products

We have now calculated the CO_2 equivalents (i.e. the global warming potential) for the production of 1 kWh electricity and a corresponding amount of heat by the PEFC system. If one asks you: how does that compare with the electricity generation by a coal power plant, what would you answer? Well, so far, it would be difficult to answer this question because we have two useful products from the fuel cell system, and we must find a way to calculate the emissions associated with *one* product only.

This kind of problem can arise whenever a system or company produces more than one product. Take a farmer raising cows. The cow produces milk, but eventually it will be slaughtered and converted into meat. How can the farmer allocate the costs of feeding the cow to produce the milk (daily) and the meat (at the end of the cow's life)?

There are two main ways to deal with this problem. One is called *allocation* (see the Appendix at the end of the book) whereby an appropriate basis is sought for allocating costs between the products. In the case of the former, this might be the relative nutritional values of milk and meat, or the prices of the milk and the meat on the market.

For the case of the cogeneration system, one allocation basis could be the energy generated. Take the example of an electrical efficiency of 40% and a thermal efficiency of 40%. Thus, for each kWh of electricity, 1 kWh of heat is produced. The allocation basis would thus be 50:50, that is 50% of the CO_2 emissions are allocated to the electrical output and 50% to the heat output.

However, this allocation basis does not really represent the "value" of the products. Instinctively, 1 kWh electricity seems more valuable than 1 kWh low-temperature heat. And in fact, as we know from thermodynamics, only a fraction of the heat can be converted into electricity. Therefore, many people use exergy as the allocation basis. Exergy describes the amount of useful energy that is contained within the product; the exergy of electricity is equal to its energy. The exergy of heat, in contrast, is given by the Carnot efficiency multiplied by the energy value.

The second way to deal with co-products is to estimate the "avoided burden". If the cow, for instance, had not produced milk, it would have been necessary to buy some substitute for milk, such as soya milk. The total cost of the feed for the meat would then be the sum of the feed cost over the lifetime of the cow minus the avoided costs for the soya milk.

In the case of the fuel cell system this means that we have to identify the heating systems that would actually be replaced by such fuel cell systems. This will depend on a number of factors, for instance the country, the type and age of the houses, the preferred fuels and so on. It also depends on the perspective of the decision-maker: from the perspective of a house owner, it is the individual house heating system that might be superseded by a fuel cell system. Boiler manufacturers might compare fuel cells with other modern heating systems. A politician who has to decide which heating system to subsidise financially will have to consider, for instance, a fuel cell domestic energy system or a modern condensing boiler.

Questions

1. Allocate the emissions of CO_2 equivalents between the electricity and heat from the fuel cell system considered in this case study by using exergy as the allocation basis. Assume a temperature of 80 °C for the heat output. The Carnot efficiency is equal to:

$$\eta_{Carnot} = 1 - T_s/T$$

where T is the operating temperature and T_s is the average temperature of the surroundings (see Appendix 5.A for the Carnot efficiency). Calculate the emissions of CO_2 equiv. per kWh_{el} by multiplying the calculated allocation factor with the total CO_2 emissions determined in the previous section.

2. Now calculate the CO_2 equivalent emission per kWh_{el} using the avoided burden approach. Assume that as a competing system, a condensing boiler is being replaced and that the production of 1 MJ of heat from the condensing boiler (including the fuel supply and production of the system) leads to the emissions of 75 g CO_2 equivalent.

3. In the avoided burden approach, when would you assume that a mix of technologies (e.g. the overall electricity mix or an average heat production system) is being substituted and when a single technology (e.g. a coal power plant, a gas-combined cycle or a condensing boiler)? Under what circumstances it is appropriate to base the avoided burdens estimates on future technologies and when on marginal technologies being shut down and leaving the market?

4. Which approach do you consider to be more appropriate: allocation or avoided burden? What are the advantages and disadvantages of the two approaches? Is there the "best" approach?

5. Now compare your LCA results for CO_2 equiv. to the CO_2 emissions from different sources of electricity (see the table below).

Electricity generation system	CO_2 equiv. emissions (g CO_2 equiv./kWh_{el} on a life cycle basis)
Coal power plant	980
Gas combined cycle (without cogeneration)	434
Reciprocating engine (cogeneration; avoided burden approach)	370
Wind power	20
River-flow hydroelectric power	20

6. Now assume that instead of the PEFC investigated, you have a 1 MW SOFC system. Such a system might achieve an electric efficiency of 60% when it is

coupled with a gas turbine. The thermal efficiency is then of the order of 20%. Assume no changes in the CO_2 emissions of the power plant production. How does this SOFC perform with respect to the CO_2 equiv.?

10.3.2   Social and Economic Considerations

"Dollars + Time = Fuel Cell". This was the headline in a German newspaper article on the future of stationary fuel cells. This concise quotation highlights the two severe limitations of stationary fuel cells.

Because of their higher efficiencies and thus reduced fuel costs, fuel cells can still be competitive with higher capital costs than the competing technologies. For example, estimates of capital costs have shown that even with 20–30% higher costs per kW_{el} fuel cells could still compete with other energy systems. Even so, the costs of current systems are still prohibitively high: fuel cells in stationary applications are still a factor 10–50, which is too expensive. This is partly due to the current low production volume; if their production increased significantly, learning[2] and economies of scale[3] would lead to reduction in cost. But in addition to this, research and development are needed to reduce material costs and quantities used, to enhance performance and enable production of more integrated systems with standardised power-plant components.

Because of their potential to revolutionarise the energy systems, fuel cells have attracted much public attention and raised expectations. These expectations have also been promoted by early announcements by fuel cell manufacturers that the fuel cell systems would be available in the near future. However, as mentioned above, fuel cells need much more technical development and reduction of capital costs and are therefore far from commercialisation. Another issue yet to be solved is the question of longevity. Due to material and component degradation, the lifetime of fuel cell systems is still well below target. This also means that fuel cells will come too late to enable rapid climate protection measures demanded by the Kyoto Protocol.

Given the marketing efforts of big companies and the good image of fuel cells, it is not surprising that customer acceptance of this technology is high. In some cases, utility companies have been overrun by interested people who wanted to have a fuel cell installed in their home. Customer interviews even showed that a great percentage of people would not refuse a little fuel cell power plant in their own basement.

The fuel cell as a new product also needs new distribution channels. Particularly for small residential applications, but also for larger systems, service contracting will be required (Chapter 11); that means that the utility or another service company owns the fuel cell systems and leases it to the customer, to provide a package of services consisting, for instance, of electricity, heat, financing and maintenance of the system. Thus, fuel cells not only might conceivably lead to a technical transformation,

---

[2] "Learning curves" reflect cost reductions due to increased production and technological innovation as a function of cumulative production.

[3] The economies of scale refer to the relationship between the size of a plant and its capital and operating costs. Normally, the larger the capacity of the plant, that is the larger the economies of scale, the lower the capital and operating unit costs.

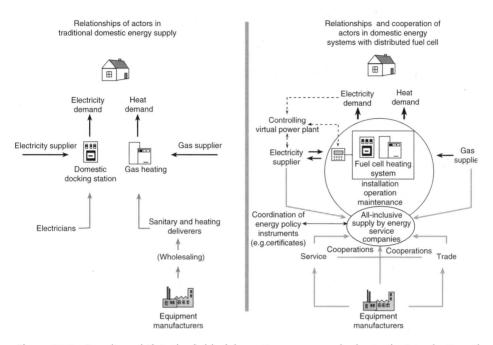

Figure 10.5 *Paradigm shift in the field of domestic energy supply due to the introduction of fuel cells (Pehnt and Ramesohl, 2003)*

but might also fundamentally change the way the heat and electricity markets and domestic energy supply are organised (Figure 10.5). For instance, utilities might offer fuel-cell-related energy services, in heat supply and district heating systems and reinforce relationship with their customers by long-term contracts. These new models of commercial relationships also imply new skills needs, with craftsman needing skills which cut across the traditional trades of electrician, plumber and so on. Thus, once fuel cells are sufficiently developed for widespread use, they will need to be supported by the new modes of training.

Questions

1. What problems arise from the discrepancy between public perception of product's maturity and its actual readiness for the market?
2. Comment on the readiness of the public to accept fuel cells in "their back yard". How does that compare with the public reaction to some other energy technologies, such as incineration and the NIMBY syndrome (Chapter 5)?
3. Advances in information and communication technology might make it possible for small distributed power systems to act as one large power plant, that is to be centrally controlled. This is sometimes referred to as a "virtual power plant" (Figure 10.5). Discuss the advantages of this concept.
4. Based on your findings in this case study, the information given above and Table 10.1, try to develop a marketing strategy or a commercial case for a fuel cell in an

application of your choice. Which aspects would you highlight? How would you visualise this information? Compare this to any advertisements you might have seen with respect to fuel cells or hydrogen.
5. An effective introduction strategy for fuel cells needs to recognise potential bottlenecks or time-limiting factors. Try to design a table similar to Table 10.1 to show the barriers to and challenges for the fuel cells systems.
6. Now imagine you work for a Non-Governmental Organisation (NGO) dealing with environmental protection. What would be your position with respect to stationary fuel cells? Take into consideration actual and recent political developments, such as the Kyoto Protocol, the Iraq war, and events such as tanker oil spills which attract public attention.

Conclusions

Fuel cells are an emerging energy technology being developed by a number of companies and research organisations worldwide. Currently, fuel cells are much more expensive than the conventional energy systems and that makes their commercialisation difficult and slow. Further problems that are yet to be solved include design improvements, hydrogen storage and provision of infrastructure. However, environmentally, fuel cells appear to offer significant advantages over the competing technologies despite the fact that they are at this stage of development still dependent on the fossil fuels. It is expected that in the future the growth of the solar hydrogen economy will make fuel cells even more sustainable.

As in other areas of technology development, the future of fuel cells will not be determined by any one single factor but rather a combination of (often unpredictable) technological, economic, environmental and social considerations. Although speculating on the future of anything and particularly on a technology is a futile job, one thing at least seems to be certain: fuel cells have come back and are set to continue growing. We await with interest to see whether they grow up.

Acknowledgement

The author would like to acknowledge support for parts of this publication from the German Federal Ministry of Education and Research under the socio-ecological research framework.

References

EEA (2002) Energy and Environment in the European Union. Environmental Issue Report No 31. Copenhagen, European Environment Agency.
EU (2000) Towards a European Strategy for the Security of Energy Supply. Green Paper, European Commission, COM(2000)769 final.
IEA (2002) World Energy Outlook 2002. Paris, International Energy Agency.

Pehnt, M. (2002) Ganzheitliche Bilanzierung von Brennstoffzellen in der Energie- und Verkehrstechnik (Life Cycle Assessment of Fuel Cells in Stationary and Mobile Applications). Düsseldorf, VDI Verlag Fortschritt-Berichte Reihe 6 Nr. 476 ISBN 3–18–347606–1.

Pehnt, M. and Ramesohl, S. (2003) Market Introduction of Stationary Fuel Cells for Distributed Power: Benefits, Barriers, and Drivers. Study Commissioned by the World Wide Fund for Nature (WWF). Heidelberg, Wuppertal, IFEU Institut für Energie- und Umweltforschung, Wuppertal Institut für Klima, Umwelt, Energie.

Internet Links for Further Information

www.hyweb.de
www.h2cars.de/
www.fuelcells.org
http://fuel-web.net/
http://www.hfcletter.com
http://www.eyeforfuelcells.com/
http://www.h2fc.com/
www.eren.doe.gov/hydrogen
www.fuelcellworld.org
www.enaa.or.jp/WE-NET
http://americanhistory.si.edu/csr/fuelcells/

11

Towards Sustainable Process Contracting: The Case of the Glass Industry

Michael J. Nicholas

Summary

This chapter examines the process-contracting industry and the way the sustainability agenda is influencing it. The first part of the chapter reviews the implications of sustainable development for industry in general and then focuses on the sustainability challenges facing the process-contracting industry. The case study, presented in the second part of the chapter, considers a typical process-contracting sector in the glass industry. The reader is asked to take on the role of a process contractor who, in response to an invitation to tender from a glass manufacturing company, is required to design, cost out and submit a proposal for the supply of sustainable gas cleaning equipment.

11.1 Sustainable Development and Industry

11.1.1 The General Implications of Sustainability for Industry

As discussed in Chapter 1, there is currently a great deal of activity within governments worldwide to develop policies that will initiate a move towards more sustainable practices. However, the impact on and requirements for individual sectors of industry are not readily defined. Many governments encourage sustainable business

Sustainable Development in Practice: Case Studies for Engineers and Scientists
Edited by Adisa Azapagic, Slobodan Perdan and Roland Clift
© 2004 John Wiley & Sons, Ltd   ISBNs: 0-470-85608-4 (HB); 0-470-85609-2 (PB)

and outline generic potential benefits, but the direct implications for individual companies can be difficult to interpret in practice (Azapagic and Perdan, 2000). At a general level, sustainable development requires the satisfaction of the three objectives of social equity, economic prosperity and environmental protection (Chapter 1). It has been highlighted that for individual organisations to address such issues it will be necessary for commitments to be made at the highest level of management, so that 'the bottom line' of profitability is converted to a 'triple bottom line' in order to create 'win-win-win solutions' (SustainAbility, 1999). It has also been stressed that the economic sacrifices implied by 'balancing' or 'trading off' the three core aspects need no longer exist since the adoption of more sustainable practices actually involves an 'integration' of the three aspects to create environmentally and socially sustainable industries (DTI, 2000).

Whilst economic considerations are currently the cornerstone of business management systems, much effort has been expended to raise the profile of environmental and social management issues within industry. In 1991, the International Chamber of Commerce (ICC) developed the Business Charter for Sustainable Development with the aim of providing a foundation for businesses to build an Integrated Environmental Management System (ICC, 2000). This establishes 16 key principles that can be used as a guide to organisations in the establishment of environmental policies. McIntosh *et al.* (1998) note that most of these principles are included within the requirements of ISO 14001 (ISO, 1996), the international standard for Environmental Management Systems (EMS) and within the European Eco-Management and Audit Scheme (EMAS). The now widely recognised business benefits of EMS include lower resource costs, less-expensive waste disposal, increased markets, improved employee relations and decreased liabilities. Many governments are strongly encouraging larger companies to adopt a certified EMS in order to identify and manage their impacts and are themselves implementing EMS within government departments (DTI, 2000).

With respect to social issues, in 1997 the Council on Economic Priorities Accreditation Agency launched a global standard for Social Accountability: SA 800. The basis of SA 800 is the International Labour Organisation conventions such as those on forced labour and freedom of association and on the UN's Declaration of Human Rights and its convention on Rights of the Child (McIntosh *et al.*, 1998). Moreover, the approach to management of Occupational Health and Safety issues, which has for a long time been integrated within industrial working policies, is now being standardised at the international level by the International Organisation for Standardisation under the designation ISO 18000.

Question

1. With reference to the ICC's Business Charter for Sustainable Development and established management systems (e.g. ISO 14001 and EMAS), discuss the main issues associated with integrating more sustainable practices into industry. Give examples of initiatives taken by leading companies in adopting more sustainable practices.

11.1.2 Sustainable Development and the Process-Contracting Industry

Companies can now do much to move towards more sustainable practices. Their efforts can be enhanced by developing an integrated business management system to manage economic, environmental and social issues (Azapagic, 2003). But although the guiding principles are in place, the question remains: What does sustainable development mean in practice for specific sectors of industry? This chapter focuses on the process-contracting industry in an attempt to explore the meaning of sustainability for this sector.

A typical construction site during construction of a new plant. Photograph courtesy of Priroda.

There is currently little guidance for process contractors willing to improve their social and environmental performance. However, the industry can be thought of as analogous to the construction industry (building and civil works), for which there have been various initiatives in different countries to develop a sustainability strategy. For example, during 1998 the UK Government consulted on a Sustainable Construction Strategy (DETR, 1998). From this consultation, three broad socio-environmental themes have been identified:

1. The construction industry is a significant polluter and consumer of resources. Increasing material reuse and recycling or avoidance and minimisation of pollution could contribute significantly to sustainable development. These issues are discussed in section 'Direct Aspects of a Process-Contracting Company' in terms

of the 'direct' aspects of a process-contracting company. Here, 'direct' refers to aspects that are associated with specific activities carried out by the company and not associated with its products or services.

2. Buildings and installations, in operation or at the end of their life, consume energy and materials and create wastes and pollution. Improving energy and resource efficiency of processes and buildings are key issues. This is discussed in section 'Indirect Aspects of Existing Technology Portfolio' with respect to the 'indirect' aspects of the existing technology portfolio of a process-contracting company. Indirect aspects are those associated with activities over which the company has control or influence but which are not activities of the company itself (e.g. those related to the use of its processes, or those related to its suppliers/subcontractors).

3. The overall design and type of building supplied should meet the needs of society. Ensuring that the type of product or service supplied enhances the quality of life is a key issue for a more sustainable business. This is discussed in section 'Direct and Indirect Aspects of Future Technology Portfolios' with respect to the direct and indirect aspects of possible future technology portfolios.

Direct Aspects of a Process-Contracting Company

The process-contracting industry supplies process equipment to chemical and manufacturing companies. The EC Directive on Integrated Pollution Prevention and Control (EC, 1996) highlights that there are five main stages in the life of a process plant: comprising design, construction, operation, maintenance and decommissioning (see Chapter 6 for more detail on the life cycle of a plant; further detail on the IPPC Directive can be found in Chapters 4 and 5). For the process-contracting company, its direct aspects[1] are associated with the design and construction (including commissioning) of the process plant that they supply. These direct aspects range from those associated with the design of process and plant, such as office activities (paper, energy use, etc.) and travel, to the various activities associated with a construction site and commissioning of an installation. Included are several socio-environmental aspects such as stakeholder communication (client, regulator and community relationships) and the environmental awareness of employees or subcontractors.

A common requirement within EMS is that a company must continually improve both its environmental performance and the way in which environmental issues are managed. As a minimum, companies are required to control their activities in a way such as to ensure compliance with all relevant legislation. For a process-contracting company, relevant environmental legislation is mainly associated with the construction and commissioning of the process plant. During the construction phase, impacts arise from planned activities, which require specific licensing (e.g. disposal of construction waste), to possible unplanned or emergency situations which may cause pollution (e.g. silt pollution of controlled waters). The construction industry is one of the highest polluting industrial sectors, as exemplified by the majority of prosecutions in 1999 in England and Wales concerning waste and water offences (Environment

---

[1] Note that 'direct' and 'indirect' aspects are equivalent to 'foreground' and 'background' impacts respectively, the terms used in Chapters 4, 5 and 6.

Agency, 1999). Improving management practice to ensure compliance and to reduce the frequency and severity of incidents would, in some measure, contribute towards sustainable development (DETR, 1998). Further guidance on such improvements has been published by the Environment Agency (EA) for England and Wales in the form of a Pollution Prevention Guideline (PPG) for working at construction and demolition sites – PPG6 (Environment Agency, 2000).

Commissioning brings further potential for impact and must be carried out in accordance with the requirement of any permits or authorisations which the client may possess. For example, conditions within permits issued to industry under the Integrated Pollution Prevention and Control (IPPC) regulations in the EU. Again impacts can be planned (e.g. emissions, waste, noise and odour) or unplanned incidents. When commissioning new installations or individual plant items, there is increased potential for accidents. In the extreme, major accidents, which can result in substantial environmental harm or possible fatalities, can pose a threat to the success of a company (Hobbs and Stevens, 2003).

Questions

1. This section discussed environmental issues for the process-contracting industry. What do you think are other sustainability issues, including economic and social, related to this type of industry?
2. The EA for England and Wales publishes regular press releases concerning prosecutions on its website, in addition to an annual report on business environmental performance known as 'Spotlight'. Examine the EA's relevant web pages and produce a table which lists the key environmental offences committed by contracting/construction companies, indicating the number of companies prosecuted for each type of offence. What do you conclude: is the sector environmentally offensive?
3. What are the most frequent types of offence you found in the previous question and how does this compare with the guidance given in the EA's PPG6?
4. Do you think it is a good practice to publicise environmental prosecutions in the way the EA does (see the previous two questions)? Explain why.

Indirect Aspects of Existing Technology Portfolio

Whilst direct impacts are undeniably an important area that needs to be addressed when making a company more sustainable, the indirect aspects – those associated with its products or services – often far outweigh the direct aspects in terms of total impact caused. With respect to the impact of buildings, it has been demonstrated that the energy consumed during the lengthy use phase outweighs any other impacts including those associated with construction (Horsley *et al.*, 2000). For the manufacturing and process industries, the use phase is also the 'hot spot' in the life cycle of an installation, as verified for the glass industry (Nicholas *et al.*, 2000). Other indirect aspects are associated with other companies in the supply chain; for example, pollution due to raw material extraction and processing or incidents due to failure to manage subcontractors (Beale, 2003). Arguably, the greatest environmental benefits will be gained from reducing indirect burdens of the process-contracting company.

The impacts of indirect aspects must be included within an EMS – they must meet legislative requirements and must be subject to continual improvement. For process contracting, the indirect burdens are strongly influenced by the process design of the installation, which determines the way it can be operated, maintained and decommissioned. Additional indirect burdens are influenced by aspects such as the degree of client training provided by the contractor and the depth of information, together with consequences of mal-operation, included within operating manuals. If a process-contracting company can make improvements in plant design, so as to reduce their indirect burdens, significant contribution would be made to sustainable development of this sector.

Technological improvements are driven by the established legal mechanisms for pollution control. The basis of such legislation is continual improvement to ensure the use of the best technique within given cost restraints. A typical example is Best Available Technique (BAT) regulated by the IPPC Directive (EC, 1996). In addition to increasingly strict legislation at least in developed countries, the scope of pollution control is also becoming more holistic; for example, the IPPC Directive requires consideration of the whole life cycle of an installation, from design to decommissioning, when choosing BAT. The process-contracting companies play an essential role in the improvement process throughout the life cycle of an installation. Through the provision of research and development facilities and the promotion of improved technologies, the boundaries of environmental protection can be continually moved forward. All process-contracting companies, and not just those engaged in the environmental technology market, have a key role to play in advancing BAT through global dissemination of knowledge concerning cleaner technology. In this respect, process-contracting companies play a key role in contributing to the transfer of environmentally sound technology and management methods throughout the industrial and public sectors, as promoted by the ICC's Business Charter for Sustainable Development (ICC, 2000).

Whilst the tightening of legislation ensures that a process-contracting company is able to achieve some degree of continual improvement in the environmental performance of technology supplied, achieving improvements which go beyond BAT can be difficult. Prior to and during the tendering process, the contracting company will usually enter into dialogue with the client to discuss available techniques and technologies. At this stage, the process-contracting company can do much to stress the advantages of going beyond the legal minimum, for example, preparedness for more stringent legislation within the lifetime of the installation. In addition, clean technologies can be promoted which have the added benefits of improved efficiencies and reduced operating costs. The final specification of technology to be supplied, however, will always be selected by the client, with decision-making strongly influenced by costs.

Traditional economic procurement procedures can hinder the implementation of environmentally beneficial technologies. End-of-pipe solutions are perceived as costly, and generally involve a net investment. Where these technologies are required, the winning contractor will often be the one with the Cheapest Available Technique Not Incurring Prosecution (CATNIP). With respect to clean technologies, there is potential for payback through improved efficiencies. However, operating costs are not always included within procurement procedures. Even when lifetime costs are considered, the traditional discounting approaches to cash flow and the immediate requirements of shareholders are biased towards short-term decisions, with the result that lower capital costs will still be favoured above the long-term benefits of resource and energy efficiency. Therefore, with respect to continual improvement of indirect burdens, the process-contracting company is dependent on the willingness of its clients to improve their own sustainability performance and their willingness to consider the lifetime cost of the proposed technique.

The challenge facing contracting companies who wish to improve their indirect burdens is to develop solutions that result in reduced environmental and social impact and which are competitive on a capital cost basis. To achieve this could involve moving beyond their existing technology portfolios to develop new technologies or move into new market areas.

Direct and Indirect Aspects of Future Technology Portfolios

In terms of long-term strategic planning, how can a process contracting company improve its technology portfolio and progress towards sustainability? It is generally agreed that sustainable development requires significant change. Whether the improvements in eco-efficiency required are in the magnitude of Factor 4 or Factor 10 (Chapter 1), the change required is likely to involve step changes in technology, as opposed to incremental improvements in existing practice. The move towards a service-based or knowledge-based economy has been cited as an example of such a step change (DTI, 2000). Therefore, process-contracting companies must examine the technologies within their portfolios and the manner by which their business is carried out, in order to seek opportunities to develop clean technology solutions to meet the needs of both their clients and society as a whole (Christie *et al.*, 1995).

Whilst some leading process-contracting groups have identified the potential for the development of new, cleaner solutions, for the kind of change required by sustainable development, the entire contracting sector must improve. An overall improvement may not be achieved if 'dirty' technologies are divested to another company that continues their marketing (i.e. shifting the burden and responsibility elsewhere). Also, contractors supplying state-of-the-art technology and trying to recoup development costs are at risk of loosing out to contractors supplying established, well-proven and possibly cheaper technology. Overall improvement will be achievable only if clients and their regulators are willing to accept novel process solutions, to ensure that clean technology displaces traditional processes. This must occur on both the national and the global scale, so that developing countries avoid the implementation of 'dirty' technologies, in effect learning from the mistakes of developed countries (Munasinghe, 1995). As with improvements to existing technology, process contractors play an essential role in promoting the global transfer of new, cleaner technologies (ICC, 2000).

In order to implement novel techniques, it may be necessary for contractors to adopt new forms of relationship with their clients. Moving towards sustainability will require stable collaboration between the project stakeholders (Turton, 1998). Within process contracting, this could be achieved through building alliances between process engineering and client companies for the provision of long-term service contracts whereby project profits (or losses) are shared between alliance members. Such arrangements would allow the process-contracting company to enjoy a greater depth of knowledge relating to the client's processes. This would enable the contractor to establish a long-term programme of research and development in order to provide integral process solutions, as opposed to short-term benefits by virtue of minor refits; that is moving from end-of-pipe design to clean technology. The distribution of project risk through the alliancing approach may allow easier implementation of novel solutions and encourage active cooperation between alliance partners to overcome any difficulties during the project execution, including the avoidance of pollution and maintaining good stakeholder relations. This is because all alliance members would have a direct interest in the outcome of the project and would therefore be more likely to work together to achieve success. For example, one group of companies in the oil and gas sector successfully used the alliancing approach for an off-shore oil field development in the UK. Because both the risk and the benefits from the project were shared by all in the alliance, any challenges to the project were quickly overcome so that the project was brought to a successful conclusion. This can be contrasted with traditional supply chains where contractors and subcontractors have little or no incentive to do anything more than fulfil the requirements within their own limited scope of supply.

Bennett (1998) highlights that a barrier to the formation of long-term partnerships has traditionally come from 'competitive bidding' for procurement processes. These requirements are common within quality management systems and in some cases are required by law. For example, the EU rules on procurement of assets and services for the public sector require tenders to be put out for competitive bidding, including advertising through a dedicated Internet site (Tenders Electronic Daily, 2000). Bidding procedures are established to prohibit corruption and ensure good competition and hence good value; however, they are not suited to the complex issues involved when establishing partnerships. Whilst traditional tendering procedures are applicable to the pre-defined contractual requirements of specific projects (e.g. 'turnkey' contracting), they do not allow for the evolution of the project and the flexibility that is required in the provision of a service. Therefore, new procurement practices must be developed based on open negotiations, performance standards and shared risk.

Questions

1. Compare and contrast the traditional approach to 'turnkey' contracting with new alliancing approaches. How may new approaches help move the process-contracting industry towards sustainable development?
2. Why is supply chain management important for the implementation of sustainable solutions within the contracting industry?

11.2   Case Study: Process Contracting in the Glass Industry

We will now consider a case study related to process contracting in the glass industry. The aim is to illustrate the complexity of the contracting process and the sustainability issues faced by both the contractors and the clients, in this case the glass manufacturers. Although the case study is based around a hypothetical contractor and equally hypothetical glass manufacturer, the contracting process and sustainability issues are real enough to provide an insight into the process-contracting sector.

The case study starts with an invitation to a leading process-contracting company ConCo by a glass manufacturer Glass Bottle Co. to prepare a quotation for a gas cleaning system. The glass company must upgrade its existing gas cleaning system to meet the new requirements of the IPPC Directive. Both the contracting and the glass company are based in Europe.

Having received the letter from the glass company (Appendix 11.A), ConCo puts together a team to design the gas cleaning system and prepare a preliminary budget proposal. If successful in the first stage of the bidding process, this preliminary proposal will be followed by a final design and budget estimate. ConCo is very interested in this project but they are aware that they are not the only company that has been invited to bid so that if they want to win this contract, they will have to provide a very competitive proposal. They will have to anticipate what their competitors are likely to propose and then go beyond that. Having read the Glass Bottle Co. Sustainability Policy that the company sent to ConCo (Appendix 11.B), the bidding team agree that one way to increase their chances of winning the contract is to consider all three aspects of sustainability in their design. To achieve this aim, ConCo will have to enter discussions with the glass company, equipment manufacturers, the glass company's regulators and the local community.

In preparing their preliminary and then, if successful, a final design, the ConCo design team will use and rely on the following sources of information:

- covering letter from the Glass Bottle company (Appendix 11.A);
- Glass Bottle Co. Sustainability Policy (Appendix 11.B);
- glass plant layout (Appendix 11.C);
- glass furnace specification and air emission limits (sections 'Glass Manufacturing Process and Air Emission Limits');
- ConCo's own in-house design data and practices (section 'Technical Information for Gas Cleaning Systems' and 'Further Plant Information and Design Requirements');
- cost data (section 11.2.2);
- legislation and regulation acts (section 11.2.3); and
- stakeholder consultation and subcontractor history (section 11.2.4).

The reader is invited to join the ConCo team and help them to design a sustainable gas cleaning system in order to win the contract.

11.2.1   Technical and Design Specifications

Glass Manufacturing Process and Air Emission Limits

Before the team can start on the design, they need to understand better the glass manufacturing process used by the glass company. The company has provided them with the following information.

The glass plant consists of two horizontal furnaces, each with a capacity of 200 t of glass per day. The glass furnace design is illustrated in Figure 11.1. The manufacturing

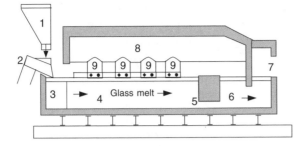

(1) glass batch container; (2) batch feeder; (3) batch feeding compartment - 'dog house'
(4) melting and refining tank; (5) tank throat; (6) forehearth; (7) feeder to glass forming;
(8) roof or 'crown' of the melting tank; and (9) burner ports.

Figure 11.1   *Cross section of the glass furnace melting tank (Schott Guide to Glass, 2nd edition, 1996, p. 37, Pfeander, figure 3.2. With kind permission of Kluwer Academic Publishers.)*

process involves heating the raw material batch (mainly silica, lime, soda and recycled glass – cullet) to the molten state at 1400–1600 °C, and maintaining that temperature to allow the homogeneous formation of the glass. The molten glass then flows from the furnace to be formed into the packaging containers, that is bottles. The furnace melting energy (7.8 MJ/kg glass) is supplied by firing via burners with either natural gas or fuel oil. Combustion products (N_2, H_2O, CO_2, O_2, NO_x, SO_x and particulates) together with products from the glass melt reactions (particulates, CO_2, SO_x, HCl, HF and small quantities of other compounds) are emitted from the furnace. Prior to being released in to the atmosphere, energy is recovered from the waste gas by using it to preheat combustion air.

The glass company has summarised the operating conditions of the two furnaces and the waste gas composition in Table 11.1. They have also specified the emissions limits that the regulator will expect them to meet if they are to renew their permit to operate. These limits are shown in Table 11.2.

Further Plant Information and Design Requirements

Plant battery limits
The plant battery limits are shown in the plant layout in Appendix 11.C. The ducting from furnaces to chimneys is rectangular with dimensions of 1.5×1.5 m. Two 1×1 m take-off points have also been installed to allow future retrofit of cleaning equipment – these are the plant battery limits.

Dust recycle to furnace
The company is keen to minimise waste and therefore recycle the dust from the dust cleaning equipment to a furnace. However, it is not possible to send dust collected from the green furnace to the flint furnace (though flint furnace dust can be returned to the flint furnace). In addition, the green furnace can accept a maximum of 150 kg/h of waste dust and the raw material composition can be adjusted so that only

Table 11.1   *Furnace specification and waste gas composition data*

	Furnace No. 1	Furnace No. 2
Glass type	Flint (colourless glass)	Green
Glass melted	200 t/day	200 t/day
Temperature at battery limit[a]	550 °C	550 °C
Pressure at battery limit[a]	−5 mbar	−5 mbar
Cullet	40 t/day	100 t/day
Other raw materials	182 t/day[b]	114 t/day[b]
Furnace fuel	Natural gas	Natural gas
Melting energy	6.2 GJ/t melt	5.5 GJ/t melt
Waste gas flow[c]	23 000 Nm³/h[d]	21 000 Nm³/h[d]
Waste gas composition		
Nitrogen	73.5%	73.5%
Carbon dioxide	6.8%	6.7%
Oxygen	6%	6.2%
Water	13.2%	13.1%
NO_x[e]	750 mg/Nm³	745 mg/Nm³
SO_x[e]	855 mg/Nm³	845 mg/Nm³
Particulate matter[e]	130 mg/Nm³	115 mg/Nm³
Metals (total solid & gaseous)[e,f]	4 mg/Nm³	6 mg/Nm³

[a] Battery limits indicated on plant layout diagram (Appendix 11.C).
[b] Excess material lost as gases due to melt reactions.
[c] Nm³ = volume normalised to dry, 0 °C (273 K), 101.3 kPa.
[d] Difference in gas flows due to lower energy usage in furnace No. 2 due to higher rate of cullet usage.
[e] Concentration expressed at 8% O_2, dry, 0 °C (273 K), 101.3 kPa.
[f] Selenium (a decolourising agent) is the most significant emission from furnace No.1 whilst lead (from cullet impurities) is significant in furnace No. 2.

Table 11.2   *Maximum allowable emission levels from the stack*

NO_x	800 mg/Nm³
SO_x	300 mg/Nm³
Particulate matter	20 mg/Nm³
Metals (total solid & gaseous)	<1 mg/Nm³

a slight increase in SO_x emissions occurs (maximum by 20 mg/Nm³). A quotation is required for two options:

1. separate gas cleaning systems, one for each furnace; and
2. a single system treating the combined gases from both furnaces.

Cullet preheater

By cooling the waste gas exiting the furnace from 550 °C to approximately 200 °C, the batch material in the furnace can be heated to typically 270 °C. This greatly improves the energy efficiency of the plant as it reduces fuel consumption. The company has also found that a waste gas temperature of above 600 °C may cause the batch to become sticky, leading to problematic batch feeding.

Whilst they have not specifically required a cullet preheater in the Invitation to Bid, the Glass Bottle Co. is very keen to reduce the fuel (natural gas) consumption as part of its negotiated agreements under the climate change programme. However, this would require an alliancing type approach with shared risks or would make contractors to take on all risks and use the plant as a demonstration. 'Turnkey' approach is not an option in this case.

Technical Information for Gas Cleaning Systems

In designing their gas cleaning system, the ConCo team will have to look into both the primary and the secondary measures for reducing the emissions from the glass furnace. The former include in-furnace measures to prevent or reduce the formation of pollutants. Secondary measures involve the use of 'end-of-pipe' techniques such as acid gas scrubbing and particulate removal in an electrostatic precipitator or bag filter (Chapter 5). A typical gas cleaning system is illustrated in Figure 11.2.

In addition to the information provided by the glass company and their own experience, the ConCo design team has access to the following information within their company regarding the design procedures for gas cleaning systems.

Removal of acid gases

Acid gases can be removed by several techniques but dry and semi-dry absorption are typically used with lime [$Ca(OH)_2$] being the preferred absorbent for both techniques (see Chapter 5 for more detail on semi-dry sorption). The theoretical amount of lime required for the removal of acid gases can be estimated from the Ca/S molar ratio. Typically, an excess of 10% above the estimated theoretical amount is used. The removal efficiencies for SO_x and other acid gases for different Ca/S ratios are summarised in Table 11.3.

The required lime-dosing rate is therefore dependent on the required abatement rate. At Ca/S > 1, it can be assumed that all unreacted lime forms calcium carbonate ($Ca(CO_3)$). For example, for Ca/S = 2:

$$2Ca(OH)_2 + SO_2 + CO_2 \rightarrow CaSO_3 + CaCO_3 + 2H_2O$$

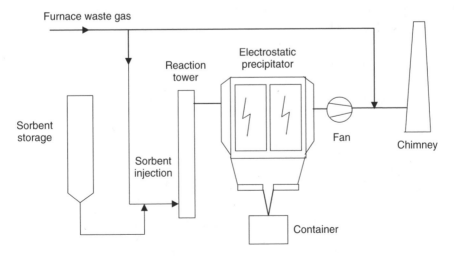

Figure 11.2   *Flue gas cleaning by dry absorption*

Table 11.3   *Removal efficiencies with lime for SO$_x$ and other acid gases*

Ca/S ratio	SO$_x$ removal efficiency (%)	
	Dry scrubbing	Semi-dry scrubbing
4.4 (@400°C)	65	
1 (@200°C)	22 (Removal efficiency of other acid gases for Ca/S = 1:70%)	80 (Removal efficiency of other acid gases for Ca/S = 1:90%)
1.5 (@200°C)	n/a	90
2 (@200°C)	40	92
3 (@200°C)	55	n/a

Dry scrubbing is normally carried out in a vertical cyclindrical tower or duct (Figure 11.2). The dimensions of the tower must be such as to allow sufficient residence times for the reaction between the acid gases and the lime. From experience, the design team assumes that a 15-m high tower with an effective upflow velocity of 5 m/s will ensure the sufficient residence time. If a horizontal duct is used, then a minimum velocity of 15 m/s is required for the dust-laden gas.

Removal of particulates
Electrostatic precipitators (ESPs) are the preferable technology in the glass industry for the removal of particulates. The maximum allowable gas temperature for entry into an ESP is usually 400°C (unless exotic materials of construction are used). Waste gases leaving the furnaces can be cooled either by ingress of ambient air or by radiative cooling from the ductwork, or a combination of both (which may be required for optimum filter size). Some gas cooling takes place from ambient air due to lime injection. The gas can also be cooled down by cullet preheat, if this option is used.

After the scrubbing tower phase, the gas is laden with the particulates generated in the furnace and with the spent absorbent from acid gas scrubbing. Therefore, the ESP collecting plates will have to be sufficiently large to ensure the required particulates collection efficiency.

The required collecting area for ESP can be found from the Deutsch–Anderson equation:

$$\eta = 100(1 - \exp(-AW_e/Q)) \quad (\%) \qquad (11.1)$$

where:
  η efficiency of removal of particulates (%)
  A area of the collecting plates (m^2)
  W_e effective particle migration velocity (normally taken to be 7 cm/s)
  Q gas flow rate (m^3/s)

A minimum of two fields is required in order to minimise the effect of emission spikes during rapping (cleaning of ESPs). All fields must be of the same size (type). The field sizes available are summarised in Table 11.4. Gas velocity within the ESP must be less than 1.5 m/s.

Table 11.4 *Field sizes available for electrostatic precipitators*

Type	Collecting area per field (m²)	Field width W (m)	Field length Lª (m)	Field height H (m)
A	700	4	6	5.5
B	1000	4.5	6	7
C	1300	5	6	8
D	1600	5.5	6	9
E	1900	6	6	10

ª direction of gas flow is along length L.

To calculate power consumption by ESP, the following can be assumed:

– current of $0.5\,mA/m^2$ of collecting electrode;
– voltage of $50\,kV$; and
– transformer efficiency of 85%.

Collected dust can in most cases be recycled to the glass furnace, with the interim storage in silo within the batch house. In specific cases where a common cleaning system serves two different furnaces it may not be possible to recycle dust to one or other furnace due to quality requirements. In such cases, all the dust may be able to go to one furnace or separate systems may be necessary, otherwise some dust may require landfill. This is the case with the Glass Bottle Co. furnaces.

Removal of metals
In addition to the acid gases, the scrubbing process also captures metals. Dry scrubbing by lime, for example, captures approximately 80% of gaseous metals. The ratio of metals adsorbed on the dust to those in gaseous state can be assumed to be 1:1.

Pressure drop
The typical pressure drop across a system with average length ducting, scrubbing tower and ESP is in the region of 15–20 mbar. The pressure drop is significantly higher if a bag filter is used.

Cullet preheater
Due to the drive towards energy efficiency, the Research & Development (R&D) Department in ConCo has been developing a new cullet preheater. This works by allowing raw materials to come into contact with the hot waste gases in a counter-current flow, after they have been used to heat the combustion air. Neither ConCo nor anyone else has built a full-scale plant to date.

Typical performance characteristics of a cullet preheater retrofit into a 200 t/day furnace are expected to be:

– reduction in energy consumption of approximately 15–20%, leading to direct cost savings;
– reduced gas flow rate (due to lower fuel and combustion air rates and additional gas cooling) allows for smaller gas cleaning plant; typically 15% reduction in gas volume leaving the furnace can be achieved;

- raw materials remove some acidic compounds (around 60% of SO_2), thus reducing or eliminating the need for sorbent injection;
- cullet preheater introduces dust to the waste gas (the waste gas takes up additional dust of between 0.5 (with 80% cullet) and 1% of the batch charge (with 50% cullet)). At less than 30% cullet, there is too much batch carry over for the system to work effectively.

11.2.2 Project Cost Data

The only Main Plant Item (MPI) that can be supplied in-house by ConCo is the ESP. Costs of design, supply and erection of ESP and related control equipment are given in Table 11.5. Furthermore, the ConCo knows that capital cost of a cullet preheater is around £850 000 with annual operating costs of £40 000, including additional energy cost due to pressure drop.

All other MPIs must be subcontracted, with delivery to site and erection included in the costs quoted by the subcontractors. The ConCo's subcontractors include:

- Ducting and absorption tower:
    - UK Steelwork Co.
    - EC Metals GmbH
    - Euro Pipework Co.
- Fans:
    - UK Pumps and Blowers Ltd
    - UK Fan Company
    - Big Blowers.
- Storage Facilities:
    - Silo Co.
    - Dust Storage Solutions Ltd
    - Solid Storage and Handling Ltd
- Civil engineering:
    - Smith and Sons Bricks Ltd
    - Cement and Sand Co.
    - Bob and Sons Building Contractors.

The costs quoted by these contractors are summarised in Appendix 11.D.

Table 11.5 *Costs of design, supply and erection of ESP*

Type	Collecting area per field (m²)	Cost for 2 field ESP £000s	Cost per additional field £000s
A	700	326	49
B	1000	404	61
C	1300	473	71
D	1600	535	80
E	1900	594	89

Although ConCo has worked with these subcontractors before, in view of the Glass Bottle Co. Sustainability Policy, in addition to the cost considerations, they will have to evaluate their subcontractors on environmental and social performance and decide whether they are suitable for this contract. This is further discussed in section 11.2.4.

Once the MPI costs have been established, the total project costs are calculated according to the formula:

$$C_T = [1 + f_1 + f_2 + f_3 + f_4 + f_5] \cdot \Sigma C_{MPI} \tag{11.2}$$

where:

C_T total cost
ΣC_{MPI} total cost of MPIs
f_1 cost factor for piping, instrumentation and electrical ($f_1 = 0.2$)
f_2 cost factor for design and engineering ($f_2 = 0.15$)
f_3 cost factor for site supervision ($f_3 = 0.05$)
f_4 cost factor for safety, health and environmental costs ($f_2 = 0.02\text{--}0.05$)
f_5 contingency cost factor ($f_2 = 0.1$)

Finally, accounting for profit of 5%, ConCo envisages the total project cost as:

$$C_p = 1.05 \, C_T \tag{11.3}$$

11.2.3   Environmental Legislation

Having obtained most of the technical information they will need for the preliminary and later stages of the final design, the next task for the ConCo team is to review the legislative requirements for air emissions from the glass industry so that they can design the system that meets these requirements.

The glass plant is subject to the EC Directive on IPPC. The Directive requires the glass industry to control not only emissions to air but also emissions to water and land. In addition to emissions and pollution, however, IPPC also requires consideration of additional aspects including noise reduction, energy efficiency, use of raw materials, off-site waste disposal, accident prevention and the protection of the environment as a whole (see Chapters 4 and 5 for more detail on the IPPC requirements). It requires glass manufacturers to use the BAT for protection of the environment and to apply to the regulator for a permit to operate. Within the permit, various conditions are set which establish how the manufacturing process should be operated, including limits on emissions to air.

The ConCo team has also found out that, to guide the regulators when determining permit conditions, the EC has developed Best Available Techniques Reference (BREF) document for the glass manufacture (EC, 1999). This document gives detailed descriptions of glass furnaces, their emissions and pollution control techniques so that the team will use it as the main guiding document in preparing a design for the gas cleaning system.

11.2.4   Social Considerations

To ensure that they take into account the relevant social concerns in their preliminary design and therefore minimise any design changes and costs in the final stage, the ConCo has approached the local residents to discuss their concerns with respect to the construction and operation of the new gas cleaning system.

Two concerns have been expressed by the local resident group: one over increased noise levels and another over increased transport. The resident group has in particular highlighted that A37 is already busy and dangerous and that the construction and use of the gas cleaning equipment would make the transport situation in that area even worse.

Secondly, following the Glass Bottle Co. Sustainability Policy, ConCo has reviewed the subcontractors on their social responsibility and has found out the following:

Steelwork: Both EC Metals and Euro Pipework have been removed from the Glass Bottle Co. suppliers list by their purchasing department. ConCo could not find out the exact reason for this, but has heard rumours that these companies have had problems with respect to Union action on the EC Working Time Legislation.

Fans: Big Blowers is rumoured to be exploiting women and under-age workers in its Asian factories.

Civil Engineering: Cement and Sand Co. has been prosecuted during the past 2 years in connection with water pollution. Bob and Sons is being investigated by Health and Safety Executive as his sons working in the company are thought to be under-aged. Furthermore, Smith and Sons has had financial problems lately from which they are still recovering.

The ConCo team now has most of the technical, economic, environmental and social data so that they can begin their preliminary design. After providing an initial quote to the Glass Bottle Co., they hope to proceed to the final design.

Questions

1. Use the information provided in this case study to produce first a preliminary and then a final design of a sustainable gas cleaning system for this glass manufacturing process.
2. How would you explore the alliancing approach to design a more sustainable gas cleaning system used in this case study?

There are many ways to go about this design – there is no single answer nor approach to this problem. This is a complex task which requires a multidisciplinary team work. Bear in mind that you will not need all the information given here for the preliminary design so that you need to decide which level of detail is required for which type of design. You will also need to do some research by yourself to find out the missing data.

Conclusions

Companies can do much to move towards more sustainable practices. Their efforts can be enhanced by developing an integrated business management system to manage economic, environmental and social issues. But although the guiding principles are in place, the question remains: What does sustainable development mean in practice for specific sectors of industry?

This chapter and the case study have focused on the process-contracting industry in an attempt to explore the meaning of sustainability for this sector. A case study of process contracting in the glass industry has been used to illustrate the complexity of the problem and to provide an insight into the way of addressing the sustainability challenge for the industry. It has been argued that the current contracting and bidding practices are unsustainable as they are focused on short-term economic gains with little consideration of environmental and social aspects. An alliancing approach in which partnerships are formed between the stakeholders in the contracting industry may help to move the sustainability agenda in the contracting industry further. However, this requires a close collaboration between contractors, clients, regulators and local communities. The role of engineering teams within these partnerships is to demonstrate that it is possible to deliver more sustainable designs not only by using the available and well-established techniques but also by considering innovative solutions and approaches.

Appendix 11.A: Invitation to Bid – Letter from Glass Bottle Co. to ConCo

Glass Bottle Co.
2 Furnace Drive
Glasstown 1BY 0B

FAO Director of Sales
ConCo
1 Deal Close
Tendertown 2E 1S

Dear Sir,

Re: Supply of emissions abatement system

Subsequent to our previous discussions, I invite you to tender for the 'turnkey' supply of an emissions abatement system (including civil engineering works) for our glass furnace waste gas.

I can confirm that our recently obtained IPPC permit includes an improvement condition requiring upgrade of the current techniques for control of our glass furnace emissions. As part of this process we intend to install pollution abatement equipment to our glass bottle furnaces Nos. 1&2. I have enclosed a plant layout diagram along with the relevant technical details for the two furnaces, including the required future emission limits. In addition I must draw your attention to our Sustainability Policy Statement which requires all suppliers to demonstrate their commitment to environmental protection, Health and Safety, and to reducing the impact of their operations on the community surrounding Glass Bottle Co.

In order for us to set aside the required funding and to shortlist proposed solutions, would you please supply us initially with a Budget quotation ($\pm 20\%$) of the abatement system that you propose. This should include:

(i)   A basic process description with process flow diagram;
(ii) Emissions performance and material/energy consumption values; and
(iii) List of proposed subcontractors.

Within your Firm quotation, please include the following:

– Process description with piping and instrumentation diagram;
– Plant layout diagram;
– Description of proposed locations and methods for monitoring and sampling emissions with reference to relevant standards (CEN/ISO/BS);
– Guarantees to cover emissions, material and energy consumption;
– Total cost and cost breakdown;
– Justification for choice of subcontractors;
– Justification as to why your proposal is BAT (refer to Article 3 and Annex IV of the IPPC Directive and the glass BREF);
– Discussion of arrangements and provisions concerning the prevention of pollution on site and the maintenance of good relations with local residents adjacent to the Glass Bottle Co. site; and
– Your sustainability or environmental, health and safety policy statements if available.

Please contact me to discuss a suitable date for submission of Budget and Firm quotations – we will be requiring you to make a presentation at both stages of your proposal. In addition, should you wish to clarify any issues do not hesitate to arrange a further meeting with my colleagues or myself.

Yours faithfully
Mr I.B. Green
Plant Engineering Manager

Appendix 11.B

Glass Bottle Co. Sustainability Policy Statement

The Glass Bottle Co. is a leading multi-national company concerned with the worldwide manufacture and supply of glass containers for a wide range of uses. We recognise the need for companies to develop in such a way that they improve people's standard of living, wherever they are in the world. To achieve this, the Glass Bottle Co. is actively involved in promoting adoption of the principles linked to Sustainable Development. We ensure that measures to improve quality of life are integrated throughout our business activities, from the concerns of senior management to the heart of its manufacturing facilities.

In particular we have identified the following responsibilities.
Our environmental responsibilities:

- As a minimum we seek to comply with all the environmental legislation within the countries we operate and where possible to adopt best practice for environmental protection.
- In developing new products and processes and in reviewing existing ones, we seek to minimise their environmental impacts, to prevent pollution and to reduce the impact of all activities associated with their construction, manufacture, use and disposal.
- We seek to continuously improve our environmental performance and the way we manage our environmental responsibilities. This is achieved through the identification and management of all environmental aspects associated with our products, processes and associated services.
- We actively encourage the recycling of our products and are working closely with those who use our containers to establish a network so that they can be collected for recycling after use.
- We require that all our suppliers demonstrate their commitment to environmental issues and we encourage suppliers to improve their own environmental performance.
- We strive to demonstrate the importance of environmental protection to our employees and those involved with our business. We encourage suggestions for improvement of our environmental performance.

Our social responsibilities:

- We regularly consult our neighbours on the issues that concern them, with the aim of reducing our impact upon local neighbourhoods.

- We provide a safe and healthy working environment for all our employees and all those entering our sites and encourage employees to highlight ways in which improvements can be made.
- We recognise that everyone has an equal opportunity to work and ensure that there is no discrimination of employees or their representatives.
- We abide by and promote the fundamental international laws concerning human rights and in particular the rights of children.
- We encourage all suppliers to adopt these responsibilities as their own and to ensure that they plan their activities so as to minimise risk to their employees, our employees and to our neighbours.

We are accountable for all these responsibilities and publish an annual Sustainability Report to demonstrate our achievement of these goals.

Mr G.C. Goodfellow   Dr I. Care
CEO   Director for Sustainability

Appendix 11.C: The Layout of the Glass Bottle Plant

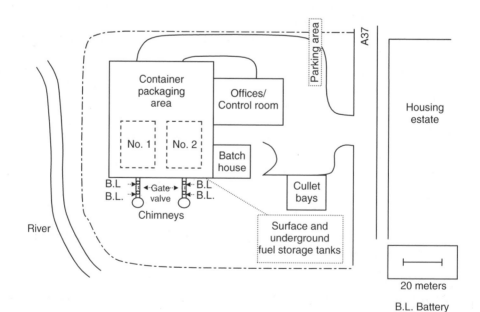

Appendix 11.D: Costs of the Equipment and Subcontracting

Ducting and absorption tower   Costs based on duct cross-sectional area A (m^2)
UK Steelwork Co. $C_{D\&T} = 2000\,A^{0.6}$ (£/m)
EC Metals GmbH $C_{D\&T} = 1800\,A^{0.6}$ (£/m)
Euro Pipework Co. $C_{D\&T} = 1750\,A^{0.6}$ (£/m)

Fans   Costs based on flow Q (m^3/s)
UK Pumps and Blowers Ltd $C_F = 5400\,Q^{0.8}$ (£)
UK Fan Company $C_F = 5700\,Q^{0.8}$ (£)
Big Blowers $C_F = 4400\,Q^{0.8}$ (£)

These costs are for a fan serving a standard gas cleaning system (pressure drop $\Delta P_1 = 15\text{–}20\,\mathrm{mbar}$). The cost is adjusted for pressure drop according to:

$$C_{\Delta P_2} = C_{\Delta P_1}(\Delta P_2/\Delta P_1)^{0.8}$$

To reduce noise, a silencer can be added; this increases fan costs by 20%.

Dust/lime storage facilities   Costs based on the storage volume V (m^3)
(incl. discharge equipment)
Silo Co. $C_S = 5400\,V^{0.6}$ (£)
Dust Storage solutions Ltd $C_S = 5300\,V^{0.6}$ (£)
Solid storage and handling Ltd $C_S = 5450\,V^{0.6}$ (£)

Civil engineering	Roadways/parking	Plant foundations*
Smith and Sons Bricks Ltd	$C_{CE} = 500$ (£/m^2)	$C_{CE} = 1100$ (£/m^2)
Cement and Sand Co.	$C_{CE} = 450$ (£/m^2)	$C_{CE} = 1000$ (£/m^2)
Bob and Sons Building Contractors	$C_{CE} = 550$ (£/m^2)	$C_{CE} = 1110$ (£/m^2)

*Civil contractor requires ConCo to supply structural details (i.e. plant height, type and materials) to calculate loads (static and wind) for foundations.

References and Further Reading

Azapagic, A. (2003) Systems Approach to Corporate Sustainability: A General Management Framework. *IChemE Trans. B.* **81**, 303–316.

Azapagic, A. and Perdan, S. (2000) 'Indicators of Sustainable Development for Industry: A General Framework', Process Safety and Environmental Protection, *IChemE Trans.*, **78**, Part B, July, 243–261.

Beale, C.J. (2003) Factors Influencing the Safe Management of Contractors on Major Hazard Installations. In: *Hazards XVII: Process Safety – Fulfilling Our Responsibilities.* IChemE Symposium Series No. 149, Institution of Chemical Engineers, Rugby.

Bennett, E. (1998) Contract procurement solutions for public–private partnerships, UNDP/Yale collaborative programme http://ww3.undp.orp/ppp/library/files/bennet03.txt (January 2001).

Christie, I., Rolfe, H. and Legard, R. (1995) *Cleaner Production in Industry.* Policy Studies Institute, London.

DETR (1998) Sustainable Development: Opportunities for Change – Sustainable Construction, Department of the Environment, Transport and the Regions: London. http://www.environment.detr.gov.uk/sustainable/construction/consult/index.htm (January 2001).

DoE (1994) Energy Efficiency Office Good Practice Guide 127. Energy Efficient Environmental Control in the Glass Industry. ETSU, Harwell.

DoE (1995) Secretary of State's Guidance under EPA90 PG 3/3(95) Glass (Excluding Lead Glass) Manufacturing Processes. Her Majesty's Stationery Office: London.

DTI (2000) DTI Sustainable Development Strategy Department of Trade and Industry. http://www.dti.gov.uk/sustainability/index.htm.

Environment Agency (1999) Spotlight on business environmental performance – 1999. http://www.environment-agency.gov.uk/envinfo/spotlight/index.htm.

Environment Agency (2000) Working at Construction and Demolition Sites: PPG6, from: http://www.environment-agency.gov.uk/business/ppg/?lang=_e&region=.

EC (1996) Council Directive 96/61/EC of 24/9/96. Concerning Integrated Pollution Prevention and Control. *Official Journal of the European Communities*, L257 10/10/996. Her Majesty's Stationery Office, London.

EC (1999) Reference Document on Best Available Techniques in Glass Manufacturing Industry, European Commission Directorate-General JRC Joint Research Centre, Institute for Prospective Technological Studies: Seville. http://eippcb.jrc.es/pages/FActivities.htm (August 1999).

Goode, G.A.A., Kannahand, K. and Copley, G.A. (1996) EPA90 – the Options for Large Scale Glass Melting. *Glass Technology*, 37(6) 188–191.

Hobbs, M. and Stevens, G.C. (2003) How Does Safety Performance Affect Corporate Value? In: Hazards XVII Process safety – fulfilling our responsibilities. IChemE Symposium Series No. 149, Institution of Chemical Engineers: Rugby.

Horsley, A., France, C. and Quatermass, B. (2000) Turning up the Heat: Improving The Energy Performance of UK Building through Public/Private Partnership. Proceedings of the Engineering Doctorate in Environmental Technology Annual Conference. Centre for Environmental Strategy, University of Surrey, Guildford.

ICC (2000) Business Charter for Sustainable Development, International Chamber of Commerce. http://www.iccwbo.org/sdcharter/charter/principles/principles.asp (January 2001).

IChemE (2000) Future Life: Engineering Solutions for the Next Generation. Institution of Chemical Engineers: Rugby. http://www.icheme.org/publicity/publications/futurelife/futurelife.pdf (January 2001).

ISO 14001 (1996) *Environmental Management Systems – Specification with Guidance for Use*. British Standards Institution, London.

Kiely, G. (1997) *Environmental Engineering*. McGraw-Hill International (UK).

McIntosh, M., Leipziger, D. Jones, K. and Coleman, G. (1998) *Corporate Citizenship: Successful Strategies for Responsible Companies*. Financial Times Professional Ltd, London.

Munasinghe, M. (1995) Making Economic Growth More Sustainable. *Ecological Economics*, **15**, 121–124.

Nicholas, M.J., Clift, R., Walker, F.C., Azapagic, A. and Porter, D.E. (2000) Determination of Best Available Techniques for Integrated Pollution Prevention and Control: A Life Cycle Approach. Process Safety and Environmental Protection, *Trans. IChemE*, **78**, Part B, May, 193–203.

Perry, R.H. (ed.) (1984) *Perry's Chemical Engineer's Handbook*, Sixth Edition. McGraw-Hill International Editions.

Pfaender, H.G. (1996) *Schott Guide to Glass*. Chapman and Hall, London.

SustainAbility (1999) *SustainAbility Headlines*. SustainAbility Ltd, London.

Turton, P. (1998) Business Opportunities in Sustainability. Environment Agency. http://www.environment-agency.gov.uk//modules/MOD31.107.html (January 2001).

Tenders Electronic Daily (2000) Public Tenders. Internet version of the Supplement to the Official Journal of the EC, http://eur-op.eu.int/general/en/b7.htm (January 2001).

12

Multi-Criteria Decision Analysis: The Case of Power Generation in South Africa

Jim Petrie, Lauren Basson, Philippa Notten and Mary Stewart

Summary

Chapters 9 and 10 considered future energy scenarios and technologies respectively. In this chapter we explore an old and well-established energy technology based on coal. However, we look into the future of this industry and use the South African example to analyse how this well-established sector can become more sustainable. Coal is likely to continue to be a dominant source of energy in South Africa (and in some other developing countries, including China). We seek to understand the broader consequences of coal-fired power generation in terms of regional sustainable development. We argue that there is a need for more transparent, legitimate and defensible decision-making processes to ensure that stakeholder concerns are captured in the process, and that the implications of any trade-offs which ensue from decision outcomes are made explicit. We in particular address the issue of management of uncertainty in the decision-making process. We make use of a technology design case study to demonstrate some decision-support tools which meet these objectives.

12.1 Introduction

It is not an unreasonable comment to suggest that South Africa's economic development, like development of any other developing country, is tied inextricably to the cost

Sustainable Development in Practice: Case Studies for Engineers and Scientists
Edited by Adisa Azapagic, Slobodan Perdan and Roland Clift
© 2004 John Wiley & Sons, Ltd   ISBNs: 0-470-85608-4 (HB); 0-470-85609-2 (PB)

of energy. Politicians, economic planners and the parastatal electrical utility alike all make much of the current low cost of electricity and the critical role this has played to date in attracting economic investment to the country. In recent years, much of this investment has been in the primary resources sector, including aluminium, zinc and steel. This has been enabled, in part, by innovative electricity-pricing contracts, often tied to commodity prices on the London Metals Exchange. This trend is set to continue for the foreseeable future, with several other large minerals refining projects in the planning stages. At the same time, the national electrical utility has embarked on a highly ambitious programme to improve domestic (including rural) access to electricity, resulting in an annual increase in new connections of 200 000–250 000 over the last 5 years, and, through the African Energy Fund, promoting partnerships with other regional utilities to "light up Sub-Saharan Africa". This is occurring at a time when the industry itself is earmarked for deregulation and privatisation, and it is likely that independent power producers will enter the market in the medium term.

Together, these trends have placed significant strain on the electricity network, and considerable increase in generation capacity is being contemplated over the next 5–15 years. The challenge is how best to meet this increased demand – what supply-side generation strategies should be employed and how should these be balanced with a comprehensive set of demand-side management strategies. Electrical power generation is predominantly coal-based, and the vast reserves of coal will ensure that coal-fired generation will continue to dominate into the medium term. This is not to suggest that other forms of electricity generation are not in an advanced state of development (including renewables), merely that the size of the demand, the investment in existing infrastructure and current energy minerals pricing policies will ensure that coal retains its dominance.

In this chapter, we seek to understand the broader consequences of this commitment to coal-fired power generation in terms of regional sustainable development. We argue that there is a need for more transparent, legitimate and defensible decision-making processes to ensure that stakeholder concerns are captured in the process, and that the implications of any trade-offs which ensue from decision outcomes are made explicit. A particular challenge is to understand the implications of uncertainty in the various sub-models of the system under investigation (the issue also raised in Chapter 2). We make use of a technology design case study to demonstrate some decision-support tools which meet these objectives.

Questions

1. Why does the cost of energy influence development of developing countries?
2. How are developed countries affected by the cost and availability of energy?
3. Where are the largest mineral reserves found: in developed or developing countries? How do you think the mineral reserves have helped the economic development of these countries?
4. Do your own research on the energy situation in the Sub-Saharan Africa. What do you conclude: what are the priorities in this region with respect to energy?
5. What are the main sustainability issues for South Africa? What is the role of energy in the development of South Africa?

12.2 Coal Mining and Environmental Challenges in South Africa

The official estimate indicates *in situ* coal resources of $121\,218 \times 10^6$ t in South Africa, of which $55\,333 \times 10^6$ t are classified as economically recoverable (DME, 2003a). Low-grade bituminous coal constitutes about 80% of the reserves (Bredell, 1987). Opinions as to how long these reserves will last differ widely because of the difficulty in predicting future export and usage figures. Assuming an annual increase in coal production of 1.8%, Surridge *et al.* (1995) predicted that coal production would peak by 2050, and then tail off over the next two centuries.

Coal mining is an important contributor to South Africa's GDP, with total local and export sales amounting to R9564 million[1] (152×10^6 t) and R16 956 million (69×10^6 t) respectively in 2001 (Prevost, 2002).

Over the years, coal mining has been a cause of major environmental degradation in South Africa (Van Horen, 1996). Coal mining, particularly opencast mining, is associated with massive surface disruption. This results in changed land use and water catchment patterns, in addition to the noise, visual intrusion, dust and water contamination typically accompanying surface mining operations. Opencast mining accounts for nearly 50% of South Africa's coal production (Prevost, 2002). Underground mining is generally less disruptive. Water contamination, surface subsistence and underground fires are some of the major impacts of underground mines (Wells *et al.*, 1992). Only the environmental impacts of coal mining are considered here, although considerable social impacts also accompany coal mining, including the problems of migrant labour and the high number of injuries and fatalities occurring in coal mines (Van Horen, 1996). In the first three quarters of 2002 (the most up-to-date information available), 11 workers had died on South African coal mines and 115 had been injured (DME, 2003b). Social and ethical aspects of mining are considered further in Chapter 13.

Major environmental impacts stem from the high ash content of Southern Hemisphere coals, which require beneficiation to produce coals of acceptable quality for the world markets. The resultant discard dumps are responsible for some of the most serious environmental effects of coal mining, including land sterilisation and groundwater contamination. On exposure to air and water, the pyrites oxidise to form sulphuric acid, and iron oxides and hydroxides, which cause the pH to drop. The acid produced reacts with basic minerals in the rock to form salts, in the process of mobilising any heavy metals present. The resultant acid mine drainage (AMD) contains elevated levels of salts (mainly calcium and magnesium sulphates) and metals (predominantly iron, manganese and aluminium). The pyrite-rich discard is also susceptible to low-temperature oxidation (the so-called spontaneous combustion) and subsequent release of toxic air pollutants. AMD and spontaneous combustion can be minimised by preventing water and air getting to the pyrite and other sulphidic minerals. The power stations mostly burn Run-Of-Mine (ROM)[2] coal, so are not responsible for discard production, although some power stations are supplied by dual-product mines. These mines maximise their coal production by producing

---

[1] 1R = 0.1 US$ in 2001.
[2] Coal produced at the mine before any cleaning or preparation.

a high-quality coal for export (which must be cleaned) and a medium-quality power station coal which contains a portion of the washing discard blended with the ROM coal.

The location of South Africa's coalfields is significant. The Mpumalanga/Eastern Gauteng/Northern Free State region, where 65% of the reserves are to be found, has been extensively farmed, with little natural environment remaining. Coal mining therefore has little residual impact on natural ecosystems and land rehabilitation is usually able to restore the land to an acceptable state (Wells *et al.*, 1992). However, from a water quality perspective, the coalfields occur in the worst possible location, since most mines are situated in the vulnerable upper reaches of South Africa's major river systems (Wells *et al.*, 1992). In addition, regional air quality is adversely compounded by the large number of minerals refining plants also present.

Questions

1. Why are underground mines generally less disruptive environmentally than the surface mines? Discuss the differences in environmental impacts from these two types of mine.
2. Find out what are the main environmental and social issues associated with mining (you may wish to consult Chapter 13 for more detail on this topic). How do these issues affect developing countries such as South Africa?
3. Discuss the importance of coal for energy generation in South Africa. How easy would it be for this country to switch to a cleaner source of energy such as natural gas or renewable sources? Discuss the socio-economic implications of these changes.
4. How could fuel cells be used in a country such as South Africa to provide energy to remote rural areas? Would this be an "appropriate" technology for South Africa? You may wish to consult Chapter 10 for discussion on fuel cells.

12.2.1   Discard Coal as a Resource

In 2001, ROM coal production was 290×10^6 t of which 223.5×10^6 t was saleable (Prevost, 2002), the balance being described as "discard". Cumulative stocks of discard coal exceed 800×10^6 t (DME, 1998). The percentage of these discard stocks which are burning spontaneously at any one time is variable, but estimates in excess of 30% have been tabled (DMEA, 1985). The economic value and environmental impact of coal discards have been well documented.

> Coal discards form a valuable reserve, even though they are of low quality. Since they are located above ground they can be reclaimed by beneficiation at a competitive cost as they do not incur a further mining cost.

> There are at least two potential means of making use of discard coal, firstly the beneficiation of discards to yield conventional coal products and, secondly, the combustion of raw discards, for example in a fluidised bed combustor. Research has indicated that approximately 60% of the accumulated discards can be used for energy application purposes.

Government is in support of current techno-economic investigations for power production from discard coal. Government will continue to investigate and encourage options for the utilisation of coal discard streams and stockpiles and will promote appropriate options for the resultant energy and environmental benefits.

DME, 1998

We will return to the potential of fluidised bed combustion (FBC) of discards in the subsequent case study.

Questions

1. Explain how waste from coal production can be used as a resource. Suggest what this might mean in the South African context. What are the barriers to this? How can the use of coal waste be encouraged by governments?
2. Find out how the beneficiation of coal discards could be carried out to recover more coal. How can combustion in fluidised bed help reduce the problem of coal discards?

12.3   Coal-based Power Generation

South Africa's electrical power industry is dominated by coal, a situation which will remain for the foreseeable future, given the cheap and plentiful supply available and the strong political drive to keep electricity prices low (Notten, 2002). Significant environmental, social and economic effects stem from this large-scale mining and combustion of coal.

Eskom, South Africa's electrical utility company, is the fifth largest in the world (rated according to both sales and capacity), with a nominal installed capacity of 40 GW (Eskom, 2002). In 1999, it supplied 95% of South Africa's total available electricity, with the balance supplied by municipalities and industries that generate part of their electricity requirements. This translated to a total of nearly 188 TWh (net) produced in Eskom stations, with a small percentage (1.4%) of the electricity sold imported from neighbouring countries (Eskom, 1999). Eskom also dominates the Sub-Saharan electricity supply, and is responsible for 76% of installed capacity and 83% of production and trade of electricity in this region (Lennon, 1997). Eskom's capacity is heavily reliant on coal, with 89% of the total nominal capacity being provided by coal-fired stations, which consumed 96.5×10^6 t of coal in 2001 (Eskom, 2002). The ability of the modern power stations to burn low-grade coals means that primary energy costs can be kept very low, making it extremely difficult for other fuels to penetrate the market. In addition, these coals are relatively low in sulphur compared to world averages, so the stations are run without flue gas desulphurisation (FGD) units.

Eskom's integrated strategic electricity planning process (ISEP) has predicted a 50% increase in energy demand between the years 2000 and 2015, assuming a long-term economic growth rate for South Africa of between 1.5 and 3.5% (Lennon, 1997).

Eskom is considering a number of established and new technologies to meet this demand, guided by the following factors (Lennon, 1997):

- capital and operating cost;
- plant reliability and availability;
- access to indigenous, low-cost fuel;
- lead times;
- operations flexibility (base load vs peaking);
- water availability;
- environmental considerations (likely to move up in importance with pending legislation);
- security of fuel supply;
- local capacity to sustain technology;
- funding availability; and
- political considerations.

The continued dominance of coal is evident from the above list, that is an emphasis on keeping costs low and using an indigenous fuel supply. Any anticipated technology intervention (whether of a "supply-side" or "demand-side" management nature) needs to be assessed in terms of these potentially conflicting criteria, both at a design stage and throughout its operation. This suggests the need for a rigorous framework within which the requisite information can be analysed to explore trade-offs between competing objectives. In this case study, we identify such a Decision Support Framework (DSF), populate it with the required arguments and demonstrate the use of several tools to support decision making around technology selection. Underpinning all these tools is a commitment to the philosophy of life cycle thinking and the general management science of Multi-Criteria Decision Analysis (MCDA). The DSF should elicit all the relevant information about the problem at hand, and, through a set of systematic (and defensible) constructs and arguments, facilitate the transformation of this information into a decision with (hopefully) sustainable outcomes.

Questions

1. Taking a life cycle approach, identify economic, environmental and social issues associated with power generation from coal, from its extraction to delivery of electricity to end user. Discuss in turn how these issues affect developing and developed countries.
2. What is the role of large energy companies such as Eskom in sustainable development of developing countries? Visit Eskom's website to see what the company is doing for sustainable development in South Africa.
3. What decision criteria should be considered when deciding on new energy technologies in a developing country such as South Africa? Which of these criteria do you think are likely to be more important for an energy company such as Eskom? Why?
4. Which decision criteria might be important to a local community who would be beneficiaries of this electricity generation, but whose residences are adjacent to the proposed new power station complex?

12.4   A Decision Support Framework

Decision making in the face of multiple objectives, uncertainty and different stake-holder values (Chapter 13) is a challenging activity, generally undertaken without adequate consideration of these defining characteristics. As industry, including the electrical utility sector, seeks to align its practices with the goals of sustainable development (Chapter 1), there is increasing pressure to ensure that decision making embraces the "triple bottom line" of techno-economic efficiency, environmental stewardship and social acceptability (as discussed in Chapter 11). The challenge for decision makers is to choose the appropriate system boundary for planning and decision making – not only in the temporal and spatial domains, but also in a social sense, where the latter requires a sensitivity to the needs and perspectives of all those who may be affected by the decision outcomes. Of significance here is the issue of legitimacy, where the emphasis is often not so much on the outcome of the decision or who makes it, but rather on the *process* by which decisions are made. Particularly for decisions that may affect many people with different perspectives and which may have ramifications over large areas and for long periods, discursive and participatory approaches to decision making are essential (as clearly demonstrated in Chapter 13). At the same time, an overwhelming number of guiding concepts (e.g. pollution prevention, cleaner production, waste minimisation, industrial ecology, etc.) and decision-support tools (e.g. Life Cycle Assessment, Environmental Risk Assessment, Social Impact Assessment, etc.) have been developed. Decision makers may find it very difficult to know when it is appropriate to use a particular tool and how to integrate information from several tools to ultimately make a decision with some degree of confidence. Before considering how this approach might be developed in practice, it is first necessary to outline some of the constructs of decision analysis.

Questions

1. Describe the following approaches: pollution prevention, cleaner production, waste minimisation and industrial ecology. What can be achieved by these approaches and what are the main differences between them?
2. Describe the following decision-support tools: Life Cycle Assessment, Environmental Risk Assessment, Environmental Impact Assessment and Social Impact Assessment. Explain in which decision-making context each of these tools can be used and summarise the main differences between them.
3. Why do we need a more formal approach to decision making in the context of sustainable development?

12.5   Structured Approaches to Decision Making

Decision analysis provides a structured approach to decision making (von Winterfeldt and Edwards, 1986; Keeney, 1992). The first stage of this systematic approach to decision making is called *problem structuring* – the aim of which is to identify the stakeholders and obtain agreement about the exact decision at hand, the objectives that need to be satisfied by the decision outcome, the alternatives available, how to assess these (i.e. to what extent they meet decision objectives) and to elicit the preferences of stakeholders for particular decision outcomes. The next step in the decision-making process – *problem analysis* – involves the evaluation of the alternatives under consideration to determine to what extent these satisfy the decision objectives. This is followed by the selection of a preferred alternative and sensitivity analyses to ensure that the conclusion is robust. The decision-making process described above is not linear. Iterations occur both between steps in the cycle and in the cycle as a whole, as more information becomes available or further clarity is obtained about the information that is required in each step. This structured approach to decision making can be applied in all decision contexts and is the basis for the DSF used here.

Problem structuring is essentially a discursive and deliberative process, and is best done through direct interaction between stakeholders. Rosenhead (1989) provides a review of tools to assist in problem structuring. An important assumption of the decision analysis methodology is that those participating in the decision-making process are willing to engage in discussion and to reach consensus position on the problem structuring elements, to facilitate subsequent analysis of the problem – in other words, these participants are interested in rational decision outcomes. In general, strategic and tactical problems tend to require more discussion and deliberation than operational ones, since the former often involve a variety of stakeholders with divergent interests, while, in the latter, the focus is more on the decision for a single entity, where there is a clearer basis for consensus. The outcome of a problem structuring exercise is often summarised by way of an objectives hierarchy, which shows the criteria that will be used to evaluate the alternatives under consideration and the attributes (expressed quantitatively or qualitatively) that will be enumerated (where appropriate) to determine the relative performance of the alternatives. The issue of stakeholders' interests and the decision attributes has also been discussed in Chapter 2.

During problem analysis it is necessary to obtain data on the performance of the alternatives in all the criteria. This can be done by simply rating options relative to each other based on experience, or could involve more extensive data gathering and modelling to obtain more accurate performance information. A variety of methods and tools are available to provide environmental performance information. Important aspects include the choice of system boundary for modelling and the quality of the performance indicators used. To avoid merely transferring environmental impacts to other stages of a production chain or to other media, the importance of more systemic models of industrial production systems is recognised. As discussed in many other chapters in this book, the philosophy of life cycle thinking can be applied to guide the scope of this analysis and provide the spatial and temporal boundaries for modelling. Life Cycle Assessment (LCA) provides a range of environmental indicators based on aggregated mass and energy balance data (see the Appendix at the end of the book). These can be interpreted as highly aggregated impact indicators at a global and regional level. Site-specific Environmental Assessment and Ecological Risk Assessment provide more accurate environmental impact information. The type of indicators used will be largely determined by the type of decision sought. In general, more aggregated indicators are used for making strategic decisions and at the early stages of tactical project development decisions, and indicators based on more detailed (often site specific) modelling are used for later project stages and operational decision making.

The challenge for decision makers is to evaluate the alternatives based on a large number of attributes expressed in incommensurate units. In the DSF, the recommended approach to resolving this problem is to use a range of MCDA methodologies (Stewart, 1992; Belton and Stewart, 2002). In MCDA, each decision criterion is given due consideration, that is the performances in different criteria are not converted to a common scale (e.g. monetary units), nor is a single criterion selected as most important, thereby allowing the performance in all other criteria to be defined in terms of constraints. Instead, MCDA methods enable simultaneous comparison of performances in all criteria. Where the focus in the project is on the evaluation of finite sets of alternatives, Multiple Attribute Decision Analysis (MADA) methods have been applied. The choice of MADA method is based, amongst others, on the type of decision, the stakeholders involved in the decision-making process and the information available to support decision making. The approach taken here is based on Multi-Attribute Value Function Theory (MAVT), which requires explicit statements of acceptable trade-offs between performance in different criteria and aggregates the performance information across all criteria to create a single index for each alternative. This index reflects the extent to which the alternative meets the decision objective. The intuitive nature of this single index approach makes it more accessible to stakeholders involved in technology selection projects, as is the case here. We will now briefly introduce the value function approach before proceeding to discuss the case study.

12.5.1 Value Function Approach

Value function methods aggregate the information about preferences for different levels of performance in each criterion (represented as marginal or partial value functions) with information about the relative importance of the criteria, in order to provide an overall evaluation of each alternative in terms of the preferences of those involved in the decision-making process. Value function methods have been discussed in detail by many authors (e.g. Keeney and Raiffa, 1976; von Winterfeldt and Edwards, 1986; Keeney, 1992; Beinat, 1997; Belton and Stewart, 2002). The most commonly used aggregation model is the additive aggregation in which the value function $V(a_i)$ is constructed from the partial value functions $v_j(a_i)$ defined over the set of criteria j:

$$V(a_i) = \sum_{j=1}^{n} w_j v_j(a_i)$$

(12.1)

where w_j is known as the "weight" of criterion j and a_i is a particular alternative within the set of alternatives under consideration. In turn, the partial value functions,

$v_j(a_i)$, are constructed from a sense of the inherent "value" of the performance of alternatives in specific criteria. It is this mapping exercise which enables performance scores to be translated from incommensurate units into a common "value" score, thereby allowing for aggregation of scores for a given alternative across all criteria. This is the single index, $V(a_i)$. Partial value functions are usually standardised so that the "worst" and "best" outcomes in each criterion are assigned a value of 0 and 1 (or 100) respectively. When these standardising conventions are applied, the weight of a criterion is in fact a scaling constant with a very specific meaning, that is it indicates the relative gain associated with an improvement from the worst to the best outcome in the criterion.

Two points are noteworthy from the above. First, the shape of the value function relation for each criterion is a modelling choice for the decision maker, and reflects a strength of preference which is informed by the range of performance scores in a particular criterion. This suggests a relation between the construction of such preference relations and the choice of any data normalisation rules. Secondly, whilst weights are scaling constants in the value function method, they still involve value judgements, and are thus sources of inherent uncertainty. Both these features of the value function method suggest that there is a need for any DSF employing this technique to look critically at management of uncertainty within the decision-making process (e.g. Notten, 2002; Seppala *et al.*, 2002; Basson, 2003). We will return to this consideration of valuation uncertainty in the case study which follows.

Questions

1. Develop a flow diagram which identifies all the key steps in a structured approach to decision making. Distinguish between those which pertain to *problem structuring* and those relevant to *problem analysis*.
2. Problem structuring is regarded by many as the most valuable and significant part of decision support, and particularly for decision contexts involving multiple stakeholders and potentially conflicting points of view, interaction and deliberation are essential. List three methods which could be used to identify the key elements that inform the decision process and organise these to enable further discussion and analysis.
3. A distinction is often made between "means" objectives and "fundamental" objectives. Returning to the objectives list of the previous section, characterise these according to this distinction.
4. What performance measures could be used to quantify the degree to which these objectives might be met by a particular course of action (or decision)?
5. Value functions are a method by which performance scores (in arbitrary units) can be converted to a commensurate "value" scale which reflects the decision maker(s)' preferences. Explain the relationship between the decision maker's sense of "risk" and "value" for three common value functions – linear, sigmoidal, convex. For environmental criteria, can you suggest whether particular value function shapes are more meaningful than others?

12.6   Case Study: Using Decision Support Framework for Technology Choice

12.6.1   Problem Structuring: The Decision Context

The DSF is really a structure within which various models – of problem structure, of the alternatives under consideration, of preferences and aggregation models – are brought together into a systematic assessment, within which various forms of uncertainty can be identified and their residual influence on decision outcomes identified. The above discussion has highlighted the importance of problem structuring, and identified an approach for consideration of stakeholders' preferences (assuming these can be articulated as part of the process). It is time now to turn our attention to the technology case study, and develop appropriate models of the alternatives to be considered.

The problem structuring exercise generated the following statement of the problem to be investigated. The potential of FBC as a technology for reducing SO_2 emissions during coal combustion is well known. Of particular importance in this context is its potential for burning colliery discards, thereby avoiding the significant environmental impacts of stockpiling the discard. However, burning discard in a fluidised bed results in a trade-off between impacts, primarily between the water and air pollution from the stockpiled discard, and the emissions to air and ash waste produced when the discard is burned. This case study investigates the combustion of discard coal in a reconditioned power station. The study again takes place at an early stage in the design process, and the operating conditions of the system are not yet fixed, although the environmental profile of the system is expected to vary considerably with differing operating conditions. The study has therefore been reformulated to some degree, and aims to determine the conditions under which the system need operate to achieve a particular level of certainty in net environmental benefit, rather than characterising the environmental performance of a "typical" operation. The key question to be answered has therefore been formulated as:

> Under what operating conditions is it environmentally beneficial to re-power an old pulverised fuel (PF) station with an FBC boiler burning discard coal?

This particular formulation of the question focuses the study on a parameter analysis, rather than trying to pre-define a number of tightly defined scenarios (you may recall the scenario approach that has been discussed in Chapter 9). In this way, significant decision variables (e.g. the quality of the discard sourced, the type of sorbent used, etc.) are investigated as part of the model parameter uncertainty analysis, rather than specified in discrete scenarios "up front".

Question

1. Describe in your own words the decision-making context in this case study. Who are the decision makers?

12.6.2   Problem Structuring: System Definition and the Alternatives

The primary system to be modelled is an old station with reconditioned boiler units burning discard coal. Also requiring definition are the alternatives for comparison. To determine whether the FBC system is "environmentally beneficial" requires comparison against the power generating options it is displacing. Different scenarios are possible, as the comparative basis changes depending on the driver for the project. Most likely is that the station is being re-commissioned because the additional capacity is required for the grid, that is if the station is not re-powered using FBC technology, the capacity will be supplied from some other source. Other possible sources include re-commissioning the station as a conventional PF station, building a new PF station or operating the existing stations at higher loads. The first alternative is complicated by the fact that the extent to which the station is refurbished will significantly influence its environmental performance, and the comparison will have to take this into account. Alternatively, the driver behind the project may not be the requirement of new capacity, for example, the primary aim of the project could be to remove the discard dumps, or a political drive to demonstrate a "clean coal" technology. In this case, re-powering the station would displace existing power off the grid, and a relevant comparison would be between the re-powered FBC station and the average grid mix. In this case study, we consider only the former possibility. The systems to be modelled are thus:

- an old plant re-commissioned with FBC boiler units; and
- the plant re-commissioned with the original PF boiler units.

Although the case study is conducted without a specific power station in mind, some site specificity is introduced, as the locations of the power stations currently in storage are known. The older stations that are no longer operating, but have the potential for being reconditioned and brought back into service, all fall into a fairly localised region of the country, which mirrors the localised coal-producing region. Site-specific considerations therefore play a more significant role than usually found in tactical studies in the selection of the relevant impacts to be considered, as well as in the importance attached to these impacts.

12.6.3   Problem Analysis

The LCA Approach

Suitable models must be constructed to determine the environmental profile of the alternatives. We have elected to use LCA as the support tool for generating this environmental information (see the Appendix at the end of the book). Since the study involves the comparison of alternative systems, it is also necessary to define criteria against which they can be rated (e.g. impact categories or selected environmental interventions). This section presents the major considerations in the definition of these structures. The system models consist of two main components: a life cycle inventory (a complete list of all material and energy entering or leaving the system under study) and the extrapolation of the inventory data to potential environmental impacts. Coal mining and all waste disposal steps are explicitly considered. The life cycle covered by the model is that of coal; its extraction, processing, combustion and disposal of its residues. Transmission, distribution and use of the power are not covered. This model thus provides an inventory of *undelivered* electricity. In addition, only process-related emissions are assessed. Burdens associated with the running and maintenance of offices, workshops and so on at the power station are not incorporated in the assessment. The life cycle model is for an operating power station and mine. Building and commissioning the plants are not included, neither are the burdens associated with the materials for construction. Maintenance materials are also not included, and only consumable materials are included in the inventory.

The flowsheet for the coal-electricity life cycle is given in Figure 12.1. This shows the flow of coal through its life cycle and all the associated processes. The groupings of colours indicate the top level of breakdown in the model and coincide with the major technology combinations available at the mines and power stations. The flowsheet is broken down into these sub-steps primarily for clarity and ease of assessment, and the sub-processes do not necessarily stand-alone. The breakdown allows a single flowsheet to encompass all the technology combinations possible, and the sub-processes are mixed and matched to represent the various technology combinations of the plants. These combinations are:

- underground or opencast mining;
- stockpile at the mine or at the power station;
- boiler and particulate removal equipment type;
- wet or dry cooling; and
- wet or dry ashing.

The case study only considers discard sourced directly from the coal washing plant, and not that reclaimed from a dump. The study is limited to a consideration of discard produced within a fairly close radius of the power station (approximately 12 km). The coal supply is assumed to be from dual-product mines, since the study considers a reconditioned station (i.e. its dedicated colliery is assumed to have stopped operating and it is supplied by an existing nearby mine adjusting its coal product to also produce a power station feed, or the dedicated mine subsequently started producing a high-quality coal product to sustain itself when the power station ceased operating). This introduces the problem of allocating the mining burdens between the power station and high-quality coal product.

Factor-based models are used to generate inventory data for the foreground system (the processes shown in Figure 12.1). The simple input/output models are based on mass balance principles. Factors derived predominantly from process data essentially act as splitter functions that steer an input to its respective output streams (e.g. the percentage of sulphur in ash determines the partitioning of sulphur in coal between stack emissions and retention in ash). An important feature of the process models is therefore that they are not based on any fundamental chemical or physical modelling, but on characterisation factors derived from process data. The models are thus very data intensive, and the accuracy of the calculated inventory data is very much dependent on the applicability of the data used. Where process data were not available, recourse has been made to data from process simulation models, literature, experimental data, or in the worst case, rough assumptions made.

The Eco-indicator 99 (EI99) method (Goedkoop and Spriensma, 1999) was chosen to illustrate the transformation from inventory data to impact indicators, primarily

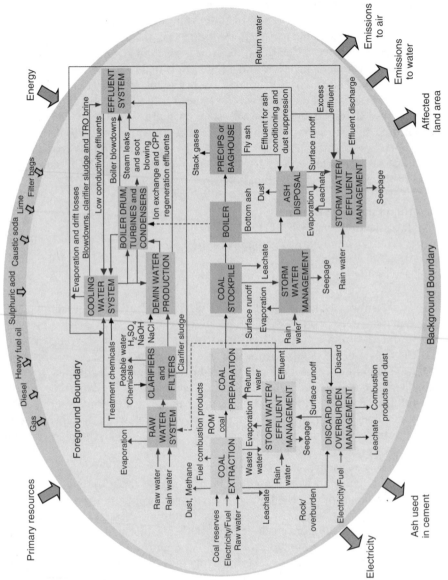

Figure 12.1 Life cycle of electricity from coal

because data on the uncertainty of the equivalency factors are available for most of the impact categories. This method allows for a number of valuation scenarios to be explored based on Cultural Theory arguments. In this case study, we consider only the "Hierarchist's" perspective.[3] Two additional criteria reflecting burdens considered important in the context of the study, but not captured by the EI99 damage categories, are included. Water use is included as a criterion because of its known importance in the regional context of the study. This includes raw water purchased by the mine and power station, as well as the water "consumed" by the process by virtue of its impact on the catchment area. Also of importance in the regional context of the study is the effect of the systems on regional water quality. A key aspect of the study is the trade-off between the emissions from the discard dump, and those from the ash/gypsum dump. The level of detail at which the mine and power station inventories are constructed is not sufficient to capture the water quality impacts as reflected in the EI99 toxicity categories, so the impacted land footprint indicator (Hansen, 2003) is used to give an indication of the potential of solid waste deposits to contaminate water bodies through leachate generation. It incorporates the land occupied by the dump and its leachate potential into a single indicator.

In addition to the removal of the discard dump, a key aspect of the FBC system is the energy savings resulting from producing useful energy from an otherwise wasted energy source. The functional unit needs to reflect this, as well as compare the systems on an equivalent basis. A dual time and product basis is therefore taken, in which the burdens calculated for an average year's operation are normalised to the total power produced in the year. The normalisation is necessary because without it a more efficient system merely reflects increased burdens and not an increased energy product.

Questions

1. Use the information presented in the previous section and in Figure 12.1 and consult the Appendix at the end of the book to answer the following questions:

   (a) What is the goal and scope of the LCA carried out in this case study?
   (b) What is the functional unit?
   (c) Sketch the system boundary for the system under study. Which activities in the life cycle of coal electricity are included in and which are excluded from the consideration in this case study? Do you think the assumptions made are justified given the goal of the study?
   (d) Find out how the environmental burdens are translated into environmental impacts within the EI99 approach? How is that different from the problem-oriented approach described in the Appendix on LCA?
   (e) What impacts do you think are likely to be important in the life cycle of coal electricity?

---

[3] The EI99 approach to Impact Assessment in LCA considers three general types of impact: damage to human health; damage to ecosystem quality; and resource use. There are three ways to aggregate these impact categories by using "weights" of importance. The "Hierarchist's" approach is one of the three in which the weights are assigned in the following way: human health, 40%; ecosystem quality, 30%; and resource use, 30%.

2. What are the advantages and limitations of using LCA as the basis for environmental assessment in this case study?
3. Is the problem definition, as defined, capable of answering the question of whether fluidised bed technology with discard coal is genuinely a "clean coal technology"?

Reducing the Number of Possible Alternatives

The various combinations of technologies and operating conditions found within this case study, compounded by uncertainties in empirical parameters, model parameters and model choices, together suggest an infinite number of alternatives for consideration. The effort required to fully characterise and explore such a decision space to identify preferred alternatives using MCDA tools or similar is a daunting task. In this case study, we look to reduce the number of alternatives to a manageable number, and explore their performance using uncertainty propagation tools (including scenario analysis).

The certainty required in the results depends on how conservative or "risk averse" the decision makers are. However, the level of confidence acceptable to the decision makers is also influenced by the variance exhibited by the system (that due to both empirical and model parameters), that is "high" confidence limits required may be unachievable in the context of the study. The uncertainty is primarily a function of the complexity, depth and data accuracy of the models used, which, in turn, are functions of the goals and scope of the study. The level of uncertainty with which the decision makers are comfortable is therefore inextricably linked to the decisions taken during goal and scope definition. The level of variance able to be tolerated in the results is also a function of the extent of the differences between the options.

Decision variables comprise the majority of model parameters investigated in this study. The choice of these variables is under the direct control of the decision makers, and is predominantly related to the degree of refurbishment of the plant (i.e. the specification of the boiler and water plant) and to the choice of mine supplying the coal or discard. A model parameter sensitivity analysis enabled the important parameters to be grouped into "best", "worst" and "most likely" scenarios. This information was used to define scenario states for each of the two main technologies (i.e. PF or FBC). This results in a discrete set of alternative "states" for consideration as part of the decision analysis, according to Table 12.1. The uncertainty in empirical parameters for each of these alternative "states" can be addressed through probabilistic techniques. A framework for such an integrated approach has been developed by Notten (2002).

Question

1. Why is it important to address uncertainty in decision making? Where do the uncertainties arise? What can be done to reduce the level of uncertainty?

Decision Criteria

Table 12.2 lists the full set of environmental indicators considered in this case study. The indicators have been calculated based on EI99 mid-point choices.

Table 12.1 *Decision variable values for three extreme scenario "states"*

	Worst (Little refurbishment)	Most likely	Best (Significant investment)
Maximum unit capacity (MW)	125	200	200
Number of generator sets	4	2	2
Load factor (%)	64	80	80
Sorbent type	dolomite	limestone	limestone
SO_2 removed (%)	30	60	90
Particulate control	ESP	ESP	FF
Mine type	opencast	underground	underground
Mine power source	adjacent station	grid	grid
Coal bypassing washing plant (%)	15	20	25
Station, stockpile and mine life (years)	35	20	15
Stormwater and effluent management	poor	average	good
Distance coal transported (km)	25	10	3
Method of coal transport	rail	conveyor	conveyor
Transport distances (km)	850	500	150
Transport mode	road	road	rail
Ashing method	wet	wet	dry
Water plant configuration	un-optimised	optimised	optimised, and adjusted for dry ashing
Stockpile size (reserve time)	3 years	3 months	3 weeks

Table 12.2 *Decision criteria*

Criterion	Units
Generating cost	[a]R(1996)/GWh
Carcinogenic effects on humans	[b]DALYs/GWh
Respiratory effects on humans caused by organic substances (summer smog)	DALYs/GWh
Respiratory effects on humans caused by inorganic substances (winter smog)	DALYs/GWh
Climate change	DALYs/GWh
Ecotoxic emissions	PDF $\times$ m^2 $\times$ yr/GWh
Combined effect of acidification and eutrophication	[c]PDF $\times$ m^2 $\times$ yr/GWh
Extraction of fossil fuels	MJ surplus energy/GWh
Water use	Ml/GWh
Affected land footprint	km^2/GWh
Number of jobs created	total number

[a] R: South African rands.
[b] DALY: Disability Adjusted Life Years. This indicator measures ill health, disability and premature death attributable to environmental pollution.
[c] PDF: Potentially Disappeared Fraction of vascular plant species.

The use of the EI99 impact assessment method is attractive as it allows consideration of different cultural perspectives as part of an exercise to unpack the significance of valuation choices in decision outcomes. However, this aspect of valuation is not considered here, and only the EI99 default "Hierarchist's" perspective is used. The uncertainty in the characterisation factors for impact categories is explored using probability distributions rather than single point estimates.

In addition to the environmental decision criteria, the economic criterion "generating cost" (cost of electricity generation) and the social criterion "number of jobs created" have also been included as decision criteria.

Questions

1. Analyse the decision criteria in Table 12.2 and explain the meaning of each. You may wish to consult Goedkoop and Spriensma (1999) for more detail on the Eco-indicator approach.
2. What other criteria would you consider and why?

Normalisation

When considering familiar decision criteria such as "generating cost" and "number of jobs created", those involved in the decision-making process are able to express their preferences for different levels of performance directly, hence for these, the absolute numbers are of interest. However, when considering performance in the environmental criteria, it is necessary to provide a reference base in order for those involved in the decision-making process to express their preferences. The performances in the environmental criteria have thus been normalised relative to the average performance considering all the power stations owned by the company.

Performance Ranges

Table 12.3 shows the attribute ranges for each criterion considering the uncertainty in the performance information (i.e. lowest and highest likely performance scores in each criterion).

Table 12.3 *Performance ranges for six alternatives under consideration*

Criterion	Units	Minimum value	Maximum value
Generating cost	R(1996)/MWh	30[a]	100[a]
Carcinogenic effects (humans)	relative to company average	0.0001	13
Summer smog	relative to company average	0.05	177
Winter smog	relative to company average	0.04	20
Climate change	relative to company average	0.32	4.1
Ecotoxic emissions	relative to company average	0.0008	6.3
Combined effect of acidification & eutrophication	relative to company average	0.05	4.4
Extraction of fossil fuels	relative to company average	0.03	3
Water use	relative to company average	1	4.5
Affected land footprint	relative to company average	−6	11
Number of jobs created	total number	55	165

[a] Data scaled to protect confidential information.

Questions

1. The performance of options in the environmental criteria are expressed "relative to company average". This reduces numerical sensitivity. Explain the challenges in normalisation to ensure that stakeholder preference information can be meaningfully derived from performance scores.
2. Examine the minimum and maximum values for the criteria in Table 12.3. What do you conclude: which criteria are associated with the largest level of uncertainty?

Value Functions

Two sets of value functions were considered:

1. a set in which all the value functions were assumed to be linear (set A); and
2. a set in which sigmoidal value functions were selected for those criteria (other than generating cost) in which the performance scores across the set of alternatives could be differentiated (set B).

The second set of value functions would thus ensure that greater value scores were assigned to those alternatives that did well in those criteria in which the alternatives could be differentiated. The linear value function for "generating cost" was retained since this was expected to be more consistent with the attitude to improvements in generating cost. A summary of the value function shapes is provided in Table 12.4.

Questions

1. Why were two different sets of value functions considered?
2. Examine the value functions in Table 12.4. What is the significance of the linear and sigmoidal shapes of the value functions respectively ?
3. Why is shape of the value functions for sets A and B similar for most of the decision criteria?

Table 12.4   *Summary of value function shapes*

Criterion	Value function set A	Value function set B
Generating cost	Linear	Linear
Carcinogenic effects on humans	Linear	Linear
Summer smog	Linear	Linear
Winter smog	Linear	Linear
Climate change	Linear	Linear
Ecotoxic emissions	Linear	Linear
Combined effect of acidification & eutrophication	Linear	Linear
Extraction of fossil fuels	Linear	Sigmoidal
Water use	Linear	Linear
Affected land footprint	Linear	Sigmoidal
Number of jobs created	Linear	Sigmoidal

Weight Elicitation

The attribute ranges for the environmental criteria spanned orders of magnitude due to the uncertainty in the environmental performance information (Table 12.3). Experience in similar situations suggested that those involved in the decision-making process are not able to express preferences with confidence when faced with trade-offs which span such large ranges. Under these circumstances, it was regarded as more meaningful to do a sensitivity analysis for the weights rather than attempt the direct elicitation of weights from stakeholders. Two approaches were used to consider the sensitivity of the rank of the alternatives to the relative weighting of the criteria:

1. comparison of two nominal weight sets; and
2. varying the weights of each criterion in turn, keeping the ratio of the other weights constant.

The nominal weighting sets consisted of a set in which the criteria were weighted equally (i.e. trade-off across the entire attribute range of all the criteria was regarded as equally acceptable) and one in which emphasis was placed on those criteria in which the set of alternatives could be differentiated easily, despite inherent uncertainty in the information set. A summary of the weights is provided in Table 12.5.

Questions

1. How can preferences be elicited from decision makers? Explain how different decision contexts affect the choice of the preference elicitation method.
2. Why do decision makers (and people in general) have difficulties in expressing their preferences when the values of decision criteria span large ranges (e.g. several orders of magnitude)?
3. What is the implication, if any, of having multiple environmental criteria, but only one economic and one social criterion? Does this suggest any form of bias towards environmental concerns? Explain this in terms of the objectives hierarchy.

Table 12.5   *Summary of weighting sets*

Criterion	Equal weights	Alternative weighting set
Generating cost	0.09	0.215
Carcinogenic effects on humans	0.09	0.020
Summer smog	0.09	0.020
Winter smog	0.09	0.020
Climate change	0.09	0.020
Ecotoxic emissions	0.09	0.020
Combined effect of acidification & eutrophication	0.09	0.020
Extraction of fossil fuels	0.09	0.215
Water use	0.09	0.020
Affected land footprint	0.09	0.215
Number of jobs created	0.09	0.215

4. Instead of a parametric sensitivity study of "weighting", direct elicitation of weights could be attempted by all stakeholders. It has been suggested here that this is particularly difficult given the range of performance scores in each criterion. However, it appears that the reported ranges are indicative more of inherent uncertainty than they are of real performance differences for the options. Explain how one could target critical uncertainties to explore their systematic reduction.

Case Study Results

The strongest differences between the PF and FBC systems are in their fossil fuel use and their land footprint. The considerable savings in fossil fuel resources by using FBC reflect the use of a "waste" energy source to generate power. The discard is defined as a waste from the mining system and, as such, is not allocated any mining burdens other than the "avoided" burdens resulting from the removal of the dumps (see Chapter 10 for the "avoided burdens" approach). It therefore does not reflect any fossil fuel resource consumption, as all fossil fuels consumed and extracted during mining are allocated to the coal product. Also caused by the avoidance of mining burdens are the lower contributions to climate change, water use and summer smog of the FBC system relative to the PF system. This is less marked for climate change, because if compared on the basis of the power station alone (i.e. without the effects of mining), the FBC system has a slightly higher climate change burden than the PF system (caused predominantly by the use and transport of limestone in the FBC system).

The lower contribution to the combined effect of acidification and eutrophication by the FBC system stems from the far lower NO_x emissions from the FBC boiler. The effect is much more marked for a consideration of NO_x alone, as SO_2 emissions are not always lower in the FBC system (they depend on the degree of desulphurisation). The SO_2 emissions of the "worst" FBC scenario (with only 30% SO_2 removal) are higher than those of the PF scenarios, whilst those of "best" FBC system are significantly lower.

Winter smog is shown to be ambivalent between the PF and FBC systems (i.e. neither system plots strongly with or against the winter smog vector). Although the FBC system always causes an increase in particulate emissions, the volume of SO_2 emitted can "swing" winter smog to being significantly worse or slightly better than the PF system. The toxicity categories also do not show a strong tendency to be better or worse in either of the systems.

A full consideration of empirical parameter uncertainty is beyond the scope of this case study. Interested readers are referred to Notten (2002), where this is explored in some depth. What is more relevant here is to explore the significance of valuation choices in the decision outcomes. This approach is taken not only to emphasise the importance of valuation arguments in decision making of this nature, but also to demonstrate that such perspectives can be accommodated within a decision analysis framework as part of a rational approach to complex decision situations. This is detailed below, including consideration of model parameter uncertainty.

Question

1. What do you conclude: which system is preferable environmentally: PF or FBC? Why?

Overall Value Scores

The overall value scores for the two-criteria nominal weighting sets are presented in Figure 12.2. These figures show the cumulative probability distribution functions for each of the alternative "states" as a function of the overall desired value. In other words, these figures provide evidence of the confidence the decision maker can place in the separation of alternatives, despite the inherent valuation uncertainty. The options which are further to the right in the figures, that is those with the highest value scores, are preferred overall. Detailed consideration of this approach is given by Basson (2003).

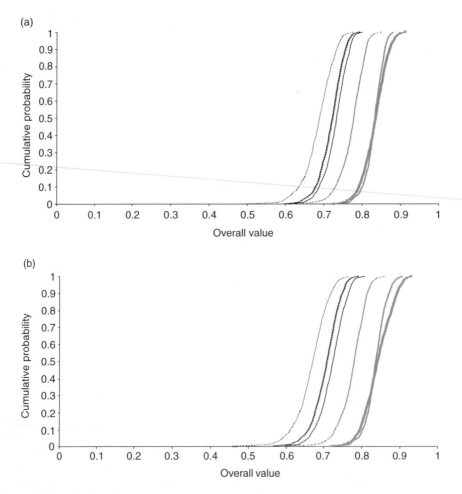

Figure 12.2 *Continued*

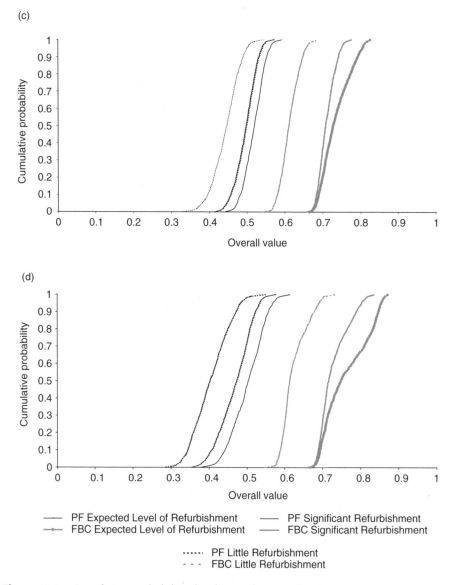

Figure 12.2 *Cumulative probability distribution for overall value score: (a) value function set A, equal weights; (b) value function set B, equal weights; (c) value function set A, alternative weighting set; and (d) value function set B, alternative weighting set*

As can be seen from the cumulative distributions for the overall value score presented in Figure 12.2, the greatest degree of separation is achieved for the value function and weight sets which place emphasis on those criteria in which the alternatives show the greatest differences in performance scores (Figure 12.2[d]). However, in all cases, the FBC alternatives obtain higher overall value scores than the PF alternatives, with the best scores being obtained by the FBC system for the greatest extent of refurbishment. The evaluation suggests that, despite the extensive uncertainty present

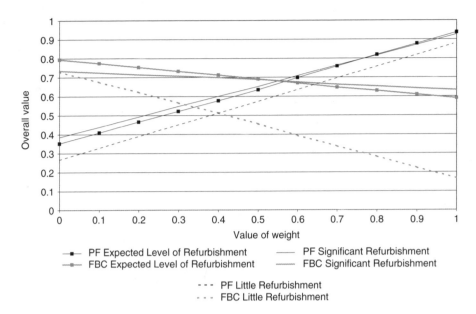

Figure 12.3   *Effect on median value of overall value of varying weight on generating cost (value function set B, alternative weighting set)*

in both the performance and the preference information, it can be concluded that re-powering the power station with a fluidised bed boiler system would be the more preferable approach.

The sensitivity analysis conducted by varying the weights of each criterion in turn, keeping the ratio of the other weights constant, showed that the FBC alternatives would be preferred to the PF alternatives in all cases except where there was marked variation in the generating cost weight. This was the case regardless of value function set or weighting set. Figure 12.3 shows that when the weight placed on the generating cost exceeds a value of about 0.56, the FBC options with the expected level of refurbishment, and that with significant refurbishment, would no longer be preferred over some of the PF options.

Questions

1. Examine the results shown in Figures 12.2 and 12.3 and identify the preferred option for different value functions and weights. What do you conclude: how do they affect the choice of the preferred technology in this case?
2. Do you think this type of analysis is useful for decision makers? Why? What can they gain from it?

Results of Uncertainty Analysis

Rank correlation analyses were carried out to determine which of the uncertain performance scores made the most significant contribution to the uncertainty in the overall value scores of the alternatives. The results for the different value functions and weighting sets are presented in Figure 12.4. In these graphs the larger the "Overall Value Importance", the more significant is the contribution of the uncertainty in the input parameter to the uncertainty in the overall value score.

The results of the uncertainty analysis presented above indicate that when greater weights are placed on those criteria in which the performance scores of the alternatives differ distinctly (Figure 12.4 [c] and [d]), the uncertainty in the overall value scores is dominated by a few criteria (i.e. uncertainty relating to "fossil fuel consumption" in the case of the PF alternatives and uncertainty relating to the "number of jobs created" in the case of the FBC alternatives). In contrast, when equal weights are placed on the criteria (Figure 12.4 [a] and [b]), uncertainty in the performance information in a larger number of criteria make similar contributions to the uncertainty in the overall value scores. Furthermore, when relative preference for performance in

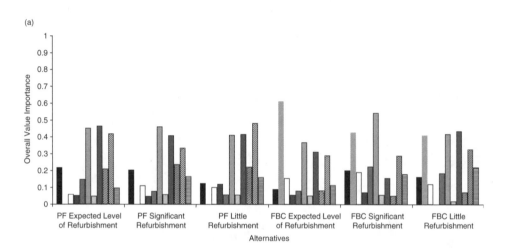

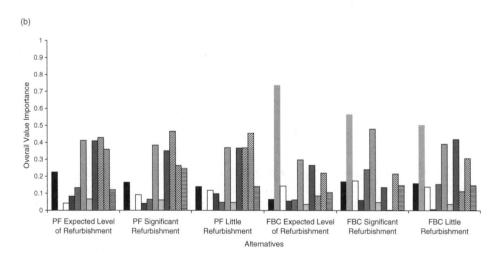

Figure 12.4   *Continued*

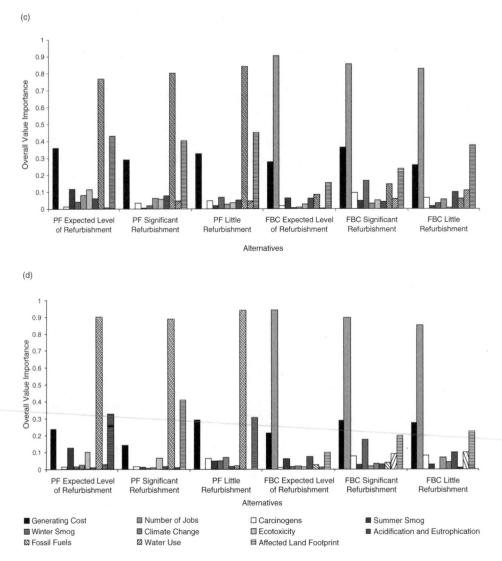

Figure 12.4 *Relative significance of uncertainties in performance scores for the uncertainty in the overall value scores: (a) value function set A, equal weights; (b) value function set B, equal weights; (c) value function set A, alternative weighting set; and (d) value function set B, alternative weighting set*

the individual criteria are modelled using sigmoidal value functions in those criteria (other than "generating cost") in which the performance scores of the alternatives differ distinctly, the uncertainty in "fossil fuel consumption" (PF alternatives) and uncertainty relating to the "number of jobs created" (FBC alternatives), which are both allocated sigmoidal value functions, make a more significant contribution to the uncertainty in the overall value scores. This effect is more distinct for the alternative weighting set. These results are perhaps not unexpected. Performance scores in criteria which have large weights are expected to make a larger contribution to the overall value score. Furthermore, sigmoidal value functions allow alternatives which span the attribute range to have a much larger range of potential value scores. This is the case for "fossil fuel consumption" (PF alternatives) and "number of jobs created" (FBC alternatives).

Question

1. Examine the results presented in Figure 12.4. What are the findings of the uncertainty analysis? Can the decision makers be confident in their technology choice? What strategies do you suggest the company to adopt to improve its confidence in the decision outcome?

Observation of Uncertainty and Sensitivity Analyses

The results of the sensitivity analysis for weights indicate that the FBC alternatives are expected to be preferred in all circumstances considered, other than when a large weight (>0.56) is placed on the "generating cost". The uncertainty analysis indicates that if a distinction is to be made between the performances of the individual PF and FBC alternatives, information leading to the estimates of "fossil fuel consumption" (PF alternatives) and "number of jobs created" (FBC alternatives) should be the first areas of focus of efforts to reduce the uncertainty in the relative ranking of the alternatives. What is perhaps striking about this conclusion is that it highlights the fact that the ability to make an informed decision about this technology choice requires more detailed and accurate information about two aspects of the problem which, in a narrow economic assessment, run the risk of being overlooked completely.

Questions

1. Summarise step by step the decision-making process carried out in this case study. Comment on the practicality of such a process: how long would it take, who would be involved and how much would it cost?
2. Comment on the necessity of the formal approach to decision making: what are the main advantages of the formal DSF as used in this case study? Comment in particular on the stakeholder engagement process. What are the disadvantages of such a formal approach? Do you think that the decision makers could have reached this decision without using a formal decision-making approach?
3. How important is it in your opinion to reduce uncertainty in decision making in the context of sustainable development? How much effort should be put in reducing uncertainty and carrying out sensitivity analyses? Why?
4. Do you think that the decision makers who participated in the decision-making process presented in this case study can be assured that they have identified a truly

more sustainable technological option given the alternatives that they considered? Why?

5. Given the iterative and discursive nature of decision making, how would you suggest this analysis be communicated to the broad range of stakeholders to ensure their continued participation in the decision process?
6. If this had been your decision, what would you do next, and why?

Conclusions

This case study has considered the various challenges faced by decision makers within the resources sector (in this case, coal-based power generation) in choosing technologies best suited to promoting sustainability. Based on the philosophy of life cycle thinking and structured around the tools of decision analysis, the approach developed here affords decision makers the opportunity to engage all stakeholders in a decision, thereby improving the transparency of the process and leading, hopefully, to better decisions with more robust outcomes.

The DSF places emphasis on information gathering and management of uncertainty. It should be emphasised that decision analysis allows for the incorporation of information from a variety of sources (i.e. based on many of the decision-support tools already in existence and used routinely). Additionally, it suggests that it is the decision-making process (and its underlying constructs) which is most important – not the methods of data collection themselves. That said, it is important to understand the underlying uncertainties in the information used to characterise a decision situation, without which, our experience suggests, it is often impossible to arrive at meaningful decision outcomes. In all decision situations, it is a case of ensuring that the requisite set of performance information is collected. This point is not to be understated. Too many researchers and practitioners in the field of environment and sustainability are bent on measurement and monitoring, when perhaps a focus on decision objectives and desired outcomes might be more helpful in advancing the sustainability agenda.

The case study itself generates some interesting observations. Fluidised combustion of discard coals does offer advantages over refurbished PF technology when looking, from the context of sustainability, at re-powering mothballed stations. This is not an immediately obvious conclusion, given the complexity of the situation and the inherent uncertainties in the empirical quantities and decision variables which define the problem. Focusing on valuation-type uncertainties, the case study highlighted the importance of job creation and resource depletion in determining a preferred technology alternative.

It is not a coincidence that these two criteria reflect some of the more pressing development issues within emerging economies – that of employment creation and resource management. Our opening statement that South Africa's economy continues to be driven, in large measure, by the availability of low-cost energy raises an additional challenge – how do we engage with the interconnectedness of energy–minerals networks to deliver an analysis which is meaningful in a macro-sense? It is our belief that the approach reflected in this case study has more general applicability and can engage this larger perspective also.

References and Further Reading

Basson, L. (2003) Context, Compensation and Uncertainty in Multi-Criteria Decision Making. PhD Dissertation, University of Sydney, Australia.

Baxter, B. (1993) Cleaning up the Act. *SA Mining, Coal, Gold and Base Minerals*, September 1993, pp. 14–15.

Belton, V. and T.J. Stewart (2002) *Multi Criteria Decision Analysis*. Kluwer Academic Publishers, Boston.

Beinat, E. (1997) *Value Functions for Environmental Management*. Dordrecht, Kluwer Academic Publishers.

Bredell, J.H. (1987) South African Coal Resources Explained and Analysed; Geological Survey of South Africa.

Department of Minerals and Energy (DME) (1998) White Paper on Energy Policy of the Republic of South Africa. Government Printer.

Department of Minerals and Energy (DME) (2001) Report Number D2/2001: Operating and Developing Coal Mines in the Republic of South Africa, 2001. Department of Minerals and Energy, South Africa.

Department of Minerals and Energy (DME) (2003a) Coal Reserves; http://www.dme.gov.za/energy/coal_resources.htm (April 2003).

Department of Minerals and Energy (DME) (2003b) Quarterly Statistics: Mine Accidents 1 January to 30 September 2002; http://www.dme.gov.za/mhs/mine_quarterly_stats.htm (April 2003).

DMEA (1985) South African Discard and Duff Coal – National Inventory 1985. Department of Mineral and Energy Affairs, South Africa.

Energy Information Administration (2002) Country Analysis Briefs: South Africa. September 2002; http://www.eia.doe.gov/emeu/cabs/safrica.html (April 2003).

Energy Research Institute (2001) *Preliminary Energy Outlook for South Africa*. ERI, The University of Cape Town, South Africa.

Eskom (1999) Annual Report 1998. ESKOM Corporate Communication Department.

Eskom (2001) Environmental Report 2000. ESKOM Corporate Communication Department; http://www.eskom.co.za/enviroreport01/resource.htm (April 2003).

Eskom (2002) Annual Report 2001. ESKOM Corporate Communication Department; http://www.eskom.co.za/about/Annual%20Report%202002/index.html; accessed April 2003.

Goedkoop, M. and R. Spriensma (1999) *The Eco-Indicator 99: A Damage Oriented Method for Life Cycle Impact Assessment*. Pre Consultants, the Netherlands.

Hansen, Y. (2003) Leachate Generation and Mobility in Coal-based Solid Wastes – Impact Prediction and Environmental Assessment. PhD Dissertation, University of Sydney, Australia.

Keeney, R.L. (1992) *Value-focused Thinking*. Harvard University Press, Cambridge, Massachusetts.

Keeney, R.L. and Raiffa, H. (1976) Decisions with Multiple Objectives. *Preference and Value Tradeoffs*. New York, Wiley.

Lennon, S.J. (1997) Clean Coal Technology Choices Relating to the Future Supply and Demand of Electricity in Southern Africa. *J. Energy S. Afr.* (May 1997), 45–51.

MEI Online (2002) US grants $500 000 for South African Plant. 1 March 2002; http://www.min-eng.com/enviro/37.html (April 2003).

Notten, P. (2002) Life Cycle Inventory in Resource Based Industries – A Focus on Coal-based Power Generation. PhD Dissertation, University of Cape Town, South Africa.

Prevost, X.M. (2002) Coal. In: *South Africa's Mineral Industry 2000/01*. Department of Minerals and Energy, Mineral Economics Directorate and Mineral Bureau, South Africa.

Rosenhead, J. (ed.) (1989) *Rational Analysis for a Problematic World*. John Wiley & Sons, New York.

Seppala, J., L. Basson and G. Norris (2002) Decision Analysis Frameworks for Life Cycle Impact Assessment. *J. Industrial Ecology*, **5**(4), 45–68.

Surridge, A.D., C.J. Grobbelaar and J.K. Asamoah (1995) On South African Coal Reserves/Resources and their Utilisation. Colloquium: Coal Processing, Utilisation and Control of Emissions. South African Institute of Mining and Metallurgy, Randburg, South Africa.

Stewart, T.J. (1992) A Critical Survey of the Status of Multiple Criteria Decision Making Theory and Practice. *Omega, Int. J. Mgmt. Sci.*, **20**(5–6), 569–586.

Van Horen, C. (1996) Counting the Social Costs. *Electricity and Externalities in South Africa.* UCT and Elan Press.

von Winterfeldt, D. and W. Edwards (1986) *Decision Analysis and Behavioural Research.* Cambridge Univ. Press, Cambridge, England.

Wells, J.D., L.H. Van Meurs and M.A. Rabie (1992) Terrestrial Minerals. In: *Environmental Management in South Africa* (eds R.F. Fuggle and M.A. Rabie), Juta.

13

Social and Ethical Dimensions of Sustainable Development: Mining in Kakadu National Park

Slobodan Perdan

Summary

This case study examines a controversy concerning the proposal to open a uranium mine in Kakadu National Park in Australia, involving several stakeholders with diverse and conflicting views. Sustainability issues raised by the proposal are complex: there are varied cultural, ethical and social concerns entangled with economic and environmental issues, as it happens in so many development projects. The aim of the case study is to highlight a wide range and the complexity of sustainability concerns that emerge from such and similar controversies, and to illustrate how different cultures, value systems and worldviews influence one's perception of appropriate development.

Throughout the case study the reader is invited to reflect on the issues raised, and to deploy critical (and reflective) thinking about different stakeholders, their interests and values. The case study is not designed to offer a decisive calculus to assists us in deciding whether the mining should proceed, but rather to pose some important questions about our fundamental values and priorities. In this respect, the case study is less concerned with the scientific or engineering aspects of sustainability than with its social and ethical sides. There is at least one important benefit of viewing the challenge of sustainability from this perspective: it brings it into the domain of dialogue, discussion and participation. Rather than being a "technical" or

Sustainable Development in Practice: Case Studies for Engineers and Scientists
Edited by Adisa Azapagic, Slobodan Perdan and Roland Clift
© 2004 John Wiley & Sons, Ltd   ISBNs: 0-470-85608-4 (HB); 0-470-85609-2 (PB)

"management" problem that technology, experts or the government can solve for us, when seen as an ethical or social issue, sustainability becomes the concern for all of us.

13.1 Introduction

Mining, as an important economic activity, has a significant role to play in achieving sustainable development. In the context of the mining and mineral sector, the goal of sustainable development should be to maximise the contribution to the well-being of the current generation in a way that ensures an equitable distribution of its costs and benefits, without reducing the potential for future generations to meet their own needs (IIED and WBCSD, 2002). Yet, as our case study will demonstrate, on its road to sustainable development, the mining industry faces a range of challenges. The following section gives a brief overview of these challenges.

13.2 Mining and Sustainable Development

Mining, defined simply as "the extraction of minerals from the earth", is of funda-mental importance in the economy of a number of countries, both developed and developing. It is estimated that 30 million people are involved in large-scale mining, representing 1% of the world's workforce, with a further 13 million involved in small-scale mining (IIED and WBCD, 2002). It is therefore likely that, including dependants, 250–300 million people rely on mining. Many other people are also directly or indirectly employed in the rest of the minerals supply chain.

Mining, together with oil and gas extraction, creates most of the energy and resources needed to meet society's needs. Minerals are essential to everyday life, making up numerous products we all use. They are also vital raw materials in a large number of industries including ceramics, construction, cosmetics, deter-gents, drugs, electronics, glass, metal, paint, paper and plastics (Azapagic, 2003). The mining industry generates wealth in direct and indirect ways, and creates many opportunities including jobs and the development of local infrastructure and services.

Mining activities, however, also result in serious consequences for the environment and society – locally and globally. Mining has had adverse impacts on local com-munities and cultures, destroyed natural habitats, polluted the air, soil and water, and produced enormous amounts of waste that can have environmental impacts for decades after mine closure. Problems have resulted from land clearance, particularly in the case of strip mining, processing of ore and from the "tailings" or waste products that many mines produce (WWF, 2002). Mining therefore carries a range of present and future environmental and social costs, both direct and indirect, which need to be balanced against the benefits it brings.

Until relatively recently, mining companies did not give great importance to these environmental and social impacts. In many ways the picture today is already more positive than it was a decade ago, and environmental and social concerns are now increasingly integrated in the planning and operation of mines. However, many operations, particularly in developing countries, still need to be upgraded in order to meet current expectations of sustainable practice. Concerns about the social and environmental effects of mineral developments and disparities in the distribution of costs and benefits are still very real (IIED and WBCSD, 2002). In short, there remains much to be done for improving the sector's contribution to all aspects of sustainable development.

Following a widely accepted categorisation of sustainability concerns, the key sustainability issues for the mining and minerals sector can be classified into three major categories: economic, environmental and social (Azapagic, 2003). These issues are discussed briefly below.

13.2.1 Economic Issues

Economic viability and competitiveness of the mining and minerals sector is important for sustainable development as the industry brings various economic benefits to society, including provision of employment and generation of wealth. To provide economic benefits to society, a mineral company must, like any other business, perform well at the micro-economic level by minimising costs and maximising profits and shareholder returns. This may lead to macro-economic benefits through various investments and injection of "hard" currency (particularly in poorer countries), contribution to Gross Domestic Product (GDP) and tax, royalty and other payments to the public sector. However, a number of factors can influence the ultimate returns to society from mineral developments.

One of these factors is the management and distribution of mineral wealth and revenues. The micro-economic issues have traditionally dominated business decision-making with a focus on short-term returns, which is in the mining and minerals industry often based on production volumes rather than on value-added products and services. This, combined with price volatility of some minerals, has in some cases led to a profligate use of mineral resources and a faster depletion of mineral reserves, therefore causing greater environmental damage and returning little economic benefit to society.

One of the ways to partly offset this unsustainable resource depletion is to increase the value added of minerals by further processing the raw materials closer to the front end of the supply chain (Azapagic, 2003). This would not only maximise financial returns to the industry, but would also enable producer countries to derive more benefits from their resources. However, one of the great obstacles to adding more value to minerals at source is the tariffs imposed by industrial countries on imports of processed goods. For example, exporting copper wire or aluminium tubes into European Union, USA, Japan, Canada and Australia is on average 3.2 and 5.3% more expensive respectively than exporting unprocessed copper and aluminium ores (IIED and WBCSD, 2002).

A further challenge is the distribution of revenues from minerals among private sector, central government and local communities (Azapagic, 2003). This is a contentious issue which has often created tension, political controversy and sometimes even armed conflicts. The common practice has been to split the earnings between the company and the central government, thus bringing little benefit to the local communities. Governments often use corporate taxation and royalty payments to gain an adequate share of revenues from a mineral development. Developing countries as a whole derive 80% of their mineral revenues from taxes on corporate profits (Cawood, 2001).

However, this approach can deprive these economies of valuable income in case of non-profitable mineral developments. Royalty payments and other taxes (e.g. value-added, stamp duty and fuel) are also used to further increase government's gains from mineral resources. However, high taxes can also deter investors thus depriving a country of perhaps a vitally important income. To encourage investments, some countries introduce subsidies; this approach has often been criticised for under-pricing mineral resources and stimulating unsustainable levels of production, thus leading to a faster depletion of mineral reserves.

Although many countries are now trying to address this issue, few have been able to institute policy and regulatory frameworks which enable more equitable sharing of the wealth generated from minerals. Yet, equitable distribution of wealth is one of the prerequisites for more sustainable societies, making this not only an important economic but also a social issue.

13.2.2 Environmental Issues

Given the scale of mining activities, it is not surprising that they have a wide range of environmental impacts at every stage of operation. Depletion of non-renewable resources and environmental impacts as a result of air emissions, discharges of liquid effluents and generation of large volumes of solid waste are the most important environmental issues for the mining and minerals industry (Azapagic, 2003). Energy consumption and contribution to global warming are also considered to be significant. Some estimates show that the mining and minerals industry consumes 4–7% of the energy used globally (IIED and WBCSD, 2002).

Mining activities such as extraction have a visual impact on the landscape and lead to destruction or disturbance of natural habitats, sometimes resulting in the loss of biodiversity. Mining of some types of minerals (e.g. some metals) is also associated with the acid drainage problem which can cause a long-term acidification of waterways and can affect biodiversity. Furthermore, some effluents generated by the metal mining industry can also contain large quantities of toxic substances, such as cyanides and heavy metals, which can pose significant human health and ecological risks. This was demonstrated by the two most recent incidences of the tailing dams' failures, at the Baia Mare gold mine in Romania and at the Aznalcollar zinc, lead and copper mine in Spain. In general, the environmental impacts of metal mining are likely to be greater than that of other minerals because of toxic chemicals that are often used in minerals separation (Azapagic, 2003).

A number of environmental issues can also arise in the rest of the life cycle of mineral products, including the use and disposal stages. For instance, the use of some minerals can have toxic effects on humans and the environment. The most drastic examples here are asbestos, lead and uranium. Other issues include generation of solid waste and loss of valuable resources at the end of the product's useful life. Some minerals can be recovered and recycled to increase their eco-efficiencies.

At the end of their useful life, the mine and production facilities can also pose several environmental problems including water contamination due to acid mine drainage and other toxic leachates, irreversible loss of biodiversity, loss of land and visual impact. A number of abandoned mine sites and unrestored quarries are a testimony to the unsatisfactory environmental performance of the industry in the past (EC, 2000). This practice is set to change as modern development projects increasingly include plans for decommissioning and rehabilitation. However, a recent PriceWaterCoopers survey revealed that, although 88% of surveyed companies have environmental post-closure mitigation plans, only 45% have detailed socio-economic plans that are regularly reviewed and have updated cost estimates (PWC, 2001).

13.2.3 Social Issues

In addition to more conventional socio-economic concerns related to employees (wages, benefits, occupational health and safety, education and skills development, equal opportunities, etc.), mining companies have to deal increasingly with a set of wider social issues. Many mining companies see the emergence of those wider social issues as by far the most difficult part of the sustainability agenda. They particularly point with some anxiety to the complexity of relations with communities, indigenous peoples and with NGOs at both the local and the international levels.

Employment opportunities in the local area, capacity-building, involvement in decision-making and distribution of wealth and revenue between company and local community are some of the issues that can arise in relations of the mining companies with local communities in which they operate.

Employment in the mining sector is generally falling in most parts of the world. However, employment opportunities provided by the mining industry can be substantial, and in some cases a mining company is the main employer in the area. This cannot only bring wealth and prosperity to communities, but can also cause considerable disruption to the social life and structure. An increasing trend in the industry is contracting out or outsourcing which means that local communities are less likely to benefit from new jobs and business opportunities (Azapagic, 2003). A typical example of this is "fly-in, fly-out" operations which bring workforce from different parts of the world to exploration sites. Lack of locally available skilled workforce is often quoted as a reason for outsourcing. Yet, capacity-building through education, training and skills development of the local labour force could help overcome the skills shortage problems, and at the same time contribute towards more sustainable communities, even after mine closure.

In addition to jobs and training, mining companies frequently build schools and hospitals or health facilities for workers and their families. Their investments and activities usually produce significant economic and social benefits. Yet, many mineral-rich areas have traditionally been inhabited or used by indigenous peoples. If mining takes place in such an area, contacts with the exogenous mining personnel and a foreign culture have sometimes unintentional consequences for the local community, such as the influx of diseases against which indigenous groups do not have natural immunity (sexually transmitted diseases being only a minor component of the problem), and the devaluing or even disappearance of indigenous traditions and cultures. It is therefore of critical importance for the mining industry that in its relationship with indigenous peoples, it is guided by the principle of respect for their cultural values and ways of life.

The challenge for the mining companies at the community level, as elsewhere, is to maximise the benefits and to avoid or mitigate any negative impacts of mining. Determining the best way of doing this should be through participatory processes involving all relevant actors, including members of the affected community, and in accord with the local context. This requires appropriate processes for participation and dialogue, involving all relevant stakeholders. Particular attention should be paid to including not only potentially disadvantaged groups such as already mentioned indigenous peoples, but also women and minorities.

Protection of human rights is another relevant social concern that should be addressed when considering sustainability of the mining and minerals sector. There have been accusations that some mining companies abuse human rights, in actions taken either independently or in collusion with governments (IIED and WBCSD, 2002). This includes paying unfairly low wages, denying the right to employees to organise in trade unions, the use of child labour, abuse of women, forced and compulsory labour, violation of indigenous rights and use of force to gain control over land. These are all serious sustainability issues which require a concerted action of the industry and national and international community.

This is also true for corruption, which is one of the main obstacles to equitable distribution of wealth from minerals (Azapagic, 2003). Some companies in the sector have been involved in bribing officials, for example to secure or speed up the permitting process. Although in many cases these payments are done in the interests of business efficiency, bribery and corruption are damaging the economy and human development as they divert revenue away from the government priorities and bring little benefit to local communities. A recent survey by Transparency International, a German NGO, found out that out of 32 leading countries with mineral deposits, 23 appear to have some kind of corruption problem (Hodess *et al.*, 2001). This, like the human rights abuse, is a large-scale problem which cannot be addressed by the mining companies alone, but only in collaboration and partnership with all relevant stakeholders.

To sum up, the mining and minerals sector is facing a range of sustainability challenges, and if the mining industry is to contribute positively to sustainable development, it needs to demonstrate continuous improvement of its economic, environmental and social performance.

Most of the sustainability challenges mentioned above are reflected in the case study discussed below. The case study is concerned with the issue of mining in Kakadu National Park in Australia's Northern Territory. Kakadu is a place of immense ecological and cultural significance, which also happens to be very rich in minerals. The latest proposal to explore the Jabiluka uranium deposit, considered to be one of the largest undeveloped uranium ore body in the world, has caused a great controversy, which is the main focus of the case study. Before we explore the Jabiluka mining proposal in more detail, to understand better why the project has caused such a controversy, let us first see why is Kakadu so ecologically important and culturally sensitive place.

13.3   Case Study: Mining in Kakadu National Park

13.3.1   The Background

Kakadu National Park is a unique archaeological, ethnological and ecological reserve, located in the tropics at the northern end of Australia's Northern Territory, 120 km east of Darwin, covering a total area of $19\,804\,km^2$. Kakadu has been inhabited continuously for more than 40 000 years. The cave paintings, rock carvings and archaeological sites present a record of the skills and the ways of life of the region's inhabitants, from the hunters and gatherers of prehistoric times to the Aboriginal people still living there. It is a unique example of a complex of ecosystems, including those of tidal flats, floodplains, lowlands and plateau, providing habitat for a wide range of rare or endemic species of plants and animals.

Kakadu has a monsoonal climate, and during the wet season, rivers and creeks flood and spread out over the broad floodplains to form vast wetlands. These extensive wetlands, which include floodplains, billabongs, rivers, coastal and estuarine areas, are recognised internationally as being significant for migratory birds, and are listed under the Convention on Wetlands of International Importance (the Ramsar Convention).

Kakadu is rich in mineral resources such as uranium which have been exploited. The photograph shows the existing Ranger uranium mine. Photograph by S. Perdan.

Kakadu protects the entire catchment of a large tropical river, the South Alligator, and examples of most of Australia's Top End habitats. From this range of habitats stems a remarkable abundance and variety of plants and animals. Many are rare or not found anywhere else, such as the black wallaroo, chestnut-quilled rock pigeon, and the white-throated grass wren.

The Alligator Rivers region, which encompasses the park, is considered to be the most floristically diverse area of monsoonal northern Australia. More than 1600 plant species have been recorded from the park, reflecting the variety of major landform types and associated plant habitats in the region. Of particular importance is the diverse flora of the sandstone formations of the western Arnhem Land escarpment, where many species are endemic. Based on recent surveys and records of the Northern Territory, some 58 plant species occurring in the park are considered to be of major conservation significance.

Kakadu is also one of the few places in Australia where there have been limited, if any, extinctions of plants or animals over the last 200 years. New species continue to be discovered in Kakadu, and the area remains a stronghold for some globally threatened species such as ghost vampire bat, estuarine crocodile, loggerhead turtle and hooded parrot. Kakadu also contains an extremely rich bird fauna of 274 species. This biological diversity makes Kakadu a place of immense ecological significance.

Kakadu is also extremely important to Aboriginal people who regard it as a place of special spiritual significance. There are several places in Kakadu which are regarded as "sacred and dangerous" by Aborigines (Box 13.1).

Kakadu's wetlands provide habitats for a wide range of rare or endemic species of plants and animals, and are recognised internationally as being significant for migratory birds. Photograph by S. Perdan.

Box 13.1   *Sacred and dangerous sites (AAPA, 2003)*

"What is a Sacred Site?

Aboriginal people believe that the entire world, including the seas, continents, living things, and human beings, originates in the deeds of Ancestral Spirits. These Spirit Ancestors were active in the past, in the time often referred to as 'the Dreamtime', but are also present in the landscape today. They continue to influence all aspects of the natural and social worlds. The rules governing human life are grounded in the deeds and continuing presence of these Ancestors.

Features in the landscape mark episodes in the deeds associated with these Ancestors. Some Ancestors became transformed into physical features such as mountains, rocks or celestial objects. Others became species of plants and animals. While the Ancestors traveled across the whole landscape, the strongest concentration of their powers can be found in places where they created a landform, left an object behind, or remain in the ground. These are sacred sites. Sometimes these are obvious features, but in other places they may not be spectacular or interesting to non-Aboriginal eyes.

Aboriginal people know that sacred sites are dangerous places. They are concerned to protect ignorant people, including non-Aboriginals, from hurtful contacts with such places. Some activities, such as lopping a sacred tree or digging into sacred ground, may disturb the Spirit Ancestors, with grave consequences both for the person causing the disturbance, and for the Aboriginal people who are custodians for that place. In some cases, custodians believe that if they allow a site to be damaged, other Aboriginal people will hold them responsible, and will invoke powerful supernatural punishments."

– by Aboriginal Areas Protection Authority,
Northern Territory Government

Kakadu has some very significant Aboriginal archaeological sites, and one of the finest and most extensive collection of rock art in the world, a tangible reminder of Aboriginal people's long and continuing association with the area. The art sites, concentrated along the Arnhem Land escarpment and its outliers, display a range of art styles including naturalistic paintings of animals. The most significant art sites are those associated with "Bula", a Creation Time being who created a number of sacred and potent sites that, even today, are considered by Aborigines to be dangerous. The art also includes more recent "contact" images of European items and people. The numerous Aboriginal art sites not only represent a unique artistic achievement, but also provide an outstanding record of human interaction with the environment over tens of thousands of years.

The art sites of Kakadu are recognised as a major international cultural resource and are part of the reason that Kakadu is inscribed on the United Nations List of World Heritage properties. Sites nominated for World Heritage listing are inscribed on the List only after carefully assessing whether they represent the best examples of the world's cultural and natural heritage.

Kakadu National Park was inscribed on the World Heritage List in three stages, in 1981, 1987 and 1992. It is one of the few sites included in the List for both outstanding cultural and natural universal values (EA, 2003):

1. Natural

    (a) as an outstanding example representing significant ongoing ecological and biological processes;
    (b) as an example of superlative natural phenomena; and
    (c) containing important and significant habitats for *in situ* conservation of biological diversity.

2. Cultural

    (a) representing a unique artistic achievement; and
    (b) being directly associated with living traditions of outstanding universal significance.

Kakadu's outstanding scenery, numerous recreational opportunities, significant archaeological sites and Aboriginal rock art attract over 200 000 visitors every year, making it a significant tourist attraction and an important contributor to Australian tourist industry.

Kakadu is also rich in mineral resources such as gold, platinum, palladium and uranium, which some think should be mined. Mining already goes on in the Kakadu area and there is pressure to allow more. The most recent mining proposal concerns the Jabiluka uranium deposit. An economics study commissioned by the company that owns the deposit, Energy Resources of Australia (ERA), indicates that Jabiluka will contribute A$6.2 billion to Australia's GDP over 28 years. According to ERA, all Australians will benefit directly from the royalties and taxes flowing from Jabiluka. ERA also estimates that the Jabiluka mine will provide jobs and benefits for the local community, and will generate $210 million in royalties for the Northern Territory Aboriginal community (ERA, 1998, 2002).

The local Aborigines supported by various environmental and social justice groups are strongly opposed to the mine. They are concerned over threats to the natural and cultural values of Kakadu National Park. Concerns over the effects of the mine on the cultural values include the concerns about over 200 sacred sites within the lease area, including burial sites, creation sites, living areas and art sites. Concerns over the potential impact of the mine on the natural values of the park include the possibility of escape of radioactive materials into Kakadu's ecosystems, the lack of information on whether the mine will affect any rare or endangered species and the necessity of building an access road to the mine.

Before we consider the latest mining proposal in more detail, let us pause here for a moment to reflect first on some general questions.

Questions

1. Should more mining be allowed in Kakadu? Could mining in ecologically and culturally important places such as Kakadu be regarded as an appropriate or sustainable economic activity? How do we compare the benefits of protecting

Kakadu with the economic benefits of the mine which might improve the lives of a number of people, including the lives of the local Aboriginal people? How exactly might we reach answers to these questions?

2. If you are concerned about environmental and/or cultural and/or other impacts of the mine, and think that protecting Kakadu is more important than the potential economic benefits of the mine, explain the reasons behind your concerns? What influences your views?

3. If you think that the benefits of mining outweigh environmental or other concerns in this case, explain why you hold such a position? What influences your views?

In answering the above questions, you might have felt that you needed more "facts" to reach an appropriate decision. It is indeed essential to acquire knowledge and understanding about potential social and environmental impacts of the project as well as about economic and wider social benefits from the mining. This however may, in itself, be a difficult task. As we shall see later in the chapter, technical data and information concerning the Jabiluka mining proposal and its environmental and cultural impacts are voluminous and complex. Different stakeholders hold different and often conflicting views on the potential impacts of the mining proposal. This should not be surprising since the knowledge surrounding many development projects is contested and open to diverse interpretations.

For example, the opponents of the mining proposal may claim that it is likely that the mine will pollute the waters of Kakadu, greatly disturb the ecosystems, endanger some species and generally have adverse impacts on the cultural and natural values of Kakadu. The opposition to mining will therefore rely on empirical claims: that is, claims about what will in fact happen. The proponents may dispute these claims, for instance, by pointing out that only a small piece of land will be affected. Some may think that even if the opposition claims are true, it is better to go ahead with the development of the mine because benefits from the project outweigh the costs. It is, therefore, important to bear in mind that even if the facts are settled, the issue will not necessarily be resolved. In this case we shall have to pay attention not only to factual evidence, but also to different value systems and cultural contexts which influence stakeholders' perception of benefits and costs involved in this project. The controversy of mining in Kakadu is an example of situations in which "facts are uncertain, values in dispute, stakes high and decisions urgent" (Funtowitcz and Ravetz, 1992).

The key question will therefore be: how do we reconcile different and conflicting value judgements and worldviews? We shall return to this question at the end of our case study. Let us now turn our attention to the Jabiluka mining proposal and examine the controversy in more detail.

13.3.2   The Jabiluka Uranium Deposit

The Jabiluka uranium deposit is situated inside the World Heritage-listed Kakadu National Park, about 230 km east of Darwin and 20 km north of the existing Ranger uranium mine. The Jabiluka uranium deposit is considered to be one of the largest undeveloped ore bodies of its type in the world, with 19.5×10^6 t of ore and the potential to yield more than 90 400 t of uranium oxide over 28 years. Uranium oxide production is expected to peak at 4600 t per annum.

As already mentioned, the mining company, ERA, which is majority owned by London-based mining multinational Rio Tinto, holds the Jabiluka Mineral Lease. Although within the outer boundaries of Kakadu National Park, the lease is not legally part of the park and therefore not subject to the legal prohibition on mining within Kakadu.

The Jabiluka uranium deposit was discovered in 1971. The proposal to mine the deposit was first submitted in 1979 by the initial leaseholder Pan Continental Ltd, and the Australian government approvals were granted in 1982. The original Jabiluka mining project, however, did not go ahead. Between 1983 and 1996 a "three mines policy" was in operation in Australia with respect to uranium mining. This policy limited the number of operational uranium mines in Australia to three (including the Ranger mine located within, but excised from, Kakadu National Park), and therefore effectively excluded the possibility of uranium ore extraction at the Jabiluka Mineral Lease. With a change in policy in March 1996, this limitation on the construction of new uranium mines in Australia came to an end.

In 1991, ERA bought the lease from Pan Continental Ltd for A$125 million. After the change in the mining policy in 1996, ERA lodged its new application to mine Jabiluka and the government approvals were granted in 1997.

The Jabiluka uranium mine had originally been proposed as an open cut mine by Pan Continental Ltd, which had potential for serious environmental management problems. ERA has proposed an underground mine with two options for progressing the Jabiluka mine. Under the Ranger Mill Alternative (RMA) (the company's preferable option), Jabiluka ore is to be transported to the existing Ranger mine (20 km south of Jabiluka) for milling and processing, and tailings are to be disposed of in surface pits, and covered on the mine's closure. This project option, however, requires the traditional owner's consent under the 1992 Deed of Transfer of the Jabiluka lease. The second option, known as the Jabiluka Mill Alternative (JMA), involves constructing and operating a mill on site at Jabiluka and disposing of tailings via a combination of surface pits and underground storage.

According to ERA, it is estimated that the operation of the Jabiluka mine will increase Australia's national economic welfare by $3.8 billion over its 28-year life. This amount represents the economic benefit of the mine, but excludes any environmental costs associated with mine development or operation. The operation of the mine is also estimated to increase economic activity in Australia by a $6.2 billion increase in real GDP over the mine's 28-year life.

However, there is a very strong opposition to the Jabiluka mining proposal. The Mirrar Aboriginal people, Australian and international environmental NGOs, and individuals and groups speaking on behalf of the Aboriginal people have opposed the mining proposal because they believe that the Jabiluka mine threatens the people, culture and environment of Kakadu. They think that "one of Australia's most beautiful places is in danger of being sacrificed to Australia's ugliest industry". Mining at Jabiluka, according to the opponents, will have an irreversible impact on the integrity of the World Heritage cultural and natural values of Kakadu National Park and the Mirrar community. Under Australian law, the Mirrar people are recognised as the traditional owners of the land, and their senior member has responsibility for the care of the land and the people. The traditional lands of the Mirrar people cover the Ranger and Jabiluka Mineral Leases, the Jabiru township and other surrounding areas within the World Heritage property.

Environmental and other NGOs worked with the Mirrar people to blockade the mine site in 1998. This initiative gained significant media coverage and placed the issue of Jabiluka firmly on the public agenda. In 1998, the UN World Heritage Committee sent a special mission to Kakadu to investigate claims by traditional owners and environmental groups that Kakadu was "in danger" from the impact of the Jabiluka mine, and to assess "ascertained and potential threats to the World Heritage values of Kakadu National Park posed by the Jabiluka mining proposal" (UNESCO, 1998).

The mission delivered its report in November 1998 finding that Jabiluka posed serious threats to the cultural and natural values of Kakadu and made 16 recommendations including: "that the proposal to mine and mill uranium at Jabiluka should not proceed" (UNESCO, 1998). However, after a successful lobbying by the Australian government (the opponents of the mine called it "political bullying"), the World Heritage Committee ruled against placing Kakadu on its "In Danger List", which means that the uranium mining option has remained open.

Construction work at the Jabiluka mine began in June 1998, and it had been expected that the first uranium oxide would be recovered in 2001. ERA completed the core sampling drilling work and construction of the tunnel into the Jabiluka ore body in September 1999. The Jabiluka mine was then placed on standby and environmental monitoring mode, meaning that no construction activity is occurring until the issue concerning where to mill the uranium and store the tailings could be resolved.

In October 1999, ERA formally sought approval for the RMA from the Northern Land Council. The Northern Land Council, operating on behalf of the Mirrar traditional owners and acting on their instruction, vetoed further discussions of the RMA for a period of 5 years (because of the Mirrar's fundamental opposition to mining). This means that if ERA are to pursue the development of Jabiluka in the next 5 years, their only project option is the JMA which would probably greatly increase the project's environmental and cultural impacts. Following the moratorium on consideration of the RMA for 5 years, ERA is undertaking a strategic review and evaluation of the Jabiluka mine, focusing on progressing the JMA. In order to progress the JMA in stages and have a mill operating at commercial levels, ERA needs to conduct further site-assessment work to develop specifications and tender for supply of mill equipment. Construction of the mill will then progress in stages, in accord with the Australian government's regulations. It could take up to 3–4 years to build and commission the new mill, and will involve planning and associated above- and bellow-ground works. ERA is now expecting that full-scale commercial mining at Jabiluka will be reached by about 2009.

Protest actions against the project and the companies involved have continued in both Australia and overseas, and Jabiluka remains one of Australia's most controversial industrial developments.

The two following sections provide some insight into the conflicting views of the key stakeholders. Section 13.3.3 outlines ERA's views and section 13.3.4 summarises the opposition's standpoint.

Questions

1. Draw up a comprehensive list of the interest groups (stakeholders) involved in the Jabiluka case.
2. Specify what are, in your opinion, the major concerns of each group.
3. Identify potential conflict of interests, and analyse what may cause it.

13.3.3   The Proponent's Position

The Company's Profile

ERA is a uranium enterprise selling uranium oxide from the Ranger mine in the Northern Territory and sources of uranium concentrates outside Australia to nuclear energy utilities in Japan, South Korea, Europe and North America. The company is currently producing ore from its Ranger 3 open pit and is proceeding with the development of the new Jabiluka mine. The company is intent on maximising profitable sales with a secure portfolio of medium- and long-term sales contracts and, as the third-largest uranium mining company in the world, has maintained a good reputation within the marketplace. ERA is a 68.4% owned subsidiary of North Limited, recently acquired by Rio Tinto Australia, and has strong shareholder–customer links with electricity utilities in Japan, France and Sweden. The following pages, based on the documents produced by ERA (1998, 2002), offer the company's perspective on the Jabiluka uranium mine proposal.

ERA's Proposal to Mine Uranium at Jabiluka

ERA claims that:

– the proposal offers a balanced approach to resource development;
– the Jabiluka uranium lease is outside the World Heritage-listed Kakadu National Park;
– strict international safeguards have been put in place to prevent the use of the uranium from Jabiluka for military purposes;
– the use of existing infrastructure at Ranger allows a considerable reduction in the scale, complexity and environmental impact of the Jabiluka mine;
– the mine operation will be designed in such a way as to protect ecosystems in the area and will have minimal visual or physical impact on the surrounding environment;
– the World Heritage values of Kakadu National Park will not be adversely affected;
– Jabiluka will not be a health risk;
– it will provide additional benefits such as jobs, training opportunities, new housing and so on to the local Aboriginal community over and above the $210 million in royalties the Jabiluka mine is expected to generate for the Northern Territory Aboriginal community;

– the Jabiluka project will provide significant benefits for the local and regional population, as well as the nation; and
– the Jabiluka proposal provides significantly more benefits for the local community than the "no project" option.

These key points are expanded below.

A balanced approach to resource development
The Jabiluka development has been planned to minimise impact on the environment while providing major economic benefits for Traditional Aboriginal Owners and all Australians. Jabiluka's Mineral Lease Number 1 was granted in August 1982 and covers an area of 7275 ha. The original proposal to mine the Jabiluka deposit has changed dramatically in response to concerns of local traditional owners and the environmental movement. ERA's preferred option involves 75.5 ha, less than 1% of the lease and less than 10% of the previously approved Pan Continental proposal.

Jabiluka is outside Kakadu
The Ranger and Jabiluka uranium leases are outside the World Heritage-listed Kakadu National Park. Kakadu was created progressively after the leases were granted. The Jabiluka operation will be an underground mine. It will be built on the opposite side of the hill from tourist viewpoints and the Magela Wetlands and the intended mine site is tiny – smaller than the area covered by the Parliament House in Canberra.

Strict international safeguards
Uranium from Australia is sold only to make electricity. ERA will export uranium to electricity utilities in Europe, the United States and Asia. Strict international safeguards have been put in place to prevent the use of ERA's uranium for military purposes. The safeguards take the form of legally binding agreements between Australia and countries to which it exports the mineral. No uranium has ever been diverted from a genuine civil reactor to weapons.

Two alternatives for milling
The Ranger mill alternative.   Under ERA's preferred milling option, there will be minimal surface facilities because the ore will be milled at nearby Ranger. The use of existing infrastructure at Ranger allows a considerable reduction in the scale, complexity and environmental impact of the Jabiluka mine. This option is called the Ranger Mill Alternative. Under the RMA, Jabiluka will produce about 90 400 t of uranium oxide over 28 years. There is enough energy contained in that tonnage to generate electricity equal to 20 times Australia's current annual needs. Ore will be mined at a rate of 100 000 t/yr increasing to 900 000 t/yr midway through the mine's life. A stockpile pad for the placement and handling of ore and waste rock, a retention pond to collect run-off water from the stockpiles and the mine's operation areas, a small administration and amenities block and a mine portal entrance will be built at Jabiluka. A 22.5-km haul road will also be built to transport ore from Jabiluka to Ranger, and back-haul low-grade uneconomic ore from the Ranger stockpiles to be used underground as cemented fill. Once at Ranger, the Jabiluka

ore will be blended with material from Ranger Pit 3 and processed through the Ranger mill which is currently designed to produce over 5000 t of U_3O_8 a year, but with Jabiluka ore, will be capable of producing over 6000 t of U_3O_8 a year. Approximately 17 ha of land will be required for the Jabiluka mine site, plus 54 ha for the haul road between Jabiluka and Ranger. This is 1% of the Jabiluka Mineral Lease. Tailings – the dewatered slurry left at the end of the milling process – will be permanently stored in the mined-out (closed for operation) Ranger Pit 1 and later in the mined-out Ranger Pit 3. The pits will be specially treated to ensure there is no leakage into the environment.

The Jabiluka mill alternative.   A second proposal for Jabiluka – the Jabiluka Mill Alternative – has been put forward by ERA for consideration in recognition of the opposition by some Traditional Aboriginal Owners to the company's preferred option of transporting Jabiluka ore to the existing Ranger operation for treatment and milling. The JMA is a small-scale, stand-alone mine and mill which will incorporate the latest technology in water and waste management. This alternative would require an area of 135 ha. As with the RMA, the JMA will not be visible from tourist viewpoints or the Magela Wetlands. If the JMA is adopted, the ore production rate will increase and reduce the mine life to 26 years. Production would commence at a rate of 450 000 t of ore a year, corresponding to an annual output of about 2500 t of uranium until 2008, and then to a maximum of 900 000 t of ore a year, corresponding to an annual output of about 4000 t of uranium. As with the RMA, tailings will be buried deep underground in pits designed to prevent leakage into the environment. ERA is committed to a programme of "zero release" of any mine water at the Jabiluka mine, mill and tailings facility.

The JMA would require the establishment of a new milling and processing plant instead of using the Ranger facilities. However, the improved stand-alone option offers a feasible alternative development strategy that delivers real benefits to the local and national economies.

ERA also has the option to provide further environmental assessment to the government on "cemented past-fill technology" which could be adopted for the disposal of mill tailings. Tailings would be dewatered and treated with cement to form a paste and used as backfill first in the underground development and then in the below-ground storage area. Two disposal pits would be built to accommodate tailings not disposed of underground. Negotiations with traditional owners will be undertaken to decide where the processing will take place. ERA would prefer to process the ore at Ranger.

Minimum impact on the environment
The JMA was the subject of detailed technical studies in the Environmental Impact Assessment (EIA) (see Chapter 6 for the requirements of EIA) and a Public Environment Report (PER). These are the key findings of the EIA and PER:

– Jabiluka will have no detrimental impact on Kakadu. The World Heritage values of Kakadu National Park will not be adversely affected. In addition, the mine's facilities and operations will not be visible from tourist routes.

– Jabiluka will not disturb areas of cultural or biological importance. No items of significant cultural value or areas of notable biological value will be disturbed.
– Jabiluka will not be a health risk. Predicted radiation levels from the mine will be well within the international guidelines, with no health risk to the general public or employees.

The proposed Jabiluka mine will operate according to strict internationally recognised requirements that protect the environment. The mine operation will be designed in such a way as to protect ecosystems in the area and will have minimal visual or physical impact on the surrounding environment. Jabiluka will be subject to stringent environmental requirements and will be strictly monitored by two independent authorities, the Commonwealth Supervising Scientist Group and the Northern Territory Department of Mines.

ERA has a long-standing commitment to high environmental values with an 18-year record of responsibility, accountability and environmental sensitivity at the Ranger mine. Ranger is one of the most highly regulated mines in the world and is governed by more than 50 Commonwealth and Northern Territory pieces of legislation. The environmental practice, standards and compliance established by ERA coupled with government regulation of Ranger are world-class. Similarly, Jabiluka will set a very high environmental benchmark. ERA has made guarantees about the operation of the Ranger mine, to ensure that the fragile and pristine ecosystems within the park are not disturbed, these guarantees will continue. No mining, or activities associated with mining, will be carried out in the park. ERA has shown at Ranger that it is committed to excellent environmental management. Stringent safeguards will be put in place at Jabiluka to protect the water quality, and constant monitoring and measuring will take place to detect any adverse effects downstream. In the unlikely event of environmental problems, immediate remedial action will be taken. ERA is committed to a "zero-release" mine water management programme in the Jabiluka mine. This means only clean water will be released and all stormwater run-off within the "Total Containment Zone" will be contained in a 9-ha retention pond and treated. The pond will be lined with a synthetic membrane which will prevent seepage to groundwater. The pond is designed to withstand a one in 10 000-year rainfall event. When mining is completed at Jabiluka, the site will be rehabilitated. Over time, it will be difficult to detect evidence of mining activity.

Health and safety
The Jabiluka mine will set a new standard in health and safety practices. Stringent international requirements will not just be met, but built upon. ERA will put in place safeguards and work practices, which ensure radiation exposure for employees is less than 20 millisieverts (mSv) per annum. This is below the level set by the International Commission on Radiological Protection (ICRP), where there is minimal health risk to workers or the general public. The ICRP recommendation allows for an exposure of 100 mSv to be averaged over 5 years and that the exposure in any one year must not exceed 50 mSv. With multi-skilling, management and control of the ventilation system and a number of special design features and practices, the Jabiluka mine will be safe for workers and the general public. With the use of appropriate equipment, the annual exposure for the most exposed workers, that is those working

underground, will be approximately 12 mSv/yr – well below the internationally recommended levels of 20 mSv/yr. All other workers will have even lower exposure. ERA has an excellent record in mine-radiation safety. In its 18 years of operation at Ranger, no worker has been exposed to excess radiation. Stringent international workplace health and safety standards will be implemented at Jabiluka to ensure this proud record is repeated at Jabiluka.

Aboriginal owners

A key concern of ERA is the possible impact of mining on Traditional Aboriginal Owners in the region. To ensure these issues are fully addressed, a comprehensive social and cultural impact study of the region was undertaken by a group of Aboriginal people within the Kakadu region and a group of stakeholder representatives. ERA contributed half the funding for the Kakadu Region Social Impact Study (KRSIS). The study was an independent assessment of the impact of mining on Aboriginal groups and tourism in the region and provides a community action plan to deal with the regional impacts on the Aboriginal community. ERA has already implemented a number of initiatives recommended in the KRSIS report. ERA acknowledges that concern about the impact of mining on the social and cultural fabric of the Aboriginal community has been expressed by a Senior Traditional Aboriginal Owner of the Jabiluka and Ranger sites. The company wants to address the concerns of Aboriginal Owners and is working with the community to help it to achieve social and economic independence. Following consultations with the Northern Land Council, the company has agreed to provide additional benefits to the local Aboriginal community over and above the $210 million in royalties the Jabiluka mine is expected to generate for the Northern Territory Aboriginal community.

These benefits include:

- employment and training opportunities for local Aboriginal people, with approximately 20% of the people working on the Jabiluka project to be Aboriginal;
- provision of new housing for approximately 65 Aboriginal families;
- assistance in Aboriginal businesses;
- funding for a Women's Resource Centre;
- funding for a bridging education unit for local Aboriginal children;
- traineeships for Aboriginal students.

The company, with the support of the Gunbang Action Group which represents 18 community groups, has also stopped take-away alcohol sales from the Jabiru Sports and Social Club. This reduced alcohol intake in Jabiru by 30% in the first six months. To support this initiative, ERA also funded the appointment of an alcohol counsellor for the Jabiru region.

Employment, training and education

The Jabiluka project will provide significant benefits for the local and regional population, as well as the nation. Targeted employment, training, education and investment opportunities, as well as increased income for the local people will assist in helping to eliminate some of the social disadvantages experienced by members of the Aboriginal community. The Social Impact Assessment in the EIS found that the impacts of the Jabiluka mine were likely to be relatively limited. Although the Aboriginal community in Jabiru currently experiences some social disadvantages, it is not anticipated that these conditions will be exacerbated by the small population change associated with the mine development. The assessment found that Jabiru provided a full range of community facilities and services that would normally be expected of a much larger town. Furthermore, the assessment found that the principal social impact of the development may occur in the medium to longer term, as the benefits from investment of the substantial compensation payments made to the Aboriginal community associations were realised. If the Jabiluka project did not go ahead, the life of the Ranger operation would be significantly shortened and would adversely impact the long-term viability of the township of Jabiru. Mining is the single largest employer in the area, accounting for 37% of the employed labour force. It is likely that most people employed by ERA would leave the area when mining ceased. This would place considerable strain on the viability of community services, such as health and education, and the local and regional economy. This reduced level of service and amenity would impact on the quality of life of those living in the region.

Economic benefits
Mining continues to be one of Australia's most important export industries and, as such, is fundamental to national prosperity. Jabiluka and Ranger will generate more than $12 billion as revenue during the next 28 years. At least 87% of this revenue will be distributed within Australia. Access Economics estimates Jabiluka will increase economic activity in Australia by a $6.2 billion in real GDP. Throughout the staged development of Jabiluka, ERA will employ a total of 380 people, of which 110 will be at Jabiluka itself, 230 at Ranger, 20 in Darwin and 20 in Sydney. Under the JMA, a workforce of up to 170 people will be required at Jabiluka. All Australians will benefit directly from the royalties and taxes that will flow from Jabiluka. In fact, the money ERA will pay to the Commonwealth and Northern Territory Governments is estimated to be the equivalent of 1500 jobs per year. As well as jobs, the Traditional Aboriginal Owners will receive royalties and rent from ERA. Total royalties from the Jabiluka development are expected to be approximately $210 million, plus $9 million as benefits.

"No project" option
While it could be argued that the "no project" option could lead to a strengthening of traditional Aboriginal community values and culture, this option would also result in the cessation of royalty payments to Aboriginal communities. This would mean that approximately $63 million in financial benefits from Jabiluka would not be paid to the local Aboriginal owners. This amount is on top of more than the $37 million already paid to the Aboriginal community in royalties from Ranger. Royalties have provided wide-ranging community services, facilities and businesses, such as the Cooinda Lodge and Crocodile Hotel, the establishment of an endowment fund for children, and health, food and other support services for outstations. The Social Impact Assessment concluded that the Jabiluka proposal provides significantly more benefits to the local community than the "no project" option.

Questions

1. What are the main social and environmental concerns related to uranium mining in general? What are specific concerns raised by the Jabiluka mining proposal? How does the company propose to address those concerns? In your opinion, does the company cover all the important sustainability aspects in its proposal?
2. What is your view on the company's proposal? To what extent does the Jabiluka mining project correspond to or differ from your vision of "appropriate" development?
3. Is mining, and particularly uranium mining and milling, in such close proximity and upstream from a World Heritage property, compatible with the protection of its natural and cultural values? Should World Heritage properties be recognised as "no-go" areas?
4. Australia has no nuclear power plants so that uranium from Jabiluka will be exported to nuclear utilities in Europe, the United States and Asia, and used to generate electricity. Australia has only one nuclear reactor (at Lucas Heights in southern Sydney) which is used mostly to generate isotopes for X-ray machinery, sterilisation equipment and smoke alarms. In your opinion, should Australia be exporting uranium to other countries to use in their nuclear facilities while refusing to have nuclear plants itself?
5. What is your position on nuclear power? What are the advantages and disadvantages of nuclear power? Why is nuclear power so controversial? Is this controversy justified or simply the result of some people's ignorance of the technology involved? Should nuclear power be actively promoted as a clean source of energy?
6. The company promises to deliver various mine-derived benefits to the local community, including housing and education for the Aborigines. That could be seen as an example of corporate social responsibility in practice. Yet, the critics would say that the company should not assume the role and responsibilities of government. If you were an ERA manager, how would you answer the following question: "How many communities in Sydney or Melbourne (or, for that matter, in any other city in the world) would accept a situation where their children received education only if they agreed to their local park being excavated for a uranium mine, and the funding for the school being controlled by the mining companies?"
7. Take the position of an ERA's engineer/shareholder. What do you think their benefit/cost assessment criteria would be? Where do your criteria fit in relation to their position? What criteria do you think are relevant for assessing the costs and benefits associated with the Jabiluka mine? Compare your criteria with those of your colleagues.
8. Put yourself in the position of an ERA manager. What challenges would you face in trying to explain the project to local people?

13.3.4   The Opponents' Position

There is a very strong opposition to the Jabiluka uranium mining proposal. Environmental and other NGOs and the Mirrar Aboriginal people, traditional owners of the Jabiluka Mineral Lease, have opposed the mining proposal because they believe that mining activity within the external boundaries of Kakadu National Park poses a direct threat to the natural and cultural values of the Kakadu World Heritage area, and has been responsible for significant adverse environmental and social impacts.

The opposition to mining argues that the original Jabiluka mining agreement was unfair and unjust. They claim that the agreement, signed in 1982 by the Northern Land Council, representing the Mirrar people, and Pan Continental Ltd, the first mining company to own the mining lease, emerged from the "bad old days" of Aboriginal mining agreements, when alcohol, duress, complex legal concepts, the exploitation of language difficulties, unconscionable conduct and outright lies were used to gain the "consent" of Aboriginal land owners.

The opposition to mining has also expressed many specific concerns raised by the proposal to mine uranium at Jabiluka. Australian Conservation Foundation, one of the most active conservationist groups in the campaign to stop mining at Jabiluka, claims that there are very solid arguments as to why Jabiluka should not be mined, including (ACF, 2000):

- There have been serious procedural irregularities in the government approval of JMA – including that this was done without an EIA despite a written assurance from the Supervising Scientist to the contrary.
- The project design that received approval was not that which was presented in the Jabiluka Mining Alternative PER or that which received any public examination. Rather it was developed during dialogue between the government and the project proponent.
- A number of dangerous sacred sites will be disturbed by any exploration and mining in the Jabiluka area, and damage would be done to the areas with World Heritage-listed cultural values.
- The social and economic problems facing the Aboriginal community in the Kakadu region are complex and ongoing. Industry research prepared as part of the Kakadu Regional Social Impact Study has shown that there has been no net economic benefit for Aboriginal people in the region from uranium mining operations.
- The Jabiluka mine would have a significant and long-term impact on the cultural and natural World Heritage values of Kakadu National Park. The Ranger/Jabiluka project areas would be a uranium development province within Kakadu for an additional quarter of a century.
- Mining operations at Jabiluka would result in the creation of an additional 20×10^6 t of radioactive tailings. Over time, these will seep and erode into Kakadu and contaminate the natural resources of the region. These tailings retain almost all their radioactivity for hundreds of thousands of years.
- The nearby Ranger mine has been plagued with significant water management problems since the mine began and regularly releases contaminated water into Kakadu against the wishes of the Aboriginal people. This has again happened in early 2000 – mining operations at Jabiluka would add to this pressure.
- The Jabiluka ore body is a health and safety hazard for workers because of its high radioactivity and the special problems of underground uranium mining. Proposals by ERA to address this are not internationally best practice and are insufficient to guarantee worker health and safety.

Kakadu has some very significant Aboriginal archaeological sites, and one of the finest and most extensive collection of rock art in the world. Photograph by S. Perdan.

Other NGOs such as Friends of the Earth and Wilderness Society share these views. They all express serious concerns about potentially damaging social and environmental impacts of the Jabiluka mine, including the concerns about potential leaks of radioactive materials into the thriving Kakadu ecosystem, radioactive waste and associated environmental and health hazards, and adverse social impacts on the local Aboriginal community. In their report to the World Heritage Committee of UNESCO, Australian environmental NGOs argued that mining operations at Jabiluka pose "both ascertained and potential dangers" to the World Heritage values and properties of Kakadu National Park. These dangers include (ACF, 2000):

- disregard for traditional owners and their cultural values;
- inadequate piecemeal and inconsistent approval process for the mine;
- inadequate regulatory framework for mining in the region; and
- limited detail and public disclosure about the project, for instance, important details regarding tailings disposal remain unavailable to the public.

The Mirrar people, Aboriginal traditional owners of the area, are unequivocally opposed to the project. The most pressing concern of the Aboriginal traditional owners is the destruction of their living tradition which will result from continued mining in their land (GAC, 1999). The Mirrar believe that mining and its associated impacts (such as the establishment of the mining town of Jabiru) is destroying their culture and society, and that the development of another uranium mine will have a continuing "genocidal impact on Aboriginal people in the region" (Mirrar, 2003). Specific concerns have been expressed about sacred sites. The Mirrar believe that the Jabiluka uranium mine will directly interfere with sacred sites which "will result in cataclysmic consequences for people and country". An additional mine, the Mirrar argue, will push their culture "past the point of cultural exhaustion to genocidal decay" (Mirrar, 2003).

In a joint letter of concern the Mirrar Gundjehmi, Mirrar Erre, Bunitj and Manilakarr clan leaders have stated:

> A new mine will make our future worthless and destroy more of our country. We oppose any further mining development in our country...We have no desire to see any more country ripped up and further negative intrusions on our lives...If the project is completed, the total loss of cultural value will be inevitable. The loss of cultural value encompasses both the destruction of cultural sites of significance by specific mining activity and a structural decline in the Mirrar living tradition resulting from imposed industrial development manifested as an attack on the rights of Mirrar.

Through the Mirrar and NGOs' concerns and action, the Jabiluka mine is currently stalled.

Questions

1. What are the opponents' main concerns about the proposed development? In your opinion, are their concerns justified? What evidence do they present to support their claims that the Jabiluka mine threatens "the people, culture and

environment of Kakadu"? You may wish to visit their respective websites to find more information on this.

2. If Jabiluka is not part of Kakadu National Park, how can the mine project affect the World Heritage area?

3. Suggest an economically viable alternative to the mining in Kakadu. Is it more sustainable than the proposed development? If you think so, explain why?

4. Some Mirrar people are fundamentally fearful of the possible destructive impact of the Jabiluka uranium mine on the "sacred and dangerous" sites. Should their beliefs be allowed to stand in the way of modern development that might improve the lives of many people?

5. What is, in your opinion, a role that NGOs play in this controversy? Has their contribution been helpful or has their involvement made the agreement less likely? Do NGOs have a legitimate role to play in projects like the mining at Jabiluka?

6. The NGOs involved in the Jabiluka controversy are actively campaigning to stop uranium mining and Australia's involvement in the nuclear industry. They reject nuclear power as unsafe and argue that there is still no long-term, totally satisfactory method of disposing of radioactive wastes. If you were an anti-nuclear campaigner how would you dispute the following claims:

   – "Nuclear power is the safest form of large-scale commercial power generation, much safer (in terms of human lives lost) than fossil fuel-burning power plants".
   – "Nuclear power is cleaner and less damaging to the environment than other sources of energy – it does not produce harmful, carbon-based greenhouse gases such as carbon dioxide, nor does it emit particulates, sulphur dioxide and similar harmful substances into the environment."

13.4   Role-Play Exercise

Share and compare your views on this proposed development at Jabiluka with that of your colleagues, classmates or friends. Carry out the following tasks:

1. Indicate in the matrix below which position you hold.

I believe that...	There should be no mining at Jabiluka	There should be no mining unless maintenance of critical ecological and social values can be guaranteed.	The mining should proceed with responsible management.	The mining should proceed.
Your position				

2. Take one of the following roles:

   (a) an ERA engineer;
   (b) an ERA shareholder;

    (c) the Mirrar traditional owner;

    (d) an environmental activist;

    (e) an independent scientist/environmental consultant;

    (f) an Australian Federal Government official from the Department of Industry, Tourism and Resources;

    (g) an official from the Northern Territory Government's Department on Infrastructure, Planning and Environment; and

    (h) a UNESCO–World Heritage commissioner.

3. Get into a group with seven others, preferably with those of whom have supported a position different to yours, and discuss the case. Before the group discussion, identify what would influence your views in your new role, and analyse your strong and weak points. Represent your position forcefully and with as much detail as you can summon. If it is not possible to reconcile your views with the views of those who oppose them, question their premises and assumptions. At the same time, try to understand the views of other parties involved. Make, as a group, a list of issues on which you agree and on which you do not. Suggest a way to overcome the identified differences and disagreements.

4. When you have finished the above group discussion, indicate in the matrix above your current position. Have you changed the viewpoint you had held before discussion? If so, explain how and why?

5. Based on all what has been presented in this chapter and the discussions you have had with your colleagues, write a short essay answering the following questions:

    (a) What are, in your opinion, the main sustainability issues raised by the Jabiluka mine proposal?

    (b) What are the contentious issues? How deep are the differences expressed?

    (c) Is it possible to reach a win-win solution? If not, what are the trade-offs involved?

    (d) If you agree that the main conflict is between the different values and worldviews, can you suggest a way of reconciling those conflicting views?

    (e) What "sustainability" lessons can we learn from the Jabiluka mining controversy?

Conclusions

We live in a highly differentiated, pluralistic society which involves different cultures with not only different but also conflicting values and interests. Indigenous peoples and their cultures are part of the fabric of modern society. As the Johannesburg Declaration on Sustainable Development has reaffirmed, they play "the vital role in sustainable development". We recognise that, for thousands of years, many indigenous groups worldwide have been living in harmony with their natural environment, and we have been starting to re-evaluate the significance of their cultures and traditions and incorporate their knowledge and expertise into our own. We increasingly support the rights of indigenous peoples to self-identification and their rights to preserve their collective identity and living culture.

Yet, what should we do in a situation where at stake is a huge economic benefit from a mine that happens to be on the land owned by an indigenous group, and they happen to be opposed to the development? How are we to reconcile their rights to preserve their collective identity and living culture with legitimate economic interests of the mining industry? Moreover, should certain areas be beyond reach any human activity that will disturb them, including mining, because they contain critical natural and cultural values? In which circumstances, if any, should cultural, environmental or other factors override access to valuable minerals?

These are difficult questions. They are not just about the decision on whether or not to explore and mine minerals in a certain area. These questions go to the heart of sustainable development, and concern our fundamental values and priorities. They remind us that on our path towards sustainable development we shall have to make many complex decisions. In some cases, we shall have to decide whether it is acceptable to suffer minor environmental damage in exchange for major social and economic gain, or whether it is worth sacrificing economic and social benefits for a significant environmental goal. There may be a conflict between global, national and local priorities, or between long-term sustainability objectives and short-term imperatives. In many cases, a majority perhaps, reaching a consensus will not be possible, and we shall have to resort to compromises. Our decisions will have to involve trade-offs: between different stakeholders' interests, and between different objectives and dimensions. And in some cases, we shall have to make decisions not to proceed with a certain project because it may go past some widely accepted limits such as transgressing fundamental human rights or destroying biological diversity.

How we deal with these questions is critical for sustainable development. The aim of sustainable development is to improve the quality of life for all people in ways which simultaneously protect and enhance the environment. It is an ethical vision, confronting us with the question of our responsibilities towards nature, to the world's poor and to future generations. Realising this ethical vision will be difficult without a set of values which promote social equity, respect for cultural and biological diversity, and a culture of cooperation and shared responsibility in achieving sustainability.

As we have pointed out in Chapter 1, one of the core principles of sustainable development is greater equity in access to opportunities and in the distribution of costs and benefits. The importance of equity considerations in assessing "sustainability" of a mining project has been clearly demonstrated in our case study. Who will benefit from it, and how the costs and benefits (not only economic but also environmental and social) should be distributed are the questions that have polarised the parties involved.

The Jabiluka mining controversy has also raised the issue of biological and cultural diversity and its relation to sustainable development. It should be said that, in many ways, biological and cultural diversity are essential for achieving sustainable development. Various forms of cultures and institutions in human society – political, religious, social or economic – have been built upon services provided by natural resources arising from biological diversity. Innumerable cultural practices depend upon specific elements of biodiversity for their continued existence and expression. At the same time, significant groups of biological diversity are developed, maintained and managed by cultural groups. The biologically diverse landscapes created and maintained by Aboriginal Australians through their astute use of fire is but one well-documented example.

There is therefore a mutual dependency between biological diversity and human culture, and the Aboriginal culture in Kakadu is a good example of that dependency. Over the course of their history, Aboriginal people have developed the lifestyle and culture which are intricately tied to nature. Their value and belief systems have evolved to enable them to respect and live in harmony with nature, conserving the diversity of life upon which they depend. The species-diverse environment in which Aboriginal people live has shaped their productive activities and spiritual values. This relationship is expressed in Aboriginal art, music, song, dance, ceremonial body painting, craft and storytelling.

The way of life of indigenous peoples depends on biological diversity, and the way of life of Aboriginal Australians is not an exception to this. Their cultural and religious beliefs and traditional spiritual values have often served to prevent overexploitation of resources and sustain the systems in which their communities live for their own benefit and that of future generations. The concept of the sustainable use of biological diversity, one of the objectives of sustainable development, is inherent in the value systems of indigenous and traditional societies.

Unfortunately, both biological and cultural diversity are now in imminent danger owing to present-day human activities. Not only biological species, but also many ethnic groups around the world are now faced with extinction. The causes and consequences of this loss lie in the increasingly unsustainable exploitation of the earth's natural resources and the growing marginalisation and dispossession of indigenous and minority groups. The causes of loss of biodiversity are also major causes of depletion of the foundations of peoples' lives and their distinct cultures.

This aspect of sustainability appears particularly important for the mining industry since mining often takes place in biologically diverse areas inhabited or used by indigenous peoples. The activity of mining almost inevitably involves altering the landscape and disturbing the flora and fauna, and has significant impacts on the indigenous communities. Concerns about these environmental and social impacts feature prominently in the case of mining in Kakadu. We have seen that the major concern of the Mirrar people is the threat the mine poses to their culture and way of life. Their concerns have been expressed very strongly – they even talk about possible "exhaustion" and "decay" of their culture. Additionally, the environmental groups involved have been warning us about the adverse impacts the mining will have on Kakadu's biodiversity and unique ecosystems.

These concerns over biological and cultural diversity present a huge challenge to the mining company involved. Here, as in many other mining projects, the challenge for the industry is to find a way of contributing positively to "sustainability imperatives": the economic imperative to raise the standard of living and quality of life, the environmental imperative to protect the natural environment and respect biodiversity, and the social and ethical imperative to maintain harmonious relationships and respect cultural diversity and human rights. And, as our case study confirms, these are not easy tasks at all. Yet, as already mentioned, it is of critical importance for the mining industry that, in its relationship with indigenous peoples and when operating in biologically important places such as Kakadu, it is guided by the principle of respect for the cultural and biological diversity.

Indeed, there are no simple solutions to the problems raised by the Jabiluka mining proposal. There is, however, at least one important lesson to be learned. A well-thought framework for consultation, benefit sharing, dispute resolution and involvement of local communities and the key stakeholders in decision-making at the earliest possible stages of a mining project appear to be critical for success. This early involvement of the people and communities most directly affected is also an appropriate way for the mining sector to deal with the complexity of social and cultural issues raised by their activities. Bringing decision-making process as close as possible to the people and communities most affected and making decisions in cooperation with them secure the rights of the people to be informed about issues and conditions that influence their lives, and ensure recognition of diverse values. Public participation in decision-making processes is also consistent with equity, because it provides every individual an equal and fair chance to defend his or her personal interests and values, and to contribute to the definition of the collective goal of sustainable development (Perdan and Azapagic, 2000). In its deepest form, cooperation and public participation should involve local community in all steps of planning, implementation and evaluation of projects, in order to enlist people's support and commitment, and increase their awareness of shared responsibility in delivering sustainable development.

As we have seen, the Jabiluka mining proposal raises many important and fundamental questions. There is no decisive calculus available to assists us in answering these questions. There are many different sets of values at play which makes finding the right decision more complicated. But, as Andrew Brennan put it, "life is complicated, and we will not make progress in tackling the grave difficulties we face unless we learn to avoid shallow thinking and simple solutions".

Finally, however difficult is to decide whether or not to explore and mine uranium at Jabiluka, the ultimate decision must be based on an integrated assessment of economic, environmental, cultural and social impacts, and thus be governed by the principles of sustainable development.

Post Scriptum

1 Aug 2003: The Northern Territory government has given the go-ahead for a clean-up of the controversial Jabiluka uranium mine, ending a long row which pitted conservation groups and Aboriginal people against mining company ERA. Under the clean-up program, ERA (Energy Resources Australia) will backfill the 1.8 kilometre decline located next to the world heritage-listed Kakadu National Park in the Northern Territory. ERA, majority owned by mining giant Rio Tinto, will retain the lease on the mine but will sign a formal agreement with traditional owners, the Mirrar people, undertaking no future development without their explicit permission.

The Age, 1 Aug 2003

References and Further Reading

AAPA (2003) Aboriginal Sacred Sites. Aboriginal Areas Protection Authority, http://www.nt.gov.au/aapa/text/sites1.htm.

Aboriginal Art (2003) "Dreaming", http://www.aboriginalart.com/arn_pages/dreamings.html.

ACF (2001) Ten Reasons Why Jabiluka Should Not be Mined, Australian Conservation Foundation, http://www.acfonline.org.au/asp/pages/document.asp?IdDoc=110, March, 2001.

ACF (Australian Conservation Foundation), Environment Centre of the NT, and Friends of the Earth Australia (2000) Kakadu: World Heritage under threat – Report to the World Heritage Committee of UNESCO by Australian environment NGO's, ACF, Victoria.

Azapagic, A. (2003) Developing a Framework for Sustainable Development Indicators for the Mining and Minerals Industry, *Journal of Cleaner Production* (in press).

Cawood, F. (2001) Aligning Mineral Wealth with Sustainable Development: The South African Perspective. Paper prepared for MMSD Southern Africa. In: IIED and WBCSD (2002). Mining, Minerals and Sustainable Development Project: Final Report, Ch. 8.

EA (2003) "Kakadu – World Heritage Site", Environment Australia, http://www.ea.gov.au/heritage/awh/worldheritage/sites/kakadu/index.html, March, 2003.

EC (2000) Communication from the Commission on Promoting Sustainable Development in the EU Non-energy Extractive Industry. The European Commission, Brussels, 3.5.2000, COM(2000) 265 final.

ERA (1998) The Jabiluka Report, Energy Resources of Australia, Sydney.

ERA (2002) Jabiluka Overview, Energy Resources of Australia, http://www.energyres.com.au/jabiluka/overview.shtml, January 2002.

Funtowitcz, S.O. and Ravetz, J.R. (1992) "*Environmental Problems, Post-Normal Science, and Extended Peer Communities*" (Read to the Environment Department, The World Bank, Washington DC, October 26, 1992).

Hodess, R., Banfield, J. and Wolfe, T. (eds) (2001) Global Corruption Report 2001. Transparency International, Berlin. http://www.globalcorruptionreport.org/#download (7 November 2002).

IIED and WBCSD (2002) Breaking New Ground: Mining, Minerals and Sustainable Development. Final Report on the Mining, Minerals and Sustainable Development Project (MMSD). International Institute for Environment and Development and World Business Council for Sustainable Development. www.iied.org/mmsd. (30 October 2002).

GAC (1999) Mirrar Fighting for Country: Information Kit, Gundjehmi Aboriginal Corporation, 1999.

Mirrar (2003) The Mirrar oppose the Jabiluka uranium mine, http://www.mirrar.net/jabiluka.html, March 2003.

Perdan, S. and Azapagic, A. (2000) Sustainable Development and Industry: Ethical Indicators. Environmental Protection Bulletin, Issue 066, May 2000, IchemE.

PWC (2001) *Mining and Sustainability: Survey of the Mining Industry*. PricewaterhouseCoopers/MMSD, London.

The Age (2003) Nod to clear Mine, www.theage.com.au, 1 August 2003.

UNESCO (1998) Bureau of the World Heritage Committee – Report on the mission to Kakadu National Park Australia, 26 October to 1 November 1998.

WSSD (2002) The Johannesburg Declaration on Sustainable Development, World Summit on Sustainable Development, Johannesburg, September 2002, http://www.johannesburgsummit.org (downloaded, October 2002).

WWF (2002) To Dig or Not to Dig: Criteria for Determining the Suitability or Acceptability of Mineral Exploration, Extraction and Transport from Ecological and Social Perspectives, WWF International & WWF-UK, Gland.

Appendix: Life Cycle Thinking and Life Cycle Assessment (LCA)

Adisa Azapagic

A.1 Life Cycle Thinking

In attempts to reduce environmental impacts of industrial and human activities, scientists and engineers have traditionally concentrated on one life cycle stage of a particular activity. For example, in trying to protect the environment from the emissions from an industrial installation, we have often resorted to an end-of-pipe technology to clean up air emissions or liquid effluents. Although clean-up technologies do reduce the immediate pollution from the installation, the use of energy and chemicals and the need to further treat and dispose of the wastes generated in the clean-up process often lead to additional pollution further up- or down-stream of that industrial facility. Thus, instead of protecting the environment, we may inadvertently increase the impacts from that installation. Therefore, we can be sure that we are protecting the environment as a whole only if we adopt a systems approach to consider the whole life cycle of an activity. This is known as life cycle thinking. It is also referred to as a 'cradle-to-grave' approach because it follows an activity from the extraction of raw materials ('cradle') to the return of wastes to the ground ('grave'). It is now widely accepted that environmentally sustainable solutions can be found only by taking a life cycle approach to environmental systems analysis (Azapagic, 2002). In this way, we can obtain a full picture of human interactions with the environment and avoid shifting of environmental impacts from one life cycle stage to another.

An important step in trying to understand the impacts of human interactions with the environment is the identification and quantification of environmental impacts of an activity from 'cradle to grave'. Life Cycle Assessment (LCA) is one of the tools that can help us do that.

A.2 Life Cycle Assessment

Life Cycle Assessment (LCA) is an environmental management tool underpinned by life cycle thinking. The International Organisation for Standardisation (1997) defines LCA as:

> a compilation and evaluation of the inputs, outputs and the potential environmental impacts of a product throughout its life cycle.

Sustainable Development in Practice: Case Studies for Engineers and Scientists
Edited by Adisa Azapagic, Slobodan Perdan and Roland Clift
© 2004 John Wiley & Sons, Ltd   ISBNs: 0-470-85608-4 (HB); 0-470-85609-2 (PB)

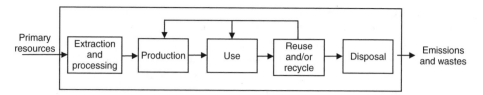

Figure A.1 *Stages in the life cycle of an activity considered by LCA*

As shown in Figure A.1, LCA considers the following stages in the life cycle of an activity:

– extraction and processing of raw materials;
– manufacturing;
– transportation and distribution;
– use, reuse and maintenance;
– recycling; and
– final disposal.

The LCA methodology is standardised by a series of ISO standards (ISO, 1997; 1998a–c) and includes the following phases:

1. Goal and scope definition (ISO 14041);
2. Inventory analysis (ISO 14041);
3. Impact assessment (ISO 14042); and
4. Interpretation (ISO 14043).

A.2.1 Goal and Scope Definition

This first phase of LCA includes definition of:

– the purpose of the study and its intended use;
– the system and system boundaries;
– the functional unit; and
– data quality, the assumptions and limitations of the study.

The process of conducting an LCA as well as it outcomes are largely determined by the goal and scope of the study. For example, the goal of the study may be to identify the 'hot spots' in a manufacturing process and to use the results internally by a company to reduce the environmental impacts from the process. Alternatively, the company may wish to use the result externally, either to provide LCA data to their customers who use their product in their manufacturing process or perhaps to market their product on the basis of environmental claims. In each case the assumptions, data and system boundaries may be different so that it is important that these are defined in accordance with the goal of the study.

In full LCA studies, the system boundary is drawn to encompass all stages in the life cycle from extraction of raw materials to the final disposal. However, in some cases, the scope of the study will demand a different approach, where it is not appropriate to include all stages in the life cycle. This is usually the case with commodities, for instance, which can have a number of different uses so that it is not possible to follow their numerous life cycles after the production stage. The scope of such studies is from 'cradle to gate' (as opposed to 'cradle to grave'), as they follow a product from the extraction of raw materials to the factory gate.

One of the most important elements of an LCA study is a functional unit. The functional unit represents a quantitative measure of the output of products or services which the system delivers. In comparative LCA studies, it is crucial that the systems are compared on the basis of equivalent function, that is functional unit. For example, comparison of different beverage packaging should be based on their equivalent function which is to contain a certain amount of beverage. The functional unit is then defined as 'the quantity of packaging necessary to contain the specified volume of beverage'.

This phase also includes an assessment of the data quality and establishing the specific data quality goals. 'Goal and scope definition' are constantly reviewed and refined during the process of carrying out an LCA, as additional data become available.

A.2.2   Inventory Analysis

The purpose of the 'Inventory analysis' is to identify and quantify the environmental burdens in the life cycle of the activity under study. The burdens are defined by material and energy used in the system and emissions to air, liquid effluents and solid wastes discharged into the environment. 'Inventory analysis' includes the following steps:

– detailed definition of the system under study;
– data collection;
– allocation of environmental burdens in multiple-function systems; and
– quantification of the burdens.

Following a preliminary system definition in the 'Goal and scope definition phase', detailed system specification must be carried out in the 'Inventory phase' to identify data needs. A system is defined as a collection of materially and energetically connected operations (including, e.g., manufacturing process, transport or fuel extraction) which performs some defined function. The system is 'separated' from the environment by a system boundary; this is illustrated in Figure A.2.

Detailed system characterisation involves its disaggregation into a number of interlinked subsystems; this is represented by flow diagrams (as shown in Figure A.2). Depending on the data available, the subsystems can represent the unit operations or a group of units. Environmental burdens are then quantified for each subsystem according to the formula:

$$B_j = \sum_{i=1}^{i} bc_{j,i}\, x_i \tag{A.1}$$

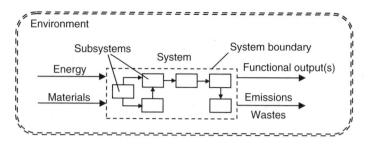

Figure A.2 *Definition of system, system boundary and the environment*

where, $bc_{j,i}$ is burden j from process or activity i and x_i is a mass or energy flow associated with that activity. A simple example in Box A.1 illustrates how the burdens can be calculated.

Box A.1 *Calculating environmental burdens and impacts in LCA – an example*

The system shown below has one functional output (product) and each activity i from extraction of raw materials to final disposal generates a certain amount of CO_2 and CH_4. For example, the output from the activity 'Extraction' (x_1) is 2 t of raw materials per functional unit (FU). This activity is associated with the emissions of 0.2 kg of CO_2 and 0.1 kg of CH_4 per tonne of raw materials extracted. The product output from activity 'Use' (x_3) is defined as the functional unit and is equal to 1 t.

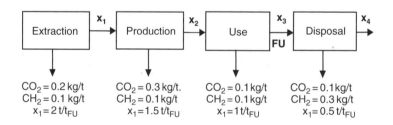

Using equation (A.1), the total environmental burdens per functional unit related to the emissions of CO_2 and CH_4 are therefore:

$$B_{CO_2} = \sum bc_{CO_2} \cdot x_i = 0.2 \cdot 2 + 0.3 \cdot 1.5 + 0.1 \cdot 1 + 0.1 \cdot 0.5 \Rightarrow B_{CO_2} = 1.0\,kg/t_{FU}$$
$$B_{CH_4} = \sum bc_{CH_4} \cdot x_i = 0.1 \cdot 2 + 0.1 \cdot 1.5 + 0.1 \cdot 1 + 0.3 \cdot 0.5 \Rightarrow B_{CH_4} = 0.6\,kg/t_{FU}$$

Global warming potential related to these two greenhouse gases can be calculated by applying equation (A.2) and the classification factors given in Table A.1:

$$E_{GWP} = ec_{CO_2} \cdot B_{CO_2} + ec_{CH_4} \cdot B_{CH_4} = 1 \cdot 1 + 11 \cdot 0.6 \Rightarrow E_{GWP} = 7.6\,kg\,CO_2\,equiv./t_{FU}$$

Table A.1 Classification factors for selected burdens*

Burdens	Resource depletion (world reserves)	Global warming GWP 100 years (equiv. to CO_2)	Ozone depletion ODP (equiv. to CFC-11)	Acidification AP (equiv. to SO_2)	Eutrophication EP (equiv. to PO_4^{3-})	Photochemical smog POCP (equiv. to ethylene)	Human toxicity	Aquatic toxicity (m^3/mg)
Coal reserves	8.72E+13 t							
Oil reserves	1.24E+11 t							
Gas reserves	1.09E+14 m^3							
CO							0.012	
CO_2		1						
NO_x				0.7	0.13		0.78	
SO_2				1			1.2	
HC excluding CH_4						0.416	1.7	
CH_4		21				0.007		
Aldehydes						0.443		
Chlorinated HC		400	0.5				0.98	
CFCs		5000	0.4				0.022	
Other VOCs		11	0.005			0.007		
As							4700	
Hg							120	
F_2							0.48	
HCl				0.88			0.48	
HF				1.6			0.02	
NH_3				1.88				
As							1.4	1.81E+08
Cr							0.57	9.07E+08
Cu							0.02	1.81E+09

Fe		0.0036	4.54E+11
Hg		4.7	2.99E+08
Ni		0.057	1.81E+09
Pb		0.79	3.45E+08
Zn		0.0029	
Fluorides		0.041	
Nitrates	0.42	0.00078	
Phosphates	1	0.00004	
Oils & greases			4.54E+07
Ammonia	0.33	0.0017	
Chlor. solv./comp		0.29	5.44E+07
Cyanides		0.057	
Pesticides		0.14	1.18E+09
Phenols		0.048	5.35E+09
COD	0.022		

*all classification factors are expressed in kg/kg, unless otherwise stated.

If the system under study produces more than one functional output, then the environmental burdens from the system must be allocated among these outputs. This is the case with co-product, waste treatment and recycling systems; in LCA such systems are termed multiple-function systems. Allocation is the process of assigning to each function of a multiple-function system only those environmental burdens that each function generates. An example of a co-product system is a naphtha cracker which produces ethylene, propylene, butenes and pyrolytic gasoline. The allocation problem here is to assign to each of the products (functional outputs) only those environmental burdens for which each product is 'responsible'. The simplest approach is to use either mass or economic basis, allocating the total burden (e.g. emission of CO_2) in proportion to the mass output or economic value of each product. More sophisticated and realistic allocation requires mathematical modelling and allocation based on physical causality which reflects the underlying physical relationships between the functional units (Azapagic and Clift, 1999). The allocation method used will usually influence the results of the LCA study so that the identification of an appropriate allocation method is crucial. To guide the choice of the correct allocation method, ISO recommends a three-step allocation procedure (ISO, 1998a); this is explained in Box A.2.

Box A.2   The ISO allocation procedure

The international standard ISO 14041 (1998a) prescribes a three-step procedure for avoiding or handling allocation:

1. Where possible, allocation is to be avoided by subdividing the process by analysis at a greater level of detail, or by system expansion. System expansion is more commonly applicable. The figure below illustrates the principle. Process 1 produces two outputs, A and B. Product A can also be produced by process 2, which does not produce B. Allocation of environmental impacts from process 1 between products A and B is avoided by expanding the system to include process 3 which produces only product B, at a rate equal to that from process 1. The two systems now produce the same outputs and can be compared directly. For more complex applications of this approach, see Tillman et al. (1994).

A principal difficulty with system expansion lies in the selection of the additional process 3. Should this be the average of current processes making B, or the current best processes, or likely future processes, or the current least economic processes (on the argument that these are the processes which will be displaced if process 1 is brought into operation)? Appropriate selection of the expanded system depends on the goals and scope of the LCA study (Weidema, 2001).

2. Where allocation cannot be avoided, the environmental impacts should be partitioned between the system's 'different products or functions in a way which reflects the underlying physical relationships between them' (ISO 14041, 1998a).

In other words, allocation should reflect the way the system in question actually functions by allocating an environmental impact to a functional output according to how much the impact changes with change in that output while others are kept constant. This is known as the marginal allocation approach. For examples of the application of this approach, see Azapagic and Clift (1999) and Baumann and Tillman (2003).

3. If neither of these approaches is possible, allocation should be on a basis 'which reflects other relationships' between the products. This default is most commonly necessary when two or more products must be produced together in fixed proportions: chlorine and sodium hydroxide by electrolysis of brine, for example. The 'other relationships' are most commonly the economic values of the co-products as they leave the process in question.

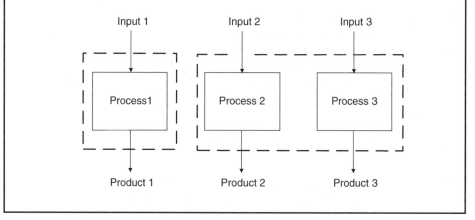

A.2.3   Impact Assessment

The environmental burdens quantified in 'Inventory analysis' are then translated into the related environmental impacts. This is carried out within the following steps in the 'Impact assessment' phase:

– classification;
– characterisation;
– normalisation; and
– valuation.

Classification involves aggregation of environmental burdens into a smaller number of environmental impact categories to indicate their potential impacts on human and ecological health and the extent of resource depletion. The aggregation is done on the basis of the potential impacts of the burdens, so that one burden can be associated with a number of impacts; for example, Volatile Organic Compounds (VOCs) contribute to both global warming and ozone depletion. The approach used most widely for classification of the impacts is known as 'problem-oriented', whereby the burdens are aggregated according to their relative contributions to the environmental effects that they may have. The impacts most commonly considered in LCA are:

- non-renewable resource depletion;
- global warming;
- ozone depletion;
- acidification;
- eutrophication;
- photochemical oxidant formation (photochemical or summer smog);
- human toxicity; and
- aquatic toxicity.

These impacts are defined in Box A.3.

The identification of the impact of interest is then followed by their quantification in the next, characterisation, step. In the problem-oriented approach, the impacts are calculated relative to a reference substance. For instance, CO_2 is a reference gas for determining the global warming potential of the other greenhouse gases such as CH_4 and VOCs. The environmental impacts can be calculated by using the following general formula:

$$E_k = \sum_{j=1}^{j} ec_{k,j}\, B_j \qquad (A.2)$$

where $ec_{k,j}$ represents the relative contribution of burden B_j to impact E_k, as defined by the problem-oriented approach. The specific environmental impacts can be calculated using the formulae given in Box A.3 and the relative impact factors for different burdens given in Table A.1. A simple example of how to calculate global warming is illustrated in Box A.1.

The impacts can be normalised with respect to the total emissions or extractions in a certain area and over a given period of time. This can help to assess the extent to which an activity contributes to the regional or global environmental impacts. However, normalisation results should be interpreted with care because of the lack of reliable data for many impacts on both the regional and the global scales.

The final stage within 'Impact assessment' is valuation in which each impact is assigned a weight which indicates its relative importance. As a result, the environmental impacts are aggregated into a single environmental impact function, EI:

$$EI = \sum_{k=1}^{k} w_k E_k \qquad (A.3)$$

where w_k is the relative importance of impact E_k.

A number of techniques have been suggested for use in valuation. They are mainly based on expressing preferences either by decision-makers, 'experts' or by the public. Some of these methods include Multiattribute Utility Theory (MAUT), Analytic Hierarchy Process (AHP) and Cost–Benefit Analysis (CBA). However, because of a number of problems at both philosophical and practical levels associated with using these techniques, there is no consensus at present on how to aggregate the environmental impacts into a single environmental impact function. Furthermore, some people argue that valuation should not be carried out at all as it obscures information and that considering the impact in a disaggregated form enhances transparency of decision-making based on LCA results.

Box A.3 *Definition of environmental impacts: problem-oriented approach*

Non-renewable resource depletion includes depletion of fossil fuels, metals and minerals. The total impact is calculated as:

$$E_1 = \sum_{j=1}^{j} \frac{B_j}{ec_{1,j}}$$

where, B_j is the quantity of a resource used per functional unit and $ec_{1,j}$ represents the estimated total world reserves of that resource.

Global warming potential (GWP) is equal to the sum of emissions of the greenhouse gases (CO_2, N_2O, CH_4 and VOCs) multiplied by their respective GWP factors, $e_{2,j}$:

$$E_2 = \sum_{j=1}^{j} ec_{2,j} B_j \quad (kg)$$

where B_j represents the emission of greenhouse gas j. GWP factors $ec_{2,j}$ for different greenhouse gases are expressed relative to the GWP of CO_2, which is therefore defined to be unity. The values of GWP depend on the time horizon over which the global warming effect is assessed. GWP factors for shorter times (20 and 50 years) provide an indication of the short-term effects of greenhouse gases on the climate, while GWP for longer periods (100 and 500 years) are used to predict the cumulative effects of these gases on the global climate.

Ozone depletion potential (ODP) indicates the potential of emissions of chloro-fluorocarbons (CFCs) and other halogenated HCs for depleting the ozone layer and is expressed as:

$$E_3 = \sum_{j=1}^{j} ec_{3,j} B_j \quad (kg)$$

where B_j is the emission of an ozone-depleting gas j. The ODP factors $ec_{3,j}$ are expressed relative to the ODP of CFC-11.

Acidification potential (AP) is based on the contributions of SO_2, NO_x, HCl, NH_3 and HF to the potential acid deposition, that is on their potential to form H^+ ions. AP is calculated according to the formula:

$$E_4 = \sum_{j=1}^{j} ec_{4,j} \, B_j \quad (kg)$$

where, $ec_{4,j}$ represents the AP of gas j expressed relative to the AP of SO_2, and B_j is its emission in kg per functional unit.

Eutrophication potential (EP) is defined as the potential of nutrients to cause over-fertilisation of water and soil, which can result in increased growth of biomass. It is calculated as:

$$E_5 = \sum_{j=1}^{j} ec_{5,j} \, B_j \quad (kg)$$

where, B_j is an emission of species such as N, NO_x, NH_4^+, PO_4^{3-}, P, and COD and $ec_{5,j}$ are their respective EPs. EP is expressed relative to PO_4^{3-}.

Photochemical oxidants creation potential (POCP) is related to the potential of VOCs and nitrogen oxides to generate photochemical or summer smog. It is usually expressed relative to the POCP classification factors of ethylene and can be calculated as:

$$E_6 = \sum_{j=1}^{j} ec_{6,j} \, B_j \quad (kg)$$

where, B_j is the emission of the species participating in the formation of summer smog, and $ec_{6,j}$ is the classification factor for photochemical oxidation formation.

Human toxicity potential (HTP) is calculated by taking into account releases to three different media toxic to humans, that is air, water and soil:

$$E_7 = \sum_{j=1}^{j} ec_{7,jA} B_{jA} + \sum_{j=1}^{j} ec_{7,jW} B_{jW} + \sum_{j=1}^{j} ec_{7,jS} B_{jS} \quad (kg)$$

where $ec_{7,jA}$, $ec_{7,jW}$, and $ec_{7,jS}$ are human toxicological classification factors for substances emitted to air, water and soil respectively, and B_{jA}, B_{jW} and B_{jS} represent the respective emissions of different toxic substances into the three media. The toxicological factors are calculated using scientific estimates for the acceptable daily intake or the tolerable daily intake of the toxic substances.

Aquatic toxicity potential (ATP) can be calculated as:

$$E_8 A = \sum_{j=1}^{j} ec_{8,jA} B_j \quad (m^3)$$

where, $ec_{8,jA}$ represents the toxicity classification factors of different aquatic toxic substances and B_{jA} is the respective emissions to the aquatic ecosystem. ATP is based on the maximum tolerable concentrations of different toxic substances in water by aquatic organisms.

A.2.4   Interpretation

This phase is aimed at system improvements and innovation, and it includes the following steps:

– identification of major burdens and impacts;
– identification of 'hot spots' in the life cycle;
– sensitivity analysis; and
– evaluation of LCA findings and final recommendations.

Quantification of environmental impacts carried out in 'Impact assessment' phase enables identification of the most significant impacts and the life cycle stages that contribute to these impacts. This information can then be used to target these 'hot spots' for system improvements or innovation.

Before the final conclusions and recommendations of the study are made, it is important to carry out sensitivity analysis. Data availability and reliability are some of the main issues in LCA since the results and conclusions of an LCA study will be determined by the data used. Sensitivity analysis can help identify the effects that data variability, uncertainties and data gaps have on the final results of the study and indicate the level of reliability of the final results of the study.

References

Azapagic, A. (2002). Life Cycle Assessment: A Tool for Identification of More Sustainable Products and Processes, pp. 62–85. In: *Handbook of Green Chemistry and Technology* (eds J. Clark and D. Macquarrie), Blackwell Science, Oxford.

Azapagic, A. and R. Clift (1999). Allocation of Environmental Burdens in Multiple-function Systems. *J. Cleaner Prod.*, **7**(2), 101–119.

Baumann, H. and A.-M. Tillman (2003). *The Hitch-hiker's Guide to LCA*, Studentlitteratur, Lund.

ISO (1997). ISO/DIS 14040: Environmental Management – Life Cycle Assessment – Principles and Framework. ISO, Geneva.

ISO (1998a). ISO/DIS 14041: Environmental Management – Life Cycle Assessment – Goal and Scope Definition and Life Cycle Inventory Analysis. ISO, Geneva.

ISO (1998b). ISO/CD 14042: Environmental Management – Life Cycle Assessment – Life Cycle Impact Assessment. ISO, Geneva.

ISO (1998c). ISO/CD 14043: Environmental Management – Life Cycle Assessment – Life Cycle Interpretation. ISO, Geneva.

Tillman, A.-M., T. Ekvall, H. Baumann and T. Rydberg (1994). Choice of System Boundaries in Life Cycle Assessment. *J. Cleaner Prod.*, **2**(1), 21–29.

Weidema, B. (2001). Avoiding Co-product Allocation in Life-cycle Assessments, *J. Ind. Ecol.*, **4**(3), 11–33.

Index

Sustainable Development in Practice: Case Studies for Engineers and Scientists
Edited by Adisa Azapagic, Slobodan Perdan and Roland Clift
© 2004 John Wiley & Sons, Ltd   ISBNs: 0-470-85608-4 (HB); 0-470-85609-2 (PB)